The 60s

FEB 21 201

D0463186

THE

60s

THE STORY OF A DECADE

THE
60s
THE STORY OF
A DECADE

THE NEW YORKER

Edited by Henry Finder
Introduction by David Remnick

RANDOM HOUSE
NEW YORK

Published in the United States by Random House, an imprint and division
of Penguin Random House LLC, New York.

RANDOM HOUSE and the HOUSE colophon are registered trademarks of
Penguin Random House LLC.

All pieces in this collection were originally published in *The New Yorker*.

The publication dates are given at the beginning or end of each piece.

LIBRARY OF CONGRESS CATALOGING-IN-PUBLICATION DATA
Names: Finder, Henry, editor.
Title: The 60s: the story of a decade / The New Yorker; edited by
Henry Finder; introduction by David Remnick.
Description: First edition. | New York: Random House, 2016.
Identifiers: LCCN 2016013617 | ISBN 9780679644835 | ISBN 9780679644842 (ebook)
Subjects: LCSH: United States—Civilization—1945– | Nineteen sixties.
Classification: LCC E169.12 .A188 2016 | DDC 909.82/6—dc23
LC record available at http://lccn.loc.gov/2016013617

Printed in the United States of America on acid-free paper

randomhousebooks.com

2 4 6 8 9 7 5 3 1

FIRST EDITION

Book design by Simon M. Sullivan

CONTENTS

YOUTH IN REVOLT

PART THREE · AMERICAN SCENES

A Note by Jill Lepore 197

PRESSURE AND POSSIBILITY

SHOTS WERE FIRED

PART SIX · ARTISTS & ATHLETES
A Note by Larissa MacFarquhar 397

PART SEVEN · CRITICS
A Note by Adam Gopnik 489

THE CURRENT CINEMA

ART & ARCHITECTURE

TELEVISION

THE THEATRE

PART NINE · FICTION

A Note by Jennifer Egan   637

INTRODUCTION

THE NEW YORKER IN THE SIXTIES

David Remnick

T's DIFFICULT TO think of William Shawn, the reserved and courteous man who edited *The New Yorker* from 1952 to 1987, as a figure of the sixties. If he wore a tie-dyed T-shirt, he kept it well hidden. Most days, he wore a dark wool suit, a necktie of subdued color, and a starched white shirt, sometimes adding one or two sweater vests to the ensemble when it was chilly. He was soft-spoken and addressed his colleagues with the formality of an earlier time. Nearly everyone in the office referred to him, even when he was out of earshot, as "Mr. Shawn." He was already well into middle age when that decisive decade came roiling in, and although there is no definitive way to fact-check this, I would bet the house that he did not partake of the hallucinogens that helped define the era.

Yet this volume represents a magazine that, under his guidance, became more politically engaged, more formally daring, more vivid, and more intellectually exciting than it had ever been or wished to be. The world was changing, and Shawn was determined to change *The New Yorker*. In the early days of the magazine, Shawn's predecessor, Harold Ross, had preferred to minimize politics in what he referred to as a "comic weekly." When Dorothy Parker wanted to write a piece about the civil war in Spain that was sympathetic to the Loyalists, Ross told her wryly that he would print it, but only if she would come out in favor of Generalissimo Franco. "God damn it," he told her, "why can't you be funny again?"

Shawn, who had been Ross's longtime deputy, helped deepen the magazine with its coverage of the Second World War, but *The New*

Yorker tended to steer clear of the most vexed of many political questions, including that of race. There were exceptions, including "Opera in Greenville," Rebecca West's 1947 account of a lynching in South Carolina; Richard H. Rovere's occasional coverage of the movement to desegregate American schools; and Joseph Mitchell's "Mr. Hunter's Grave," which portrayed an elderly man living in Sandy Ground, one of the oldest communities founded by free African Americans. But such instances were infrequent.

In 1959, Shawn gave James Baldwin an advance to make a trip to Africa and write about it for the magazine. Baldwin was then thirty-five, and celebrated for his novels *Go Tell It on the Mountain* and *Giovanni's Room,* and for the essays that formed the collections *Notes of a Native Son* and *Nobody Knows My Name.* He was a consistent presence at civil-rights rallies, and he spoke with eloquence and penetration from stages and on television about the realities of white supremacy. Baldwin, accompanied by his sister Gloria, finally made the trip in the summer of 1962. He made stops over a period of a few months in Guinea, Senegal, Ghana, Liberia, Ivory Coast, and Sierra Leone. But, when he returned, he failed to concentrate for long on the writing he was meant to do about his journey. He was too absorbed by what was going on at home.

A few years earlier, Baldwin had agreed to write an article on Elijah Muhammad's separatist movement, the Nation of Islam, for Norman Podhoretz, the editor of *Commentary.* Baldwin set to work on "Down at the Cross," a discursive and powerful twenty-thousand-word essay on race, the church of his Harlem childhood, and the Black Muslims. He gave it to *The New Yorker.* Podhoretz never forgave Baldwin or Shawn.

Baldwin's essay confronted the "cowardly obtuseness of white liberals"—that is, much of the magazine's readership—and acted as a kind of spur to the next phase of the civil-rights movement, black power. Shawn was well aware that such an intensely personal and polemical essay, which did not permit an easy complacency, was a mold breaker for a magazine that had thrived for so long on reportage, humor, fiction, and, for the most part, a generalized equanimity. As if to domesticate the essay, to keep it within the bounds of his readers' expectations, Shawn retitled it "Letter from a Region in My Mind." (It appeared the following year in the book *The Fire Next Time.*)

Baldwin's masterpiece was one of a number of ambitious works in the sixties that reshaped the tenor of the magazine, expanding its sense of the possible. Rachel Carson's environmental manifesto, "Silent Spring";

Hannah Arendt's coverage of the trial of one of the engineers of the Holocaust, "Eichmann in Jerusalem"; Dwight Macdonald's assessment of American poverty; Jonathan Schell's dispatches from Vietnam; Calvin Trillin's and Renata Adler's coverage of the student movements; and Ellen Willis's essays on feminism and rock music were among the pieces that provoked the kind of rancorous debates that were part of the sixties soundtrack. For a magazine that had long had a distinct antipathy toward intellectual seriousness, Arendt, a German émigré philosopher with a Germanically heavy prose style, was an especially unlikely addition to the table of contents. Arendt's assessment of the trial, her phrase "the banality of evil," and her interpretation of Holocaust history, particularly her seeming disdain for the behavior of the victims, would be debated for years afterward.

Perhaps the most sensational publication of the decade for the magazine was one that Shawn quietly came to regret. In 1959, Truman Capote, who had failed as a young assistant in *The New Yorker*'s art department before becoming famous for his short fiction, came across a brief clipping about the murder of the Clutter family in Holcomb, a small town in Kansas. Shawn was under the impression that Capote was going to write a "Letter from . . ." describing how the people of Holcomb reacted to the grisly murders. Capote, occasionally joined by his friend Harper Lee, spent years interviewing countless sources, particularly the two suspects, and the manuscript he turned in, which was several times longer than John Hersey's *Hiroshima,* was far more lurid than Shawn, who was averse to violence, could ordinarily stomach. Still, despite his misgivings, he published the series, and *In Cold Blood* was a newsstand phenomenon and remains a model of the "nonfiction novel."

Shawn came to adore the Beatles, though the astute archivist will note scant coverage of the band in the magazine. Such are the curiosities—the misses among the hits—in any publication. But what was more remarkable was how many of the cultural touchstones of the time the magazine, which was not exactly *Rolling Stone* or *Creem,* did cover well. Nat Hentoff's 1964 Profile of Bob Dylan, Jane Kramer's Profile of Allen Ginsberg, Pauline Kael's essays on the films of that time, and Michael Arlen's Vietnam-focused television criticism all hold up for their vitality. In poems like W. S. Merwin's "The Asians Dying," the politics, the catastrophe, of the sixties was never far away. As a vehicle for fiction, *The New Yorker* widened its scope, including not only the suburban-based classicists Updike and Cheever, mainstays of the magazine, but also the

Yiddish-language tales of Isaac Bashevis Singer, the Paris-based stories of Mavis Gallant, and the formal experiments of Donald Barthelme. William Shawn did not look the part, and his voice was barely a whisper in a raucous time, but this book demonstrates that he, too, was a man of the turbulent sixties and that his *New Yorker* was equal to the moment.

PART ONE
RECKONINGS

A NOTE BY GEORGE PACKER

THESE DAYS, THE quarter century between the Second World War and the 1970s seems like at least an American silver age. The middle class was big and prosperous. Leaders in government, business, and labor worked out compromises that kept the deal table level and the payout fair. National institutions worked pretty well, and under stress they didn't collapse. Congress responded to civil-rights protests with sweeping, bipartisan legislation; environmental awareness produced the Clean Air and Clean Water Acts. As Richard H. Rovere wrote in "Half Out of Our Tree," even the protests over the war in Vietnam showed that American democracy still had a pulse—a strong one by today's standards.

Read the journalism of the 1960s and you might not think so. If the country now seems to be painfully breaking down, in the sixties it was quite dramatically exploding. The sense of continuous crisis forced a change in the journalism that appeared in *The New Yorker*. The magazine lost its habitual cool, its restraint. It began to publish big, ambitious reports and essays that attempted to meet the apocalyptic occasion. These pieces were intended to make noise, even to shock the national mind, and they dominated conversation for weeks or months. In the sixties, *The New Yorker* acquired a social consciousness. It went into opposition, challenging the complacent postwar consensus that had prevailed across American culture, including in its pages. The result was some of the most famous and influential journalism ever to appear in the magazine.

This work occupied so much territory—paid for by the voluminous and high-end advertising that used to fill *The New Yorker*'s pages—that some of the pieces took up an entire issue, or else spread themselves out over two, three, or even five in succession. Ambitious work had often appeared in the magazine, but the pieces from the sixties were something more than stories enjoying the luxury of a lot of space to be well and fully told. This was journalism as event. Sometimes the events arrived so fast and thick that readers could barely catch their breath. Rachel Carson's warning of the effects of chemical spraying on birds, trees, and other living things—published in the late spring of 1962—is now credited with starting the environmental movement. Five months later, James Baldwin's autobiographical essay on the black church, the Nation of Islam, and the racial crisis detonated, making him a prophet of the civil-rights era, Jeremiah to Martin Luther King, Jr.'s Moses, and that rare thing in American letters—the writer as national oracle. No less a personage than Bobby Kennedy felt prompted to answer "Letter from a Region of My Mind," privately, leading to an angry exchange between the two in Kennedy's midtown Manhattan apartment.

Just a few months later, in early 1963, *The New Yorker* published a report on the trial in Jerusalem of the Nazi criminal Adolf Eichmann, by the German-Jewish writer Hannah Arendt: a piece of political philosophy that simultaneously raised the repressed horror of the Holocaust and interrogated its perpetrators and victims alike—the former for their supposed banality, the latter for failing to put up a fight. Nor did Arendt try to conceal her contempt for the new state of Israel. From an Olympian perch, she flung down complex, razor-edged sentences that couldn't fail to hurt. The writers known as the New York intellectuals were thrown into an uproar, published replies, replied to the replies, broke into pro- and anti-Arendt camps, and debated the piece at a legendary town-hall meeting that Arendt herself disdained to attend.

In the middle of the decade came Truman Capote's *In Cold Blood*, about the killing of a family of four in Kansas. The murders had taken place in 1959, and the story of lonely, doomed small-town Americans feels as if it's in black and white, not Technicolor. But Capote's literary method helped define the experimental journalism of the sixties. *In Cold Blood* was shocking above all for its style, which dared to enter the dream life of a killer, to flirt dangerously along the borderline between fact and fiction. Jonathan Schell's "The Village of Ben Suc" was more conventional in its reportorial approach—dispassionate and meticulous—but devastating in its description of the American war machine turned loose on one corner of South Vietnam. The piece conveys the madness of overpowering technology and geopolitical dogma wreaking havoc, with no ability to see or understand the targets of destruction.

The sixties introduced the idea, reluctantly acknowledged in Rovere's essay "Half Out of Our Tree," that something had gone wrong with America—that we could no longer assume ourselves to be good. *The New Yorker* registered this change in many departments, but nowhere more memorably than in its journalism. These heavyweight pieces did not just record the decade's drama—they became part of it.

SILENT SPRING—1

Rachel Carson

JUNE 16, 1962

THERE WAS ONCE a town in the heart of America where all life seemed to be in harmony with its surroundings. The town lay in the midst of a checkerboard of prosperous farms, with fields of grain and hillsides of orchards, where white clouds of bloom drifted above the green land. In autumn, oak and maple and birch set up a blaze of color that flamed and flickered across a backdrop of pines. Then foxes barked in the hills and deer crossed the fields, half hidden in the mists of the mornings. Along the roads, laurel, viburnum, and alder, great ferns and wild flowers delighted the traveller's eye through much of the year. Even in winter, the roadsides were places of beauty, where countless birds came to feed on the berries and on the seed heads of the dried weeds rising above the snow. The countryside was, in fact, famous for the abundance and variety of its bird life, and when the flood of migrants was pouring through in spring and fall, people came from great distances to observe them. Other people came to fish streams, which flowed clear and cold out of the hills and contained shady pools where trout lay. So it had been from the days, many years ago, when the first settlers raised their houses, sank their wells, and built their barns.

Then, one spring, a strange blight crept over the area, and everything began to change. Some evil spell had settled on the community; mysterious maladies swept the flocks of chickens, and the cattle and sheep sickened and died. Everywhere was the shadow of death. The farmers told of much illness among their families. In the town, the doctors were becoming more and more puzzled by new kinds of sickness that had appeared among their patients. There had been several sudden and unexplained deaths, not only among the adults but also among the children, who would be stricken while they were at play, and would die within a few hours. And there was a strange stillness. The birds, for example—where had they gone? Many people, baffled and disturbed, spoke of them. The feeding stations in the back yards were deserted. The few birds to be seen anywhere were moribund; they trembled violently and could not fly. It was a spring without voices. In the mornings, which had once throbbed with the dawn chorus of robins, catbirds, doves, jays, and wrens, and scores of other bird voices, there was now no sound; only silence lay over the fields and woods and marshes. On the farms, the hens brooded but no chicks hatched. The farmers complained that they were unable to raise any pigs; the litters were small, and the young survived only a few days. The apple trees were coming into bloom, but no bees droned among the blossoms, so there was no pollination and there would be no fruit. The roadsides were lined with brown and withered vegetation, and were silent, too, deserted by all living things. Even the streams were lifeless. Anglers no longer visited them, for all the fish had died. In the gutters under the eaves, and between the shingles of the roofs, a few patches of white granular powder could be seen; some weeks earlier this powder had been dropped, like snow, upon the roofs and the lawns, the fields and the streams. No witchcraft, no enemy action had snuffed out life in this stricken world. The people had done it themselves.

This town does not actually exist; I know of no community that has experienced all the misfortunes I describe. Yet every one of them has actually happened somewhere in the world, and many communities have already suffered a substantial number of them. A grim spectre has crept upon us almost unnoticed, and soon my imaginary town may have thousands of real counterparts. What is silencing the voices of spring in countless towns in America? I shall make an attempt to explain.

. . .

The history of life on earth is a history of the interaction of living things and their surroundings. To an overwhelming extent, the physical form and the habits of the earth's vegetation and its animal life have been molded and directed by the environment. Over the whole span of earthly time, the opposite effect, in which life modifies its surroundings, has been relatively slight. It is only within the moment of time represented by the twentieth century that one species—man—has acquired significant power to alter the nature of his world, and it is only within the past twenty-five years that this power has achieved such magnitude that it endangers the whole earth and its life. The most alarming of all man's assaults upon the environment is the contamination of the air, earth, rivers, and seas with dangerous, and even lethal, materials. This pollution has rapidly become almost universal, and it is for the most part irrecoverable; the chain of evil it initiates, not only in the world that must support life but in living tissues, is for the most part irreversible. It is widely known that radiation has done much to change the very nature of the world, the very nature of its life; strontium 90, released into the air through nuclear explosions, comes to earth in rain or drifts down as fallout, lodges in soil, enters into the grass or corn or wheat grown there, and, in time, takes up its abode in the bones of a human being, there to remain until his death. It is less well known that many man-made chemicals act in much the same way as radiation; they lie long in the soil, and enter into living organisms, passing from one to another. Or they may travel mysteriously by underground streams, emerging to combine, through the alchemy of air and sunlight, into new forms, which kill vegetation, sicken cattle, and work unknown harm on those who drink from once pure wells. As Albert Schweitzer has said, "Man can hardly even recognize the devils of his own creation." It took hundreds of millions of years to produce the life that now inhabits the earth—aeons of time, in which that developing and evolving and diversifying life reached a state of adjustment to its surroundings. To be sure, the environment, rigorously shaping and directing the life it supported, contained hostile elements. Certain rocks gave out dangerous radiation; even within the light of the sun, from which all life draws its energy, there were short-wave radiations with power to injure. But given time—time not in years but in millennia—life adjusted, and a balance was reached. Time was the essential ingredient. Now, in the modern world, there is no time. The speed with which new hazards are created reflects the impetuous and heedless pace of man, rather than the deliberate pace of nature. Radiation is no longer merely the background radiation of rocks, the bombardment of cosmic rays, the ultraviolet of the sun, which existed before there was any life on earth; radiation is now also the unnatural creation of man's tampering with the atom. The chemicals to which life is asked to make its adjustment are no longer merely the calcium and silica and copper and the rest of the minerals washed out of the rocks and carried in rivers to the sea; they are also the synthetic creations of man's inventive mind, brewed in his laboratories and having no counterparts in nature. To adjust to these chemicals would require time on the scale that is nature's; it would require not merely the years of a man's life but the life of generations. And even this would be futile, for the new chemicals come in an endless stream; almost five hundred annually find their way into actual use in the United States alone. The figure is staggering and its implications are not easily grasped: five hundred new chemicals to which the bodies of men and all other living things are required somehow to adapt each year—chemicals totally outside the limits of biological experience.

Among the new chemicals are many that are used in man's war against nature. In the past decade and a half, some six hundred basic chemicals have been created for the purpose of killing insects, weeds, rodents, and other organisms described in the modern vernacular as "pests." In the form of sprays, dusts, and aerosols, these basic chemicals are offered for sale under several thousand different brand names—a highly bewildering array of poisons, confusing even to the chemist, which have the power to kill every insect, the "good" as well as the "bad," to still the song of birds and to stop the leaping of fish in the streams, to coat the leaves with poison and to linger on in soil. It may prove to be impossible to lay down such a barrage of dangerous poisons on the surface of the earth without making it unfit for all life. Indeed, the term "biocide" would be more appropriate than "insecticide"—all the more appropriate because the whole process of spraying poisons on the earth seems to have been caught up in an endless spiral. Since the late 1940s, when DDT began to be used widely, a process of escalation has been going on in which ever more toxic chemicals must be found. This has happened because insects, in a triumphant vindication of Darwin's principle of the survival of the fittest, have consistently evolved super-races immune to the particular insecticide used, and hence a deadlier one has always had to be developed—and then a deadlier one than that. It has happened also that destructive insects often undergo a "flareback," or resurgence, after spraying, in numbers greater than before. The chemical war is never won, and all life is caught in its cross fire.

Along with the possibility of the extinction of mankind by nuclear war, a central problem of our age is the contamination of man's total environment with substances of incredible potential for harm—substances that accumulate in the tissues of plants and animals, and even penetrate the germ cells, to shatter or alter the very material of heredity, upon which the shape of the future depends. Some would-be architects of our future look toward a time when we will be able to alter the human germ plasm by design. But we may easily be altering it now by inadvertence, for many chemicals, like radiation, bring about gene mutations. It is ironic to think that man may determine his own future by something so seemingly trivial as the choice of his insect spray. The results, of course, will not be apparent for decades or centuries. All this has been risked—for what? Future historians may well be amazed by our distorted sense of proportion. How could intelligent beings seek to control a few unwanted species of weeds and insects by a method that brought the threat of disease and death even to their own kind?

The problem whose attempted solution has touched off such a train of disaster is an accompaniment of our modern way of life. Long before the age of man, insects inhabited the earth—a group of extraordinarily varied and adaptable beings. Since man's advent, a small percentage of the more than half a million species of insects have come into conflict with human welfare, principally in two ways—as competitors for the food supply and as carriers of human disease. Disease-carrying insects become important where human beings are crowded together, especially when sanitation is poor, as in times of natural disaster or war, or in situations of extreme poverty and deprivation. As for insects that compete with man for food, they become important with the intensification of agriculture—the devotion of immense acreages to the production of a single crop. Such a system sets the stage for explosive increases in specific insect populations. Single-crop farming does not take advantage of the principles by which nature works; it is agriculture as an engineer might conceive it to be. Nature has introduced great variety into the landscape, but man has displayed a passion for simplifying it. Thus he undoes the built-in checks and balances by which nature holds the various species within bounds. One important natural check is a limit on the amount of suitable habitat for each species. Obviously, an insect that lives on wheat can build up its population to much higher levels on a farm devoted solely to wheat than on a farm where wheat is intermingled with crops to which the insect is not adapted. In all such circumstances, insect control of some sort is necessary and proper. But in the case of both types of insect—the disease-carrying and the crop-consuming—it is a sobering fact that massive chemical control has had only limited success, and even threatens to worsen the very conditions it is intended to curb.

Another aspect of the insect problem is one that must be viewed against a background of geological and human history—the spreading of thousands of different kinds of organisms from their native homes into new territories. This worldwide migration has been studied and graphically described by the British ecologist Charles Elton in his recent book *The Ecology of Invasions by Animals and Plants*. During the Cretaceous period, some hundred million years ago, flooding seas created many islands within continents, and living things found themselves confined in what Elton calls "colossal separate nature reserves." There, isolated from others of their kind, they developed large numbers of new species. When some of the land masses were joined again, about fifteen million years ago, these species began to move out into new territories—a movement that not only is still in progress but is now receiving considerable assistance from man. The importation of plants is the primary agent in the modern spread of species, for animals have almost invariably gone along with the plants—quarantine being a comparatively recent and never completely effective innovation. The United States government itself has imported approximately two hundred thousand species or varieties of plants from all over the world. Nearly half of the hundred and eighty-odd major insect enemies of plants in the United States are accidental imports from abroad, and most of them have come as hitchhikers on plants. In new territory, out of reach of the natural enemies that kept down its numbers in its native land, an invading plant or animal is able to increase its numbers enormously. Realistically speaking, it would seem that insect invasions, both those occurring naturally and those dependent on human assistance, are likely to continue indefinitely. We are faced, according to Dr. Elton, "with a life-and-death need not just to find new technological means of suppressing this plant or that animal" but to acquire the basic knowledge of animal populations and their relations to their surroundings that will "promote an even balance and damp down the explosive power of outbreaks and new invasions." Much of the necessary knowledge is now available, but we do not use it. Have we fallen into a mesmerized state that makes us accept as inevitable that which is inferior or detrimental, as though we had lost the will or the vision to demand that which is good? Such thinking, in the words of the American ecologist Paul Shepard, "idealizes life with only its head out of water, inches above the limits of toleration of the corruption of its own environment," and he goes on to ask, "Why should we tolerate a diet of weak poisons, a home in insipid surroundings, a circle of acquaintances who are not quite our enemies, the noise of motors with just enough relief to prevent insanity? Who would want to live in a world which is just not quite fatal?"

Yet such a world is pressed upon us. For the first time in history, virtually every human being is subjected to contact with dangerous chemicals from birth to death. In the less than two decades of their use, DDT and other synthetic pesticides have been thoroughly distributed over all but a few corners of the world. They have been recovered from many of the major river systems, and even from the streams of ground water flowing unseen through the earth. They have been found in soil to which they were applied a dozen years before. They have lodged in the bodies of fish, birds, reptiles, and domestic and wild animals to the point where it is now almost impossible for scientists carrying on animal experiments to obtain subjects free from such contamination. They have been found in fish in remote mountain lakes, in earthworms burrowing in soil, in the eggs of birds, and in man himself. These chemicals are now stored in the bodies of the vast majority of human beings, regardless of their age. They occur in mother's milk, and probably in the tissues of the unborn child.

All this has come about because of the prodigious growth of an industry for the production of synthetic chemicals with insecticidal properties. This industry is a child of the Second World War. In the course of developing agents of chemical warfare, some of the chemicals created in the laboratory were found to be lethal to insects. The discovery did not come by chance; insects were widely used to test chemicals as agents of death for man. In being man-made—by the ingenious laboratory manipulation of molecules, involving the substitution of atoms or the alteration of their arrangement—the new insecticides differ sharply from the simpler ones of prewar days. These were derived from naturally occurring minerals and plant products: compounds of arsenic, copper, lead, manganese, zinc, and other minerals; pyrethrum, from the dried flowers of chrysanthemums; nicotine sulphate, from some of the relatives of tobacco; and rotenone, from leguminous plants of the East Indies. What sets the new synthetic insecticides apart is their enormous biological potency. They can enter into the most vital processes of the body and change them in sinister and often deadly ways. Yet new chemicals are added to the list each year, and new uses are devised for them. Production of synthetic pesticides in the United States soared from 124,259,000 pounds in 1947 to 637,666,000 pounds in 1960—more than a fivefold increase. In 1960, the wholesale value of these products was well over a quarter of a billion dollars. But in the plans and hopes of the industry this enormous production is only a beginning. . . .

. . .

Over increasingly large areas of the United States, spring now comes unheralded by the return of the birds, and the early mornings, once filled with the beauty of bird song, are strangely silent. This sudden silencing of the song of the birds, this obliteration of the color and beauty and interest they lend to our world, has come about swiftly and insidiously, and has gone unnoticed by those whose communities are as yet unaffected. From the town of Hinsdale, in northeastern Illinois, in 1958, a housewife wrote in despair to one of the world's leading ornithologists, Robert Cushman Murphy, Lamont Curator Emeritus of Birds at the American Museum of Natural History: "Here in our village the elm trees have been sprayed for several years. When we moved here six years ago, there was a wealth of bird life; I put up a feeder and had a steady stream of cardinals, chickadees, downies, and nuthatches all winter, and the cardinals and chickadees brought their young ones in the summer. After several years of DDT spray, the town is almost devoid of robins and starlings; chickadees have not been on my shelf for two years, and this year the cardinals are gone, too; the nesting population in the neighborhood seems to consist of one dove pair and perhaps one catbird family. It is hard to explain to the children that the birds have been killed off, when they have learned in school that a federal law protects the birds from killing or capture. 'Will they ever come back?' they ask, and I do not have the answer."

One story might serve as a tragic symbol of the fate of the birds—a fate that has already overtaken some species and threatens all. It is the story of the robin, the bird known to everyone. To millions of Americans, the season's first robin means that the grip of winter is broken. Its coming is an event reported in newspapers and described eagerly at the breakfast table. And as the number of arrivals grows and the first mists of green appear in the woodlands, thousands of people listen for the dawn chorus of the robins, throbbing in the early-morning light. But now all is changed, and not even the return of the birds may be taken for granted.

The fate of the robin, and indeed of many other species as well, seems linked with that of the American elm, a tree that is part of the history of thousands of towns within its native range, from the Atlantic to the Rockies, gracing their streets, their village squares, and their college campuses with majestic archways of green. Today, the elms are subject to a disease that afflicts them throughout their range—a disease so serious that many experts believe all efforts to save the elms will in the end be futile. The so-called Dutch elm disease entered the United States from Europe in 1930, in elm-burl logs imported for the veneer industry. It is a fungus disease; the organism invades the water-conducting vessels of the tree, spreads by spores carried in the flow of sap, and, by mechanical clogging and also by poisons it secretes, causes the branches to wilt and the tree to die. The disease is spread from diseased trees to healthy ones by elm-bark beetles. The insects tunnel out galleries under the bark, and these become a favorable habitat for the invading fungus. As the insects move through the galleries, they pick up the spores, and later carry them wherever they fly. Efforts to control the disease have concentrated on achieving control of the carrier insect, and in community after community, especially throughout the strongholds of the American elm, the Middle West and New England, intensive spraying with DDT has become a routine procedure.

What this spraying could mean to bird life, and especially to the robin, was first made clear by the work of two ornithologists at Michigan State University, Professor George Wallace and one of his graduate students, John Mehner. In 1954, when Mr. Mehner began work toward his doctorate, he chose a research project that had to do with robin populations. This came about entirely by chance, for at that time no one suspected that the robins were in danger. But even as he undertook the work, events occurred that were to change its character—and, indeed, to deprive him of his material. Spraying for Dutch elm disease began in a small way on the university campus that very year. In 1955, the city of East Lansing, where the university is situated, joined in; spraying on the campus was expanded; and, with local programs for control of the gypsy moth and the mosquito also under way, the chemical rain increased to a downpour. In 1954, the year of the first, light spraying, all seemed to be well. The following spring, the migrating robins returned to the campus as usual. Like the bluebells in H. M. Tomlinson's haunting essay "The Lost Wood," they were "expecting no evil" as they reoccupied their familiar territory. But soon it became evident that something was wrong. Dead and dying robins began to appear on the campus. Few birds were seen engaging in their normal foraging activities or assembling in their customary roosts. Few nests were built; few young appeared. The pattern was repeated with monotonous regularity in succeeding springs. In the sprayed area, each wave of migrating robins would be eliminated in about a week. Then new arrivals would come in, only to add to the numbers of birds seen on the campus in the agonized tremors that precede death. "The campus is serving as a graveyard for most of the robins that attempt to take up residence in the spring," Dr. Wallace noted. But why? At first, he suspected some disease of the nervous system, but soon it became evident that "in spite of the assurances of the insecticide people that their sprays were 'harmless to birds,' the robins were really dying of insecticidal poisoning; they invariably exhibited the well-known symptoms of loss of balance, followed by tremors, convulsions, and death." Several circumstances suggested that the robins were being poisoned not so much by direct contact with the insecticides as indirectly, by eating poisoned earthworms. Campus earthworms had been fed to crayfish in a research project, and all the crayfish had quickly died. A snake kept in a laboratory cage had gone into violent tremors after being fed such worms. And earthworms are the principal food of robins in the spring.

A key piece in the jigsaw puzzle of the doomed robins was presently supplied by Dr. Roy Barker, of the Illinois Natural History Survey. Dr. Barker's work, published in 1958, traced the intricate cycle of events by which the robins' fate is linked to the elm trees by way of the earthworms. The trees are sprayed in the spring or early summer and often again a few months later. Powerful sprayers direct a stream of poison toward all parts of the tallest trees, killing directly not only the target organism—the bark beetle—but other insects, including pollinating species and predatory spiders and beetles. The poison forms a tenacious film on the leaves and bark. Rains do not wash it away. In the autumn, the leaves fall to the ground, accumulate in sodden layers, and begin the slow process of becoming one with the soil. In this they are aided by the toil of the earthworms, which feed in the leaf litter, for elm leaves are among their favorite foods. In feeding on the leaves, the worms, of course, also swallow the insecticide. Dr. Barker found deposits of DDT throughout the digestive tracts of the worms, and in their blood vessels, nerves, and body wall. Undoubtedly some of the earthworms themselves succumb, but those that survive become "biological magnifiers" of the poison—that is, the concentration of insecticide builds up in their bodies. Then, in the spring, the robins return. As few as eleven large earthworms can transfer a lethal dose of DDT to a robin. And eleven worms form a small part of a robin's daily ration; in fact, a robin may easily eat eleven earthworms in as many minutes.

Not all robins receive a lethal dose, but another consequence of poisoning may lead as surely to the extinction of their kind. The shadow of sterility lies over all the bird studies—and, indeed, lengthens to include all living things. There are now only two or three dozen robins to be found each spring on the entire hundred-and-eighty-five-acre campus of Michigan State University, compared with a conservatively estimated three hundred and seventy adults before spraying. In 1954, every robin nest under observation by Mehner produced young. In 1957, Mehner could find only one young robin. Part of this failure to produce young is due, of course, to the death of one or both of a pair of robins before the nesting cycle is completed. But Dr. Wallace has significant records that point toward something more sinister—the actual destruction of the birds' ability to reproduce. He has, for example, "records of robins and other birds building nests but laying no eggs, and others laying eggs and incubating them but not hatching them." In 1960, he told a congressional committee that was holding hearings on a bill for better coordination of spraying programs, "We have one record of a robin that sat on its eggs faithfully for twenty-one days and they did not hatch. The normal incubation period is thirteen days. . . . Our analyses are showing high concentrations of DDT in the testes and ovaries of breeding birds."

The robins are only one element in the complex pattern of devastation arising from the spraying of the elms, even as the elm program is only one of the multitudinous spray programs that spread poison over our land. Heavy mortality has occurred among about ninety species of birds, including those most familiar to amateur naturalists, and in some of the sprayed towns the populations of nesting birds in general have declined as much as 90 percent. All the various types of birds are affected—ground feeders, treetop feeders, bark feeders, predators. Among them is the woodcock, which includes earthworms in its diet and which winters in southern areas that have recently been heavily sprayed with chemicals. Two significant discoveries have now been made about the woodcock. The numbers of young birds in New Brunswick, where many woodcocks breed, have definitely been reduced, and adult birds that have been analyzed contain heavy residues of both DDT and a chlorinated hydrocarbon called heptachlor. Already there are disturbing records of mortality among more than twenty other species of ground-feeding birds, including three of the thrushes whose songs are among the most exquisite of bird voices, the olive-backed, the wood, and the hermit. And the sparrows that flit through the shrubby understory of the woodlands and forage with rustling sounds amid the fallen leaves—the song sparrow and the whitethroat—have also been found among the victims of the sprays.

All the treetop feeders—the birds that glean their insect food from the leaves—have disappeared from heavily sprayed areas, including those woodland sprites the kinglets, both ruby-crowned and golden-crowned; the tiny gnat-catchers; and many of the warblers, whose migrating hordes flow through the trees in spring in a multicolored tide of life. In Whitefish Bay, Wisconsin, in the years before 1958, at least a thousand myrtle warblers could be seen in migration; after the spraying of the elms in that year, observers could find only two. So, with additions from other communities, the list grows, and the warblers killed by the spray include those that most charm and fascinate all who are aware of them: the black-and-white, the yellow, the magnolia, and the Cape May; the ovenbird, whose call throbs in the Maytime woods; the Blackburnian, whose wings are touched with flame; the chestnut-sided, the Canada, and the black-throated green. These treetop feeders are affected either directly, by the eating of poisoned insects, or indirectly, by a shortage of food.

The loss of food has also struck hard at the swallows, which cruise the skies straining out the aerial insects as herring strain out the plankton of the sea. A Wisconsin naturalist has reported, "Swallows have been hard hit. Everyone complains of how few they have compared to four or five years ago. Our sky overhead was full of them only four years ago. Now we seldom see any. . . . This could be both lack of insects because of spray, or poisoned insects." Of other birds this observer wrote, "Another striking loss is the phoebe. Flycatchers are scarce everywhere, but the early common phoebe is no more. I've seen one this spring and only one last spring. Other birders in Wisconsin make the same complaint. I have had five or six pair of cardinals in the past, none now. Wrens, robins, catbirds, and screech owls have nested each year in our garden. There are none now. Summer mornings are without bird song. Only pest birds, pigeons, starlings, and English sparrows remain."

The sprays applied to the elms in the fall, sending the poison into every little crevice in the bark, are probably responsible for severe reductions observed in the numbers of bark feeders—chickadees, nuthatches, titmice, woodpeckers, and brown creepers. During the winter of 1957–58, Dr. Wallace for the first time in many years saw no chickadees or nuthatches at his home feeding station. Three nuthatches that he came upon later provided a sorry little step-by-step lesson in cause and effect: one was feeding on an elm, another was found dying, and the third was dead. The loss of all these birds is deplorable for economic reasons as well as for less tangible ones. The summer food of the white-breasted nuthatch and the brown creeper, for example, includes the eggs, larvae, and adults of a very large number of insect species injurious to trees. About three-quarters of the food of the chickadee is animal, including all stages of the life cycle of many insects. The chickadee's method of feeding is described in Arthur Cleveland Bent's *Life Histories of North American Jays, Crows, and Titmice*: "As the flock moves along, each bird examines minutely bark, twigs, and branches, searching for tiny bits of food (spiders' eggs, cocoons, or other dormant insect life)." Various scientific studies have established the critical role of birds in insect control in a variety of situations. Thus, woodpeckers are the primary factor in the control of the Engelmann spruce beetle, reducing its populations by a minimum of 45 percent and a maximum of 98 percent, and are also important in the control of the codling moth in apple orchards. Chickadees and other winter-resident birds can protect orchards against the cankerworm. But what happens in nature is not allowed to happen in the modern, chemical-drenched world, where spraying destroys not only the insects but their principal enemy, the birds. When, as almost always happens, there is a resurgence of the insect population, the birds are not there to keep their numbers in check.

To the public, the choice may easily appear to be one of stark simplicity: Shall we have birds or shall we have elms? But it is not as simple as that, and, by one of the ironies that abound throughout the field of chemical control, we may very well end by having neither. Spraying is killing the birds but is not saving the elms. The theory that the survival of the elms lies in spraying is a dangerous illusion, leading one community after another into a morass of heavy expenditures without producing lasting results. Greenwich, Connecticut, sprayed regularly for ten years. Then a drought year brought conditions especially favorable to the beetle, and the mortality of elms went up a thousand percent. In Toledo, Ohio, a similar experience caused the city's Superintendent of Forestry, Joseph A. Sweeney, to take a realistic look at the results of spraying. Spraying of elms was begun there in 1953 and continued through 1959. Meanwhile, however, Mr. Sweeney had noticed that a citywide infestation of the cottony maple scale was worse after the spraying recommended by "the books and the authorities" than it had been before. He decided to review for himself the results of spraying for Dutch elm disease. His findings shocked him. In the city of Toledo, he found, "the only areas under any control were the areas where we used some promptness in removing the diseased or brood trees. Where we depended on spraying, the disease was out of control. In the county, where nothing has been done, the disease has not spread as fast as it has in the city. This indicates that spraying destroys any natural enemies. We are abandoning spraying for the Dutch elm disease. This has brought me into conflict with the people who back any recommendations by the United States Department of Agriculture, but I have the facts and will stick with them."

In the spraying of the elms, the birds are the incidental victims of an attack directed at an insect, but in other situations they are now becoming a direct target of poisons. There is a growing trend toward aerial applications of deadly poisons, like parathion, a member of the family of organic-phosphate insecticides, for the purpose of "controlling" concentrations of birds distasteful to farmers. The Fish and Wildlife Service has expressed serious concern over this trend, pointing out that "parathion-treated areas constitute a potential hazard to humans, domestic animals, and wildlife." In southern Indiana, for example, a group of farmers joined forces in the summer of 1959 to engage a spray plane to treat an area of river-bottom land with parathion. The area was a favored roosting site of thousands of blackbirds, which were feeding in nearby cornfields. The problem could have been solved easily by a slight change in agricultural practice—a shift to a variety of corn with deep-set ears, inaccessible to the birds—but the farmers had been persuaded of the merits of killing by poison, and so they sent in the plane. The results probably gratified them, for the casualty list included some sixty-five thousand red-winged blackbirds and starlings. The question of other wildlife deaths that may have occurred was not considered. Parathion is not a specific for blackbirds; it is a universal killer. But such rabbits or raccoons or opossums as roamed those bottom lands, and perhaps never visited the farmers' cornfields, were doomed by a judge and jury who neither knew nor cared about their existence. And what of human beings? In orchards sprayed with this same parathion, workers handling foliage that had been treated a month earlier have collapsed and gone into shock, escaping severe injury only by a small margin, thanks to skilled medical attention. Does Indiana still raise boys who roam the woods and fields, and might even explore the margins of a river? If so, who guarded the poisoned area to keep out any boys who might wander in? Who kept watch to tell the innocent stroller that the fields he was about to enter were deadly, their vegetation coated with a lethal film? No one. Yet it was at so fearful a risk that the farmers waged their war on blackbirds.

LETTER FROM A REGION IN MY MIND

James Baldwin

NOVEMBER 17, 1962

Take up the White Man's burden—
Ye dare not stoop to less—
Nor call too loud on Freedom
To cloak your weariness;
By all ye cry or whisper,
By all ye leave or do,
The silent, sullen peoples
Shall weigh your Gods and you.

> —Kipling

Down at the cross where my Saviour died,
Down where for cleansing from sin I cried,
There to my heart was the blood applied,
Singing glory to His name!

> —Hymn

I underwent, during the summer that I became fourteen, a prolonged religious crisis. I use "religious" in the common, and arbitrary, sense, meaning that I then discovered God, His saints and angels, and His blazing Hell. And since I had been born in a Christian nation, I accepted this Deity as the only one. I supposed Him to exist only within the walls of a church—in fact, of our church—and I also supposed that God and safety were synonymous. The word "safety" brings us to the real meaning of the word "religious" as we use it. Therefore, to state it in another, more accurate way, I became, during my fourteenth year, for the first time in my life, afraid—afraid of the evil within me and afraid of the evil without. What I saw around me that summer in Harlem was what I had always seen; nothing had changed. But now, without any warning, the whores and pimps and racketeers on the Avenue had become a personal menace. It had not before occurred to me that I could become one of them, but now I realized that we had been produced by the same circumstances. Many of my comrades were clearly headed for the Avenue, and my father said that I was headed that way, too. My friends began to drink and smoke, and embarked—at first avid, then groaning—on their sexual careers. Girls, only slightly older than I was, who sang in the choir or taught Sunday school, the children of holy parents, underwent, before my eyes, their incredible metamorphosis, of which the most bewildering aspect was not their budding breasts or their rounding behinds but something deeper and more subtle, in their eyes, their heat, their odor, and the inflection of their voices. Like the strangers on the Avenue, they became, in the twinkling of an eye, unutterably different and fantastically *present*. Owing to the way I had been raised, the abrupt discomfort that all this aroused in me and the fact that I had no idea what my voice or my mind or my body was likely to do next caused me to consider myself one of the most depraved people on earth. Matters were not helped by the fact that these holy girls seemed rather to enjoy my terrified lapses, our grim, guilty, tormented experiments, which were at once as chill and joyless as the Russian steppes and hotter, by far, than all the fires of Hell.

Yet there was something deeper than these changes, and less definable, that frightened me. It was real in both the boys and the girls, but it was, somehow, more vivid in the boys. In the case of the girls, one watched them turning into matrons before they had become women. They began to manifest a curious and really rather terrifying single-mindedness. It is hard to say exactly how this was conveyed: something implacable in the set of the lips, something farseeing (seeing what?) in the eyes, some new and crushing determination in the walk, something peremptory in the voice. . . .

And I began to feel in the boys a curious, wary, bewildered despair, as though they were now settling in for the long, hard winter of life. I did not know then what it was that I was reacting to; I put it to myself that they were letting themselves go. In the same way that the girls were destined to gain as much weight as their mothers, the boys, it was clear, would rise no higher than their fathers. School began to reveal itself, therefore, as a child's game that one could not win, and boys dropped out of school and went to work. My father wanted me to do the same. I refused, even though I no longer had any illusions about what an education could do for me; I had already encountered too many college-graduate handymen. My friends were now "downtown," busy, as they put it, "fighting the man." They began to care less about the way they looked, the way they dressed, the things they did; presently, one found them in twos and threes and fours, in a hallway, sharing a jug of wine or a bottle of whiskey, talking, cursing, fighting, sometimes weeping: lost, and unable to say what it was that oppressed them, except that they knew it was "the man"—the white man. And there seemed to be no way whatever to remove this cloud that stood between them and the sun, between them and love and life and power, between them and whatever it was that they wanted. One did not have to be very bright to realize how little one could do to change one's situation; one did not have to be abnormally sensitive to be worn down to a cutting edge by the incessant and gratuitous humiliation and danger one encountered every working day, all day long. The humiliation did not apply merely to working days, or workers; I was thirteen and was crossing Fifth Avenue on my way to the Forty-second Street library, and the cop in the middle of the street muttered as I passed him, "Why don't you niggers stay uptown where you belong?" When I was ten, and didn't look, certainly, any older, two policemen amused themselves with me by frisking me, making comic (and terrifying) speculations concerning my ancestry and probable sexual prowess, and, for good measure, leaving me flat on my back in one of Harlem's empty lots. Just before and then during the Second World War, many of my friends fled into the service, all to be changed there, and rarely for the better, many to be ruined, and many to die. Others fled to other states and cities—that is, to other ghettos. Some went on wine or whiskey or the needle, and are still on it. And others, like me, fled into the church.

For the wages of sin were visible everywhere, in every wine-stained and urine-splashed hallway, in every clanging ambulance bell, in every scar on the faces of the pimps and their whores, in every helpless, newborn baby being brought into this danger, in every knife and pistol fight on the Avenue, and in every disastrous bulletin: a cousin, mother of six, suddenly gone mad, the children parcelled out here and there; an indestructible aunt rewarded for years of hard labor by a slow, agonizing death in a terrible small room; someone's bright son blown into eternity by his own hand; another turned robber and carried off to jail. It was a summer of dreadful speculations and discoveries, of which these were not the worst. Crime became real, for example—for the first time—not as *a* possibility but as *the* possibility. One would never defeat one's circumstances by working and saving one's pennies; one would never, by working, acquire that many pennies, and, besides, the social treatment accorded even the most successful Negroes proved that one needed, in order to be free, something more than a bank account. One needed a handle, a lever, a means of inspiring fear. It was absolutely clear that the police would whip you and take you in as long as they could get away with it, and that everyone else—housewives, taxi-drivers, elevator boys, dishwashers, bartenders, lawyers, judges, doctors, and grocers—would never, by the operation of any generous human feeling, cease to use you as an outlet for his frustrations and hostilities. Neither civilized reason nor Christian love would cause any of those people to treat you as they presumably wanted to be treated; only the fear of your power to retaliate would cause them to do that, or to seem to do it, which was (and is) good enough. There appears to be a vast amount of confusion on this point, but I do not know many Negroes who are eager to be "accepted" by white people, still less to be loved by them; they, the blacks, simply don't wish to be beaten over the head by the whites every instant of our brief passage on this planet. White people in this country will have quite enough to do in learning how to accept and love themselves and each other, and when they have achieved this—which will not be tomorrow and may very well be never—the Negro problem will no longer exist, for it will no longer be needed. . . .

Perhaps the whole root of our trouble, the human trouble, is that we will sacrifice all the beauty of our lives, will imprison ourselves in totems, taboos, crosses, blood sacrifices, steeples, mosques, races, armies, flags, nations, in order to deny the fact of death, which is the only fact we have. It seems to me that one ought to rejoice in the *fact* of death—ought to decide, indeed, to *earn* one's death by confronting with passion the conundrum of life. One is responsible to life: It is the small beacon in that terrifying darkness from which we come and to which we shall return. One must negotiate this passage as nobly as possible, for the sake of those who are coming after us. But white Americans do not believe in death, and this is why the darkness of my skin so intimidates them. And this is also why the presence of the Negro in this country can bring about its destruction. It is the responsibility of free men to trust and to celebrate what is constant—birth, struggle, and death are constant, and so is love, though we may not always think so—and to apprehend the nature of change, to be able and willing to change. I speak of change not on the surface but in the depth—change in the sense of renewal. But renewal becomes impossible if one supposes things to be constant that are not—safety, for example, or money, or power. One clings then to chimeras, by which one can only be betrayed, and the entire hope—the entire possibility—of freedom disappears. And by destruction I mean precisely the abdication by Americans of any effort really to be free. The Negro can precipitate this abdication because white Americans have never, in all their long history, been able to look on him as a man like themselves. This point need not be labored; it is proved over and over again by the Negro's continuing position here, and his indescribable struggle to defeat the stratagems that white Americans have used, and use, to deny him his humanity. America could have used in other ways the energy that both groups have expended in this conflict. America, of all the Western nations, has been best placed to prove the uselessness and the obsolescence of the concept of color. But it has not dared to accept this opportunity, or even to conceive of it as an opportunity. White Americans have thought of it as their shame, and have envied those more civilized and elegant European nations that were untroubled by the presence of black men on their shores. This is because white Americans have supposed "Europe" and "civilization" to be synonyms—which they are not—and have been distrustful of other standards and other sources of vitality, especially those produced in America itself, and have attempted to behave in all matters as though what was east for Europe was also east for them. What it comes to is that if we, who can scarcely be considered a white nation, persist in thinking of ourselves as one, we condemn ourselves, with the truly white nations, to sterility and decay, whereas if we could accept ourselves *as we are,* we might bring new life to the Western achievements, and transform them. The price of this transformation is the unconditional freedom of the Negro; it is not too much to say that he, who has been so long rejected, must now be embraced, and at no matter what psychic or social risk. He is *the* key figure in his country, and the American future is precisely as bright or as dark as his. And the Negro recognizes this, in a negative way. Hence the question: Do I really *want* to be integrated into a burning house?

White Americans find it as difficult as white people elsewhere do to divest themselves of the notion that they are in possession of some intrinsic value that black people need, or want. And this assumption—which, for example, makes the solution to the Negro problem depend on the speed with which Negroes accept and adopt white standards—is revealed in all kinds of striking ways, from Bobby Kennedy's assurance that a Negro can become President in forty years to the unfortunate tone of warm congratulation with which so many liberals address their Negro equals. It is the Negro, of course, who is presumed to have become equal—an achievement that not only proves the comforting fact that perseverance has no color but also overwhelmingly corroborates the white man's sense of his own value. Alas, this value can scarcely be corroborated in any other way; there is certainly little enough in the white man's public or private life that one should desire to imitate. White men, at the bottom of their hearts, know this. Therefore, a vast amount of the energy that goes into what we call the Negro problem is produced by the white man's profound desire not to be judged by those who are not white, not to be seen as he is, and at the same time a vast amount of the white anguish is rooted in the white man's equally profound need to be seen as he is, to be released from the tyranny of his mirror. All of us know, whether or not we are able to admit it, that mirrors can only lie, that death by drowning is all that awaits one there. It is for this reason that love is so desperately sought and so cunningly avoided. Love takes off the masks that we fear we cannot live without and know we cannot live within. I use the word "love" here not merely in the personal sense but as a state of being, or a state of grace—not in the infantile American sense of being made happy but in the tough and universal sense of quest and daring and growth. And I submit, then, that the racial tensions that menace Americans today have little to do with real antipathy—on the contrary, indeed—and are involved only symbolically with color. These tensions are rooted in the very same depths as those from which love springs, or murder. The white man's unadmitted—and apparently, to him, unspeakable—private fears and longings are projected onto the Negro. The only way he can be released from the Negro's tyrannical power over him is to consent, in effect, to become black himself, to become a part of that suffering and dancing country that he now watches wistfully from the heights of his lonely power and, armed with spiritual traveller's checks, visits surreptitiously after dark. How can one respect, let alone adopt, the values of a people who do not, on any level whatever, live the way they say they do, or the way they say they should? I cannot accept the proposition that the four-hundred-year travail of the American Negro should result merely in his attainment of the present level of the American civilization. I am far from convinced that being released from the African witch doctor was worthwhile if I am now—in order to support the moral contradictions and the spiritual aridity of my life— expected to become dependent on the American psychiatrist. It is a bargain I refuse. The only thing white people have that black people need, or should want, is power—and no one holds power forever. White people cannot, in the generality, be taken as models of how to live. Rather, the white man is himself in sore need of new standards, which will release him from his confusion and place him once again in fruitful communion with the depths of his own being. And I repeat: The price of the liberation of the white people is the liberation of the blacks—the total liberation, in the cities, in the towns, before the law, and in the mind. Why, for example—especially knowing the family as I do—I should *want* to marry your sister is a great mystery to me. But your sister and I have every right to marry if we wish to, and no one has the right to stop us. If she cannot raise me to her level, perhaps I can raise her to mine.

In short, we, the black and the white, deeply need each other here if we are really to become a nation—if we are really, that is, to achieve our identity, our maturity, as men and women. To create one nation has proved to be a hideously difficult task; there is certainly no need now to create two, one black and one white. But white men with far more political power than that possessed by the Nation of Islam movement have been advocating exactly this, in effect, for generations. If this sentiment is honored when it falls from the lips of Senator Byrd, then there is no reason it should not be honored when it falls from the lips of Malcolm X. And any Congressional committee wishing to investigate the latter must also be willing to investigate the former. They are expressing exactly the same sentiments and represent exactly the same danger. There is absolutely no reason to suppose that white people are better equipped to frame the laws by which I am to be governed than I am. It is entirely unacceptable that I should have no voice in the political affairs of my own country, for I am not a ward of America; I am one of the first Americans to arrive on these shores.

This past, the Negro's past, of rope, fire, torture, castration, infanticide, rape; death and humiliation; fear by day and night, fear as deep as the marrow of the bone; doubt that he was worthy of life, since everyone around him denied it; sorrow for his women, for his kinfolk, for his children, who needed his protection, and whom he could not protect; rage, hatred, and murder, hatred for white men so deep that it often turned against him and his own, and made all love, and trust, all joy impossible—this past, this endless struggle to achieve and reveal and confirm a human identity, human authority, yet contains, for all its horror, something very beautiful. I do not mean to be sentimental about suffering—enough is certainly as good as a feast—but people who cannot suffer can never grow up, can never discover who they are. That man who is forced each day to snatch his manhood, his identity, out of the fire of human cruelty that rages to destroy it knows, if he survives his effort, and even if he does not survive it, something about himself and human life that no school on earth—and, indeed, no church—can teach. He achieves his own authority, and that is unshakable. This is because, in order to save his life, he is forced to look beneath appearances, to take nothing for granted, to hear the meaning behind the words. If one is continually surviving the worst that life can bring, one eventually ceases to be controlled by a fear of what life can bring; whatever it brings must be borne. And at this level of experience one's bitterness begins to be palatable, and hatred becomes too heavy a sack to carry. The apprehension of life here so briefly and inadequately sketched has been the experience of generations of Negroes, and it helps to explain how they have endured and how they have been able to produce children of kindergarten age who can walk through mobs to get to school. It demands great force and great cunning continually to assault the mighty and indifferent fortress of white supremacy, as Negroes in this country have done so long. It demands great spiritual resilience not to hate the hater whose foot is on your neck, and an even greater miracle of perception and charity not to teach your child to hate. The Negro boys and girls who are facing mobs today come out of a long line of improbable aristocrats—the only genuine aristocrats this country has produced. I say "this country" because their frame of reference was totally American. They were hewing out of the mountain of white supremacy the stone of their individuality. I have great respect for that unsung army of black men and women who trudged down back lanes and entered back doors, saying "Yes, sir" and "No, Ma'am" in order to acquire a new roof for the schoolhouse, new books, a new chemistry lab, more beds for the dormitories, more dormitories. They did not like saying "Yes, sir" and "No, Ma'am," but the country was in no hurry to educate Negroes, these black men and women knew that the job had to be done, and they put their pride in their pockets in order to do it. It is very hard to believe that they were in any way inferior to the white men and women who opened those back doors. It is very hard to believe that those men and women, raising their children, eating their greens, crying their curses, weeping their tears, singing their songs, making their love, as the sun rose, as the sun set, were in any way inferior to the white men and women who crept over to share these splendors after the sun went down. But we must avoid the European error; we must not suppose that, because the situation, the ways, the perceptions of black people so radically differed from those of whites, they were racially superior. I am proud of these people not because of their color but because of their intelligence and their spiritual force and their beauty. The country should be proud of them, too, but, alas, not many people in this country even know of their existence. And the reason for this ignorance is that a knowledge of the role these people played—and play—in American life would reveal more about America to Americans than Americans wish to know.

The American Negro has the great advantage of having never believed that collection of myths to which white Americans cling: that their ancestors were all freedom-loving heroes, that they were born in the greatest country the world has ever seen, or that Americans are invincible in battle and wise in peace, that Americans have always dealt honorably with Mexicans and Indians and all other neighbors or inferiors, that American men are the world's most direct and virile, that American women are pure. Negroes know far more about white Americans than that; it can almost be said, in fact, that they know about white Americans what parents—or, anyway, mothers—know about their children, and that they very often regard white Americans that way. And perhaps this attitude, held in spite of what they know and have endured, helps to explain why Negroes, on the whole, and until lately, have allowed themselves to feel so little hatred. The tendency has really been, insofar as this was possible, to dismiss white people as the slightly mad victims of their own brainwashing. One watched the lives they led. One could not be fooled about that; one watched the things they did and the excuses that they gave themselves, and if a white man was really in trouble, deep trouble, it was to the Negro's door that he came. And one felt that if one had had that white man's worldly advantages, one would never have become as bewildered and as joyless and as thoughtlessly cruel as he. The Negro came to the white man for a roof or for five dollars or for a letter to the judge; the white man came to the Negro for love. But he was not often able to give what he came seeking. The price was too high; he had too much to lose. And the Negro knew this, too. When one knows this about a man, it is impossible for one to hate him, but unless he becomes a man—becomes equal—it is also impossible for one to love him. Ultimately, one tends to avoid him, for the universal characteristic of children is to assume that they have a monopoly on trouble, and therefore a monopoly on you. (Ask any Negro what he knows about the white people with whom he works. And then ask the white people with whom he works what they know about him.)

How can the American Negro past be used? It is entirely possible that this dishonored past will rise up soon to smite all of us. There are some wars, for example (if anyone on the globe is still mad enough to go to war) that the American Negro will not support, however many of his people may be coerced—and there is a limit to the number of people any government can put in prison, and a rigid limit indeed to the practicality of such a course. A bill is coming in that I fear America is not prepared to pay. "The problem of the twentieth century," wrote W. E. B. Du Bois around sixty years ago, "is the problem of the color line." A fearful and delicate problem, which compromises, when it does not corrupt, all the American efforts to build a better world—here, there, or anywhere. It is for this reason that everything white Americans think they believe in must now be reexamined. What one would not like to see again is the consolidation of peoples on the basis of their color. But as long as we in the West place on color the value that we do, we make it impossible for the great unwashed to consolidate themselves according to any other principle. Color is not a human or a personal reality; it is a political reality. But this is a distinction so extremely hard to make that the West has not been able to make it yet. And at the center of this dreadful storm, this vast confusion, stand the black people of this nation, who must now share the fate of a nation that has never accepted them, to which they were brought in chains. Well, if this is so, one has no choice but to do all in one's power to change that fate, and at no matter what risk—eviction, imprisonment, torture, death. For the sake of one's children, in order to minimize the bill that *they* must pay, one must be careful not to take refuge in any delusion—and the value placed on the color of the skin is always and everywhere and forever a delusion. I know that what I am asking is impossible. But in our time, as in every time, the impossible is the least that one can demand—and one is, after all, emboldened by the spectacle of human history in general, and American Negro history in particular, for it testifies to nothing less than the perpetual achievement of the impossible.

When I was very young, and was dealing with my buddies in those wine- and urine-stained hallways, something in me wondered, *What will happen to all that beauty?* For black people, though I am aware that some of us, black and white, do not know it yet, are very beautiful. And when I sat at Elijah's table and watched the baby, the women, and the men, and we talked about God's—or Allah's—vengeance, I wondered, when that vengeance was achieved, *What will happen to all that beauty then?* I could also see that the intransigence and ignorance of the white world might make that vengeance inevitable—a vengeance that does not really depend on, and cannot really be executed by, any person or organization, and that cannot be prevented by any police force or army: historical vengeance, a cosmic vengeance, based on the law that we recognize when we say, "Whatever goes up must come down." And here we are, at the center of the arc, trapped in the gaudiest, most valuable, and most improbable water wheel the world has ever seen. Everything now, we must assume, is in our hands; we have no right to assume otherwise. If we—and now I mean the relatively conscious whites and the relatively conscious blacks, who must, like lovers, insist on, or create, the consciousness of the others—do not falter in our duty now, we may be able, handful that we are, to end the racial nightmare, and achieve our country, and change the history of the world. If we do not now dare everything, the fulfillment of that prophecy, re-created from the Bible in song by a slave, is upon us: *God gave Noah the rainbow sign, No more water, the fire next time!*

EICHMANN IN JERUSALEM

Hannah Arendt

FEBRUARY 16, 1963

E VERY MORNING, THE words *"Beth Hamishpath"* ("The House of Jus
tice"), shouted by the court usher at the top of his voice, make us
jump to our feet as they announce the arrival of the three judges,
who, bare-headed and in black robes, walk into the courtroom from a
side entrance to take their seats on the highest tier of the raised platform
at the front of the long hall. They sit at a long table, which is eventually
to be covered with innumerable books and more than fifteen hundred
documents. Immediately below the judges are the translators, whose services are needed for direct exchanges between the defendant or his coun
sel and the court; otherwise, Adolf Eichmann, the German-speaking
accused party, like all the other foreigners in the courtroom, follows the
Hebrew proceedings through the simultaneous radio transmission,
which is excellent in French, bearable in English, and sheer comedy—
frequently incomprehensible—in German. (In view of the scrupulous
fairness of all the technical arrangements for the trial, it is among the
minor mysteries of the new State of Israel that, with its high percentage
of German-born people, it was unable to find an adequate translator into
the only language the accused and his counsel could understand. The old
prejudice against German Jews, once very pronounced in Israel, is no
longer strong enough to account for it.) One tier below the translators are
the glass booth of the accused and the witness box, facing each other.
Finally, on the bottom tier, with their backs to the spectators, are the
prosecutor, Attorney General Gideon Hausner, with his staff of four assistant attorneys, and Dr. Robert Servatius, counsel for the defense—

a lawyer from Cologne, chosen by Eichmann and paid by the Israeli government (just as at the Nuremberg Trials all attorneys for the accused were paid by the tribunal of the victorious powers), who during the first weeks is accompanied by an assistant. Whoever planned this auditorium in the newly built House of the People, *Beth Ha'am*—now guarded from roof to cellar by heavily armed police, and surrounded by high fences, as well as by a wooden row of barracks in the front courtyard, in which all comers are expertly frisked—obviously had a theatre in mind, complete with orchestra and balcony, with proscenium and stage, and with side doors for the actors' entrances.

At no time, however, is there anything theatrical in the conduct of the judges—Moshe Landau, the presiding judge, Judge Benjamin Halevi, and Judge Yitzhak Raveh. Their walk is unstudied; their sober and intense attention, visibly stiffening under the impact of grief as they listen to the tales of suffering, is natural; their impatience with the prosecutor's attempt to drag out the hearings is spontaneous and refreshing; their attitude toward the defense is perhaps a shade over-polite, as though they had it always in mind that, to quote the judgment they handed down, "Dr. Servatius stood almost alone in this strenuous legal battle, in an unfamiliar environment"; their manner toward the accused is always beyond reproach. They are so evidently three good and honest men that one is not surprised to see that none of them yields to the greatest of all the temptations to play-act in this setting—that of pretending that they, all three born and educated in Germany, must wait for the Hebrew translation of anything said in German. Judge Landau hardly ever waits to give his answer until the translator has done his work, and he frequently interrupts the translation to correct and improve it, appearing grateful for this bit of distraction from the grim business at hand. In time, during the cross-examination of the accused, he even leads his colleagues to use their German mother tongue in the dialogue with Eichmann—a proof, if proof were still needed, of his remarkable independence of current public opinion in Israel.

There is no doubt from the very beginning that it is Judge Landau who sets the tone, and that he is doing his best—his very best—to prevent this trial from becoming a "show" trial under the direction of the prosecutor, whose love of showmanship is unmistakable. Among the reasons he cannot always succeed is the simple fact that the proceedings happen on a stage before an audience, with the usher's marvellous shout at the beginning of each session producing the effect of a rising curtain. Clearly, this courtroom is well suited to the show trial that David Ben-Gurion, Prime Minister of Israel, had in mind when he decided to have Eichmann kidnapped in Argentina and brought to the District Court of Jerusalem to answer the charge that he had played a principal role in "the Final Solution of the Jewish question," as the Nazis called their plan to exterminate the Jews. And Ben-Gurion, who has rightly been given the title of "architect of the state," is the invisible stage manager of the proceedings. He does not attend a single one of the sessions; in the courtroom, he speaks with the voice of his Attorney General, who, representing the government, does his best—his very best—to obey his master. And if his best often turns out not to be good enough, the reason is that the trial is presided over by someone who serves Justice as faithfully as Mr. Hausner serves the State of Israel. Justice demands that the accused be prosecuted, defended, and judged, and that all the other questions, though they may seem to be of greater import—of "How could it happen?" and "Why did it happen?," of "Why the Jews?" and "Why the Germans?," of "What was the role of other nations?" and "What was the extent to which the Allies shared the responsibility?," of "How could the Jews, through their own leaders, cooperate in their own destruction?" and "Why did they go to their death like lambs to the slaughter?"—be left in abeyance. Justice insists on the importance of Adolf Eichmann, the man in the glass booth built for his protection: medium-sized, slender, middle-aged, with receding hair, ill-fitting teeth, and nearsighted eyes, who throughout the trial keeps craning his scraggy neck toward the bench (not once does he turn to face the audience), and who desperately tries to maintain his self-control—and mostly succeeds, despite a nervous tic, to which his mouth must have become subject long before this trial started. On trial are his deeds, not the sufferings of the Jews, not the German people or mankind, not even anti-Semitism and racism.

And Justice turns out to be a much sterner master than the Prime Minister. The latter's rule, as Mr. Hausner is not slow in demonstrating, is permissive; it permits the prosecutor to give press conferences and interviews for television during the trial (the American program, sponsored by the Glickman Corporation, is constantly interrupted—business as usual—by real-estate advertising), and even "spontaneous" outbursts to reporters in the court building (he is sick of cross-examining Eichmann, who answers all questions with lies); it permits frequent side glances into the audience, and the theatrics characteristic of a conspicuous vanity, which finally achieves its triumph in the White House with a compliment on "a job well done" by the President of the United States. Justice does not permit anything of the sort; it demands seclusion, it requires sorrow rather than anger, and it prescribes the most careful abstention from all the nice pleasures of putting oneself in the limelight.

Yet no matter how consistently the judges shun the limelight, there they are, seated at the top of the platform, facing the audience as from a stage. The audience is supposed to represent the whole world, and in the first few weeks it indeed consisted chiefly of newspapermen and magazine writers who had flocked to Jerusalem from the four corners of the earth. They were to watch a spectacle as sensational as the Nuremberg Trials; only this time, Mr. Hausner noted, "the tragedy of Jewry as a whole was the central concern." In fact, said Hausner, "if we charge him [Eichmann] also with crimes against non-Jews . . . this is" not because he committed them but, surprisingly, *"because we make no ethnic distinctions."* That was certainly a remarkable sentence for a prosecutor to utter in his opening speech; it proved to be the key sentence in the case for the prosecution. For this case was built on what the Jews had suffered, not on what Eichmann had done. And, according to Mr. Hausner, that amounted to the same thing, because "there was only one man who had been concerned almost entirely with the Jews, whose business had been their destruction, whose role in the establishment of the iniquitous regime had been limited to them. That was Adolf Eichmann." Was it not logical to bring before the court all the facts of Jewish suffering (which, of course, were never in dispute) and then look for evidence that, in one way or another, would connect Eichmann with what had happened? The Nuremberg Trials, where the defendants had been "indicted for crimes against members of many and various nations," had left the Jewish tragedy out of account, Hausner said, for the simple reason that Eichmann had not been there. Did Hausner really believe the Nuremberg Trials would have paid greater attention to the fate of the Jews if Eichmann had been in the dock? Hardly. Like almost everybody else in Israel, he believed that only a Jewish court could render justice to Jews, and that it was the business of Jews to sit in judgment on their enemies.

If the audience was to be the world and the play was to be the huge panorama of Jewish suffering, the reality was falling short of expectations and failing to accomplish its purpose. The journalists remained faithful for no more than two weeks, and then the audience changed drastically. It was now supposed to consist of Israelis, and, specifically, of those who were too young to know the story or, as in the case of Oriental

Jews, had never been told it. The trial was supposed to show them what it meant to live among non-Jews, to convince them that only in Israel could a Jew be safe and live an honorable life. (For correspondents, the lesson was spelled out in a little booklet on Israel's legal system, which was handed to the press. Its author, Doris Lankin, cites a decision of Israel's Supreme Court whereby two fathers who had "abducted their children and brought them to Israel" were directed to send them back to their mothers, living abroad, who had a legal right to their custody. This, says the author—no less proud of such strict legality than Hausner of his willingness to prosecute a murder charge even when the victims of the murder were non-Jews—"despite the fact that to send the children back to maternal custody and care would be committing them to waging an unequal struggle against the hostile elements in the Diaspora.") But in actuality there were hardly any young people in the audience, and it did not consist of Israelis, as distinguished from Jews. It was filled with "survivors"—middle-aged and elderly people, immigrants from Europe, like myself—who knew by heart all that there was to know, and who were in no mood to learn any lessons and certainly did not need this trial to draw their own conclusions. As witness followed witness and horror was piled upon horror, they sat there and listened in public to stories they would hardly have been able to endure in private, when they would have had to face the storyteller. And the more "the calamity [in Hausner's words] of the Jewish people in this generation" unfolded, and the more grandiose Hausner's rhetoric became, the paler and more ghostlike became the figure in the glass booth, and no finger-wagging ("And there sits the monster responsible for all this") could summon him back to life.

It was precisely the play aspect of the trial that collapsed under the weight of the hair-raising atrocities. A trial resembles a play in that both focus on the doer, not on the victim. A show trial, to be effective, needs even more urgently than an ordinary trial a limited and well-defined outline of what the doer did, and how. In the center of a trial can only be the one who did—in this respect, he is like the hero in the play—and if he suffers, he must suffer for what he has done, not for what he has caused others to suffer. No one knew this better than the presiding judge, before whose eyes the trial began to deteriorate into a bloody spectacle, or, as the judgment called it, "a rudderless ship tossed about by the waves." But if his efforts to prevent this were often defeated, the defeat was, strangely, in part the fault of the defense, which hardly ever rose to challenge any testimony, no matter how irrelevant or immaterial it might be. *Dr.* Servatius (as everybody invariably addressed him) was a bit bolder when it came to the submission of documents, and the most impressive of his rare interventions occurred when the prosecution introduced as evidence the diaries of Hans Frank, wartime Governor General of Poland and one of the major war criminals hanged at Nuremberg. "I have only one question," Dr. Servatius said. "Is the name Adolf Eichmann, the name of the accused, mentioned in those twenty-nine volumes [in fact, it was thirty-eight]? . . . The name Adolf Eichmann is not mentioned in all those twenty-nine volumes. . . . Thank you, no more questions."

Thus, the trial never became a play, but the show that Ben-Gurion had had in mind did take place—or, rather, the "lessons" he thought should be offered to Israelis and Arabs, to Jews and Gentiles; that is, to the whole world. These lessons to be drawn from an identical show were meant to be different for the different recipients. Ben-Gurion had outlined them before the trial started, in a number of articles that were designed to explain why Israel had kidnapped the accused. There was the lesson to the non-Jewish world: "I want to establish before the nations of the world how millions of people, because they happened to be Jews, and one million babies, because they happened to be Jewish babies, were murdered by the Nazis." Or, in the words of *Davar*, the organ of Ben-Gurion's *Mapai* party: "Let world opinion know this, that not Nazi Germany alone was responsible for the destruction of six million Jews of Europe." Hence, again in Ben-Gurion's own words, "We want the nations of the world to know . . . and they should be ashamed." The Jews in the Diaspora were to remember how "four-thousand-year-old Judaism, with its spiritual creations, its ethical strivings, its Messianic aspirations, had always faced a hostile world," how the Jews had degenerated until they went to their death like sheep, and how only the establishment of a Jewish state had enabled Jews to hit back, as Israelis had done in the War of Independence, in the Suez adventure, and in the almost daily incidents on Israel's unhappy borders. And if the Jews outside Israel had to be shown the difference between Israeli heroism and Jewish submissive meekness, there was a complementary lesson for the Israelis; for "the generation of Israelis who have grown up since the holocaust" were in danger of losing their ties with the Jewish people and, by implication, with their own history. "It is necessary that our youth remember what happened to the Jewish people. We want them to know the most tragic facts in our history." Finally, one of the motives in bringing Eichmann to

trial was "to ferret out other Nazis—for example, the connection between the Nazis and some Arab rulers."

If these had been the only justifications for bringing Adolf Eichmann
to the District Court of Jerusalem, the trial would have been a failure on
most counts. In some respects, the lessons were superfluous, and in others they were positively misleading. Thanks to Hitler, anti-Semitism has
been discredited, perhaps not forever but certainly for the time being,
and this is not because the Jews have become more popular all of a sudden but because not only Ben-Gurion but most people have "realized
that in our day the gas chamber and the soap factory are what anti-
Semitism may lead to." Equally superfluous was the lesson to the Jews in
the Diaspora, who hardly needed a great catastrophe in which a third of
their people perished to be convinced of the world's hostility. Not only
has their conviction of the eternal and ubiquitous nature of anti-Semitism
been the most potent ideological factor in the Zionist involvement since
the Dreyfus Affair; it must also have been the cause of the otherwise
inexplicable readiness of the German-Jewish community to negotiate
with the Nazi authorities during the early stages of the regime. This
conviction produced a fatal inability to distinguish between friend and
foe; the German Jews underestimated their enemies because they somehow thought that all Gentiles were alike.

The contrast between Israeli heroism and the submissive meekness
with which Jews went to their death—arriving on time at the transportation points, walking under their own power to the places of execution,
digging their own graves, undressing and making neat piles of their
clothing, and lying down side by side to be shot—seemed a telling point,
and the prosecutor, asking witness after witness, "Why did you not protest?," "Why did you board the train?," "Fifteen thousand people were
standing there and hundreds of guards facing you—why didn't you revolt
and charge and attack these guards?," harped on it for all it was worth.
But the sad truth of the matter is that the point was ill taken, for no non-
Jewish group or non-Jewish people had behaved differently. Sixteen
years ago, while still under the direct impact of the events, a former
French inmate of Buchenwald, David Rousset, described, in *Les Jours de
Notre Mort*, the logic that obtained in all concentration camps: "The
triumph of the S.S. demands that the tortured victim allow himself to be
led to the noose without protesting, that he renounce and abandon himself to the point of ceasing to affirm his identity. And it is not for nothing. It is not gratuitously, out of sheer sadism, that the S.S. men desire

his defeat. They know that the system which succeeds in destroying its victim before he mounts the scaffold . . . is incomparably the best for keeping a whole people in slavery. In submission. Nothing is more terrible than these processions of human beings going like dummies to their death." The court received no answer to this cruel and silly question, but one could easily have found an answer had he permitted his imagination to dwell for a few minutes on the fate of those Dutch Jews who in 1941, in the old Jewish quarter of Amsterdam, dared to attack a German security police detachment. Four hundred and thirty Jews were arrested in reprisal, and they were literally tortured to death, being sent first to Buchenwald and then to the Austrian camp of Mauthausen. Month after month, they died a thousand deaths, and every single one of them would have envied his brethren in Auschwitz had he known about them. There exist many things considerably worse than death, and the S.S. saw to it that none of them was ever very far from the mind and imagination of their victims. In this respect, perhaps even more significantly than in others, the deliberate attempt in Jerusalem to tell only the Jewish side of the story distorted the truth, even the Jewish truth. The glory of the uprising in the Warsaw ghetto and the heroism of the few others who fought back lay precisely in their having refused the comparatively easy death that the Nazis offered them—before the firing squad or in the gas chamber. And the witnesses in Jerusalem who testified to resistance and rebellion, to "the small place the uprising had in this history of the holocaust," confirmed the known fact that only the very young had been capable of taking the "decision that we cannot go and be slaughtered like sheep."

In one respect, Ben-Gurion's expectations for the trial were not altogether disappointed, for it did indeed become an important instrument for ferreting out other Nazis and criminals—but not in the Arab countries, which had openly offered refuge to hundreds of them. The wartime relationship between the Grand Mufti of Jerusalem and the Nazis was no secret; he had hoped they would help him in the implementation of some "Final Solution" of the Jewish question in the Near East. Hence, newspapers in Damascus and Beirut, in Cairo and Amman, did not hide their sympathy for Eichmann or their regret that he had not "finished the job"; a broadcast from Cairo on the day the trial opened went as far as to inject a slightly anti-German note into its comments, complaining that there was not "a single incident in which one German plane flew over one Jewish settlement [in Palestine] and dropped one bomb on it throughout the last world war." That Arab nationalists have been in sympathy with Nazism is notorious, and neither Ben-Gurion nor this trial was needed "to ferret them out"; they were never in hiding. The trial revealed only that all rumors about Eichmann's connection with Haj Amin el Husseini, the wartime Mufti of Jerusalem, were unfounded. (Along with other departmental heads, he had once been introduced to the Mufti during a reception at an S.S. office in Berlin.) Documents produced by the prosecution showed that the Mufti had been in close contact with the German Foreign Office and with Himmler, but this was nothing new. But if Ben-Gurion's remark about "the connection between the Nazis and some Arab rulers" was pointless, his failure to mention present-day West Germany in this context was surprising. Of course, it was reassuring to hear that Israel "does not hold Adenauer responsible for Hitler," and that "for us a decent German, although he belongs to the same nation that twenty years ago helped to murder millions of Jews, is a decent human being." (There was no mention of decent Arabs.) While the German Federal Republic has not yet recognized the State of Israel—presumably out of fear that the Arab countries might thereupon recognize Ulbricht's Germany—it has paid seven hundred and thirty seven million dollars in reparation to Israel during the last ten years; the reparation payments will soon come to an end, and Israel is now trying to arrange with West Germany for a long-term loan. Hence, the relationship between the two countries, and particularly the personal relationship between Ben-Gurion and Adenauer, has been quite good, and if, as an aftermath of the trial, some deputies in the Knesset, the Israeli Parliament, succeeded in imposing certain restraints on the cultural-exchange program with West Germany, this certainly was not hoped for, or even foreseen, by Ben-Gurion. It is more noteworthy that he did not foresee, or did not care to mention, the fact that Eichmann's capture would trigger the first serious effort made by West Germans to bring to trial at least those war criminals who were directly implicated in murder. The Central Agency for the Investigation of Nazi Crimes, which was belatedly set up by the eleven West German states in 1958 (barely two years before—in May, 1960—the West German statute of limitations wiped out all offenses except first-degree murder, for which the time limit is twenty years), and of which Prosecutor Erwin Schüle is the head, had run into all kinds of difficulties, caused partly by the unwillingness of German witnesses to cooperate and partly by the unwillingness of the local courts to prosecute on the basis of material sent to them from the Central Agency. It was not that the trial in Jerusalem produced any important new evidence of the kind needed for the discovery of Eichmann's associates but that the news of Eichmann's sensational capture and the prospect of his trial had an impact strong enough to persuade the local courts to use Mr. Schüle's findings and to overcome the native reluctance to do anything about the "murderers in our midst" by the time-honored expedient of posting rewards for the capture of well-known criminals.

The results were amazing. Seven months after Eichmann's arrival in Jerusalem—and four months before the opening of the trial—Richard Baer, successor to Rudolf Höss as commandant of Auschwitz, was finally arrested. Then, in rapid succession, most of the members of the so-called Eichmann Commando—Franz Novak, Eichmann's transportation officer, who had been living as a printer in Austria; Dr. Otto Hunsche, his legal expert and his assistant in Hungary, who had settled as a lawyer in West Germany; Hermann Krumey, Eichmann's second in command in Hungary, who had become a druggist; Gustav Richter, former "Jewish adviser" in Rumania; and Dr. Günther Zöpf, who had filled the same post in Amsterdam—were arrested, too. (Although evidence against these five had been published in Germany years before, in books and magazine articles, not one of them had found it necessary to live under an assumed name.) For the first time since the close of the war, German newspapers were full of stories about trials of Nazi criminals—all of them mass murderers—and the reluctance of the local courts to prosecute these crimes still showed itself in the fantastically lenient sentences meted out to those convicted. (Thus, Dr. Hunsche, who was personally responsible for a last-minute deportation of some twelve hundred Hungarian Jews, of whom at least six hundred were killed, received a sentence of five years of hard labor; Dr. Otto Bradfisch, of the *Einsatzgruppen,* the mobile killing units of the S.S. in the East, was sentenced to ten years of hard labor for the killing of fifteen thousand Jews; and Joseph Lechthaler, who had "liquidated" the Jewish inhabitants of Slutsk and Smolevichi, in Russia, was sentenced to three years and six months.) Among the new arrests were people of great prominence under the Nazis, most of whom had already been denazified by the German courts. One was S.S. *Obergruppenführer* Karl Wolff, former chief of Himmler's personal staff, who, according to a document submitted in 1946 at Nuremberg, had greeted "with particular joy" the news that "for two weeks now a train has been carrying, every day, five thousand members of the Chosen People" from Warsaw to Treblinka, one of the Eastern killing centers. He still awaits trial. The trial of Wilhelm Koppe, who had at first managed the gassing of Jews in Chelmno and then become the successor of Friedrich-Wilhelm Krüger in Poland, in a high post in the S.S. whose duties included making Poland *judenrein* (Jew-clean)—in postwar West Germany, he was the director of a chocolate factory—has not yet taken place. Occasional harsh sentences were even less reassuring, for they were meted out to offenders like Erich von dem Bach-Zelewski, a former S.S. *Obergruppenführer.* He was tried in 1961 for his participation in the Röhm rebellion in 1934, was sentenced to four and a half years, and then was indicted again in 1962 for the killing of six German Communists in 1933, tried before a jury in Nuremberg, and sentenced to life. Neither indictment mentioned that Bach-Zelewski had been anti-partisan chief on the Russian front or that he had participated in the Jewish massacres at Minsk and Mogilev, in White Russia. Should a German court, on the pretext that war crimes are no crimes, make "ethnic distinctions"? And is it possible that what was an unusually harsh sentence (for a German postwar court) was arrived at because Bach-Zelewski was among the very few Nazi leaders who had tried to protect Jews from the *Einsatzgruppen,* suffered a nervous breakdown after the mass killings, and testified for the prosecution in Nuremberg? (He was also the only such leader who in 1952 had denounced himself publicly for mass murder, but he was never prosecuted for it.) There is little hope that things will change now, even though the Adenauer administration has been forced to weed out of the judiciary a hundred and forty–odd judges and prosecutors, along with many police officers, with a more than ordinarily compromising past, and to dismiss the chief prosecutor of the Federal Supreme Court, Wolfgang Immerwahr Fränkel, because, his middle name notwithstanding, he had been less than candid when he was asked about his Nazi past. It has been estimated that of the eleven thousand five hundred judges in the *Bundesrepublik,* five thousand were active in the courts under the Hitler regime. In November, 1962, shortly after the purging of the judiciary and six months after Eichmann's name had disappeared from the news, the long-awaited trial of Martin Fellenz took place at Flensburg in an almost empty courtroom. The former Higher S.S. and Police Leader, who had been a prominent member of the Free Democratic Party in Adenauer's Germany, was arrested in June, 1960, a few weeks after Eichmann's capture. He was accused of participation in, and partial responsibility for, the murder of forty thousand Jews in Poland. After more than six weeks of detailed testimony, the prosecutor demanded the maximum penalty—a life sentence, to be served at hard labor. And the court sentenced him to four years, two and a half of which he had already served while waiting in jail.

Nevertheless, there can be no doubt that the Eichmann trial had its deepest and most far-reaching consequences in Germany. The attitude of the German people toward their own past, which all experts on the German question had puzzled over for fifteen years, could hardly have been more clearly demonstrated: they themselves did not care much about it one way or the other, and did not particularly mind the presence of murderers at large in the country, since none of these particular murderers were likely to commit murder now, of their own free will; however, if world opinion—or, rather, what the Germans call *das Ausland*, collecting all countries outside Germany into a singular noun—became obstinate and demanded that these people be punished, they were perfectly willing to oblige, at least up to a point. When Eichmann was captured, Chancellor Adenauer had foreseen embarrassment and had voiced a fear that the trial would "stir up again all the horrors" and produce a new wave of anti-German feeling throughout the world—as it did. During the ten months that Israel needed to prepare the trial, Germany was busy bracing herself against its predictable results by showing an unprecedented zeal for searching out and prosecuting Nazi criminals within the country. At no time, however, did either the German authorities or any significant segment of public opinion demand Eichmann's extradition, which seemed the obvious move, since every sovereign state is jealous of its right to sit in judgment on its own offenders. (The official objection of the Adenauer government that such a move was not possible because there existed no extradition treaty between Israel and West Germany is not valid; it meant only that Israel could not have been forced to extradite. Fritz Bauer, Attorney General of Hessen, applied to the federal government in Bonn to start extradition proceedings. But Mr. Bauer's feelings in this matter were the feelings of a German Jew, and they were not shared by German public opinion. His application was not only refused by Bonn, it was hardly noticed and remained totally unsupported. Another argument against extradition, offered by the observers the West German government sent to Jerusalem, was that Germany had abolished capital punishment and hence was unable to mete out the sentence Eichmann deserved. In view of the leniency shown by German courts to Nazi murderers, it was difficult not to suspect that this objection was made in bad faith. Surely, the greatest political hazard of an Eichmann trial in Germany would have been that a German court might not have given him the maximum penalty under German law.)

Another aspect of the matter was at once more delicate and more relevant to the political situation in Germany. It was one thing to ferret out mass murderers and other criminals from their hiding places, and it was another thing to find them prominent and active in the public realm—to encounter innumerable men in the federal and state administrations whose careers had bloomed under the Hitler regime. To be sure, if the Adenauer administration had been too sensitive in employing officials with a compromising Nazi past, there might have been no administration at all. For the truth is, of course, the exact opposite of what Dr. Adenauer asserted it to be when he said that only "a relatively small percentage" of Germans had been Nazis, and that "a great majority were happy to help their Jewish fellow-citizens when they could." (At least one West German newspaper, the *Frankfurter Rundschau*, asked itself the obvious question, long overdue—why so many people who must have known, for instance, the record of Wolfgang Immerwahr Frankel had kept silent—and then came up with the even more obvious answer: "Because they themselves felt incriminated.") The logic of the Eichmann trial, as Ben-Gurion conceived of it—a trial stressing general issues, to the detriment of legal niceties—would have demanded exposure of the complicity of all German bureaus and authorities in the so-called Final Solution of the Jewish question; of all civil servants in the state ministries; of the regular armed forces, with their General Staff; of the judiciary; and of the business world. But although the prosecution went as far afield as to put witness after witness on the stand who testified to things that, while gruesome and true enough, had only the slightest connection, or none, with the deeds of the accused, it carefully avoided touching upon this highly explosive matter—upon the almost ubiquitous complicity, stretching far beyond the ranks of the Party membership. (There were widespread rumors prior to the trial that Eichmann had named "several hundred prominent personalities of the Federal Republic as his accomplices," but these rumors were not true. In his opening speech, Mr. Hausner still mentioned Eichmann's "accomplices in the crime [who] were neither gangsters nor men of the underworld," and promised that we should "encounter them—the doctors and lawyers, scholars, bankers, and economists—in those councils that resolved to exterminate the Jews." This promise was not kept—nor could it have been kept in the form in which it was made, for in the Nazi regime there were no "councils that resolved" anything, and the "robed dignitaries with academic degrees" made no decision to exterminate the Jews; they came together only to plan the necessary steps in carrying out an order given by Hitler.) Still, one case of complicity was brought to the attention of the court—that of Dr. Hans Globke, who, more than twenty-five years ago, was co-author of an infamous commentary on the Nuremberg Laws and, somewhat later, author of the brilliant idea of compelling all German Jews to take "Israel" or "Sarah" as a middle name, and who is today one of Adenauer's closest advisers. And Globke's name—and only his name—was inserted into the proceedings by the defense, and probably only in the hope of "persuading" the Adenauer government to start proceedings to extradite Eichmann. Still, former Ministry Official and present Undersecretary of State Globke doubtless had more right than the former Mufti of Jerusalem to figure in the history of what the Jews had actually suffered at the hands of the Nazis.

And it was history that, as far as the prosecution was concerned, stood at the center of the trial. "It is not an individual that is in the dock at this historic trial, and not the Nazi regime alone," Ben-Gurion said, "but anti-Semitism throughout history." The tone set by Ben-Gurion was faithfully followed by Hausner. He began his opening address (which lasted through three sessions) with Pharaoh In Egypt and Haman's decree "to destroy, to slay, and to cause them [the Jews] to perish." He then proceeded to quote from Ezekiel's words "And when I passed by thee, and saw thee polluted in thine own blood, I said unto thee: 'In thy blood, live!,'" explaining that they must be understood as "the imperative that has confronted this nation ever since its first appearance on the stage of history." It was bad history and cheap rhetoric; worse, it was clearly at cross-purposes with putting Eichmann on trial at all, since it suggested that perhaps he was only an innocent executor of some mysteriously foreordained destiny, or even, for that matter, of anti-Semitism, which had been necessary to blaze the trail of "the bloodstained road travelled by this people" to fulfill its destiny. A few sessions later, after Salo W. Baron, Professor of Jewish History at Columbia University, had testified to the more recent history of Eastern European Jewry, Dr. Servatius could no longer resist temptation and asked the obvious questions: "Why did all this bad luck fall upon the Jewish people?" and "Don't you think that irrational motives are at the basis of the fate of this people? Beyond the understanding of a human being?" Is not there perhaps something like "the spirit of history, which brings history forward . . . without the influence of men?" Is not Mr. Hausner basically in agreement with "the school of historical law"—an allusion to Hegel—and has he not shown that what "the leaders do will not always lead to the aim and destination they wanted?" And Dr. Servatius added, "Here the intention was to destroy the Jewish people and the objective was not reached and a new flourishing state came into being." The argument of the defense had now come perilously close to the newest anti-Semitic theory about the Elders of Zion, which had been set forth in all seriousness a few weeks earlier in the old Egyptian National Assembly by Hussain Zulficar Sabri, Nasser's Deputy Foreign Minister: Hitler was innocent of the slaughter of the Jews; he was a victim of the Zionists, who had compelled "Hitler to perpetrate crimes and to create the legend that would eventually enable them to achieve their aim—the creation of the State of Israel." Except that Dr. Servatius, following the philosophy of history expounded by the prosecutor, had put History in the place of the Elders of Zion.

Despite the intentions of Ben-Gurion and the efforts of the prosecution, there remained an individual in the dock, a person of flesh and blood, and even if Ben-Gurion, as he claimed, did not "care what verdict is delivered against Eichmann," it was undeniably the sole task of the Jerusalem court to deliver one.

FROM

IN COLD BLOOD: THE CORNER

Truman Capote

OCTOBER 16, 1965

NSTITUTIONAL DOURNESS AND cheerful domesticity coexist on the fourth floor of the Finney County Courthouse, in Garden City, Kansas. The presence of the county jail supplies the first quality, and the so-called Sheriff's Residence, a pleasant apartment separated from the five cells that make up the jail proper by steel doors and a short corridor, accounts for the second. For the last three years, the Sheriff's Residence has in fact been occupied not by the sheriff, Earl Robinson, but by the under-sheriff and his wife, Wendle and Josephine—or Josie—Meier. The Meiers have been married more than twenty years. They are much alike—tall people with weight and strength to spare, with wide hands, with square and calm faces, and a kindly look, the last being especially true of Mrs. Meier, a direct and practical woman who nevertheless seems illuminated by a quite mystical serenity. As the under-sheriff's helpmate, she puts in long hours; between five in the morning, when she begins the day by reading a chapter in the Bible, and 10 P.M., her bedtime, she cooks for the prisoners, sews and darns for them, does their laundry, takes splendid care of her husband, and looks after the five-room Sheriff's Residence, with its *gemütlich* mélange of plump hassocks and squashy chairs and cream-colored lace window curtains. The Meiers have one child, a daughter, who is married to a Kansas City policeman, so the couple live alone—or, as Mrs. Meier more correctly puts it, "alone except for whoever happens to be in the ladies' cell."

The jail actually contains six cells. The sixth, the one reserved for female prisoners, is actually an isolated unit situated inside the Sheriff's Residence; indeed, it adjoins the Meiers' kitchen. "But that don't worry me," says Josie Meier. "I enjoy the company. Having somebody to talk to while I'm doing my kitchen work. Most of those women, you got to feel sorry for them. Just met up with Old Man Trouble is all. Course, Smith and Hickock was a different matter. Far as I know, Perry Smith was the first man ever stayed in the ladies' cell. The reason was the sheriff wanted to keep him and Hickock separated from each other until after their trial." Perry Edward Smith and Richard Eugene Hickock were a young pair of ex-convicts who had confessed that in November of 1959 they murdered in his home a prominent Finney County farm rancher, Herbert W. Clutter, and three members of his family: his wife, Bonnie; their sixteen-year-old daughter, Nancy; and a son, Kenyon, fifteen. Smith and Hickock were arrested on December 30, 1959, in Las Vegas, Nevada; on January 6, 1960, they were returned to Garden City to await trial. Robbery and a desire to avoid the consequences of possible identification were the confessed motives for the crime.

"The afternoon they brought them in, I made six apple pies and baked some bread and all the while kept track of the goings on down there on Courthouse Square," Josie recalls. "My kitchen window overlooks the square; you couldn't want a better view. I'm no judge of crowds, but I'd guess there were several hundred people waiting to see the boys that killed the Clutter family. I never met any of the Clutters myself, but from everything I've ever heard about them they must have been very fine people. What happened to them is hard to forgive, and I know Wendle was worried how the crowd might act when they caught sight of Smith and Hickock. He was afraid somebody might try to get at them. So I kind of had my heart in my mouth when I saw the cars arrive, saw the reporters—all the newspaper fellows running and pushing. But by then it was dark, after six, and bitter cold, and more than half the crowd had given up and gone home. The ones that stayed, they didn't say boo. Only stared. Later, when they brought the boys upstairs, the first one I saw was Hickock. He had on light summer pants and just an old cloth shirt. Surprised he didn't catch pneumonia, considering how cold it was. But he looked sick, all right. White as a ghost. Well, it must be a terrible experience—to be stared at by a horde of strangers, to have to walk among them, and them knowing who you are and what you did. Then they brought up Smith. I had some supper ready to serve them in their cells—hot soup and coffee and some sandwiches and pie. Ordinarily, we feed just twice a day—breakfast at seven-thirty, and at four-thirty we serve the main meal—but I didn't want those fellows going to bed on an empty stomach; seemed to me they must be feeling bad enough without that. But when I took Smith his supper—carried it in on a tray—he said he wasn't hungry. He was looking out the window of the ladies' cell. Standing with his back to me. That window has the same view as my kitchen window—trees and the square and the tops of houses. I told him, 'Just taste the soup—it's vegetable, and not out of a can. I made it myself. The pie, too.' In about an hour, I went back for the tray, and he hadn't touched a crumb. He was still at the window. Like he hadn't moved. It was snowing, and I remember saying it was the first snow of the year, and how we'd had such a beautiful long autumn right till then. And now the snow had come. And then I asked him if he had any special dish he liked—if he did, I'd try and fix it for him the next day. He turned round and looked at me. Suspicious. Like I might be mocking him. Then he said something about a movie; he had such a quiet way of speaking— almost a whisper. Wanted to know if I had seen a movie—I forget the name. Anyway, I hadn't seen it; never have been much for picture shows. He said this show took place in Biblical times, and there was a scene where a man was flung off a balcony, thrown to a mob of men and women, who tore him to pieces. And he said that was what came to mind when he saw the crowd on the square. The man being torn apart. And the idea that maybe that was what they might do to him. Said it scared him so bad his stomach still hurt. Which was why he couldn't eat. Course, he was wrong, and I told him so—nobody was going to harm him, regardless of what he'd done; folks around here aren't like that. We talked some—he was very shy—but after a while he said, 'One thing I really like is Spanish rice.' So I promised to make him some, and he smiled, kind of, and I decided—well, he wasn't the worst young man I ever saw. That night, after I'd gone to bed, I said as much to my husband. But Wendle snorted. Wendle was one of the first on the scene after the crime was discovered. He said he wished I'd been out at the Clutter place when they found the bodies. Then I could've judged for myself just how *gentle* Mr. Smith was. Him and his friend Hickock. He said they'd cut out your heart and never bat an eye. There was no denying it. Not with four people dead. And I lay awake wondering if either one was bothered by it—the thought of those four graves."

. . .

A month passed, and another, and it snowed some part of almost every day. Snow whitened the wheat-tawny countryside, heaped the streets of the town, hushed them. The topmost branches of a snow-laden elm touched the window of the ladies' cell. Squirrels lived in the tree, and Perry, after weeks of tempting them with scraps left over from breakfast, lured one off a branch onto the window sill and through the bars. It was a male squirrel, with auburn fur. He named the squirrel Big Red, and Big Red soon settled down, apparently content to share his friend's captivity. Perry taught him several tricks—to play with a paper ball, to beg, to perch on his shoulder. All this helped to pass time, but still there were many hours the prisoner had somehow to lose. He was not allowed to read newspapers, and he was bored by the magazines Mrs. Meier lent him—old issues of *Good Housekeeping* and *McCall's*. But he found things to do: file his fingernails with an emery board and buff them to a silky pink sheen; comb and comb his lotion-soaked-and-scented hair; brush his teeth three and four times a day; shave and shower almost as often. And he kept the cell, which contained a toilet, a washbasin, a shower stall, a cot, a chair, and a table, as neat as his person. He was proud of a compliment Mrs. Meier had paid him. "Look!" she had said, pointing at his bunk. "Look at that blanket! You could bounce dimes." But it was at the table that he spent most of his waking life. He ate his meals there; it was where he sat when he sketched portraits of Big Red and did drawings of flowers, and the face of Jesus, and the faces and torsos of imaginary women; and it was where, on cheap sheets of ruled paper, he made diarylike notes of day-to-day occurrences.

"*Thursday 7 January. Dewey here. Brought carton cigarettes. Also typed copies of Statement for my signature. I declined.*" The "Statement," a seventy-eight-page document he had dictated to the Finney County court stenographer, recounted admissions—including the murder of the Clutter father and son—that he had already made to Alvin Dewey and Clarence Duntz, Special Agents of the Kansas Bureau of Investigation, who had questioned him in Las Vegas after his arrest. Dewey, speaking of his encounter with Perry Smith on January 7th, remembered that he had been "very surprised" when Perry refused to sign the statement. "It wasn't important," Dewey said. "I could always testify in court as to the oral confession he'd made to Duntz and myself. And, of course, Hickock had given us a signed confession while we were still in Las Vegas—in which he accused Smith of having committed all four murders. But I was curious. I asked Perry why he'd changed his mind. And he said, 'Everything in my statement is accurate except for two details. If you'll let me correct those items, then I'll sign it.' Well, I could guess the items he meant. Because the only serious difference between his story and Hickock's was that he denied having murdered the Clutters singlehanded. Until now, he'd sworn Hickock killed Nancy and her mother. And I was right! That's just what he wanted to do—admit that Hickock had been telling the truth, and that it was he, Perry Smith, who had shot and killed the whole family. He said he'd lied about it because, in his words, 'I wanted to fix Dick. For being such a coward. Dropping his guts all over the goddam floor.' And the reason he'd decided to set the record straight wasn't that he suddenly felt any kinder toward Hickock. According to him, he was doing it out of consideration for Hickock's parents—said he was sorry for Dick's mother. Said, 'She's a real sweet person. It might be some comfort to her to know Dick never pulled the trigger. None of it would have happened without him—in a way, it was mostly his fault—but the fact remains I'm the one who killed them.' But I wasn't certain I believed it. Not to the extent of letting him alter his statement. As I say, we weren't dependent on a formal confession from Smith to prove any part of our case. With or without it, we had enough to hang them ten times over." Among the elements contributing to Dewey's confidence was the recovery of a radio and a pair of binoculars that the murderers had stolen from the Clutter house and eventually disposed of in Mexico City (where a K.B.I. agent named Harold Nye, having flown there for the purpose, traced them to a pawnshop). Moreover, Perry, while dictating his statement, had revealed the whereabouts of other potent evidence. "We hit the highway and drove east," he'd said, in the process of describing what he and Dick had done after leaving Holcomb, the village where the murders took place. "Drove like hell, Dick driving. I think we both felt very high. I did. Very high, and very relieved at the same time. Couldn't stop laughing, neither one of us. Suddenly it all seemed very funny—I don't know why, it just did. But the gun was dripping blood, and my clothes were stained—there was even blood in my hair. So we turned off onto a country road, and drove maybe eight miles, till we were way out on the prairie. You could hear coyotes. We smoked a cigarette, and Dick went on making jokes. About what had happened back there. I got out of the car and siphoned some water out of the water tank and washed the blood off the gun barrel. Then I scraped a hole in the ground with Dick's hunting knife—the one I used on Mr. Clutter—and buried in it the empty shells and all the leftover nylon cord and adhesive tape. After that, we drove till we came to U.S. 83, and headed east toward Kansas City and Olathe [Hickock's home town]. Around dawn, Dick stopped at one of those picnic places—what they call rest areas—where they have open fireplaces. We built a fire and burned stuff. The gloves we'd worn, and my shirt. Dick said he wished we had an ox to roast; he said he'd never been so hungry. It was almost noon when we got to Olathe. Dick dropped me at my hotel, and went on home to have Sunday dinner with his family. Yes, he took the knife with him. The gun, too." K.B.I. agents were dispatched to Hickock's home, a four-room farmhouse near Olathe, and they found the knife inside a fishing-tackle box and the shotgun casually propped against a kitchen wall. (Hickock's father, who refused to believe that his "boy" could have taken part in such a "horrible crime," insisted that the gun hadn't been out of the house since the first week in November, and therefore couldn't be the death weapon.) As for the empty cartridge shells, the cord, and the tape, these were retrieved with the aid of Virgil Pietz, a county-road worker, who, using a road grader in the area pinpointed by Perry Smith, shaved away the earth inch by inch until the buried articles were uncovered. Thus the last loose strings were tied. The K.B.I. had now assembled an unshakable case, for the tests established that the shells had been discharged by Hickock's shotgun, and the remnants of cord and tape were of a piece with the materials used to bind and silence the victims.

"*Monday 11 January. Have a lawyer. Mr. Fleming. Old man with red tie.*" Having been informed by the defendants that they were without funds to hire legal counsel, the court, in the person of District Judge Roland H. Tate, appointed as their representatives two local lawyers, Arthur Fleming and Harrison Smith. Fleming, who was seventy-one, was a former mayor of Garden City, a short man who habitually enlivened an unsensational appearance with rather conspicuous neck-wear. He resisted the assignment. "I do not desire to serve," he told the judge. "But if the court sees fit to appoint me, then, of course, I have no choice." Hickock's attorney, Harrison Smith, was forty-five, six feet tall, a golfer, and an Elk of exalted degree. He accepted the task with resigned grace: "Someone has to do it. And I'll do my best. Though I doubt that'll make me too popular around here."

"*Friday 15 January. Mrs. Meier playing radio in her kitchen and I heard man say the County Attorney will seek Death Penalty. 'The rich never hang. Only the poor and friendless.'"* In making his announcement, the County Attorney, Duane West, an ambitious, portly man of twenty-eight who looks forty, told newsmen that day, "If the case goes before a jury, I will request the jury, upon finding them guilty, to sentence them to the death penalty. If the defendants waive right to jury trial and enter a plea of guilty before the judge, I will request the judge to set the death penalty. This was a matter I knew I would be called upon to decide, and my decision has not been arrived at lightly. I feel that, due to the violence of the crime and the apparent utter lack of mercy shown the victims, the only way the public can be absolutely protected is to have the death penalty set against these defendants. This is especially true since in Kansas there is no such thing as life imprisonment without possibility of parole. Persons sentenced to life imprisonment actually serve, on the average, less than fifteen years."

"Wednesday 20 January. Asked to take lie-detector in regards to this Walker deal." A case like the Clutter case—a crime of such magnitude—arouses the interest of law-enforcement men everywhere, and particularly those investigators burdened with similar but unsolved crimes, for it is always possible that the solution to one mystery will solve another. Among the many officers alert to events in Garden City was the sheriff of Sarasota County, which includes Osprey, Florida, a fishing settlement not far from Tampa, and the scene, slightly more than a month after the Clutter tragedy, of a quadruple slaying on an isolated cattle-raising ranch. Again the victims were four members of a family—a young couple, Mr. and Mrs. Clifford Walker, and their two children, a boy and a girl, all of whom had been shot in the head with a rifle. Parallels aside, there was another circumstance that made Smith and Hickock first-class suspects: on the nineteenth of December, the date of the Walker murders, the Clutter murderers had spent the night in a Tallahassee hotel. Not unnaturally, Osprey's sheriff, who had no other leads whatever, was anxious to have the two men questioned and a polygraph examination administered. Dick consented to take the test, and so did Perry, who told Kansas authorities he had seen reports of the slaying in a Miami newspaper: "I remarked at the time, I said to Dick, I'll bet whoever did this must be somebody that read about what happened out here in Kansas. A nut." The results of the test—to the dismay of Alvin Dewey, who does not believe in extraordinary coincidences—were decisively negative. The murderer of the Walker family remains unknown.

"Sunday 31 January. Dick's dad here to visit Dick. Said hello when I saw him go past [the cell door] *but he kept going. Could be he never heard me. Understand from Mrs. M* [Meier] *that Mrs. H* [Hickock] *didn't come because she felt too bad to. Snowing like a bitch. Dreamed last night I was up in Alaska with Dad—woke up in a puddle of cold urine!!!"* Mr. Hickock spent three hours with his son. Afterward, he walked through the snow to the Garden City depot, a work-worn old man, stooped and thinned down by cancer, which would kill him a few months later. At the station, while he was waiting for a homeward-bound train, he spoke to a reporter: "I seen Dick, uh-huh. We had a long talk. And I can guarantee you it's not like people say. Or what's put in the papers. Those boys didn't go to that house planning to do violence. My boy didn't. He may have some bad sides, but he's nowhere near bad as that. Smitty's the one. Dick told me he didn't even know it when Smitty attacked the man [Mr. Clutter]— cut his throat. Dick wasn't even in the same room. He only run in when he heard them struggling. Dick was carrying his shotgun, and how he described it was 'Smitty took my shotgun and just blew that man's head off.' And he says, 'Dad, I ought to have grabbed back the gun and shot Smitty dead. Killed him 'fore he killed the rest of that family. If I'd done it, I'd be better off than I am now.' I guess he would, too. How it is, the way folks feel, he don't stand no chance. They'll hang them both. And having your boy hang, knowing he will—nothing worse can happen to a man."

Perry Smith's only living relatives were his father and a sister, and neither of them wrote to him or came to see him. The father, Tex John Smith, was presumed to be prospecting for gold somewhere in Alaska— though investigators, despite great efforts, had been unable to locate him. The sister, on the other hand, had told investigators that she was afraid of her brother, and requested that they please not let him know her address. (When Perry was informed of this, he smiled slightly and said, "I wish she'd been in that house that night. What a sweet scene!") Except for the squirrel, and except for the Meiers and an occasional consultation with his lawyer, Mr. Fleming, he was very much alone. He missed Dick. *"Many thoughts of Dick,"* he wrote in his makeshift diary one day. Since their arrest, they had not been allowed to communicate, and, freedom apart, that was what he most desired—to talk to Dick, be with him again. Dick was not the "hard rock" that Perry had once thought him— "pragmatic," "virile," "a real brass boy." He had proved to be "pretty weak and shallow," "a coward." Still, of everyone in all the world, this, for the moment, was the person to whom he was closest, for at least they were of the same species, brothers in the breed of Cain, and, separated from Dick, Perry felt "all by myself. Like somebody covered with sores. Somebody only a big nut would have anything to do with."

But then, one morning in mid-February, Perry received a letter. It was postmarked Reading, Massachusetts, and it went, "Dear Perry, I was sorry to hear about the trouble you are in and I decided to write and let you know that I remember you and would like to help you in any way that I can. In case you don't remember my name, Don Cullivan, I've enclosed a picture taken at about the time we met. When I first read about you in the news recently I was startled and then I began to think back to those days when I knew you. While we were never close personal friends I can remember you a lot more clearly than most fellows I met in the Army. It must have been about the fall of 1951 when you were assigned to the 761st Engineer Light Equipment Company at Fort Lewis, Washington. You were short (I'm not much taller), solidly built, dark with a heavy shock of black hair and a grin on your face almost all the time. Since you had lived in Alaska quite a few of the fellows used to call you 'Eskimo.' One of my first recollections of you was at a Company inspection in which all footlockers were open for inspection. As I recall it all the footlockers were in order, even yours, except that the inside cover of your footlocker was plastered with pictures of pin-up girls. The rest of us were sure you were in for trouble. But the inspecting officer took it in stride and when it was all over and he let it pass I think we felt you were a nervy guy. I remember that you were a fairly good pool player and I can picture you quite clearly in the Company day room at the pool table. You were one of the best truck drivers in the outfit. Remember the Army field problems we went out on? On one trip that took place in the winter I remember that we each were assigned to a truck for the duration of the problem. In our outfit, Army trucks had no heaters and it used to get pretty cold in those cabs. I remember you cutting a hole in the floorboards of your truck in order to let the heat from the engine come into the cab. The reason I remember this so well is the impression it made on me because 'mutilation' of Army property was a crime for which you could get severely punished. Of course I was pretty green in the Army and probably afraid to stretch the rules even a little bit, but I can remember you grinning about it (and keeping warm) while I worried about it (and froze). I recall that you bought a motorcycle, and vaguely remember you had some trouble with it—chased by the police?—crackup? Whatever it was, it was the first time I realized the wild streak in you. Some of my recollections may be wrong; this was over eight years ago and I only knew you for a period of about eight months. From what I remember, though, I got along with you very well and rather liked you. You always seemed cheerful and cocky, you were good at your Army work and I can't remember that you did much griping. Of course you were apparently quite wild but I never knew too much about that. But now you are in real trouble. I try to imagine what you are like now. What you think about. When first I read about you I was stunned. I really was. But then I put the paper down and turned to something else. But the thought of you returned. I wasn't satisfied just to forget. I am, or try to be, fairly religious [Catholic]. I wasn't always. I used to just drift along with little thought about the only important thing there is. I never considered death or the possibility of a life hereafter. I was too much alive: car, college, dating etc. But my kid brother died of leukemia when he was just 17 years old. He knew he was dying and afterward I used to wonder what he thought about. And now I think of you, and wonder what you think about. I didn't know what to say to my brother in the last weeks before he died. But I know what I'd say now. And this is why I am writing you: because God made you as well as me and He loves you just as He loves me, and for the little we know of God's will what has happened to you could have happened to me. Your friend, Don Cullivan."

The name meant nothing, but Perry at once recognized the face in the photograph—a young soldier with crew-cut hair and round, very earnest eyes. He read the letter many times; though he found the religious passages unpersuasive ("I've tried to believe, but I don't, I can't, and there's no use pretending"), he was thrilled by it. Here was someone offering help, a sane and respectable man who had once known and liked him, a man who signed himself "friend."

Gratefully, in great haste, he started a reply: "Dear Don, Hell yes I remember Don Cullivan. . . ."

. . .

Dick Hickock's cell had no window—he faced a wide corridor and the façades of other cells—but he was not isolated. There were people to talk to—a plentiful turnover of drunkards, forgers, wife beaters, and Mexican vagrants—and Dick, with his light-hearted "con-man" patter, his sex anecdotes and gamy jokes, was popular with the inmates. (There was one, though, who had no use for him whatever—an old man who yelled at him, "Killer! Killer!," and who once drenched him with a bucketful of dirty scrub water.) Outwardly, Hickock seemed to one and all an exceptionally untroubled young man. When he was not talking or sleeping, he lay on his cot smoking or chewing gum and reading sports magazines or paperback thrillers. Often, he simply lay there whistling old favorites ("You Must Have Been a Beautiful Baby," "Shuffle Off to Buffalo") and staring at an unshaded light bulb that burned day and night in the ceiling of the cell. He hated the light bulb's monotonous surveillance; it disturbed his sleep and, more explicitly, endangered the success of a private project—escape. For the prisoner was not as unconcerned as he appeared to be, or as resigned; he intended taking every step possible to avoid "a ride on the Big Swing." Convinced that such a ceremony would be the outcome of any trial—certainly any trial held in the State of Kansas—he had decided to "bust jail, grab a car, and raise dust." But first he must have a weapon, and, over a period of weeks, he had been making one: a shiv, an instrument very like an icepick—something that would fit with lethal niceness between the shoulder blades of Under-sheriff Meier. The components of the weapon—a piece of wood and a piece of hard wire—were originally part of a toilet brush he had appropriated, dismantled, and hidden under his mattress. Late at night, when the only noises were snores and coughs and the lugubrious whistle-wailings of Santa Fe trains rumbling through the darkened town, he honed the wire against the concrete floor of the cell. And while he worked he schemed.

Once, the winter after he finished high school, he had hitchhiked across Kansas and Colorado. "This was when I was looking for a job," he recalled one day. "Well, I was riding in a truck, and the driver, me and him got into a little argument, no reason exactly, but he beat up on me. Shoved me out. Just left me there. High the hell up in the Rockies. It was sleeting, like, and I walked miles, my nose bleeding like fifteen pigs. Then I come to a bunch of cabins on a wooded slope. Summer cabins, all locked up and empty that time of year. And I broke into one of them. There was firewood and canned goods, even some whiskey. I laid up there over a week, and it was one of the best times I ever knew. Despite the fact my nose hurt so and my eyes were green and yellow. But when the snow stopped, the sun came out. You never saw such skies. Like Mexico. If Mexico was in a cold climate. I hunted through the other cabins and found some smoked hams and a radio and a rifle. It was great.

Out all day with a gun. With the sun in my face. Boy, I felt good. I felt like Tarzan. And every night I ate beans and fried ham and rolled up in a blanket by the fire and fell asleep listening to music on the radio. Nobody came near the place. I bet I could've stayed till spring." That, provided the escape succeeded, was the course he had determined upon: to head for the Colorado mountains, and find there a cabin where he could hide until spring—alone, of course. (Perry's future did not concern him.) The prospect of so idyllic an interim added to the inspired stealth with which he whetted his wire, filed it to a limber stiletto fineness.

• • •

"Thursday 10 March. Sheriff had a shake-out. Searched through all the cells and found a shiv tucked under D's mattress. Wonder what he had in mind (smile)." Not that Perry really considered it a smiling matter, for Dick, flourishing a dangerous weapon, could have played a decisive role in plans he himself was forming.

As the weeks went by, Perry had become familiar with life on Courthouse Square—its habitués and their habits. The cats, for example, the two thin gray toms who appeared with every twilight and prowled the square, stopping to examine the cars parked around its periphery: behavior puzzling to him until Mrs. Meier explained that the cats were hunting food—dead birds caught in the vehicles' engine grilles—and thereafter it pained him to watch their mancuvers, "because most of my life I've done what they're doing, the equivalent." And there was one man of whom he had grown especially aware: a robust, upright gentleman with hair like a gray-and-silver skullcap; his face, filled out, firm-jawed, was somewhat cantankerous in repose, the mouth down-curved, the eyes downcast as though in mirthless reverie—a picture of unsparing sternness. And yet this was at least a partly inaccurate impression, for now and again the prisoner glimpsed him as he paused to talk to other men, joke with them, and laugh, and then he seemed carefree, jovial, generous, "the kind of person who might see the human side"—an important attribute, for the man was Roland H. Tate, Judge of the Thirty-second Judicial District, the jurist who would preside at the trial of the State of Kansas vs. Hickock and Smith. The name Tate, as Perry soon learned, was an old and awesome one in western Kansas. The judge was rich, he raised horses, he owned much land, and his wife was said to be very beautiful. He was the father of two sons, but the younger had died—a tragedy that had greatly affected the parents and had led them to adopt a small boy who appeared one day in court as an abandoned, homeless child. "He sounds softhearted to me," Perry once said to Mrs. Meier. "Maybe he'll give us a break." But that was not what Perry really believed. He believed what he'd written to Don Cullivan, with whom he now corresponded regularly: his crime was "unforgivable," and he fully expected to "climb those thirteen steps." However, he was not altogether without hope, for he, too, had plotted an escape. It depended upon a pair of young men whom he had often observed observing him. One was red-haired, the other dark. Sometimes, standing in the square under the tree that touched the cell window, they smiled and signalled to him—or so he imagined. Nothing was ever said, and always, after perhaps a minute, they drifted away. But the prisoner had convinced himself that the young men, possibly motivated by a desire for adventure, meant to help him escape. Accordingly, he drew a map of the square, indicating the points at which a "getaway car" could most advantageously be stationed. Beneath the map he wrote, "I need a Hacksaw Blade 5." Nothing else. But do you realize the consequences if you get caught (nod your head if you do)? It could mean a long stretch in prison. Or you might get killed. All for someone you don't know. YOU BETTER THINK IT OVER!! Seriously! Besides, how do I know I can trust you? How do I know it isn't a trick to get me out there and gun me down? What about Hickock? All preparations must include him." He kept this document on his desk, wadded and ready to drop out the window the next time the young men appeared. But they never did; he never saw them again. Eventually, he wondered if perhaps he had invented them. (He once mentioned a notion that he "might not be normal, maybe insane." This had troubled him "even when I was little," he said, recalling, "My sisters laughed because I liked moonlight. To hide in the shadows and watch the moon.")

Whether the young men were phantoms or not, he ceased to think of them. Another method of escape, suicide, replaced them in his musings, and despite the jailer's precautions (no mirror, no belt or tie or shoelaces), he had devised a way to do it. For in his cell, too, was a ceiling bulb that burned constantly; also, unlike Hickock, he had in his cell a broom, and by pressing the broom brush against the bulb he could unscrew it. One night, he dreamed that he had unscrewed the bulb, broken it, and, with the broken glass, cut his wrists and ankles. "I felt all breath and light leaving me," he said, in a subsequent description of his sensations. "The walls of the cell fell away, the sky came down, I saw the big yellow bird." Throughout his life—as a child, poor and meanly treated; as a foot-loose youth; as an imprisoned man—the yellow bird, huge and parrot-faced, had soared across his dreams, an avenging angel who savaged his enemies or, as now, rescued him in moments of mortal danger. "It lifted me," he said. "I could have been light as a mouse. We went up, up. I could see the square below, men running, yelling, the sheriff shooting at us, everybody sore as hell because I was free, I was flying, I was better than any of *them*."

FROM

THE VILLAGE OF BEN SUC

Jonathan Schell

JULY 15, 1967

U P TO A few months ago, Ben Suc was a prosperous village of some thirty-five hundred people. It had a recorded history going back to the late eighteenth century, when the Nguyen Dynasty, which ruled the southern part of Vietnam, fortified it and used it as a base in its campaign to subjugate the natives of the middle region of the country. In recent years, most of the inhabitants of Ben Suc, which lay inside a small loop of the slowly meandering Saigon River, in Binh Duong Province, about thirty miles from the city of Saigon, were engaged in tilling the exceptionally fertile paddies bordering the river and in tending the extensive orchards of mangoes, jackfruit, and an unusual strain of large grapefruit that is a famous product of the Saigon River region. The village also supported a small group of merchants, most of them of Chinese descent, who ran shops in the marketplace, including a pharmacy that sold a few modern medicines to supplement traditional folk cures of herbs and roots; a bicycle shop that also sold second-hand motor scooters; a hairdresser's; and a few small restaurants, which sold mainly noodles. These merchants were far wealthier than the other villagers; some of them even owned second-hand cars for their businesses. The village had no electricity and little machinery of any kind. Most families kept pigs, chickens, ducks, one or two cows for milk, and a team of water buffaloes for labor, and harvested enough rice and vegetables to sell some in the market every year. Since Ben Suc was a rich village, the market was held daily, and it attracted farmers from neighboring villages as well as the Ben Suc farmers. . . .

Troops of the Army of the Republic of Vietnam (usually written "ARVN" and pronounced "Arvin" by the Americans) maintained an outpost in Ben Suc from 1955 until late 1964, when it was routed in an attack by the National Liberation Front (or N.L.F., or Vietcong, or V.C.), which kidnapped and later executed the government-appointed village chief and set up a full governing apparatus of its own. The Front demanded—and got—not just the passive support of the Ben Suc villagers but their active participation both in the governing of their own village and in the war effort. In the first months, the Front called several village-wide meetings. These began with impassioned speeches by leaders of the Front, who usually opened with a report of victories over the Americans and the "puppet troops" of the government, emphasizing in particular the downing of helicopters or planes and the disabling of tanks. Two months after the "liberation" of the village, the Front repelled an attack by ARVN troops, who abandoned three American M-113 armored personnel-carriers on a road leading into the village when they fled. The disabled hulks of these carriers served the speakers at the village meetings as tangible proof of their claimed superiority over the Americans, despite all the formidable and sophisticated weaponry of the intruders. Occasionally, a badly burned victim of an American napalm attack or an ex-prisoner of the government who had been tortured by ARVN troops was brought to Ben Suc to offer testimony and show his wounds to the villagers, giving the speakers an opportunity to condemn American and South Vietnamese–government atrocities. They painted a monstrous picture of the giant Americans, accusing them not only of bombing villages but also of practicing cannibalism and slitting the bellies of pregnant women. The speeches usually came to a close with a stirring call for support in the struggle and for what was sometimes called "the full cooperation and solidarity among the people to beat the American aggressors and the puppet troops." The speeches were often followed by singing and dancing, particularly on important National Liberation Front holidays, such as the founding day of the Front, December 20th, and Ho Chi Minh's birthday, May 19th. . . .

People from many villages around Ben Sue who had been left homeless after ground battles, bombing, and shelling migrated to the comparative safety of other villages, to live with relatives or just fend for themselves. When the small village of Mi Hung, across the river from Ben Suc, was heavily bombed, at least a hundred of its people moved into Ben Suc. During 1966, a scattering of refugees from other bombed villages had also found their way there. Then, in the second week of the month of January, 1967—when the population of Ben Suc was further swollen by relatives and friends from neighboring villages who had come to help with the harvest, which was exceptionally abundant that season, despite the war—the Americans launched in Binh Duong Province what they called Operation Cedar Falls. It was the largest operation of the war up to that time.

· · ·

For the Americans, the entire Saigon River area around Ben Suc, including particularly a notorious forty-square-mile stretch of jungle known as the Iron Triangle, had been a source of nagging setbacks. Small operations there were defeated; large operations conducted there turned up nothing. The big guns shelled and bombed around the clock but produced no tangible results. The enemy "body count" was very low, and the count of "pacified" villages stood at zero. In fact, a number of villages that had been converted into "strategic hamlets" in Operation Sunrise, launched three years earlier, had run their government protectors out of town and reverted to Front control. Late in 1966, the American high command designed the Cedar Falls operation as a drastic method of reducing the stubborn resistance throughout the Iron Triangle area. Named after the home town, in Iowa, of a 1st Division lieutenant who had been posthumously awarded the Medal of Honor, Operation Cedar Falls involved thirty thousand men, including logistical support, and it was planned and executed entirely by the Americans, without the advance knowledge of a single Vietnamese in the province. The decision that *no* Vietnamese was a good enough security risk was based on previous experiences, in which the enemy had learned about operations ahead of time and had laid traps for the attackers or simply disappeared. It also reflected the Army's growing tendency to mistrust all Vietnamese, regardless of their politics. On several American bases, entrance is forbidden to all Vietnamese, including ARVN soldiers, after a certain hour in the evening. During Cedar Falls, security was particularly tight. . . .

The attack on Ben Suc was planned for January 8th—the day before the thrust into the Triangle. I joined a group of six newsmen outside a field tent on the newly constructed base at the village of Lai Khé, to hear Major Allen C. Dixon, of the 173rd Airborne Brigade, outline the plan and purpose of this part of the operation. "We have two targets, actually," he explained, pointing to a map propped on a pile of sandbags.

"There's the Iron Triangle, and then there's the village of Ben Suc. This village is a political center, as far as the V.C. is concerned, and it's been solid V.C. since the French pulled out in '56. We haven't even been able to get a census taken in there to find out who's there." Most of the American officers who led the operation were not aware that ARVN had had an outpost in Ben Suc for the nine years preceding 1964. They saw the village as "solid V.C. as long as we can remember." Major Dixon continued, "Now, we can't tell you whether A, B, and C are at their desks or not, but we *know* that there's important infrastructure there—what we're really after here is the infrastructure of the V.C. We've run several operations in this area before with ARVN, but it's always been hit and run—you go in there, leave the same day, and the V.C. is back that night. Now, we realize that you can't go in and then just abandon the people to the V.C. This time we're really going to do a thorough job of it: we're going to clean out the place completely. The people are all going to be resettled in a temporary camp near Phu Cuong, the provincial capital down the river, and then we're going to move *everything* out—livestock, furniture, and all of their possessions. The purpose here is to deprive the V.C. of this area for good. The people are going to Phu Cuong by barge and by truck, and when they get there the provincial government takes over—it has its own Revolutionary Development people to handle that, and U.S. AID is going to help."

A reporter asked what would happen to the evacuated village.

"Well, we don't have a certain decision or information on that at this date, but the village may be levelled," Major Dixon answered, and went on to say, "The attack is going to go tomorrow morning and it's going to be a complete surprise. Five hundred men of the 1st Infantry Division's 2nd Brigade are going to be lifted *right into* the village itself in sixty choppers, with Zero Hour at zero eight hundred hours. From some really excellent intelligence from that area, we have learned that the perimeter of the village is heavily mined, and that's why we'll be going into the village itself. Sixty choppers is as large a number as we've ever used in an attack of this nature. Simultaneous with the attack, choppers with speakers on them are going to start circling over the village, telling the villagers to assemble in the center of the town or they will be considered V.C.s. It's going to be hard to get the pilots on those choppers to go in low to make those announcements audible, but everything depends on that. Also, we're going to drop leaflets to the villagers." (Later, I picked up one of these leaflets. On one side, the flags of the Republic of Vietnam, the United States, the Republic of Korea, New Zealand, and Australia were represented in color; on the other side was a drawing of a smiling ARVN soldier with his arm around a smiling soldier of the National Liberation Front. The text, written in English, Vietnamese, and Korean, read, "Safe conduct pass to be honored by all Vietnamese Government Agencies and Allied Forces." I learned that the Chieu Hoi, or Open Arms, program would be in operation during the attack. In an attempt to encourage defections from the Front, the government was opening its arms to all *hoi chanh,* or returnees who turned themselves in. Hence the unusually friendly tone of the leaflets.)

About the encirclement of the village, Major Dixon said, "There are going to be three landing zones for the choppers. Then the men will take up positions to prevent people from escaping from the village. Five minutes after the landing, we're going to bring artillery fire and air strikes into the whole area in the woods to the north of the village to prevent people from escaping by that route. At zero eight thirty hours, we're going to lift in men from the 2nd Brigade below the woods to the south to block off that route. After the landing is completed, some of our gunships are going to patrol the area at treetop level to help keep the people inside there from getting out. After the area is secure, we're lifting a crew of ARVN soldiers into the center of the village to help us with the work there. We want to get the Vietnamese dealing with their own people as much as we can here. Now, we're hoping that opposition is going to be light, that we're going to be able to get this thing over in one lightning blow, but if they've got intelligence on this, the way they did on some of our other operations, they could have something ready for us and this *could* be a hot landing. It could be pretty hairy."

For several reasons, the plan itself was an object of keen professional satisfaction to the men who devised and executed it. In a sense, it reversed the search-and-destroy method. This time, they would destroy first and search later—at their leisure, in the interrogation rooms. After all the small skirmishes and ambushes, after months of lobbing tons of bombs and shells on vague targets in Free Strike Zones, the size, complexity, and careful coordination of the Cedar Falls operation satisfied the military men's taste for careful large-scale planning. Every troop movement was precisely timed, and there would be full use of air support and artillery, in a design that would unfold over a wide terrain and, no matter what the opposition might be, would almost certainly produce the tangible result of evacuating several thousand hostile civilians, thereby depriving the V.C. of hundreds of "structures," even if the "infrastructure" was not present. This time, unless the entire village sneaked off into the forest, the objective of the operation could not wholly elude the troops, as it had in previous campaigns. Thus, a measure of success was assured from the start. In concluding his briefing to the newsmen, Major Dixon remarked, "I think this really ought to be quite fascinating. There's this new element of surprise, of going right into the enemy village with our choppers and then bringing in our tremendous firepower. Anyway, it ought to be something to see."

That evening, I was sent by helicopter to a newly constructed base ten miles north of Ben Suc, at Dau Tieng, where Colonel James A. Grimsley, commanding officer of the 2nd Brigade, 1st Infantry Division, was winding up his briefing of his officers on the next morning's attack on Ben Suc. The officers were assembled in a tent, in which a single light bulb hung from the ceiling. "The purpose of this operation is to move in there absolutely as fast as we can get control of the situation," Colonel Grimsley said. "I want to emphasize that you're going to have only about ten seconds to empty each chopper, because another chopper will be coming right in after it. A last word to men landing below the southwest woods: Your job is to keep anyone from escaping down that way. Now, of course, if it's just a bunch of women and children wandering down through the woods, who obviously don't know what they're doing, don't fire, but otherwise you'll have to take them under fire. The choppers will be taking off at zero seven twenty-three hours tomorrow morning. Are there any questions?" There were no questions, and the officers filed out of the tent into the darkness.

. . .

The men of the 1st Division's 2nd Brigade spent the day before the battle quietly, engaging in few pep talks or discussions among themselves about the dangers ahead. Each man seemed to want to be alone with his thoughts. They spent the night before the attack in individual tents on the dusty ground of a French rubber plantation, now the Americans' new base at Dau Tieng. The airstrip was complete, but not many buildings were up yet, and construction materials lay in piles alongside freshly bulldozed roads. The men were brought in by helicopter in the afternoon from their own base and were led to their sleeping area among the rubber trees. Most of the transporting of American troops in Vietnam is done by helicopter or plane. So the men, hopping from American base to

American base, view rural Vietnam only from the air until they see it through gunsights on a patrol or a search-and-destroy mission.

Darkness fell at about six-thirty. Thanks to a cloudy sky over the high canopy of rubber leaves, the area was soon in perfect blackness. A few men talked quietly in small groups for an hour or so. Others turned to their radios for company, listening to rock-'n'-roll and country-and-Western music broadcast by the American armed-services radio station in Saigon. The great majority simply went to sleep. Sleep that night, however, was difficult. Artillery fire from the big guns on the base began at around eleven o'clock and continued until about three o'clock, at a rate of four or five rounds every ten minutes. Later in the night, along with the sharp crack and whine of outgoing artillery the men heard the smothered thumping of bombing, including the rapid series of deep explosions that indicates a B-52 raid. Yet if the outgoing artillery fire had not been unusually near—so near that it sent little shocks of air against the walls of the tents—the sleepers would probably not have been disturbed very much. Because artillery fire is a routine occurrence at night on almost every American base in Vietnam, and because everyone knows that it is all American or Allied, it arouses no alarm, and no curiosity. Furthermore, because most of it is harassment and interdiction fire, lobbed into Free Strike Zones, it does not ordinarily indicate a clash with the enemy. It does make some men edgy when they first arrive, but soon it becomes no more than a half-noticed dull crashing in the distance. Only the distinctive sound of mortar fire—a popping that sounds like a champagne cork leaving a bottle—can make conversations suddenly halt in readiness for a dash into a ditch or bunker. Throughout that night of January 7th, the roaring of one of the diesel generators at the base served as a reminder to the men that they were sleeping on a little island of safety, encircled by coils of barbed wire and minefields, in a hostile countryside.

The men got up at five-thirty in the morning and were guided in the dark to a mess tent in a different part of the rubber grove, where they had a breakfast of grapefruit juice, hot cereal, scrambled eggs, bacon, toast, and coffee. At about six-thirty, the sky began to grow light, and they were led back to the airstrip. Strings of nine and ten helicopters with tapered bodies could be seen through the treetops, filing across the gray early-morning sky like little schools of minnows. In the distance, the slow beat of their engines sounded soft and almost peaceful, but when they rushed past overhead the noise was fearful and deafening. By seven o'clock, sixty helicopters were perched in formation on the airstrip, with seven men assembled in a silent group beside each one. When I arrived at the helicopter assigned to me—No. 47—three engineers and three infantrymen were already there, five of them standing or kneeling in the dust checking their weapons. One of them, a sergeant, was a small, wiry American Indian, who spoke in short, clipped syllables. The sixth man, a stocky infantryman with blond hair and a red face, who looked to be about twenty and was going into action for the first time, lay back against an earth embankment with his eyes closed, wearing an expression of boredom, as though he wanted to put these wasted minutes of waiting to some good use by catching up on his sleep. Two of the other six men in the team were also going into combat for the first time. The men did not speak to each other.

At seven-fifteen, our group of seven climbed up into its helicopter, a UH-1 (called Huey), and the pilot, a man with a German accent, told us that four of us should sit on the seat and three on the floor in front, to balance the craft. He also warned us that the flight might be rough, since we would be flying in the turbulent wake of the helicopter in front of us. At seven-twenty, the engines of the sixty helicopters started simultaneously, with a thunderous roar and a storm of dust. After idling his engine for three minutes on the airstrip, our pilot raised his right hand in the air, forming a circle with the forefinger and thumb, to show that he hoped everything would proceed perfectly from then on. The helicopter rose slowly from the airstrip right after the helicopter in front of it had risen. The pilot's gesture was the only indication that the seven men were on their way to something more than a nine-o'clock job. Rising, one after another, in two parallel lines of thirty, the fleet of sixty helicopters circled the base twice, gaining altitude and tightening their formation as they did so, until each machine was not more than twenty yards from the one immediately in front of it. Then the fleet, straightening out the two lines, headed south, toward Ben Suc.

In Helicopter No. 47, one of the men shouted a joke, which only one other man could hear, and they both laughed. The soldier who had earlier been trying to catch a nap on the runway wanted to get a picture of the sixty helicopters with a Minolta camera he had hanging from a strap around his neck. He was sitting on the floor, facing backward, so he asked one of the men on the seat to try to get a couple of shots. "There are sixty choppers here," he shouted, "and every one of them costs a quarter of a million bucks!" The Huey flies with its doors open, so the men who sat on the outside seats were perched right next to the drop. They held tightly to ceiling straps as the helicopter rolled and pitched through the sky like a ship plunging through a heavy sea. Wind from the rotors and from the forward motion blasted into the men's faces, making them squint. At five minutes to eight, the two lines of the fleet suddenly dived, bobbing and swaying from the cruising altitude of twenty-five hundred feet down to treetop level, at a point about seven miles from Ben Suc but heading away from it, to confuse enemy observers on the ground. Once at an altitude of fifty or sixty feet, the fleet made a wide U turn and headed directly for Ben Suc at a hundred miles an hour, the helicopters' tails raised slightly in forward flight. Below, the faces of scattered peasants were clearly visible as they looked up from their water buffalo at the sudden, earsplitting incursion of sixty helicopters charging low over their fields.

All at once, Helicopter No. 47 landed, and from both sides of it the men jumped out on the run into a freshly turned vegetable plot in the village of Ben Suc—the first Vietnamese village that several of them had ever set foot in. The helicopter took off immediately, and another settled in its place. Keeping low, the men I was with ran single file out into the center of the little plot, and then, spotting a low wall of bushes on the side of the plot they had just left, ran back there for cover and filed along the edges of the bushes toward several soldiers who had landed a little while before them. For a minute, there was silence. Suddenly a single helicopter came clattering overhead at about a hundred and fifty feet, squawking Vietnamese from two stubby speakers that stuck out, wing-like, from the thinnest part of the fuselage, near the tail. The message, which the American soldiers could not understand, went, "Attention, people of Ben Suc! You are surrounded by Republic of South Vietnam and Allied Forces. Do not run away or you will be shot as V.C. Stay in your homes and wait for further instructions." The metallic voice, floating down over the fields, huts, and trees, was as calm as if it were announcing a flight departure at an air terminal. It was gone in ten seconds, and the soldiers again moved on in silence. Within two minutes, the young men from No. 47 reached a little dirt road marking the village perimeter, which they were to hold, but there were no people in sight except American soldiers. The young men lay down on the sides of embankments and in little hollows in the small area it had fallen to them to control. There was no sign of an enemy.

For the next hour and a half, the six men from No. 47 were to be the masters of a small stretch of vegetable fields which was divided down the center by about fifty yards of narrow dirt road—almost a path—and bounded on the front and two sides (as they faced the road and, beyond it, the center of the village) by several small houses behind copses of low palm trees and hedges and in back by a small graveyard giving onto a larger cultivated field. The vegetable fields, most of them not more than fifty feet square and of irregular shape, were separated by neatly constructed grass-covered ridges, each with a path running along its top. The houses were small and trim, most of them with one side open to the weather but protected from the rain by the deep eaves of a thatch-grass roof. The houses were usually set apart by hedges and low trees, so that one house was only half visible from another and difficult to see from the road; they were not unlike a wealthy American suburb in the logic of their layout. An orderly small yard, containing low-walled coops for chickens and a shed with stalls for cows, adjoined each house. Here and there, between the fields and in the copses, stood the whitewashed waist-high columns and brick walls of Vietnamese tombs, which look like small models of the ruins of once-splendid palaces. It was a tidy, delicately wrought small-scale landscape with short views—not overcrowded but with every square foot of land carefully attended to.

Four minutes after the landing, the heavy crackle of several automatic weapons firing issued from a point out of sight, perhaps five hundred yards away. The men, who had been sitting or kneeling, went down on their bellies, their eyes trained on the confusion of hedges, trees, and houses ahead. A report that Mike Company had made light contact came over their field radio. At about eight-ten, the shock of tremendous explosions shattered the air and rocked the ground. The men hit the dirt again. Artillery shells crashed somewhere in the woods, and rockets from helicopters thumped into the ground. When a jet came screaming low overhead, one of the men shouted, "They're bringing in air strikes!" Heavy percussions shook the ground under the men, who were now lying flat, and shock waves beat against their faces. Helicopter patrols began to wheel low over the treetops outside the perimeter defended by the infantry, spraying the landscape with long bursts of machine-gun fire. After about five minutes, the explosions became less frequent, and the men from the helicopters, realizing that this was the planned bombing and shelling of the northern woods, picked themselves up, and two of them, joined by three soldiers from another helicopter, set about exploring their area.

Three or four soldiers began to search the houses behind a nearby copse. Stepping through the doorway of one house with his rifle in firing position at his hip, a solidly built six-foot-two Negro private came upon a young woman standing with a baby in one arm and a little girl of three or four holding her other hand. The woman was barefoot and was dressed in a white shirt and rolled-up black trousers; a bandanna held her long hair in a coil at the back of her head. She and her children intently watched each of the soldier's movements. In English, he asked, "Where's your husband?" Without taking her eyes off the soldier, the woman said something in Vietnamese, in an explanatory tone. The soldier looked around the inside of the one-room house and, pointing to his rifle, asked, "You have same-same?" The woman shrugged and said something else in Vietnamese. The soldier shook his head and poked his hand into a basket of laundry on a table between him and the woman. She immediately took all the laundry out of the basket and shrugged again, with a hint of impatience, as though to say, "It's just laundry!" The soldier nodded and looked around, appearing unsure of what to do next in this situation. Then, on a peg on one wall, he spotted a pair of men's pants and a shirt hanging up to dry. "Where's *he*?" he asked, pointing to the clothes. The woman spoke in Vietnamese. The soldier took the damp clothing down and, for some reason, carried it outside, where he laid it on the ground.

The house was clean, light, and airy, with doors on two sides and the top half of one whole side opening out onto a grassy yard. On the table, a half-eaten bowl of rice stood next to the laundry basket. A tiny hammock, not more than three feet long, hung in one corner. At one side of the house, a small, separate wooden roof stood over a fireplace with cooking utensils hanging around it. On the window ledge was a row of barely sprouting plants, in little clods of earth wrapped in palm leaves. Inside the room, a kilnlike structure, its walls and top made of mud, logs, and large stones, stood over the family's bedding. At the rear of the house, a square opening in the ground led to an underground bomb shelter large enough for several people to stand in. In the yard, a cow stood inside a third bomb shelter, made of tile walls about a foot thick.

After a minute, the private came back in with a bared machete at his side and a field radio on his back. "Where's your husband, huh?" he asked again. This time, the woman gave a long answer in a complaining tone, in which she pointed several times at the sky and several times at her children. The soldier looked at her blankly. "What do I do with her?" he called to some fellow-soldiers outside. There was no answer. Turning back to the young woman, who had not moved since his first entrance, he said, "O.K., lady, you stay here," and left the house.

Several other houses were searched, but no other Vietnamese were found, and for twenty minutes the men on that particular stretch of road encountered no one else, although they heard sporadic machine-gun fire down the road. The sky, which had been overcast, began to show streaks of blue, and a light wind stirred the trees. The bombing, the machine-gunning from helicopters, the shelling, and the rocket firing continued steadily. Suddenly a Vietnamese man on a bicycle appeared, pedalling rapidly along the road from the direction of the village. He was wearing the collarless, pajamalike black garment that is both the customary dress of the Vietnamese peasant and the uniform of the National Liberation Front, and although he was riding away from the center of the village—a move forbidden by the voices from the helicopters—he had, it appeared, already run a long gantlet of American soldiers without being stopped. But when he had ridden about twenty yards past the point where he first came in sight, there was a burst of machine-gun fire from a copse thirty yards in front of him, joined immediately by a burst from a vegetable field to one side, and he was hurled off his bicycle into a ditch a yard from the road. The bicycle crashed into a side embankment. The man with the Minolta camera, who had done the firing from the vegetable patch, stood up after about a minute and walked over to the ditch, followed by one of the engineers. The Vietnamese in the ditch appeared to be about twenty, and he lay on his side without moving, blood flowing from his face, which, with the eyes open, was half buried in the dirt at the bottom of the ditch. The engineer leaned down, felt the man's wrist, and said, "He's dead." The two men—both companions of mine on No. 47—stood still for a while, with folded arms, and stared down at the dead man's face, as though they were giving him a chance to say something. Then the engineer said, with a tone of finality, "That's a V.C. for you. He's a V.C., all right. That's what they wear. He was leaving town. He had to have some reason."

The two men walked back to a ridge in the vegetable field and sat down on it, looking off into the distance in a puzzled way and no longer bothering to keep low. The man who had fired spoke suddenly, as though coming out of deep thought. "I saw this guy coming down the road on a bicycle," he said. "And I thought, you know, Is this it? Do I shoot? Then some guy over there in the bushes opened up, so I cut loose."

The engineer raised his eyes in the manner of someone who has made a strange discovery and said, "I'm not worried. You know, that's the first time I've ever seen a dead guy, and I don't feel bad. I just don't, that's all." Then, with a hard edge of defiance in his voice, he added, "Actually, I'm glad. I'm glad we killed the little V.C."

Over near the copse, the man who had fired first, also a young soldier, had turned his back to the road. Clenching a cigar in his teeth, he stared with determination over his gun barrel across the wide field, where several water buffaloes were grazing but no human beings had yet been seen. Upon being asked what had happened, he said, "Yeah, he's dead. Ah shot him. He was a goddam V.C." . . .

. . .

With the attack over, the tricky task of distinguishing V.C.s from the civilians moved from the battlefield into the interrogation room. First, under the direction of the Americans, ARVN soldiers segregated the villagers by age level, sex, and degree of suspiciousness. All males between the ages of fifteen and forty-five were slated to be evacuated to the Provincial Police Headquarters in the afternoon. From among them, all who were suspected of being Vietcong and a smaller group of "confirmed V.C.s" were singled out. Some of these men were bound and blindfolded, and sat cross-legged on the ground just a few yards from the large assemblage of women, children, and aged. They were men who had been caught hiding in their bomb shelters or had otherwise come under suspicion. One group, for example, was unusually well dressed and well groomed. Instead of bare feet and pajamalike garb, these men wore Japanese foam-rubber slippers and short-sleeved cotton shirts. Standing over them, his arms akimbo, an American officer remarked, "No question about these fellas. Anyone in this village with clothes like that is a V.C. They're V.C.s, all right." A group of about a dozen men categorized as defectors were singled out to be taken to the special Open Arms center near Phu Cuong.

The Americans interrogated only the prisoners they themselves had taken, leaving the prisoners taken by the Vietnamese to the Vietnamese interrogators. The American interrogations were held in a large, debris-strewn room of the roofless schoolhouse. Four interrogating teams worked at the same time, each consisting of one American and an interpreter from the Vietnamese Army. The teams sat on low piles of bricks, and the suspects sat on the floor, or on one brick. These sessions did not uncover very much about the enemy or about the village of Ben Suc, but I felt that, as the only extensive spoken contact between Americans and the Ben Suc villagers throughout the Cedar Falls operation, they had a certain significance. Approximately forty people were questioned the first day.

In one session, a stout American named Martinez questioned, in a straightforward, businesslike manner, a small, barefoot, gray-haired man with a neat little gray mustache, who wore a spotlessly clean, pure-white loose-fitting, collarless shirt and baggy black trousers. First, Martinez asked to see the old man's identification card. By law, all South Vietnamese citizens are required to carry an identification card issued by the government and listing their name, date and place of birth, and occupation. (The Americans considered anyone who lacked this card suspicious, and a man who last registered in another village would have to supply a reason.) This suspect produced an I.D. card that showed him to be sixty years old and born in a village across the river. A search of his pockets also revealed an empty tobacco pouch and a small amount of money.

"Why did he come to Ben Suc?" Throughout the session, Martinez, who held a clipboard in one hand, spoke to the interpreter, who then spoke to the suspect, listened to his reply, and answered Martinez.

"He says he came to join relatives."

"Has he ever seen any V.C.?"

"Yes, sometimes he sees V.C."

"Where?"

"Out walking in the fields two weeks ago, he says."

"Where were they going?"

"He says he doesn't know, because he lives far from the center of the village. He doesn't know what they were doing."

"Does he pay any taxes?"

"Yes. The V.C. collect two piastres a month."

"What's his occupation?"

"He says he is a farmer."

"Let's see his hands."

Martinez had the man stand up and hold out his hands, palms up. By feeling the calluses on the palms, Martinez explained, he could tell whether the man had been working the fields recently. Aside from asking questions, Martinez employed only this one test, but he employed it on the majority of his suspects. He squeezed the old man's palms, rubbed the calves of his legs, then pulled up his shirt and felt his stomach. The old man looked down uneasily at Martinez's big hands on his stomach. "He's not a farmer," Martinez announced, and then, with a touch of impatience and severity, he said, "Ask him what he does."

The interpreter talked with the suspect for about half a minute, then reported, "He says that recently he works repairing bicycles."

"Why did he say he was a farmer?"

"He says he has repaired bicycles only since he finished harvesting."

Deliberately accelerating the intensity of the interrogation, Martinez narrowed his eyes, looked straight at the suspect crouching below him, and, in a suddenly loud voice, snapped, "Is he a V.C.?"

"No, he says he's not," the interpreter answered, with an apologetic shrug.

Martinez relaxed and put his clipboard down on a table. A weary smile took the place of his aggressive posture. "O.K. He can go now," he told the interpreter.

The interpreter, a thin young man with sunglasses, who had spoken to the suspect in a courteous, cajoling manner throughout the questioning, seemed pleased that the interrogation was to involve nothing more unpleasant than this. He gave the old man a smile that said, "You see how nice the Americans are!" and then patted him on the shoulder and delivered him into the hands of a guard.

After the old man had gone, Martinez turned to me with the smile of a man who has some inside information and said confidentially, "He was a V.C. He was probably a tax collector for the V.C." After a moment, he added, "I mean, that's my supposition, anyway."

The other interrogations were very similar. Martinez asked the same questions, with little variation: "Where does he live?" "Is he a farmer?" (Then came the touch test.) "Has he seen any V.C.?" And, finally, "Is *he* a V.C.?" And the suspects, instead of insisting that the National Liberation Front actually governed the village and involved the entire population in its programs, supported him in his apparent impression that the Front was only a roving band of guerrillas. To judge by their testimony to Martinez, the villagers of Ben Suc knew the Front as a ghostly troop of soldiers that appeared once a fortnight in the evening on the edge of the forest and then disappeared for another fortnight. When one young suspect was asked if he had "ever seen any V.C.s in the area," he answered that he had seen "fifty armed men disappearing into the forest two weeks ago." Another man, asked if he knew "any V.C.s in the village," answered in a whisper that he knew of *one*—a dark-complexioned man about forty-five years old named Thang. Still another man said that he had been "taken into the jungle to build a tunnel a year ago" but couldn't remember where it was. I had the impression that the suspects were all veterans of the interrogation room. For one thing, they were able to switch immediately from the vocabulary of the Front to the vocabulary of the American and South Vietnamese–government troops. It is a measure of the deep penetration of propaganda into every medium of expression in wartime Vietnam that few proper names serve merely as names. Most have an added propagandistic import. Thus, to the Americans the actual *name* of the National Liberation Front is "Vietcong" (literally, "Vietnamese Communists")—a term that the Front rejects on the ground that it represents many factions besides the Communists. Likewise, to the Front the actual *name* of the Army of the Republic of Vietnam is "Puppet Troops." Even the names of the provinces are different in the two vocabularies. The Front refuses to comply with a presidential decree of 1956 renaming the provinces, and insists on using the old names—calling Binh Duong, for instance, by its old name of Thu Dau Mot. There is no middle ground in the semantic war. You choose sides by the words you use. The suspects made the necessary transitions effortlessly. (Confronted with this problem myself, I have tried in this article to use for each organization the name that its own side has chosen for it.)

Several women were brought into the schoolhouse for interrogation, sometimes carrying a naked child balanced astride one hip. Unlike the men, they occasionally showed extreme annoyance. One young woman only complained loudly, and did not answer any of the questions put to her. Her baby fixed the interrogator with an unwavering, openmouthed stare, and an old woman, squatting next to the suspect, looked at the ground in front of her and nodded in agreement as the young mother complained.

"Do you know any V.C.s in this village?" the interrogator, a young man, asked.

The interpreter, having tried to interrupt the woman's complaining, answered, "She says she can't remember anything. She doesn't know anything, because the bombs were falling everywhere."

"Tell her to just answer the question."

"She says she couldn't bring her belongings and her pig and cow here." The interpreter shook his head and added, "She is very angry."

The interrogator's face grew tense for a moment, and he looked away, uncertain of what to do next. Finally, he dismissed the woman and impatiently turned his pad to a fresh sheet.

The Vietnamese troops had their own style of interrogation. At eleven o'clock that morning, an ARVN officer stood a young prisoner, bound and blindfolded, up against a wall. He asked the prisoner several questions, and, when the prisoner failed to answer, beat him repeatedly. An American observer who saw the beating reported that the officer "really worked him over." After the beating, the prisoner was forced to remain standing against the wall for several hours. Most of the ARVN interrogations took place in a one-room hut behind the school where the Americans were carrying on their interrogations. The suspects, bound and blindfolded, were led one by one into the hut. A group of ten or twelve fatherless families sitting under the shade of a tree nearby heard the sound of bodies being struck, but there were no cries from the prisoners.

As one young man was being led by one arm toward the dark doorway of the interrogation hut, a small boy who was watching intently burst into loud crying. I went inside after the suspect, and found that three tall, slender, boyish Vietnamese lieutenants, wearing crisp, clean American-style uniforms crisscrossed with ammunition belts, and carrying heavy new black pistols at their hips, had sat the young man against the wall, removed his blindfold, and spread a map on the floor in front of him. Pointing to the map, they asked about Vietcong troop movements in the area. When he replied that he didn't have the answers they wanted, one lieutenant beat him in the face with a rolled-up sheet of vinyl that had covered the map, then jabbed him hard in the ribs. The prisoner sat wooden and silent. A very fat American with a red face and an expression of perfect boredom sat in a tiny chair at a tiny table near the door, looking dully at his hands. The three lieutenants laughed and joked among themselves, clearly enjoying what seemed to them an amusing contest of will and wits between them and the silent, unmoving figure on the floor in front of them. Looking at the prisoner with a challenging smile, the lieutenant with the map cover struck him again, then asked him more questions. The prisoner again said he couldn't answer. Suddenly noticing my presence, all three lieutenants turned to me with the wide, self-deprecating grins that are perhaps the Vietnamese soldiers' most common response to the appearance of an American in any situation. Realizing that I could not speak Vietnamese, they called in an American Intelligence officer—Captain Ted L. Shipman, who was their adviser, and who could speak Vietnamese fluently. They asked him who

I was, and, upon learning that I was not a soldier but a reporter, they looked at each other knowingly, saluted me, and continued their interrogation, this time without beatings. A few minutes later, however, Captain Shipman, who had been standing beside me, said that he was extremely sorry but they wanted me to leave. When we were outside, Captain Shipman, a short man with small, worried eyes behind pale-rimmed glasses, drew me aside and, shaking his head, spoke with considerable agitation. "You see, they *do* have some—well, methods and practices that *we* are not accustomed to, that we wouldn't use if we were doing it, but the thing you've got to understand is that this is an Asian country, and their first impulse is force," he said. "Only the fear of force gets results. It's the Asian mind. It's completely different from what we know as the Western mind, and it's hard for us to understand. Look— they're a thousand years behind us in this place, and we're trying to educate them up to our level. We can't just do everything for them ourselves. Now, take the Koreans—they've got the Asian mind, and they really get excellent results here. Of course, we believe that that's not the best way to operate, so we try to introduce some changes, but it's very slow. You see, we know that the kind of information you get with these techniques isn't always accurate. Recently, we've been trying to get them to use some lie detectors we've just got. But we're only advisers. We can tell them how we think they should do it, but they can just tell us to shove off if they want to. I'm only an adviser, and I've made suggestions until I'm *blue in the face*! Actually, though, we've seen some improvement over the last year. This is a lot better than what we used to have."

I asked if the day's interrogations had so far turned up any important information.

"Not much today," he answered. "They're not telling us much. Sometimes they'll just tell you, 'Hey, I'm a V.C., I'm a V.C.' You know—proud. Today, we had one old man who told us his son was in the V.C. *He* was proud of it." Then, shaking his head again, he said with emphasis, as though he were finally putting his finger on the real cause of the difficulty, "You know, they're not *friendly* to us at this place, that's the problem. If you build up some kind of trust, then, once some of them come over to your side, they'll tell you anything. Their brother will be standing near them and they'll tell you, 'Him? He's my brother. He's a V.C.' It's hard for us to understand their mentality. They'll tell you the names of their whole family, and their best friends thrown in." Of the Front soldiers he said, "They don't know what they're doing half the time. Outside of the hard-core leaders, it's just like those juvenile delinquents back home, or those draft-card burners. They're just kids, and they want excitement. You give those kids a gun and they get excited. Half of the V.C.s are just deluded kids. They don't know what they're doing or why. But the V.C. operates through terror. Take this village. Maybe everybody doesn't want to be a V.C., but they get forced into it with terror. The V.C. organizes an association for everyone—the Farmers' Association, the Fishers' Association, the Old *Grandmothers'* Association. They've got one for everybody. It's so mixed up with the population you can't tell who's a V.C. Our job is to separate the V.C. from the people."

At that moment, a helicopter came in sight five hundred yards away, cruising low over the woods and emitting a steady chattering sound that was too loud to be the engine alone. Breaking off his explanation to look up, Captain Shipman said, "Now, there's a new technique they've developed. That sound you hear is the 7.62-calibre automatic weapon on the side. They have a hell of a time finding the V.C. from the air, so now when they hear that there's a V.C. in the area they'll come in and spray a whole field with fire. Then, you see, any V.C.s hiding below will get up and run, and you can go after them."

Captain Shipman went off to attend to other business, and I walked back to the interrogation hut. The fat American in the tiny chair was still looking at his hands, and the prisoner was still sitting stiff-spined on the floor, his lips tightly compressed and his gaze fixed in front of him. The young lieutenant with the map cover held it above the suspect's face and stared intently down at him. All three lieutenants were wholly engrossed in their work, excited by their power over the prisoner and challenged by the task of drawing information out of him. After twenty seconds or so, the American looked up and said to me, "They been usin' a little water torture." In the water torture, a sopping rag is held over the prisoner's nose and mouth to suffocate him, or his head is pushed back and water is poured directly down his nostrils to choke him. Again the lieutenants had not noticed me when I entered, and when the American spoke one of them looked up with a start. The tension and excitement in his expression were immediately replaced by a mischievous, slightly sheepish grin. Then all three lieutenants smiled at me with their self-deprecating grins, inviting me to smile along with them.

Captain Shipman came in, looking even more harried than before. One of the lieutenants spoke to him in a sugary, pleading tone, and Captain Shipman turned to me with a fatalistic shrug and said, "Look, I'm really sorry, but I get it in the neck if I don't take you away." Glancing over my shoulder as I left, I saw that the lieutenants were already crouching around their prisoner again and were all watching my exit closely. Outside again, Captain Shipman explained that this was only a preliminary interrogation—that a more extensive session, by the Province Police, would be held later. He pointed out that American advisers, like him, would be present at the police interrogation.

At the end of an interrogation, the questioner, whether American or Vietnamese, tied an eight-inch cardboard tag around the neck of the bound prisoner. At the top were the words "Captive Card," in both Vietnamese and English, and below were listed the prisoner's name, address, age, occupation, and the kind of weapon, if any, he was carrying when caught. None of the captive cards on the first day listed any weapons.

At one o'clock, the official count of "V.C.s killed" stood at twenty-four, with no friendly casualties reported. Soldiers on the spot told me of six shootings. I learned that three men had crawled out of a tunnel when they were told that the tunnel was about to be blown up. "One of them made a break for it, and they got him on the run," the soldier said. An officer told me that a man and a woman were machine-gunned from a helicopter while they were "having a picnic." I asked him what he meant by a picnic, and he answered, "You know, a *picnic*. They had a cloth on the ground, and food—rice and stuff—set out on it. When they saw the chopper, they ran for it. They were both V.C.s. She was a nurse—she was carrying medical supplies with her, and had on a kind of V.C. uniform—and he was, you know, sitting right there with her, and he ran for it, too, when the chopper came overhead." A soldier told me that down near the river three men with packs had been shot from a distance. Inspection of their packs revealed a large quantity of medical supplies, including a surgical kit, anti-malaria pills, a wide assortment of drugs, and a medical diary, with entries in a small, firm hand, that showed the men to have been doctors. (The *Stars and Stripes* of January 12th gave an account of seven additional shootings: "UPI reported that Brigadier General John R. Hollingsworth's helicopter accounted for seven of the Vietcong dead as the operation began. The door gunner, personally directed by the colorful assistant commander of the 1st. Inf. Div., shot three V.C. on a raft crossing the Saigon River, another as he tried to sneak across camouflaged by lily-pads, and three more hiding in a creek nearby.")

I asked the officer tabulating the day's achievements how the Army disposed of enemy corpses. He said, "We leave the bodies where they are and let the people themselves take care of them." It occurred to me that this was going to be difficult, with only women and children left in the area. Later in the afternoon, I heard the following exchange on the field radio:

"Tell me, how should we dispose of the bodies, sir? Over."

"Why don't you throw them in the river? Over."

"We can't do that, sir. We have to drink out of that river, sir."

The captured-weapons count stood at forty-nine—forty booby traps, six rifle grenades, two Russian-made rifles, and one American submachine gun. All were captured in caches in tunnels.

In the early afternoon, I went over to the field where the Americans were resting to ask them about the attack in the morning and what their feelings were concerning it. When I told one soldier that I was interested in finding out what weapons, if any, the Vietnamese dead had been carrying, he stiffened with pride, stared me straight in the eye, and announced, "What do you mean, 'Were they carrying weapons?' Of course they were carrying weapons! Look. I want to tell you one thing. *Anyone killed by this outfit was carrying a weapon.* In this outfit, no one shoots unless the guy is carrying a weapon. You've got to honor the civilian, that's all." With that, he terminated our conversation. Later, he and I walked over to a small tent where several men sat on the ground eating Spam and turkey from canned rations. They ate in silence, and, in fact, most of the men preferred to be alone rather than talk over the morning's attack. The men who did say anything about it laconically restricted themselves to short statements—such as "C Company had some light contact in the woods over there. Snipers mainly"—usually brought out in an almost weary tone, as though it were overdramatic or boastful to appear ruffled by the day's events. Nor did they kid around and enjoy themselves, like the ARVN soldiers. One young soldier, who looked to be not out of his teens, did come riding by on a small bicycle he had found near one of the houses in the village and cried out, with a big, goofy smile, "Hey! Look at this!," but the other men ignored him coldly, almost contemptuously.

I entered into conversation with Major Charles A. Malloy. "We're not a bunch of movie heroes out here," he said. "I think you'll find very few guys here who really hate the V.C. There's none of that stuff. I'll tell you what every soldier was thinking about when he stepped out of the helicopter this morning: Survival. Am I going to make it through? Am I going to see my wife and kids again? O.K., so some people without weapons get killed. What're you going to do when you spot a guy with black pajamas? Wait for him to get out his automatic weapon and start shooting? I'll tell you I'm not. Anyway, sometimes they throw away their weapon. They'll throw it into the bushes. You go and look at the body, and fifty yards away there's the weapon in the bushes. You can't always tell if they were carrying a weapon. Now, this man here has just heard that his wife had his first kid, a baby girl." He indicated a short, young-looking soldier with bright-red hair. "Now, if I told any one of these men they could go home tomorrow, they'd be off like a shot." The men listened with quiet faces, looking at the ground. "No, there's very little fanatic stuff here," he went on. At that moment, a middle-aged Vietnamese wearing the customary black floppy clothing was led by, his arms bound behind his back. Major Malloy looked over his shoulder at the prisoner and remarked, "There's a V.C. Look at those black clothes. They're no good for working in the fields. Black absorbs heat. This is a hot country. It doesn't make any sense. And look at his feet." The prisoner had bare feet, like many of the villagers. "They're all muddy from being down in those holes." In a burst of candor, he added, "What're you going to do? We've got people in the kitchen at the base wearing those black pajamas."

At three-forty-five, the male captives between the ages of fifteen and forty-five were marched to the edge of the helicopter pad, where they squatted in two rows, with a guard at each end. They hid their faces in their arms as a Chinook double-rotor helicopter set down, blasting them with dust. The back end of the helicopter was lowered to form a gangplank, leading to a dark, square opening. Their captive cards flapping around their necks, the prisoners ran, crouching low under the whirling blades, into the dim interior. Immediately, the gangplank drew up and the fat bent-banana shape of the Chinook rose slowly from the field. The women and children braved the gale to watch its rise, but appeared to lose interest in its flight long before it disappeared over the trees. It was as though their fathers, brothers, and sons had ceased to exist when they ran into the roaring helicopter.

Inside the Chinook, the prisoners were sitting on two long benches in a dim tubular compartment, unable to hear anything over the barely tolerable roaring of the engines, which, paradoxically, created a sensation of silence, for people moved and occasionally talked but made no sound. Many of the prisoners held their ears. Up front, on each side, a gunner wearing large earphones under a helmet scanned the countryside. The gunners' weapons pointed out, and there was no guard inside the helicopter. A few of the prisoners—some bold and some just young—stood up and looked out of small portholes in back of their seats. For the first time in their lives, they saw their land spread below them like a map, as the American pilots always see it: the tiny houses in the villages, the green fields along the river pockmarked with blue water-filled bomb craters (some blackened by napalm), and the dark-green jungles splotched with long lines of yellow craters from B-52 raids, the trees around each crater splayed out in a star, like the orb of cracks around a bullet hole in glass.

REFLECTIONS: HALF OUT OF OUR TREE

Richard H. Rovere

OCTOBER 28, 1967

WHETHER OR NOT they mean it, the leaders of the Administration miss no opportunity to wring their hands and insist that it is peace, and not victory, they seek, and that they are ready at any time to sit down with anyone anywhere, and so on. ("I would depart today for any mutually convenient spot," Rusk said, "if I could meet a representative of North Vietnam with whom I could discuss peace in Southeast Asia.") *Do* they mean it? Who knows? If they don't mean it, why are they saying it? If they didn't talk so much, the credibility gap might narrow. But they go on. Week after week, the Secretary of Defense, the master of the greatest war machine in history, seems to be trying to signal to us, his countrymen, that the damned thing isn't working, that the bombing is pointless, that it should be stopped. Does he speak for the President? Evidently not, but he still has the job. As for the President, speaking of mankind's behavior in this century, he said earlier this month, in Williamsburg, Virginia, "We can take no pride in the fact that we have fought each other like animals." He added that it "is really an insult to the animals, who live together in more harmony than human beings seem to be able to do." After some generalizations on other failures of statesmanship, he said, "Shame on the world and shame on its leaders." Those who support the war, like those who oppose it, appeal not to the patriotic heart but to the bleeding one. This is without precedent.

Consider, also, the attitudes toward civilian deaths, and casualties, and the general human suffering brought by the war to the Vietnamese, North and South. These, too, are without known precedent. Whether this war is like or unlike any earlier one, it resembles all modern wars in that noncombatants are killed, the innocent suffer greatly, and there is much cruel and needless destruction. In Korea, we bombed and shelled villages, killed countless women and children. No Senate committees pestered the generals to learn how many civilians had been killed or what steps were being taken to avoid the slaughter of the innocents. *C'est la guerre.* We killed a great many civilians in the Second World War. If they were Germans or Japanese, it served them right. (Hiroshima produced some immediate revulsion, but it was the newness and hideousness of the weapon employed that affected us, who had been little moved by wider killing with mere TNT.) If they were Italians or Frenchmen, we thought of their deaths as gallant sacrifices they made happily for the liberation of their soil. To be sure, civilized people have always felt that noncombatants should be spared to the greatest extent consistent with military needs, but until now there was no doubt in anyone's mind that the military needs—provided, of course, they were our own—should be the first consideration. Any sense of outrage over atrocities and dead civilians was directed at the enemy. Now, for the first time, the conscience of a large part of the nation has been aroused by agonies for which our own forces are responsible.

All wars are brutalizing, and perhaps in the random violence of the past few years (not merely the riots—not even so much the riots as the murders and assassinations) we are paying part of the price for sanctioned murder in the name of anti-Communism, self-determination, and democracy. But what seems already clear—from the size of the anti-war movements, from the muting of the eagles, from the outrage over atrocities and civilian losses—is that there is building up in this country a powerful sentiment not simply against the war in Vietnam but against war itself, not simply against bombing in Vietnam but against bombing anywhere at any time for any reason, not simply against the slaughter of innocents in an unjust conflict but also against the slaughter of those who may be far from innocent in a just conflict. The youthful protesters would probably acknowledge this without hesitation, only asking themselves why anyone should labor the point so heavily. (Some would no doubt go further, and say that they oppose not only the wars this government runs but everything else it does.) Their elders, thinking of a past they find it necessary to be true to, cannot turn pacifist overnight. They must distinguish between this war and the wars they have supported in the past—up to and including the war in the Middle East a few months ago. But in fact our present war is different mainly in that it seems endless and hopeless.

. . .

Is it possible for us to come through this experience, if we come through at all, as a pacifist nation? I suppose not. "Pacifist nation" seems a contradiction in terms. If all of us, or most of us, were pacifists, we would have little reason to be a nation. Defense is the fundamental raison d'être for the modern state. And if a pacifist nation didn't come apart at the seams, some non-pacifist nation would tear it apart. It seems to me, though, that if the war goes on and if opposition to it continues to increase at the present rate, there will in time be a testing of this whole proposition. No government that is not totalitarian can go on indefinitely fighting a hard war that its people hate. Something has to give. Either the government yields to the popular will or it becomes oppressive and stifles the protest by terror. Thus far, there is no sign that our government has faced the question. With very few exceptions, as far as the anti-war movement is concerned, police power has been used sparingly and in the interests of domestic tranquillity. Few other governments, even when they were not at war, would be as restrained as this one has been in dealing with protest movements, including violent ones. It seems to me that this is in part because we are waging the Vietnam war with an essentially professional military force. Its morale is said to be high and not to be much affected by what is going on here. This state of affairs cannot last indefinitely. Morale will be affected, and then the test will be made. I cannot figure the odds on the outcome. On the one hand, repression is the safest, surest, cheapest course for any government to take. I can imagine the coming to power of an American de Gaulle, or even of someone a lot more authoritarian than de Gaulle. Much of the troublemaking in the months and years ahead will be the work of Negroes, and I can even imagine the imposition of a kind of American apartheid—at least in the North, where Negroes live in ghettos that are easily sealed off. If there should be the will to do it, it could be done quite "legally" and "Constitutionally." There are enough smart lawyers around to figure out how. On the other hand, there is unprecedented opposition to the war inside the odious "power structure" itself. There is much opposition in Congress and in every department of the federal government. The governors of large states and the mayors of great cities—among them the Mayor of New York—are opposed to the war. The Supreme Court, which was such a bastion of liberty in the McCarthy years, would make things as hard as possible for all the smart lawyers. The government could, of course, ignore, or even abolish, the Supreme Court. But the Court is not the only American institution that has proved quite resilient in periods of stress. The churches, the press, the universities—all are centers of dissent. It could prove to be crucial that the American middle class—as despicable as the Establishment in the minds of the young and alienated—is also a center of dissent. The proletariat may not be willing to call off strikes or accept pay cuts because of the war, but it offers little support to the protest movements. If we are now undertaking, or are about to undertake, a radical alteration in values, support for it will come not from the workers but from an unproclaimed, and even unwanted, alliance between relatively affluent whites, of whom I happen to be one, and what Daniel P. Moynihan calls the "underclass," consisting mainly of unemployed Negroes, many of whom want to kill me.

I want American democracy to survive. It is in many ways a fraud. It is not keeping its promises to the American Negroes. It has abused them and many other people. It has very little aesthetic or intellectual appeal. But under it there is at least a hope of redemption. Things do get done here that don't get done under other systems. But it now seems clear to me that if American democracy does survive it will be something quite different from what we have known. I find it hard at this stage to see how a victory for democracy will not also be a victory for pacifism. Those who will lead the struggle are, whether they acknowledge it or not, renouncing war as an instrument of policy. They may insist that of course they would fight the enemy at the gates, or perhaps take arms against a new Hitler if one should arise. But the wars of the future—at least, those that would have any ideological content—are not going to be like the wars of the past. India and Pakistan or India and China may fight over bits and pieces of territory, but the Soviet Union and the United States are agreed on the need for common efforts to cool it when such disputes get hot. Most future wars are apt to be like the war in Vietnam—wars that will be called by their instigators "wars of national liberation." The Soviet Union, as Nikita Khrushchev long ago informed us, will support them. From its point of view, they are irresistible. They cost next to nothing and drive us Americans out of our minds. But if we survive as anything like a free society, we will not be entering them. I simply cannot imagine this country, under any President chosen in a free election, taking on another Vietnam. If this is so, it may be good news. But it means that we won't have much in the way of a foreign policy. We will draw back from all difficult situations. We will leave the field to those who have not renounced war.

. . .

I hold a kind of Tolstoyan view of history, and believe that it is hardly ever possible to determine the real truth about how and why we got from here to there. Since I find it extremely difficult to uncover my own motives, I hesitate to deal with those of other people, and I positively despair at the thought of ever being really sure about what has moved whole nations and whole generations of mankind. No explanation of the causes and origins of any war—of any large happening in history—can ever be for me much more than a plausible one, a reasonable hypothesis. But if we cannot answer the "how" and "why" questions with anything like certitude, we can answer a good many of the "what" ones, and this sometimes enables us to eliminate at least some of the suggested "how"s and "why"s. In regard to Vietnam, I feel confident in isolating certain noncauses and non-origins. We did not go into Vietnam spoiling for a war. It was not the American attitude at the Geneva Conference in 1954 that made what everyone now speaks of as the "Geneva agreements" unworkable. A far more likely thesis is that they proved unworkable because the Russians gave the French (and the South Vietnamese) better terms than they needed to, in the expectation that the French would on this account decide not to enter the proposed European Defense Community. However that may be, those so-called agreements were not a diplomatic settlement of any kind but simply a document setting forth the terms of a cease-fire. To quote John McAlister again:

> There were only three documents signed at Geneva, and only four signatories were involved: France, the royal governments of Laos and Cambodia, and the Vietminh. [The Vietminh was an army, not a government. What we think of as the South Vietnamese, or anti-Communist Vietnamese, were never consulted.] These agreements were not treaties and they were not formally ratified by any government by any process. They were simply agreements between the opposing military commands to stop the fighting in Indo-China and to take measures to prevent the fighting from being re-

sumed. Some confusion has resulted because the "Final Declaration of the Geneva Conference," which "noted" the key provisions of the various cease-fire agreements, seemed to emanate from all nine conference participants. However, this "Final Declaration" was not signed by *any* of the participants. It was yet another cold-war device to mask the lack of consensus among the major powers—an "unsigned treaty."

We have sinned greatly and frequently since 1954, but not always in the ways that we think we have. We did not go into Vietnam hoping for a war; after all, we had just passed up a splendid opportunity to join the fighting with our then friends the French at our side. But we were not taken altogether by surprise at discovering that nothing really had been settled by Geneva. Two-fifths of our aid in the early days was military, but something beyond this figure persuades me that we were after something a bit more decent than the opening of a new firing range. The non-Communist state that came into being as a consequence of the Geneva Conference looked to our foreign-aid people as if it might actually work, as if it might turn out to be a nice, prosperous, well-behaved little democracy. In the bright light of hindsight, this seems a ridiculous dream. And what may have been ridiculous about it was not that people like the Emperor Bao Dai and Ngo Dinh Diem would never let it happen but, rather, that Ho Chi Minh would never let it happen. We are always being told what awful people we have supported in Saigon while all along there has existed the alternative of supporting the Vietnamese Thomas Jefferson, Ho Chi Minh, and having him on our side. Ho sounds a lot more attractive than most of the types we have lately been dealing with, and it might have been very smart of us back before 1950, say, to try to strike up some sort of deal with him. And Ho could not have been much interested in us in the early fifties (and anyway think of what McCarthy would have said), and Diem then did not have, or was concealing, his cloven hoof. Diem never seemed a Thomas Jefferson, or even a Lyndon Johnson, but he looked no worse than our man in Korea, Syngman Rhee. And one can at least advance the hypothesis that our troubles have grown not out of Diem's "failure" and ours to create a good society in South Vietnam but out of a certain amount of early success, or, if not that, out of Ho's fear that we might somehow succeed someday. It could also be that he was not unmindful of the possibilities for looting. The Americans had put a good many desirable things—including a lot of expensive and well-made weaponry—in South Vietnam, and if he could knock over the government without too much difficulty they would all be his.

Senator Fulbright has been saying for years that foreign aid is dangerous, because it can lead to war. I think he is right. We invest money and, more important, hope in a country, and when some thugs threaten to wreck the country and dash its hopes and ours we are tempted to police the place. Some of the most promising governments in Africa are likely to go to pieces because the leaders of less hopeful neighboring states either can't stand the thought that the people across the way are going to make it or feel that neighbors ought to share and share alike. In the late fifties and early sixties, many Americans who had no appetite for war and no thought that there would be one urged that we give Saigon enough military assistance to put down the Vietcong and enable the government at least to stand on its feet and have enough time and energy to make something of itself. They should have known better. But there was no reason then to think of the difficulties with the Vietcong as having much to do with the balance of power in Asia. Indeed—and here, perhaps, is another important difference between this war and Korea—it seems to have been *our* intervention on a large scale that gave the war a real balance-of-power meaning. In the early sixties, when Laos was a more troublesome place than Vietnam, the Russians were looking the other way. In that period, too, the "domino theory" was generally discredited. There may then have been a chance for a President to reappraise—agonizingly, of course—the whole affair and order a phase-out. Vietnam was still an obscure place, and with us no longer involved it would have been still more obscure. I speak of a time when Kennedy was alive. He could probably have de-escalated, but instead he escalated. If he had lived, and if he had beaten Goldwater or some other Republican in 1964, he might have altered his strategy at some later point. But he died, and Johnson pursued his policy with a vengeance, thereby, in my view, giving the domino theory a strange validity it had earlier lacked: *The dominoes might fall in a certain way because we set them up that way.* If we had got out of Vietnam five years ago, the balance of power in Asia might have been affected only insignificantly and imperceptibly. If we got out tomorrow, the consequences might be very serious indeed. We have painted ourselves in.

Until early in 1965, I felt that our role in Vietnam was defensible. The rulers of the country seemed an untrustworthy lot, but that did not appear a good reason for turning the place over to the Vietcong. Knowing that a developing nation cannot possibly manage war and reform at the same time without assistance, I felt that our assistance in putting down an insurgency was helpful. The fact that the insurgents were natives did not bother me; so were their antagonists, and I have never believed that civil wars are somehow more virtuous and rational than wars of any other kind. From my point of view, the operations of the Vietcong were, and still are, every bit as irrational as I now believe ours are. They don't seem to mind destroying their country any more than we do. I can understand why some Americans should be indifferent to the fate of Vietnam—to a certain degree, and to my own dismay, I am coming to feel that way myself—but I cannot understand why any Vietnamese should be indifferent to it. I wish Johnson would swallow his pride, whatever the consequences, but it seems to me it is positively idiotic for Ho Chi Minh not to take Johnson and Rusk at their word and, if what they are saying is all a bluff, call it. Why not set a place and a date, and see whether Rusk shows up? Everybody knows that unless American forces stay in Vietnam for the rest of history the Vietcong are going to have their triumphs anyway; if they negotiated us out of there tomorrow on any terms at all, the country would be theirs before long. (Tran Van Dinh, a former South Vietnamese diplomat, at odds with the Saigon regime, has speculated that this very knowledge may be a reason for Ho's not negotiating. Our departure would create a vacuum that would for a time be filled by the Vietcong but would ultimately be vulnerable to Chinese pressure. Tran Van Dinh believes that one of the last things Ho really wants is a complete American pullout.) If the Vietcong can remain as strong as they seem to be with all the Americans chasing them around the country, they should have no trouble at all seizing power after they sat down and told us enough lies about the future to make it impossible for us not to agree to get out. The American people love to be lied to at peace conferences, and if that happened in this instance the guerrilla could put away his shooting irons, turn respectable, run for office, and run the country. General Ky could get a job with Pan American World Airways or just loll about on the Riviera, where he would be an authentic part of the scene and would find a lot of his old friends as well as many new ones.

Nothing so agreeable is going to happen. It is up to us to make the first move. Until recently, I felt that the best first move would be a relatively small one—small but visible: not necessarily putting an end to the bombing but announcing a plan for scaling it down. I know Air Force officers who wouldn't object to this. Why, it may be asked, should they, since the targets are mostly gone anyway? But many other Air Force people would not object to something of the sort being done for political reasons even if they had strategic reservations. I did not think such a move would be of the least help in "bringing Hanoi to the conference table," but I thought that almost any deescalation would put an end to our scaring everyone else about our intentions, particularly toward the Chinese, and would help prepare us for the inevitable. In time, Johnson or some other President may begin a phased withdrawal in that way. But I now fear that it will soon be too late—by which I mean too late to undo the damage to us. And it is we ourselves in this moment of history that we must think of before we think of anyone or anything else. This is a terrible thing to feel compelled to say. Edwin Reischauer, in his *Beyond Vietnam: The United States and Asia*, argues that of the three options he thinks we have—escalation and a likely war with China, complete withdrawal as soon as possible, and plodding along on our present bloody and repugnant course—the last is the least disastrous and hence the most acceptable. Reischauer, who was until recently our Ambassador in Japan, is a fine scholar and humanist who has great respect and affection for the people of Asia, among whom he lived and studied for many years before John F. Kennedy persuaded him to leave scholarship for diplomacy. He is no hawk, no imperialist, no warrior of any kind. He thinks we were crazy ever to get into this and crazy to have let it reach this point. But what he fears most of all is that if we abandon this undertaking now, we will tell ourselves that Asia is impossible, that we should never again have anything to do with it, and will abandon not only Vietnam but all of Asia, with the likely exception of Japan. I share his fear. We might treat Asia as we treated Europe after 1918. We must ask ourselves right now whether that wouldn't be a pretty good idea. From some points of view, it might be an excellent idea. If our foreign policy in Asia produces such a monstrosity as the Vietnam war, why not get out? But, as Reischauer sees it, and as I would like to see it, our foreign policy in Asia is more than just the war in Vietnam. Most of Asia needs our help desperately, and we can perhaps use a good deal of Asian help in growing up. I want to go on having an American presence in Asia, because I don't want people to starve to death if we can prevent it, and I don't want Asians to despise my children and grandchildren and plot to destroy them.

Anyway, the thing wouldn't work. In recent years, a good many people have urged the dismantling of NATO, on the ground that it is no longer needed and that what is sometimes called "the European system" can work on its own. Whenever such proposals were brought to the attention of George Ball, the former Under-Secretary of State and a dedicated Europeanist, he would ask their sponsors if they remembered what had happened to "the European system" in 1914 and in 1939. Things may have changed in Europe lately, but there has never been anything anyone could call "the Asian system," capable of settling what diplomats call "regional" problems—usually meaning wars. Even if China managed to contain itself, which doesn't seem very likely, there would still be a good deal of unpleasantness between India and Pakistan. Making their own nuclear weapons might seem more important to them than it does now. And there would be unpleasantness elsewhere in Southeast Asia. And who knows whether some of Japan's long-range planners might not start casting a speculative eye on the "power vacuums" we would be creating?

Until very recently, these considerations put me in substantial agreement with Reischauer that perhaps Johnson's way offers fewer dangers than any of the others. But now I think we have reached—or are just about to reach—a point at which the argument no longer holds water. For one thing, if we continue much longer we may pull out of Asia whether we win, lose, or draw in Vietnam. It happens to be the view of our people that they don't want their kids to be killed so that Asians can go on eating. Most of them would see no logic in saying there is a necessary connection between starvation in India and Americans getting shot in Vietnam, but even if the logic were self-evident they would reject it. Beyond all that, however, we seem as incapable as the South Vietnamese of running a war—or, at any rate, *this* war—and doing anything worthwhile at the same time. Congress insists on cutting our decent programs elsewhere in the world—to say nothing of those in this country—almost to the point of absurdity. In a literal sense, it is finding a way to make the wretched of the earth foot the bill for Vietnam. This isn't its intention, and as a nation we are still more generous than most, yet not only are innocent people dying in Vietnam but, because of the dollars-and-cents cost of the war, they are dying in Africa.

The war in Vietnam is heading too many of us for the loony bin. People who could once talk sensibly about politics are becoming unhinged and disoriented by it. Some are really thinking seriously of running Ronald Reagan for President. A young man who used to be a provocative analyst now screwily and oracularly proclaims that "morality, like politics, starts at the barrel of a gun." This is printed in a local high-brow journal, and it takes a professor from California to remind this well-educated ex-humanist, now evidently en route to some kind of New Left Fascism, that politics *ends* at the barrel of a gun. Not long ago, a highly intelligent and attractive young Negro spokesman for a radical organization said that he couldn't see any reason anyone should write a book about poverty—he was talking of Michael Harrington's *The Other America*—because anyone who was really poor and had lived in a ghetto knew all there was to know about it anyway. He said he himself could tell it like it is, but thought a book about it was a waste of anyone's time. The land is filling up with cranks and zanies—some well intentioned, some vicious. It can be contended that Vietnam is not the only cause of goofing off, of alienation. Of course it isn't. But it provides the occasion, and it heightens the degree. And so it seems to me that if we stay on in Vietnam we will render ourselves incapable of being of much help to Asians or anyone else. We will need all the help we can get ourselves. If Ronald Reagan became President, I'd say by all means let's not have a foreign policy.

. . .

I want us to get out, and then try to recover our sanity, so that we may face the consequences. Some of them cause me almost no concern. The spread of Communism bothers me very little. It may be bad in some places and not so bad in others, but we can live with it just about anywhere—even ninety miles from Key West. Once, it was, or seemed to be, a world movement, and it was surely a brutally expansionist one. But its adventures in expansionism blunted its threat as a world movement. By 1948, when Tito broke with Stalin, it should have been clear that ideology was no match for nationalism—at least in Europe. When China broke with Russia, it was obvious that the same thing went for Asia. Perhaps if we had borne in mind the history of earlier religious movements we could have seen all this fifty years ago. But we didn't see it, and neither, of course, did they. At any rate, we now know that the mere circumstance that a piece of real estate falls under Communist control doesn't constitute a threat to our existence, and doesn't even mean there is no more hope for the people involved. Nor, with things as they are, can my first concern be with the indisputable fact that by pulling out we would be breaking our pledge not only to the Vietnamese but to the Thais and others to whom what would follow might be quite painful.

We are going to get out sooner or later anyway, and when we do we will not go back in, so, no matter what happens in the near future, they are going to have to work out their relations with China without much support from us. But some of the consequences of withdrawal disturb me greatly. By and large, I think that most of American foreign policy for the last thirty years has been admirable. I want us to continue to be part of the world and to use our considerable talents for the benefit of all mankind. I suspect that if we get out of Vietnam we won't have much left in the way of a foreign policy. And, most of all, I fear what will happen right here if we withdraw. Theodore C. Sorensen writes that since Khrushchev could admit a mistake in the missile crisis five years ago, and Kennedy could acknowledge one at the Bay of Pigs a year before that, Lyndon Johnson ought to be able to do the same thing now. Here are two analogies that do not work at all. The missile crisis was over in a few days, the Bay of Pigs in a few hours. No Russian soldiers died in the missile crisis, no American ones at the Bay of Pigs. It would take greater magnanimity and a greater dedication to the truth than we have any right to expect of any politician on earth for Lyndon Johnson to say that this whole bloody business is a mistake, and was from the start. He just cannot and will not do it. If he did, he would throw this country into worse turmoil than it has known at any time since the Civil War. Could he pull out and either say nothing or tell some lies? Could he possibly use Senator Aiken's ploy and announce that we had achieved our ends in Vietnam and were withdrawing? Perhaps, but there would still be turmoil. There will be turmoil whether we stay or go, and I dread it. But, between the two, I have less fear of the consequences of withdrawal than of those of perseverance.

This war is intolerable. What does it mean to say that? Not much—talk is cheap. I haven't a clue as to how we can get out, and I have never much liked the idea of proposing without knowing of a means of disposing. I don't think we can write our way out, and I doubt very much if we can demonstrate our way out. But out is where I want us to be, and I don't know what a man can do except say what he thinks and feels.

PART TWO
CONFRONTATION

A NOTE BY KELEFA SANNEH

URING CHARLAYNE HUNTER-GAULT's time at the University of Georgia, plenty of reporters interviewed her, but Calvin Trillin is the only one who regularly offered to deliver her lunch. Those were exhausting years: in 1961, she and her classmate Hamilton (Hamp) Holmes became the first black students to attend the university; their presence on campus marked the end of a long battle over integration at U.G.A., which is not to say that the losing side stopped fighting. In those days, Trillin was working as a reporter for the Atlanta bureau of *Time*, filing long, discursive dispatches that were used (or, sometimes, ignored) by the people in New York who actually wrote the stories. Hunter-Gault recalls, "He would call me at night, in my dorm, and say, 'Hi, Charlayne, it's Bud—how would you like a hot pastrami sandwich right about now?' And people would be shouting outside my window, doing all sorts of things."

When Trillin was ready to leave *Time*, he found a new home—a life-long home, it turned out—at *The New Yorker*, which was eager to increase its coverage of race and the South. This, in any case, was Trillin's impression; like many staff writers over the years, he has never been entirely sure why he was hired. "An Education in Georgia," about the integration battle and its aftermath, was Trillin's first article for the magazine and his longest, stretching over three issues, in July, 1963. (It remains his only multi-part article for *The New Yorker*.) He remembers sitting on a sofa in William Shawn's office during the editing process, which was gentle but exacting. "He always seemed to put his finger on that limping cow that you thought would be lost in the herd," Trillin says.

Trillin chose as his protagonist his old acquaintance Charlayne Hunter (as she was then), a journalism major with an analytical sensibility—a participant who also happened to be a keen observer. Readers who devoured his story knew that Hunter was remarkably unflustered by the chaos and the violence that she faced. What they didn't know was that, by the time the piece was published, Hunter was not only Trillin's subject but also his colleague. That spring, she had been scouted by Shawn and his deputy, Leo Hofeller, who had offered her an entry-level position. Hunter was hired by *The New Yorker,* as an editorial assistant, in June, 1963, and one of her first tasks was to submit to an interrogation by a member of the fact-checking department, down the hall, in connection with Trillin's piece, which was published the next month. A few years later, she was promoted to reporter, and spent a couple of years contributing to the Talk of the Town section; she established for herself an unofficial Harlem bureau, and became its chief correspondent. Hunter was, in fact, the first black writer ever hired by the magazine as a regular contributor, although of course others (including James Baldwin, in 1962) had been published on a freelance basis. This is the subtext of "An Education in Georgia": in retrospect, it is actually, and covertly, a story about two integrations at once.

Trillin spent much of the summer of 1963 writing about race and politics, a topic that took him to Washington, in August, for the March on Washington. His dispatch captures both the seriousness of the attendees—he noticed "surprisingly few knapsacks and sandals in the crowd"—and the sprawling nature of the event itself. The piece ends, rather tantalizingly, with a moment of expectant silence, as we await Martin Luther King, Jr., who goes unseen and unmentioned. Katharine T. Kinkead, observing the integration fight in Durham, North Carolina, in 1961, used small moments to create a portrait of the civil-rights movement in miniature. We hear the organizers debate how much to provoke the local police force and how to stay safe, or as safe as possible; as the group pickets a segregated cinema, we see "older white theatre patrons, who walked through the lines as though they were mist." But perhaps the most memorable image comes near the end, as a *New Yorker* reporter, "dressed warmly, in boots and a fur coat," but still shivering, is led to a radiator-warmed corridor indoors, alongside some protestors who are much younger, and much colder, than she is.

A couple of years later, Trillin was planning to go to Stanford to talk to a dream researcher when Shawn prevailed on him to stop by Berkeley—he was curious about the students who were causing such a fuss. Trillin's "Letter from Berkeley," from 1965, captures a scene that seems strikingly familiar: the students are deeply skeptical of so-called liberal values, but equally skeptical of any grand ideology that might offer itself as a replacement. He notes that "quite a few of the leaders of the Free Speech Movement are, in the words of one participant, 'between movements.'" Later that year, in "The Price of Peace Is Confusion," Renata Adler chronicled a chaotic antiwar demonstration in Washington, incisively arguing that by lionizing "individualism, privacy, personal initiative," and "isolationism and a view of the federal government as oppressive," the protesters were reviving a long-dormant strain of "right-wing consciousness." Richard H. Rovere, writing from the 1968 Democratic National Convention, in Chicago, and E. J. Kahn, writing from semi-occupied Harvard, in 1969, considered the possibilities and the limits of radical violence, a phrase that some people considered a contradiction in terms. Writing in 1967, Jacob Brackman considered a different kind of violence: rhetorical violence, as manifest in "the put-on," an emerging form of conversational sabotage, well-suited to a generation seeking new ways to express its skepticism.

Half a century later, we have learned to live with many forms of weaponized irony, although, of course, new ones spring up all the time. One thinks of the "gaunt, bespectacled Negro man with white hair" whom Kinkead observed shouting encouragement to a column of protesters. "Here come the kids again!" he cried, and they are coming still.

CIVIL RIGHTS

FROM

IT DOESN'T SEEM QUICK TO ME

Katharine T. Kinkead

APRIL 15, 1961 (DESEGREGATING DURHAM)

A NEGRO FRIEND OF mine remarked to me a few weeks ago that whether America is ultimately able to adjust its culture so as to provide equality for its colored citizens will depend mostly on the nation's Negro young people. "If you're white, it's easy to avoid the problem altogether, while if you're colored and past twenty-five, you're well along the road to accommodating yourself to second-class citizenship," he said. "But these young people today, sitting in at lunch counters and kneeling in at churches, are different from my generation. They aren't afraid and they aren't bitter. They know what they want and they're determined to get it."

I asked him whether he thought that, if I made a trip to a Southern city, there was a way I could meet some of these youths who, in the year since four boys from the Agricultural and Technical College of North Carolina had almost diffidently taken seats at a "White Only" lunch counter in Greensboro, not only had forced the country to reexamine the judicial concept of integration "with all deliberate speed" but had aroused some of the supposedly "silent generation" of their white contemporaries to join their demonstrations. When I had convinced my friend, who had tended to regard me as a complacent white Northerner, that I was serious about wanting to visit one of the groups that had mounted this sustained and remarkably peaceable offensive, he promised he would inquire for me among acquaintances in the National Association for the Advancement of Colored People and the Congress of Racial Equality, which have been providing the young Negroes with organizational and legal help.

A week later, he phoned to say that if I could take a plane to Durham, North Carolina, the next afternoon, a local Negro attorney named Floyd B. McKissick, who was active in the N.A.A.C.P. and had been giving guidance and legal aid to local sit-in demonstrators, would meet me at the airport there and put me in touch with a group that was on the verge of starting a new sort of protest action. I agreed to this plan. My friend and I were both pleased—although for different reasons—that it was to be Durham I would visit. He had told me, "The kids there were the first to take up lunch-counter sitting-in after the start at Greensboro. In fact, the whole sit-in movement caught fire from Durham a week or so later." My own pleasure at going to Durham stemmed more from selfish awareness of my age. North Carolina, I knew, was more liberal in its attitude toward Negroes than the Deep South, having started voluntary integration of its schools in 1957; I felt that in a demonstration there a middle-aged woman would be considerably safer than in, say, Alabama or Mississippi.

· · ·

Durham, which likes to be known as the Friendly City, is four hundred miles south of Washington in the north-central section of North Carolina. A guidebook told me that it is a city of about eighty thousand, the second-largest manufacturing center in the state, the home of furniture and textile firms, as well as of both the American Tobacco and the Liggett & Myers companies, which together make 19 percent of the cigarettes smoked in the United States. In Durham also are the seventy-five-hundred-acre campus and ornate Gothic buildings of Duke University, which at present has no Negroes in its student body of six thousand, and the fifteen-acre campus of North Carolina College, a four-year Negro liberal-arts institution with sixteen hundred students. Ten miles to the south, in Chapel Hill, is the University of North Carolina (eight thousand five hundred students, thirty-three of them Negroes); fifty-five miles to the west, in Greensboro, are Bennett College, for Negro women, and the Agricultural and Technical College of North Carolina, a coeducational Negro state institution; and thirty miles to the south, in Raleigh, is the North Carolina State College of Agriculture and Engineering, which has a largely white student body with a very few Negroes.

When I reached the Durham airport, which lies south of the town in a wide stretch of sandy soil and pines, there, waiting for me in the wind and bright cold sunshine, was Mr. McKissick, a round-faced, erect, keen-eyed man in his late thirties. Beside him stood three youths, all with thin mustaches and all wearing trim topcoats, scarves, and narrow-brimmed Rex Harrison hats. McKissick introduced them—John Edwards, nineteen years old, a student at Durham Business College, which is a one-year private Negro school, and president of an N.A.A.C.P. Youth Council group called the Crusaders; Claude Daniels, also nineteen, also a student at the business college, and also a Crusader; and Bruce Baines, eighteen, a senior at the all-Negro Hillside High School and treasurer of the Crusader group. With awkward, elaborate courtesy, the boys took my bags and, after practically dusting off the front seat of McKissick's car for me, handed me into the vehicle, then themselves got into the back.

As we rode toward Durham, through a countryside of small tobacco farms, the boys' conversation slowly expanded from the "No, Ma'am"s and "Yes, Ma'am"s of which it had at first been solely composed. They told me that although Durham had been the fourth town in the state to desegregate its schools, it had not done so until September, 1959. "If you call desegregation having eight Negroes in with fifteen hundred whites in the junior and senior high schools. We call it just one bean in a basket," said John, a long-lipped boy with bright eyes, who often interspersed his rapidly spoken remarks with drolleries in a heavy Southern accent, to the delight of both himself and his listeners. He went on to tell me that McKissick's next-to-youngest daughter was one of the integrated students at the junior high school, and that an older sister of hers, now in college, had been admitted to the high school. Local newspaper stories that I subsequently looked up described the integration of the high school as "uneventful"; it had come about by the decision of the school board, acting on what the press called "the overwhelming volume of 225 Negro reassignment requests"—the largest number of such requests ever sent in by Negroes in a Southern community. Accompanying one newspaper account was a photograph of McKissick's daughter walking into school escorted by her mother and father, past some jeering white students. The lawn was strewn with leaflets that the newspaper said contained such exhortations as "Remember Little Rock. The people there at least had the guts to fight. Does Durham have less Courage?" The source of the leaflets was not identified, but opposing the enlightened influence of the many higher educational institutions about Durham, I later learned, is an inflammatory weekly entitled the *Public Appeal*, which specializes in long outpourings by Gerald L. K. Smith, among others.

. . .

I asked the boys to tell me about the Crusaders, and Claude, a tall, handsome youth with sharply cut features, large and somewhat mournful eyes, and an antique, daguerreotype kind of dignity in his manner, told me that the organization had been established at Hillside High about four years ago and now also included groups in Bull City Barber College and De Shazer's Beauty College, as well as in the Durham Business College. "Besides the Crusaders, the movement's got men and women students in the N.A.A.C.P. group at North Carolina College, and some Duke students," he said. "There's even a white Durham High School girl in it—she made all our picket signs. All told, there's about a thousand of us in the movement." (All of the organized local activity for desegregation was, I discovered, usually lumped under the heading of "the movement"—or more formally, in the printed literature, the Protest Movement.)

"Last August, our big chain-store lunch counters—Kress's, Woolworth's, and Walgreen's—were officially desegregated," said John. "And every few weeks two or three of us keep testing around, dropping into other lunch counters to see if they'll serve us. There are over half a dozen places where we can eat now in the main downtown business district. Before that, if you had a job downtown and didn't want to go way back over the tracks to the Negro section, the only warm food you could buy was hot dogs at a couple of places that'd let you stand up and eat them. You get *awful* sick of hot dogs. A few other places would serve you sandwiches wrapped up but wouldn't let you eat them there." I asked the boys if, in addition to lunch counters, any white restaurants with table service had been desegregated. "Oh, no," they said, looking at me in astonishment.

When I asked what the task of getting the lunch counters integrated had been like, the boys were silent for a moment. Then Bruce—who, in spite of his hat and his mustache, looked absurdly young—spoke up. "We started sitting in and picketing on February 8, 1960, and except for Sundays and a few times when the stores closed, we didn't miss a day until six months later, when the counters were desegregated."

"How many days did you fellows actually sit in?" McKissick asked.

After some figuring, the boys said that in their case the average was probably fifteen days or so, although much additional time had, of course, been spent picketing.

"Also, you might say they had some casualties," McKissick told me. "These young fellows are known among the Crusaders as the Jailbirds. They've each been arrested at least once. Bruce is under a thirty-day sentence to work on the roads—suspended on condition of two years of good behavior—for assaulting a white man."

"There was a lot of pushing one day we were sitting in, and this big man fell off his stool and yelled for the police," explained Bruce. "I was lucky I only got a month."

"John and Claude are out on bail on a trespass charge," said McKissick. "During two days in May, we had two mass arrests, and eighty kids were indicted. Seven of them were convicted and given both fines and jail sentences. We've consolidated the seven cases and appealed to the state Supreme Court. What happens to them will decide what happens to the seventy-three others. You've been arrested two other times, haven't you, John?"

"They didn't amount to much," said John. "They were squashed in court."

"Douglas Thompson, who was killed last summer in a car accident, he's got on his gravestone that he was a Crusader. He was arrested, too," said Claude.

· · ·

I now inquired about the new protest the group was planning. In unison, the youths opened their topcoats to show small white tags bearing the legend, in red, "I do not attend segregated movies. DO YOU?"

"At four o'clock tomorrow afternoon, we start picketing the theatres," John said. For a long while, he continued, the younger Negroes had been restive about theatre segregation. The city has five motion-picture houses, I was told. Two admit only whites. A third is run by a Negro in a slum section of town, and is out of bounds for college students. "You wouldn't want to take a young lady there, and she couldn't go there alone," Claude said. "It usually books only second- or third-rate shows, anyway." The two other theatres admit Negroes, via separate ticket booths and entrances, to what John called their "buzzards' roosts," one a second balcony, the other a third balcony. "That third balcony is at the Carolina," said John. "It's a tall building, and the balcony is over six stair flights up. Even if your eyes are good enough to see the movie, it's likely you're too tired when you get up there to enjoy it. And old folks can't make it at all." None of the boys had been to the movies for about four years. It was four years earlier that the idea of protesting the theatre situation had been conceived and the tags that the boys now wore had been printed. "Before we used the tags, we wanted to give the city a chance to do something," John said. "So we wrote a letter to the city manager telling him how dissatisfied we were. But nothing ever happened. We were about to start against the theatres last year when the lunch-counter sit-in began." In July, he went on, in negotiations with the Mayor's Committee on Human Relations—a nine-member biracial advisory group of merchants, professors, ministers, and civic leaders appointed by the mayor—the Negro students had agreed that if the lunch counters were desegregated, there would be no new demonstrations of any sort "until it was felt that reasonable adjustment to this move had been made by the community."

"The college students started the lunch-counter protest," said McKissick, "but it was the Crusaders who put it over. The college kids had to slack off when they began using up their classroom cuts, and a lot of them were away during the summer."

"This time, *we're* starting the demonstration, and we hope it's going to spread all over the South," Claude said. "The college students are studying for exams, so we've told them we'll keep the lines going for two weeks by ourselves, till they can join us."

"The Carolina and the Center—the two segregated theatres—are the ones we're going to picket," John said. "We intend to keep it up until they get desegregated. Over at Chapel Hill, there's *no* theatres admit Negroes. *Porgy and Bess* is showing there, and the students are picketing to let colored people see it."

"You'd think they'd let Negroes into *Porgy and Bess*, wouldn't you, man?" Bruce put in.

"The Chapel Hill manager says he'll have an extra ten-o'clock showing, but we don't want that kind of token arrangement," said Claude.

"Over near the coast, I hear there's a theatre has three separate entrances—one for Negroes, one for whites, and one for Indians. That must be *mighty* confusing," said John.

"Like the old blind folks in an institution I hear tell about," said Claude. "It's got white people in one section and Negroes in another. People take them out together to visit other blind folks' homes, and when they get there, they're all supposed to right away segregate themselves." . . .

. . .

The next day, the temperature was down in the low twenties, and a bitter wind was fitfully swirling flakes of snow about. McKissick's offices, where I had arranged to meet the boys after lunch, turned out to be a pleasant set of rooms up a flight of wooden stairs in one of a row of old buildings not far from my hotel. Scrubbed, combed, and pressed, John, Claude, Billy, and Bruce were waiting for me. Their scarves were arranged carefully around their necks and their anti-segregated-movie tags fluttered from their lapels. Except for their frequent consultation of note pads that they kept pulling out of their pockets, their behavior seemed calm and normal. With them were two white Duke students—Franklin Ingram, a blond, bespectacled Southerner majoring in sociology, and Ned Opton, a tall, dark-haired Yale graduate who was studying for a Ph.D. in psychology. After introducing them, Claude triumphantly held up a car key. "I have the use of a car for the day," he said. "We have some errands to do before we go to St. Joseph's Church, where we've asked people to meet about three, when we'll get ready for our movie-theatre protest. If you'd like to come along, we can show you some more of the town. But please don't expect modern transportation." Leaving Ingram and Opton, who were to rejoin us at the church, we started off in a sedan that was several years old.

"We wanted to begin our demonstration with a solemn march from St. Joseph's to the City Hall, where we would recite a prayer before going to the theatres," said Billy. "So we asked for an appointment with the assistant chief of police. He talked real nice. But he said he had to deny us a permit in the public interest. 'We don't want a race riot, and I know you don't,' he said. 'We're only trying to keep law and order. The police is neutral.'"

"The police *always noo*tral," said John, winking.

We were driving through residential streets lined with modest, nicely kept houses—low-roofed double dwellings of white clapboard, each in its own yard, where, in many instances, there stood magnolias or other ornamental trees. "We think this is the garden spot of Durham," Claude said. "We all grew up here, within a few blocks of each other." He pointed out a large red brick school with white pillars, which the boys had all attended, and farther along, in a newer section, we came to the Durham Business College, which is housed in a former grade-school building. We stopped at a white cottage with an old spinning wheel decorating its porch to pick up a well-dressed and exceedingly high-spirited lad named McKinley Cates.

As we drove along, Claude asked John if he knew whether or not a certain girl would be at the church.

"Now, man, don't mix business and pleasure in the movement," said John.

Claude protested, "I just want to ask her something about school"—a remark the other boys found very amusing.

"This afternoon is *business*," said John sternly.

At John's house, we waited for some time while he collected some articles for the demonstration, did a couple of chores, and changed into a warmer sweater. Once, we saw him walk across his yard, looking pre-occupied and carrying a load of kindling. As we waited, Billy and McKinley were talking quietly in the back seat.

"Did you see that television show from Georgia last week?" asked Billy.

"Pertainin' to what?" said McKinley.

"They had some Ku Klux Klanners on, and they told how they felt about colored people. You know, you could tell by their manner of speaking those guys were *businessmen*. They were important and educated."

"I can believe it, man," said McKinley. "I can even believe one of them might be a policeman."

"It just don't seem right for a bunch of adults, *businessmen*, to talk that way, McKinley," said Billy.

"Someday it won't be that way any more," Claude put in.

"Man! I would live one thousand years to see that time come, man," said McKinley.

When John had rejoined us, and we were on our way to the church, I asked him if his parents had had anything special to say about his again participating in a protest.

"'Get your chores finished first, boy,' they say, same as always. And then, 'Be careful, Son,'" he replied.

"Mine always say, 'Remember, prayer is the most important thing,'" said Billy.

. . .

It was now two o'clock. I was feeling a little tense, and said so. "You're shaky because it's the first time," Billy told me comfortingly. "I was, too, my first time. But just a turn or two up and down the line and you feel all right again. What's real hard, and you have to *learn* to do, is to accept inside of you all those things people do to you that you ordinarily wouldn't take. They call you names. They throw ammonia on you. They even spit in your face—that's the worst."

"Don't the police make them stop?" I asked.

"The police don't see so good," said Claude.

"The police is *noo*tral," said John.

"One time we felt real bad," Billy said. "It was real cold, and a white man with a long scraggly beard and a raggedy coat came up to us on the line with a carton of hot coffee and cups, and wanted to treat us. We had to refuse him. We didn't know what might be in that coffee, and we just couldn't trust *anybody* we didn't know."

On Fayetteville Street, the main artery of the Negro section, Claude stopped the car before St. Joseph's Church, a large brick building with tall stained-glass windows. We all got out, and I followed the boys through the swirling snow into a windowless room in the basement of the parish house, which served as their headquarters. It contained rows of folding chairs facing a long table; a battered piano; a mantel with a tissue-paper rose stuck in a mirror over it; and a counter, behind which were an icebox and a stove. On the front wall, between a conventional-ized pastel picture of Christ and an American flag, was a blackboard chalked with "Rules for Decorum Around the Church." Against one wall stood three or four dozen hand-lettered signs. Claude began exam-ining them. "These are the ones we used in the sit-ins," he said. "We've changed a word here and there so we can use them again." The other boys busied themselves at the long table. Billy and Ned, the white Duke student, who had just arrived, were trying to remember the exact word-ing of the oath the students had taken the previous year, before the sit-ins began, because they were to repeat it today. John was outlining the statements that he and Claude, as the group's spokesmen, would make to reporters. Other problems were swiftly solved. It was decided that John, Billy, Claude, and Ned were to superintend the picketing, while Bruce was to stay at the church and move the shifts of pickets off to the theatres at the proper intervals. There was to be a maximum of around forty pickets at one time, divided between the two theatres, but this strength would probably not be reached until the college students joined in. "We're going to have mostly young ladies at first, and it's going to be pretty cold on those lines, so we'll have to use half-hour shifts," John said.

The problem that now concerned the boys most was how to get the pickets from the church to the theatres, almost a mile away. Billy still had his heart set on the "solemn march" that the police had forbidden. "Not down the middle of the street," he said, renewing his appeal, "but just two by two, quiet and serious and peaceful along the sidewalk. You couldn't call that a parade."

"The police could," said Claude.

"Suppose we don't have a parade," someone said. "Suppose we just go over to the other side of town separately. If we don't have a parade, we don't get arrested."

"If we don't do nothin', we don't get arrested, either," said Billy. "Attorney McKissick says no matter how hard we try not to, we'll probably have some arrests eventually. If a lot of people collect, there's jostling, and then we can get arrested for obstructing the sidewalk."

"I don't anticipate trouble or arrests at first," said Ned. "Not till the news gets around."

"We don't want arrests *any* time," said John. "We got to be especially careful to keep moving and not block anybody when we change shifts—that's the bad time."

Finally, it was agreed that the pickets would proceed to the theatres more or less as Billy had proposed—"quiet and serious and peaceful along the sidewalk," but not in any formation the police could object to, and with no overt demonstrations.

· · ·

It was now a little after three o'clock, and young people with schoolbooks under their arms were beginning to arrive. They stood around chatting in groups, or sat down on the straight chairs with sober expectancy. There were girls dressed in wool plaid skirts, gay sweaters, and warm, bright-colored coats, and others wearing much washed cotton frocks and thin, unlined raincoats. There were a few North Carolina College girls with stylish coiffures and costume jewelry, and junior-high-school students with braids and bobby socks. Boys wearing fur-lined gloves and sturdy new parkas greeted lads in frayed slacks and grimy pullovers. On one side of me, a tall, gangling youth in ill-fitting clothes was studying a chemistry book. On the other side, bouncing about on her chair in a high state of excitement, a plump teenager chattered with three companions. A young man with a large, handsome head and sad, staring eyes slowly pushed his way through the crowd, a white cane in his hand. He was guided to a seat in the row behind me by a spindly boy in glasses, who told me later that his friend had a beautiful singing voice, and also that he had learned at Durham Business College to take dictation on the typewriter at the rate of fifty words a minute. The blind boy, though he would not be able to join the picket line, stayed throughout the meeting, his head cocked to the discussion.

A very young white girl with blond hair and a demure, animated face, framed by a little black hood, had come in, and now stood laughing with Claude and Billy. Presently, Claude led her over to me. She was the Durham High School girl who had originally made all the picket signs. I complimented her on her work, and asked her how she had happened to become interested in the desegregation activities. Last spring, she said, one of the Negro girls at her school had invited her to a meeting at which Roy Wilkins, the Executive Secretary of the N.A.A.C.P., had spoken. "I have awfully strong feelings about this," she said. "I moved here from New Jersey, and there's a lot of injustice back there, too, you know. Why, you can tell when you are in the Negro section of a town just by the condition of the sidewalks. Quite a few white kids at our school feel bad, too, but not enough to risk their popularity. I just feel much better when I'm doing something about it."

A dozen white students from Duke had arrived, in spite of a mimeographed appeal, which one of them showed me, issued by the predominantly anti-segregation Christian Action Commission of the university's Methodist Student Center, suggesting that sympathetic students wait until after exams to picket, because "academic failure on the part of any student involved would enable the university legitimately to call the protests into question." Among those from Duke was a lively, dark-eyed young woman who, I learned, was the co-chairman of a Human Relations Coordinating Committee made up of undergraduates from Duke and North Carolina College. She had taken part in both the picketing and the sit-ins of the past year, and she told me about the attention given to the Duke girls involved in the demonstrations. "People decided we were either riffraff or Communists," she said. "The old ladies with pursed-up mouths were the worst. 'She's just trying to get men,' they'd say, or, 'Poor thing, I guess she doesn't have a mother.' Sometimes they'd even shout, 'Who are you sleeping with?' The times we were most apt to have serious trouble were Saturdays, when people from the back hills came to town. Still, you'd be surprised at the number of white women who whispered, 'Keep it up. I'm for you!'" Though the Duke girls had occasionally undergone some heckling at college from male students, and particularly from those who were members of the more fashionable fraternities, she went on, many Southern girls had expressed their regret that, out of loyalty to their parents—who were, after all, paying for their education—they could not join the movement. "But they'd do without Cokes or movies, and contribute that money to our fund," she said. The police, she felt, had on the whole behaved correctly. "Of course, tempers got short sometimes when the weather was hot, and then there were little harassments. We were nagged to shorten or lengthen our lines, to slow up or speed up, and so on. Sometimes new policemen were a little rough. But we finally learned to report such incidents. We got results, too."

A Negro man sitting nearby, who, I learned, was a member of the North Carolina College Education Department and had accompanied his daughter to the church, began chatting with the Duke girl about the college students' part in the movement. When the white girl remarked that she hoped to bring Duke and North Carolina College students together in greater numbers, he said, "Don't do anything special. Let it come naturally. There's been too much special done for too long." The girl looked a little surprised, and he explained, "For two hundred years now, the American Negro has been assigned a special position. People do special things for us, pay us special attention. We don't want special attention any more. All we ask is to be recognized as just Americans—free to be accepted or rejected on an individual basis, like other Americans, and not because we are part of a particular group."

• • •

Now John, sitting at the center of the long table, with Claude, Bruce, Billy, and Ned about him, raised his hand for silence. He looked very serious. First he asked everyone to recite the Lord's Prayer, and then, when silence had fallen once more, he announced, "Mr. Ned Opton, Bruce Baines, Billy Thorpe, Claude Daniels, and myself will serve as your leaders until the college students' exams are over. As you know, we have two social-action projects for this year—to break down the barriers of segregation in movie theatres, and to gain employment in private business and local, state, and national government. We'll start the first project by picketing the Center and Carolina Theatres. Our purpose in doing it isn't just to get to see a movie but to break down another barrier of segregation. How many of you have picketed with us before?" About seventy-five people, or three-fourths of the audience, raised their hands. "Good," said John. "Now, how many of you would like to go right down to the theatres this afternoon and start picketing?"

There were gasps of surprise and titters of nervous laughter. Eventually, almost everyone present raised his hand.

"I need ten young ladies to leave immediately for the Carolina and Center Theatres as our scouts," John said. "They are to try to buy tickets at the main entrances. If refused, they are to ask to see the manager. They are to be *very* polite to him, and say, 'Good afternoon, we want to buy tickets at your main ticket booth and sit in the orchestra.' If the young ladies don't call us back in half an hour after leaving here, we'll know they are sitting downstairs in the theatres." The audience hooted at this supposition. If the managers refused, John continued, the girls were to call the church immediately, then gather on a designated corner between the theatres and wait for the pickets. John then selected the ten girls, including a well-dressed child in a red coat, sitting in front of me, who got up, the picture of frightened determination, and almost visibly forced herself to join the others as they left the room.

John rapidly explained the picketing procedure. Since the group was not yet at its full strength, thirty pickets at a time would be divided between the two movie houses. The first group, accompanied by the four watchers, would leave for downtown, carrying the picket signs, as soon as the scouts phoned. Mondays through Thursdays, the picketing schedule would be from four o'clock in the afternoon to eight at night; on Fridays it would be from four to nine; and on Saturdays it would be from one to nine. It was especially important, John said, that on this first day the pickets be present for the start of the last show, at nine o'clock, and he asked everyone to stay for as many rounds of picketing as he could manage.

"There's a very important oath that you are asked to take. Brother Daniels here will explain it to you," John said, introducing Claude.

"This oath is to cover your conduct for the entire period of the movement, whenever you are participating in it," Claude said. "First I'm going to read it. Then I ask you to stand and repeat it phrase by phrase after me, raising your right hand to God. Then I want you each to come and sign your name right here on the piece of paper the oath is written on."

The students fell into deep silence as Claude slowly read the oath. Then they raised their hands, and, in strong, clear tones that made the room reverberate, they echoed the phrases: "I do solemnly swear that while serving as a student protester I will demean myself in an orderly manner. I will refrain from taking any mental or physical action against anyone even to protect my person. I will not use profane language. I will not talk to anyone nor carry any sharp weapons while serving as a student protester. I will conduct myself in a Christian non-violent manner, and I will love all persons, even the ones I protest against. I do solemnly swear to uphold the above oath while I am a student protester, notwithstanding any circumstances that may occur. Amen."

Before Claude administered the oath, mimeographed sheets of regulations for pickets had been passed out, and now Ned rose to ask that everyone read them attentively and be careful to observe them. The first rule was "There shall be no violence displayed in any way, physically, mentally, or morally, within the Protest Movement." A number of the succeeding rules arose from this basic precept: "Carry no type of object, sharp or otherwise, that can be used for a weapon," "Do not take advantage of a situation or a person," and "Assume a respectful and sympathetic attitude toward the opinions, beliefs, shortcomings, and mistakes of others." Some regulations concerned general conduct, which was to be that of "young ladies and young men" at all times: "Do not tell questionable jokes," "There should be no petty grievances among the group. If some should arise, please contact your leaders at once, privately," "Refrain from showing discord with leaders publicly," and "Please do not walk in the street or public places eating and smoking."

Now Billy issued final instructions. No one was to go downtown to join the protest until he had checked with Bruce. Since a parade permit had been denied, the members of each shift leaving the church must be careful to walk close to the curb and remain well separated, so as not to obstruct pedestrian traffic. "Once on the theatre line, keep five feet apart and close to the curb, but not close enough for a car to run into you," he warned. "At each theatre, the two lines will walk toward each other, pivot at a spot we will show you, and then walk away from each other. Don't *ever* stop moving, even after leaving the line. The sidewalk is public, and if we follow these rules we can have the use of it. We won't go into any part of the theatre itself—not even near its walls for shelter from the weather, or into its doorway to get warm. Remember, too, not to jaywalk or break any other minor regulations. People will be watching to tell the police on us." Finally, he said, "When the first shift goes downtown, only the two students at the head of the column are to hold up their picket signs."

McKissick had been standing at the back of the room, and now John asked him to say a few words. The lawyer briefly outlined the kind of conduct that might lead to arrests, then said he knew that no one in the movement would be guilty of behavior that could lead to arrests for disorderly conduct or the use of obscene language. "You'll be all right if you remember always to conduct yourself, both within and without, in a Christian, gentle, and loving manner," he finished. "What you are doing is far-reaching in effect. Whether you know it or not, when you carry that picket sign you are carrying it for every black man who walks the face of the earth, whether in the Congo, in Johannesburg, or in New Orleans. If a man happens to spit on you, remember that what you are doing is far more important than what he is doing. If we speak quietly and act quietly, God will be with us. Nothing can hurt us if we march with dignity, hold our heads high, and remember our oath. God bless you!"

There was a second of silence, and then the young people, their faces aglow, broke into applause. Through it came the ring of a telephone. John hurried off to answer it, and returned a moment later to report that the scouts had been refused admission to the orchestra seats of the theatres. He swiftly chose thirty boys and girls for the first shift, and in a few minutes, outside in the cold wind and still swirling snow, they formed into pairs, tucked their signs under their arms, and, with the four leaders consulting lists and giving instructions as they kept alongside them, started the long walk downtown.

• • •

At the head of the column, which was strung out for half a block, two boys carried signs reading, "Don't Attend Segregated Theatres," and "Segregation Is the Negroes' Burden and America's Shame.—M. L.

King." As I walked along, keeping beside or behind the pickets, I watched both their young, solemn faces and the faces of the people they passed on the crumbling, uneven sidewalks of the Negro part of town. Upon the approach of the column, people stopped, with almost comic abruptness, whatever it was they were doing to stare for a second or two; then their faces broke into expressions of emotion. Most often, the first emotion was amazement. Then, usually, came pleasure. A gaunt, bespectacled Negro man with white hair took off his hat and flourished it. "Here come the kids again!" he cried exultantly. A woman called up to a friend gaping out of a second-story window, "It's the theatres they're after now! Whee!" Half a mile away, near the railroad tracks, as we hurried through a shabby district where knots of people were lounging in front of stores and bars, a large black woman smelling heavily of beer stomped out of a saloon and for a while walked beside me at the end of the line. "Good for them! God, if I was only that young again to join them," she kept mumbling.

When we had gone through an underpass beneath the tracks and emerged in the white district, there were no more smiles. On the contrary, the faces that turned to stare seemed to freeze in an identical expression—a rigid, hostile look of worry. As we approached a large building on Main Street, Billy dropped back to walk with me. "That's where we were put in the clink," he said. I saw a motorcycle policeman emerge from the building and, with his back to us, walk over to his machine. He had swung one leg over it when the column came into his line of vision. Without wasting a motion, he smoothly swung his leg back again and, at a measured pace, reentered the building. At an intersection up ahead of us, a white-capped traffic patrolman turned to signal waiting cars, spotted our column, put his hands on his hips in a gesture that was almost an audible exclamation, and left his post to stride down the sidewalk ahead of us, in the direction of the theatres.

"I feel bad," Billy suddenly said to me as the column split into two sections, one bound for the Center and the other, which we followed, for the Carolina. "I just remembered I forgot to introduce you to our meeting."

I said it was the last thing I would have expected him to do at so tense a time.

"I do apologize," he said. "We like to respect our visiting guests."

At the theatres, which were a few blocks apart, policemen were now collecting like flies around a pudding. Ahead of us walked an assistant police chief; patrolmen were standing before the movie houses; and several motorcycle officers hovered in the offing. The Carolina, a cliff-like building, stood on a windy corner at the bottom of an incline. As I followed the column toward it, I heard raucous laughter. At the rear entrance of a store, peering down an alley at us, stood a crowd of smirking men and women. "Hi, you niggers—" someone started to call out, and then the door was suddenly banged shut.

Before the lighted theatre marquee, announcing *The Grass Is Greener,* with Cary Grant, Deborah Kerr, and Robert Mitchum, about half of the column halted at Billy's order; the rest, led by Claude, went around the corner to the colored entrance. Calmly, Billy and Claude instructed their pickets while the theatre manager and his assistants, crowded into the ticket booth, watched, as did the policemen and a number of men in some garages across the street. Then the pickets began their slow march back and forth. "Democracy Lies Buried Here," proclaimed the first sign, which bore a white cross. It was carried by the boy who had been the blind student's escort at the church. Now a faded stocking cap was pulled down over his ears, and the collar of his outer garment—an old suit jacket—was turned up against the strong wind. I also recognized the young girl who headed Claude's column, and many of the other marchers. As they passed me, they did not so much as look at me. Each was withdrawn far back into his own loneliness.

Before long, four white teen-age boys, slack-jawed and leather-jacketed, appeared and, grinning widely, began circling the lines. The pickets paid no attention to them, and kept to their silent, expressionless march.

The biggest teen-age boy accosted Billy. "We going to kick up a little trouble with you," he said.

"Go right ahead," Billy replied. "I'll get you a little help—a police escort."

At that, the white boys sauntered away.

A little later, a newsboy who had ridden up on a bicycle began arranging bundles of papers on the sidewalk so as to increasingly confine the space in which the pickets walked. One of the policemen ordered him on.

After I had watched a couple of changes of shift, I decided to walk over to the Center and see how things were going there. On the way I met Ned, looking elated. "All is well," he said. Through the lighted windows of several stores, I could see white salesmen selling goods to Negro customers. At the corner, where the Center's marquee announced "Roaring Action, Excitement, Thrills, Stirring Adventure!"—provided by the ubiquitous Miss Kerr and Mr. Mitchum in *The Sundowners*—the picket lines were being photographed by a man crouching in the street under the watchful eyes of several policemen. On the corner directly opposite, John was being interviewed by a reporter. His hands fumbling in the cold, the man was writing down on a pad the wordings of the picket signs, which John obligingly read off to him: "We Hold These Truths to Be Self-Evident, That All Men Are Created Equal," "Why Feed Red Propaganda by Making Democracy a Lie?," and "This Generation Will Not Tolerate Segregation." When the reporter asked if it was true that the pickets were being paid two-fifty an hour, John denied it with dignity. "We expect someday to be paid in being recognized as first-class citizens," he said.

The picketing seemed to have little effect on most older white theatre patrons, who walked through the lines as though they were mist. One white woman, however, who had a Cub Scout in tow, crossed the street to offer an apology to John before entering the Center. "My sympathies are with you," she said, "but I promised Sonny I'd let him see the kangaroos. He'd make himself sick if I took him home now." The picket lines seemed to disturb quite a few white adolescent couples. They would halt their conversation for a moment when they spied the pickets, and then, looking straight ahead, would proceed into the theatre with elaborate nonchalance. Two young Negro couples, whose battle with their consciences had begun almost a block away from the theatre, stood under the lighted sign "Colored Entrance" for almost ten minutes, and at last walked hurriedly away.

Not long afterward, two young white men emerged from the theatre and, walking up to John and Ned, asked to take a turn on the picket line. They identified themselves as Duke graduate students. One revealed that he was from the Deep South, and Ned asked how his friends at home felt about such protests. "My own family is against integration," the student said. "The thing you notice most now down home is the fear among the white people. The old patterns of habit and trust that held them together seem to be breaking up."

A burly white man who had been standing nearby for some time, looking on with a preoccupied, troubled air, came over. He had just returned to North Carolina after ten years with the armed services in Japan, he said, and went on, "Over there, we were trying to tell people how liberal and democratic America is. The first day I got back, I stopped off at the courthouse on some business, and what did I see? All these kids filling the courtroom—on trial. It grated on me. I was going to go back into the service, but now I think maybe I can do more by staying right here."

Just then, two big, husky white men stopped before him. "Ed, for God's sake, where did you turn up from?" one of them shouted jubilantly.

After several minutes of loud, back-pounding reunion, one of the men stared at the picket line and said, "What do you know—what the jigs up to now?"

"They're trying to get the theatres desegregated," the man said stiffly.

His two friends broke into incredulous laughter. The man spoke to them earnestly for a while. Finally, with uneasy glances at each other, they bade him goodbye and moved on.

It was now past seven o'clock, and though I was dressed warmly, in boots and a fur coat, I was shivering. At this point, I encountered Billy, who noticed my plight, and told me to follow him. He led me down a side street and into an ancient office building. In its first-floor corridor, sitting on a flight of wooden stairs or huddled over a radiator, were about twenty of the pickets, trying to get warm while they waited their third or fourth turn on the line. A Negro attorney, Billy said, had allowed them the use of the hall for the evening, and it was hoped that, upon evidence of their good behavior, he would repeat his gesture on following nights. A few minutes after I arrived, a boy entered and stood near me, beating his gloveless hands together, his face stiff with cold. He told me it was his first experience in the movement, though his three brothers had picketed last year, and the oldest of his four sisters, a North Carolina College student, hoped to join the lines next week. His father was a bulldozer operator, he said. "The only thing bothering me is my homework," he went on. "I want to go either to Michigan State or U.N.C. I got to make good grades for that. I want to teach chemistry or math. *Nothing's* going to keep me from it, *nothing*. But I've got to do my share in this movement, too."

The door opened again and John came in, holding up a box of vanilla wafers and a bag of sugar cookies, which he passed around. A somewhat unkempt boy in sneakers and a frayed windbreaker stuffed a cookie into his mouth and then began talking to me in a burst of expansive confidence. "It's not right that we can't see movies except in the balcony," he said. "But I understand why white folks don't want to sit down and eat with Negroes. Not *sit down* and *eat* right beside them."

A girl sitting on the steps, thumbing a textbook, her thin raincoat pulled over her cotton dress, looked up at him calmly. "Under the skin, same bony structure, Joe, same organs, same heart," she said.

"I suppose when we're old, and all this segregation gone, we'll say, 'Gee, that was done quick,'" the boy said.

"It doesn't seem quick to me, Joe," the girl replied.

A little later, I said good night to John and Billy, and told them I would look in at the church the next afternoon before they left for the theatres.

Back at the hotel, I bought a copy of the Durham evening paper. There on the front page were the headlines "N.C. HIGH COURT BACKS CONVICTIONS HERE—SIT-IN TRESPASS VERDICTS UPHELD." The court held that "no statute in this state forbids discrimination of people on account of race or color, or white people in company with Negroes" by the owner of a privately owned restaurant in a privately owned building, and concluded that the defendants "have not shown the violation of any of their rights, or the rights of any one of them," as guaranteed by the state and federal constitutions.

I decided to walk over to McKissick's office, on the chance that he might still be there. I found him alone and looking tired, at work over a stack of documents on his desk. The next week, he said, he would start the necessary steps to carry the trespassing case to the United States Supreme Court. I had been told that a clear decision on this particular issue had so far been sidestepped by the highest court, and I also knew that there were several similar cases pending. When I spoke of this, McKissick summarized his legal view for me. "The stores have been licensed to serve the public by the state," he said. "When they refuse service in one part of the store on the basis of race alone, and call in the police and courts to enforce that refusal, the aid of the state is being used to enforce racially discriminating policies contrary to the due-process and equal-protection clauses of the Fourteenth Amendment." If the Supreme Court refused to review the case, he added, the seven defendants, as well as, presumably, the other seventy-three students under trespass charges, would go to jail.

• • •

When I arrived at St. Joseph's the next afternoon, many of the protesters were gathered before the bulletin board, which bore newspaper stories and photographs of the theatre picketing. I heard no mention of the court decision, but, possibly because of that news, or because of the continued unusual cold, or, as Claude suggested, because there were double chores to do, noticeably fewer people had turned up than on the previous day. As they waited for more to arrive, those on hand struck up some songs. One of these was a tune called "Freedom," whose title they chorused again and again, while single voices came in with lines such as "We'll sit at the counters all day long!" There was a now mournful, now serene piece called "We Shall Overcome," which concluded with the phrase "Deep in my heart I do believe we'll walk hand in hand someday." The singing ended with

> We shall not, we shall not be moved.
> Just like a tree
> Planted by the water,
> We shall not be moved.
>
> Black and white together,
> We shall walk together.
> We shall not be moved.
> Just like a tree
> Planted by the water,
> Oh, let's tell the Saviour,
> We shall not be moved.

"We'd better get ready to start," John said, finally. "You did a splendid job yesterday. But we must watch out for two things. First, the police warned us that unless we keep five feet apart on the picket lines they will take action. And, second, no young lady—or young man, either—is to leave from downtown alone. Last night, a young lady left the line by herself and was followed by a white man and given a bad scare. We will see that you leave either in a group or by bus or taxi or private car. Now let us pray." All heads were bowed. "Thank You for the things You have done for us, O Lord," John began. "We ask that You watch over us, guide us, and make us strong and able, so that You may be pleased with us. Make us like Moses when he led his people out of the wilderness. We don't ask You to make the road easier for us, God, but only to always let us know You in our hearts."

Back in New York, a few weeks later, I phoned McKissick to find out how the protest was coming. "All right," he said. "The Crusaders kept the line going till the college students came in. One day, twenty-five faculty members from Duke and North Carolina College joined them. Groups like ours are now picketing theatres in five other North Carolina towns, and in more than a half-dozen places outside this state, including Dallas and Oklahoma City. Around here, it's been the darnedest coldest weather since people can remember, but these kids have staying power; the picket lines haven't missed a day. There have been no major incidents. But there have been no signs of theatre desegregation, either."

FROM

AN EDUCATION IN GEORGIA

Calvin Trillin

JULY 13, 1963 (INTEGRATING A PUBLIC UNIVERSITY)

B Y MAY 17, 1954, when the United States Supreme Court declared racial segregation in public education unconstitutional, most Southern states had already desegregated their state universities, some voluntarily and some under a prophetic series of Supreme Court rulings on the practical inequality of "separate but equal" education. After the 1954 decision, some of the states had to pretend that the Negroes attending their universities with whites did not exist; otherwise, a good deal of the oratory of the late fifties would have been impossible. In 1957, for instance, when Governor Orval Faubus, of Arkansas, decided that the enrollment of a dozen Negro students in Central High School in Little Rock would result, as surely as election follows the Democratic nomination, in a breakdown of public order, the University of Arkansas had been integrated for nine years. Jimmie Davis promised the voters of Louisiana in 1959 that he would go to jail before allowing a Negro to attend classes with whites, and was elected governor on that platform, in a state whose university had been integrated for eight years. And a year later, when the Louisiana legislature passed a whole string of bizarre bills designed to prevent even the token integration of the New Orleans public schools, four hundred and twenty-five Negroes were attending the New Orleans branch of Louisiana State University.

In the states of the Deep South where no Negroes attended white universities before 1954, the first assault on segregation came in higher education, and came after the battle lines were drawn, with the result that it was considered as much of a threat to the system as if it had come in the grade schools or the high schools. The Negro students involved had none of the anonymity of those who had integrated the universities of Arkansas, Louisiana, Virginia, North Carolina, and Tennessee, nor were they blurred by inclusion in a group, like the teenagers in Little Rock or the four first-graders in New Orleans. One after another, they became famous, but only for two or three weeks, their names, in some cases, fading so quickly from the news that many people now find it hard to keep them straight: Autherine Lucy, at the University of Alabama; Charlayne Hunter and Hamilton Holmes, at the University of Georgia; James H. Meredith, at the University of Mississippi; Harvey Gantt, at Clemson College, in South Carolina. Student Heroes of a strange new kind, they were famed for no achievements in athletics or scholarship but merely for showing up to attend classes. Their presence was the test of the desegregation order, whether the test resulted in successful defiance, as in Alabama, where Autherine Lucy was expelled after three days for accusing the university administration of complicity in the riots that accompanied her arrival, or in peaceful compliance, as in South Carolina, where the state authorities decided in advance that upon Harvey Gantt's admission to Clemson order would be self-consciously maintained. Nowhere was the test more decisive than in Georgia, where Charlayne Hunter and Hamilton Holmes, two Negroes from Atlanta, entered the state university, in Athens, in January of 1961. During their first week at the university—which began in relative calm, was climaxed by their both being suspended "for their own safety" after a riot, and ended with their both returning to the campus, under a new court order—Georgia abandoned its policy of all-out resistance and accepted desegregated education.

According to the lawyer for the plaintiffs, an Atlanta Negro named Donald Hollowell, the University of Georgia case was "the case that turned the state around and allowed them to start, or at least to *see,* what was in the other direction." Few would disagree with his belief that the enrollment of Charlayne and Hamilton in the university was the turning point for Georgia, being accomplished in a way and at a time that made it inevitable (a word formerly scorned and now almost popular in Georgia) that the state would move forward rather than backward. The walk out of the Deep South mentality has been accelerated a good deal since then by a federal-court ruling against the County Unit System, which formerly made Georgia the only state to elect not only its legislature but its governors, senators, and congressmen by a voting system designed to favor the rural voter, and the atmosphere in Georgia now is far different from what it was when Charlayne and Hamilton showed up in Athens on a cold Monday morning two and a half years ago. Among the Student Heroes, Charlayne and Hamilton have another distinction, too. They are the first to have completed their education, or at least their undergraduate education. Since both entered the University of Georgia after completing the first half of their sophomore year elsewhere—Hamilton had gone to Morehouse, a private Negro men's college in Atlanta, and Charlayne to Wayne University, in Detroit, during the year and a half it took them to get into Georgia after first applying for admission—they graduated this June, both in good standing and Hamilton as a Phi Beta Kappa. As a reporter then based in Atlanta, I had covered both the weeklong trial that resulted in their admission and the events that followed their arrival on campus in 1961, and this spring, ten weeks before Charlayne and Hamilton graduated, I returned to Georgia from New York, where I had been living, to see how integration had worked out at the University of Georgia—whether or not the Student Heroes had ever become simply students. And because this question involved not only the university's attitude toward them but their attitude toward the university, I began by trying to find out how these two young people had happened to become Student Heroes in the first place. Both had always been considered perfectly cast for the role. Good-looking and well dressed, they seemed to be light-complexioned Negro versions of ideal college students—models for an autumn Coca-Cola ad in a Negro magazine. Both had attended Turner High School in Atlanta, and Charlayne, a slim, attractive girl with striking hazel eyes, had edited the school paper, had been crowned Miss Turner, and had finished third in her graduating class. The valedictorian that year was Hamilton, who had been president of the senior class and, as a promisingly shifty halfback, co-captain of the football team. Since Charlayne and Hamilton had been such unlikely targets for abuse from the start, and had eventually been joined at the university by several other Negro undergraduates, the situation, looked at from a distance, seemed rather heartening. None of the stories from Georgia about school integration had mentioned any violence done to the pioneers. They had dealt instead with the peaceful integration of public schools in Atlanta and the admission of Negroes to Georgia Tech in September of 1961 without even the pressure of a court case. The atmosphere was such that Emory University, a private school in Atlanta, had been able to desegregate its nursing school voluntarily and was planning the integration of its medical school, having already chosen Hamilton Holmes as its first Negro medical student. But I knew from occasional communications I had had from Charlayne and Hamilton since they entered the university that the general progress of the State of Georgia often did not seem closely related to the day-to-day problems facing the first Negroes at the University of Georgia. I was reminded of this again by Charlayne's reply to a letter I wrote her announcing my plans to revisit the campus. "Well, this is Brotherhood Week in Athens," she concluded, with characteristic irony, "and I'm going out to stand on the street corner and wait for an invitation to lunch." . . .

. . .

The Atlanta Negro community has traditionally been led by the wealthy businessmen who run the insurance companies, banks, and real-estate offices on Auburn Avenue, and by the presidents of the six private Negro colleges that make up Atlanta University Center, and it has long had a considerable middle class, whose level of prosperity and education is the highest in the Negro South. Negroes have registered freely since 1944, when the white primary was declared unconstitutional, and in the last two mayoral elections in Atlanta the candidate who was elected did not have a white majority. But even though Atlanta was a relatively enlightened city—"too busy to hate," a former mayor used to say—it had achieved little integration by the late fifties. The traditional leaders of the Negro community, usually called the Old Leadership, seemed to have settled into the belief that the white businessmen, always called the Power Structure, would take care of everything in time if the boat remained unrocked and the voting coalition remained unbroken. "Atlanta was comparing itself to Mississippi and saying how enlightened it was," says Whitney Young, Jr., the executive director of the National Urban League and a former dean of the Atlanta University School of Social Work. "Nothing was really integrated, not even the library or the buses, but the people were beginning to believe their own press clippings— even the Negroes." Early in 1958, to make a study of just what had been done in Atlanta toward equality for the one out of every three citizens who was a Negro, Young and several other Negroes, most of whom were in their forties and most of whom had their headquarters on Hunter Street, in the newer Negro district, rather than on Auburn Avenue, started an informal group called the Atlanta Committee for Cooperative Action, or A.C.C.A. The editor of the study, which was published eight months later under the title "A Second Look," was Carl Holman, who was then an English professor at Atlanta University Center's Clark College, and is now the public-information officer for the Civil Rights Commission in Washington. From 1960 to 1962, Holman was also editor of the Atlanta *Inquirer*, a lively weekly founded during the Atlanta sit-ins by him and some other Negroes who were fed up with the cautious policies of Atlanta's Negro daily newspaper. By the time "A Second Look" was published, it had the backing and financial assistance of the Old Leadership, and it immediately became a guide to the action that was needed. The younger men, working through existing organizations whenever that was possible and forming new ones when it wasn't, initiated the action, pulling the Old Leadership behind them—the pattern that integration activities in Atlanta have followed ever since. The man from the A.C.C.A. group who was most concerned with school integration was Jesse Hill, Jr., the energetic young chief actuary of the Atlanta Life Insurance Company, which is the second-largest life-insurance company in Georgia and one of Auburn Avenue's most solid institutions. In 1957, Hill, who was a member of the education committee of the local chapter of the National Association for the Advancement of Colored People, had enlisted the help of two or three other Negro leaders in an attempt to desegregate the Georgia State College of Business Administration, in Atlanta. Georgia State had the advantages of being a city college with no dormitories, which obviated travel and rooming problems, and of having night sessions. "In those days," Hill told me when I visited him in Atlanta, "people hesitated to send a seventeen-year-old kid into that hostility, and we were working mainly to get older people to try for the night school. Frankly, we did some real campaigning. We tried to enlist some of the people in our own office, for instance. We got three girls to apply, and we won our court case, although the judge didn't order the plaintiffs admitted. By that time, the state had investigated the girls who were applying and found some illegitimate births and that kind of thing with two, and so they could have been turned down on so-called moral grounds. Also, the state passed a law that said nobody over twenty-one could start as an undergraduate in a Georgia college, which eliminated the third girl and, of course, ended any chance of having older people apply for Georgia State."

In 1958, working quietly (in anti-integration laws passed after the 1954 decision, Georgia strengthened its laws against barratry, or incitement of litigation), Hill and some of the other younger men compiled a list of outstanding seniors in the city's Negro high schools and began to approach those whose academic records were so good that a college would have to find other reasons for rejecting them. Hill talked to about a dozen students, some of whom agreed to consider Georgia State and some of whom were more interested in the University of Georgia or Georgia Tech or the state medical college at Augusta. Ultimately, either because something in their backgrounds made them vulnerable to one kind of attack or another, or because of a final unwillingness to go through with it, none of these actually applied. Then, in June of 1959, Hill found Charlayne and Hamilton.

"Ordinarily, this is a selling job," Hill told me. "You have to go seek out and work with these people and do quite a bit of selling. That's how it's been with the other kids at Georgia and those at Tech and all. But not Hamilton and Charlayne. They had an almost normal desire to go to the University of Georgia—as normal as you could expect from a Negro in a segregated community. They both knew something about the school; Hamilton had followed the football team, and Charlayne knew all about the journalism school. They were almost like two kids from Northside." Northside is a formerly all-white high school in Atlanta's best residential district, and it may be a sign of progress that one of the Negro freshmen at Georgia Tech last year actually *was* from Northside, having entered it as one of the nine Negro seniors who integrated Atlanta high schools in 1961. "Hamilton Holmes was on the list," Hill went on. "But I really didn't have to recruit those kids; they almost recruited me. They knew just what they wanted. I took them over to Georgia State. We were after a breakthrough, and we had a good chance there. The judge had retained jurisdiction in the case, and Georgia State had plenty of vacancies, because of this age law. The Atlanta *Journal* had run pictures of almost empty classrooms. That was important; after all, the University of Georgia kept Charlayne and Hamilton out for a year just by saying they were overcrowded, and it sounded pretty legitimate, on the face of it. Anyway, Charlayne and Hamilton wouldn't hear of going to Georgia State. Both of them wanted to go to Georgia. Why they wanted to go I'll never know, but it happened that that was the right thing. It got straight to the heart of the matter. I think the Governor might have closed Georgia State or the Atlanta high schools if they had come first, but Georgia, with all those legislators' sons over there, and the way everybody in the state feels about it, was different. He wouldn't dare close it."

Once Charlayne and Hamilton had decided to go to Georgia, Hill set out to do battle again with the system that had defeated him in the Georgia State case. He fired the first volley of letters and phone calls through the facilities of Atlanta Life, and then got the local N.A.A.C.P. chapter to put up the money for the legal expenses that were necessarily incurred before the litigation got far enough along to be eligible for aid from the N.A.A.C.P. Legal Defense & Educational Fund, Inc. (a separate corporation from the N.A.A.C.P. itself, and usually called the Inc. Fund, or the Ink Fund). Hill had to make a lot of long-distance calls to find the Turner High School principal, whose signature was required on the application forms and who had left for the summer. Hill went to the Fulton County Courthouse with Charlayne and Hamilton, towing their pastors along as references, and was passed from judge to judge until the clerk of the Fulton County Superior Court finally agreed to certify that both of the young people were residents of the State of Georgia—documentation that the federal court ruled was adequate without the addition of alumni recommendations, which were formerly required and which, naturally, were not easy for Negro applicants to obtain. Hill, Holman, and Young met with Charlayne and Hamilton to warn them of what to expect from Georgia admissions officials and Georgia students. "I had sent for application blanks and a catalogue and hadn't got them," said Hill. "We wanted to make sure we had them in time. Like most places, the University of Georgia has Negroes to do the cleaning up, and one of the janitors got application blanks and catalogues for us. Every time we took a step, we double-checked. I must have written a hundred letters to the university; they wouldn't tell you anything. Don Hollowell checked every letter. We had to certify it and send it registered mail, receipt requested. Anything that got lost, that was the end of that for another year. It was just like pulling teeth. Carl Holman checked and double-checked the applications. We didn't leave anything to chance. And still, it took a year and a half."

The energy was provided by the same men who had published "A Second Look." In the first weeks after Charlayne and Hamilton applied, the A.C.C.A. group even maintained a nightly patrol of Charlayne's house. (Atlanta has always had more bombings than Southern cities with otherwise less progressive race relations; there were a dozen in the twelve months prior to public-school integration.) Support from the rest of the Negro community varied greatly. Some members thought that Georgia Tech or the Atlanta public schools would be a better place to begin. Others believed that it was rather early to begin anywhere. "A lot of people were opposed to this," Hill told me. "They said, 'These people are going to take reprisals on us. There'll be a loss of jobs, and all.' During the Georgia State case, one leader of the Negro community said, 'Why'd you take those unwed mothers over there?' After Charlayne and Hamilton applied at Georgia, he said, 'Why'd you take those two fine kids over there?' All we ever got from the older leaders was 'You're going to mess up some kids.'"

. . .

Just why "two fine kids" like Hamilton and Charlayne should want to go to any Southern white college is a question that is often asked in the North, where many people take it for granted that a Negro student would go to jail for the right to eat a dime-store hamburger but must have an elaborate motive for going to a formerly all-white school. Most white Southerners have already settled the question to their own satisfaction. They believe that the students are chosen by the N.A.A.C.P.—hand-picked by one of the crafty operators from New York, where all evil finds its source, and probably paid handsomely for their services. The New York–based N.A.A.C.P. conspiracy remains a strong vision to most white Southerners, even though it should be apparent by now that if the N.A.A.C.P. had a tenth of the resources and efficiency they credit it with, segregation would have been eradicated years ago. As for Negroes in Atlanta, when they talk about why Hamilton went to the University of Georgia they usually begin by mentioning his family, and especially his grandfather, Dr. Hamilton Mayo Holmes, who is an Atlanta physician and the family patriarch. Hamilton is not only a third-generation college graduate; he is also a third-generation integrationist. His grandfather, his father, and one of his uncles filed suit to desegregate the Atlanta public golf courses in 1955, and, through a 1956 Supreme Court decision on their case, the courses became the first integrated public facility in Atlanta. I had spent some time with Hamilton's father, Alfred Holmes, during the integration in Athens, and on one of my first days in

Atlanta this spring I arranged to talk with him at his office about both his son and his father. Alfred Holmes, who is known in Atlanta as Tup, is a short, chunky man with a breezy manner and a cheerful, chipmunk-ish expression. He seems to know everybody on the street, whether it is Hunter Street or Auburn Avenue, in Atlanta, or Hancock Street, in Athens, where he worked for six or eight months as an embalmer early in his career. Almost everybody he sees gets a cheery "How you makin' it?" or "You makin' it O.K.?" Strictly Hunter Street in philosophy himself, Tup Holmes shares an office building there with the Atlanta *Inquirer*, the law offices of Donald Hollowell and his associates, the local branch of the N.A.A.C.P. (which disturbed some of the Old Leadership by moving there from Auburn Avenue not long ago), the Southeastern Regional Office of the N.A.A.C.P., and a school for beauticians. Holmes has been in several businesses, mostly selling one thing or another, and the office he ushered me into—a small one—was devoted to the sale of real estate and insurance. Having assured him that I was making it O.K., I asked him about Hamilton's decision to go to the University of Georgia.

"The aggressiveness of the family might have influenced him, but Hamp's a steady sort of boy," Holmes said. "He's always thought deeply and on his own. Jesse Hill asked if I would mention Georgia to Hamp, because he was just about perfect, with his grades and his personality. That's all I had to do was mention it; before I could do anything else, he had already talked to Jesse. I went down to Athens once or twice, and I tell you he's two different people when he's there and when he's in Atlanta. He lives for Friday afternoon, when he can come home. There's really no one in that town for him to talk to, and he's not the kind to do much visiting. He sticks to his lessons. He made up his mind he was going to make those crackers sit up and take notice. You know, I travel around the state quite a bit in my business, and sometimes I talk in the high schools or the churches. I didn't realize for quite a while what a hero this boy is to those people in the backwoods. When I'm being introduced to a group of people, sooner or later the man introducing me gets around to saying, 'This is the father of Hamilton Holmes.' And they say, 'You mean the Hamilton Holmes up at Georgia? Let me shake your hand.' I think he means so much to those people because of his grades. The white man in the South has always accepted the Negro as his equal or superior physically, because he figures we're not far removed from the jungle and we've had to do physical work for so long that our muscles have got hard.

But the whites never have accepted us as their equal or superior mentally. They have always said that the Negro is only good for plowing. Well, Hamp is destroying all those myths. He's made the Phi Kappa Phi honor society, you know, and we hope he'll make Phi Beta Kappa. When those people in the backwoods see those A's, they stand up. That's why he means more to them than James Meredith, or even Charlayne."

After we had talked a while longer, Holmes said, "Well, if you're going to get in to see Daddy, we'd better get over there. If you come after eleven-thirty, there's so many patients you can't get near the place." On the drive from Hunter Street to Auburn Avenue, where Dr. Holmes has his office, Tup Holmes told me about his father, whose prowess as a doctor, a golfer, and a speaker makes him almost as popular a subject for conversation in the Holmes family as Hamilton. "My daddy's a real scrapper," Tup Holmes said. "He ran away from home when he was twelve to go to school. He was from Louisiana. The backwoods. And I mean the real backwoods. He worked in the sugar mills in New Orleans and went to school at night in a small school that's now part of Dillard. Then he worked his way through Shaw Medical School, in North Carolina, and came to Atlanta to practice—that was in 1910. He's a real scrapper. Daddy was a pioneer on this golf-course thing. It required a lot of courage on his part, especially considering all the training and inhibitions of his generation. You have to remember that when he was coming up he would have to tip his hat and move to the side every time he saw a white lady on the street."

When we arrived at Dr. Holmes' office, on the fourth floor of an old building, it was half an hour before his office hours began, but six or eight patients were already sitting in the waiting room, watching television. They hardly looked up as Holmes and I walked into the Doctor's office, where a nurse from the treatment room, adjoining, told us to make ourselves comfortable until the Doctor arrived. Dr. Holmes' office was a small room, containing an old-fashioned desk, a refrigerator, a day bed, a floor safe with a filing cabinet on top of it, and two or three tables. Almost every flat surface was covered with golfing trophies, and the walls were covered with a staggering collection of plaques, pictures, and framed prayers. There were several religious pictures, some family pictures, and numerous plaques from golf organizations and fraternities. In one frame were three glossy prints of Hamilton and Charlayne and a letter from the Half Century Alumni Club of Shaw University. The wall decorations also included a chart showing the postal zone of every street in Atlanta, a sports award from radio station WSB for a hole-in-one made on January 1, 1961, and a cardboard reprint of the Prayer for Physicians by Maimonides. Between a plaque signifying life membership in the United Golfers Association, which is the Negro equivalent of the U.S. Golfers Association, and a poem about medicine from the Fifty Year Club of American Medicine hung an eye chart.

After a few minutes, Dr. Holmes bustled in. A jolly man, shorter, chunkier, and darker than his progeny, he had a tiny gray mustache and a tiny gray goatee. Since he also had tufts of gray hair on the sides of his head and more tufts of gray hair for eyebrows, he looked like a tiny Uncle Remus. He wore a three-piece blue suit, a diamond stickpin, and a watch chain. When Dr. Holmes heard that I was there to ask about Hamilton, he could hardly wait to begin.

"I trained my children from infancy to fear nothing, and I told my grandson the same thing," Dr. Holmes said. "I told him to be meek. Be meek, but don't look too humble. Because if you look too humble they might think you're afraid, and there's nothing to be afraid about, because the Lord will send his angel to watch over you and you have nothing to fear. I'm glad Hamp has faith; you have to have faith. Science is not enough; you have to have more than science. You have to know the Lord is watching over you. Hamp is a religious boy and he's a natural-born doctor. He's wanted to be a doctor since infancy. I told his mother before he was born, I said, 'You just think on medicine and if it's a boy maybe the prenatal influence will make him a natural-born doctor.' And she did think on it, and sure enough, that's what he is, a natural-born doctor."

Dr. Holmes talked a bit about his own practice. "I've been practicing medicine here for fifty-three years, and I'm busier now than I've ever been," he said. "I come in at eleven-forty-five and I stay until four-thirty or five. I come back at seven and stay till ten-thirty or eleven. I don't much like to work past eleven any more. I try to treat everybody as an individual. Once, a lady came in and said, 'You sure took a long time with that last patient,' and I said, 'O.K., if you want, I'll hurry on you.' She said, 'Don't hurry on me. Oh, no!' Well, I treat them all like individuals, but I still see fifty or sixty patients a day. I work every day but Wednesday and Sunday. I play golf on Wednesdays, and on Sundays I go to church. Then I play golf."

I asked Dr. Holmes if his game was still as good as the trophies indicated.

"I beat nearly everybody I play with, young and old alike," he admitted. "They say, 'I'm waiting for you to get tired.' I tell them they better beat me now, because I'm not going to get tired. I'll be seventy-nine on the fourth of April, but not an ache, not a pain, not a stiffness in the joints. Not a corn, not a callus, not a bunion on my feet. And my memory is as good as it was fifty years ago." And Dr. Holmes stretched his muscles and his joints to demonstrate their efficiency. I certainly had no reason to doubt it, or to doubt his memory. ("Hamp's granddaddy is quite a character," Charlayne told me a day or two later. "He called up once and said he'd decided Hamp and I should get married, and he'd give me any kind of convertible I wanted for a wedding present. He hadn't consulted Hamp, of course. I explained to him that Hamp and I were more like brother and sister, and that Hamp had a girl. But he said we would just have to get married, because we'd have such smart children.")

Charlayne, unlike Hamilton, is rarely explained as the logical result of a family tradition. In fact, even at the age of eighteen, when she entered the University of Georgia, she seemed remarkably independent. "She's always wanted to be out front," I was once told by her mother, a pretty, retiring woman who works as a secretary in a Negro real-estate company. "When she was a little girl, I never had to get after her to do her lessons, or anything. She's just always been that way." Charlayne's poise during the first days of integration was occasionally attributed to her having spent her eighth-grade year as one of only a few Negroes in an integrated Army school in Alaska, where her father, Charles Hunter, a career Army chaplain, was stationed. Now retired, with the rank of lieutenant colonel, he was often the first Negro to hold whatever post he was assigned to, but the extent of his influence on Charlayne is not certain. He and Mrs. Hunter separated after the year in Alaska, and Charlayne, who had previously gone for long stretches without seeing her father while he was overseas, rarely saw him after that, for she returned to Atlanta to live with her mother, her two younger brothers, and her grandmother. Charlayne's father is a Methodist minister and her mother is also a Methodist, but Charlayne became a Catholic when she was sixteen. At Georgia, Charlayne continued to look at things from a point of view of her own. In fact, because she was a journalism student, she had a kind of double vision for those two and a half years. During her first week or two at Georgia, she sometimes seemed to be watching the reporters watch her integrate the university, occasionally making notes on both phenomena for one of the articles on the integration she was later to write for the Atlanta *Inquirer*. According to Carl Holman, who, as editor of the *In-*

quirer, had also found that covering the integration news often meant observing his own activities, "It gave her a detachment she might not have had otherwise. Hamilton has the views of the average citizen on the subject; that is, he regards reporters as just as dangerous as anyone else. But Charlayne was always studying them, and I think it made her feel better that they were around."

One day last March, while Charlayne was at home for several days after her next-to-last round of final examinations at Georgia, she and I met for lunch at a restaurant on Hunter Street, and I found that she was still able to see her experience as a news story. Although she had always received more attention in the press than Hamilton, she assured me that Hamilton made a better study. "He's consistent and I'm not," she said. "He knows what he wants and where he's going and how he's going to get there. We're a lot different. For instance, he can't wait for Friday. He comes back to Atlanta every weekend. He has a girl here, and his family. I think my mother and brothers are great, but that's the only reason I come home at all. I'd just as soon stay in Athens and sleep or read. Hamp's very uncomfortable there. For one thing, he's not crazy about white people. And he loves Atlanta. I guess I'm just as comfortable there as I am anyplace else. Hamp and I were sort of rivals at Turner, but we usually agreed on big things. I wanted to go to journalism school, and I had considered Georgia, but not really seriously. It seemed such a remote possibility. I had just about decided to go to Wayne, for no special reason except they had a journalism department and had answered my letters and I wanted to go to school away from home. When Hamp brought up Georgia—I think it was while we were posing together for a yearbook picture—I said sure, I'd like to go. It seemed like a good idea. I can't stress enough that I didn't ponder it. I guess it always was in my mind that I had the right, but Hamp and I never had any discussions about Unalienable, God-given Rights. We just didn't speak in those terms. It sounded like an interesting thing to do, and in the back of my mind I kept thinking this would never really happen; it was just something we were doing. I guess at that stage of the game we thought that anything we wanted to do was possible. Each step got us more involved, but we didn't think of it that way. We just went step by step, and it seemed kind of like a dream. When we got together with Jesse Hill and Hollowell and Carl and Whitney Young, they thought we ought to go to Georgia State. It also had journalism courses, and I really didn't know the difference. Negro kids don't know anything about white colleges. We figured if it was white it was good. We picked up applications at Georgia State, but neither one of us really liked the place; the catalogue showed they really didn't offer much. We went out on the steps and stood around, and Hamp said, 'I want to go to Athens. That's the place to go.' And he pointed right in the direction of Athens. I said, 'I'm with you,' and they said, 'O.K., you'll go to Athens.' I think a lot of it was Hamp's having always taken an interest in the Georgia football team."

. . .

One reason for the dreamlike quality of the eighteen months that followed was that, except for two or three hearings they had to attend, Charlayne and Hamilton were merely spectators of the complicated maneuvers that Jesse Hill and Donald Hollowell—eventually joined by Constance Baker Motley, associate counsel of the Inc. Fund—were carrying on with the state. Charlayne and Hamilton regularly submitted applications, which were regularly turned down, usually on the ground of a space shortage, and all they had to do to be rejected again was to submit their college transcripts each semester. They did have to appear in federal district court in Macon, in the summer between their freshman and sophomore years, but at that time Judge William Bootle refused to order them into the university through a temporary restraining order, ruling that they had not exhausted their administrative remedies. He did, however, schedule a December trial on a motion for a permanent injunction. Under Judge Bootle's orders, Charlayne and Hamilton both went to Athens for admission interviews that November. At these, Charlayne was treated politely, and Hamilton, appearing before a three-man panel, was asked such questions as whether or not he had ever been to a house of prostitution or a "tea parlor" or "beatnik places"—questions that, Bootle later noted in a judicial understatement, "had probably never been asked of any applicant before." . . .

. . .

Although Hamilton's high-school record indicated that he was likely to have an outstanding academic career at Georgia, he was found unqualified before he went to court, and not, said the officials, because he was a Negro. Shortly before the trial in Athens federal court in December of 1960, at which I first met Charlayne and Hamilton, the university Registrar and Director of Admissions, Walter Danner, having considered the interviews with both students, wrote Charlayne that she would be considered for admission the following fall—there was no room for transfer students in her category before then—and wrote Hamilton that he had been rejected on the basis of his interview. Hamilton, the Registrar said, had been "evasive" in answering the questions put to him by the three-man panel, and had left its members in "some doubt as to his truthfulness." As Hollowell later brought out in the trial, these were almost exactly the same reasons that a special interviewing board had given eight years before for deciding that Horace Ward was unqualified to be a lawyer and should therefore be rejected by the University of Georgia Law School. (Ward had gone on to Northwestern Law School, had returned to join Hollowell's office in Atlanta, and must have derived a good deal of satisfaction from assisting Hollowell and Mrs. Motley in the trial, not to mention escorting Hamilton into the admissions office to register a month later.) The charge of untruthfulness was based on Hamilton's having given a negative reply to the board's question of whether or not he had ever been arrested. The admissions office, Danner said in court, just happened to know that Hamilton had once been fined and had had his license suspended for speeding, and the office considered that an arrest.

Before the trial, Mrs. Motley and three assistants spent two weeks going through the Georgia admissions files, which had been opened by court order. By comparing the treatment given Charlayne and Hamilton with that given other students, they had no difficulty in demonstrating that the whole business was a subterfuge, that the only real category the university had was white, and that the interviewers were less interested in Hamilton's speeding ticket than in the impossibility of stalling him any longer by claiming that the dormitories were overcrowded, since university rules permitted male students to live off campus after their freshman year. In any event, the housing problem was not so acute that the university had to refrain from sending a dean of the agriculture school to upstate New York that year to recruit students for its food-technology program. Moreover, the interview that had been considered so important in Hamilton's case was given to some students *after* they were already attending the university. The university, then, had been double-dealing for a year and a half, and it was instructive to see the double-dealing presented as a legal defense by a state that had vowed open resistance to integration. In the effort to correct the false notion that the South has a monopoly on bigotry, the equally false notion has been created that the North has a monopoly on hypocrisy, and I had often heard it said that "in the South at least everybody knows where he stands and people are honest about it." According to this way of thinking, the resistance promised on the campaign stump by politicians should have been continued in court by state officials. But the university officials I listened to for a week in Athens, testifying about their overcrowded dormitories and their administrative problems, sounded less like Southerners fighting a holy crusade than like Long Island real-estate brokers trying to wriggle out of an anti-discrimination law. After one has spent a few minutes listening to a desegregation trial, the reason for this shift becomes clear. It is a simple matter of law. In federal court, where the case must be tried, the issue has already been decided: segregation in the public schools is unconstitutional. The only possible defense is that segregation does not exist. When politicians say they will resist integration "by all legal means," they can only be implying that they will try to prolong litigation by any available dodge, since the issue has already been settled by all legal means. In Georgia, in 1960, a trial had to be held. It was demanded by what had evolved into a ritual of combatting integration even when it was obvious that the combat would do no good. . . .

To anybody who had sat through the trial in the Athens Federal Building—to the reporters, who sat in the jury box, or to the university and town people, who segregated themselves by race the first day or two, even though they were in a federal court, and only gradually got used to sitting wherever there was a place—it was no surprise to read Judge Bootle's decision that "although there is no written policy or rule excluding Negroes, including plaintiffs, from admission to the University on account of their race or color, there is a tacit policy to that effect," and that the plaintiffs "would already have been admitted had it not been for their race and color." However, Bootle's decision, issued one Friday afternoon in early January, 1961, a month after the trial ended, did contain one surprise; it ordered the students admitted not by the following fall, as had been predicted, or for the spring quarter, beginning in March, but, if they so desired, for the winter quarter, for which registration closed the following Monday. . . .

. . .

The University of Georgia was desegregated with unusual suddenness. Only a weekend separated Judge Bootle's surprise order and the appearance of Charlayne and Hamilton on the campus—not enough time for either the side of law or the side of violence to marshal its forces. A succession of contradictory or ambiguous court orders and executive acts added to the confusion. At one point, Judge Bootle stayed his own order, to allow time for an appeal, only to have Elbert Tuttle, chief judge of the Fifth Circuit, rescind the stay within a couple of hours. From the vague statements of Governor Vandiver and the refusal of President Aderhold to say anything at all, there was some doubt whether the university would remain open or not. The result of all the confusion was three relatively non-violent, if chaotic, days on campus for Charlayne and Hamilton, and a spate of congratulations to the university from television newscasters and Northern newspapers on how well everybody had behaved. Some of the undergraduates at Georgia had spent the weekend rounding up signatures for petitions to keep the university open—the dominant concern of most students. Others had engaged in some minor effigy and cross burning, including a sorry demonstration I witnessed on the football practice field the Saturday night before Charlayne and Hamilton arrived. Twenty-odd students wanted to burn a cross made of two-by-fours, but, owing to a lack of kerosene and a lack of experience in this kind of endeavor, they were unable to get it ablaze. Most of the demonstrations against integration during the two new students' first three days on the campus seemed to be in that tradition. When Charlayne and Hamilton showed up at nine o'clock Monday morning, they were met only by a small group of curious students and a few reporters. In fact, throughout the first day, as Hamilton and his father and Horace Ward walked around campus going through the registration process, they often met with nothing more than some stares or a muttered "Hey, there's that nigger." The crowds around Charlayne were larger, but they seemed almost playful, even when they began to bounce a car she was riding in, or swarmed into the Academic Building, where she was registering, to yell "2-4-6-8! We don't want to integrate!"—a chant they had borrowed from the women screaming at six-year-olds outside the integrated schools in New Orleans. A large crowd, triggered by a speech of Vandiver's that seemed to say the school would close, marched through downtown Athens on Monday night behind a Confederate flag. On Tuesday night, the first night Charlayne spent on campus, some of those who had found out which dormitory she had been assigned to—Center Myers—gathered on the street in front of it to chant, push around some television cameramen there, and throw some firecrackers. It was a rowdier crowd, but, like the rest, it was broken up by Dean Tate, who, working singlehanded, confiscated some university identification cards and told some of the boys he knew to go home.

In a special issue of the campus newspaper Tuesday, ten student leaders issued a warning that violence could only mar the image of the university. By Wednesday, just about everybody on the campus knew there was a riot scheduled in front of Charlayne's dormitory after the basketball game that night. It had been organized by a number of law-school students. All day Wednesday, the organizers scurried around making plans and bragging about the promises of help and immunity they had received from legislators. Some students got dates for the basketball game and the riot afterward. Reporters, faculty members, and even some students warned Joseph Williams, the dean of students, about the riot and suggested that he ban gatherings in front of the dormitory, or at least cancel the basketball game. But Williams said that neither step was necessary. Just after ten, a small crowd of students gathered on the lawn in front of Center Myers and unfurled a bed-sheet bearing the legend "Nigger Go Home." Then three or four of them peeled off from the group, ran toward the dormitory, and flung bricks and Coke bottles through the window of Charlayne's room. Dean Tate had been assigned by Williams to remain with the crowd at the gymnasium after the basketball game, and Williams himself, standing in front of the crudely lettered sign, made no attempt to break up the group. As more people came up the hill from the basketball game—a close loss to Georgia Tech—and a few outsiders showed up, the mob grew to about a thousand, many of whom threw bricks, rocks, and firecrackers. The few Athens policemen present were busy directing traffic, and after about thirty minutes Williams finally agreed to let a reporter phone the state police, who had a barracks outside Athens. Although the university understood that thirty state troopers would be standing ready in the barracks, the desk sergeant said that he could not send the troopers without the permission of the captain. But the captain said he had to have authority from the Commissioner of Public Safety, and the Commissioner, in turn, said he could not make a move without an order from the Governor. (In a failure of communications that still fascinates students of Georgia back-room shenanigans, it was so long before the Governor gave the order that the state police did not arrive until an hour after the riot was over and two hours and twenty minutes after they were called. Then a carload of them came to take Charlayne and Hamilton back to Atlanta.)

The riot was finally broken up by the arrival, together, of Dean Tate, who waded in and started grabbing identification cards, and of more Athens cops, who started fighting back when they were pushed, and then drove everybody away with tear gas. It had been a nasty riot, but the group courage that sometimes comes to mobs had never infected it. Although the students could have stormed the dormitory several times without meeting any effective defense, they never did. A few hours after the television newscasters had congratulated Georgia on its behavior, the area around Center Myers looked like a deserted battlefield, with bricks and broken glass on the lawn, small brush fires in the woods below the dormitory, and the bite of tear gas still in the air. The casualties were several injured policemen, a girl on the second floor who had been scratched by a rock, and, as it turned out, the university's reputation. Dean Williams suspended Charlayne and Hamilton, informing them that it was "for your own safety and the safety of almost seven thousand other students," and they were driven back to Atlanta. Williams' on-the-spot decision to suspend the target of the mob, rather than those in the mob itself, seemed unrelated to anybody's safety, since it was made after the last rioter had gone home and after university and Athens officials had assured Williams that order had been restored and that giving in to the mob would only mean going through the whole experience again. Dean Williams and Charlayne, who was crying by this time and clutching a statue of the Madonna, walked right out of the front door of Center Myers into the state-police car, watched only by a few straggling reporters.

• • •

From the moment the two arrived on campus, Charlayne attracted much more attention than Hamilton. At the time, some onlookers explained this by devising complicated anthropological theories about the greater interest in the enemy female. Others said it was only natural that unfriendly students should believe the girl more likely to be frightened away by their presence and that friendly students should think her more in need of their support. Dean Tate's answer is that it was merely a matter of convenience. He calculated that two or three times during the day there were two thousand students within two hundred yards of Charlayne, whose classes at the Henry W. Grady School of Journalism kept her on the busiest part of the campus, whereas there were far fewer students around the science center (which is removed from the main campus), where Hamilton spent most of the week. The fact that Charlayne took a dormitory room, while Hamilton moved in with a Negro family in Athens, made the difference even greater. Then, after the riot, stories about it, including a widely published picture of Charlayne leaving the dormitory in tears, made her better known to people outside Athens as well. The immediate result of Charlayne's publicity was that in her first week or two at Georgia she received about a thousand letters—three or four times the number Hamilton got—from all over the United States and several foreign countries. Charlayne's mother filed all the letters by states, the Georgia and New York folders ending up the fattest, and later sent each of the writers a reprint of an article Charlayne wrote about her experience for a now defunct Negro magazine called the *Urbanite*. I was interested in seeing just what people wrote in such letters, and during my trip this spring I borrowed the folders from Mrs. Hunter, who has them stored in a big pasteboard box. Charlayne told me later that the University of Georgia library would like to have the letters eventually but that she hesitated to give them up, especially while some of the writers might be embarrassed by even a historian's perusal of their names and opinions. That was an understandable objection, I thought, but it did seem like the justice of scholarship for the university to end up with nearly a thousand expressions of outrage at its behavior. There were only fifteen or twenty abusive letters, I discovered, and this surprised me, but I was more surprised to find that most of the particularly foul ones were from the North. The unfriendly letters from the South, even if they were written in the guise of kindly advice, were instantly recognizable, since in almost every case they contained no conventional salutation. "Dear Charlayne" would have been too chummy, and anybody willing to say "Miss Hunter" apparently would not have written a letter in the first place. Most of the writers solved the problem by starting out with a flat "Charlayne Hunter," as if they were beginning a formal proclamation. There were also surprisingly few crank letters, although some of the writers were obviously just lonely people who wanted somebody to write to, and a few of the letters, like one from Italy that began, "Dear Little Swallow," reflected emotions other than sympathy. A number were from Negro undergraduates (their own experiences with separate but equal education revealed in their spelling) who sent along a picture and hoped that a correspondence might develop. Many of the writers told Charlayne they were praying for her; many of the Catholics mentioned her conversion to Catholicism. She received dozens of prayer cards, copies of sermons by Harry Emerson Fosdick and Norman Vincent Peale, Seventh Day Adventist tracts, and two books by Gandhi. Several letters were from college student councils or N.A.A.C.P. chapters that had taken resolutions supporting Charlayne and deploring the action of those who persecuted her. Most of the letters from individuals also expressed admiration for Charlayne's "courage and dignity"—the phrase was used almost as one word—and outrage at the mob. There was often a mention of helplessness in the letters from Northerners, which included phrases like "This must be small comfort" and "Of course, I can never really understand." Some of those who believed they could never really understand nevertheless tried to establish their credentials for understanding, listing personal experiences with prejudice or with Negroes. A girl at the University of Connecticut told Charlayne that her high school had a Negro teacher, who was considered by all the students to be the best teacher in the school; the yearbook had been dedicated to him four out of the five years he had been there, she said. A young white woman in West Virginia wrote that she was attending a formerly all-Negro college. "Your people are teaching me," she noted. But the great majority of the letters from the North had no personal experiences to offer. In many of them, a picture of Charlayne cut from a newspaper was enclosed, and most of them seemed to be from sensible, decent people who were appalled by the picture of a pretty girl being bullied by a mob and felt they had to write, even if they didn't know quite what to say.

The letters from Georgia had a different theme. Many of them were from University of Georgia alumni, who seemed to have a very specific and compelling reason for writing. They wanted to tell Charlayne that all of them were not like the mob or the people who permitted it to form. As I read through their letters, it seemed to me that each person who wrote felt he had to assure Charlayne of that or she might not know. On the whole, of course, the Georgia letters were also more realistic. But none quite captured the plain realism of a young boy in Rochester, New York, one of two dozen pupils in a parochial-school eighth grade who had apparently written to Charlayne as a class project. "Dear Miss Hunter," he said. "I am very sorry for the way you are being treated. I hope you have the courage to take this treatment in the future. Respectfully yours."

I had first discussed the letters with Charlayne two years before, when she was back in Atlanta for the weekend after her second week at the university. Since her return to the campus following the riot, she had been under police protection, and in consequence she was now cut off from the rest of the students even more sharply than she had been during the chaotic first week. She seemed amazed and moved by the number of people who had written to her, but she found some of their letters slightly off the subject. "All these people say 'Charlayne, we just want you to know you're not alone,'" she said, smiling. "But I look all around and I don't see anybody else." . . .

. . .

The pattern of the students' attitude toward Charlayne and Hamilton emerged during the week of their return. The fraternities and sororities let it be known that anybody interested in his own position on campus would be wise not to talk to the two Negroes. Another group of students, most of them associated in one way or another with Westminster House, the campus Presbyterian organization, formed a group called Students for Constructive Action. They posted signs about the Golden Rule in the classroom buildings and arranged to take turns walking with Charlayne and Hamilton on their way to classes. The girls in Center Myers had all trooped down to visit Charlayne the first night she was in the dormitory, reinforcing a widely held opinion that girls would always be kind to a new girl, even a new Negro girl, but on the following night—that of the riot—their behavior changed drastically. After the first brick and the first Coke bottle had crashed into her room, Charlayne went to a partly partitioned office, ordinarily used by one of the student counsellors, and stayed there during most of what followed. A group of Center Myers coeds soon formed a circle in front of the office and marched around, each screaming an insult as she got to the door. "They had been told to strip their beds, because tear-gas fumes might get into the sheets," Charlayne said to me later. "They kept yelling that they would give me twenty-five cents to make their beds, although at the hourly rate I was being paid by the N.A.A.C.P., according to them, it wouldn't have made much sense for me to work for a quarter. They kept yelling, 'Does she realize she's causing all this trouble?' Out of all the girls who had visited me the night before, only one girl came in and stayed in the office with me. But I finally made her go to bed. After a while, Mrs. Porter, the housemother, told me to get my things together, because I was going back to Atlanta, and that's when I started to cry. Dean Williams carried my books and my suitcase, which was pretty nice. He could have made me carry them. When we went by to pick up Hamp, he wanted to drive his own car back. I guess by then my imagination was running wild; I could imagine K.K.K. all up and down the highway. I didn't want Hamp to drive, and I almost got hysterical. Finally, he said O.K., he'd go with the troopers. Dean Tate went with us, and talked all the way back about the little towns we went through—things like why 'Dacula' is pronounced 'Dacula,' instead of 'Dacula.' The next day, at home, the lights were low, and people kept coming by saying how sorry they were. It felt as if I had been ill for a long time and was about to go, or as if somebody had already died. I was going back to Athens, but I was glad we didn't have to go back for two or three days."

MARCH ON WASHINGTON

Calvin Trillin

SEPTEMBER 7, 1963

W E FLEW TO Washington the day before the march and, early the next morning, walked from Pennsylvania Avenue past the side entrance of the White House and toward the lawn of the Washington Monument, where the marchers were gathering. It was eight o'clock—three and a half hours before the march was scheduled to move from the Washington Monument to the Lincoln Memorial—and around the Ellipse, the huge plot of grass between the White House grounds and the lawn of the Washington Monument, there were only about half a dozen buses. Most of them had red-white-and-blue signs saying "Erie, Pa., Branch, N.A.A.C.P.," or "Inter-Church Delegation, Sponsored by National Council of Churches of Christ in the U.S.A. Commission on Religion and Race," or "District 26, United Steelworkers of America, Greater Youngstown A.F.L.-C.I.O. Council, Youngstown, Ohio." On a baseball field on the Ellipse, three men were setting up a refreshment stand, and on the sidewalk nearby a man wearing an N.A.A.C.P. cap was arranging pennants that said "March on Washington for Jobs and Freedom. Let the World Know We Want Freedom."

Most of the buses were nearly full, and many of the occupants were dozing. Sitting on a bench in front of one of the buses, some teen-agers were singing, "Everybody wants freedom—free-ee-dom."

On the lawn of the Washington Monument, a group of military police, most of them Negroes, and a group of Washington police, most of them white, were getting final instructions. Women dressed in white, with purple armbands that said "Usher" and blue sashes that said "Pledge Cards," were handing out cards to everybody who passed. "I've already contributed to this," a man near us told one of the women. But the card asked for no money; it asked instead that the signer commit himself to the civil-rights struggle, pledging his heart, mind, and body, "unequivocally and without regard to personal sacrifice, to the achievement of social peace through social justice."

Outside march headquarters—a huge tent with green sides and a green-and-white striped roof—workers were setting up a rim of tables. One table held a display of pennants, offering a large one for a dollar and a small one for fifty cents. Inside the tent, a man wearing a CORE overseas cap, a blue suit, an armband with the letter "M" on it, and a badge saying "Assistant Chief Marshal," was testing a walkie-talkie, and another man was issuing instructions to a group of program salesmen. "Now, everybody report back by nine-fifteen, or whenever they give out," he said. Two or three Negroes were sorting signs that said "The Southern Christian Leadership Conference of Lynchburg, Virginia." In a roped-off area near one end of the tent, the official signs for the march were stacked face down in large piles, most of them covered by black tarpaulins. Next to the signs, in an enclave formed by a green fence, half a dozen women sat behind a long table. Two signs on the fence said "Emergency Housing." Nearby, three or four television crews had set up their cameras on high platforms.

By this time, there were several thousand people on the lawn, many of them gathered around the Monument. An ice-cream truck had managed to drive to within a hundred feet of the Monument and was starting to do an early-morning business. Many of those gathered near the Monument were sitting on the grass, and some were sleeping. Three boys dressed in khaki pants and shirts with button-down collars were using their knapsacks for pillows and had covered their faces with black derbies. There were, we thought, surprisingly few knapsacks and sandals in the crowd. Most of the people were neatly dressed, and as they waited for the pre-march program to start, they acted like ordinary tourists in

Washington, or like city people spending a warm Sunday in the park. A man took a picture of a couple standing in front of a sign that said "New Jersey Region, American Jewish Congress"; a policeman was taking a picture of two smiling Negro couples; a woman who was selling programs balanced her programs and her purse in one hand and, with the other, took pictures of the sleepers with derbies over their faces.

By nine o'clock, a group of marchers had congregated outside a green fence surrounding a stage that had been set up several hundred yards from the Monument; they were standing six or eight deep against the fence. More people were arriving constantly—some in couples and small groups, others marching in large contingents. A group of young Negroes walked behind a blue-and-gold banner that said "Newman Memorial Methodist Church School, Brooklyn, N.Y., Organized 1900." Another group of Negroes—older, and wearing yellow campaign hats that bore the letters "B.S.E.I.U."—followed four boys who were carrying a long banner that said "Local 144" and two flag-bearers, one carrying the American flag and one carrying a flag that said "Building Services Employees International Union."

In front of the headquarters tent, a group of young people in overalls and T-shirts that said "CORE" were marching around in a circle, clapping and singing.

"I'm going to walk the streets of Jackson," one girl sang.

"One of these days," the others answered.

"I'm going to be the chief of police," another sang.

"One of these days," the crowd answered.

Near the singing group, a double line of Negro teen-agers came marching across the lawn. All of them were dressed in black jackets. They had no banners or pennants, and they filed by in silence.

"Where y'all from?" a Negro girl in the CORE group asked one of them.

"From Wilmington, North Carolina," one of the boys replied, and the black-jacketed group walked on silently.

We started toward the stage and happened to come across Bayard Rustin, the deputy director of the march, heading that way with Norman Thomas. Following them up to the stage, we found two other members of the march committee—Courtland Cox, of the Student Non-Violent Coordinating Committee, and Norman Hill, of the Congress of Racial Equality—looking out at the people between the stage and the Monument and talking about the crowd.

At exactly nine-thirty, Ossie Davis, serving as master of ceremonies, tried to begin the pre-march program, but it had to be postponed, because Rustin and Thomas were the only two dignitaries on the stage and many more were expected.

"Oh, freedom," said a voice over a loudspeaker a little later. The program had started, and Joan Baez began to sing in a wonderfully clear voice. "Oh, freedom," she sang. "Oh, freedom over me. Before I'll be a slave, I'll be buried in my grave . . ."

Then came folk songs by Miss Baez; Peter, Paul, and Mary; Odetta; and Bob Dylan. Davis made the introductions, occasionally turning the microphone over to a marshal for an announcement, such as "Mr. Roosevelt Johnson. If you hear me, your child, Larry Johnson, is in the headquarters tent." By ten-thirty, the expanse of grass that had been visible between the crowd around the stage and the crowd around the Monument had almost disappeared, and more people were still marching onto the lawn, carrying signs and banners. Most of the signs identified groups—such as the Alpha Phi Alpha Fraternity and the Detroit Catholics for Equality and Freedom—but some had slogans on them, and one, carried by a white woman who marched up and down the sidewalk in back of the stage, said "What We All Need Is Jesus and to Read the Bible." Another folk singer, Josh White, arrived on the stage while Odetta was singing. White didn't wait for an introduction. He merely unpacked his guitar, handed the cigarette he had been smoking to a bystander, and walked up to the microphone to join Odetta in singing "I'm on the Way to Canaan Land." In a few moments, Miss Baez was also singing, and then all the folk singers gathered at the microphone to finish the song.

At about eleven, Davis announced that the crowd was now estimated at ninety thousand. From the stage, there was no longer any grass visible between the stage and the Monument. Next, Davis introduced a representative of the Elks, who presented the organizers of the march with an Elks contribution of ten thousand dollars; a girl who was the first Negro to be hired as an airline stewardess; Lena Horne; Daisy Bates, who shepherded the nine teen-agers who integrated Central High School in Little Rock; Miguel Abreu Castillo, the head of the San Juan Bar Association, who gave a short speech in Spanish; Bobby Darin; and Rosa Parks, the woman who started the Montgomery bus boycott by refusing to move to the back of the bus.

The official march signs had been passed out, and they began to bob up and down in the crowd: "No U.S. Dough to Help Jim Crow Grow," "Civil Rights Plus Full Employment Equals Freedom."

At about eleven-forty-five, Davis told the crowd that the march to the Lincoln Memorial was going to begin, and suggested that people standing near the Monument use Independence Avenue and people standing near the stage go down Constitution Avenue. We were closer to Constitution Avenue, and as we got onto the street there was a crush of people that for a moment brought back stories of the dangers inherent in a crowd of such a size. But almost immediately the crush eased, and we walked comfortably down shady Constitution Avenue. We noticed that practically nobody was watching the march from the sidelines, and that in the march itself there was a remarkable lack of noise. Occasionally, a song would start somewhere in the crowd, but to a large extent the marchers were silent. A few hundred yards from the Monument, the march was stopped by a man who was holding a sign that said "Lexington Civil Rights Committee" and wearing an armband that said "Mass. Freedom Rider." He asked the people in the front row to link arms, and, beginning to sing "We Shall Overcome," they moved on down the street.

"Slow down, slow down!" the man from Massachusetts shouted as he walked backward in front of the crowd. "Too fast! You're going too fast! Half steps!"

A few hundred feet farther on, a policeman and an M.P. stood in the middle of the street and split the crowd down the middle. We followed the group to the left, and in a few minutes found ourself standing in a crowd, now even quieter, to the left of the reflecting pool in front of the Lincoln Memorial.

YOUTH IN REVOLT

FROM

LETTER FROM BERKELEY

Calvin Trillin

MARCH 13, 1965 (THE FREE SPEECH MOVEMENT)

MARCH 3

ONE AFTERNOON JUST after the spring semester began at the University of California, I paused on my way to the Berkeley campus to make a tour of the card tables that had been set up that day by student political organizations on the Bancroft strip—a wide brick sidewalk, outside the main entrance to the campus, that had been the original battlefield of a free-speech controversy that embroiled and threatened the university for the entire fall semester. There were half a dozen tables, lined up, as usual, along the campus edge of the sidewalk, and hundreds of students were streaming past them onto the campus. By the time I had crossed the sidewalk to the tables, standup hawkers had presented me with a flyer announcing the picketing of Oakland restaurants by the Congress of Racial Equality, a flyer asking for contributions to raise bail for some earlier demonstrators from the Ad Hoc Committee to End Discrimination, and a homemade pamphlet called "Some Organizing Ideas: Excerpts from Idea Essay by Lee Felsenstein." The table at one end of the line was sponsored by the Young Socialist Alliance, an organization that is ordinarily referred to as Trotskyist, though few people seem to know just what the implications of that position are in Berkeley, California, in 1965. The Y.S.A. table was being watched over rather casually by a collegiate-looking young man in a blue blazer; he was reading a book, but would glance up occasionally at students who stopped to look at his display, which included leaflets in support of a local City Council candidate, pamphlets introducing the Y.S.A., and a number of booklets on the order of "Fidel Castro Denounces Bureaucracy and Sectarianism, Speech of March 26."

The Y.S.A. table was separated from the table of Slate, a campus political party of left-wing but non-sectarian views, by a cardboard sign announcing that placards for the CORE picketing of Oakland restaurants would be made on the steps of Sproul Hall, the administration building, the following afternoon. A young man wearing a lapel button reading "Free Oakland Now" was sitting behind the Slate table and calling out at intervals that he was selling the "Slate Supplement," a student critique of the university's courses. His table held not only a pile of "Slate Supplement"s but also leaflets protesting discrimination in Oakland, a mailing list to be added to by those interested in receiving Slate literature, a stack of pamphlets about Mississippi put out by the Student Nonviolent Coordinating Committee, and a pile of buttons that included two varieties of the "One Man, One Vote" buttons produced by S.N.C.C., along with several of the "Free Speech" buttons worn by supporters of Berkeley's Free Speech Movement, a few "Free Oakland Now" buttons, and one button that said "Slate." A student stopped at the Slate table and, indicating a sign that asked for contributions to the bail fund for the Ad Hoc Committee demonstrators, asked the Slate representative, "Did you hear about the DuBois Club pulling out of the Ad Hoc Committee?"

"That's not what happened at all," the Slate representative replied. "The Ad Hoc Committee broke up. They're having a press conference at one o'clock, and Mike Myerson's going to explain it."

"Do you expect me to believe anything in the press?" the student asked.

"It's *their* press conference," said the Slate man. "Mike Myerson is the president of the Ad Hoc Committee."

"That doesn't make any difference," said the student, and wandered off.

The DuBois Club had the table on the other side of Slate's. A couple of students were looking over the literature available there—mostly pamphlets describing the DuBois Club, plus the various magazines of the American Communist Party—while the young man in charge discussed the relative merits of two sociology courses with a friend. At the table next to his, a representative of the California College Republican Club was explaining to a passing student that that club was the only moderate Republican club on campus, and, at the table beyond, the Independent Socialist Club was selling "The Mind of Clark Kerr," a pamphlet criticizing the president of the university, by the Independent Socialist Club's leader, Hal Draper, which had been one of the popular pamphlets of the free-speech controversy. At the end of the row, a girl wearing a button that said "I Care" was sitting behind a table sponsored by the Student Committee for Agricultural Labor arguing patiently with a young man who had stopped by to offer his suggestions. "I think we have to concentrate on organization at this stage," the girl was saying.

"No, no, no!" the young man exclaimed. "The thing to do now is to picket the grocery stores. Then we sit in at the factories."

In addition to stacks of literature and a paper to be signed by those interested in becoming members of the organization or receiving its mail, nearly every one of the tables set up on the Bancroft strip has a pile of political buttons, the sale of buttons having become a popular way to raise money for student organizations at Berkeley. Students who want to protest against the House Un-American Activities Committee—and that seems to include most of the students who stop at the Bancroft strip—can usually buy a "Sack HUAC" button from the University Society of Libertarians or a "HUAC Eccch!" button from the Bay Area Council for Democracy; some of them already have a button that says "I Am Not Now Nor Have I Ever Been a Member of the House Un-American Activities Committee." Another popular button says "A Free University in a Free Society," and is sold by Students for a Democratic Society, an organization affiliated with but often to the left of the League for Industrial Democracy, and someone has attempted the succinct approach with a button that says simply "I am an Enemy of the State." The Cal Conservatives for Political Action, who are sufficiently outnumbered to find humor their most effective weapon, wear buttons that say "I Am a Right Wing Extremist." During my stay in Berkeley, one of the most popular new buttons has been one saying "Abolish the Regents." It is being sold by Ed Rosenfeld, a young man with a shaggy beard who has been an active worker in the Free Speech Movement. Rosenfeld ordinarily mans a table of his own, holding up a sign decorated with covers of

"The Regents"—a pamphlet that the F.S.M. published during the controversy in an attempt to show that the University Board of Regents represented corporate wealth in the state rather than the people—and shouting, "'Abolish the Regents,' twenty-five cents!"

"Does this money go for political activity?" a prospective customer asked while I was standing at Rosenfeld's table.

"Clearly," said Rosenfeld, who was himself wearing a "Get Out of Vietnam" button on one lapel and, on the other, the pin of the National Liberation Front, which is also known as the Vietcong, though rarely in Berkeley. "In this case, it will go to send a student to the Youth Festival in Algeria next summer."

"Who is the student?" asked the customer.

"I am the student," Rosenfeld said. "Naturally."

The customer bought a button, and Rosenfeld continued his chant. "'Abolish the Regents,' twenty-five cents!" he called out. "Send your favorite regent to Vietnam!"

· · ·

With the start of the spring semester, the leaders of the Free Speech Movement find themselves in a perhaps unexpected position—that of revolutionaries whose revolution has succeeded. The F.S.M. headquarters—a casually furnished storefront office where businesslike girls carefully compile logs of phone calls and cover the wall with messages written in marker pencil—bears a startling resemblance to the headquarters of the Council of Federated Organizations in Jackson, Mississippi. But, unlike COFO workers, who still can't be sure that their civil-rights campaign has made any significant change in conditions in Mississippi, F.S.M. workers need only walk a block or two to witness unrestricted campus political activity of the kind that was the goal of their movement, and, to anyone who has spent some time listening to their reminiscences, the F.S.M. headquarters, which is a relatively recent acquisition, seems to be a make-work echo of the days when the F.S.M. had a series of command posts, with names like Strike Central and Press Central—a system of walkie-talkies for communication among its scouts on the campus—and an emergency telephone number, called Nexus, to be used when the regular number was busy. During the fall semester, the free-speech controversy demanded the attention, and often the full-time participation, of a large number of Berkeley students, administrators, and faculty members; it involved an unprecedented use of mass action by students and two potentially disastrous confrontations between hundreds of students and hundreds of policemen; and it eventually produced a situation in which a distinguished university of twenty-seven thousand students nearly came to a halt—a situation that the chairman of the Emergency Executive Committee of the Academic Senate called, with little disagreement from anybody who spent the fall in Berkeley, "one of the critical episodes in American higher education." Those events are in the past, however, and unless another issue involving free speech arises on the campus—or, as many F.S.M. adherents would put it, "unless the administration commits another atrocity"—quite a few of the leaders of the Free Speech Movement are, in the words of one participant, "between movements."

According to the best-known F.S.M. leader, an intense, intellectually aggressive young man named Mario Savio, who was studying philosophy before he became involved in the controversy, "All that's left is the trial—legal and political defense—and making sure that the final rules on political activity are acceptable. Then, as far as the F.S.M. goes, that's it, we disband." The trial he referred to is that of some eight hundred students who were arrested, on the orders of the governor of California, when they refused to leave Sproul Hall during the protest sit-in that is generally considered to have been the climactic event of the controversy. Political defense can be carried out through activities familiar to participants in mass movements (during the first week of the new semester, the F.S.M. held a rally on "The Berkeley Trials: Justice or Vengeance"), but legal defense is another matter. The same students who, wearing blue jeans and singing hymns, had to be carried out of Sproul Hall by the police have conscientiously presented themselves, in quiet, well-dressed groups of fifty, in a makeshift courtroom in the auditorium of the Berkeley Veterans Building to enter their pleas. (For making a comment to the judge about "shameless hypocrisy" that would have been only a warmup for stronger language on the steps of Sproul Hall, Savio was given a two-day jail sentence for contempt.) The defendants have had to elect a Council of Twenty to deal with their staff of attorneys, who number at least twenty themselves, and F.S.M. leaders have acknowledged, with some embarrassment, that their movement, which once attacked the computer as the symbolic agent of its followers' alienation and which adopted "Do Not Fold, Spindle, or Mutilate" as one of its war cries, has lately been borrowing the university's I.B.M. machine to keep track of all the people involved in its legal affairs.

Officially, the issues that divided the Free Speech Movement and the university administration have not yet been completely settled. The Board of Regents, which has final authority over Berkeley and the eight other campuses of the University of California, still has a committee working to determine what its final policy on political activity should be; the Berkeley chancellor's office has yet to announce permanent campus regulations governing the precise times and places for holding the demonstrations that are now allowed, and ways of holding them that will not interfere with education; and the final point at issue between the administration and the F.S.M.—whether the university would discipline those who advocate or organize illegal actions on its campuses—is settled mainly by the willingness of both sides to interpret each other's ambiguous statements with a minimum of conflict. However, there is so little disagreement left about the basic changes made in university policy during the controversy that President Kerr, who became the chief adversary of the F.S.M., has lately acknowledged in several speeches that the rules in effect before this fall—rules that prohibited students from planning, soliciting for, or advocating off-campus causes on university property—were of "doubtful legality." The dispute actually arose over the sudden application of these rules to the Bancroft strip—where until last September they had been unenforced, in the belief (or pretense) that the property belonged to the city—but before it ended the regents had officially removed such restrictions entirely. The Bancroft strip, where thousands of students enter the busiest plaza of the campus every day, has remained the area of greatest political activity, but now there is also a line of tables near the fountain in front of the Student Union, a group of three buildings that stand on one side of the plaza, and on the other side of the plaza political rallies are held on the steps of Sproul Hall itself. Martin Meyerson, a social scientist who was formerly dean of the College of Environmental Design and in January was appointed acting chancellor, has gained wide confidence among students and faculty—around the university the belief is widespread that his appointment was one of the chief benefits to come out of the dispute—and he is considered quite unlikely to commit an atrocity. Under the regents' new policy, the Berkeley campus is now operating peacefully, and, all in all, most people look upon the free-speech controversy as settled. . . .

. . .

The Free Speech Movement was originally formed in the early fall by a decision to unite all the groups that had a stake in using the Bancroft strip for political activity, whether they were interested in distributing pamphlets for the Young Socialist Alliance or in recruiting students to ring doorbells for Barry Goldwater. It is now agreed in Berkeley that the F.S.M. eventually had the participation of a large number of the university's outstanding students—not to mention many of the ex-students, part-time students, and non-students who make up what is sometimes called the Hidden Community in Berkeley—and that although it had the almost constant opposition of the student newspaper and the student government, it attracted wide support within the student population. The Sociology 105 poll indicates that two-thirds of the Berkeley students approved of the F.S.M.'s goals and one-third of them approved of both its goals and its methods. It is also agreed that despite the presence of a representative of Students for Goldwater among the twelve members of F.S.M.'s Steering Committee, the committee was considerably more radical than most of its supporters. Although radicalism during the controversy was more a matter of tactics than of political beliefs, a good deal of attention was given to the left-wing politics of those who led the F.S.M. There was wide circulation of a statement, credited to President Kerr, that 40 percent of the F.S.M.'s members were Maoists or Castroites—he later denied having made such a statement—and wide discussion, some of it in a humorous key, of the exotic political beliefs of some of those involved. "I'd considered my views rather far to the left until I went to an F.S.M. meeting after Kerr's statement," I was told by an English girl doing graduate work. "Some speaker was saying that it was actually Kerr who was using Maoist tactics. The conservatives—the Young Democrats, for instance—were applauding, but then some people started booing. They were angry at what they considered a slur on Mao." In actuality, the only Steering Committee member who has been known, on occasion, to refer to himself as a Maoist is Art Goldberg, a large, amiable, sleepy-looking young man from Los Angeles, and his commitment to Peking is not taken very seriously, despite such gestures as carrying a sign at the CORE picketing which said "Racism Is a Paper Tiger."

Savio's usual reply to remarks about left-wing influence in the F.S.M. was the statement that its Executive Committee, consisting of fifty members, included only four "revolutionary Socialists"—a figure he arrived at by adding the two representatives of the Young Socialist Alliance to the two from the DuBois Club. Savio now acknowledges that the figure was irrelevant, since membership in an organization with a revolutionary ideology was no measure of tactical radicalism within the

F.S.M.; moreover, it was so far from encompassing all those who considered themselves revolutionary Socialists that he was later approached by a number of people who wanted to know why they had been left out of the count. The Berkeley campus has organizations representing just about all forms of Socialist ideology, and it is possible to hear references to people who are "rather fond of the Togliatti deviation" or are "hung up on democratic centralism." But student radicalism at Berkeley cannot be interpreted as if it were composed of the kind of disciplined ideological warring factions that dominated the radicalism of the thirties. It is believed in some quarters that the organizations themselves are less disciplined and less ideological than those of the past. What is far more important is that the tone of student radicalism at Berkeley is set not by the old ideological groups but by people whose approach is sufficiently different from that of the thirties that they have come to think of themselves as embracing a New Radicalism. New Radicals don't ordinarily use the term, but they constantly stress that they have a new approach to radical politics—and it was this approach that dominated the Steering Committee of the Free Speech Movement. Most F.S.M. leaders make no attempt to disguise their deep alienation from American society, but they regard allegiance to any specific alternative as utopian, divisive, immobilizing, and—perhaps most significant—not their "style." The word "style" is widely used among the New Radicals—most of whom are indeed admirers of Fidel Castro, often because of *his* style—and in giving reasons for their avoidance of the old radical organizations they are as likely to cite distaste for the style of their jargon and theoretical debate as disgust with the futility of what Savio has called "spending hours trying to invent a motto that makes you different from other sects." While part of this preference for dissociation is undoubtedly a desire to avoid tarnished labels, the New Radicals consciously avoid in their own activities the automatic condemnation of Communists—"pathological anti-Stalinism," in their phrase—that has come to characterize the non-Communist left in the United States during the Cold War, and they count it as one of the accomplishments of the F.S.M. that the DuBois Club could be represented on the Steering Committee without any more objection than was made.

In place of ideology, the New Radicals tend to rely on action. "The word 'existential' is used a lot," Jack Weinberg told me. Weinberg, who is twenty-four, is a full-time unpaid activist; he wears a droopy mustache and work clothes, and in the pictures taken during his imprisonment in The Police Car he somehow managed to resemble both Sacco *and* Vanzetti. "You could call it an affirmation of self," he went on. "Just because we can't see what the end might be doesn't mean we're going to sit here. It's a matter of screaming. We have to justify everything in terms of the act itself. The trouble with being ideologically oriented is that it's immobilizing; you have to justify all kinds of things in terms of the ideology. We're really problem-oriented. Utopia is too far away to worry about. F.S.M. had a limited goal, but look what happened. Look at the effect it could have on educational policy and student activism across the country. Who could have planned that?"

Although Savio is considered the most moralistic of the New Radicals, all of them explain their conclusion that America is "sick" or "evil" at least partly in moral terms—emphasizing that American society is not what it claims to be, that it engages in sham and hypocrisy, that those in control are not concerned with "telling it like it is" (a phrase borrowed from the S.N.C.C. workers in Mississippi). The New Radicals ordinarily share the views of the far left on foreign affairs, but more orthodox leftists are sometimes dismayed to find Savio and Weissman, for instance, apparently more concerned with the idea that the American government is being hypocritical about why it is fighting in Vietnam than with the idea that the United States is engaging in an "imperialistic colonial war." Suzanne Goldberg, a graduate student in philosophy from New York, who is a member of the F.S.M. Steering Committee, has explained this moral tone by saying, "It's really a strange kind of naïveté. What we learned in grammar school about democracy and freedom nobody takes seriously, but we do. We really believe it. It's impossible to grapple with the problem of the structure of the whole world, but you try to do something about the immediate things you see that bother you and are within your reach."

Because of this approach, the New Radicals often engage in a kind of ad-hoc activism directed at specific problems whose solutions are no more than the stated goals of American democracy—free speech, the right to vote, the right to fair employment and housing. Obviously, it is in the field of civil rights that the most inconsistency is to be found between what the American structure says it is and what it is, and often the New Radicals work in Mississippi with S.N.C.C., as Savio did last summer, or work with some of the more radical CORE chapters or with ad-hoc committees on such projects as rent strikes and sit-ins over hiring policy, or organizing ghetto communities. Since they take the position of demanding only what society claims to be giving in the first place, they tend to be contemptuous of gradualism or of compromise in negotiations. "We ask for what we should get, not for what we could get," Miss Goldberg says. Their techniques are often extra-legal, and they save their ultimate contempt for people who express agreement with their goals but not with their methods. "'Liberal' is a dirty word here," Weinberg told me. "Liberalism is a trap. It's the impotence of having principles that make you opposed to something and other principles that keep you from doing anything about it." New Radicals ordinarily have little faith that anything can be accomplished by the "Liberal Establishment." Any mention of the American Communist Party is usually greeted with the scornful remark that the Party backed Lyndon Johnson in the last election, and the same kind of criticism is made of the DuBois Club—which, one of its members admitted to me half apologetically, "does believe in cooperation with non-Socialist groups." At Berkeley, where a number of the students are the children of Communists and other radicals of the thirties—they are often called "red-diaper babies"—a conversation about a member of the DuBois Club sometimes sounds like the sort of conversation that is held at other state universities about people who felt compelled to join Sigma Chi because of a family tradition. The one organization whose style seems to be almost universally respected among the New Radicals is S.N.C.C.; its project in Mississippi is admired for its moral tone, for its patient organizing of impoverished Negroes, for its activism, and for its frequent refusal to accept the advice of liberals.

One evening, I asked Savio for a description of the New Radicalism, and he said, "Certain words are more useful. Maybe they're a bit too theatrical. Words like 'moral protest,' 'existential revolt,' 'alienation'—as opposed to 'class conflict' or 'forces of proletarian revolution.' We're talking about the same objective reality, but it's a question of being more tentative. I don't know if all our problems would vanish if we had a state monopoly on production and distribution. I don't have a Utopia in mind. I know it has to be a good deal more egalitarian than it is now. Maybe the classic Marxist models and the classic Adam Smith models don't apply anymore. There are a lot of people who have enough to eat who are incredibly resentful, because their lives are meaningless. They're psychologically dispossessed. There's a feeling that they have nothing to do; the bureaucracy runs itself. Why are we so alienated? I would say for three reasons: depersonalization, hypocrisy, and the unearned privilege that comes with great wealth. The country's forms aren't so bad, if we would take them seriously, if somebody were willing to say the Emperor had no clothes. The worst thing about the society is that it lies to itself. Look at the last election. The two subjects that were not issues in the campaign were Vietnam and civil rights. What's the choice? What can you do in a situation like that? Oh, add to the good words 'anti-bureaucratic tendency.' American radicals are traditionally anarchistic, and that tendency is very strong here."

People here who try to define the New Radicalism in traditional terms usually say it resembles anarcho-syndicalism more than anything else, since it is characterized by a belief that laws and regulations have to be justified and by a dislike for centralized bureaucracy. The ideological radical who has been closest to the radical student leaders at Berkeley is Hal Draper, a long-time Socialist editor, in his fifties, who now works in the university library. Draper's Independent Socialist Club, according to its statement of principles, stands for "a Socialist policy which is completely independent of and opposed to both of the reactionary systems of exploitation of man by man which now divide the world: capitalism and Communism." In discussions with the New Radicals, Draper often argues that however much they insist on avoiding labels, their views amount to what in any other country would be called Left Wing Socialism. But although Weinberg belonged for a time to Draper's Independent Socialist Club (it has many members in common with CORE), and although Weissman has said that Draper's ideas come closer to making sense to him than those of any other ideologist, the New Radicals insist that programs and theories cannot express their style, and they deny that this leaves them with nothing but negativism. "I think the student activist movement does offer new ideas," I was told by Martin Roysher, a polite, articulate, scholarly-looking sophomore from southern California, who transferred to Berkeley from Princeton because he wanted more political activity. "When the structure is challenged, the response may not often be exactly what we want, but it's helpful. Take the wide range of student demonstrations—sit-ins, rent strikes, organizing the communities. They definitely bring about changes in the power structure. It doesn't take the students very long to realize that the structure is pretty corrupt when it has to bring in the cops."

Many Berkeley people who are well acquainted with the Free Speech

Movement say that the most "political"—and some say the most influential—of the F.S.M. leaders is Steve Weissman, a twenty-five-year-old graduate student from Tampa who has red hair and a pointed red beard and usually dresses in Ivy League style. Weissman told me he had considered becoming a full-time organizer for Students for a Democratic Society this semester but had decided to continue studying history instead. "I think we are arriving at a philosophy," he said. "There aren't many people, but it is a new voice. I think it represents the thinking of a lot more people, and thirty percent of the student body bought our style. It's exemplified by S.N.C.C. in Mississippi; about the only other people working full time are forty or fifty Students for a Democratic Society people in the slum-organization projects. Politically, there's a feeling that while other groups may be necessary sometimes, there's no use celebrating coalitions. You take a direct line outside the normal arena and force the liberals to make a choice. What we're against is consensus politics— the idea of finding out what the regents will give before you ask for it. That's one thing. Something we're for is certain values for the future—a kind of democratic participation, letting people have some control over their lives, the way S.N.C.C. is organizing people in the Freedom Democratic Party right at the ward level, or the way students are asking for participation in the university, or the way we're trying to get poor people involved in the war on poverty, instead of just professors. In a way, the people we're closest to are the Populists, or the *narodniki*—the intellectuals in Russia who went out and worked with the peasants. Sure, we see connections from different issues. Our values are radical. We don't automatically accept the value of institutions, and we admit going beyond the normal American equality, because we include economic equality. We do accept the Socialist criticism of American capitalism, but that doesn't mean we buy any particular solution."

I asked Weissman about the charge sometimes made that many of the New Radicals have so profound a distaste for the society that the immediate goal of their action is less important to them than fomenting trouble or demonstrating the sickness of the society or, as some critics at Berkeley have asserted, attempting to undermine faith in the democratic processes.

"You're not naïve enough not to realize that there's a grain of truth in that," Weissman said. "And I'm willing to grant that our alienation is deep enough so that we underrate the possibility of channels sometimes.

But the conspiracy theory really comes down to Red-baiting or bed-baiting; it's either an attempt to make people think it's all a Communist plot or some Freudian theory that we're all just revolting against our parents. The criticism that it's a conspiracy would be valid only if we didn't make any progress toward our ostensible goals, and I don't think they can show any place where we haven't."

I suggested to Weissman that one reason for the conspiracy theory might be that there appears to be a gap between what one professor has called "working for liberal goals with radical methods" and changing the structure of society.

"It bothered me for a while that the end of radical politics seems to be increasing the welfare state," Weissman said. "Breaking down of hiring-policy rights with demonstrations just means some kind of federal fair-employment agency. Well, some changes are made and we're doing what has to be done. Maybe we're developing constituencies; that's more than the idcologists are doing. Maybe it means that the people are there to make a revolution if we ever decide that's what's needed."

It is generally agreed at Berkeley that the membership of the ideo-logical clubs is more than matched by the students who fall roughly into the category of New Radicals. It is the New Radicalism, rather than the old, that comes near to expressing some of the dissatisfaction felt by students who would not consider themselves radicals, and it was the New Radicalism that led to the Free Speech Movement. Some professors were disturbed by what they felt was a tone of near anti-intellectualism in the F.S.M., and this seems closely related to the New Radicals' tendency to emphasize action at the expense of theorizing, to explain themselves in moral rather than intellectual terms, to stress political rights rather than academic disciplines, and to insist that an issue is more important than an institution. Critics of the New Radicals have said that their style works best against liberals—who have a respect for institutions and for channels, and who also have a distaste for meeting mass action with force—and it is true that liberals seem to have extraordinary difficulty in communicating with them, or, to use a phrase often heard in Berkeley, "tuning in on them." For many observers, one of the ironies of the con-troversy lay in the fact that the chief villain was Clark Kerr, a man of widely praised liberal accomplishments, who had himself been given an award for liberalizing the regulations concerning free speech at the Uni-versity of California, and who had himself—in a series of Godkin lectures at Harvard, later published as *The Uses of the University*—pointed out the elements of the modern American "multiversity" that would cause alienation and perhaps revolt among the students. But the F.S.M. leaders seemed not at all surprised to find Kerr their bitterest opponent, for without some special effort at understanding a liberal would find that many of his tenets were handicaps in dealing with the New Radicals. A liberal's faith that wrongs can eventually be adjusted within the democratic processes is treated with contempt by people who believe the ends of channels to be tokenism or hypocrisy; the argument that a noisy free-speech controversy would serve the ends of right-wing opponents of the university is of no concern to people who have no great faith in institutions and consider such thinking the worst kind of "consensus politics." The style of the New Radicals is not to avoid controversy by compromise but to keep a controversy going until they have won their point. In December, Weissman told a gathering of graduate students that if Kerr had managed to carry the day at The Greek Theatre with a rousing speech, he would have taken the platform and used whatever oratory might have been necessary "to break the thing open again." He has told me that if the university had not itself broken the thing open again the week before The Greek Theatre by its disciplinary action against four of the F.S.M. leaders, the students would have acquired a print of *Un Chant d'Amour*—a Genet film that had been banned as obscene from a student film series that week—set up a portable projector and loudspeaker, and shown the film on the wall of Sproul Hall.

Although the campus is now comparatively peaceful, President Kerr is concerned about how a university is to handle people who, for instance, equate any compromise in negotiations with selling out. According to a young philosophy professor named John Searle, who has probably been the faculty member closest to the F.S.M., the problem should be stated another way. "The militants were forced into the leadership of the F.S.M. because of the intransigence of the administration on an issue on which they were clearly in the wrong," Searle says. "Of course these people are absolutists. They are radicals. They perform a useful function in society as gadflies, but they have no loyalty to the structure, and once you've forced the population to adopt them as leaders, you have trouble. The problem is not how to handle them. The problem is how not to get in a position where a mass movement has to turn to them for leadership."

THE PRICE OF PEACE IS CONFUSION

Renata Adler

DECEMBER 11, 1965

T ALMOST EVERY major university in the country, mimeograph machines operate by night in cluttered student apartments, coffeehouses are filled by day with animated political debate, an outdoor platform is occupied nearly every afternoon by speakers deploring some aspect of American foreign policy, and students rush home each evening to pore over copies of the *Times, Le Monde,* and the *Congressional Record* as if they contained reviews of a production in which the students themselves were playing a major part. The source of this activity is a student protest movement that offers, as the students are fond of saying, "not an ideology but a rallying cry." And the cry itself is vague and changeable enough to reflect a curious fact about America in the sixties: there are very few revolutionary positions that the Establishment does not already, at least nominally, occupy. Students who are revolutionary in spirit, however, after protesting a bit for mere protest's sake, have come up with real social criticism in three phases: the Free Speech Movement, which began as an attack upon the bureaucracy of the large university and turned into a protest against the impersonality of all institutions that, like the government welfare program, have lost contact with the people and values they were designed to serve; the Civil Rights Movement, which began as a campaign for Negro rights and turned into a campaign for eliminating local pockets of poverty; and the Peace Movement, which has begun as a protest against American military involvement in Vietnam and is turning into an attempt to influence all of foreign policy. On many campuses, all factions of the peace movement are united in an Independent Committee to End the War in Vietnam—a frail, tangled coalition of forces and personalities that includes groups ranging from religious pacifists to militant supporters of the Vietcong;

sociological types ranging from children of left-wingers of the thirties to what one student called "some of your preppier New Englanders, who are in it for moral reasons"; a few students who simply hope to evade the draft; a few representatives of national, local, and ad-hoc committees; a few hard-line members of the Young Socialist Alliance (Y.S.A.), who are commonly referred to as Trotskyists and are known within the movement, familiarly, as the "Trots"; and a new breed of lonely hangers-on and demonstration enthusiasts who might be described as Sunday Outing Radicals. Most of the students involved regard the United States position in Vietnam as at best unjust, and most of them feel that a post-Nuremberg ethic requires them to oppose a war that they cannot in conscience support. How to go about it is another matter. Since there has been, for good or for ill, no long-standing tradition of student protest in this country (as there is in France, and in other countries that do not regard college students as children), American students seem to have borrowed their tactics from several contemporary sources. From Aldermaston and, more recently, from the civil-rights movement comes the protest march. From the Johannesburg Negroes' burning of their identity cards stems, apparently, the American students' draft-card burning. And the extreme form of Buddhist protest against the Diem regime seems to have inspired at least one American student to burn himself to death.

These manifestations, quite naturally, have caused alarm. The possibility that a generation of young might refuse to carry on the military business of their generally permissive society seemed, for a time, to threaten the nation in a not yet demilitarized world. There was also concern for the fact that, in their enthusiasm for the movement, many students were leaving their studies and shuttling back and forth among the campuses of the nation as vagabond dropouts in a vaguely academic orbit. And the unkempt appearance, condescending manner, and frequent acts of civil disobedience of many of the demonstrators added to an impression that this particular lot had spoiled, and that something must be done to keep the rest from being ruined. Militant countermovements quickly sprang up on many campuses. In August, Congress passed legislation that provides a maximum penalty of five years in prison for draft-card burners. In October, Attorney General Katzenbach said that the Justice Department had found in the peace movement evidence of Communist infiltration. These developments, coupled with a certain predisposition on the part of student revolutionaries to draw a sense of risk from somewhere, confirmed in the minds of students an already widespread suspicion that the government was conspiring against them. Few demonstrators at Columbia now, to take one example, have any doubt that their telephones are being tapped; anyone who brings a camera or a notebook to a demonstration is immediately pointed out to all bystanders as an agent of the F.B.I.; and students seem to stand in hourly expectation of an academic purge of dissidents, followed by a rapid punitive draft. But the peace movement has also matured. Most of the early leaders now concede that radical action on the peace issue was a tactical mistake. (The disruption of an R.O.T.C. ceremony at Columbia last May 7th, for instance, which was once thought of as "a milestone," or "a hairy idea," is now spoken of on campus simply as an "aberrant demonstration.") As for the charge that the peace movement inadvertently prolongs the war by misrepresenting American public opinion, it has been treated in several of the movement's countless "position papers"—most recently in "A Position Paper on Tactics," by a student named Robert E. Bogosian, who suggests that communiqués be sent at once to Peking, Hanoi, and the Vietcong informing them that the demonstrators speak only for themselves and that theirs is a minority position, which, obviously, it is. As for the charge of Communist infiltration, the demonstrators tend to dismiss it (Students for a Democratic Society has dropped its anti-Communist clause) as "irrelevant." Post-Stalinist Communism no longer seems to these well-travelled children of prosperity a monolith, or even a particularly potent expansionist force. "If an American still wants to be a Communist, we think that's his business," says David Gilbert, a leader of the peace movement at Columbia. The charge of Communist *inspiration* for the movement, however, seems particularly wide of the mark. If anything has characterized the movement, from its beginning and in all its parts, it has been a spirit of decentralization, local autonomy, personal choice, and freedom from dogma. On many campuses, even simple majority rule is regarded as coercive of the minority; policy decisions require a "consensus." As a result, very few policy decisions are made. In fact, it often appears that the movement may be, in the end, more right than left—that it may have picked up a dropped conservative stitch in the American political tradition. Individualism, privacy, personal initiative, even isolationism and a view of the federal government as oppressive—these elements of the right-wing consciousness have not been argued in such depth (least of all by the right wing itself, with its paradoxical insistence on domestic police expansion and on military intervention abroad) since 1932.

. . .

Over the Thanksgiving weekend, the student peace movement and many other groups of diverse moral and political persuasions—all apparently united by an overriding concern that the United States get out of Vietnam—converged upon Washington. By Sunday night, the student demonstrators had divided into several major factions, and the student peace movement faced a crisis that had very little to do with its attitudes toward the war in Vietnam. The first split, which occurred well before the march, was down the middle, between a liberal institution and the student groups. In August, more than three hundred demonstrators calling themselves the Congress—and, later (to avoid the acronym "COUP"), the Alliance—of Unrepresented Peoples staged a sit-in on the steps of the Capitol in a protest that combined the causes of peace and civil rights. When the demonstration was over, some of the participants met to form a new group, the National Coordinating Committee to End the War in Vietnam. The Coordinating Committee was to be situated centrally, in Madison, Wisconsin. It was to have no membership and no specific policy. Its function, under its chairman, Frank Emspak (a recent graduate of the University of Wisconsin), and a secretarial staff of four, was to issue a weekly newsletter and facilitate communication among the members of various far-flung organizations—an alphabet heap that included, among others, YAWF, W.F.P., W.I.L.P.F., P.L.P., M. 2 M. (for the May 2nd Movement), C.P., S.P.U., W.R.L., Y.P.Y.F., T.U.P., C.F.R., I.W.W., C.F.IV.I. (for something called the Committee for a Fourth International), Y.S.A., I.S.C., C.N.V.A., M.F.D.P., S.S.O.C., V.D.C., and S.D.S., together with numerous local "independent" and ad-hoc committees. The Coordinating Committee successfully coordinated a number of nationwide activities, most notably the marches on October 15th and 16th (the International Days of Protest). It was decided to hold a national five-day convention of the Coordinating Committee in Madison over the Thanksgiving holidays. Then it was learned that Sanford Gottlieb, political director of SANE (the Committee for a Sane Nuclear Policy), and other sponsors were urging a national peace march on Washington on the Saturday after Thanksgiving. Since the Coordinating Committee wanted no conflict between the two events, it decided to move its convention to Washington. In time, however, it became apparent that SANE's invitation to march had been what the students refer to as an "exclusionist call." Although anyone might march, sane reserved the right to authorize the slogans that the marchers could carry. Any poster that could, in SANE's judgment, politically compromise the movement would be excluded from the demonstration. The Coordinating Committee, which had always stressed its non-exclusionist, non-centralized, laissez-faire character, expressed outrage ("They're leaning over backwards to define not what they are but what they're not," said one student), and the march organizers, having no practical means to censor the posters anyway, capitulated. The rift between SANE and the Coordinating Committee, however, was established almost from the outset—if not in official policy, then certainly in spirit. The next jolt to the student movement came not from what it looks upon as the creeping, ineffectual liberalism of SANE but from the thirties, and from within the Coordinating Committee itself.

The first few hours of the convention in Washington ran smoothly, with the arrival on Wednesday of delegates from all over the country at convention headquarters—a basement in a predominantly Negro neighborhood of Washington. There were a few cheerful posters taped to the bleak stone walls ("God Bless This Office and All the Revolutionaries Who Work Here" and "The Price of Peace Is Confusion"), but the room was basically an office devoted to the serious business of registering fifteen hundred delegates and alternates, and assigning them—two or three to a room, if necessary—to the Harrington Hotel, where twelve workshops, or discussions, on such subjects as Peace and Freedom, National Program, Organization Structure, the Draft, and Community Organization were to be held. A few arriving delegates began to confer in the strange, conditional idiom of Anglo-American dialecticians ("I would be prepared to argue that . . ." and "Yes, well, in that case I might want to maintain that . . ."), but, perhaps because the room was overheated, most of the delegates left the basement as soon as they had registered.

Late Wednesday evening, at the Second Act Coffee Shop, around the corner from headquarters, a crowd of delegates gathered, and a kind of civil-rights alumni reunion appeared to be taking place. Ray Robinson, a tall, handsome Negro veteran of countless civil-rights and peace campaigns, seemed to know almost everyone from somewhere or other. He was telling of his participation in a protest march from Canada toward Guantanamo ("Uncle Sam said, 'Man, you can't go 'cross that water.

Cuba's over there'") when Stephen Frumin, an intense young delegate who had attended the University of Wisconsin, broke in. "The war and my perception of things have escalated," he said.

"We may be a minority, but at least the press is giving us equal time," said another delegate. "They think the fact that some of us have beards is interesting. It's a sign of the boredom and banality of American life."

"I hope we get some things decided at this convention," said Vicki Cooper, a delegate from Pittsburgh. "There are so many issues that are still receiving much heated debate. If we could get some of this clarified, maybe the press would stop describing the *people* involved in the movement and pay some attention to our ideas. We might even put up political candidates, although it would have to be in a participatory, democratic way. I couldn't permit any major decisions to be made for me. If I couldn't have a major say, I wouldn't follow them."

At nine o'clock Thursday morning, at the Harrington Hotel, a meeting of the Coordinating Committee's presiding committee was held, at which, with a great deal of gravity and circumspection, very little was accomplished. Emspak conducted a low-keyed discussion of whether rigid standards should be set up for delegate credentials. It was decided that since few, if any, delegates would want to falsify their registration, standards should be loose.

When the committee adjourned, a young man from Youth Against War and Fascism tried to sell a "Support the National Liberation Front" button to Mary Walker, a middle-aged delegate from the Committee on Non-Violence of Denver. "No, thank you," she said. "I have a thousand 'Stop the War' buttons back in Denver. I think that gets the message across."

• • •

"A Reverent Silence Is Requested," said an old sign above the door to the nave of the Lincoln Memorial Congregational Temple, where the first plenary session of the convention was held, at twelve-thirty on Thanksgiving Day. Within moments, however, there was neither silence nor reverence anywhere in the building, for a power struggle, in a completely unexpected form and at a completely unexpected time, threatened to split the Coordinating Committee. What started it was a leaflet signed by thirty-three delegates and alternates, most of whom identified their local committees as either the Committee to End the War in Vietnam (C.E.W.V.) or the Vietnam Day Committee (V.D.C.), proposing an additional workshop "that would provide an opportunity for the independent committees to discuss their own programs, structure, and tasks." The workshop, the thirteenth, was to meet concurrently with the twelve others, which were preoccupied with essentially the same problems. This may have struck some of the delegates as strange, but only the most knowledgeable at once besieged the platform with cries of "Point of order!," "Amendment takes precedence!," "Sit down!," "Shut up!," "Let him speak!," and "Two-thirds of us don't know what's going *on*!" (At one point, Emspak actually had to restrain someone intent on wresting the microphone from him.)

As Jens Jensen, a delegate from Cambridge, Massachusetts, rose to say that "no one wants to be divisive in the slightest," Marilyn Milligan, Jack Weinberg, and Jerry Rubin—all members of the Berkeley V.D.C. and signers of the controversial document—gathered around Steve Weissman, a Californian, also of the V.D.C., and one of the early leaders of the Berkeley free-speech movement. "What have I signed?" asked Marilyn Milligan. "I knew we shouldn't have signed. Those so-called members of independent committees aren't independents at all. They're Y.S.A. The Trots seem to be trying to steal the movement."

"Every generation has got to learn," said Weissman. "The Trots have still got their sense of *imminence*. They're still listening to history and not to people."

Aside from a few converts to the Young Socialist Alliance, it was difficult to imagine what the "Trots" hoped to gain from splitting and undermining the National Coordinating Committee. Some delegates thought Y.S.A. was trying to bring the whole movement into its own sectarian line. Others thought Y.S.A. was maneuvering to form a hardcore cadre of extreme radicals within the non-exclusionist N.C.C., and others speculated that the urge to take over an organization—no matter how formless that organization might be—was simply a reflex acquired from the bitter struggles of the thirties.

The delegates on the floor, however, most of them still unaware of what was going on, voted to adjourn and to give the thirteenth workshop permission to meet after the plenary session if it chose. The meeting was held briefly in the basement of the church. There were some impassioned appeals to disband, and the workshop voted to adjourn until seven-thirty that night, when it would decide whether to adjourn for good.

The rest of the afternoon was devoted to the twelve scheduled workshops and, for those who wanted them, seething discussions about "structure." The anti-draft workshop, under the leadership of Staughton Lynd, a professor of history at Yale, began in the church balcony, with a series of reports from various regions: "I'm from New Orleans, and the consensus out there seemed to be that a person should do anything that he feels he can do in conscience," and "I'm from Chicago, and we simply could not get even a simple majority to endorse any organized program of draft opposition. We don't feel that without an extreme consensus we ought to get into the anti-draft bag." Another workshop met in the nave of the church, in full view of the balcony. Practically every remark there was greeted with tempestuous applause, and at one point Professor Lynd leaned over the balcony to shout, "Friends, do you think you could *not* applaud every time somebody says something?" This was greeted by the first laughter of the afternoon.

At seven-thirty, when the meeting of the thirteenth workshop was slated to begin, the room was packed and overflowed into the hallway. Jerry Rubin rescinded his endorsement of the leaflet and pronounced it "beyond my comprehension" that he should ever have signed such a thing. Then, having moved that the meeting adjourn and having lost by a small margin, Rubin led the Berkeley delegation and many of the real independents out of the meeting and to Room 407, where the Berkeley delegation held a meeting of its own.

"That was stylishly done," said Steve Weissman in Room 407. "But now, as I see it, the Berkeley delegation, as one of the oldest, truly independent committees here, should draft the strongest statement possible denouncing the attempt to split the movement."

"Do you think we should lay it on the line that Y.S.A. is behind it?" asked Rubin. "In a way, they've packed the delegations and we're faced with a *fait accompli*. Y.S.A. chairs the independent committees from San Francisco, Los Angeles, and Cleveland, just for a beginning, and they've got ten years of political indoctrination behind them."

Ray Robinson bounded angrily into the room. "I've just been caucusing with the Mississippi people downstairs, and they're going to resign this goddam thing," he said. "They're cutting out. *Three times* now, they've been asked to come up to Washington for peace and they have just been *used*. The infighting has got to stop. One of the girls from down there asked me a simple question. She asked what she came up here for— you dig? She didn't come here to *meet* people, and listen to Y.S.A. interpret ideology for the ones who don't know where they're at. You college people messed up again, I tell you that, brother."

"We know, Ray," said Weissman. "And we're trying to draft a statement. But is that all—is there a bitch besides that?"

"Yeah," said Robinson. "The Mississippi people just aren't being made to feel welcome."

"I know just what they mean, and it isn't just the Mississippi people, either," said Beverly Sterner, a member of C.N.V.A. "The opening of the session was so sterile and so cold. No orientation. No word of welcome."

The Berkeley delegation didn't draft a statement that night. It didn't have to. Word came upstairs that the thirteenth workshop's meeting had been persuaded to adjourn, after all, by Rubin, who had gained admission, recanted his endorsement yet again, and confessed that he had been "taken in by Y.S.A." This last remark was pronounced "not in good taste" by members of the Y.S.A., but for the moment they gave in.

Late Thursday night, the Mississippi delegation, having decided not to leave, was holding the first of its "soul sessions" at the hotel. The soul session, which has become a tradition of the movement in the South, is a kind of marathon group therapy, with a dash of mysticism. Participants have described it as a drugless "high on talk." The Mississippi people, who were likely to have experienced more suffering at the hands of society than any of the other delegates, were trying to demonstrate that a revolution can originate in the personal sufferings of people, freely expressed, rather than in a few directives from the top. "Don't think you have to talk," Delmar Scudder, a Negro student from Swarthmore, said at the beginning of the session, "until you feel that you can get out some of the pain, and find out where it is."

In a room marked "Ideological Overflow," Al Johnson, a Negro worker for the Mississippi Freedom Democratic Party in Washington, said to Weissman, "I'm not sure what this convention has to offer the movement in the South. The argument about structure—we had it all in S.N.C.C., and look where it led. No more local autonomy. Every worker has to file a weekly *report*. Man, that's what I'd call a co-*er*cive structure."

"That's just what I think the movement is all about," said Weissman. "To see if we can find any structures that are not coercive. Maybe it can't be done. Maybe there can't be any participatory democracy in a mass society. But you M.F.D.P. people, and the chapters of S.D.S., and the movement in New York, and we in Berkeley ought to be able to talk to each other about that."

The conversations and caucuses and soul sessions went on at the Harrington far into the night.

. . .

Breakfast on Friday in the Harrington cafeteria was a time for introspection and political realignment. ("The trouble with national structures is just what's happening here. They can be taken over." "Yes, but how can you confront a national government without a national structure?") In the lobby of the Harrington, photographers were gathering some of the more bizarre-looking people around and posing them on a sofa as a cross-section of the movement.

Very few people went to any of the workshops on Friday, and the Students for a Democratic Society held a caucus to plan its own convention in December. "I suggest that we get away from the smoke-disaster syndrome," said one delegate. "All this boring dialectic in smoke-filled rooms. I think this time we ought to go someplace where we can run in the fields." The S.D.S. discussed the meeting place for several hours and then reached a consensus: Antioch, if the delegate who had suggested it could get use of the campus.

"I think S.D.S. ought to stay away from protest for a while," said Weissman. "The other groups have taken it up, and I'm less concerned with anything we can do about Vietnam now than I am about how we can affect foreign policy seven wars from now. It's hard for a democratic group to find the levers of foreign policy. In a way, M.F.D.P. and S.D.S. have the same problem about the convention. We don't want or need a strong central structure at present. We've got our local community-action constituencies."

That evening, at a plenary session, a delegate from Mississippi read a transcript of ten single-spaced pages of soul session, taken down the previous night. He told the delegates, "Don't applaud. We don't care if you agree. The issue is whether we can speak to one another." The delegates gave him a standing ovation. Immediately thereafter, however, the Young Socialist Alliance broke forth with a complicated new issue, concerning credentials. There was a long and bitter floor fight, which the Y.S.A. lost but which caused one Mississippi delegate to tear up his delegate card in chagrin and another to suggest the possibility of a delegate-card burning. The Y.S.A. made still another attempt to take over, through the seemingly harmless maneuver of suggesting that the movement adopt three slogans—"Let's Bring the Troops Home Now," "Self-Determination in Mississippi and Vietnam," and "Freedom Now, Withdrawal Now"—for the march the following morning. But David

Gilbert, of Columbia, among others, pointed out that the "Withdrawal Now" slogan would be unacceptable to SANE and also to many constituents of the Coordinating Committee (who believe in negotiated withdrawal); that the ensuing split would simply feed the movement's enemies; and that the convention was, in any case, not empowered to adopt slogans without a mandate from the local committees. Throughout this discussion, there were jeers, cries of "Parliamentary nincompoop!," "Ideologue!," and "Let him finish!" In the end, the convention allowed each marcher to adopt the slogan of his choice.

· · ·

On Saturday, the march itself went off almost without a hitch, and without much excitement, either. Veterans in the vanguard of the procession were shouting, "No more vets! No more vets!" The flags at the base of the Washington Monument made their usual applauding noise. In front of the stage below the monument, a special section was roped off by SANE monitors, to be reserved for veterans, clergymen, writers, celebrities, and, "in case there should be enough room," the old and the infirm. There were speeches of varying quality, leading up to an appearance by Sanford Gottlieb, who seemed to be showing a certain hostility toward the marchers when he asked, "How many of you can't hear me back there? Raise your hands," and then continued, "Oh, well, I see a lot of raised hands. That must mean you can hear just fine." (As it happened, owing to quirks of the wind, the marchers back there could hear perfectly at times and sometimes not at all.) But the high point for most of the students, and for some of the older people as well, was the speech by the president of Students for a Democratic Society, Carl Oglesby, who had held himself aloof all week from the Coordinating Committee infighting and who now delivered a scathing yet considered attack not on the administration in Washington but on the institution of American liberalism itself, which, he said, had become so entrenched as to be, in an almost entirely new sense, complacent and reactionary. A bearded young man himself, he said that America had become "a nation—may I say it?—of beardless liberals." He went on, "There is simply no such thing for the United States now as a just revolution," and he deplored the government's determination to "safeguard what they take to be American interests around the world against revolution or revolutionary change, which they always call Communism—as if it were that." Later, he said, "Then why can't we see that our proper human struggle is not with

Communism or revolutionaries but with the social desperation that drives good men to violence, both here and abroad?" The rhetoric of Oglesby's speech was strangely old-fashioned, but the young people present were moved, and even the older people seemed to feel reassured. The scene ended with Sanford Gottlieb advancing and raising Oglesby's arm in triumph, like a prizefighter's, to volleys of cheering.

At the Harrington, however, many students, who had not bothered to march, were locked in caucus about structure. (The issue of Vietnam, never very clearly in focus at the convention, seemed to have been eclipsed entirely.) Immediately after the march, the presiding committee met in a room at the hotel, while in another room the thirteenth workshop had reconvened and was making a last-ditch effort to form a movement of its own, in a meeting that was turning really ugly. Three young members of the Y.S.A. stood guard outside the door, and unlocked it only for members of independent committees who pledged themselves to vote in favor of founding a separate national committee. When one delegate, remarking that the room had been paid for by the Coordinating Committee, attempted to meet force with force and enter, he was caught for some time in the door, which the guards were pushing shut, and then was forcibly dragged some distance down the hallway.

"Goons and Storm Troopers," said one dismayed independent. "This is supposed to be a *peace* movement."

"*We've* never advocated non-violence," said one member of Y.S.A.

"And furthermore, there has *been* no violence here," said a middle-aged woman emerging from the door. "You didn't see any, there wasn't any, and if you insist on misrepresenting things that way I'll have you escorted out of here."

The final plenary session—the meeting on structure—was held on Sunday morning, in a room at the New Dunbar Hotel. Dave Dellinger, the editor of *Liberation* and a pacifist loved and admired by almost all factions, presided. The Y.S.A. caucus had come up with its own proposals on structure. But Jack Weinberg received permission to make an opening statement and set what he called a "tone" to the meeting. He said that he knew some delegates had reached "the conclusion that we are going to come out of here divided," and he asked them to "destroy the split before it is carried home to every chapter and there is a vote— a majority and a minority, with two separate affiliations and no consensus—in every community and on every campus." Then a man leaped to his feet, identified himself as Albert Nelson, of the Spartacist

Movement, and, in the first really open allusion in the plenary session to anything that was going on behind the scenes, claimed that "the political infighting ought to be hitting the floor," that someone was "gutting the convention of its real political issues." Condemning the Young Socialist Alliance and the Coordinating Committee for their "lack of candor" and loss of the personal touch, he announced that he would abstain from voting for the proposals made by either one. Here Dellinger interposed. "A common interest has reasserted itself," he said, "but if there are any jokers here we are trying to bring them out. If they take over the national organization, it will be only the shell, because the rest of us will continue under other auspices."

After all the votes had been cast (the Coordinating Committee's proposal on structure was adopted), Elizabeth Fusco, a worker for M.F.D.P. in S.N.C.C. overalls, asked, and received, permission to speak. She announced that the Mississippi delegation had just completed another soul session, said that "they felt they were the only people in the convention dealing with something warm—the pain they feel," and asked that everyone remain after the plenary to join in. "Will you stay?" she cried. "Will you stay?" Delmar Scudder then climbed to the stage to announce that the Mississippi people were so pleased with their sessions that they were planning to hold a "soul press conference" and to look into "travelling soul workshops and soul education and soul recreation," adding, "Maybe that's what we have to offer the American people."

. . .

When the last soul session of the convention took place, in a room at the Statler Hilton, it was packed, not only with S.D.S. and Mississippi people but with other independents. The Y.S.A. (who were caucusing again) didn't attend, nor did Emspak, who was on his way back to Madison. The session lasted for a full thirty-six hours, after which everyone claimed to feel refreshed. The Mississippi people returned to their work in their Mississippi counties, and S.D.S. organizers, who were concentrating on community action, returned to their communities and campuses.

"I guess if you take the soul sessions, and the ideologues, and the kids who just can't sleep on account of Vietnam, you can get a pretty clear idea which way all this churning up of institutions in search of values is going to lead," said one delegate, enigmatically, as he boarded a bus to return in time for a class on Monday morning.

THE PUT-ON

Jacob Brackman

JUNE 24, 1967

The put-on is becoming a major communication option in intercourse between artist and critic, or, for that matter, between artist and society at large. This option has been, in some respects, overdue. Artists get asked a lot of stupid questions they don't feel like answering. Before the advent of the put-on, however, outright reluctance garnered an artist a reputation for surliness; playing along, on an interviewer's own terms, made him appear shallow or inarticulate. *The Interview*, a brilliant Ernest Pintoff–Mel Brooks animated cartoon of a few years back, epitomized this hangup. A Monk-type jazz musician, asked questions like "What does your piece express?," mumbled involuted hipster incoherencies: "You know, man, I start wailing, I'm into that groove, I listen to the other cats, I just *blow*—you dig, man?" Recently, on a Channel 13 television broadcast, members of the Blues Project were asked this same question. Traditionally, musicians have prided themselves on their inability to talk with civilians. But, without hesitation, a member of the Project replied, "Man, this piece expresses what *every*body feels about *every*thing." Asked how the group got together, he replied, "We're *still* not together." (A classic put-on ploy: knowingly embracing a wrong but semantically plausible meaning—the chief bravura of John Lennon's prose.) When pressed, the Project member said they met as trolls in the Black Forest.

In another recent Channel 13 interview, the jazz bass player Charlie Mingus was asked by Dennis Azzarella (who seemed almost a parody of unhip ofay) whether a violent Harlem ballet, *Long Hot Summer*, contained anti-white feeling.

"There weren't even any white people in it," Mingus replied. "I didn't see anything hostile, did you? Just a happy little Negro community beating each other up."

When pressed about the ballet's "message," Mingus said, "When I see *your* people dance, girls jumping around on the *Ed Sullivan Show*, I can't see no messages."

"Are you putting me on?" Azzarella whined helplessly, glancing over at his cameraman.

Ernst von Salomon achieved a masterpiece through the form of interview put-on in his novel *Der Fragebogen*, which he constructed as a detailed reply to a questionnaire that the Allies circulated in Germany as part of their de-Nazification program.

The interview, indeed, offers a prime matrix for the put-on. This may be a perverse rejection of the interview process as a social symbol. (So one enters schools, jobs, the Army, etc.) It is also, surely, a pragmatic response to the difficulty of questions in general. Honest answers are hard, because they can be disadvantageous (How much money are you entitled to deduct from your income tax?), because they are unknown (What do you believe?), or because they are boring (What have you been doing with yourself?). The put-on resolves all difficulties—it breaks up sets, disorients the interviewer, ridicules the interview process, communicates "real" ideas and feelings yet deflates the seriousness of questions and replies. The now classic *Playboy* interview with Bob Dylan, by Nat Hentoff, must represent the apogee of this option. Hentoff deliberately "chose to play straight man in [my] questions, believing that to have done otherwise would have stemmed the freewheeling flow of Dylan's responses." Some excerpts from their dialogue may illustrate the complexity of put-on technique:

PLAYBOY: What about [your old fans'] charge that you vulgarized your natural gifts?

DYLAN: It's like going out to the desert and screaming, and then having little kids throw their sandbox at you. I'm only twenty-four. These people that said this—were they Americans?

PLAYBOY: What made you decide to go the rock-'n'-roll route?

DYLAN: Carelessness. I lost my one true love. I started drinking. The first thing I know, I'm in a card game. Then I'm in a crap game. I wake up in a pool hall. Then this big Mexican lady drags me off the table, takes me to Philadelphia. She leaves me alone in her house, and it burns down. I wind up in Phoenix. I get a job as a Chinaman. . . . Needless to say, he burned the house down and I hit the road. The first guy that picked me up asked me if I wanted to be a star. What could I say?

PLAYBOY: And that's how you became a rock-'n'-roll singer?

DYLAN: No, that's how I got tuberculosis.

PLAYBOY: Let's turn the question around: Why have you stopped composing and singing protest songs?

DYLAN: The word "protest," I think, was made up for people undergoing surgery. It's an amusement-park word. A normal person in his righteous mind would have to have the hiccups to pronounce it honestly. The word "message" strikes me as having a hernia-like sound. It's just like the word "delicious." Also the word "marvellous." You know, the English can say "marvellous" pretty good. They can't say "raunchy" so good, though. Well, we each have our thing.

PLAYBOY: Can't you be a bit more informative?

DYLAN: Nope.

PLAYBOY: How do you get your kicks these days?

DYLAN: I hire people to look into my eyes, and then I have them kick me.

PLAYBOY: And that's the way you get your kicks?

DYLAN: No. Then I *forgive* them; that's where my kicks come in.

PLAYBOY: Did you ever have the standard boyhood dream of growing up to be President?

DYLAN: No. When I was a boy, Harry Truman was President. Who'd want to be Harry Truman?

PLAYBOY: Well, let's suppose that you *were* the President. What would you accomplish during your first thousand days?

DYLAN: Well, just for laughs, so long as you insist, the first thing I'd do is probably move the White House. Instead of being in Texas, it'd be on the East Side in New York. McGeorge Bundy would definitely have to change his name, and General McNamara would be forced to wear a coonskin cap and shades.

In conversation, the put-on nearly always arises in response to questions. When the questioner and questionee represent opposing philosophies, invocation of the put-on precludes any possible agreement. Even though it's really a defensive weapon, the put-on almost always provides an offensive for the questionee, representative of the smaller, more helpless faction, making his group appear In and the larger, more powerful group of the questioner appear Out. Because the put-on is a close-range weapon, it is usually, by a curious mechanism, employed against the most sympathetic elements among the enemy. One might almost say that it is invoked when the moment of reconciliation is in sight, at the point when dialogue might begin—to prevent dialogue, to guarantee continued estrangement, and to protect the integrity of a beleaguered minority position. Thus, a bohemian delinquent will usually treat policemen with careful deference, but he will mercilessly put on a friendly probation officer or social worker. An artist will put on a dumb but eager fan who inquires about his creative methods but not a total boor who evinces no interest in art whatever. By the same token, Negroes commonly put on white liberals. As an exception, Stokely Carmichael built up a nearly legendary reputation in S.N.C.C. by putting on Southern bigots (subtly sassing Lowndes County deputies, mimicking their swaggers, addressing them in Yiddish)—an almost unheard-of practice. He could get away with it simply because the form of the put-on is so elusive; the victim is never sure precisely what's happening. In this manner, the put-on brings the submerged antagonisms of a relationship perilously close to the surface—*without actually allowing them to come into the open*. If the victim chooses to notice the put-on, the perpetrator can always feign absolute innocence. A put-on may even be veiled in expressions of injured purity:

A: What are you trying to do—make fun of me, nigger?
B: Oh *no*, suh. No *suh*, Boss.

In less explosive situations, this impalpable quality prevents forthright discussion of the resentments that may have produced the put-on in the first place:

A: Why are you treating me contemptuously?

B: Contemptuously? That's just a hostile projection. What ever are you talking about? You must be paranoid.

A: Well, perhaps I am oversensitive. Perhaps I'm imagining things.

The victim is often at least a partially willing victim; a bewildered guilt makes him reluctant to press the issue. But his vague feeling of having been placed at an unfair disadvantage, of having been ridiculed, persists semi-consciously. He may subsequently take indirect revenge.

Although there may be as many variations as practitioners, the extended in-group put-on usually improvises on two classic formats:

(1) Relentless Agreement: The perpetrator beats his victim to every low cliché the latter might possibly mouth.

(2) Actualization of the Stereotype: The perpetrator *personifies* every cliché about his group, realizes his adversary's every negative expectation. He becomes a grotesque rendition of his presumed identity, faking heated emotion.

Either of these options—caricaturing the victim or caricaturing the victim's image of oneself—is called into play when an out-group representative attempts to engage an in-group representative on the subject of their estrangement. The second option, being more *obviously* hostile, is more often taken at face value by the victim, but both options serve to affirm the belief that communication between disparate worlds is impossible—to affirm in-group solidarity and isolation. Both types grow progressively more extravagant. Here are some examples:

I. Young vs. Old: A well-disposed but bewildered adult tries to talk with a "rebellious adolescent" about generational gap. The young man responds:

(1) "Ah, I don't know. . . . Kids today—they're always running. But who knows where they're going? Crazy clothes, loud music—if you wanna call it music—fast cars, drinking, smoking, drugs. The next thing you know, we'll be going out with girls."

(2) "Why don't you go play with your mutual funds or something? Why don't you get off my back? I just want to bug out on your nowhere scene, nowhere man. Excuse me, I gotta go dig some groovy sounds and sniff a pot of airplane glue. Lemme peel out on my boss Harley."

II. Black vs. White: A benevolent progressive tries to express his questioning support of civil rights. The militant Negro responds:

(1) "You're two hundred percent right. I mean, with freedom goes responsibility. You can't just grab everything right off. Some demonstrations can only hurt our cause, you know what I mean? Like Dr. King says, our people've got to meet body force with Soul Force. He sets a good example. Like Joe Louis. He was a helluva fighter, huh? But he knew his place. Now, a man like Adam Clayton Powell, he's overstepping his bounds. He takes advantage. Ralph Bunche. That was a good nigger. 'Cept he couldn't sing and dance. What do you think?"

(2) "Don't make your superego gig with me, ofay baby. Your granddaddy rape my grandmammy, and now you tell me doan sleep with your daughter? Well, beat up side my black head and whup my humble black back, but don't offer me none of the *supreme* delectafactotory blessings of equalorama, 'cause when this bitch blows you gonna feel black man's machete in the soft flesh of your body, dig?"

III. Dove vs. Hawk: A patriotic Republican tries to start a serious conversation on the Southeast Asian situation. The subversive responds:

(1) "Absolutely. We're just making the same mistake we made in Korea, pussyfooting in those jungle swamps like gorillas. Our country's going to lose its first war unless we go on up North and nuke 'em and nape 'em. That's the only language those Commies understand, those Red butchers. We should throw all our pinko bleeding heart draft-card burners in jail, or ship 'em over to Ho Chi Minh, where they belong."

(2) "Sure, I'd just love to go into the military myself, start a little education program of my own. Maybe take a squadron out to defoliate Central Park and burn down Rockefeller Center. Give you imperialist warmongers and your Texas Führer in the White House something to think about."

IV. Hip vs. Square: A Sunday Villager from uptown seeks illumination on the bohemian mystique. The hippie responds:

(1) "Yeah, well, you know if we could get jobs we'd lap 'em up, but who'd hire us, man? Like we're *dirty*. I haven't had a bath since last February. And you should see the chick that shares my pad—freaky little mind-blower. You really got the life, Charlie—kids, a couple parakeets, a beer and a ball game. You don't worry about nothin', hear? You're on the right track. Listen, could you spare a quarter? I haven't had breakfast."

(2) Sullen silence interspersed with incoherent grunts. Hippie finally

grins sardonically and offers the square a reefer. "Somethin' is happening here, but you don't know what it is. *Do* you, Mistah Jones?"

V. Homosexual vs. Heterosexual: A straight (another meaning of this protean word) but enlightened man, evincing his enlightenment, seeks data. The homosexual responds:

(1) "Why, of *course* it's a *sickness,* there's no *question.* Take me. My father was *weak, hen*pecked. It's psycho*log*ical. My mother wouldn't let me wear long *pants* till I was fourteen. And then the *Army.* Well, *you* know. It's better than *an*imals. My analyst thinks I'm progressing toward a real adj*ust*ment."

(2) Mock flirtation; strokes the victim, bats eyelashes, dentalizes or lisps. "You sure know how to dress. And you're so under*standing.* Why don't you loosen up a little, Mary?"

In less threatening situations, the put-on itself can become the basis of the come-on. Such cases prostitute the form: genuine transaction is avoided (cop-out), but time passes and nothing real or interesting happens. Asked about his background at a party, a young man replies in a Westbrook Van Vorhis voice, "I was born of rich but humble parents in a little mining town called Juarez. . . ." There is no promise of engagement in what is to come, because there is no potential for fake-out. Is the truth so boring or embarrassing? This species of ersatz put-on lacks the element of tension. It is, at bottom, only a "bit," and occurs when the put-on itself becomes an established set—when a person begins actually to put himself on, and can no longer betray *any* straight feelings. Once the put-on is explicitly labelled (as by a new comedian, who titled his first record album *Take-Offs and Put-Ons*), uncertainty dissolves and old-fashioned kidding takes over.

Like sentimentality, the put-on offers a lazy man's substitute for feeling as well as for thought. Again, the form contains a built-in escape clause. People are not so much unsure of their feelings as unsure what feeling may be appropriate. Thus, a trite expression of feeling now has the advantage of being equivocal.

"How did you like the play?"

"Very moving."

Perfect, take it how you will. Whether the play was moving, corny, or itself a put-on, the question has been answered—assuming a slightly ambiguous intonation—appropriately.

A related but more calculated and aggressive dodge involves, quite simply, replying in gibberish when no honest response springs to mind.

"How did you like the play?"

"It was over the bush, man."

This sort of remark is seldom challenged. On the rare occasion when a victim asks, "What does 'over the bush' mean?," the perpetrator assumes a vaguely irritated tone and replies, "You know, man, it's like funk, only trippier," or some such nonsense. It takes a hardy victim to press the matter further.

Another subtle, and eventually devastating, ploy might be called the "silent put-on." Its perpetrator sits in rapt attention—nodding vigorously, asking occasional questions—as his victim pontificates. Gradually, the victim begins to suspect, rightly or wrongly, that his silent audience knows a good deal more about the subject at hand than he's letting on ("Here I've been running on about modern art on the basis of catalogue blurbs, and this fellow is obviously an important critic or painter himself"). As the perpetrator begins to reinforce this suspicion with improbable expressions of awe, the victim dimly perceives that, having been given enough rope to hang himself, he has behaved like a pompous, ignorant ass. Typically, he tapers off in embarrassment and excuses himself.

Not all conversational put-ons are so viciously intended. Some, particularly those employed by people who are either high on mind-affecting chemicals or have experimented considerably with such drugs, are simply a form of exploratory play—the interpersonal equivalent of set-breaking put-ons in serious art. LSD and, to a lesser extent, marijuana and hashish continuously dissolve and re-form the structure of reality, until being put through changes—and following these changes wherever they may lead—constitutes the drug user's most real and pleasurable sort of experience. The word "straight," therefore, denotes both not going through changes (not appreciating put-ons) and not being under the influence of drugs. Hallucinogens subject one's world of static reality (the Comprehensive Come-On) to constant fake-outs—transform it, indeed, into a gigantic put-on. The psychedelic solution to this flux: embrace every tangent, every fake-out with the same zeal. A conversational digression, perhaps initiated by a pun or misunderstanding, becomes altogether as important as the "main" conversation, and may supersede it entirely. When "heads" relate to one another, they perpetually put each other through changes, bust up each other's sets before sets can solidify. Flowing downstream with these changes is, for these people, serious fun. When heads relate to straight people, however, this set-breaking activity is experienced as put-on. A head's deliberately inappropriate behavior at a party—ranting, or talking nonsense, or demonstrating disproportionate affection toward strangers, or radically shifting the mood and emotional intensity of discourse—subjects his victims to a kind of involuntary "acid test." Either they are able to follow him through his changes—neutralizing and appreciating them with their own consciousnesses—or they persist in their straightness and are "freaked"; i.e., respond, by leaving or fighting, as if they were under attack. If they do the first, they are said to have been turned on; if the second, they can have quite a bad time. Hence the positive or negative reactions on the part of reporters interviewing creative performers who have been influenced by mind-bending drugs. A non-psychedelic illustration of the same principle turns up in *Don't Look Back,* D. A. Pennebaker's *cinema-vérité* movie of Dylan's London tour, a prolonged documentary of Dylan putting on the British—or, rather, putting them through changes. Some get turned on, some completely fail to perceive what's happening, and many get freaked.

Heads try to break up sets without malevolence, but their put-ons are sometimes so extreme that straight people mistake them for "scoring"—the sort of derision that Negroes call "signifying" and adolescents call "chopping," "ranking," or "sounding." Non-heads also may employ the put-on without malice. Sometimes understated facetiousness seems the only way to keep the ball rolling in a conversation that would be otherwise devoid of interest and amusement. When such put-ons pass unrecognized over the heads of one's companions, all parties can enjoy the proceedings on different levels and no feelings are ruffled.

FROM

LETTER FROM CHICAGO

Richard H. Rovere

SEPTEMBER 7, 1968

I T IS CLEAR to everyone in retrospect—as it was clear to many in prospect—that it was a dreadful mistake to hold this gathering in Chicago in August of 1968. "We knew this was going to happen," the

186 · THE 60S: THE STORY OF A DECADE

Vice-President said as he turned away from the ugly picture in his picture window to the exhilarating one on the tube. "It was programmed." Everyone knew that it was programmed. The Republicans, ingloriously but nonetheless wisely, withdrew to Miami Beach, a community—if it deserves any such designation—in many ways more obscene than this one but at least a place in which bloodshed was unlikely. As it turned out, there was bloodshed across the bay—probably, though not certainly, related to their Convention—but there is blood running in the streets of many cities now, and although there were deaths in Miami proper, as there have not been in Chicago so far, there was no programmed confrontation there, and there could not have been one unless the demonstrators had chosen to form an invading armada. Holding the Democratic Convention in Chicago was in itself an act no less provocative than the actions of some of the demonstrators who wished, above all else, to have things work out exactly as they did. The Democrats stuck to Chicago for some reasons that were terrible and for some that were not. The President, who had planned the Convention he did not dare attend at a time when he still expected to be its candidate, did not wish the sessions to be held in Republican territory; that ruled out New York, California, Florida, and a good many other states. A commitment was made to Mayor Daley, who sealed the deal with a bundle of cash. But the seal could have been broken and the cash returned as recently as a month ago for reasons both honorable and humane. No doubt a reluctance to offend the Mayor played a part in the decision not to change the site. But by that late date the pride of other Party leaders had also become involved. "It would be an act of pure chicken to run away from Chicago now," one Party spokesman said at the end of July. "Chicago is where the people live, and if Democrats are afraid to face them, we might as well fold up the Party."

It can be argued that only in a few other places—Miami Beach, Honolulu, and Fairbanks seem to just about exhaust the list—could a confrontation have been avoided. Transportation is relatively cheap in this country now, and a lack of money was not, in any case, what primarily afflicted those who spent their days in the parks by the lake and their nights doing battle in the nearby streets; the few who were poor and hardy made it to Chicago free, by hitchhiking. They would have assembled in any city in the country about as they did here. But one cannot avoid the conclusion that almost anywhere else would have been better. This is a peculiarly violent city; there may be no higher ratio of brutes among the police here than among the police anywhere, though it certainly seemed as if there were to those who watched them in action the last two nights. But there is violence in the politics of this place. Long before the Convention, the Mayor gave his sanction to the use of the gun, and he exhibited this week—as he moved through the heavily policed hotel lobbies surrounded by a large personal guard—nothing but pride when asked by newspapermen to comment on the work of his force. The most shocking thing of all, however, was not the lack of restraint on the part of the police but the obvious preparations for violence among the citizens. In the days before the Convention, the papers were full of stories about the outrage of the people living in the neighborhoods between the Loop and the stockyards at the prospect of their streets' becoming a parade route for anti-war protesters headed for the International Amphitheatre. "If they just march through quietly, we'll ignore it," one man said, "but if they bring a Viet Cong flag on this block, we'll tear them apart—we'll kill them." Newspapers tend to play up the extravagant and inflammatory. Yet a tour of the streets in question—the old Studs Lonigan neighborhood, and still Mayor Daley's, but nowadays predominantly peopled by industrial workers of Eastern European background—seemed to show that there was little overstatement in the stories. For block after dismal block, there was scarcely a house—one in twenty, perhaps—without an American flag and a portrait of Mayor Daley in the window. On Union Avenue, a main thoroughfare of the section, sandwich men paraded up and down with anti-Communist slogans, and one could not help feeling that perhaps it was best, after all, not to grant a parade permit to the demonstrators. It would have been one thing, of course, if a permit had been issued and the police instructed to protect the protesters. But this might have required the police to deal with the burghers as they had been dealing with the demonstrators. This they would never have done. It would have been like clubbing their fellow-cops.

HARVARD YARD

E. J. Kahn, Jr.

APRIL 19, 1969

T HE PREVAILING MOOD at Harvard the day after Crimson blood was spilled was one of sadness. There was disbelief, too, but to a lesser degree. Belief has been suspended, if not shattered, on many campuses of late. Still, Harvard was, and probably is, and maybe will even continue to be, something different—the quintessential university, the very symbol of higher learning. One junior faculty member we ran into in the Yard at noon on Thursday, twenty-four hours after the students had occupied University Hall and seven hours after the police had bludgeoned them out, declared sadly, "Some of us are suffering today from the kind of hangover that comes only from over-indulgence in hubris." He went on, "It's all so irrational. It's surrealistic. A photographer who loves Harvard was roughed up first by the demonstrators and then by the cops. After that, he couldn't focus his camera, because he was crying. A dean who told me about this started crying, too. And the mere telling you about it is putting me in tears."

There were those in Cambridge who were saying, perhaps not without hindsight, that Harvard had been overdue for trouble; it had been lucky too long, it was too prominent, too inviting a target to be further spared. The Students for a Democratic Society had been muttering about occupying a Harvard building, but threat-making is the principal S.D.S. line of business, and few thought that what happened would happen. Indeed, at an evening meeting on Tuesday, April 8th, the S.D.S. had voted not to occupy. But its leaders had swiftly announced a meeting at noon the next day to reconsider, and even as that session was getting under way members of its more militant faction—including many students affiliated with the all-out-revolutionary Progressive Labor Party—were moving into University Hall. They were well prepared, with chains and padlocks and placards reading "Fight Capitalists—Running Dogs" and "Put Your Body Where Your Head Is." They had the occupants of the building hustled out within the hour. The evictions were accomplished without injury, except to pride. There was some pushing and jostling, and one frail, quiet, nonviolent assistant dean was carried out slung over a student's back, because he refused to leave under his own steam. He was James E. Thomas, an ordained minister who is also a nuclear physicist and a graduate student in philosophy, and who has long been acclaimed as one of the most liberal-minded Harvard administrators. His nickname is Jet. When a student he knew ordered Thomas out, he refused to go. "This building is occupied," he was told. "But surely it's big enough for both of us to occupy," Thomas said. "Oh, come on, Jet," said the student, and hoisted him onto his shoulders. As Thomas was being carted off, another student walked behind him, solicitously picking up the things that fell out of his pockets.

The S.D.S. had long since made known its demands, which, like many student demands these days, were proclaimed to be non-negotiable. The principal one was that Harvard abolish its Reserve Officers Training Corps. The Harvard administration had already stripped the R.O.T.C. of its academic standing and its instructors of their professorial rank; the faculty had voted by a ten-to-one ratio *not* to abolish the R.O.T.C. The S.D.S. apparently didn't really care. It was not the issue that mattered but the event. By midafternoon, the S.D.S. had the situation well in hand. Its occupation was reasonably orderly. Early on, the students voted against doing willful damage to the building, and against smoking marijuana while inside. Some filing cabinets were moved around, to serve as barricades, and the contents of a few of them were inspected. (On Friday, an underground paper sold in Harvard Square published some documents that purported to reveal an unsavory connection between the University and the C.I.A.) Finding a batch of blank identification cards for freshman proctors, a few students at once conferred proctorial status upon themselves; others, aware that Ivy League acceptances were about to be mailed to high-school seniors, whiled away the hours by typing on Harvard letterheads warm notes to young men around the country, congratulating them on their admission as freshmen next fall. Still others typed stencils, and one mimeograph machine churned forth a manifesto that concluded, "This is the first action of many to build a strong anti-imperialist movement in this country." Somebody painted an obscenity on a wall of the office of Fred L. Glimp, the Dean of the College; somebody else Scotch-Taped a note alongside it saying, "Dear Sir, We apologize for whoever did this. This vandalism was not a purpose of our protest." At one point, there were at least four hundred students in University Hall, perhaps half of them observers. One of the latter, a senior, told us afterward, "There were more beautiful girls at this Harvard function than at any other I've ever been to. One of them lent me a book to read. It was *Cuba: Anatomy of a Revolution.* The thing that worried me most about many of the people in there was their ego-building. They seemed to spend half the day congratulating themselves on what they were doing."

From time to time during the afternoon and evening, the occupiers held a more or less formal meeting in the spacious faculty room, from which they voted to bar the faculty; they would communicate with the faculty, and with the administration, they further voted, only by public statements. Their friends outside provided them with food and with bedding. Other friends, and spectators, swarmed outside, in a blaze of television lights. One camera crew, it developed, was filming background scenes for a movie about a fictitious campus revolt. "Here we are in front of Jenkins Hall at Metropolitan University," an actor impersonating a television commentator was saying. "The atmosphere here is like a carnival."

Eventually, many of the two hundred students who remained in the building went to sleep. Quite a few of them still expected no trouble. They were wrong, of course. The administration had already decided—without consulting the faculty—to have them routed out at five in the morning. Some four hundred policemen were converging on the Yard. At four o'clock, to summon other students to the scene, fire alarms were set off—presumably by the S.D.S.—throughout the Harvard community. The students inside University Hall had been told by Franklin L. Ford, the Dean of the Faculty of Arts and Sciences, within a short time of their taking it over that if they didn't clear out in fifteen minutes they would be liable to charges of criminal trespass. Now, at 4:55 A.M., Dean Glimp warned them by bullhorn that they had exactly five minutes to get out with impunity. Apparently, nobody inside heard him. At five, the police moved in. There were two kinds—dark-blue shirts and light-blue shirts. The dark-blues were municipal police; their job was to clear students off the four flights of steps leading into University Hall. The light-blues were state police; their job was to get the students inside the building out. It is generally conceded that the dark-blues were the less disciplined and the more brutal. As they converged on the steps, clubs in hand, a few students inside the building leaped from windows and ran to freedom. Dozens of boys and girls were clubbed. One student in a wheelchair was hit. "I had to leave," a Radcliffe girl told us. "I thought it was too voyeuristic to stick around and watch students bare their skulls to nightsticks."

A hundred and ninety-six boys and girls were bundled into police vans and taken off to jail. Some forty were injured. The cops were gone by six-fifteen. The Yard was littered with trash and rutted by police vehicles. Buildings and Grounds men moved swiftly into University Hall and painted over Dean Glimp's profaned wall. All morning long, students milled about the Yard, in a daze compounded of sleeplessness and shock. "Whatever I think about seizing buildings—and I don't think much of it—I keep reminding myself that human beings perform these acts, not three guys whose initials are S., D., and S.," one of them told us. Some classes went on as scheduled. One bitterly anti-S.D.S. student reacted to the tumult by attending a course he hadn't been to in three months.

At eleven, while the students who had been arrested were being arraigned and, in most instances, released on their own recognizance, between fifteen hundred and two thousand moderate students held a meeting at the Memorial Church, in the Yard. The church had never before been so crowded; there were students perched atop the reredos. One of the undergraduate leaders invited his fellow-students to turn to and reflect on Hymn 256 in the hymnals on hand: "O God of earth and altar, / Bow down and hear our cry. / Our earthly rulers falter. / Our people drift and die." Professor Stanley H. Hoffmann, the social scientist, got up to speak on behalf of rationality. "This is the only university we've got," he said. "It could be improved. It can be improved. But it cannot be destroyed." He was loudly cheered. He advocated changes in Harvard's decision-making processes, but he warned against changing the processes so much that the will of a minority could prevail. "No university can function if the minority insists on winning all the time," he said. More cheers. The assembled students began debating what course of action they should take. They finally decided on a three-day strike, and they passed a number of resolutions—among others, condemning the administration for unnecessarily summoning the police, condemning the police for their brutality, and calling for the resignation of President Pusey if he didn't meet student demands. "This is the most impressive and most exciting thing I've seen in four years at Harvard," a Radcliffe senior said after the meeting. "It's the first time that moderates have dealt with radicals on their own terms. There's no longer a murky atmosphere here. The way the moderate students have reacted is electrifying." A resolution to condemn the S.D.S. was tabled. Nonetheless, some of the S.D.S. people who had got out of jail had hastened to the church and were already crying "Foul!" They said that the administration had purposely delayed their release so they couldn't get to the Memorial Church meeting in time to vote. The meeting broke up at two o'clock, amid ringing, responsible cries of "Clean the church! Clean the church!" Outside, a girl screamed "Bail money!" into the ears of a haggard passing dean. He winced. "Women shouldn't be allowed to talk in public," he said, not ill-naturedly. We caught sight of a student we know, a junior who hadn't missed a demonstration throughout his stay at Harvard. He looked crestfallen. "My alarm clock didn't go off," he said. "I slept through the bust. I've lost my honor."

The Yard was still full of clusters of disputants. Graduate students from the Business School and the Medical School had drifted over to see what was going on. A Divinity School student came by and asked no one in particular if it was all right for a lady organist to practice in the church, between meetings, for an imminent recital. Two S.D.S. members ripped an orange sign off a tree. "Hey, that's my sign!" yelled a student. "You wrote that?" one of the rippers asked scornfully. "Yeats did," said the sign's owner, even more scornfully. "The ceremony of innocence is drowned," the sign read. "The best lack all conviction, while the worst are full of passionate intensity." The S.D.S. men shrugged and yielded up the sign.

We had a word with an instructor in government. He had a booklet in one hand entitled "After Harvard—What?" He asked us if we were going to the faculty meeting. "What faculty meeting?" we asked. "There are meetings all over today," he said. "This one's at Sever Hall."

We headed toward Sever. On the way, we were stopped by an undergraduate with a solemn expression. "Would you like to hear the views of an ordinary, middle-of-the-road student?" he asked. We said we would. "I have always been incensed by the moral arrogance of S.D.S., but I'm afraid that this morning they scored a brilliant victory," he said. "Because of the administration's response to their totally unwarranted action, the issue, God help us, is no longer what S.D.S. did. The issue is cracked heads. It puts moderates like me in an uncomfortable position. I won't absolve S.D.S. of responsibility, and I won't support any strike, but I'll sign all the petitions in the world to disapprove of calling in the cops that way. Most of all, I am deeply concerned about the future of Harvard University."

So were the eighty faculty members who had gathered in Sever Hall. George Wald was there, and James D. Watson, and John Kenneth Galbraith, and everybody was sitting facing a blackboard on which someone had chalked "on strike." As we entered, a man we didn't recognize was saying, "For heaven's sake, let's 'reject,' or let's 'repudiate,' but, whatever we do, let's do anything but 'deplore.'" They agreed that the sense of their meeting was that they repudiated the occupation of University Hall, the eviction of the deans, the calling of the police, and the failure to inform the faculty that the police were being called. Professor Daniel Seltzer spoke up. "The primary purpose of this university is to teach," he said. "As long as one single student shows up for any of my classes, I'll teach him." Most of his colleagues nodded approvingly.

PART THREE

AMERICAN SCENES

A NOTE BY JILL LEPORE

THE SOUND YOU hear reading these pieces is the sound of shattering. It's unmistakable but faraway, like a rustle in the woods or a whistle in the distance. "We strain our ears, but we hear no bugles, no sounds of fifes and drums," Michael J. Arlen wrote in a Comment about the Vietnam War, at the end of 1965. Arlen later said that when he sent in more powerful stuff about the war, more damning stuff, noisier stuff, William Shawn would say things like, "This is a Comment piece. It represents the magazine. We're not ready to say that this is wrong." And so there is, instead, this unnerving sound of shattering, muffled.

"John Kennedy was killed, his life made to disappear right there before us, frame by frame," Arlen wrote, in a piece about bearing witness to violence by watching television, and you can almost hear the screen cracking, breaking like a heart. There's cut glass all over these essays: lenses and panes and, on the ground, shards as sharp as spikes. Especially, there are panes, and reporters peering through them. Here's Daniel Lang, visiting a missile silo that reminds him of an operating room: "Through windows I could see two small rooms, one containing double-decker beds and the other a library of technical manuals stamped 'SECRET.'" And here's Charlayne Hunter, the first black student to graduate from the University of Georgia, walking through Harlem: "In the window of the meat market were rows of ox tails, turkey wings, and chops, and a sign on the window advertised chitterlings and hog maws at bargain prices." More often, though, it's the absence of glass that draws attention: "He was shot in secrecy, away from cameras," Arlen writes about the assassination of Martin Luther King, Jr., on the balcony of a motel in Memphis. Then there's E. B. White on the assassination of J.F.K., shot while riding through the streets of Dallas in a car with the windows rolled down: "He died of exposure."

The pieces gathered here aren't investigative: they're not exposés. They're scenes. They're mainly letters from this place or that, chronicling one kind of fracture or another. (The historian Daniel T. Rodgers has called the 1980s the "age of fracture," but, arguably, it was the 1960s.) Whether at Woodstock or in the White House, these writers are more likely to stare than to pry. Jonathan Schell attends a rally in 1968: "The crowd, which grew to well over a thousand as the evening progressed, was composed mostly of people whom we took to be in their twenties. There was a noticeably large proportion of college-age girls, and a peppering of Africans and American Negroes. Some people carried signs consisting of large photographs of half-starved Biafran children, and others carried signs saying, among other things, 'Stop Man's Inhumanity.'" Ellen Willis goes to a hearing before an eight-member committee—"all male"—of the New York State Legislature. The subject is abortion. Willis writes, "Of the fifteen witnesses listed on the agenda, fourteen were men; the lone woman was a nun." Women who've had abortions turn up and insist on speaking. The committee hardly listens to these women. But Willis does. "We're probably the first women ever to talk about our abortions in public," one of them says, wandering out.

Rovere doesn't stare so much as glare, writing from Washington with wry and even cynical detachment about everything from the Cuban missile crisis ("there are dark hints that Moscow may be dissembling") to Lyndon B. Johnson's first hundred days ("it is entirely possible that things were livelier in this city in the middle years of the Pierce administration"). Charlayne Hunter was only twenty-five when she wrote about a block in Harlem where she found, more or less, a mirror: "Near us, a young Negro woman who looked to be in her early twenties stood leaning against a car with a sketch pad and pencil in her hands." When two men ask the woman with the sketch pad what she's doing there, she says, "I'm a student, and I'm doing a paper for one of my classes on the changing face of Harlem." The face of the United States was changing in the 1960s. The question was: Who was drawing those faces? Who was really looking?

The New Journalism that *The New Yorker* disavowed was loud, a yelp and a howl, a bellow and a grunt. It didn't stare so much as it leered. You can see and hear something very different in the best and quietest moments of these American scenes. "Our last glimpse of President Kennedy was in Miami," Lillian Ross wrote, the week after the assassination. Hundreds of people went out to the Miami airport, hoping to meet the

President. That number, Ross wrote, included, "a pretty young Negro woman, who was herding a small group of Negro children," her fourth-grade class. A girl named Barbara Laidler wore a green ribbon in her hair.

We noticed that Mrs. Peterson and her fourth-graders were crowded against the wire fence, their hands outstretched, and we noticed that the President kept trying to pull away from the Secret Service men and head in their direction. A white man was holding Barbara up high to get a better look (her green hair ribbon was now untied and fluttering), so that she could give a responsible report to the rest of her class and share with them everything she saw that day.

The next day, Lillian Ross called Mrs. Peterson on the telephone, and Mrs. Peterson read to Ross the papers her students had been assigned to write. Little Barbara Laidler reported: "The President has reddish hair and had on a suit." It was the last time she ever saw him.

PRESSURE AND POSSIBILITY

LETTER FROM WASHINGTON

Richard H. Rovere

NOVEMBER 3, 1962 (THE CUBA CRISIS)

OCTOBER 28

THE WHITE HOUSE has not, at this writing, received the latest Khrushchev note, but the world has, and to everyone here it appears that all of the essential requirements—as distinct from the formal demands—of American policy are about to be satisfied. If the Soviet technicians are in fact dismantling the medium- and intermediate-range missile installations and withdrawing their components, on-site inspection and verification can be arranged at a later date, and in all probability no harm would come of it if there never were any inspection. The United States had little difficulty in detecting the construction of the bases; it can surely verify their destruction—and, thanks to the conveniently slim and elongated contours of the Pearl of the Antilles, without the need for overflights. Most of the surveillance we have thus far conducted has required no violation of Cuban air space. Nuclear warheads are, of course, another matter, but nuclear warheads in a Cuba with no effective launching systems endanger only Cuba. The latest news released by the Pentagon suggests that, like the President, the Soviet technicians in Cuba have not as yet got Khrushchev's message. They are still building, and there are dark hints that Moscow may be dissembling. This is hard to credit; enough has already happened in this extraordinary week to suggest that Khrushchev remains a true Leninist to the extent that it offends him very little to make strategic withdrawals when survival seems to require them, and that bourgeois notions of pride never put him off. "If you are not able to adapt yourself," Lenin told his comrades after the humiliation of the Brest-Litovsk Treaty, "if you are not ready to crawl in the mud on your belly, you are not a revolutionist but a chatter-box." Lenin, of course, recommended retreat only when it was necessary to preserve the opportunity for bringing up "fresh forces [and] renewing the attack." Khrushchev's crawl may be a prelude to a renewed attack, but it hardly seems likely to come in Cuba—or, indeed, in the Western Hemisphere.

Throughout the week, the principal anxiety in American diplomatic and military circles here was not that the Cuban crisis, whether it ended in an American invasion or a Soviet withdrawal, would be a prelude to an attack elsewhere but that it would be a dangerous distraction from what was regarded as the central crisis—Berlin. During the late summer and the early autumn, the administration kept insisting that the Soviets would deliver an ultimatum on Berlin this year, and that a final showdown could not be avoided. It interpreted the first Soviet maneuvers in Cuba as an effort to draw American attention away from Berlin, and possibly to provoke the United States into an invasion. The tendency in most Allied capitals and among a good many observers here was to feel that the Berlin crisis the administration was talking about was of local rather than of Soviet manufacture. On the surface, it was lent an air of reality only by Khrushchev's statement in September that he would not "embarrass" the President by bringing the matter up before the Congressional elections. The British took this to be nothing more than a convenient procrastination. The French held, as usual, that Khrushchev was a windbag who would never dare make a move that would incur the displeasure of General de Gaulle. The West Germans said that they saw no particular evidence of Soviet impatience. Russian diplomats and correspondents here went about town asking Americans why they were stirring up trouble with all their talk of the imminence of a crisis. Was it to help the Democrats in the November elections? Was it because the American government feared that the American people were growing bored with Berlin? It was only when it became clear that Cuba was being converted into a base for Soviet weapons of a flagrantly and devastatingly offensive character that the administration's sense of urgency about Berlin was taken with much seriousness; the haste in October to outflank our thermonuclear deterrent to the south seemed to explain Khrushchev's curious reference to the elections in November. It appeared to be a classic instance of second-front strategy, and one that, if it had worked, might have rendered completely ineffective what we call our "second-strike capability"—that reserve of nuclear striking power which, according to the theory of deterrence, would restrain any sane commander from making nuclear war, because his own society would be destroyed even if he had, moments earlier, destroyed the enemy. By the middle of last week, there seemed nothing in the least preposterous about saying that the successful emplacement in Cuba of a large number of medium- and intermediate-range missiles would result in the unilateral disarmament of the United States at the hands of the Soviet Union. No other policy objective could be brought forward to account for the nature of the Soviet presence in Cuba. Had the Soviet objective been attained, it seemed clear, and had a Berlin ultimatum been issued, the choice of the West would have been between abandonment of Berlin and destruction.

There has not yet been time for anyone to address himself to the question of whether Khrushchev's hasty withdrawal requires some new reading of his original motives. The text of the President's message of last night has not yet been released. It may have contained an ultimatum that left Khrushchev no time for procrastination or maneuver. The speed with which he met the American terms, though, suggests either that he had miscalculated on an incredible scale by supposing it was possible to set up Cuban bases without American detection, or that he had never been up to anything more than a test of the President's will and courage. If he was indeed conducting a probe, that, too, involved a huge miscalculation, for there could surely have been ways of learning what he wanted to know without unifying, as he did, the Organization of American States, without accepting for the first time the authority of the United Nations, without demonstrating to the satellites and to the neutrals he has sought to befriend how quickly he will run out on an ally, and without destroying the political value of his rocket-rattling. (Between August, 1957, the month in which the Soviets announced their first successful firing of "a super-long-distance intercontinental multistage ballistic missile," and the end of 1961, there were twenty-three distinct occasions upon which Khrushchev employed the threat of his missile power as an instrument of his aggressive diplomacy. State Department disarmament experts, who keep records of this sort, did not this past week have complete figures for the first ten months of 1962, but they said that if Khrushchev's known threats—made mainly to representatives of NATO countries, who were told that their continued association with the United States invited their destruction by Soviet weapons—were combined with those made since 1957 by his direct subordinates and by official publications of his government, the figure would be well over a hundred.) His losses seem to be staggering in their dimensions, and it is almost impossible to imagine how they might be offset by any seen or unseen gains. He has won high praise from Bertrand Russell, and he has been complimented by the President for a "statesmanlike" act. He has the world's gratitude for playing a large role in preserving the peace that he had threatened in the first place. These things cannot be begrudged him, but they butter no parsnips for a Communist politician. He has perhaps stored up a certain amount of credit with Western leaders, who may feel that they ought to follow the amiable customs of their craft and do Khrushchev some kind of favor that will make him look better with the people back home. If what he would like is Berlin, however, he will not get it, nor is he likely at any early date to persuade NATO to give up any considerable part of its installations in Turkey. He can probably get a summit meeting if he wants one, and he can expect not to be pressed too hard by the West for further concessions on his part.

. . .

The week has provided a display of the ruthlessness of Soviet diplomacy and of what appears to be its gross miscalculation. It has also provided a display of its extraordinary flexibility and virtuosity. Since American diplomacy has succeeded, its critics will be few and their strictures mild. No one who watched developments here failed to be impressed by the forethought, precision, subtlety, and steady nerves of the President and those around him in preparing our bold and ultimately successful initiative. The week had hardly begun, though, when it became apparent that if much was required of us in the way of flexibility, we would not have much to give. Khrushchev was able to play for time in ways that would have been available to President Kennedy only if he had elected to run risks of internal dissension that might in the end have caused him to lose his control over events. Had the Soviet and American roles been reversed in the middle of the week, it is doubtful whether—no matter what prudential or tactical considerations recommended it—the President could have made a decision comparable to Khrushchev's decision not to run the Caribbean blockade. The Soviet leaders are possessed by an ideology that is unyielding on all questions other than those of tactics and strategy, where, as Lenin's words about crawling through the mud so clearly reveal, it is infinitely pragmatic. The American leaders are unideological and essentially pragmatic on nearly all questions other than those of tactics and strategy, where they tend to be hobbled by the demonologies and tribal memories of our society, as well as by its democratic morality. If the President had made miscalculations as basic as those made by Khrushchev, and if he had subsequently decided to pull back and save the peace of the world, he would, even if he escaped impeachment, have lost the better part of his Presidential authority. Khrushchev's words and his actions can be at complete—and, from the world's point of view, useful—variance; he can conceal the contradictions from his own people if he chooses to, or he can expect them to be acceptable to Leninist morality if his case for retreat is a strong one. Dealing with a free, informed, articulate, and highly concerned constituency, Mr. Kennedy cannot revert to the doctrine that consistency may be—on occasion, at least—a mean and dangerous virtue.

The next period is likely to show the weaknesses as well as the strengths of the American practice. It may very well be that a time has arrived for broad and advantageous settlements. The world has been frightened as it had never been frightened before, and the Soviet leaders may have been the most frightened men of all. A chance may exist, as the President has said, for a genuine *détente* and for important steps toward general disarmament. The President found it easy to get the country behind him when he seemed close to an assault on Cuba; he will find it far less easy to get it behind him if he chooses now to engage in negotiations with the Soviet Union. The mere mention, a few days back, of a summit meeting brought from Harry Truman the recollection that he had attended two of them and had learned that they weren't worth a damn, and from the less experienced Everett Dirksen, the Minority Leader of the Senate, the opinion that every one he had ever heard of was a swindle. Khrushchev is no longer asking us to dismantle our Turkish base, but Walter Lippmann had suggested a few days before Khrushchev brought it up that this might be a way out of the crisis. Had Mr. Lippmann been right in thinking it a fair deal (he characterized the proposal as an exchange of a defenseless base in Cuba for a nearly obsolete one in Turkey), it would nevertheless have been one that the President could not possibly have been party to in the atmosphere that then prevailed. The atmosphere that seems likely to prevail now will be filled with pressures not to follow victory with more negotiations but to follow the present negotiation with more victories. These would be hard to produce.

· · ·

The President said in his address to the nation last Monday evening that his first knowledge of the new and dangerous developments in Cuba had been brought to him on Tuesday, October 16th, at nine in the morning. From then until last Sunday, he managed to carry on without betraying any sense of an impending ordeal. (The White House correspondents who accompanied him on the campaign trip that ended in Chicago on the morning after it began were not satisfied with Pierre Salinger's story that the President had a head cold and one degree of fever. What they suspected was that he might have two or three degrees of fever.) On one occasion, though, he expressed an uncharacteristic sentiment in a characteristic way. In the afternoon of the day he received the first intelligence reports, he met with a group of newspaper and broadcasting people who were in Washington for some conferences organized by the State Department. At the conclusion of a short and rather routine talk on foreign policy, he said there came to his mind a poem by a Spaniard named Ortega that had been translated by Robert Graves. The text he recited was:

> Bullfight critics ranked in rows
> Crowd the enormous Plaza full;
> But only one is there who *knows*
> And he's the man who fights the bull.

Ortega is Domingo Ortega, a bullfighter. The poem appeared in the British monthly *Encounter* in December, 1961. Robert Graves quoted it as reflecting his feelings when he won the Oxford Chair of Poetry, a position he said might be called "a Siege Perilous."

AN INQUIRY INTO ENOUGHNESS

Daniel Lang

OCTOBER 10, 1964 (VISITING A MISSILE SILO)

THE ENTRANCE TO an ICBM silo—or, to give its official designation, launch-control center—is called an "entrapment area," and it
is accurately named, as I know from having stood inside one on a
day I visited an underground Atlas. The entrapment area was a hollow
cubicle of darkness, ten feet long, five feet wide, and eight feet high. The
steel door through which I had entered it, with a military escort, had
closed behind me. Before me was another steel door leading to the interior. In a corner of the ceiling was a closed-circuit television camera,
through which the invisible commanding officer of the missile team
within the silo peered at me and my escort as he challenged us, in a se-
pulchral voice. My companion, responding earnestly, identified us and
stated our business; his name was Captain Richard W. Wetzel, and he
was ordinarily a silo commander himself. Neither Wetzel's voice nor
presence, I found, did much to mitigate my sense of entrapment, and I
tried to remember the landscape I had just blotted out for myself. I was a
mile from the Canadian border, in a corner of upstate New York above
Plattsburgh that was in the nuclear domain of Colonel Stewart, and the
countryside there was sunny and verdant with maples and birches. Herds
of Jerseys were grazing in a nearby pasture, the property of a dairy farmer
who had chosen to sell the Air Force an acre of his land for this emplacement. Now, in the entrapment area, I recalled the sign at the gate leading
into the militarized acre: "It is unlawful to enter this area without authority of the Base Commander. . . . Area is patrolled by armed guards
and vicious sentry dogs."

"Fuel!" Wetzel told the television camera, giving the day's password.

The door before us was pulled open, but there were two more steel
doors to go—mammoth ones, weighing a half ton each. They were
blastproof, and had been designed to protect the ICBM from earth-
quakes and near misses. Each door was opened only long enough to

admit us, and then secured again. When we were past both of them, I found myself looking at a lounge and galley, whose stores, I was told, included a ten days' supply of emergency rations. (The silo, which had taken two years to build and cost ten million dollars, had its own water and power supply.) I followed Wetzel down a short flight of stairs to the silo's headquarters room—an area, about thirty by forty feet, that put me in mind of a hospital operating theatre, possibly because fluorescent lamps glared brilliantly against its pastel walls. The room was crammed with instrumentation, the most prominent piece of equipment being a large console covered with twinkling green, red, and amber lights. Through windows I could see two small rooms, one containing double-decker beds and the other a library of technical manuals stamped "secret." The silo's commanding officer was in the headquarters room as I entered. He was sitting in an easy chair watching television, a revolver strapped at his side. The image on the screen before him was that of his own ICBM warhead, and he was viewing it in order to make sure that it wasn't afire or being tampered with. "Channel One," he said, taking a last look at the picture before he rose to greet Wetzel and me. He introduced himself as Major Robert Carr. The officers stood side by side for a moment, two nice-looking, cheerful men in their thirties, Carr blond and Wetzel brown-haired. The working uniforms worn by Carr and his men, several of whom were on duty in the headquarters room, added to the hospital atmosphere. They were impeccable white coveralls, designed to show up any stains made by hazardous chemicals. "An ICBM silo is a spotless place," Carr remarked to me.

Before we left him to inspect the missile, he relieved us of our wristwatches; their straps, he explained, might snag on a piece of equipment or their movements might be damaged by a vagrant high-voltage current. In exchange, he gave us hard hats, and Wetzel and I clambered through a low fifty-foot tunnel that was closed off at each end by two more blastproof doors. The tunnel led to the vertical shaft that held the ICBM, and we were scarcely there when a young technical sergeant in white coveralls joined us unobtrusively. We were standing on a narrow ledge whose walls were stenciled "NO-LONE ZONE." Below us were other levels, and below them were the base of the silo and the missile's launching platform. One could descend into the silo by means of a spiral staircase or by means of an elevator that sounded a clanging, ambulancelike bell when it was in use. Around us were phones, fire alarms, fire-fighting equipment, oxygen masks, and emergency flashlights. Lining the cylindrical chamber were four sets of the most immense springs I have ever seen, their huge coils of steel extending down four levels below; they were designed to help absorb the shock of an earthquake or a near miss by an enemy weapon. The missile itself, at the center of the silo, was sheathed in an encircling wall of steel, called the crib, which was broken by apertures through which one could see the graceful stainless-steel body of the Atlas, eighty-four feet tall. My eye went to the warhead. It wasn't sharp-nosed, as I had expected, but blunt, and it had been painted a drab grayish-white.

"I can't tell you its yield or its target," Wetzel volunteered.

"Is it loaded?" I asked.

He replied pleasantly. "We're on alert, and that weapon cost a million dollars."

We descended the steep, winding staircase to the next level, which, except for glimpses of the ever-present Atlas through the apertures, was solid with panels of contacts and relays. These were crucial in governing the sequence of the missile's actions, Wetzel told me, and I could deduce their importance for myself by the open suspicion with which the sergeant eyed me. There was a constant loud, whirring noise, which Wetzel said was the sound of air being washed in a dust collector. The silo, Wetzel said, depended heavily on water; it was needed for air-conditioning, for cooling diesel generators, and for fighting the fires that might be started by diesel fumes and other hazards. As we walked to the elevator to make our next descent, Wetzel, hospitably making talk, spoke of his plans for his eventual retirement. He hadn't yet decided how to spend it, he said, sounding as though his missile days were already behind him. He rather looked forward to a second career, he went on—not that he regretted for one minute the years he had put in with the Air Force. "It's been a good way of life," he said. "I may go into animal husbandry. I majored in that at Penn State, and it's been of some use to me in my work with missiles. It helped bring out my mechanical skills, and it taught me about chemicals."

The elevator was freight-size and slow-moving, and we spent each of our downward rides listening to its clanging bell. A new sound, deep and thumping, took over as we approached Level 6, and Wetzel showed me where it was coming from—a gray diesel generator squatting massively in a corner. As we continued our inspection, I saw many other things: bottles of helium; small brass pipes, which detected noxious gases in the atmosphere; air-support cylinders, whose function, like that of the enormous springs above, was to help maintain the missile's balance in the event of violent earth shocks; emergency showers, for washing burns that the men might suffer in changing the silo's exotic fuels; and emergency eye showers—basins specially fitted out with spouts for cleansing eyes burned by acids. Here, also, was a large white cylindrical tank containing twenty-three thousand gallons of LOX (liquid oxygen), the missile's primary fuel, whose normal temperature is -297° F. "Plenty of fire in there," he said. "But when we fuel up, the LOX-loading lines get so cold you can't even tap them without injuring your finger."

Eventually, the three of us stood at the very base of the silo, well below the missile's tail. The launching platform was there—a rectangular gray metal slab—and, unaccountably, the sight of it brought back to me one of Blake's "Proverbs of Hell": "You never know what is enough unless you know what is more than enough." Our view of the Atlas was now unimpeded, the bottom of its encircling wall being ten or fifteen feet above us. I looked up toward the warhead, but it was obscured by the missile's gleaming bulk. I wondered whether the birches and dairy herds were still visible in the outdoors above, and looked at my wrist to check the time, only to be reminded that Major Carr had my watch. Wetzel smiled. "Relax," he said easily. "There's nothing to do down here but wait and hope for nothing to happen."

FROM

LETTER FROM WASHINGTON

Richard H. Rovere

DECEMBER 19, 1964 (THE GREAT SOCIETY)

December 10

A PRESIDENT WITH MATCHLESS energy, manifold skills, and an enormous desire for posterity's esteem sits in the White House preparing to exercise what he has every reason to regard as a clear and urgent mandate to get on with the building of the New Jerusalem, his vision of which he has described in almost cadenced rhetoric: "So here's the Great Society. It's the time—and it's going to be soon—when nobody in this country is poor. It's the time—and there's no point in waiting—when every boy or girl can have all the education that boy or girl can put to good use. It's the time when there is a job for everybody who wants to work. It's the time when every slum is gone from every city in America, and America is beautiful. It's the time when man gains full domination under God over his own destiny. It's the time of peace on earth and good will among men." Thus spoke the President on October 27th in Pittsburgh—an improbable but certainly an appropriate place for describing such dreams. He had little doubt then that he would be returned to office, but he could not have been certain that the electorate would give him a Congress eager to follow, and perhaps even to lead, him to the Holy City. What he did know was that throughout our present, less than great society there were hundreds of social architects and engineers working away at the design for the new order of things, and that when, or if, the opportunity he sought presented itself, he would be ready to make the most of it. Within a few weeks after he took office last year, he had instructed various aides to mobilize battalions of experts who could provide him with (as he put it in a letter to one whose cooperation he sought) "general thoughts and specific new proposals which you feel would be helpful in my efforts to give our nation the kind of vigorous and imaginative leadership which it deserves." As he knew he would be, he has been deluged not only with "general thoughts and specific new proposals" but with the most elaborate and detailed blueprints, accompanied by ingenious financing schemes and drafts of legislation. And in three weeks there will come together a Congress that, if its Democratic leaders are correct in their appraisals, will enact just about any programs the President asks for and will appropriate funds in the amounts he requests.

It might be supposed, then, that the atmosphere in this city today is one of excitement and anticipation. Here is a President who is bold enough, at least in speech, to strike out for Utopia and who has most of the basic provisions—popular support, governmental power, and money—thought to be necessary for such a journey. At his side is a brilliant team of advisers, and at their sides are the élite of the Utopian planners. How, in such extraordinary circumstances, can the air fail to be electric? It is necessary, however, to report that while excitement may break out at any moment, there is hardly a trace of it here now, nor has there been throughout the post-election period. It is entirely possible that things were livelier in this city in the middle years of the Pierce administration than they have been in the past few weeks. There is some desultory talk of whether Postmaster General Gronouski will remain in office, a bit of speculation about whether the President will junk the multilateral nuclear force, and occasional discussion of what the future holds for Robert F. Kennedy. But far more is heard of what Barry Goldwater is likely to do than of what Lyndon Johnson is likely to do. The future of Dean Burch and the past of Bobby Baker attract more attention than any fulfillment of the great expectations raised by the President.

The explanation of this state of affairs is not that a lack of interest or curiosity exists. It is simply that, outside a small circle of Presidential advisers with zippered lips, there is no information. It is impossible to discuss the future of the administration, not only because no one knows what the President plans to do but because no one has much of a clue to what he is *thinking* of doing. No one knows what proposals are under discussion—or, for that matter, what proposals have been made, or by whom. It is known that bulky reports have been turned in by Presidential "task forces" and are being studied by various members of the administration. Some of these men acknowledge—often with considerable pride—the existence of the reports. They will remove them from desk drawers to show that they are hefty. But their contents are strictly classified. Proposals regarding the form and dimensions of federal aid to education are guarded as carefully as if they were war plans or diplomatic codes. Studies of the problems of mass transit are top secret, like reports from C.I.A. agents in East Germany or the findings of reconnaissance satellites. There is much generalized talk about the scores of planners, economists, and academic specialists of every conceivable sort who are mapping the Great Society, but beyond that nothing—not even the identity of the planners—has been revealed to anyone but a handful of White House staff members, who have been given to understand that the penalties will be swift and severe if they share any part of their knowledge with others. A few names found their way into the press last fall, and the President was as outraged as if the darkest of state secrets had been handed over to an enemy. From time to time, it has been reported that Eric F. Goldman, a Princeton historian who has been a special consultant to the President since early in the year, is the coordinator of this underground brain trust, but each report has been followed by a denial, and no one seems to know what Goldman does. No one, indeed, seems to know what anyone in the White House—apart from the President and a few domestics and secretaries—does. Only today, George Reedy, the President's press secretary, provoked unrestrained hilarity when, upon announcing the appointment of Richard N. Goodwin as a special assistant to the President, he was asked what Goodwin's duties would be. He answered by saying that Goodwin had "for the past few months been detailed to the White House, working in areas similar to those he now formally undertakes." Reedy was unable to restrain himself from joining in the mirth.

It is all part of Lyndon Johnson's method. The lid is on. It will be raised from time to time by the President himself, it would seem, but rarely, if ever, by any lesser personage. And in the case of the President it is always hard to tell whether he is lifting the lid or merely playing with it. For example, at a press conference on his ranch a couple of weeks ago he said he was by no means sure that it would be possible to submit a budget of less than a hundred billion dollars for the coming fiscal year. If Dwight Eisenhower or John Kennedy had said this, correspondents would have taken it as tantamount to an announcement that he would request more than a hundred billion, and this may be what the President was trying to convey. On the other hand, many people who know him rather well were ready to bet that he would present a budget of under a hundred billion. He is a man who likes to say that the brook is far too broad for leaping, and then leap it. They recalled that he said last year he didn't see how he could trim his requests below a hundred and three billion dollars, and then presented to the Congress a budget calling for expenditures of only ninety-eight billion. If a man can define the miraculous as something he knows to be within his capabilities, he can perform miracles every day. Johnson's sleight of hand with the budget for the current fiscal year is thought to have helped greatly in persuading businessmen to subscribe to his "consensus."

Not only is the President running his own show, as Presidents are expected to do; he *is* his own show. This is all well and good, but the President cannot be onstage every minute. The Presidency, as Johnson's predecessor demonstrated, need not be a one-man act. The Kennedy administration was interesting not only because the star was interesting but because he surrounded himself with a first-rate supporting cast. From the look of things at the moment, the White House during the next few years is likely to resemble the Eisenhower White House more than the Kennedy White House. During the Eisenhower years, the place—except in moments of crisis—seemed lifeless, not worth a visit except by those whom the lessee himself would receive. (For this, it was necessary to be a soft-drink tycoon, a successful football coach, or a newspaper publisher.) This was less because the President ordered his assistants to keep their mouths shut—though on occasion he did exactly that—than because not much was going on. In the Kennedy years, there was plenty going on, and the White House was a very lively place because the President saw some value, political and otherwise, in promoting interest, encouraging speculation, and even provoking controversy over his own schemes. There is probably more astir in Johnson's White House than there was in Kennedy's. Kennedy dreamed of a Great Society—or, at any rate, of a good civilization—but he wasn't quite up to describing it, and he didn't think that a man who had beaten Richard Nixon by a hundred and thirteen thousand votes could do more than get to its frontier. But his headquarters was a noisy, vibrant place, while Johnson's is, at the moment, one from which nothing but silence issues except when the President himself speaks. When he is silent, so is most of the government that he heads.

It is not altogether clear why President Johnson wishes it to be this way. His infrequent explanations have explained rather little. He has said, for instance, that he thinks it unwise to reveal the names of his advisers outside the government because they, in turn, would be bothered by people eager to advise *them*. He has said, too, that he thinks anonymity is conducive to objectivity. All that he knows of anonymity could easily be inscribed on the head of a pin. It is a condition of which he has had absolutely no first-hand experience, and unless the people advising him differ greatly from the majority of their predecessors, it is a condition they are not likely to appreciate. It seems probable that they would put up with unsolicited advice from others (they might even be happy to receive it) in exchange for having it known that they were laying some bricks and spreading some mortar for the Great Society. It has been said that the President is the Alfred Hitchcock of politics—that he is a master of suspense, and that suspense is an essential element of the Johnson style. If details of his program leaked out from time to time, the suspense would be lost, and there would be little interest in his Inaugural Address, his State of the Union Message, and his budget. The idea is to keep it all behind a curtain, which he will pull open next year, revealing splendid vistas not piecemeal but in their gorgeous entirety. His apologists recall that he succeeded in creating interest in what would otherwise have been a spiritless ceremony at Atlantic City last August by declining to make known his Vice-Presidential choice until the Convention had only a few hours to run and then putting Hubert Humphrey's name in nomination himself. It is one thing, though, to make a cliff-hanger out of what appears to be a contest between ambitious men, and quite another to make one out of an item in a budget. (It is also easier to have an opinion about whether Senator Humphrey, of Minnesota, or Senator Dodd, of Connecticut, would make an acceptable Vice-President than it is to know how much money is required to find an acceptable solution to the problem of high-school dropouts.) In any case, a President who is as secretive as this one over matters of public policy denies himself and his programs the advantages—and they are thought by many politicians to be numerous—of widespread public discussion, examination, and criticism. And it would seem difficult to arouse much interest in programs that the public can only approve or disapprove. Johnson may have found a way of getting to the Great Society, but it is also a way of making the political process as tiresome a spectacle for onlookers as a friendly game of catch.

It is possible, of course, that the President will change his ways after he gets settled in a bit more. He has always played his cards close to his chest, but then he has always, in the past, been in a poker game of one sort or another. Now, except when outsiders like Harold Wilson and Andrei Gromyko stop by, he sits alone at the table, with no one to bluff, no one to outsmart, no one betting against him. In his present situation, the rewards of foxiness are few. He has only his "mandate" to interpret, and it is natural enough that he should wish to interpret it himself. "The people have spoken," someone remarked after the election of 1936, "and in the fullness of time Franklin Roosevelt will tell us what they have said." In a fairly short time, Johnson will do the same. He will explain what the "consensus" is that more than 60 percent of Americans subscribe to, and then, perhaps, he may come to feel a need for generating some interest in the means by which he will lead us to our noble ends. But right now, more than a month after the electorate decided to move ahead to the Great Society, about the only really definitive word we have had from the leader is that he proposes to begin the journey on January 20th in a plain business suit and that he will change, the first night out, into a dinner jacket.

LULL

Charlayne Hunter

NOVEMBER 11, 1967 (WALKING THROUGH HARLEM)

ARLY ONE AFTERNOON last week, we set out to take a final look at perhaps the most famous block in Harlem—125th Street between Seventh and Lenox—before it is levelled to make way for the much discussed new New York State office building. It was a beautiful day, with a bright sun and a blue sky, and the air, because it was cool and crisp, felt, for a change, clean. Fall, it seemed, had at last established itself. At 110th Street and Seventh Avenue, it was an easy decision to get off the bus and walk. Young boys and girls carrying book satchels and, in some cases, empty lunch pails joined our walk at various intersections. The avenue was filled with the sound of young, high-pitched voices competing to be heard. Soon we became aware of a siren in the distance, and as the shrill sound drew nearer, we encountered other, larger groups—men and women, young and old. Two fire trucks arrived at a corner of Seventh Avenue, and, from the sound of things, others were on the way. When one of the firemen opened a hydrant, great gushes of a dark, oily-looking liquid came spewing forth, and a small boy, who had probably cooled off in the spray last summer, stood staring at the stuff incredulously. After a few minutes, there were five trucks on the scene, but it became apparent that there was no fire. In spite of this, most of the crowd lingered, watching the big, clumsy trucks maneuver their way out of the narrow street.

As we resumed our walk, two boys who looked to be no more than ten darted in front of us.

"You gonna play with your racer set?" one asked the other.

"Yeah," the other replied.

"Can I play with it with you?" the first one pursued, anxiously.

"Can't get in my apartment," said the other. "My mother ain't home."

Looking disappointed, the two crossed the street and disappeared.

We walked on, passing various groups with various interests—a stalled car drew quite a crowd—and we stopped in front of a small storefront housing the Harlem Revitalization Corps. One of a number of notices in the window read:

Join the War on Apathy
Winter Is Coming in Mississippi
IGAD
(I Give a Damn)
Needs Clothes, Food, Books on Negro
History, Dictionaries
To Be Sent to
IGAD
Rev. Hickman Johnson, Chaplain
Tougaloo College
Tougaloo, Mississippi

At the bottom of the notice, John F. Kennedy was quoted: "If a free society cannot help the many who are poor, it cannot save the few who are rich."

The storefront door was open, so we stepped inside, finding ourself in a room furnished with old chairs and a conspicuously old sofa. Notes tacked on top of notes covered a bulletin board in the center of the room ("From profits made on the fish fry the weekend of Aug. 25th and 26th we will be able to pay the rent." . . . "Mrs. Smalls reports that the total of the treasury stands at $31.00"). A young woman entered from the rear, carrying a broom, and she told us that the purpose of the Revitalization Corps was to "broaden friendship." Last summer, she went on, a number of Harlem children had changed places with children from the suburbs. "The experiment worked out beautifully," she said. "We run the organization out of our own pockets." We noticed that she seemed a bit impatient to put her broom to use, so, thanking her for her time, we went back outside.

After taking a detour through A. Philip Randolph Square, we passed a building covered with posters and announcements—some out of date (Marcus Garvey Day), others yet to occur ("Naturally '67—The original African Coiffure and Fashion Extravaganza Designed to Restore Our Racial Pride and Standards! Theme: Revolution and Riot in Ghettos or Self-Determination and Repatriation in Africa? . . . We Reserve the Right to Bar Anyone Whose Presence May Cause a Disturbance!"). Then we stopped on a street where a flatbed truck, pulled up to the curb, had attracted a gathering. On the floor of the truck were pumpkins, sacks of pecans and peanuts, and jars of honey. There were also stalks of sugar cane, bundled near the front of the truck, as we noticed when we heard a man, who had just come up, laugh and say, pointing to them, "Back where I come from, they call that uba, or iron cane." He spoke with the lilt of the West Indies.

"Well, where I come from, they make some good stuff from those cane skinnin's," said another man. "Shucks, man, you drink some of that and you'd be high for a month." He spoke in a voice of the Deep South.

By the time we reached the corner of 125th Street and Eighth Avenue, the early-afternoon crowds had broken up, except for a few shoppers around a vegetable stand and meat market. A couple standing in front of an attractive array of vegetables agreed that this was the best time of the year for collards, and a woman carrying an already well-stuffed shopping bag bought some beans, a few sweet potatoes, and some beets. In the window of the meat market were rows of ox tails, turkey wings, and chops, and a sign on the window advertised chitterlings and hog maws at bargain prices.

As we moved farther down the block, we could see smoke and ash rising from what looked like the center of the demolition. One of the stores in that block is Mr. Lewis Michaux's bookstore—the National Memorial African Bookstore—and when we drew near the corner, we could see that it was still standing, and so were most of the other buildings in the block. We stopped in to see how Mr. Michaux was getting along, and found him, as usual, bouncing around the store and keeping up lively conversations with six or seven people at once. "Everything's quiet round here," he was saying. "The Man been pouring a lot of milk in the streets, and milk's what keeps the babies from squealing." Suddenly, he turned to a man in an overcoat, and, taking him gently by the lapels, said, "You know what to do with the black man on the street?" There was a pause, and Mr. Michaux, letting go of the man's coat, laughed and said, "Sell him Heaven, and if he don't buy, give him Hell."

Mr. Michaux told us that he had been promised space in the new building but that so far he didn't know what he was going to do between the time his present quarters were demolished and the time the new building was completed. "I would have preferred to stay here in this place, but the Man say he got to have his office building *here*. Well, I hear they're going to set up a cultural center in the building, and if they do, then they got to have the National Memorial Bookstore, 'cause this is the *look.*" Mr. Michaux darted off again, and as we were leaving, one of two young girls who had been having a discussion for some time in front of a group of wall posters that were for sale called out to Mr. Michaux, "We've decided. We want one Rap Brown and one Stokely, please."

Around the corner, the signs of change were somewhat more evident. Fences constructed of old doors replaced the fronts of some buildings, and in other places along the block, where demolition had been completed, were small holes floored with splinters and jagged bricks and dust, from which a moldy smell emanated. A number of the stores carried on business as usual—shoestores, record shops, clothing stores—and others, though carrying on business, were plastered with signs, such as the one in the windows of Vim (VIM for Values; VIM for Discounts; VIM for Easy Terms): "VIM has been in business since 1920 and we will continue to serve you at a new location in this neighborhood! Thank you for your patronage." Near us, a young Negro woman who looked to be in her early twenties stood leaning against a car with a sketch pad and pencil in her hands. After a few minutes, two young Negro men, who seemed to be about her age, walked up to her.

"We'd like to know what you are doing," one of them said.

"I'm a student, and I'm doing a paper for one of my classes on the changing face of Harlem. I thought I'd do a sketch of this block, too," the young woman said amiably. "Why do you want to know?"

Both of the young men smiled. "Any time you write something down in this community, *somebody's* gonna want to know what you're writing," one said. "Especially about the new building. We don't want the wrong thing getting out."

The girl asked what he meant.

"I mean, we want people to understand what this means to some of us," he replied.

"Just what does it mean?" the girl asked.

"Well, let me put it to you this way," the young man said. "The day Governor Rockefeller came up here to signal for the demolition to begin, one of the brothers came on the scene with his bugle and played 'Taps.' Now, believe me, sister, he was speaking for a lot of us. This is the beginning of the end."

At the end of the block, we turned into 126th Street—the northern border of the block, and the only part of it that is residential. We saw the same kind of splotchy destruction as on the side we had left—some brownstones completely vacated and boarded up, and, in the windows of

others, curtains and an occasional flowerpot or some other sign of oc-
cupancy. Far down the block ahead of us we could see an old woman, in
a black coat, moving slowly along the sidewalk. After a while, she came
to a stop, rested for a few moments, and then, with a great deal of effort,
started to climb the steps of a brownstone. On each step, she stopped to
get her breath. By the time we reached her, she had climbed only three
steps, and we asked her if she would like some help.

She smiled faintly. "No, thanks," she said.

We asked her how long she had lived there.

"Seventeen years," she said, looking up toward the door, which was
still six steps away.

"Will you be moving soon?" we asked.

She said that she probably would. She told us that "the people over on
a Hundred and Twenty fifth Street"—she couldn't remember exactly
where—had promised to help her find a place.

We offered again to help her up the stairs, but she seemed determined
to make it on her own. We told her as we left that we hoped she would
find a place soon.

She took another step and, while she was catching her breath, turned
to us and smiled. "I'll do the best I can," she said.

DEMONSTRATION

Jonathan Schell

AUGUST 17, 1968 (A BIAFRA RALLY)

ON THURSDAY OF last week, a group that calls itself the American Committee to Keep Biafra Alive ran a full-page ad in the
Times asking people to attend a demonstration beginning at
12:30 P.M. that day in Dag Hammarskjöld Plaza whose purpose was to
encourage world leaders and the United Nations to exert themselves
more strenuously in the search for a way to bring relief to the estimated
five million people who face starvation in Biafra. "Let's not eat lunch,"

the advertisement read. "Go to the United Nations and let the world know that no American will ever say: 'But we didn't know.'" We went over to Dag Hammarskjöld Plaza at six o'clock in the evening. There we found about seven hundred people attending the demonstration, and we were told that attendance had reached a peak of about twenty-five hundred at lunchtime. The crowd marched up and down the broad sidewalk in a long loop, keeping in the shade of two rows of trees. At the center of the loop there was a platform with a public-address system, which was playing Bach organ fugues when we arrived and later switched to Beethoven string quartets. Most of the demonstrators wore pins that said "Keep Biafra Alive." These were being sold at a table at one end of the loop, for a minimum of twenty-five cents each. (By six o'clock, a carton used to hold the proceeds from these buttons was half filled with dollar bills.) And while some people were bringing money to buy food for the Biafrans, others were donating the food itself; there were two large and steadily growing piles of canned goods and packaged food on the sidewalk in front of the platform. Occasionally, women joining the demonstration would stop to unload a few cans of tuna fish or boxes of apricots from shopping bags and add them to the piles.

We spoke to Philip Nix, a member of the American Committee to Keep Biafra Alive, who spent two years in Biafra as a Peace Corps volunteer, and he told us that the committee had been formed around eight former Peace Corps volunteers who had been in Federal Nigeria or in Biafra. He said that until the war began, the Peace Corps had sent more volunteers to Nigeria than to any other country except India, and that by the middle of 1967 over fifteen hundred volunteers had worked there. We asked Mr. Nix how the committee had got going, and he said, "Some of us just got together at a party, and others called in when they heard about it. A few of us were in the same Peace Corps group and knew each other from Nigeria. We set up an office, and people would walk in off the street and say, 'What can I do?' Or people would call up and say, 'This can't happen!' One man has taken a leave of absence from his job for the whole summer and risks losing it. A girl came in one evening and stayed and worked all night. We feel that the situation in Biafra is intolerable. We're disgusted with the use of the word 'politics' in connection with this famine. We feel that there is a point at which people cease to exist solely for the sake of their government. What we want is an immediate air-lift, by the U.N. or by whatever government has the courage to do it. We aren't taking sides politically. I think that we have to ask ourselves what the Nuremberg trials really meant. Are we willing to sit around while a whole people is destroyed?"

The crowd, which grew to well over a thousand as the evening progressed, was composed mostly of people whom we took to be in their twenties. There was a noticeably large proportion of college-age girls, and a peppering of Africans and American Negroes. Some people carried signs consisting of large photographs of half-starved Biafran children, and others carried signs saying, among other things, "Stop Man's Inhumanity." As dusk fell, the demonstrators were handed lighted candles at one end of the loop. The candles lit up their faces from underneath, and they had to walk at a slower pace to keep the candles from blowing out. It appeared that most people had come to the demonstration alone or in twos, and as they walked silently around the loop in the darkness, carrying their signs or photographs and their candles, they expressed by faintly stiff postures and uneasy glances the embarrassment and sense of vulnerability that people tend to feel when they display themselves publicly for the sake of a strictly humanitarian cause—one that has no political intent, and is backed by no continuing movement or organization that could conceivably appeal to their self-interest or personal ambition.

We joined the people walking around the loop to ask some of them what had drawn them there. Most of the ones we spoke with seemed shy about discussing their motivation, and ended up saying things like "I read the newspaper ad" or "I wanted to do *something*" or "I just came." As we walked, we overheard two young men in business suits arguing over whether they had come for truly idealistic reasons or had really just wanted to get what one of them called "ego satisfaction." They went on to discuss whether or not the demonstration would be effective. One carried a photograph of Biafran children, and the other carried a candle. We asked them what their work was, and they said they were computer consultants. We then talked with a white-haired man, who told us that he was a court stenographer, and that he had seen the ad in the paper. "I wanted to do something, but I didn't know what. This isn't much—it probably won't solve anything—but for a selfish bastard like me it's something," he said. We also spoke with three women—two Negro and one white—who were walking together. They said they were teachers, and one of the Negro women told us, "I saw the news in the papers, and from then on it was just a terrible nightmare. We just thought we had to *do* something."

HEARING

Ellen Willis

FEBRUARY 22, 1969 (FEMINISTS ON ABORTION)

I N EACH OF the past three years, the New York State Legislature has defeated proposals to liberalize the state's eighty-six-year-old criminal-abortion statute, which permits an abortion only when the operation is necessary to preserve a pregnant woman's life. Now a reform bill introduced by State Assemblyman Albert H. Blumenthal, of New York County, appears likely to pass. It would amend "life" to "health," and give relief to women who are physically or mentally unequipped to care for a child or who risk bearing a deformed child, to victims of rape and incest, and to the very young. A second bill is also pending. Sponsored by Assembly woman Constance Cook, of the 125th Assembly District, it would repeal the abortion law entirely and make abortion available on the same basis as any other medical treatment. The repeal bill has received little public attention. Newspapers that mention it at all tend to treat it as a quixotic oddity. Most people do not know that the Cook bill exists, and some legislators, when asked for their support, have professed not to have heard of it. A number of women's organizations, however, are very much aware of the repeal proposal and are determined to spread the word. These groups are part of a revived—and increasingly militant—feminist movement. They include the National Organization for Women (NOW), the radical October Seventeenth Movement (a split-off from NOW), and Women's Liberation, a collective label for radical feminist groups formed by women activists who found that men on the left too often expected them to type, make coffee, and keep quiet. Whatever their ideological differences, feminists have united on the abortion issue. They oppose Blumenthal's reforms— or any reforms—and demand total repeal. Abortion legislation, they assert, is class legislation, imposed on women by a male-supremacist society, and deprives women of control over their bodies. They argue that women should not have to petition doctors (mostly male) to grant them as a privilege what is really a fundamental right, and that only the pregnant woman herself can know whether she is physically and emo-tionally prepared to bear a child.

Last Thursday, the Joint Legislative Committee on the Problems of Public Health convened in the Public Health Building, at 125 Worth Street, to hear a panel of expert witnesses—doctors, lawyers, and clergy-men selected for their knowledge of medical, legal, and social problems connected with abortion—who were to comment on the law and suggest modifications. About thirty women, including City Councilman Carol Greitzer, came to the hearings to demonstrate against reform and for repeal, against more hearings and for immediate action, and against the committee's concept of expertise. "The only real experts on abortion are women," read a leaflet distributed by Women's Liberation. "Women who have known the pain, fear, and socially imposed guilt of an illegal abor-tion. Women who have seen their friends dead or in agony from a post-abortion infection. Women who have had children by the wrong man, at the wrong time, because no doctor would help them." The demonstra-tors, about half of them young women and half middle-aged housewives and professionals, picketed outside the building until the proceedings began, at 10 A.M. Then they filed into the hearing room. The eight members of the Joint Committee—all male—were lined up on a plat-form facing the audience. The chairman, State Senator Norman F. Lent, announced that the purpose of the meeting was not to hear public opin-ion but, rather, to hear testimony from "experts familiar with the psy-chological and sociological facts." Of the fifteen witnesses listed on the agenda, fourteen were men; the lone woman was a nun.

The first witness, the chairman of the Governor's commission on abortion reform, began enumerating the commission's recommenda-tions. Suddenly, a young, neatly dressed woman seated near the front stood up. "O.K., folks," she said. "Now it's time to hear from the real experts. I don't mean the public opinion you're so uninterested in. I mean concrete evidence from the people who really know—women. I can tell you the psychological and sociological effect the law has had on *me*—it's made me *angry*! It's made me think about things like forcing doctors to operate at gunpoint."

It took several minutes for Senator Lent to collect himself and try to restore order. By that time, several other women were on their feet, shouting.

"Where are the women on your panel?" one woman said.

"I had an abortion when I was seventeen. You don't know what that's like," another said.

"Men don't get pregnant. Men don't rear children. They just make the laws," said a third.

Senator Lent began, "If you girls can organize yourselves and select a spokesman—"

"We don't want a spokesman! We all want to testify!" a woman cried.

"But wait a minute, dear—" the Senator began.

"Don't call me 'dear'! Would you call a black person 'boy'?" the woman shouted.

The committee quickly adjourned the hearing and announced that there would be a closed executive session in an upstairs room.

Senator Seymour Thaler, who has been long associated with hospital reform, and who is himself a proponent of the Cook bill, was furious with the women. "What have you accomplished?" he called out. "There are people here who want to do something for you!"

"We're tired of being done for! We want to *do,* for a change!" one of the women replied.

Upstairs, police barred the door, and the women stood outside shouting, "We are the experts!" Women's Liberation sent in a formal request to testify, and the committee replied that two women might speak after the other witnesses had finished. The women were not satisfied ("It's a back-of-the-bus compromise!" "They just want to stall us till the newspapermen go home"), but half a dozen members of Women's Liberation decided to stick it out. All of them were under thirty, and half were married. Two had had illegal abortions; one had had a child and given it up for adoption; one had a friend who had nearly died because she hesitated to go to the hospital after a badly done seven-hundred-dollar operation.

As it turned out, the women waited for seven hours, sitting on the floor in the corridor, because the authorities, afraid of further disruption, would not let them into the hearing room. Finally, three women were permitted to speak. They talked about their experiences and demanded a public hearing that would be devoted entirely to the expert testimony of women.

The legislators would not agree to this. "Why do you assume we're against you?" one senator asked. "Four of the witnesses were for repeal. They said the same things you've been saying."

"There's a political problem you're overlooking," said the last of the women to speak. "In this society, there is an imbalance in power between men and women, just as there is between whites and blacks. You and your experts may have the right ideas, but you're still men talking to each other. *We* want to be consulted. Even if we accepted your definition of expert—and we don't—couldn't you find any female doctors or lawyers?"

"I agree with you about the law," Senator Thaler said. "But you're just acting out your personal pique against men."

"Not personal pique—*political grievance!*" the final speaker replied.

"All I can say," Senator Thaler declared, in conclusion, "is that you're the rudest bunch of people I've ever met."

The meeting broke up, and everyone began drifting out. "Well, we're probably the first women ever to talk about our abortions in public," one woman said. "That's something, anyway."

NOTES AND COMMENT

James Stevenson and Faith McNulty

AUGUST 30, 1969 (WOODSTOCK)

ED, A PORTLY, middle-aged parent, appeared in our doorway one afternoon last week, his shoes caked with dried mud, a bit of corn tassel sticking out of a trouser cuff, and a glazed look behind his glasses. "Woodstock," he gasped, leaning against the door. "I mean Walkill . . . I mean Bethel . . . I mean White Lake . . ."

"The Festival?" we asked.

Ed nodded, and handed us an unfolded, dirty cardboard box labelled "Howard Johnson's Salt Water Taffy," on which there was a lot of small, sloppy handwriting running in various directions. Then he limped away down the hall. Ed's notes seemed to begin under the word "Taffy":

"I had not planned to attend any festivals—rock, art, folk, or Aquarian—this weekend, or any *other* weekend, for that matter. I had not planned to do much of anything beyond catching an afternoon nap, actually, when my son Jimmy, aged twelve, approached me on Friday noon, suggesting that we drive up to the Catskills and attend the three-day Woodstock Festival at White Lake. We could take sleeping bags, he explained, and sleep on the ground. Jimmy was prepared to leave at a moment's notice; he was wearing a pair of blue-and-white striped bell-bottoms, a Navy work shirt, and an 'electric' hairdo. (He had spent the last of his savings to buy a Toni Home Permanent, which his mother had generously consented to apply to his hair.) I told him that going to the Festival was out of the question.

"By midafternoon, we were driving up the New York State Thruway, with two sleeping bags in the back seat and a box of Howard Johnson's Salt Water Taffy in the front. (I had consented to attend for *one* night, and one night *only*.) Frightening reports were coming in over the radio: traffic in the Bethel area backed up for twenty miles, eight-hour delay, no food, no water, etc. A quarter of a million people on the scene, and more arriving. As we turned off the Thruway for Route 17, we hit a large, ominous traffic jam—although we were still fifty miles from Bethel, or White Lake—and a fierce downpour. Turned off onto a minor road as soon as possible, and the skies cleared. Had a nice, fast ride through rolling farmland and sunshine for the next hour or so. Stopped for supplies in a village delicatessen. Jimmy did the marketing: 1 bag of pretzels, 1 bag of potato chips, 1 large jelly roll, 4 raisin cakes, six-pack of Coca-Cola, 1 box of peppermints, 2 chewing gum, 1 red gumballs. Resumed trip, and sailed along Route 52, down steep mountainsides, past lakes, big hotels, small hotels, hills, camps, farms, past Grossinger's, and through Liberty, and there the traffic slowed down. The final ten miles or so, going down toward Bethel, or White Lake, took us until near sundown—stopping and starting, starting and stopping. It was comparable to, say, the Long Island Expressway on a Friday night, except that it was devoid of car honkings and anger. Every so often, the traffic would come to a total halt, and young people in bare feet and long hair and interesting clothes would wander back along the cavalcade, greeting other people, passing along the news ('Somebody says it's eight miles to the Festival'), giving the peace sign, or whatever. Often, there would be a boarding house nearby, and as the Festival-goers walked or drove by, the guests—some in long black coats and hats and Chassidic sideburns—would cheerfully raise their hands to them in the peace sign. 'Hey, Weinstein!' an old man by the road called to another old man, who was emerging from a farmhouse. Weinstein glanced over in time to see his friend, beaming, flash him the peace sign, and Weinstein, with a smile, returned the sign with a sweeping gesture. At one point, children were stationed along the road with a large sheet on which was lettered 'peace.' There was an easy, serene give-and-take between the people on the road and the people on the roadside.

"Then, abruptly, the traffic would begin to move again—cars that had been abandoned in the grass would be started up, barefoot people would run by, and the procession would resume. Slowly, behind us, a small lake would recede into the distance; a field with large hills beyond would appear, then a valley, a turn in the road—and just when we felt we were on our way again a solid line of stopped cars would come into view, and progress would halt for another half hour. There were a few police on hand, but generally they were from somewhere else and were unable to give much information about how far down the road the Festival might be. Nobody was upset, however; everybody was cheerful.

"About an hour and a half before sunset, I lost Jimmy. He had walked on ahead several times, saying he'd see how far he could get before the traffic got moving again and I picked him up. There had been a great deal of wandering around by everybody, so I paid little attention, and assumed that I'd encounter him soon, but the traffic did not move for a long time. Finally, I set out on foot to look for him, leaving our car in line, and walked up a series of rises—a quarter or half mile, perhaps—but I couldn't find him. As I reached the highest point, and the road fell away in front of me, the traffic slowly began to move. I ran back downhill to the car, and the procession drove for several miles—but still no sign of Jimmy. Then another long halt, and I set out on foot again. I was very anxious now, because time was running out. Soon it would be night, and there were no street lights, almost no police, and where would I find him, *how* would I find him, among all the people? Well, Jimmy's account of what happened when he was 'lost' is on the other side of this cardboard."

We turned the box of taffy over and encountered a larger, messier writing:

"I got out of the car because I didn't want to sit in the hot sun, and I wanted to walk because we had been driving for a long time. We had just gone by Swan Lake and were in bumper-to-bumper traffic. I started up the hill past cars filled with all sorts of people, many of them sitting on bumpers, roofs, and hoods. I kept walking up the hill. People in jeeps, smashed-up buggies, and rented trucks. I came to a fork in the road, with a sign on one of the poles saying 'Festival.' I walked by girls, boys, and grownups waving and making peace signs at the slowly moving traffic. There was an air of happiness and gaiety, even though there was a traffic jam. I started down a hill with grassy fields on both sides filled with the loud noise of crickets chirping. I looked for the crickets but couldn't find any. People were hitchhiking and getting rides, sitting and lying on the cars, which zoomed by in the empty lane occasionally. I didn't think I should hitchhike, but I stuck out my thumb once or twice, and didn't get a ride. On the side of the road, I found a pamphlet announcing the name of the show and three days of Peace and Music and the names of the performers at the Festival. I went up a slight hill with a barn and a house on one side. You could see chickens, which were squawking. I walked a little more, and a dark-olive-green Mustang stopped with a man with a mustache and a lady, and they asked how far it was to the Festival. I said I didn't know, and they asked if I wanted a ride. I was getting tired, so I said yes. We drove along and talked about the Festival and things. When we hit more traffic, I said goodbye and thank you, and started walking again. Down the road, there were two teen-agers in a Carnival ice-cream truck. Nobody seemed to know how far it was to the place, but there was a lot of guessing. Farther along, there was a yellow school bus, which I was to see often during the time I was there. It had a big red banner with a yellow 'Peace' sign and the words 'New Orleans' on it. I kept walking and saw these men—two white, one Negro—playing with a Frisbee. The Negro had an Afro cut and a weird pipe, and a leather pouch on his belt. He smiled, and when I saw him later he remembered me and smiled again. The next ride I got was in a red car full of guys, which took me for about half a mile. I got out on a dirt road with woods on both sides, and was getting thirsty when I came in sight of a house with a little girl on the steps spraying water with a hose, so some other people and I asked her for a drink. She let us. My last ride was up a hill with a girl driving a white convertible and a man sitting on top of the back seat. I got out, finally, and walked the rest of the way to the parking lot, where there was a guy who was giving directions and looked hot and tired. I waited awhile, looking at the people, and saw a couple of choppers. I started back down the hill to look for my father, and a man was throwing leaves and flowers in the air. A few minutes after that, I found my father."

We turned the box over and returned to Ed's handwriting:

"I was so relieved to see Jimmy—even his Toni Home Permanent— that nothing else mattered. I jumped out of the car, yelling jubilantly— nobody paid any attention to that—and then we got back in the car and were directed to a parking area, which was in a vast meadow. Thousands of cars were already parked, tents were being erected in the twilight, and as we got out the ground was squishy underfoot. It occurred to me that we might be here to stay. Somebody told us the Festival was *that* way about a mile and a half, and we set off. We walked and walked—across fields and down narrow country lanes, past more and more fields filled with cars, and always accompanied by a stream of people. After perhaps an hour, it seemed we were almost there—a lot of people were sitting in a meadow, as if within earshot of a concert—so we limped into the field and looked around. We asked some reclining youths where the Festival was, and they pointed across a vast valley to some tiny lights on a distant hilltop. 'You're kidding!' said Jimmy. We sank to the grass and stared at the lights. 'What'll we do?' I asked. 'Shall we go back?' Jimmy thought for a while. 'I don't know,' he said. We just sat there. Finally, we decided we'd try to make the Festival. We cut through a muddy cornfield— Jimmy broke off an ear of corn to eat—and sank into water that was ankle-deep. We wallowed through that and reached another road. This road was really choked: cars three deep—on both shoulders as well as in the middle—almost all empty, none moving, just people streaming around them. It was pitch-dark when we climbed the final hill and found the Festival. There were no ticket-takers, or sellers—people simply poured in, free. The area was packed with people, sitting, lying down, or walking around; helicopters gargled overhead. Tim Hardin was singing—a tiny figure in a blue spotlight—but he was about as audible as a radio in a distant apartment over street noises. From time to time, a flare went up and dimly revealed the vastness of the crowd. There was no food in the area, and, apparently, no water. We sat. Somebody stepped on my hand. The people flooded in—more and more and more. I felt we would be buried any moment. Jimmy and I agreed to leave, and, using a sweater to keep us from getting separated—Jimmy holding one sleeve, I holding the other—we made our way against the oncoming tide. We retraced our steps, frequently flopping down in the grass on the roadside to rest. Jimmy never complained, although he was exhausted. But that was the spirit of the occasion. Not once did we hear anyone angry or rude or complaining—the universal attitude was one of stoicism, courtesy, good will. The benevolence was awesome. If Jimmy had been a little older or I had been a little younger, we probably would have stayed. As it was, when we reached the area where we had parked, some cars were already mired. When I stepped on the gas, the wheels of our car—for a horrible moment—spun. Then they caught, and I drove as fast as I could over the muddy field. I was sure that if I slowed down at all the car would sink in and we'd be there for a week. Jimmy went to sleep on a sleeping bag, and I drove on, stopping and starting again (the road was blocked in many places), until, about an hour later, we were in the clear. But in the opposite lane the headlights of the cars heading toward the Festival continued—on and on. I estimate we spent about fifteen minutes at the actual concert, but the next day, at home, Jimmy told everybody that the Festival was great, and he meant it, and, as a matter of fact, I think it was."

. . .

Shortly after Ed handed us his notes, we talked with a younger friend of ours—a nineteen-year-old—who had been to the Festival, and he told us he was indignant and discouraged by what the *Times* had had to say about the event. In an editorial headed "Nightmare in the Catskills," the *Times* said, "The dreams of marijuana and rock music that drew 300,000 fans and hippies to the Catskills had little more sanity than the impulses that drive the lemmings to march to their deaths in the sea. They ended in a nightmare of mud and stagnation. . . . What kind of culture is it that can produce so colossal a mess?" "It wasn't a nightmare," our friend told us. "The mud didn't matter, and it was one of the most remarkable experiences I've ever had. The big point was not that pot was passed around openly but that because there was a minimum of force and restriction— the cops were few, and they were friendly—a huge crowd of people handled itself decently. There were no fights, no hassles, no pushing, no stealing. Everybody shared everything he had, and I've never seen such consideration for others. People volunteered for all kinds of jobs— picking up trash, carrying stuff, doing whatever was needed. It was the most extraordinary demonstration of how good people can be—really *want* to be, if they are let alone. It was an ethic shared by a huge mass of people. The *Times* wants to know what kind of culture produces this. In a broad sense, Christian culture produced it."

We asked our young friend, who attends the University of Chicago and has hair neither very short nor very long, to jot down some further notes on his experience, so that, for the record, we could append them to what Ed and Jimmy had written.

"I went rather casually," he wrote, "partly because I wanted to hear the music, and partly because I knew, by word of mouth, that there would be a tremendous mass of people my age, and I wanted to be part of it. Of course, there was going to be a terrific assemblage of artists—the best this kind of event has to offer—but the main thing was that by listening to the grapevine you could tell the Festival was going to be above and beyond that. We heard it wasn't going to be like Newport, with high fences, high prices, cops shoving and cursing you. We heard that there wouldn't be any reserved seats, that we'd be free to wander, and that the townspeople weren't calling out the militia in advance. I went, like the others, to meet people, to sit on the grass and play guitars, and to be together. I also knew that people were coming from thousands of miles away, but I had no idea how tremendous the event would be. We're a car culture now, and people will travel vast distances to get something they want.

"I drove from Rhode Island with a group of friends. When we got on the New York Thruway, we began to see the first signs of how huge it would be—Volkswagens full of kids, motorcycles, hitchhikers carrying signs. Everybody waving at everybody else as people passed. The first traffic jam—about twenty miles from White Lake, on 17B—set the tone. It was a cheerful traffic jam. People talked from car to car. People came up and asked to sit on your hood. Somebody in our car spoke to a girl in a blue Volks next to us and, not having yet caught the tone, remarked that the jam was a drag. 'Oh, no,' she said quickly. 'Everyone here is so beautiful.' She gave us some wine, and we handed over peaches in exchange.

"We inched along for two hours. Cars began parking on the roadside. Boys and girls would just sit on the hillsides with a bottle of wine. They had lots of time, and they were cheerful and happy. The feeling wasn't 'Oh, God, what a jam!' but 'Wow, look how many of us there are!' There was a gathering feeling of awe that our group was this big, that the grapevine was this big. We were exhilarated. We were in a mass of *us*.

"Finally, we got to a huge parking lot. It cost five dollars and it was already full. We were the last car in. We parked and started walking. This was 10 P.M. Thursday. There would be no music until Friday afternoon. We walked along in a stream, exchanging comments with every passerby. There were no houses, no local folk staring at us. People became aware of the land around us. Somebody said, 'It's like being part of an encamped army that has won.' We felt as though it were liberated territory. We came to the top of a hill and looked down on a huge meadow—a natural amphitheatre—where the Festival would be. In the center, people were building the stage. People were lying around in sleeping bags or sitting around little fires. The grass was fresh with dew, and the stars were bright. It was wonderful. We went on and found a campground, full of people sitting around or sleeping or eating. We unpacked our gear. For fifty cents, we bought 'macroburgers' that some communal people from California had cooked. They were made of soybeans, rice, and vegetables—no meat—between slices of rye bread. The California people also gave us slices of huge cucumbers they had grown themselves. It all tasted good. The girl serving the macroburgers gave us water in a plastic cup. She said, 'Save the cup. Somebody else may want it.' The campground was full of the most ingenious shelters. One huge canopy was made of scraps of polyethylene fastened to scraps of wood. Beneath it about forty people were lying down, snuggled against each other, singing and playing music. There was a fence across the campground, and one tough guy—the only tough guy I saw—started to tear down the fence, but people remonstrated with him. They told him it was the farmer's fence and it wasn't necessary to take it down. He was only allowed to take down one panel to make an exit. It was like that through the whole Festival. Where the mass needed an opening, an opening was made. There was no needless destruction. It was a functional thing. There was a woods between us and the amphitheatre. Two paths through the woods had been marked with strings of Christmas lights. One was called the Gentle Path and the other the Groovy Way. Nobody knows who named them. Late that night, we went to sleep in our sleeping bags with the sound of singing and guitars and voices all around us. I slept well.

"In the morning, it was raining lightly, but it didn't last. I went looking for water. I found a tank truck, and there I met a Rhode Island girl I knew who was there brushing her teeth. She hugged me, and the crowd laughed. We breakfasted with some people from the Santa Fe Hog Farm Commune. They were serving out of a great vat of boiled wheat and raisins, scooped onto a paper plate with a dollop of honey on it. It was delicious. It held me all day.

"That day, I just wandered around. I found a group of people who were blowing up a red balloon five feet across, so that their friends could find them, but lots of other people had the same balloons, so these huge red globes dotted the fields. Various groups of people had put up amusement devices for everybody to use free. One was called the Bumblebee Nest. It consisted of forked branches ingeniously fastened together with wooden pegs to support a platform of hay. It was just for the pleasure of sitting on. Somebody had an enclosure of chickens and had brought chicken feed. It was fun to feed the chickens. Somebody else had brought rabbits and made a big pen with benches in it, so you could sit and watch the rabbits and feed them. There was a huge tepeelike construction with a flat stone hung from ropes that you could stand on to swing. All these were free things that people had taken the trouble to provide for others. Most of the day, people wandered around and talked. I read and played cards. In the late afternoon, the music began. The amphitheatre was a mass of people, but there was no pushing. The sound system was excellent. We listened all afternoon and evening. The music was great, and the audience sang and clapped the rhythm. The performers loved it. There was a terrific feeling of unity between the crowd and the stage.

"The next morning, we woke to find it raining hard. Some boys who had got soaked took off their clothes and walked around naked. It didn't bother anyone. It brought home the idea that this was our land. Nobody was busting them. I was struck by how harmless it was—how the violence of sexuality was missing. The naked boys looked harmless and innocent.

"The concessionaires—hot-dog stands and so on—started out with prohibitive prices, and the kids complained to the management. All day, there were announcements from the stage about where to get free food. Eventually, there was an announcement that the concessionaires had knocked their prices down to cost.

"It rained hard the early part of the day, but the reaction of the crowd was 'Don't fight it.' We sat and listened, soaking wet. The rain really did something to reinforce the spirit. There were radios on the campground, and we began to hear news reports that we were in the midst of a mass disaster. At every report, the crowd around the radio laughed. It was such a splendid example of the division between us and the outside world. It dramatized the whole crazy split that the world thought we were having a disaster and we knew we were having no such thing.

"About three o'clock, the sun came out. Everyone took off his clothes to dry. I stripped to my shorts. We lay in the sun and listened to fantastic music. The most popular song was against the Vietnam war. Just as it finished, an Army helicopter flew over. The whole crowd—all those hundreds of thousands of people—looked up and waved their forefingers in the peace sign, and then gave a cheer for themselves. It was an extraordinary thing. Soon after that, the farmer who owned the land was introduced, and he got a huge cheer, too.

"Late that afternoon, a 'free stage' began acting as a travellers' aid, where volunteers arranged free rides for people and helped to solve problems. They took up a collection for a ten-year-old boy who had lost his money. They returned a lost child to her mother. They asked for volunteers to pick up garbage, and they made announcements warning those leaving to be careful on the way out—not to take grass with them, because of busts on the highway, and so on.

"There was still another day to go, but I had to leave. We got our stuff together and jammed three hitchhikers into our car and drove it out of the mud. As we went out, people called to us, 'Don't leave! Don't leave!' Nobody wanted to let go of what we'd had there. What we'd had was a fleeting, wonderful moment of what you might call 'community.'"

SHOTS WERE FIRED

NOTES AND COMMENT

Donald Malcolm, Lillian Ross, and E. B. White

NOVEMBER 30, 1963 (THE ASSASSINATION OF JOHN F. KENNEDY)

THE DEATH OF a President enters the house and becomes a death in the family. No other public death produces so personal an alteration in one's world. Tritely, one remembers the precise spot on which one stood, resisting acceptance and grief. For us, it was a patch of crowded sidewalk. The circle of knowledge, whose center was a weak transistor radio, expanded in murmurs ("They say . . . They say . . . They say"), engulfed us, and moved on, until we were left in the silence of irrevocable fact, exchanging empty looks with our companions. Speech, when it returned, was not at first commensurate with national disaster, being little more than the incoherent responses of private pain common to all who have lost a father, a brother, or a son.

• • •

Our last glimpse of President Kennedy was in Miami, where, four days before his death, he was engaged in the same kind of mission that took him to Dallas. He was slated to arrive at Miami International Airport at

5 P.M. on Monday, November 18th, to speak there to a crowd of voters, rounded up mostly by local Democrats, and, a couple of hours later, to address a convention of the Inter-American Press Association at the Americana Hotel, with appearances at a couple of social-political gatherings squeezed in between—all this after Saturday at Cape Canaveral, Sunday at Palm Beach, and all day Monday at Tampa, there inspecting MacDill Air Force Base, lunching at Army–Air Force Strike Command Headquarters at the base, journeying by helicopter to Lopez Field, in downtown Tampa, and speaking there on the fiftieth anniversary of commercial aviation, addressing the Florida State Chamber of Commerce, addressing a meeting of the Steelworkers' Union, and riding around the Tampa streets, shaking hands through it all with everybody he could reach. The main danger that crossed our mind as we went out to the Miami airport that Monday afternoon with the press was that, in his eagerness to make himself accessible, he was probably coming in contact with scores of colds, and we marvelled at his physical stamina.

The Miami Beach *Daily Sun* had kept the public posted with banner headlines like "SPECIAL VISITOR IS COMING HERE TONIGHT," and the Miami *Herald* Spanish-language section carried a headline reading, "ARRIBA HOY KENNEDY A MIAMI—HABLARA A LOS EDITORES LATINOS." There were signs everywhere at the airport of the precautions that the Secret Service, the F.B.I., and the local police had taken to reconcile maximum handshaking with maximum security. There were also signs everywhere of Democratic Party rifts, dissatisfactions, and antagonisms, all of which the President himself would be trying, by sheer will and the force of his personal presence, to reconcile. We encountered Congressman Claude Pepper before he left Miami to meet the President in Tampa. He planned to fly back to Miami with him on the Presidential plane, along with Senator George Smathers, Governor Farris Bryant, and Congressman Dante Fascell. Pepper told us he was very hopeful that Kennedy would carry the State of Florida in 1964, having lost it by only 46,776 votes in 1960. "Some Democrats didn't fight too hard for him in 1960," he said. "I want to see the Democratic Party fight harder in '64." Pepper didn't know definitely whether he would introduce President Kennedy to the crowd at the airport. That was still to be decided, he told us—probably on the plane. He added, "All you're supposed to say is 'Ladies and gentlemen, the President of the United States.' Sam Rayburn always used to say, 'It is my distinguished honor to present the President of the United States.' What I'd like to say is 'My fellow-countrymen, it is our honor now to hear our friend the President and the *next* President of the United States.'"

The President's plane was scheduled to land in the Delta Airlines area, and a Delta hangar had been festooned with a red-and-white banner reading, "WELCOME MR. PRESIDENT." Among the Secret Service men and the police and the political planners, we came across a planner who was passing out identifying badges of various colors to members of the V.I.P., official, platform, and press groups, along with diagrams showing the position of each group (including a group of two dozen Florida mayors), and also of a hundred-and-forty-five-member band, the Band of the Hour, from the University of Miami. Another planner—a Democratic State Committeeman for Dade County, of which Miami is the seat—was passing out placards to the public, stationed behind a wire fence. The signs read, "WELCOME PRESIDENT KENNEDY BISCAYNE DEMOCRATIC CLUB" and "POLISH-AMERICAN CLUB WELCOMES PRESIDENT KENNEDY" and "SENIOR CITIZENS' COUNCIL WELCOMES PRESIDENT KENNEDY." Milling about in the V.I.P. section were a number of V.I.P. children, wearing cardboard buttons that proclaimed, "MY MOM AND DAD ARE FOR YOU PRESIDENT KENNEDY."

Just behind the wire fence stood a pretty young Negro woman, who was herding a small group of Negro children. She was Mrs. Lillian Peterson, she told us, and the children were part of her fourth-grade class at the Lillie C. Evans Elementary School. She said that no one had invited them to come to the airport; they had just come. The children looked at us solemnly and, at their teacher's prompting, identified themselves as Barbara Laidler (wearing a green ribbon bow in her hair), Anthony Shinhoster, Ietta Odom, Gregory Gill, and William Ingram. "We've just finished studying the United States of America and our three chief executives," Mrs. Peterson told us. "I drew a diagram for the children showing the Mayor in a small circle on the bottom, the Governor in a bigger circle over him, and the President in the biggest circle on top. The fourth grade, you know, is really the foundation grade for the rest of your life. These children have the responsibility of sharing the President's visit with others in the class, who could not come. They have the responsibility of writing a report about what they see today."

Around four-fifteen, four helicopters arrived and sat waiting to take the President and his party from the airport to a secret landing area near the Americana Hotel. In the V.I.P. section there appeared a group of women wearing Uncle Sam hats—red-and-white striped crowns, brims with white stars on blue, and the words "WIN WITH KENNEDY." An F.B.I. man instructed the band's conductor, a man with white hair, to play ruffles and flourishes when the President arrived, and then "Hail to the Chief." At four-twenty-two, the band broke into "On the Square," and it got through "The Colossus of Columbia March," "The Crosley March," "Nobles of the Mystic Shrine," "God Bless America," and "March of the Mighty" before the blue-and-white Presidential plane, bearing the words "UNITED STATES OF AMERICA" and the Presidential seal, finally landed, at five-twelve.

President Kennedy emerged from the tail of the plane, looking relaxed and good-humored, and got to work immediately at what he was expected to do, and more. With the Congressmen, the Senator, and the Governor sticking close to him, he extended his hand wherever he was directed to extend it, and he seemed to find a number of hands to shake on his own, too. He varied his "Hello" and "How are you?" and "Glad to see you" with an occasional "Nice going, boy." When the President appeared on the platform, there was a big cheer from the crowd (it numbered about eight thousand), and though he had yet to be introduced, he came forward eagerly to smile and wave and give a little bow. Pepper, on the platform, introduced Governor Bryant, and the Governor, it turned out, had the privilege of introducing the President. The Governor said that they were all proud of what President Kennedy had done for Florida, and that he felt a special pride and pleasure in presenting the President of the United States.

President Kennedy took it from there, in his own ebullient way. "I've been making nonpartisan speeches all day, and I'm glad to come here as a Democrat," he started off, in old-fashioned campaign style. The crowd loved it. There were cheers from both sides of the wire fence, and all the politicians on the platform appeared happy and satisfied. The President went on to talk about the national purpose—among other things, taking care of seven or eight million boys and girls who will want to go to college in the year 1970. The President said he was going to go on fighting for Congressional enactment of his program, even though certain people "oppose what I am trying to do, just as they opposed everything Franklin Roosevelt tried to do and everything Harry Truman tried to do." The crowd cheered again. The President wound up by saying that the Democrats had won in Dade County by nearly sixty-five thousand votes in the last Presidential election, and he was convinced that the State of Florida was going to be Democratic in 1964. At that, the V.I.P.s, the politicians, the public—everybody—seemed to be united in cheers and smiles.

President Kennedy then left the platform and started walking among the people, smiling, shaking hands, and saying hello. He made a special point of going over to the conductor of the Band of the Hour and thanking him. Behind the President, the politicians piled up, greeting each other joyously with cries of "Hey, Sheriff!" and "Hey, Judge!" and "Hey, Mayor!" We ran into the State President of the Young Democratic Clubs of Florida, a young man named Dick Pettigrew, who had flown in from Tampa on the President's plane. He was glowing. "I never saw so many people in my life as I did in Tampa," he told us. "The President made a brilliant speech before the Chamber of Commerce. He did a beautiful job of explaining why the administration is not anti-business. The Secret Service man next to me on the plane said that the applause the President got was not just polite applause, it was genuine." Then we ran into Congressman Pepper, and he, too, was glowing over the reception in Tampa. "If President Roosevelt, at the heyday of his popularity, had been riding through Tampa, he never would have got such a reception!" Pepper told us.

We noticed that Mrs. Peterson and her fourth-graders were crowded against the wire fence, their hands outstretched, and we noticed that the President kept trying to pull away from the Secret Service men and head in their direction. A white man was holding Barbara up high to get a better look (her green hair ribbon was now untied and fluttering), so that she could give a responsible report to the rest of her class and share with them everything that she saw that day.

The next afternoon, we telephoned Mrs. Peterson to ask her how the children had carried out their responsibilities. Barbara, she told us, reading from their reports, wrote, "The first thing we had was music. They took the President's picture many times. The President has reddish hair and had on a suit. People enjoyed seeing President Kennedy." Anthony reported that he had seen "lots of policemen," and ended up, "I enjoyed seeing our President." Ietta wrote, "We waited and waited and waited. At last we saw some airplanes and four helicopters. We saw a lot of people. John F. Kennedy finally came. He said a little speech." Gregory wrote, "I was glad to go and see our President because this was my first time seeing him and I admire him and his speeches. I think Mr. Kennedy is the greatest man in the world!" William wrote, "He went on the helicopter. Crowds and crowds of people began to say goodbye as he flew away. The crowd of people began to yell louder and louder and it sounded like one thousand people saying goodbye."

. . .

When we think of him, he is without a hat, standing in the wind and the weather. He was impatient of topcoats and hats, preferring to be exposed, and he was young enough and tough enough to confront and to enjoy the cold and the wind of these times, whether the winds of nature or the winds of political circumstance and national danger. He died of exposure, but in a way that he would have settled for—in the line of duty, and with his friends and enemies all around, supporting him and shooting at him. It can be said of him, as of few men in a like position, that he did not fear the weather, and did not trim his sails, but instead challenged the wind itself, to improve its direction and to cause it to blow more softly and more kindly over the world and its people.

VIEWS OF A DEATH

Jonathan Miller

DECEMBER 28, 1963 (J.F.K.'S TELEVISED FUNERAL)

O N NOVEMBER 22ND, when John Fitzgerald Kennedy was shot in the back of the head, he experienced, in the agonizing incommunicado of sudden death, the most public private moment of his life. The objective image of that moment was seen by a thousand people who lined the route, and a few hours later, when the negatives and prints had been washed and dried, millions more had seen it on television, or at least they had seen a grainy hieroglyph representing it, but what they saw only suggested, and could never communicate, the excruciating pith of the victim's own obliterating experience. Never was the rift between privacy and publicity so wide, and perhaps part of the shock of the event resulted from the paradox of this division. The publicity was total, and what it did was to conceal, in the very instant that it exposed, the inexorable solitude of dying.

The President's death forced television into a brief maturity. Death gagged the vulgar infant, and stifled its greedy squalling for a few days. As unvarnished metaphysical austerity flowed—undisturbed, for once—through the channels, the medium itself seemed to take on grandeur. Some of the active contributions made by the television people during this period were intelligent and restrained and technically brilliant, and some were simply drab and dutiful. There were few conspicuous lapses in taste, and there were few signs of creative inspiration. The reporting, for the most part, was direct, humane, ungaudy. There was far less false eloquence than one might have expected. Mainly, there was an unprecedented majesty about the whole affair, a harsh *mesure* that came with the endless, almost inadvertent accumulation of funereal imagery. The pure accidents of repetition and duplication proved valuable. A tic was turned to splendid advantage, allowing the instrument, as the hours wore on, to illustrate every twist and conundrum of mortality. Moreover, the repetition offered a new form of mourning and provided a crash program in grief. Unaided, the mind has a deliberate tempo in this matter, for mourning is some sort of spiritual labor, a lengthy moral exertion in which the outlets to the will are blocked as the feelings are slowly and painfully withdrawn from their familiar attachments. In the normal way of things, this ritual works to a natural andante. It is gracefully hesitant and has its own proper period. Television set a new pace. The whole process was concentrated and speeded up. The assassination, the cortege, the funeral, and the eulogies recurred in what seemed an infinite series of statements and recapitulations. Every channel was taken up with the dire scene, and even the ordinarily distracting atmospherics of television helped to create a dark new aesthetic. For instance, when a local station borrowed a transmission from one of the networks, the original picture and the reproduction, although they were essentially identical, reinforced each other's psychic effect by means of their electronically determined differences. The borrowed picture was often a blurred, Pointillist version of the original, so that as one switched from channel to channel the fact of the President's death was brutally confirmed by the electronic variations on the one, inescapable theme. It was as if, in the space of a few hours, there had been accumulated all those pictorial versions of a tragic event which usually gather in albums over the years, and which, through the myriad tiny differences within the common pattern, approach some comprehensible embodiment of the long-ago fatal incident. But the mystery of such an event can never really be embodied; it can only be approximately reconstructed, or circumscribed, by drawing innumerable pictorial tangents to the mysterious curve of the occasion. Like a computer flickering through a problem that would take a mathematician years, television did a lightning calculation and completed the spiritual algebra of grief in less than four days. As a result, the whole matter seemed to have been formulated and disposed of by the time the commercials came yapping back on Tuesday.

. . .

There were other metaphysical vignettes during that dark weekend. The display of time's arrow, for example, and of the grinding, irreversible determinism in human affairs. Most touching of all, perhaps, were those unbearable playbacks of the events leading up to, but never quite reaching, the moment of the assassination: those happy, slightly lurching newsreel shots of the Kennedys arriving at the airport, the breakfast speech at Fort Worth—all now just innocent hindsights on the approaches to a death. It all seemed so orderly—possibly still reversible—giving way only at the last instant to the photographic topsy-turvy of tragedy.

There was also that microscopic dissection of Oswald's murder, played over and over, reduced by the slow-motion camera to the actual molecules of the murder's own onward-moving process, each molecule of incident mysteriously linked to the next as they clicked, one by one, toward the detonation. And then, just as with the President's last moment, everything flies apart—a sublime dehiscence—at the moment of death itself. Images blur; the eyes of the camera roll upward and the cement ceiling of the Dallas police station streaks past; a brim of a Stetson cuts in close to the screen; there is a dilated eye, and then blackness. An hour later, on another network, the clip is screened again: the same orderly staccato, the same upward roll of the eyes, the ceiling streaking by, the Stetson, the staring eye, blackness. And again and again, as if the camera were searching out but never quite reaching the marrow of the instant. It has been said that this was the first televised murder, but there was more to it than that, for in being so inquisitive television may have become an accomplice in the crime—may actually have joggled events in the direction they took. Perception may have contributed to the act and introduced the slippery risks of Heisenberg into the Dallas police garage. One could almost feel the lens urging Ruby out of the crowd. In fact, in the pictures, it looked as if he came out of the camera itself. In a word, television has become too effective. It gets in on too much. Like some nimble amoeba, it can poke its sensitive tendrils into the world's minutest crannies, put a vast audience in touch with the world's faintest twitch. The trouble is not so much that there will be no privacy any more as that there will be no inaccessibility. The imagination will be totally usurped.

The funeral itself, the lying in state, the catafalque, provided some forceful images of death that had vanished from modern life—for, whatever else has happened, death has been bowdlerized out of the modern text. Yet suddenly, for three days, the domestic screen was almost continuously occupied with the fearful oblong simplicity of the casket. One saw, too, the dreadful heaviness of the dead as the eight enlisted men crouched and staggered under their load. One felt that not all the weight was in the bronze but that at the moment of dying some negative quantity, like phlogiston, goes out of the body, leaving it in a state of hideous density, the better to drag on the straining hawsers that lower the coffin into the grave.

NOTES AND COMMENT

Jacob Brackman and Terrence Malick

APRIL 13, 1968 (THE ASSASSINATION OF MARTIN LUTHER KING, JR.)

WE LAST SAW the Reverend Dr. Martin Luther King early last August, at the Ebenezer Baptist Church in Atlanta—a red brick building on the corner of Jackson Street and Auburn Avenue. His office, in the Sunday-school annex, to the left of the church, smelled of paraffin and linoleum glue. On the bulletin board, children's prayer cards of Jesus pointing at his heart were pinned above Southern Christian Leadership Conference posters proclaiming the summer's theme: "Black Is Beautiful." A broken Crayola popped underfoot. In the course of our conversation, Dr. King told of a recent threat against his life, in Cleveland. "It has been given to me to die when the Lord calls me," he said, digressing from his narrative. "The Lord called me into life and He will call me into death. I've known the fear of dying. Yes, I lived with that fear in Montgomery and in Birmingham, down in the State of Alabama, when brother fell upon brother in 1963." His voice was rich as his sentences rolled inexorably toward their conclusions. It had a kind of patience that was hard to distinguish from fatigue. "Since then, I've stood on the banks of the Jordan and I've looked into the promised land," he went on. "Maybe I won't make the journey, but I know that my *people* are going to make the journey, because I've stood and looked. So it doesn't *particularly* matter anymore. I've conquered the fear of dying, and a man that's conquered the fear of dying has conquered everything. I don't have to fear *any* man." He reached for a leather-bound Bible, worn to a dull shine, like an old watch, and turned to the fourth chapter of II Timothy. "'I have fought a good fight,'" he read. "'I have finished my course, I have kept the faith.'" He paused, and closed the book. (When we returned to the passage later, we noticed that it continued, "Henceforth, there is laid up for me the crown of righteousness.") Dr. King seemed embarrassed at ending the conversation there, but he had to catch a plane. As we stood with him on Auburn Avenue while he waited for his car, he mentioned that he was born "down the block." Along the avenue, modern cinder-block offices, their windows smeared with palm prints, stood beside clapboard houses. Cast-iron washtubs and rusting automobile parts lay scattered in yards. We remember that a young black girl in a stiff organdie dress was spinning a hubcap on the hot pavement.

. . .

We find ourself now, as after any disaster, investing small things with an urgent, outsize relevance. The girl in the organdie dress keeps returning to our mind; somehow she must bear for us the meaning of Dr. King's death. We haven't looked to our memory of her for meaning; her picture simply appears to us, as if through some short circuit of our intelligence. One can no longer clearly grasp the relevance of new events. They involve us all, we talk about them all day, soon we find them squeezing everything else out of our lives, but we're not sure how to weight them. This is not because one can't foresee in detail where they're leading; one never could. The frightening thing is that one can no longer *imagine* what forms the solutions to our problems will assume. One isn't even sure what a solution would look like. Ordinarily, the news media might give us clues. But the relevances we seek now aren't buried in news stories. Friday, the *Times* ran an eight-column headline on Dr. King's death. It ran eight-column headlines Monday, Tuesday, Thursday, and Saturday, too. Tucked inside Friday's paper were many stories about Dr. King's career. Their assumption seemed to be that by reentering his past we might get a running start into our future without him.

The pell-mell events of the previous weeks no doubt undermined our response to Dr. King's death. Over the past several years, we have learned to accept the fact that our destiny is not entirely what we make of ourselves. But in these last weeks, perhaps for the first time since the Second World War, we've had a sense of being submerged in history, and of becoming inured to its stupefactions. About the time of the Tet offensive, one was close to despair. Then, with Eugene McCarthy's victory in New Hampshire and Robert Kennedy's announcement that he would run for the Presidency, with President Johnson's announcement of a bombing halt and then his announcement that he would not run again, followed by a direct peace overture from North Vietnam, one began to feel that suddenly, just when things were darkest, America had found her way back to the path. Now Dr. King's death comes to us as a reproach. We had let ourselves drift away from the reality of our trouble. Finding the path will not be so easy.

Word of the assassination reached us while we were working late at our office, and we immediately switched on a television-network special report. Perhaps because we received each piece of news minutes after it happened, we came to feel that we were at the eye of a historical hurricane. Our national leaders appeared before us to guide our responses. "America is shocked and saddened by the brutal slaying tonight of Dr. Martin Luther King," the President said, in measured tones. "I know that every American of good will joins me in mourning the death of this outstanding leader and in praying for peace and understanding throughout this land." We sat, it seemed dumbly, in the gray haze of our television screen. Other notables—we can't remember which—expressed dismay. Several, staring sternly into the camera, urged viewers to "keep their cool." The argot, unfamiliar to their mouths, made it plain to whom the admonitions were addressed. Curiously, what gave us a stronger sense of tragedy than anything our leaders said was the disorder on the networks: the missed cues and fades, the A.B.C. technician who walked behind Bob Young reading a sheet of teletype paper, Keith McBee stuttering when he suddenly realized he was on camera. When our leaders did appear, their eyes glassy and focussed above the camera, we felt a strange sense of identification with the poverty of their response, and with the way they underscored one another. Too much had happened in the last week. They had been called upon too often. They could, with honor, fail to help us.

After watching the news for more than an hour, we walked out into the office corridor. The cleaning woman, an elderly Negro woman in a green shift and stretch socks, was sitting in the broom closet weeping and muttering to herself, "They're going to get him, and they're going to get everybody." We had nothing we could say to her, and, to judge by her reluctance to notice us, there was nothing she wanted to hear. When we returned to our office, Vice-President Humphrey was in the midst of dismissing predictions of violence, because, he said, no one could respond with anything but grief on this sad occasion. Even as he spoke, we could hear the wail of sirens rising through the long canyon of Sixth Avenue. Shortly afterward, we heard loud shouts and the splintering of glass. We walked onto a balcony outside our office, on the nineteenth floor, and, below, on Forty-fourth Street, saw a crowd of black youths ambling toward Times Square. One, holding a flap of his torn shirt, skipped ahead of the others and, from time to time, spun around to yell at them. We stared (we hadn't yet heard reports of trouble in New York), and said to ourself, "Now it has happened." We shut off the television set and sat in silence. The dreamy ululation of police cars racing toward Harlem continued into the night. After a while, we called a friend. If we could not define our feelings, we could at least share them, undefined. As we talked with our friend, we discovered that although in 1963 the mystery of who assassinated President Kennedy had fascinated us, there was nothing we cared to learn about the man who shot Dr. King. We knew who he was.

John Kennedy's death came like lightning from a clear sky. Dr. King's was something that for a long time we'd been hoping wouldn't happen. We would have been alarmed if Kennedy, or any President, had prophesied his own murder, yet we have grown accustomed to such predictions from civil-rights leaders. Dr. King spoke reluctantly of what he suspected would be his destiny, and most often at the prompting of journalists. Dark premonitions can easily become obsessive, as they did for Malcolm X; they never preoccupied Dr. King. Yet he was the most important example of a new kind of political leader in America—one who cannot exercise leadership without first coming to terms with the probability of his own violent death. A speech that Dr. King delivered on Wednesday evening, scarcely twenty hours before his assassination, and that the networks televised on Thursday night was notable, then, but not surprising. He spoke of having (like Moses) "been to the mountaintop" and there become reconciled. "And then I got into Memphis, and some began to talk about the threats that were out," Dr. King said. "Like anybody, I would like to live a long life. Longevity has its place. But I'm not concerned about that now. I just want to do God's will. And He's allowed me to go up to the mountain. And I've looked over, and I've seen the promised land. I may not get there with you, but I want you to know tonight that we as a people will get to the promised land." Dr. King's prophetic speech was striking only in retrospect, perhaps because we had not been duly conscious of one of his most urgent tasks: *preparing* his apostles, and his public, for their loss of him. On Tuesday night, his flight from Atlanta to Memphis was delayed by a baggage search that airline officials said resulted from threats on his life. But, as most of us have no room in our lives for much else, so Dr. King had no room for worry about himself.

• • •

Many of Dr. King's people had lately grown discontented with him. They saw him standing in the doorway he had opened, an old champion become an obstruction. He wished to solidify old gains, they imagined, while they wanted to push through the doorway. Some ridiculed the basis of his work because it was ethical and religious rather than strategic. They referred to him as "De Lawd" and spoke mockingly of his "meetin' body force with *soul* force." Some others derided what they took for rigid, irrelevant platitudes and florid plagiarisms. The week after we saw Dr. King in his office, he returned to Atlanta to address a convention of the National Association of Radio Announcers at the Regency Hyatt House. Nearly every sentence of his conversation with us recurred somewhere in that speech. Like the politicians who lamented his death, Dr. King often gave the impression of having a kind of fixed inventory of responses. His speeches, with few exceptions, seemed repetitive; they drew their resonance from the occasion that prompted them. But the inventory was a necessity. It relieved him of the distracting obligation of responding freshly, uniquely, to every new situation. It was also a source of his enormous restraint, shielding him from the temptation to vent the hot and—he thought—unconsidered feelings that were aroused in him by the whites' most dramatic outrages, such as the Birmingham bombings of 1963. Dr. King did not have to change his responses, because, from the Montgomery boycott of 1956 to the Detroit riots, the problems remained the same: hatred and fear—what he called, perhaps too abstractly, "sin." The problems were not peculiar to the White Citizens Councils or the Ku Klux Klan, he said in a famous letter from the Birmingham prison; they also afflicted "the white moderate who is more devoted to order than to justice; who prefers a negative peace, which is the absence of tension, to a positive peace, which is the presence of justice." The continuing irony of Dr. King's life was that although his simplicity sprang from the very depth at which he confronted the problems, it alienated him from many of his brothers, black and white.

The broad "coalition of conscience" with which Dr. King hoped to work was too broad, in the end, to satisfy those blacks who rejected the goal of "working into" a white society they considered malignant. A coalition that included the churches, the unions, the N.A.A.C.P., and the Liberal Democrats might effect gradual reforms, they conceded, but they, or many of them, had grown indifferent to any kind of "progress" short of radical social upheaval. Reforms did not come thick and fast enough to hold black leadership in line behind him. During the summer of 1964—which culminated, at the Democratic National Convention, in the Atlantic City compromise over the Mississippi Freedom Democrats—it became clear that the movement that Martin Luther King had fostered and unified was now polycentric. Yet large numbers of even the most militant Negroes continued to revere Dr. King. People knew that he could not be bought. Even if they themselves saw a different reality, they knew that he was true to his own vision. They knew that his caution was also tranquillity, that his arrogance came from deep within him, and that its source was the source of his humility as well. In a struggle in which hatred is often met with hatred, they knew he was genuine in loving the human being, however he deplored the deed. To the last, Dr. King assumed that when the legal and extralegal barriers to communication between races were hewn down, people would begin to see their brotherhood beneath the skin and begin to know "the majestic heights of being obedient to the unenforceable." In recent years, many blacks came to lose faith in this theory altogether. Others simply grew impatient waiting for it to come true in their own lives. But even Stokely Carmichael, who on the night of the assassination urged "retaliation by the black community," in the kind of rhetoric that Dr. King most deplored, called him the only member of the older generation whom young blacks still heard.

When Dr. King was scheduled to take part in a conference or a rally, black people of every persuasion knew it would be honest. They knew he wouldn't try to trick them. White people believed in his honesty, too. He never "told it like it is," the way Malcolm X and, later, Stokely Carmichael did—he was perhaps the most courteous revolutionary who has ever lived—but neither did he misrepresent situations by telling audiences what they wanted to hear. Radicals sometimes tried, without success, to lump Dr. King with the placators among his colleagues. A refined civility ran through him to the core; he didn't need to dissemble, to conceal hatreds, for none smoldered within him—except the hatred of evil. This is why Dr. King never frightened whites; however radical his remarks may have seemed ideologically, they were never venomous. It was a failure that cost him admiration within his own flock, perhaps, but never among those who understood that he confronted problems head on, in their total enormity, without wasting an ounce of energy on blame or vengeance. Whites could listen to him because he managed to attack evil without attacking *them*—because he always made evil seem something they could separate themselves from and join with him against.

Dr. King was a radical in the truest sense: he insisted at the same time upon the terrible reality of our problems and upon their solubility, and he rejected everything that was irrelevant to their solution. Could his death be a radicalizing event, in this same sense, for both races? Perhaps no one was completely happy with him—what he finally did was always a little different from what anyone wanted him to do—but he came closer to being a national hero for both blacks and whites than any other figure in history. Last April, when Dr. King became the first prominent American to oppose the war in Vietnam publicly, he became more than a "black leader." He made himself a leader of all men who care for peace and justice, and reluctantly estranged those of his colleagues who had focussed single-mindedly on the issue of civil rights. He served a complicated cause in a complicated time. In his life, no faction could ever fully claim him as an ally. But with his death every faction—from ghetto blacks tossing brickbats to the Administration of the United States government—loses an ally. His death is difficult for us because it deprives us of the embodiment of the cause he represented for all Americans—the more difficult because of the threat inherent in that deprivation. Incidents of arson and other violence were reported from over forty cities within twenty-four hours of his murder, and on Friday lootings occurred two blocks from the White House. Before the week-end was over, twenty-eight were dead and more than six thousand arrested across the country. But his death also forces upon us the possibility that our common need to avoid the danger of losing touch with his ideals can bring us together in a kind of desperate symbiosis. Perhaps that desperation might even draw us close enough together to see that, as one of Dr. King's annoying plagiarisms insisted, the same things make us laugh and cry and bleed.

· · ·

One tends to forget, under the pressure of events and of the fashions of political vocabulary, that most men, black or white, are essentially non-violent, and that Dr. King was trying to marshal this non-violence—to inspire and direct it, and make it count for something in the affairs of men. He brought about a sense of a black-and-white community of decent men, and until the Mississippi march of 1966 he shakily maintained it. On the day after Dr. King's death, we went to a small, dispiriting rally for him on the Mall in Central Park. As the ideologues dwelled too long and too stridently on the irony of his murder, it began to seem that the course of events would again be determined by that diffuse community of the deranged—black and white, Right and Left and apolitical—which Dr. King, at the time of his death, was again forming a community to overcome. But by Sunday—Palm Sunday—things had changed. As marchers gathered, twenty abreast and eventually seven dense blocks long, at 145th Street and Seventh Avenue, and as they marched—with few signs, and, for the most part, silently—black and white, arms linked, down Seventh Avenue, there was a sense that the non-violent, freed ever so slightly by the President's speech of last week from the dividing pressure of Vietnam, were returning in force to civil rights. It seemed that Dr. King's people, of both races, were assembling again from everywhere, to resume where they left off after Mississippi. They marched past cars whose headlights were on out of respect for Dr. King. They marched over the splinters of broken glass lining the streets of Harlem, past the churches, the abandoned houses, the stores, and the funeral homes. Some carried palm fronds; others wore armbands that read "Our King will never die." A group of the ultra-militant young Five Percenters took their places at the front of the march. No one questioned them.

They were as quiet as the rest. The march was informal—no marshals and no leaders. Bystanders on Seventh Avenue joined at the front or the sides or the rear, or did not choose to join. It was completely reflective and completely orderly. At 110th Street, the march paused, and a siren was audible in the distance. A jet passed overhead. Little boys standing at the entrance to the Park put their feet in the line of march, as though testing the water, and then joined in. Photographers were scattered on overhanging rocks. Reporters for various radio news services spoke very quietly, in their several languages, into microphones. Children gathered around them. The march entered the Park, and walked past cyclists, past very good-natured police, past players on a baseball diamond (an integrated game) near Ninety-sixth Street. Mayor Lindsay and Governor Rockefeller joined it there, and people from all over the Park, some with dogs or balloons, began to drift toward the march, inquire what it was, and then join it. The Mall, by the time the marchers got to it, was filled with a crowd several times the size of the march itself. There were hippies, two Great Danes, and several hot-dog stands, but mainly the crowd looked citywide, very mixed. We stood on the hill in back of the Mall and watched the two crowds merge. They did so almost silently, and totally, in great waves, so there was no way of knowing, from that distance, who had marched and who had been standing on the Mall waiting, and it was hard to tell who was black and who was white.

LIFE AND DEATH IN THE GLOBAL VILLAGE

Michael J. Arlen

APRIL 13, 1968

H E WAS SHOT in secrecy, away from cameras. No strange slow-motion scenes, as when the young Japanese student, sword in hand, rushed across the stage to lunge at a Socialist politician, or when Verwoerd, the South African, was shot at and for whole crazy moments (it seems so long ago; so many people shot at since then) the cameras swirled and danced around the tumbling, stampeding bodies of the crowd—and then John Kennedy was killed, his life made to disappear right there before us, frame by frame, the projector slowing down, s-l-o-w-i-n-g d-o-w-n, s . . . l . . . o . . . w . . . i . . . n . . . g d . . . o . . . w . . . n as we watched (three consecutive days we watched), gathered in little tight-gutted bands around the television set, meals being cooked somehow, children put to bed, sent out to play, our thoughts of abandonment and despair and God knows what else focussing on the images of the television set, television itself taking on (we were told later) the aspect of a national icon, a shrine, an exerciser of grief; we were never so close (we were told later) than in those days just after Dallas. It could not have been quite close enough, it seems, or lasted long enough. The man who was shot in Memphis on Thursday of last week was standing on a second-floor balcony of a motel, the Lorraine, leaning over the railing of the balcony in front of his room, which was No. 306. (We have been told it was No. 306.) He was shot once and killed by a man who fired his rifle (a Remington 30.06), apparently, from inside a bathroom window of a rooming house some two hundred feet away. The address of the rooming house is 420 South Main Street. There was no film record of the act, no attendant Zapruder to witness for us the body falling and other memorabilia, but most of us found out about it by television, and it is by television that most of us have been connected with whatever it is that really happened, or is happening now. Television connects—the global village. We sit at home—We had been out, actually, a party full of lawyers, and had come back early, and turned on the eleven-o'clock news. "I have a dream . . ." young Dr. King was chanting, "that one day on the red hills of Georgia . . ." C.B.S.'s Joseph Benti said that Dr. King had been shot and killed, was dead. The President was speaking. "I ask every citizen to reject the blind violence that has struck Dr. King, who lived by non-violence," he said. They showed us pictures of Dr. King in Montgomery. They showed us pictures of the outside of the Lorraine Motel.

The telephone rang. A friend of my wife's. "Have you heard?" she said. I said we'd heard. "It's so horrible," she said. And then, "I can't believe it." And then, "I feel we're all mad." I held the phone against my ear, mumbling the usual things, feeling, in part, her grief, her guilt, her sense of lunacy—whatever it was—and, in part, that adrenalin desire we strangers have who have been separate in our cabins all the long sea voyage to somehow touch each other at the moment that the ship goes down. She talked some more. "I'm keeping you from watching," she said at last. I mumbled protests, and we said goodbye, and disconnected. We will all meet for dinner three weekends hence and discuss summer rentals on the Vineyard.

All over the country now the members of the global village sit before their sets, and the voices and faces out of the sets speak softly, earnestly, reasonably, sincerely to us, in order once again (have four and a half years really gone by since Dallas?) to bind us together, to heal, to mend, to take us forward. The President appears. His face looks firmer, squarer, straighter now than it has looked in months. "We can achieve nothing by lawlessness and divisiveness among the American people," he says. "It's only by joining together and only by working together we can continue to move toward equality and fulfillment for all of our people." The Vice-President speaks. "The cause for which he marched and worked I am sure will find a new strength. The plight of discrimination, poverty, and neglect must be erased from America," he says. Former Vice-President Richard Nixon is expected to release a statement soon. There are brief pictures of a coffin being slid onto a plane. The Field Foundation, one hears, has just undertaken to donate a million dollars to the civil-rights movement. Dr. Ralph Bunche asks for "an effort of unparalleled determination, massiveness, and urgency to convert the American ideal of equality into reality."

The television sets hum in our midst. Gray smoke, black smoke begins to rise from blocks of buildings in Washington and Chicago. Sirens whine outside our windows in the night. The voices out of Memphis seem to be fainter now; the pictures of that little, nondescript motel, the railing, the bathroom window are already being shown to us less frequently today. Down below us on the sidewalk, six blue-helmeted policemen are gathered in a group. Three police cars are parked farther down the street. The television beams out at us a Joel McCrea movie. Detroit and Newark have been remembered. Responsible decisions have been made in responsible places. The President is working now "to avoid catastrophe." The cartoons are on this morning. The air is very bright outside. The day is sunny. All day long, the sirens sound. The television hums through its schedule. There is a circus on Channel 4. Back from the dime store, my daughter asks one of the helmeted policemen if anything has happened. He seems surprised. No, nothing, he says. A squad car drives slowly, slowly by. A bowling exhibition is taking place on Channel 7. Another movie—and then the news. Great waves of smoke, clouds, billowing waves are suddenly pouring out of buildings. The sounds of bells and sirens. Mayor Daley speaks. Mayor Daley declares a curfew. Six Negro boys are running down a street carrying armfuls of clothes. Police cars streak by. More smoke. The news is over. We are reenveloped in a movie. We sit there on the floor and absorb the hum of television. Last summer, it inflamed our passions, did it not? This time, the scenes of black men running past the smoking buildings of Chicago are handled briefly, almost dreamily—a light caress by cameras and announcers. The coffin—one wonders where the coffin is at present, who is with it. Boston University announces that ten new scholarships for "underprivileged students" have just been created. The Indian Parliament pays tribute. The voices of reason and reordering rise out of the civic temples of the land and float through the air and the airwaves into our homes. Twenty-one House Republicans have issued an "urgent appeal" for passage of the new civil-rights bill. "With whom will we stand? The man who fired the gun? Or the man who fell before it?" Senator Edward Brooke, of Massachusetts, asks. The City Council of Chicago meets and passes a resolution to build a "permanent memorial." Senator Robert Kennedy deplores the rise in violence.

There was a moment the other evening when (just for a few seconds) everybody stopped talking, when (just for a few seconds) the television stopped its humming and soothing and filling of silences and its preachments of lessons-we-have-just-learned and how-we-must-all-march-together—and (just for a few seconds) Mrs. King appeared; she was speaking about her husband, her dead husband. She spoke; she seemed so alive with him—it's marvellous how that sometimes happens between people; he really had been alive, and one knew it then—and for a few scant moments, just at that time, and afterward, sitting there looking at the set, that very imperfect icon, that very imperfect connector of people (will somebody really have the nerve to say this week that we are a nation "united in grief"?), one could almost hear the weeping out there, of real people in real villages, and the anger, this time, of abandonment.

And then the sounds came back—the sounds of one's own life. The weatherman came on. A Negro minister on Channel 13 was talking about the need to implement the recommendations of the President's new Commission on Civil Disorders. He *had* been alive . . . hadn't he?

Later that night, one could hear the sirens—very cool and clear—and, somewhere nearby (around the corner? blocks away?), the sounds of footsteps running.

LETTER FROM WASHINGTON

Richard H. Rovere

JUNE 15, 1968 (THE ASSASSINATION OF ROBERT F. KENNEDY)

JUNE 9

ROBERT F. KENNEDY, who opposed the war in Vietnam and proposed to escalate the war on poverty, was, it would appear, assassinated because he supported the Middle Eastern policy of the President he hoped to replace—a policy that is not a major, or even a minor, cause of divisiveness in this country today. Although the indicted assailant spent his adolescence here and must have been exposed to much of the worst of our commercialized popular culture, which exploits violence as it does anything else that is easily exploitable, he spent what Drs. Freud and Spock and the Roman Catholic Church assure us are the truly formative years in a part of the world where violence, organized and otherwise, has been a commonplace of life throughout much of recorded history—a part of the world, indeed, that gave our language the very word "assassin" and that, almost a millennium ago, institutionalized political and religious murder in a secret society that terrorized the Levant and parts of Europe for centuries. In this there is no vindication for our American ways. The Senator was shot in the Ambassador Hotel, Los Angeles, California, U.S.A., in the near presence of local police and other security agents. The murder weapon was no scimitar; it was an ugly little pistol of native manufacture and—if we are to credit preliminary reports released to the press by authorities in California—easily procured, thanks to the laxity of our nation's laws and those of most of the states. To the best of our present knowledge, no Arab zealot had anything to do with the killing of John F. Kennedy or Martin Luther King or Medgar Evers or Malcolm X or Mrs. Viola Liuzzo. But the extinction of an American leader by a Jordanian nationalist does seem to suggest that we cannot altogether explain our latest loss or our plight as a people by pointing to the iniquity of the war in Vietnam or by berating ourselves for letting our children play with guns and be spellbound by shoot-outs on television. It is entirely possible—it might even have been likely—that if Senator Kennedy had not been mortally wounded on June 5th, apparently for reasons having no connection with Vietnam or our domestic arrangements, he would sooner or later have been murderously assaulted by some native son inflamed by some hatred or injustice for which there would be no one to blame but ourselves. But it is every bit as possible that Sirhan Bishara Sirhan would have been moved to commit the act he is charged with if we had never intervened in Vietnam, if poverty and bigotry had been wiped out long ago, and if our popular entertainment dealt with nothing but love and gentleness and brotherhood.

Kennedy, it seems reasonable now to say, was assassinated because he sought an office of great authority and worldwide prestige and had declared his intention of continuing American friendship for and support of the State of Israel. To put it another way, he is dead today because the United States is a global power that perceives—or misperceives—a national interest in the outcome of conflicts in almost every part of the world. Thus, it becomes necessary for Americans to confront the fact that, given our ways of conducting our political affairs, our leaders are frequently at the mercy not only of the fanatics and maniacs we ourselves spawn in great profusion but also of haters and potential killers in almost every other country on earth. The mere existence of our power and of our alliances on every continent provides an almost infinite number of motivations for others to intervene in our affairs, as we are intervening in theirs. Some would no doubt argue that this is merely another way of establishing our collective guilt or our guilt as a nation. A case can certainly be made for connecting the capacity for destruction we have created for ourselves with a disposition to violence and a casual resort to it in conflicts among ourselves. But if the case against the young Jordanian is what it appears to be, he was motivated not by the malign exercise of our power but by our refusal to exercise it in behalf of the cause he espouses—or, more accurately, since we *have* sold arms to Jordan and other Arab countries, by our failure to equip his side with the quantity of power necessary for the total destruction of its enemy. A foreign policy looked upon as peaceful and benign by every American and by most of the world's people would not lack fanatical enemies. An effective policy of global reconciliation and disarmament would no more appease the Sirhans of this world than the mixed bag of policies we now pursue.

Since we are unlikely either to resolve our internal discords or to get out of the power business in the foreseeable future, the question raised by all the recent assassinations is whether we can go on choosing our political leaders by the means that are now generally regarded as traditional and are held by some to be essential to the maintenance of democracy. Senator Kennedy believed that there could be no such thing as democratic politics if candidates seeking the public favor could not freely move among the masses of the people wherever they might be encountered. This is the common view among politicians of both parties, and it has been frequently reasserted in the last few days—most strongly by Governor Rockefeller, who said, shortly after Robert Kennedy died, that he had no intention of avoiding crowds or of having any more protection than he has had in the past. It is an attractive as well as a courageous position to take, and it may be sound as political philosophy. It is certainly true that any politician who abandoned the practice of mingling at close quarters with his constituents, actual or potential, would be denying himself the enormous advantage of demonstrating his personal rapport with them and also the value of what he might learn from and about them in such encounters. In 1968, this has seemed particularly true. Senators Kennedy and McCarthy, on the Democratic side, and Governor Rockefeller, on the Republican side, mounted their respective campaigns as certifiable underdogs. It was essential to the strategy of each that he convince the ultimate nominators—the Convention delegates—that people in large numbers would welcome his presence and applaud his views. The surest, if not the only, known way of doing this is to hold open gatherings, to encourage the crowds to swell, and to allow the candidate to fraternize as much as possible with those who have troubled to join him. Moreover, when the dangers of this practice were pointed out to Senator Kennedy and others, they were able to reply that neither John F. Kennedy nor Martin Luther King had been killed while mingling with large numbers of people. Some politicians, one of them being President Johnson, have insisted that they are never safer—in the sense of immunity from assassination, if not in the sense of immunity from bruises and broken toes—than when they are in the midst of large crowds. And it can also be pointed out that Senator Kennedy was shot not while consorting with a crowd but—after several weeks of consorting with many and after having received the news that his techniques had prevailed in California—while he was seeking to avoid one.

Yet the question is not really whether one kind of exposure is more dangerous than another; it is, rather, whether our leaders are serving us or their principles well by so frequently tempting death. It is true that John F. Kennedy and Martin Luther King were shot by snipers, and that no increase in the number of bodyguards is likely to afford protection against a killer armed with a telescopic sight. But the late President would in all probability be alive today if the people on the Dallas streets had seen him through a bubbletop, and it might well have occurred to someone in the entourage of Martin Luther King, who ordinarily had more physical protection than most of our Presidential candidates, that it was imprudent for their leader to silhouette himself on a lighted motel balcony in the city of Memphis on the night of April 4th. In any case, whether or not democracy could survive the abandonment or radical reform of some of the present methods of seeking political support, it seems quite clear that it will have less hope of surviving if the acceptance of national leadership involves a high risk of death. Democracy is unquestionably diminished when there are restraints on the liberty of any citizen to go anywhere he chooses, either alone and unprotected or in the company of others. But it suffered some diminution in this country long ago; the historical fact is that nearly all our Presidents have accepted such restraints, as have most leaders of nations for as long as nations have existed. And it now seems incontestable that democracy was vastly more diminished by the death of Robert Kennedy than it would have been had he lived with more caution and more protection. He spoke for millions who are now, at least temporarily, voiceless.

The idea that democracy requires the risks our leaders run seems peculiarly American. Few presidents and prime ministers in other countries feel called upon to take so many chances. Some of them might well feel that they could afford more exposure than their American counterparts, for in no other civilized country are lethal weapons so numerous or so easily come by as they are here. Still, foreign leaders less often feel compelled to be in close and dangerous proximity with crowds that may include individuals who wish them dead, and when the need to do so seems unavoidable they have tighter (though often less visible) security. When President Eisenhower went to meet Nikita Khrushchev in Geneva in 1955, the Swiss and other Europeans—including, of course, the

Russians—professed to think that the Americans were ridiculously obsessed with security, and so it seemed when one observed six or seven Secret Service men jogging along beside the President's car as it moved through the streets of Geneva. However, the Swiss and others could afford to regard this as excessive because they had already put into effect security measures of a severeness unknown in this country. The Russians had no joggers; they simply had an enormous delegation consisting largely of strong-arm men. When President de Gaulle played host to the heads of government of this country, the United Kingdom, and the Soviet Union in 1960—for the summit conference that never took place—his police took the precaution of rounding up hundreds of persons suspected of being capable of attempting assassination and providing them with a holiday in the South of France. No such procedure would be tolerated in this country, and even if it were, a Lee Harvey Oswald or a Sirhan Bishara Sirhan might escape the dragnet. But if we are to preserve civil liberties and at the same time preserve our leaders, either our leaders will have to change their ways or their followers will have to insist that they accept more security. There can be no certain protection against determined assassins, but a bubbletop on the Presidential limousine would have spared President Kennedy, and a bodyguard of seven or eight men might have spared Senator Kennedy.

Addressing himself to this unpleasant subject a couple of nights ago, Senator Javits gave it as his opinion that the time may have come when we can no longer get along without a national police force. He was aware, he said, that the idea was abhorrent to most Americans and particularly to those of a liberal cast of mind. But he observed that other countries had managed to maintain freedom while giving broad powers of enforcement to a national police, and he did not think that the only protection from tyranny was the preservation of our tradition of local police authority. It is difficult, for example, to see how our scandalous traffic in firearms could be stopped except by a national agency. Thanks to the exertions of the National Rifle Association, Congress is still reluctant to end this traffic, but if its mood changed tomorrow and the toughest possible bill were enacted, its provisions could not and would not be enforced by our constables, sheriffs, and local police; they would lack the means and, in many parts of the country, the will to deal with a problem that might be comparable to disarming a large and hostile military force. Our technology has burdened us with many other problems that seem insoluble by means of anything short of a national police agency. One we may shortly have to face is that of the manufacture of small and not so small nuclear weapons by non-governmental organizations, and even by individuals; to tackle it with any success would require keeping track of fissionable materials all over the country. In view of our failure, even with a national agency, to do much about the circulation of narcotics, the prospect is in any case appalling, but it would be quite hopeless—as perhaps it already is—to entrust it to police responsible to thousands of local authorities.

There is an understandable tendency in this bitter and grieving city to say that there is no hope for the United States unless it quickly remakes itself in the ways that Robert Kennedy wished it to and unless it immediately equips itself with the foreign policies he urged upon it. Hope may lie where he said it lay. But the fullest and speediest realization of all his dreams would not greatly reduce the vulnerability of many of our finest spirits to the acts of deranged and desperate fanatics. If we are ever to be led to the New Jerusalem, we must do what we can to keep alive those who know the way.

· · ·

The moratorium on "politics" agreed to by all the leading candidates is not likely to endure for more than a few days. It is in no one's interest that it should. A President must be chosen in November, and unless the contenders find some way of addressing themselves to the electorate at an early date, there will be little hope in either party of challenging the front-runners, or even of negotiating any sort of policy compromises with them. It may even now be too late for this. Most people here have for some time been persuaded that neither Humphrey nor Nixon could be denied nomination. Many think that Kennedy's death has made their strength even greater than it was a week ago. In the view of a large number of Republicans, it was only the possibility of Kennedy's nomination that gave Nelson Rockefeller any kind of appeal to Republican leaders, and a big part of Kennedy's strength reflected the view of many Democratic politicians that he could run powerfully against Rockefeller. Among those who were drawn to Kennedy primarily because of his and their opposition to the war, there is a movement to transfer—or, in some cases, retransfer—their support to Senator McCarthy. But what, more than two months ago, made Kennedy seem a more hopeful candidate than McCarthy was his acceptability among such Party leaders as Jesse Unruh, of California, and Mayor Richard Daley, of Chicago. It now seems reasonable to assume that they would be more comfortable with Humphrey as the nominee than with McCarthy. The Kennedy supporters who now are moved to throw their support to McCarthy will be doing so with very little hope of wresting the nomination from Humphrey but with some expectation that anti-war sentiment could be mobilized to wring concessions on foreign policy and on Cabinet appointments. Kennedy and McCarthy, it is being pointed out, had a combined vote of 88 percent in California, and when any politician hears a figure like that he is likely to listen to reason. A similar aim is no doubt being sought by those Republicans who continue to support Rockefeller—though they, of course, can hardly lead from such strength.

The first Convention—that of the Republicans, in Miami—will get under way just two months from now. In the past, at about this stage of the Presidential year, the handicappers have become very self-assured; in the past, they have, as a rule, had good reasons to. The primaries are over. Most delegations are committed. It is hardly conceivable that any new candidates would be so foolhardy as to declare this late in the proceedings. But in 1968, two months seems a very long time indeed, and very few people are confident enough to look even two days ahead. Most are now conditioned to expect the unexpected and to acknowledge the existence of many new impulses in American life—some of them terrifying, some of them heartening, nearly all of them incalculable as to force and meaning. Moreover, there is a widespread awareness—which the latest assassination will surely increase—that we are not and never again can be in full control of our destiny. We cannot determine the course of the war in Vietnam or the course of the talks in Paris; what the Convention delegates do in August and what the voters do in November may be governed by what armies in Asia and diplomats in Europe do or fail to do in the meanwhile. But on this melancholy weekend the strongest possibility that anyone can foresee is the nomination by the Democrats of the Vice-President and by the Republicans of the last Republican holder of that office.

PART FOUR

FARTHER
SHORES

A NOTE BY EVAN OSNOS

I N THE SUMMER of 1968, William Shawn, who gave interviews as rarely as possible, conceded to a reporter that the unruly state of the world was making it impossible for *The New Yorker* to remain as merrily detached as it had once intended to be. (Harold Ross used to say, "Let the other magazines be important.") Shawn, speaking to *Women's Wear Daily*, said, "There is no question that the magazine has come to have a greater social and political and moral awareness, and to feel a greater responsibility."

Since the mid sixties, the magazine had been publishing searing reports on the growing morass in Vietnam. In December, 1965, Michael J. Arlen wrote that "we fight a ground war, but not, it would appear, in order to possess the ground." Some readers urged *The New Yorker* to return its focus to the five boroughs, or, at least, to a posture of determined disinterest; in a letter from 1970, a resident of upper Fifth Avenue cautioned, "If you subscribe to the liberalism which has done so much harm to our country, you should at least not allow it to show so obviously."

When the writers of *The New Yorker* ventured abroad in the 1960s, they found a world unfastening itself from older dispositions. It was flush with fragile new freedoms but uneasy about the passage of power into unproven hands. If the forties had presented a planet starkly divided between allies and enemies, and the fifties took shape along the battle lines of the Cold War, the sixties provided only a muddled map, in which few familiar landmarks—empires, dictators, and mores—remained untouched.

Emily Hahn, the magazine's most inveterate wanderer, arrived in Lagos in late September, 1960, primed to witness a "mystic moment of changeover," from British colony to independent nation. But when the moment arrived, at 12 A.M. on October 1st, the newly free Nigerians greeted it not with celebration but with exhaustion and a faint sense of uncertainty. "I listened expectantly for the whoops of joy," Hahn wrote. "There were none."

In many places, writers found their subjects suspended somewhere between rival ideologies. Hans Koningsberger was born in Amsterdam and fought in the Dutch Resistance and for the British Army before reaching the United States, in 1951. He spent most of the sixties on an extended political safari, writing from the Soviet Union, China, South America, and Europe. He visited Cuba in 1961, two years after Castro's ascendance, and found it rapidly, if not thoroughly, de-Americanized. "Most of the familiar signs are still there—Goodyear, Sears, Woolworth—but the subtitle 'Nacionalizada' gives them a darkly different accent," he wrote. His dinner companions were ill at ease, not yet willing to place their faith in Socialism or, for that matter, in America.

It was impossible to know which transformations were permanent. Flora Lewis, whom the *Times* editor A. M. Rosenthal once called "the world's greatest correspondent," knew too much history to suspect that the rapid Israeli victory she saw, in the Six-Day War, in 1967, would bring permanent peace. When the shooting stopped, "the new ruins I saw there were almost indistinguishable from the ancient ones," she wrote. And yet Lewis, one of the few mothers in her generation of war correspondents, never succumbed to the cynicism that might have relieved her of the urge to watch it all unfold. "When the bullets came over the King David Hotel," a friend recalled, "she was the only one left in the lounge. Everyone else was in the basement."

At times, it was difficult to know which transformations were permanent. In the spring of 1968, Joseph Wechsberg returned to Czechoslovakia, the country of his birth, to witness the first flickers of political liberalization after a "quarter of a century of fear, police brutality, and enforced ignorance." He described the head of Stalin's statue "lifted from his shoulders in broad daylight, with nearly everybody in Prague watching." Though he permitted himself to imagine that it might be "the beginning of a development that could shake the Communist world to its foundations," by the end of the year a Soviet-led invasion had stamped out the awakening. And yet the embers smoldered for decades, and when, at last, the Communists receded, in 1989, it was the end of a process that had begun during that spring two decades earlier. Wechsberg could not know that timeline, but he sensed that the eclipse would be profound. He lingered on the image of the night sky emerging over the city, "high above the river, in liquid gold, and then, suddenly, the whole thing went deep blue."

Occasionally, the pivot points of history lay in plain sight, if a writer was well placed and wily enough to witness them. Writing under the pseudonym Xavier Rynne, Francis X. Murphy was a Redemptorist chaplain and theology professor who published wry, behind-the-scenes reports from the Second Vatican Council, the first time in nearly a century that thousands of Roman Catholic religious leaders and theologians met to settle doctrinal issues. In Rynne's telling, they were negotiating nothing less than the Church's encounter with the modern world. They condemned anti-Semitism, took steps to allow languages besides Latin to be used during Mass, and encouraged Catholics to foster relations with other faiths. He chronicled the tensions between reformers and conservatives, noting that "when Pope Paul invited the aged heads of Curial offices to resign last spring, several of them . . . replied that they were prepared to serve him unto death. That is why the Pope is now seriously considering making all top positions temporary."

But the epochal shifts of the sixties did not always announce themselves on paper; more often, the writers were left to weigh the signs of progress and retrenchment with nothing but their senses and their knowledge of the terrain. Mavis Gallant, the Canadian-born writer who published a hundred and sixteen stories in *The New Yorker* between 1951 and 1995, was in her Paris apartment in the summer of 1968, when students began to march on the Left Bank. They built barricades and tore up cobblestones, raging against a patriarchal state, still so conservative that homosexuality was outlawed and women were prohibited from wearing pants to work. In the course of the next four weeks, France lurched through a moral revolution, sweeping aside constraints on education, work, family, and love.

In the clipped cadences of her diary, Gallant chronicled, with unsparing precision, those weeks and their players: the courageous, narcissistic students; the police who lobbed tear gas on to the balconies of troublesome neighbors; the intellectuals who preened on the barricades. Of one especially self-regarding professor, she wrote, "Wanted to say, 'Come off it, *vieux père.*'" Gallant is best remembered for her fiction and the densely detailed universes that she conjured. But she was, first and forever, a reporter, who sought to absorb as much as she could about the lives of those she encountered—"what they ate, and what they wore, and how they spoke, and their vocabulary, and the way they treated their children," she once told an interviewer. "I drew it all in like blotting paper."

THOUGH TRIBE AND TONGUE MAY DIFFER

Emily Hahn

DECEMBER 10, 1960 (NIGERIAN INDEPENDENCE)

THE SITE OF the Nigerian capital, which lies on the Atlantic coast just off the southwestern tip of the Nigerian mainland and is linked to it by a bridge and a ferryboat, is generally referred to as the island of Lagos, but it is really two islands, or even three, depending on how one counts. Lagos proper, also known as Eko, is separated only by a canal from a sister island called Iddo, and a bit apart from these twins is the island of Victoria, completing the Lagos group. The total area of the islands, together with a few small patches of the mainland in the immediate vicinity that are also part of the capital, is only twenty-seven square miles, and their total population is a teeming three hundred and fifty thousand. . . .

Public transport has always been one of the chief problems of existence in Lagos, and I had been given to understand that during the Independence, when the city would be seething with the excitement of entertaining special visitors, finding a taxicab might well prove impossible. It was my good fortune to be driven over this last lap by a friend, Jack, who lives near me in the English countryside and who visits Nigeria every year on business, attracted there, like the bulk of the foreigners in the nation today, by its substantial oil resources. Jack had prophesied that I would be glad of a lift into town, and he was waiting at the airport when I arrived.

In the middle of the morning, which was bright but not oppressively hot, we drove off toward the city, with Jack pointing to decorated archways along the way and talking feelingly of the traffic difficulties and the general bedlam prevailing in Lagos during the Independence. I was not surprised, having been forewarned by a Nigerian official in London that many things besides traffic were far from normal in his country just then. "We don't get any answer out of those people down there," he had said, in a rare moment of desperation. "They are not attending to business. They are all jockeying for position in the new government." Clearly obsessed with the fear of an accommodation shortage, he had added severely, "We expect many important people to attend the Independence. President Eisenhower has been invited, and no doubt he will bring a lot of people with him. The same applies to Mr. Khrushchev, not to mention other national leaders. This being so, I greatly fear there will be no room for you."

Fortunately for me, if not for President Eisenhower and Mr. Khrushchev, previous engagements with the United Nations prevented them from attending, though Governor Nelson Rockefeller did come, as head of the American delegation. I am not claiming that I got either Eisenhower's or Khrushchev's room—in fact, I'm sure I didn't, since I shared a press billet with another woman—but their failure to turn up probably helped me just the same, by relieving the general pressure all over town. . . .

Just before I got into Jack's car, a group of Nigerians—men and women—came slowly past the hotel, their bodies bent forward at a sharp angle as they strutted and danced strangely to the complicated beat of drummers in their midst; now and then one of the strutters would stop short, feet rooted to the ground, but would still keep the rhythm by jerking his or her torso this way and that. "It could be a wedding party or a funeral or anything at all," Jack said. "Nigerians dance on practically every occasion. See the drum that fellow on the left has under his arm? That's a talking drum. He can change the tone of its voice by squeezing or releasing it, and it actually does sound like talking."

A child walking by called to us "Hello! Free*dom*! Independa!" and the dancers, shouting and laughing, closed in until they surrounded us. One of the men half knelt in front of us, his head thrown back, and Jack balanced a coin on his forehead. Encouraged, another man advanced and threw his head back, but at this an ancient woman, who seemed to be in charge, scolded him sharply, and told the party to move on and stop begging. She shook hands with us both, and the others followed her example. Then they all danced away, twitching and jerking. . . .

The streets of Lagos were almost choked with disorderly lines of traffic. Garlands had been strung between lampposts, and high hoardings had been raised and decorated with bunting shields, some of these in pure blocks of green or red, others bearing the national coat of arms. Along the waterfront, a marina unrolled its length between loops of color, interspersed with great bird cages holding likenesses of parrots whose feathers ruffled realistically in the wind. Office buildings were hung with brilliant strips of cloth. At a distance, the racecourse, which was the center of the Independence celebration, could have been a great oval of fully decorated Christmas trees. . . .

. . .

The next night, for once, all the pretty green vans seemed in order, equipped with drivers, and ready to accept passengers. Loaded, they rolled in cavalcade across the bridge, across the glittering town, to the glittering racecourse. We were on our way to see the Tattoo and the flag-changing ceremony. The ships in the harbor were dressed in their finest bunting, and one, bearing on its visible side a huge emblem of the crossed flags of Nigeria and Britain, was floodlighted. Everything in town was so gaily illuminated with red and blue and green and yellow electric lights that I could have read a newspaper in the van the whole way to the racecourse. I was riding with three representatives of the American Negro press, a Nigerian from the Ministry of Information, and a woman from somewhere in Central Europe who had made her home in Africa for several years. The Nigerian and the European woman were evidently acquainted, and they plunged almost immediately into an argument concerning religion. I listened with interest, for I knew little more about religion in Nigeria than what I had read in the guidebooks; namely, that the faithful are either Christians or Moslems or adherents of one or another of the medley of aboriginal beliefs held by the people before Europe and Asia moved in on them—a medley that is called, by Europeans and Asians, "paganism." I now gathered from listening to the Nigerian that the term "paganism" is a grossly misleading simplification, a blanket term, embracing ancestor worship, pantheism, and a bewildering variety of forms of idolatry. The Nigerian scorned all the manifestations of paganism, speaking of them as if they should be eradicated as soon as possible—an attitude that enraged the European woman. "I wish you people wouldn't be like that," she burst out irritably. "I can't understand people like you, who have been educated in the Western tradition. I don't like calling these cults paganism any more than you do, because it seems to me there is something unpleasantly condescending in the term, but why must you try to destroy something so ancient, so valuable in your culture?"

"Because most of it involves unpleasant practices," the Nigerian said, speaking as if with an effort.

"When it means so much to those poor people in the villages, too," the woman hurried on. "Can't you see what a pity it is to lose such a big part of your national heritage?"

"I take it that you'd like to preserve the custom of human sacrifice?" said the Nigerian softly. "That you want our people to go on burying children alive in the mud to propitiate a god?"

The woman muttered something about carrying things to extremes, and subsided into offended silence.

We arrived at the racecourse, where solemn Girl Guides were again handing out programs and shepherding people to their seats. I reflected as I leafed through my program, elegant with shiny paper and photographs, that wherever the British have made and left their mark, tattoos are much the same, following a pattern laid down at Aldershot and exported to Africa, to India, to other parts of Asia, and, last spring, even to Madison Square Garden. Yet, unchanging though the pattern may be, I admitted to myself, a tattoo is a stirring thing.

But not to everybody, I realized, recalling a Frenchwoman I had met at lunch that day. "All this Independence seems to me too English," she said. "I saw the ceremonies in Ghana when they had theirs, and those seemed better—more African, with everyone doing just as he liked. Why, even the people directing things here are English."

"Don't forget," an Englishwoman at the table retorted, "until midnight we're still in charge—at least nominally."

I looked around at the audience. It was huge. Every space was occupied, from the padded V.I.P. chairs in the grandstand—including the Princess's—to my own hard bench. Of course, the crowd was predominantly African, but the British were out in force, the official contingent being headed by the retiring Governor-General, Sir James Wilson Robertson, G.C.M.G., G.C.V.O., K.B.E., and accompanied by a number of visitors from Britain who at one time or another had had a hand in managing Nigerian affairs. British teachers and missionaries had come to see the show, and so had British businessmen, with their wives. In fact—it dawned on me suddenly—the British were all there in perfectly ordinary, natural capacities; it was like the last day of school, or Parents' Day.

Turning back to the program, I read its outline of the midnight formalities that were to mark the mystic moment of changeover: "The Combined Guards of Honour . . . will salute in Farewell to the Union Jack of Great Britain and to honour the flag of the federation of Nigeria." It would no doubt be an emotional moment, I thought; there would surely be tears in British eyes, and the Nigerians would probably whoop for joy as their banner began flapping at the top of the tall flagpole out there in the middle of the arena, where the Union Jack was now fluttering.

The Tattoo drummed along without novelty. We had a massed-bands display ("the first time that a British Band has performed here . . . with Nigerian Bands"), and it elicited a nostalgic response from the British sitting near me, especially when the players broke into a tune that is undoubtedly regimental, although I know it as "Early One Morning." The people around me hummed the melody in such numbers and with such happy fervency that the sound dissipated the noise from the brasses and hovered over us in the still night air. I recalled the words:

> Early one morning, just as the sun was rising,
> I heard a maid sing in the valley below;
> "Oh, don't deceive me! Oh, never leave me!
> How could you treat a poor maiden so?"

Next, or soon, came a motorcycle display, a physical-training display, and so on and on—all staged in the familiar half gloom provided by the inadequate searchlights. More to my liking was the musical ride, performed by mounted police from the north—the Arab-haunted north, where emirs in white headdresses keep their wives hidden away and are born to the saddle. The riders came from Kano and Katsina and Sokoto, and they looked the part, wearing brilliant uniforms, carrying lances, and riding caparisoned steeds. As the climax of their display of skill, they thundered straight at us in a row, lifting their lances and screaming war cries. At that moment—light or no light—they really came alive.

The seamanship display, the modern battle, and at last, as smartly on the dot as any Englishman could desire, we reached the assembly and that page of history on which, with the changing of the flags, the rule of the Federation of Nigeria would begin. The massed bands marched on again, the guards of honor took their places. Two church dignitaries—one Anglican, the other Roman Catholic—walked out on the field shoulder to shoulder and mounted a rostrum that had been placed ready, and each in turn said a prayer. They were supplanted by the chief Imam of Lagos, a swathed figure who started out by praying in traditional Arabic; his syllables brought from many Nigerians in the audience an involuntary grunt of approval that seemed to roll all the way around the tiers of seats. The Imam then switched to Hausa, and again there was a rumble of response. He stopped praying. It was exactly midnight.

The bands began to play. "God Save the Queen," they played, and we all rose to our feet with an enormous rustle and looked up at the Union Jack, picked out of the darkness by one of the searchlights. But those who had tears in their eyes blinked them back instead of shedding them when, just as everybody's gaze focussed on the flag, rockets started shooting up into the air from the right of the racecourse and bursting overhead in phosphorescent green showers. At the same instant, the light trained on the flagstaff began to flutter off and on. Some people declared later that it went out entirely, but this is not true; it was snapped off and on, over and over again, so rapidly that one couldn't see a thing that was happening. Suddenly, as the last of the rockets died out, the light went on again clear and strong. The change had been made. Invisibly, the Union Jack had disappeared, and the flag of Nigeria now hung in its place. It did not actually flap in the breeze, because one end of it had been caught up in the rope in the hasty scramble to hoist it in the dark—a circumstance that worried some Nigerians a bit, I heard later, since they naturally thought of it as an omen. Still, there was the green-and-white flag, and I listened expectantly for the whoops of joy. There were none.

Oh, there was applause, all right, but only clapping of a polite sort—about as much as had been accorded the physical-training display. Then, with a bit of preliminary drumming, the bands started up again, and everyone remained standing to sing, in English, the Nigerian national anthem:

> Nigeria, we hail thee,
> Our own dear native land,
> Though tribe and tongue may differ,
> In brotherhood we stand,

Nigerians all, and proud to serve
Our sovereign Motherland.

All the Nigerians there—Hausa, Ibo, Nupe, Yoruba, and the rest, whether they came from the north, the east, or the west—sang these words, and perhaps they all meant them; it would be idle to speculate on that. Again I looked around for some sign that this was a deeply significant occasion. There was no such sign in the Nigerian faces nearest me, and the British faces all wore an expression of smiling rigidity. And then I saw one—just one. We were still standing and the last chord of the Nigerian anthem was slowly dying away when from a tier behind me came a single glad cry and a man's voice said loudly, "So we are free now! So we are free!" I stared in the direction of the voice and saw the man laugh in joy and raise clenched hands. The heavy white cloth of his sleeves slipped back and hung down from his thin black arms. That was all, but to me it was a spark that vied with the star-spreading rockets in the sky.

. . .

In the days that followed, Europeans made many guesses as to why the Nigerians had taken the ceremony so calmly. I can bear witness that the Nigerians did, by and large, take it calmly—not only at the racecourse but afterward. An hour-long rocket display followed the flag changing, and I found that the first fifteen minutes of it were about all my enthusiasm could put up with, so I rose to leave. The last thing I heard before I departed was another exchange between the Nigerian official and the European woman from my van.

"Every time one of those rockets goes off, I shudder, thinking of what it's costing the people," the woman said. "It's all got to come out of the national exchequer."

"It is only for once in history, and they love fireworks," the Nigerian replied, and I thought that his tone had become definitely impatient.

Jack saw me from his seat in the stands as I was going out, and came down to join me. Getting in his car, we drove into town to see what was going on, and found almost nothing. In the streets there was peace, even lassitude. The biggest excitement was provided by a couple of white-robed drunks, helping each other across the street and shouting cheerily for Independa. We went to a place that Jack was sure would be lively—

the popular Island Club. Though crowded and full of brilliant cotton prints and glittery evening gowns, it was not lively. A band was playing popular "high-life" music, but nobody was dancing. People came in, looked around, greeted friends and smiled, then sat down and lapsed into silence. Our table was on a balcony over the bandstand, and at the next table a man in rich draperies removed his sandals, propped his bare feet on the railing, slid comfortably down in his chair until he was balanced on his shoulder blades, and fell asleep.

"I think everybody's just shagged out, that's it," Jack said. "After all, they've been celebrating steadily for a whole week."

I said that I, too, was tired, and I went back to my hotel and to bed.

One other Nigerian's reaction to Independence comes to mind, as an Englishwoman related it to me on the day after the flag changing. "Our party was standing on a balcony of that scarcely finished new skyscraper next to the racecourse, and we had a splendid view," she said. "Some of the builders' workmen were still around, and they were standing near us. As the old flag was lowered—and that was beautifully arranged, don't you think, with the light going out and all?—I had a lump in my throat and tears in my eyes. I was expecting the workmen to behave in some wildly happy way, and I wasn't sure I could stand it without bursting into tears. But no. They did nothing. Only, I heard one say softly, 'Bye-bye.'"

FROM

LETTER FROM HAVANA

Hans Koningsberger

JUNE 10, 1961

May 21

I N SPITE OF the headlines, in spite of all the shouting, Cuba would now be the ideal vacation country for the real snobs, for that vanishing generation of travellers who refuse to hobnob with *hoi polloi* from home on any terms. Because here, for the first time since the British discovered and then ruined the French Riviera, is a country with splendid beaches, good hotels, most of the comforts of home, and not a single tourist. No English speaking guides, no shady gentlemen with dubious Parker pens for sale, no boys pursuing the visitor with the birdlike Latin-European money cry of "Mister! Hey, Mister!" In fact, one can drive from Pinar del Rio to Santiago de Cuba without hearing a word of English. Most of the familiar signs are still there—Goodyear, Sears, Woolworth—but the subtitle *"Nacionalizada"* gives them a darkly different accent. There are gas stations aplenty, but the Shell and Esso shields have been removed from their roadside signposts, and the empty curlicued frames are much more attractive than they were as supports for the signs themselves. Cuba may be only ninety miles from the United States, but now it seems like thousands. . . .

. . .

I had my first pro- and counter-revolutionary briefing on the day of my arrival—at cocktail time on the terrace of El Carmelo, still a highly fashionable café in the still fashionable quarter of Vedado. My host was a small, rather used-up old man, a retired professor at the University of Havana; his wife was much younger, and very aggressive. We spoke in French, she continually interrupting him and he almost automatically correcting her language mistakes as they came along. Against a background of waiters busy with screens to keep out a newly pouring rain, she informed me that Cuba had needed a revolution, but not this one. "Life has become so dreary," she said.

"For instance?"

For instance, El Encanto, the most splendid department store in all of Latin America, had been burned down by its personnel to protest its nationalization.

The professor snorted. Clearly enough, he said, the store had been burned down by counter-revolutionaries with professional phosphorus bombs, not by disgruntled clerks; it had been totally destroyed.

"The owner used to live right across the street from here, but he's now in Miami," his wife said. "And this restaurant used to be so crowded by six o'clock."

"Martí—" the professor began, referring to José Martí, the Cuban George Washington and Herbert Spencer rolled into one.

"Oh, Martí!" his wife exclaimed with intense boredom.

The professor became indignant. "Shall we speak of Batista, then?" he asked his wife. "This was an *indecent* country," he told me, as his wife stopped listening. "It was repugnant to be a Cuban. There was nothing but deals, nothing but corruption. Two hundred thousand people holding down *botellitas* [phony political offices], deputies receiving lifetime pensions of four hundred dollars a month. This revolution cannot be steered like an automobile, even if we want it to be. We waited four hundred years for this, and there was no more time. I am not surprised at the invasion—I *am* surprised that I should live to hear people like the American President speak about it so cynically."

I have since seen more of the professor and his wife, and have met other members of their family. He is her second husband, and she is a member of a rich family that had clearly always looked down on him as a man without means, holding a daily job for a living, and too clumsy and do-goody to get in on the various get-rich games. The professor's brother-in-law is a highly prosperous-looking man, as smooth as only Latins, very rich ones, can be; he still has a car with chauffeur. He is a physician by profession but really a politician, the professor told me—a man from the in-group in the Batista era. In a way, the revolution has been a very personal triumph for the professor.

The professor's wife lost no time getting me involved in a little plot designed to enable her to visit her nephew, who was one of the captured invaders of April 17th. She had told some official that I had come to Cuba to investigate the treatment of these prisoners for the press, and that she was needed as my interpreter, "since French is his only language." She explained this plot to me during a visit to her house on my third day in Havana. Her sister and the physician were also present. I was very much annoyed; I had come directly from New York, and surely the Cuban government would take a suspicious view of this fantastic story. I said that she should have consulted me first. "Perhaps you're a Communist?" the sister asked. I said no, but still . . . At that point, the physician tried to smooth things over by proposing that we all have lunch at La Zaragozana 1830, a wonderful restaurant. I declined, because he somehow implied that I had been holding out for just some little bribe like that. I did not go to see the prisoners with the professor's wife (they now have permission to be visited by their relatives), but I did pay another visit to the professor's house. It was late in the evening, and warm, and he and I sat out on the balcony together. The street lay silent below us as he spoke in a hoarse, hasty voice. "Latin America works for the United States," he said. "That is how the Americans can maintain their celebrated 'American way of life.'" He often used that expression—always in English, always bitterly. "That's why they're so haughty about their democracy," he went on. "That's why they fear Cuba's example." He added, in a whisper, as if to himself, "Ils vont perdre leur *way of life*." . . .

Obviously, Cuba's rich are against Castro, and to me, at least, it is also obvious that the poor are with him. The middle class here has never represented a transition between the two, the way it does in the United States and Western Europe. As part of a colonial class structure, it has reached up to the ranks of the rich but not down to those of the poor. The middle class is divided about Castro, but I couldn't begin to guess percentages, and I haven't resorted to the usual device of polling taxi-drivers. Then there are the intellectuals—the writers and artists, who in Latin countries form a rather specific group. Pablo Armando Fernandez, an editor of *Lunes*, who lived in New York for many years, wrote down the names of twelve of them for me, constituting, he said, a solid chunk of the group. (It's important to remember what a small country Cuba is.

Havana is like an eighteenth-century European town, where everyone knew everyone.) All but one of the twelve had lived in exile for some years previous to 1959; under Batista, their own country had nothing to offer them. Their average age was thirty, and they had all known one another even before they converged again on Havana. Two have since turned their backs on Castro and gone into exile again. I have had talks with several of the others. Good things were being done, they assured me; magazines with sophisticated layouts were being published, and plays like Lizarraga's *Santa Juana de America* were being produced. Most of these men did not believe in Socialist realism or any other *dirigisme*, as they called it; they did believe in the revolution, and they hoped (or doubted) that their commitment to it would carry them through the present atmosphere, which has become much more doctrinaire since the invasion attempt. One of them was the Communist political writer mentioned earlier. He started tapping his foot whenever I contradicted him, answered my questions with platitudes, and finally, when we came upon the subject of North Korea's aggression, called me a C.I.A. agent. The leader of the group, much older than the rest, is Nicolás Guillén, Cuba's poet laureate, a short, very dark, gray-haired man who reminded me of Paul Muni as Juárez and who is setting up a "writers' center" in a villa in the Vedado. "Then we can get some work done," he said. "Now we're going in all directions." Guillén clearly likes *le dirigisme*—with him doing most of it—but whether he will succeed depends on developments far from that cool white mansion on the Calle 17.

· · ·

Mother's Day may be a Yanqui invention, but that didn't spoil it for the Cuban government, which observed it by bringing to town for the day fifteen thousand mothers who had never seen Havana. While here, they visited their children, now attending school in the city, and stayed in private homes. All the preceding week, the papers were filled with saccharine drawings and stories about the glories of Cuban motherhood, and Havana's telephones carried a recorded voice which, between rings, urged the caller waiting for his party to take in a *madre campesina* as a guest. Since Cubans are never in a hurry to answer the phone, I heard this Brave New World–style message quite a few times that week. Anyway, the mothers came, and on Sunday afternoon they were packed into the Coliseo Nacional to be entertained. I went, because Castro was to come; it would be my first Castro rally. By saying *"Periodista"* ("Journalist") often enough, I worked my way up near the speakers' rostrum, where it was quite cool; in the center arena of the huge, round building and in the lower tiers of seats the heat was suffocating. Every few minutes, a couple of *milicianos* would dash for an exit with a stretcher bearing a *madre campesina* who had fainted. I have been in Hitler's Sportpalast, but the atmosphere here was more like Madison Square Garden: instead of speakers to warm up the audience, there was an endless succession of singers, television comedians, jugglers, guitar players, and all the other moth-eaten vaudeville acts that no war or revolution seems able to banish from this earth. The mothers and their children appeared to like it— those who didn't faint—and the music was Caribbean and gay. After a long while, a young woman and some young men with sports shirts hanging loose filed onto the rostrum, and an equally sloppy-looking fellow sitting beside me informed me that the girl was Celia Sanchez, a secretary of Castro's, that the beatniks were Castro's bodyguards, and that their arrival meant he was in the building.

At that moment, there was the sound of an explosion in the distance. Then, as Castro and his party entered, there was a second explosion. This was my first (and only) encounter with violence in Cuba. A great commotion arose at the exits behind us. An Indian journalist sitting next to me turned as white as his *sherwani*. Castro stopped and stood still right in front of me, and since bomb throwers traditionally kill an innocent bystander, I prayed for him to move on a bit, which he did not. The audience had gone wild, streaming down into the center arena, waving and dancing and screaming *"Paredón! Paredón!"* ("To the wall! To the wall!") Their emotion was a strange mixture of fear turned into defiance and verging on hysteria. They massed below the stand, looking up at Castro, and cheered deafeningly, waving little red-and-white flags. They started singing,

> "Somos socialistas,
> Palante y palante,
> Y al que no le guste
> Que tome purgante,"

which proclaims that they're Socialists, onward and upward, and anyone who doesn't like it can take a dose of castor oil. Slowly, some calm returned, and from a microphone on the floor the master of ceremonies, choking with emotion, reminded us and Castro that "these people [the counter-revolutionaries] do not know that he and everyone would give their lives for the revolution." Then he anticlimactically announced a team of folk dancers.

During this incredible row, Castro had looked at once distracted and very sober. He responded to the cheering only with a smile, and not at all to the m.c.'s speech. Then he sat down in a blue chair and began talking to a neighbor. After some more dances, he took his place behind the lectern and started his address. He made no reference to the explosions or the demonstrations but spoke like an earnest school-teacher; every time he was interrupted by applause, he fiddled with the microphone. His subject was illiteracy. As always, Castro repeated each idea several times in different words—a boon to the foreigners in his audience, if not to his staff, which looked slightly bored. In the center of the arena, the women and children and *milicianos* sat down on the floor, and a light buzz of conversation rose in the hall. The bodyguards on the rostrum lit cigarettes. Castro was tanned, his face without wrinkles, and I thought he looked rather like Humphrey Bogart with a beard. He has the attributes of the great orator—the voice, the pleasure in hearing himself, the gift of deliberately building sentence upon sentence, like a mason constructing a wall (Churchill does this superbly, but Castro uses no notes), and the magnetism, or star quality, as they say on Broadway. He seems possessed, or obsessed, by the need to get his thoughts across. He talked to the mothers for only an hour and a half—the equivalent for him of a few off-the-cuff remarks—and vanished with a wave of his arm, without waiting for the applause. Outside, scores of buses were lining up to cart the mothers off to their next destination—bed, one hoped for their sake. . . .

. . .

Later, driving around in a rented car of my own wherever fate and my map led me, I came upon a cooperative I.N.R.A. farm called Mamborel, near the small town of Güines. Mamborel grows rice, cane, and vegetables. All three members of the local I.N.R.A. staff insisted on showing me around. There was the filthy old settlement—not much more than a collection of African huts—and then the new I.N.R.A. one, consisting of concrete prefab houses with kitchens and bathrooms, a school, a store, a library, and all that. The village had two teachers—one for children and the other to teach the peasants how to live in houses, for until recently these people had never seen a tap, let alone a toilet. The buildings were painted in various colors and looked fresh and charming. These farms are not true cooperatives but are closer to collectives, and if it is said that the peasants would rather receive land of their own, I am ready to believe it. We had lunch afterward, and while we ate I learned that the three I.N.R.A. men were all in their early twenties—thin, eager, very hard-working. The one in charge commuted daily from Havana by bus; he was married and was waiting for a house to be built for him in Güines. I asked the two others what they did with their evenings. The movies, the bodegas, and walking, they said, and one of them had a sweetheart, a *miliciana*.

At about ten that evening, I got to Colón, a town in the heart of Matanzas Province. It was dinnertime, and the restaurant of the Santiago, clearly the leading hotel in Colón, was packed. I had my rum-and-soda and my chicken and rice, and then stood outside awhile at the intersection of two main streets. The air had the mildness it acquires only below the Tropic of Cancer. Couples walked up and down, as they do in all towns in all countries. Right next to the restaurant, in a notary's office with its door and window wide open, a wedding was taking place. The bride was in white, and quite pretty; the bridegroom had sideburns and looked extremely young and frail. The room was jammed, people made jokes, and I felt sorry for the couple, sorry for the lack of ceremony. For a moment, I thought of giving them a present, but then I realized that that was exactly what a sentimental Northern tourist would do. The mother took an endless time signing the register. Afterward, the whole party was somehow packed into three taxis and sent off. The notary stood in his doorway looking after them—an old man with a Spanish name and a Chinese face. (Cuba mixes the blood of three continents.) I asked him why the wedding had been held so late; the boy had been working in the cane fields all day, he answered.

I went back to my car, which was parked opposite a cigar-maker's workshop. The proprietor and his wife were at work there, and a child was sitting near the doorway. I watched the pair working for a while, and the man invited me in to try a cigar. Then he insisted on my taking four more. Although Colón is a town of some size, my national origin created great astonishment. The woman got up and brought a fan over to show me, on which was painted a portrait of Camilo Cienfuegos, a rebel leader who was with Castro in the Sierra Maestra in the early days; he led two columns of guerrillas down from the mountains and halfway across the island, right under Batista's nose. He was killed in a plane crash in December, 1959, and has since become a kind of people's hero; his portrait stands on the mantelpieces of farmhouses as if he were a saint. When it turned out that I knew who he was, the cigar-maker's wife began to cry.

The cigar-maker would not be paid, although I tried hard, for the family and their room looked so very poor. So finally I went to a corner stall and bought a bag of chocolates, which I took back to his wife. We all shook hands, and then I got into my Hertz *Nacionalizada* Anglia and drove back to Havana.

LETTER FROM VATICAN CITY

Xavier Rynne

DECEMBER 25, 1965

"T HE EVENT," AS theologian Karl Barth has called Vatican Council II, reached its formal close here yesterday, though it may be said that its real work is just beginning. The idea of holding the Council came to Pope John XXIII on January 20, 1959. ("The first to be surprised by this proposal of mine was myself," he wrote in his journal.) It was convened on October 11, 1962, and after Pope John's death it was reconvened by Pope Paul VI. In its four annual sessions, the Council has promulgated sixteen decrees. According to the official record-keepers, some twenty-five hundred Council Fathers cast a total of a million two hundred thousand individual ballots on the various texts put to them, and they wrote some six thousand speeches, of which fourteen hundred were delivered on the Council floor. It was not the longest Council in the history of the Church—the Council of Trent holds the record, of eighteen years—but it was beyond question the most important religious event this century has yet seen. At the beginning, Pope John declared the Council's twofold purpose to be *aggiornamento,* or the updating, of the Roman Catholic Church, and the promotion of Christian unity. The former purpose has been carried out to a considerable, though not complete, extent by the sixteen decrees, whose implementation represents the work that has only started. To symbolize the second purpose, Pope Paul in the closing days of the Council, despite protests from some Council Fathers, decided to hold a historic religious ceremony. On Saturday, December 4th, at the basilica of St. Paul's Outside the Walls, the Pope joined in an interfaith prayer service with a group of Orthodox, Protestant, and other non-Catholic churchmen who have been attending the Council as observer delegates. Many Council Fathers attended (it was not open to the public), but it was the first time that any Pope had ever participated in an interdenominational religious service. It consisted of prayers, psalms, lessons from Scripture, and hymns. The lesson in English was read by Dr. Albert C. Outler, professor of theology at Southern Methodist University, in Dallas; the lesson in French was read by Father Pierre Michalon, a Catholic priest and a Council theologian; the lesson in Greek was read by the Archimandrite Maximos Aghiorgoussis, rector of the Greek Orthodox parish church in Rome. The hymn "Now Thank We All Our God," in which all joined in English, was written by the seventeenth-century German Lutheran composer Johann Cruger. Later, Pope Paul received each of the observer delegates in the same room of the adjoining Benedictine monastery in which Pope John in 1959 first announced his idea of the Council to a group of cardinals, who greeted the news in total silence. In the course of a moving talk, delivered in French, Paul said, "We would like to have you with us always." He said that the Council had shown that reunion would eventually be achieved "gradually, loyally, and generously." In a passage that particularly impressed his hearers, he acknowledged that there had been "failures" on the part of Catholics in the past, referring to the now outmoded polemical approach to reunion and to insistence on matters of prestige. He assured them that henceforth the Roman Catholic Church would be guided by the spirit of charity proclaimed by the Apostle of the Gentiles, St. Paul. As a sign, he pointed to the fact that the Council had issued no "anathemas but only invitations." He concluded with the hope that the Council would "cause us all to recognize the blessed door of Truth." As one of the Protestant observers commented, "It was one of the most impressive moments of the whole Council." . . .

· · ·

The Pope's remarks to the Council on November 18th about the reform of the Curia and, more recently, his Motu Proprio reforming the Holy Office make it obvious that what he plans for this body is not a revolution but a gradual conversion. As he himself said, "The desired transformation will seem slow and partial, but it cannot be otherwise if due respect is to be had for persons and traditions. But this transformation will surely come." As if to put teeth into these last words, on December 6th, two days before the Council ended, he published the long-awaited new statute for the Holy Office. Not only has that formidable office been given a new name—the Congregation for the Doctrine of the Faith—but it is henceforth to be oriented not so much toward the repression and condemnation of error as toward the fostering and positive study of "new questions and opinions." It has been enjoined specifically to adopt a more positive attitude toward international theological congresses, and to establish closer ties with the Pontifical Biblical Commission—in other words, to abandon its obstructive attitude toward modern theology and theologians. The new office is also to make wider use of consultants throughout the world (no longer relying exclusively on theologians resident in Rome) and is to accord those who have been accused of error in matters of faith the opportunity of defending themselves. Two of the men who have suffered greatly at the hands of the Holy Office in recent years—Fathers John Courtney Murray, of the United States, and Henri de Lubac, of France, both of them Council *periti* and Jesuits—were pointedly invited by Pope Paul to concelebrate with him at a public session of the Council on November 18th, and the latter also dined with the Pope on the eve of the publication of the Holy Office decree. Although other details about the projected reform of the Curia have not yet been made public, it is known from interviews with Cardinal Roberti, president of the papal commission in charge of Curial reform, and from other officials that greater use will be made of laymen and that a separate congregation will probably be established staffed largely by them. There is also talk that an age limit may be set for the heads of certain offices, and that some key positions will no longer be for life. Finally, the cardinals and heads of various offices may be summoned to meet regularly with the Pope in a kind of ecclesiastical cabinet. Nothing of the kind exists at the present time. Instead, such coordination as there is has been in the hands of an unholy interlocking "directorate" of Holy Office men. It is understood that when Pope Paul invited the aged heads of Curial offices to resign last spring, several of them, including Cardinal Giuseppe Pizzardo, obstructionist head of the crucial Congregation of Seminaries and Universities, replied that they were prepared to serve him unto death. That is why the Pope is now seriously considering making all top positions temporary. . . .

· · ·

Few Council documents have aroused as much controversy or been followed with such close interest as the famous declaration on the Jews, now incorporated in a broader declaration on relations with non-Christians, including Hindus, Buddhists, and Moslems. Although the broader declaration is destined to become the Magna Carta of the newly formed Secretariat for Relations with Non-Christian Religions, under Cardinal Marella, it is the original declaration that public attention has been almost exclusively fixed on. Its history has been stormy. It originated as an idea of Pope John XXIII, who created the Secretariat for Christian Unity, presided over by Cardinal Bea. A suitable text was written early in 1961 and was presented that May to the Central Commission, which was empowered to decide what texts were to be discussed at the opening session of the Council. Bowing to pressure not only from Arab states but from reactionary forces in the Church, the Commission refused to accept the draft. So nothing was done about it during the first session. In December, 1962, after Pope John had recovered from his illness, he had Cardinal Bea revise the document, and gave the revision his approval. To avoid objections from a new reviewing body, it was decided to annex the document to the schema "On Ecumenism." When this came up for discussion at the second session, under Pope Paul, it was suddenly announced, just as Cardinal Bea was preparing to introduce the text, that the discussion would have to be postponed until the next session because of "lack of time." Pressure had again been exerted from the usual quarters. When the text actually reached the floor of the Council, at the third session, it was so altered that Archbishop Heenan, of Westminster, one of the members of the Secretariat for Christian Unity, declared it to be virtually unrecognizable. The approval of this bastardized text—to the extent that he did approve it—was probably Pope Paul's greatest tactical mistake. After two days of debate, it became clear that the previous text would have to be restored. The final version represents a compromise with the restored version, which was approved for submission to the Council on November 20, 1964. The passage rejecting the charge of "deicide" was strengthened, though the word itself was omitted. While the restored version both "deplored and condemned" hatred and persecution of Jews, the final version merely "deplores" them, but it does inveigh against "displays of anti-Semitism directed against Jews," this time mentioning the word "anti-Semitism" explicitly. While the old version warned Christians not to teach anything that could give rise to hatred and persecution of Jews, the final text urges them not to teach "anything inconsistent with the truth of the Gospel and with the spirit of Christ."

It was a foregone conclusion that the document would win a majority when it was put to a vote on October 14th and 15th, the only question being whether three groups—those disappointed by the omission of the word "deicide"; Bishop Carli's followers, who opposed the declaration on theological grounds; and those who felt that there were still political objections—would be able to register enough *non-placet* votes to impair the unanimity with which Council texts are supposed to be approved. As usual, the Fathers were deluged with literature beforehand. Bishop Carli's group urged *non-placet* votes on the grounds that the declaration favored indifferentism by tending to regard all religions as being on the same level, that it would retard the "conversion of the Gentiles," and that it would put an end to missionary work. One of the most violent pamphlets was a four-page affair signed by thirty-one so-called Catholic organizations, most of which promptly disavowed any connection with it; it turned out to be a hoax, concocted by a Latin-American crank. So much tension had been generated, however, that the authorities naturally took seriously an anonymous letter received by Cardinal Marella from a person threatening—half in French and half in German to blow up St. Peter's and the whole Council if the Jewish document was voted. Extra police were detailed to guard the building. Except for a resounding crash when some workmen's scaffolding collapsed, the voting proceeded smoothly, and the result—1,763 *placet* and 250 *non-placet*—insured that the document would be promulgated. Many bishops who disliked the omission of the word "deicide" nevertheless voted for the text, because they feared that too large a negative vote would cause the Pope to withdraw the document. They considered that the present document was better than no document at all. As one of the *periti* involved in the drafting of the various versions put the matter, "If it had not been for the publicity surrounding the previous versions, the present text would probably be regarded as excellent."

· · ·

Apart from religious liberty, the subject that caused the biggest stir during the final session of the Council was Schema 13, "On the Church in the World Today." Covering seventy-four pages in the English version, it purports to speak the Council's mind on a number of weighty problems not fully or adequately dealt with in other Council texts. The subjects include the role of man in the world today, the role of the Church, the dignity of marriage, economic and social inequalities, the advancement of culture, and international peace. Dorothy Day, an inveterate pacifist and campaigner for social justice, has well described its contents as "bits and pieces of ideas gathered from everywhere," adding, "I'm not sure that the bishops realize that the text takes in all points of view. At times, it seems contradictory. That explains why there are such varied reactions." As another commentator put it, the Church had explained its raison d'être in the schema "De Ecclesia," and Schema 13 was intended to define its *agir*, or mode of action.

The debate on Part I of the document soon narrowed down to an intense discussion of just one short paragraph, on the problem of atheism, which had been inserted to satisfy the demands of numerous bishops who wanted a clear statement condemning both atheism and Communism. The new text was carefully drafted in such a way as to avoid excessive condemnation while putting emphasis on what was lacking in atheism. No mention was made of Communism at all. The position of moderation taken by the subcommission that drafted the text was naturally supported by those who felt, like Patriarch Maximos IV and Cardinal Koenig, of Vienna, that "Christians have had a large responsibility for the rise and spread of atheism." The Patriarch said, "Condemning Marxism cannot save humanity from atheism. Rather, we must denounce the causes of atheistic Communism. . . . Many who call themselves atheists are not necessarily against the Church. In their own minds, they are only seeking for a clear idea of God. . . . They are scandalized by a Christianity that often proves itself to be so egotistical. We, too, should be opposed to the exploitation of man by man." Although some prelates from Italy and Latin America came out strongly in favor of a resounding condemnation of Communism, those from behind the Iron Curtain were generally content to endorse Cardinal Alfrink's judgment: "Since the Church has often condemned Communism, why repeat what has already been done?" A petition claiming to have four hundred and fifty signatures and asking for a declaration expressly condemning Communism, circulated by the indomitable Bishop Carli, plagued the final days of the Council. While it was true, as the Bishop argued, that previous councils had generally condemned something, the expressed intention of Vatican II was to be a pastoral, rather than a doctrinal, Council. In the end, the petition was rejected as incompatible with this aim.

A final burst of energy was generated by the debate on the morality of nuclear warfare and of conscientious objection. The wording of this section of Schema 13 was less explicit in this regard than the simple words of Pope Paul at the United Nations: "No more war! War never again." It tried to satisfy both those who feel strongly that all war should be banned and those who believe that under present circumstances an unconditional appeal of this kind would be unrealistic. To help the Council reach a right decision, twenty women, including Dorothy Day, fasted in a Roman house on the Via dell'Anima throughout the debate. The group included Catholics (the majority), Protestants, and one Christian Scientist. The attempt of Archbishop Roberts, of England, to plead on the floor for a stronger section on conscientious objection had no more success this year than last. Although he had submitted his speech to the Secretariat well in advance, in August, he was again denied the right to speak. The mood of the assembly was decidedly favorable to a strong pronouncement on peace, however, even if it was not prepared to endorse everything that the Archbishop proposed. When the aged, nearly blind Cardinal Ottaviani, of the Holy Office, rose to deliver a memorized speech in Latin pleading for the banning of war, he got a ready hearing. He wanted to ban not only all forms of violence but ideological warfare as well, "because it can so easily lead to real war." His fervently delivered peroration brought down the house: "In the spirit of a United Europe and the United States of North America as well as Brazil, I wish that there would be one world republic made up of all nations." (Significantly, this visionary speech came from one of those whom Pope John labelled "prophets of doom" at the original session of Vatican Council II.)

In the closing days, a group of American bishops attempted to change Chapter V of Schema 13, which condemned nuclear stockpiling, on the ground that it discriminated against Western nations whose possession of nuclear arms guaranteed the political freedom of large areas of the world. Archbishop Philip Hannan, of New Orleans, together with Cardinal Spellman and others, circulated a letter urging the Fathers to vote *non placet* on Chapter V, or, if their objections to it were not met, *non placet* on the schema as a whole. There were four ballots on this question. In the first, on December 4th, Chapter V received 483 negative votes, but the bishops' efforts collapsed completely in the final vote, on December 7th, when Schema 13 was approved unchanged by a vote of 2,309 to 75.

. . .

It was over birth control that the Council nearly came to grief during its closing weeks. On November 24th, two weeks before its scheduled close, it received a letter from Cardinal Cicognani, Secretary of State, containing a last-minute amendment for Schema 13: Pope Paul, it appeared, wanted a clearer reference to the present doctrine of the Church banning artificial contraception. Since the Pope had previously withdrawn the birth-control question from the jurisdiction of the Council, reserving it to himself, and had appointed a special commission of experts to advise him in making a final pronouncement on the matter, many Council Fathers felt they were now being asked to approve legislation without adequate discussion. Tempers began to soar, and for a while it looked as if the dark days that marked the close of the third session were about to be repeated. Fortunately, as a result of protests by leading commission members, such as Cardinal Léger, of Montreal, and a discreet but firm move on the part of the lay auditors, two days later another letter came from Cardinal Cicognani stating that the Pope was only offering suggestions and not ordering an amendment. The commission adroitly turned the issue by adding Pope Paul's more liberal statement of June, 1964, to the two other papal statements, and the Pope expressed himself satisfied with their work. As expected, the Council has ended with no resolution of the birth-control problem.

The Pope's reference at the U.N. to birth control, urging the world to increase the food supply and decrease poverty rather than the population, revealed his awareness that the world expects him to make a pronouncement on the subject. He stated frankly in the Cavallari interview that he did not know the answer to the problem. "The world asks us what we think about [birth control] and we must give an answer," he said. "We cannot remain silent. It is difficult to know what to say. For centuries the Church has not had to face such problems. And this matter is a little strange for churchmen to be handling, and even embarrassing from the human point of view. So the committees are meeting. Papers and reports have been piling up. We have had to do a great deal of studying, you know. But now we have to make a decision. Only we can do that. Deciding is not as easy as studying. But we have to say something. What can we say? God must enlighten us."

Paul's quandary over this problem is similar to the undogmatic and searching approach of the majority of the Council Fathers to the many new and difficult problems that confronted them. This, as we know from history, is quite unlike the juridical and dogmatic attitudes of earlier Councils. Some answers have been provided by Vatican II, but more questions have been raised. As Dr. A. C. Outler, the Methodist observer delegate, remarked before a gathering of the American hierarchy in Rome shortly before the Council's end, "Far less has been accomplished than has been made possible. More frontiers have been opened than occupied." In retrospect, Vatican II's crowning achievement will probably be to have opened doors.

ON THE SEVENTH DAY
THEY STOPPED

Flora Lewis

JULY 1, 1967 (SIX DAY WAR)

IT WILL BE some time before the precise details of how the first shots were fired in the Arab-Israeli war can be set down with full assurance. But everybody in Israel has a story about the first shots he happened to hear. They came as no real surprise, because those of us who were there had all seen fear and anger pressing, always more urgently, for release. But they still came as a shock.

A few minutes before eleven-thirty on Monday morning, June 5th, in Jerusalem, I heard rifle pings. The sound was not unusual in Jerusalem. A number of streets on the Jewish side of the city had been blocked for years by cement or metal walls, built to spoil the view of snipers from the other side. I happened to be walking down Jaffa Road, carrying my typewriter, to a car I had rented an hour earlier. Renting the car had been a precaution, but neither the solicitous girl at the rental agency nor I had mentioned the reason while we filled out the forms. The radio had broadcast a special bulletin at 8:10 A.M. announcing an outbreak of firing on the Sinai front. Shortly afterward, there had been an air-raid alert in Tel Aviv. At nine, instead of giving the news, the broadcaster had droned out a coded mobilization order, naming each unit and its station. Many men and women had already gone in the successive call-ups during three weeks of growing menace. Now there would be no more drivers and probably no more taxis, because Israel's reserve forces draw upon civilian vehicles as well as civilian manpower. But neither the broadcasts nor the first few shots really made it clear that war had started. There had been so many incidents, so many explosions. Zvi Avrami, the manager of the King David Hotel, where I was staying, had been eager to discuss the situation as he gave me street directions that morning. "It is very depressing, Madam," he had said to me. "If it comes, we'll win. But who needs it?" Then he had gone off to get his uniform and report for duty. (The next time I saw him, he was running the St. George Hotel, on the other side of Jerusalem, where occupation headquarters had been established. But that was much later—a hundred hours later.)

As I walked along Jaffa Road that morning, I became aware that the rifle fire was not stopping after two or three cracks. In a minute or so, I heard machine-gun bursts, and then there was the thud of a mortar. Some of the people on the street ran. I didn't know for sure where the car was, so I ducked into an alcove leading to a shop and found with great relief that I still had my city map in my hand. I studied it while I waited for the shooting to end. Across the street, a young man was carefully washing his store window before putting up tape.

Even the most expected of battles must take a while to penetrate the unwilling mind. That is what happened in Jerusalem. The shelters had long been prepared. A wave of panic buying of food and candles had come and gone a week before. I knew that Tamar Kollek, the wife of Jerusalem's Mayor, had had some unhappy talks with her neighbors, because, although sand had been distributed throughout the town for fire prevention in case of air raids, the Kolleks and their neighbors were still waiting for their share. "I told them our street was last," Mrs. Kollek said. "And the people weren't pleased." In her own modest apartment, the only precaution she had taken was to move her husband's collection of pre-Roman earthenware jugs down from the top of a bookshelf to the floor, along with some framed gouaches of the Marc Chagall window designs for the Hadassah Medical Center that had been given to the Kolleks by the painter. A large collection of ancient jewelry, opalescent glass, and other archeological finds that the Kolleks had assembled over the years were not moved from two crammed vitrines in the sitting room. (The Mayor, known to nearly everyone in the city as Teddy—Israel being perhaps the only country in the world to use first names even more quickly than America—told me later he had not thought Jerusalem would come under heavy attack. He had expected some shooting, of course, and quite possibly an effort to cut off the Israelis in the city, but not sustained direct shelling. "It was too obvious that it could work both ways—that the Jordanians were just as vulnerable as we," he said, in weary puzzlement when it was over. "But King Hussein put his armies under an Egyptian commander, and he lost control.")

When the attack did come, the sirens and the radio warned everyone into the shelters. There was no compulsion, no pushing, no curfew. You could roam the empty streets if you wished. But almost everybody knew just what he had to do, and did it. I never saw or heard of a case of panic—not even a forgotten dog howling in the road.

I found the car, which luckily had not been hit, and drove back to the King David Hotel. It is only a few hundred feet from the border, within easy range on three sides, but it is built of the rosy Jerusalem stone that gives the city both its beauty and its solid strength. (Throughout Jerusalem, I noticed afterward, the rough blocks of stone had resisted everything except direct shell hits.) An empty bus was standing in the middle of the road blocking the hotel's driveway, so I parked across the street in front of the Y.M.C.A. and then ran. The bus passengers, half of them children, were in the hotel. They had been coming up to Jerusalem from a village down the valley when they had suddenly found that they were being fired at. The driver, a dark Yemenite, had stomped down on the accelerator and zigzagged as evasively as possible around mountain curves until he reached the first big building. There he had slammed on the brakes and ordered everybody out to shelter. The hotel barman, Reuven Gat—formerly Robert Guth, of Vienna—was distributing free lemonade to the children.

Men in battle dress with steel helmets, barely recognizable as the clerks and waiters who had been wearing very different uniforms when I had gone out two hours before, were milling around near the door, their rifles and tommy guns tossed casually on the carpet. . . .

About twelve-thirty, a shell fell some fifteen feet in front of the hotel entrance—the one unexposed side. It smashed a tree and sent blast waves through the lobby. Fragments of the shell wounded several men. They were given first aid and taken away in an ambulance. At that point, the rest of us were urged down to the basement night club, which served as a shelter, its high windows having been sand-bagged. Some Englishmen were at the bar, drinking gin-and-tonic. To my surprise, I found that lunch was being served. It seemed a good idea to eat, because there was no telling when there would be another chance. Reuven Gat recited the menu—grapefruit or noodle soup, liver or boiled chicken, salad, pastry or compote. He was nervous, but he took all the greater care to polish the glasses, pour the wine for tasting, serve from the left, and remove plates from the right. It seemed an odd way to serve a meal under such circumstances, but he worked with the same extreme consideration all through the week. (After the war ended, he learned that his son had been knifed to death while trying to rescue some wounded friends in the Old City. I went to speak to him when I heard about it. "His name was Avraham," he told me. "We called him Avi. He was nineteen and a half. He didn't live yet. He was only starting a life." The father's face was frozen in a peculiar grimace, and he scrubbed the bar all the time he talked, rubbing so hard it seemed that he would have worn through a thinner piece of wood.) . . .

. . .

Throughout the night, we learned later, major battles were being fought at the edges of the southern desert. The Gaza Strip had been cut off, and the northernmost Israeli column had split, in order to begin encirclement of Egypt's 7th Division. To the Israeli staff's surprise, the Egyptians had diluted their tremendous force along the Sinai coastal road and the parallel inland road on the Beersheba-Ismailia line. They were moving south. The Israelis could not know whether this was the start of an Egyptian effort to drive across the southern half of Israel, possibly to link up with Jordanian forces and cut off Elath, or whether the Egyptians, believing that the Israeli main thrust would come down the coast of the Gulf of Aqaba to the Strait of Tiran and the strongpoint at Sharm-el-Sheik, were moving to block that virtually impassable route. In any case, the reason mattered less than the opportunity the Egyptian maneuvers offered.

Flexibility based on thorough planning is one of the main elements of the Israeli Army's strength. It was born of necessity. The Jewish fighters in Palestine and, since they built their state, in Israel have always been outnumbered in both men and equipment. Ben-Gurion had long before developed the concept of flexible response as the principle for protection of the early, isolated settlements. The defense forces, in those days called Hashomer, were part-time farmers and part-time soldiers. Strict economy of weapons, quick reaction and change of plan, the best possible communications and intelligence, and, above all, the use of imaginative variations on the military norm were the rules worked out to reverse the odds. Those ground rules were not changed in the nineteen-thirties, when Hashomer gave way to the Jewish underground army, Haganah, nor have they now been changed. General Yesheyahu Gavish, who commanded the entire battle against Egypt, put it simply: "All our planning has to be for a brief war—quick attack, quick advance, quick victory, and home again to work." Government officials estimate that it cost Israel fifteen to twenty million dollars a day in lost crops and production to maintain its partial mobilization in the three weeks of tension before the war. Three months of that would have ruined the state.

Brigadier General Ariel Sharon, a towering man with a soft face and a great soft middle bulging over the top of his camouflage trousers, commanded the Israeli division ordered to break through Abu Ageila on the Beersheba-Ismailia line. He met well-entrenched and superior forces, and when it was over he gave an explanation of his success in the form of a recollection of the action he had seen in an earlier campaign: "I would say the Egyptian is a good soldier, a disciplined soldier, but I think the commanders are very poor. I would not trust them. We do not think they have any fighting spirit. They are very good where everything is very simple, they are well organized, and they are very good at shooting. I must tell you a story about something that happened twelve years ago. We attacked an Egyptian battalion in the same area, at Sabha, near Nitzana, and managed in a few minutes to destroy the position. Then a few weeks later we attacked the Syrians, and we put the prisoners together, the officers separate. The Syrians asked the Egyptians how it could have happened that a battalion in a fortified defensive position, mined and equipped with heavy artillery, was defeated in a few minutes. The Egyptians answered, 'Those Jews just won't attack in proper order.' "

Attack itself, preempting the choice of time and place, is, the Israelis believe, an indispensable part of their country's defense strategy. Israel has no fallback lines, no reserves in either geography or manpower. The whole country is the front, and all that lies behind it is the sea. As the Israelis see it, if they did not fight beyond their borders, they would have little left to fight for. In the same way, the forces must all be used at once. The regular Army numbers some forty thousand. Even Jordan, the least populous and, since 1948, the least aggressive of Israel's neighbors—apart from Lebanon—had an army of fifty-five thousand. Egypt had put more than a hundred thousand men in the Sinai Desert and still had armies left to guard its Nile heartland.

I asked Major General Itzhak Rabin, the Chief of Staff, how he accounted for the vastly superior gunnery and technical expertise that enabled his tank crews of schoolteachers, businessmen, bus drivers, and waiters to pick off Egypt's professionals. (Of course, air supremacy made a crucial difference, but 90 percent of the approximately six hundred Egyptian tanks destroyed were taken out by Israeli tanks. On the second day of the war, one Israeli tank battalion finished off a brigade of a hundred and sixty-seven Egyptian tanks by what the generals call "sniping"— one shot at a time.) General Rabin said the answer was training, although most of the Israeli tankmen are civilians eleven months of the year. Then he added, "And it has something to do with the people, too."

Israel mobilized requires almost every able body, either under arms or to operate the most urgently essential services. Even children helped in the period of partial mobilization by replacing postmen and delivering milk. Of course, some exceptions have to be made in a population of two million seven hundred thousand. The quarter of a million Arabs inside Israel's borders before the war were not called to serve. Neither were members of Jerusalem's ultra-orthodox Naturei Karta sect, who preach that all violent resistance is a sin, even though they do not hesitate to stone those who violate the Sabbath by driving cars, or their codes of modesty by wearing sleeveless dresses and short skirts, or their view of chastity by permitting boys and girls to swim together. Obviously, they would be no boon to the armed forces. In many parts of the country, local rabbis of just as orthodox persuasion endorsed the government's call to defend the state, and men went off to war, but the extremists of Jerusalem would have no part in it. Some of them refuse even to recognize the State of Israel—to use its postage stamps or to pay its taxes—because they hold to the Biblical text that prophesies restoration of the Jewish nation in its ancient home by the Messiah. Since there has been no Messiah, they insist there can be no legal state. (When the Old City of Jerusalem was taken, the troops had to pass through the orthodox quarter of Mea Shearim, many of them driving captured Jordanian tanks and trucks. The people massed at the Mandelbaum Gate—the only crossing point between the two sides of Jerusalem before the war—and lined the streets to cheer. For once, the Hasidim, in the fur hats and black caftans they have copied from fourteenth-century Polish aristocrats, allowed others to mingle with them and did not cover their faces at the sight of a camera to prevent violation of the Biblical injunction against images. Their young boys, in knickers and black stockings, jumped and shouted with excitement as the victorious warriors passed. The older men watched with evidently torn feelings. They really did not approve, and their demeanor showed it. Nevertheless, for the first time in nineteen years, they would be able to make pilgrimages to the Jewish Holy Places—above all to the Wailing Wall. With mournfully ecstatic faces, even they seemed to be celebrating the fruits of the violence they condemn.)

Once the fight began, there was no pause. In the south, the Israeli columns fought for seventy-two hours without a break, day and night. When a replacement unit was needed at the vicious battle of Mitla Pass, deep in the desert, General Avram Yaffe moved one into line without a halt in firing. "It was difficult to make the maneuver without our own tanks shooting at each other," he said later, with a diffident smile to cover what seemed to be embarrassment at sounding boastful. "But we took care and we did it without a mishap." General Yaffe, a very tall and broad man who happily describes himself as more bear than man, heads Israel's Nature Conservation Board when he is not called upon to head a tank division. He knows the desert as an Englishman knows his garden. During prewar mobilization, he stopped more than once to climb out of a tank and collect a few dry seeds, which he placed tenderly in matchboxes. "This plant doesn't exist anywhere else in Israel," he remarked with delight on one occasion, according to a colleague. "It must be sturdy to live here in the desert." He has organized effective campaigns to save two species of gazelle that were on the verge of extinction in the Middle East. His great dream is to acquire eight or ten oryx—a magnificent Arabian Desert deer, very few of which are left—and turn them out to breed in a Sinai nature preserve. . . .

. . .

Late that evening, I ran into Arthur Veysey, of the Chicago *Tribune*, who had just arrived from Jordanian territory. He had staked out what might have been the royal box for the night battle, and he invited me to see some of the sights from it. It was a large balcony, complete with lounge chairs, on the fourth floor of the King David, facing the Old City wall. Reuven Gat, the barman, had waited up after the cook had gone, and he provided a bottle of well-chilled *rosé* and a stack of matzoth—all he could find—for me to take upstairs. On that we dined as we watched the spectacle that was being played out all around us.

The sense of theatre was inescapable. We knew that men were dying of real wounds, that children were hunched underground in real terror, that the earth was being heaped with the garbage of war. But all that we could actually see was a scene of incomparable drama, and even beauty. At the far right of our panorama, a whole hillside flickered in flame. The crops of Ramat Rachel, an Israeli settlement on a finger of Jewish Jerusalem surrounded by Jordan, had been set afire by shells. At center left, the tower of the Victoria Augusta Hospital was burning like a Yule log atop the Mount of Olives. There were tracers, and an occasional flash and boom, but when a non-explosive noise broke in it was always something thoroughly bucolic—a lone cock or, for a moment, a donkey. Then, suddenly, the darkness was driven back. The Israelis had mounted a giant searchlight on one of their tall buildings. Its beam flooded the entire horizon in a milky glow. Above, on a line drawn as sharply as the line of a proscenium, was black velvet sky speckled with tinsel stars— perhaps a bit too bright and too profuse for a perfectly tasteful setting. The outlines, the shadows, the mutely luminescent colors of the landscape beneath were exactly right. The Garden of Gethsemane, the village of Bethany, the towers and spires and domes and minarets that represent in stone the origin of universal faiths stood out in detail, seemingly eternal beside the cypress groves. The buzz and the racing wing lights of a pair of fighters arched overhead toward the horizon and disappeared. A minute later, two or three great orange flares dawdled down against the backdrop. The searchlight snapped off when they disappeared. It was as though the curtain had come down. But we waited, and there was more to the spectacle. First came the sound of shells being fired from big guns behind us. One—two—three—four. We counted the seconds until the explosive flashes rose behind the hills, and counted again, this time to six, for the thunder to return. It happened over and over again in that Biblical panorama, with its undelivered message of peace. Gradually, through the night, the firing toward us from the other side diminished. The rifles and machine guns never stopped altogether, but they seemed irrelevant to the spectacle. We never even thought to duck behind the balcony wall, though we took care to show no light.

The ground attack was pressed at dawn. All the hills were taken. Pushing down from just beneath the Garden of Gethsemane, the Israelis broke through the Old City wall at St. Stephen's Gate, called the Lions' Gate by the Israelis. They used tanks and mortars in support, but mainly the job had to be done by the infantry. The stones ahead were sacred to three religions. Normally, the Israeli Army is extremely stingy with the lives of its men and spendthrift with covering fire. This time, men were offered in order to spare the buildings. Nearly a third of Israel's battle dead, in a war that included a single engagement of a thousand tanks, were lost at the entrances to Jerusalem.

A few minutes after eleven on Wednesday morning, I saw a white flag flutter above the Old City wall where it makes a right-angle turn on Mount Zion. The heavy guns spoke rarely now, but the small-arms fire kept up in all directions. It was then, I learned later, that the first Israelis reached the Wailing Wall, which had belonged to Jordan since the Arab Legion took the Old City in 1948. I was told that it was a colonel who first broke through the narrow gate off Mount Temple, ran down the two flights of steep stone stairs, and threw himself at the foot of the Wall in tears. A corporal following him was shot to death by a sniper as he leaped down the last steps. The sun had dried his spilled blood into dark blotches by the time I got there.

. . .

On the afternoon of Wednesday, June 7th, I entered the Old City through the Jaffa Gate, open by then, and walked up the Via Dolorosa. All the houses were tightly shuttered. One thin and faded Jordanian woman, dressed in dust-caked black but equipped with a child's undershirt tied to a long stick as her sign of peaceful intent, came boldly up to speak to all newcomers. She was looking for her baby, she said. Had anyone seen it? She hurried off, knowing the answer before it could be translated.

There were mounds of dirt, spoiled food, scraps of burned clothing, lumps of mattress stuffing, and jumbles of wire and stone scattered in the narrow streets. The city was without water, electricity, or sanitation of any kind, and it seemed at that point to be almost without Arabs. . . . In the few hours before Israeli soldiers had been ordered to seal off all Holy Places to insure their safety, I met one Jew who, entering the Old City for the first time, had just visited the Wailing Wall. Though he was not pious, he was moved to perform the old custom of writing the name of his son on a slip of paper to push between the crevices of the ancient stones, because, he told me, "It was what my father wished to do for me, and my grandfather for him, and all the generations of my ancestors for two thousand years, and *I* am the one who has come." At the door of the Dome of the Rock, he took off his shoes, saying, "This, too, is a Holy Place, to be respected in its own way."

Israel's President, Zalman Shazar, its founder, David Ben-Gurion, its Prime Minister, Levi Eshkol, and its Minister of Defense, Moshe Dayan, all made trips to the Wall. Then the chief rabbinate of Israel met and studied the old texts and proclaimed that no Jew should set foot on

Temple Mount until the Messiah arrived to begin the promised building. No one was much troubled by the proclamation. An exaltation swept Israel at the thought that the Wall belonged to Jews once more. As Ben-Gurion reached the Wall, he said, "It is the second-greatest day of my life." The first, he added, was the day his foot touched the soil of Zion in 1906; he ignored the day in 1948 when he proclaimed the rebirth of the Jewish state. Dayan said that Israel would never give up the Wall again. A lesser government official, who could not resist sneaking away from his work for an hour on such a day, said sheepishly, on the way back, "I was so overwhelmed I didn't know what to pray. So I prayed that the Wall would remain with us forever and we could come back again and again to give the right prayers quietly."

The Army had strictly forbidden anyone without special authorization to cross from Jewish Jerusalem. Otherwise, all of Israel would have tried to crush into the stricken Old City on the day the Wall was taken. As it was, thousands straggled through, though intermittent sniping continued and some people stepped on mines in an attempt to scamper across unguarded points in no man's land. The result of all these dangerous pilgrimages was an extraordinary collection of the children of Israel before the Wall—husky, sun-tanned blondes in torn khakis; dark-skinned, smooth-cheeked young men who spoke Spanish; dignitaries with puffy pink faces; a girl with flowing red hair in an elegant beige pants suit; soldiers who were orthodox, but not to the extreme, their shoulder-length side curls hanging incongruously below Army helmets that were tilted back to leave room to strap a phylactery on their foreheads; and General Shlomo Goren, Chief Rabbi of the Army, carrying a small blue-sheathed Torah that he had taken into battle in 1948, 1956, and again in 1967. Though Israel is by proclamation a Jewish state, the bulk of its people are not customarily pious. Many are openly irritated at the theocratic rules imposed because the country has always had to have coalition governments that give the religious parties extra leverage. But the most determinedly agnostic and the most devout stood with visibly equal joy before the Wailing Wall. . . .

. . .

The war ended Saturday night in Galilee and on the Syrian front. From the Mount of Beatitudes, a plateau on a low slope north of the Sea of Galilee, you can look across to the mountain ridges where the most ferocious combat took place. Most of the Syrian emplacements were constructed of the rocks and soil of those hills, making for a perfect camouflage, and the new ruins I saw there were almost indistinguishable from the ancient ones. There are remains of British police posts, Turkish forts, Crusaders' towers, and Roman strongholds, and there are memories of conquests stretching much further back toward the origins of civilized life. The surface of the sea was tranquil, glazed a dull silver by the sun. All around it were the landmarks of ancient and modern human violence.

Near a post where there had been an artillery emplacement, I found a notebook and some letters scattered on the ground beside a burned tank, among boots, shreds of clothing, and half-eaten rations. I could not tell whether the men to whom these things had belonged had fled or were lying underground nearby; the advancing Israelis buried most of the dead very quickly—the enemy's as well as their own—to avoid epidemic diseases.

Inside the cover of the notebook, a soldier had written the names and Army post numbers of half a dozen friends. On the single sheet left in it, he had jotted—if the graceful curves of Arabic are susceptible to jotting—some notes that were apparently intended for an essay. I had a friend translate them for me, and they read:

My Life

1. The world is a playground.
2. I will not feel happy until after the fight.
3. We want to be free, not slaves.
4. Fear and fear make stronger fighting.
5. We meet events as they come.
6. I wouldn't fight if I was afraid.
7. To make a distinction between truth and falsehood.

The date set down was February 2, 1967. The letters were much older, going back to August, 1964. The shortest letter, which was undated, read:

From conscripted soldier Rashed Ghayal 3373 A.P. 886.
   To conscripted soldier Midhat Khadir 3217 A.P. 893.
   All the Arabs are united.
   Free and united and together.

To dear brother and good friend. I hope you are in the best of health. Amen. My brother Midhat, my first question is of you and your health and I ask God to treat you well. Amen. We, too, are all right. Amen. I miss your shining face. First my regards and a thousand regards. Regards to my brother Ali Rahbi if he is near to you. Best regards to any who ask about me.

And Peace.

The letter was not signed. The longer letters—one from a father to his son written by a professional scribe, others from sons to fathers—differed only in listing very many more names to whom "a thousand regards" should be sent or from whom they should be received. There were no descriptions of life, no personal comment, but there emerged both piety and an intense feeling for family and friendship. And many of them ended, as that short one did, with a formal wish that the recipient should enjoy the blessings of peace. The envelopes had been dropped on the sixth day of the war, along with the bullets, shells, and bombs that rained on the ground. On the seventh day, there was no more fighting. But neither was there peace.

LETTER FROM PRAGUE

Joseph Wechsberg

APRIL 27, 1968

April 15

ONE MORNING ABOUT a week ago, I noticed a small crowd in front of a bookstore on the Příkopy, a broad avenue leading toward Wenceslaus Square. Stepping closer, I saw in the window of the store an old photograph of Tomáš Garrigue Masaryk—Czechoslovakia's President-Liberator, as he was known until the Communists took over, in 1948. Above the picture was a sentence from one of Masaryk's books: "Our renascence must be a renascence of the soul—we must again look for the truth, listen to the truth, study the truth, love the truth, speak the truth, defend the truth until death." The hush among the people at the window seemed to shut out the noise of the street. Men and women bowed their heads; some had tears in their eyes. An elderly woman said, to no one in particular, "Thank God! I had lost hope that I would ever see *him* again." She was not exaggerating. For the past twenty years, Masaryk had officially been an un-person. It was dangerous to mention his name. Ten weeks ago, anyone publicly displaying his picture might have been arrested. When I passed the bookstore again, in the afternoon, two small water glasses had been placed below the picture, one filled with violets and one with snowdrops.

After a quarter of a century of fear, police brutality, and enforced ignorance—"first under the Nazi protectorate and then under the Stalinist protectorate," an acquaintance of mine said—many people here are having difficulty adjusting themselves to the new situation. They wake up in the morning with a sense of unreality. "When I listen to objective news reports on our radio and hear heretical questions asked on television, I feel I'm still dreaming," one man told me. An account in *Rudé Právo,* the Communist Party paper, of how eight hundred workers in an electrical-appliance factory in Pisek were led in a protest strike by the chairman of the factory's branch of the Communist Party caused people to exclaim in wonder. Only a few weeks ago, the same paper was printing ominous warnings against strikes, written by Stalinist editors. (The editors are gone, but they will get their full salaries for a few months.) For the time being, anything goes. A report in *Lidová Demokracie,* the official organ of the Catholic People's Party, read, "Young soldiers held a meeting in Pardubice and came to the conclusion that General Lomský, the Minister of National Defense, should resign and thus set an example for other Army leaders." Even in many Western countries, this would be unusual behavior. The satirical magazine *Dikobraz* ("Porcupine") captioned a cartoon of Lomský "The Minister of Self-Defense." Another paper has been running an account of former President Antonín Novotný's misdeeds, in daily installments.

Novotný's name has become the symbol of an era that is past—the Czechoslovaks hope. "I am afraid to be as happy as I would like to be," I was told by a man I have known since the thirties, when I lived in Prague. "It's almost too good to be true. After all, the police are still around, though they look the other way now, and the Stalinists haven't disappeared, though they keep quiet." On walls here and there, in fresh white paint, one sees the words "LIDÉ BDĚTE!" ("People, Be Watchful!"). This was the last message that the Czech Communist writer Julius Fučík, a national hero, smuggled out of prison before he was executed by the Germans in 1943. The people of this country have always tended to be realists, and their history has given them ample reason to be watchful. After losing the Battle of White Mountain, in 1620, they had three centuries under the Hapsburg yoke, until modern Czechoslovakia was established in 1918. Then came the Nazis, in 1938, and the Communists, in 1948. Many people here are wondering whether this exhilarating "Pražské Jaro" ("Prague Spring," the name of a world-famous music festival) will one day be known as nothing more than "an anarchist interval" in the history of the Czechoslovak Socialist Republic (as Hungary's Party theoretician Zoltán Komócsin has predicted) or whether it may be the beginning of a development that could shake the Communist world to its foundations.

. . .

People suddenly realize that unbelievable things have been happening before their very eyes, and they still don't know exactly how it all came about. "Sometime around Christmas, the Communist Party simply fell to pieces," one of the most astute Western observers here told me. "It wasn't just one event or another but a confluence of many powerful streams of thought." The beginnings of what the non-Communists here call "revolution" and the Communists call "reform" go back to the Twelfth Czechoslovak Communist Party Congress, in December of 1962, which decided to "investigate and correct" the "excesses" committed during the Stalinist era. But the investigation and correction were pretty well sabotaged by the arch-Stalinist Novotný and the people around him until last June, when the Fourth Congress of the Writers' Union, held in Prague, started a public revolt against all the "doctrine and dogma" that had been the stock in trade of Novotný's leadership. "The writer's fight to express himself will continue as long as a writer, a ruler, and a reader are left on earth," said Jan Procházka, editor of *Literární Noviny*, the Writers' Union weekly. Procházka was also a candidate-member of the Party's Central Committee. Indeed, all the writers who talked openly about freedom, tolerance, and humanity were faithful Communists, and so were the members of other groups who began to express "heretical" thoughts: the students of Prague, suddenly displaying an unusual sense of political responsibility; the young economists, dismayed at the prospect of the country's going bankrupt; the intellectuals, tired of being treated like dirt while the Novotný government gave every preference to "workers and peasants"; and the Slovaks, insisting on the full equality that the Czechs had been promising them for years. After the Writers' Union Congress, criticism of the Novotný government could be heard everywhere, but the explosions that effected the breakup of the Stalinist regime occurred at the very center of power—in the Presidium and the Central Committee of the Party. The men who lit the fuses were relatively young Communists (most of them in their forties) who wanted not to overthrow Communism but to liberalize it. . . .

. . .

"Freedom" and "democracy" are the two big words of the moment, but what do those words mean in Czechoslovakia? A few days ago, a Western journalist asked several people at random what "freedom" meant to them. The answers differed widely: "The police don't beat you up any-more, and they have to wear shield numbers and can be identified." "At last our radio has told Ulbricht what we think of him." "Now we will be able to see the movie of *Doctor Zhivago*." "My children will have religious instruction in school." "The censors themselves have asked for the complete abolition of censorship." (Kafka, who has recently been coming back into vogue in his native country, would have enjoyed the request issued by the members of the Central Publication Administration—better known as the censorship office—that "preventive political censorship be abolished at the present state of development," and he wouldn't have been at all surprised to hear that the censors were still sitting in their offices, doing no censoring.) Perhaps the clearest definition of "freedom" was "We can now openly say what before we didn't even dare think."

A third big word of the moment is "rehabilitation," and as it is defined here it often seems to involve retribution. Although Dubček has said that "no heads must roll," the new reforms have sent shock waves through the nation. "We are witnessing a terrifying study of human nature," a friend told me. "Don't forget that in this country tens of thousands of people have suffered terribly, and now they want to square accounts with those who made them suffer. And if those who suffered are dead, their widows and children and friends demand rehabilitation of the dead men's reputations and punishment of those who made them suffer." At a large public meeting, the noted writer Pavel Kohout said, "With the exception of West Germany, Czechoslovakia is the only country where a state prosecutor who murdered eleven people is walking around free." He was referring to the state prosecutor who demanded, and obtained, eleven death sentences during a political trial in 1952 in which the chief defendant was Rudolf Slánský, former First Secretary of the Party. The widow of another victim—former Foreign Minister Vlado Clementis—recently told the newspaper *Student* that she had been arrested, too, and that after her release she had asked for her husband's ashes and had been told that "they were dropped into a drain at Pankrác Prison." Mrs. Clementis has asked that "the main culprits"—former Ministers Vilém Široký and Karol Bacílek—be punished. Former President Novotný, who also had a hand in trials that are now being reviewed, declared in May, 1963, that "Clementis was not guilty of the acts with which he was charged." There have been many demands for an investigation of the mysterious death of Foreign Minister Jan Masaryk in 1948. Up to a few weeks ago, no one dared visit the small cemetery in Lány, near Prague, where the President-Liberator and his son Jan are both buried, but it has now become a place of pilgrimage for thousands of people every day. Many judges have promised to "rehabilitate people who were innocent." Dr. Jozef Břestanský, Vice-President of the Supreme Court, who was a "working-class cadre student" and rose to his eminent position in a remarkably short time, after studying law "extra-murally," is one judge who will not be able to rehabilitate anybody. He was recently found dead, his body hanging from a tree in a forest south of Prague, and the announcement that he committed suicide has led to public speculation about the sort of verdicts he may have handed down in past years. Terrible instances have become known of Czechs torturing Czechs during the Stalinist era, and there is a widespread belief that, as one man put it, "our people were sometimes more brutal than the German Gestapo."

To be sure, amid all the demands for vengeance there are also voices of moderation. Professor Goldstücker, when he was asked to join a new and militant political group made up of former political prisoners and called "K231," after the law under which they were tried during the Stalinist era, published a letter in *Mladá Fronta* explaining his position on the "rehabilitation" question. Goldstücker, to whom a great deal of the credit is due for the revival of Kafka's reputation here during the past five years, has been a leading figure in the reform movement, and he was nominated for the Presidency by the students of Prague's Philosophical Faculty. In the present climate, the fact that he is a Jew serves to strengthen his ties to the students and intellectuals, who have strongly denounced Poland's "anti-Zionist" campaign. (During the war between Israel and the Arabs last June, nearly the entire population of Czechoslovakia was on the side of Israel, though the Stalinist regime favored the Arabs. The writer Ladislav Mňačko was deprived of his citizenship when he went to Israel to demonstrate his opposition to the official policy of his country.) Goldstücker, who was sentenced to death in the early fifties and was saved only by the intervention of Khrushchev, set forth his views on vengeance in these terms:

> I have been wondering whether one can ever rehabilitate anyone who was humiliated as a political prisoner. A man who was in prison may get back his freedom, the accusations against him may be retracted, he may even get back his citizens' rights and obtain financial indemnity, but no one can indemnify him for the loss of

human dignity that he suffered. Because I belong to a minority that suffered so much, I am especially careful about looking for the guilty ones who made me suffer, and I will not summarily condemn my fellow men. Today I can understand and forgive more than before. I write to you because today it is getting very easy to become unjust and because I do believe in tolerance among men. Tolerance must begin at home.

Many people say now that they would like to forget the past, but that it is impossible to forget some of the awful things that they were exposed to only yesterday—the spies and informers, the stupidities and crimes. A man I have known since we were both boys described his feelings to me the other evening over a glass of wine. "You walk along the Moldau," he said, "and you look up to where the government ordered the enormous Stalin monument built that cost two billion *koruny* and made us a laughingstock everywhere—and then the government had to pull it down. For that money we could have built a small town, or a couple of hospitals. We are not a stupid people. We know that we are broke because the Stalinists gave away billions of goods to the Russians in ridiculous barter deals. And when you opened your mouth, some old woman who was a member of the street council might denounce you as a 'reactionary,' and you and your family would be in trouble. We have been deceived so many times that it's hard to believe *anyone*."

The fate of the huge Stalin monument on Summer Hill, overlooking the entire city, has acquired a special significance here in Prague, and it will surely stimulate generations of satirists. (In Ivan Klíma's excellent play *The Castle* there is a character known as the Head of the Commission for the Correction of the Statue.) The actual events were comic enough. Having decided, after painful deliberation, that the statue had to go, the authorities called in an English outfit to do the job in one night. But the work proved unexpectedly complicated, and eventually Stalin's head was lifted from his shoulders in broad daylight, with nearly everybody in Prague watching. Now only the empty pedestal remains. Children play around it during the day, and at night couples go there to look down at the lights of Prague reflected in the Moldau.

. . .

Western observers in Prague have been amazed by the bloodless character of the revolution and its aftermath. There has been much drama but little violence. There have been no defenestrations, and so far no one has even been arrested. "That the government didn't fall at once, which might have created chaos, is proof of our political maturity," *Rudé Právo* has declared. It is also proof of the traditional Czechoslovak dislike of melodrama and heroics. Poland's national composer is Chopin, and during the war the strains of his "Revolutionary" Étude rallied citizens in the cellars of Warsaw's bombed-out houses against the German oppressors. Czechoslovakia's national composer is Smetana, whose masterpiece, *The Bartered Bride*, is all clear-eyed happiness. The political sophistication the students here have shown in recent weeks has been very different from the behavior of their fellow-students in Warsaw or Budapest—or, for that matter, in West Berlin, Rome, or Berkeley. The students of Prague, by and large, are progressive (in the present local meaning of the word), and the radical fringe is very small. During a time of upheaval, the students here get angry, but they do not cross the boundary line between youthful indignation and uncontrolled violence. Early in March, some students started to talk about marching on the Polish Embassy to demonstrate against police brutality in Warsaw. Dubček himself went to discuss the situation with the students, and the discussion was "extremely frank," according to a girl who was there. Ultimately, he persuaded them that although their indignation was justified, they must avoid any action that might be considered a "provocation" by the country's Warsaw Pact partners. The students called off their demonstration. Some students from Slovakia who appeared at the American Embassy to submit a protest against the war in Vietnam displayed a degree of moderation and political maturity that surprised the Americans. "They showed that they understood what was going on," an Embassy official told me.

Eighteen thousand students recently attended a mass meeting at which they were able to ask questions directly of prominent Communist reformers; the meeting was televised nationally and kept people at their TV sets until one-thirty in the morning. Nearly everybody I know in Prague stayed up to look and listen, and everybody who did agreed that it was fascinating to hear the students ask questions of a sort that older and more cautious people would not dream of asking, even today. It was during this meeting that Smrkovský had the exchange with a student about Czechoslovakia's position on the map of Europe. At the end of the meeting, which became fairly vehement at times, Smrkovský told the students to "go home quietly," and they did.

What amazed the nationwide TV audience most was the absence of policemen. "Eighteen thousand demonstrators and not one policeman," I heard a middle-aged man say. "What a remarkable display of democratic discipline!"

Though the works of Tomáš Masaryk, Karel Čapek, and other writers admired by those of us who lived in the "bourgeois" Republic were officially forbidden for many years, young people apparently got hold of them somehow. Relatively few of the present generation of students are Communist Party members—possibly only one in ten—but nearly all the students I have talked with understand and accept their responsibilities as the future leaders of a Communist nation. Though there are close ties between the students and the writers, the students maintain their independence when it comes to politics. An editor of *Student* told me, "We read the writers' *Literární Listy*, but that doesn't mean that we always do what they suggest." I asked him whether they would support the reform, and he gave me the same answer I got from an editor of the writers' weekly: "For the time being, we are behind Dubček."

In a recent issue of *Literární Listy*, the playwright Václav Havel—his work (*The Garden Party* and *Memorandum*) continues the satirical tradition of Kafka, Hašek, and Čapek—began a discussion of the future role of the opposition in Czechoslovakia. Though the reformers agree that an opposition is needed, there is no agreement on who should form it or how it should work. One obvious solution would be to let the mass media—the press, radio, and television—carry out the duties of criticism. The mass media had a great deal to do with the changes that have taken place in the last few months; people in remote areas have been able to follow events in Prague, and Dubček has been supported by instantaneous "resolutions" from Party groups all over the country. In many ways, the media have already become the watchdogs of the reform. On one new TV program, people telephone in complaints, which are supposed to be taken care of immediately. While I was watching it the other day, several callers claimed that at a certain Prague post office there was still a secret unit reading letters sent abroad. Reporters in the studio telephoned the post office and various Ministries; everybody denied that there was such a unit, but the reporters promised the audience to investigate further and tell them the results within a few days. Such activities may not be welcomed in high Party circles even now. Dubček has spoken of the responsibility of the mass media in the matter of "erroneous or non-objective reports that may meet with a mass response."

Some people believe—or perhaps one should say hope—that the Social Democrats and the People's Party, both of which were permitted a moribund existence in support of the Communist Party as members of the so-called National Front, may now take over the role of a constructive opposition. But these parties have been discredited in most people's eyes by dubious accommodations they made with the Stalinists. The chairman of the People's Party, Josef Plojhar, is an unfrocked priest who served as Minister of Public Health in the Novotný regime; he is ridiculed even by the Catholics, but even after he was ousted as a member of the government he managed to get himself elected "honorary chairman" of his party. Obviously, a new generation of leaders would be needed to revive these parties. Under a proposed new law to reform electoral procedures, the names of candidates, rather than the names of parties, will appear on the ballot. And, what is more important, the new law will guarantee a secret ballot. Apparently, the Communist Party feels that it is strong enough to risk such an election; after all, it has the country's best-trained and ablest politicians. No one in Prague is apt to forget that back in 1946 38 percent of the popular (and secret) vote was cast for the Communist Party, while the party of Eduard Beneš, Tomáš Masaryk's student and successor, got only 26 percent. It was not the election of the Communist slate, headed by Klement Gottwald, but the way Gottwald took over that caused night to fall upon the city.

Among certain Communist intellectuals, an extremely interesting new method of forming a political opposition is being discussed. One of them outlined it for me this way: "Suppose that in two or three years it is realized that the events of early 1968 created a split between the conservative and the progressive wings of the Communist Party, so that there are really *two* parties, which agree on the fundamental tenets of Marxism-Leninism but disagree on methods and practical politics—just as the two big parties in the Anglo-Saxon countries agree on the fundamentals of their system but not on how it should be run. It is conceivable that Czechoslovakia could become the first Communist country with a two-party system. This would not be incompatible with the Communist gospel. Think of the abyss that divides the Communist Party in the Soviet Union from the progressive Communists in Italy—and I've read in Western papers that some of the ideas of our reformers could have been taken from Togliatti's testament. Ideally, Czechoslovakia could become the testing ground for a new, enlightened Communism."

. . .

No one in Prague expects the future to be easy. "During the honeymoon, one doesn't like to think about money," a writer said to me the other day. "As you say in America, it's 'Fly now, pay later.' But eventually the bills will come in, and they will have to be paid, and that will be the time of crisis." At the moment, people are enjoying the delightful game of publicly attacking men in high places, but what would happen if they began to attack Dubček and his supporters? Would the leaders be as tolerant of free speech as they are now? So far, the top members of the Stalinist Old Guard have been neutralized or put off by themselves in some corner, often after they have made abject apologies. But what about the vast army of bureaucrats and Party officials all over the country—the faithful Party hacks who served Novotný loyally and have now declared their loyalty to the new regime? There are said to be half a million of them. (The Czechoslovak Communist Party now has one million seven hundred thousand members. Every eighth citizen is a Party member, though a great many people joined simply out of the need to make a living.) Will it be possible to replace the "dogmatists" by able young Communists who can practice Socialist democracy as Dubček has envisioned it?

As the spring advances, many of the groups that have been supporting Dubček are sending him their demands. But, come summer and harvest time, will it be possible to meet all those demands? A case in point is offered by the Catholic Church, which has already "recognized" the regime but has expressed "expectations." Bishop František Tomášek, the Apostolic Administrator of Prague, told the papers that the Church will demand an increase in the number of bishops, expansion of the seminaries, and the removal of the obstacles to religious instruction for schoolchildren. (In the past, both parents had to sign a petition if they wanted their child to have religious instruction in school, and even then permission was not always granted.) It has already been agreed that priests who were sent to work in factories and on farms will be permitted to return to their parishes, and the Vatican may appoint a chargé d'affaires to occupy the seat of the Papal Nuncio. (The Nuncio's palace, across from the Prague Castle, has been empty for years.) The Theological Faculty of the University will be permitted to publish a magazine of its own, and the Catholic press will get a larger supply of newsprint. But it is doubtful whether Josef Cardinal Beran, who has been living as an exile in Rome, will return to Prague, and no one expects the Party to restore to the Church all the property that was seized when the Party came to power. The demands of the Church, like those of many other groups in the country, cannot be fully met. Nevertheless, anticipations are growing stronger in the spring weather here, and hopes are increasing in scope and intensity. After the long binge, there is certain to be a nationwide hangover.

But if no one can say now that the great experiment in Prague is going to succeed, it is clear that, even as an attempt, it may have tremendous consequences for other countries. The Czechoslovak reform is already a much bigger thing than János Kádár's "goulash Communism" in Hungary or even Titoism in Yugoslavia. "We made greater progress in personal freedom in twenty days than the Yugoslavs made in twenty years," a friend of mine boasted. If the Czechoslovaks prove that Communism can coexist with freedom, their success will unquestionably affect not only the intellectuals but the entire populations of other Communist countries—Poland, Hungary, East Germany, and perhaps even the Soviet Union.

The Czechoslovak movement might also have sizable repercussions in the West, where it has always been claimed that Communism is synonymous with dictatorship and terror; in no country have the Communists ever stayed in power through secret ballots that expressed the true will of the people. A Czech writer who has been in and out of jail several times in the past two decades told me the other day, "Perhaps in a few years we shall be able to create something that is acceptable to both the East and the West—a combination of enlightened Communism and Western-style personal freedom that could form a bridge between the world's two most powerful ideological systems and a basis for peace in the very heart of Europe. If anybody can do it, we can. We have the idealism and the tradition. And we are not impractical dreamers but hardheaded realists."

. . .

Now that my visit here is approaching its end, I have taken a long walk through some of the streets I knew before the war. A number of people were out enjoying the fair weather. Old men and old women sat on benches in squares and in small gardens that have been laid out in vacant lots. Even some valuable lots in the Old Town Square have been turned into improvised recreation grounds. Benches have been put up around the statue of Jan Hus—erected near the spot where twenty-seven Bohemian nobles were beheaded in 1621—and, sitting there, I had a fine view of the Old Town Hall, where in 1618 angry members of the Bohemian Diet threw two Austrian councillors out a window, in the famous defenestration that started the Thirty Years' War. Beneath the window, I noticed, there is a plaque commemorating some Czechs who were shot there by the Germans during the Occupation. The clock of the Old Town Hall struck, and a couple of sightseers photographed the medieval clockwork pageant that takes place every hour.

The Jewish quarter dates back to the ninth century, when the city became a flourishing trade center on the route that connected the Near East and the Baltic. The Nazis, who destroyed synagogues all over Europe, didn't touch the buildings in the old ghetto of Prague, because some German scholars had persuaded Hitler that the ghetto should be preserved as an ethnological museum, in which relics of the Jewish race could be shown after the race itself had been exterminated. I wanted particularly to have a look at the Pinkas Synagogue—named after a man who owned the site on which it was built, in the fifteenth century. The synagogue was rebuilt several times, and incorporates interesting late-Gothic and Renaissance elements. But few people notice the architectural details. In 1950, the Pinkas Synagogue became a memorial to the Jews of Bohemia and Moravia who died at the hands of the Nazis. The walls of the synagogue are covered with the names of men, women, and children, arranged by cities, towns, and villages, in a roll call of death. There are seventy-seven thousand two hundred and ninety-seven names. An old woman who offered me her services as a guide was quite definite about the figure: seventy-seven thousand two hundred and ninety-seven. After each name, there are two dates—the date of the victim's birth and the date he was taken away. I asked the woman to show me the names for Ostrava, and after she had pointed them out to me, she walked a little distance away. They were all there.

I walked on, in the late afternoon, past houses that seemed cold and empty to me, because the friends of mine who had lived in them were no longer there, and then I reached the Moldau and walked across Charles Bridge, the finest of Prague's fourteen bridges. It was put up by Charles IV in the fourteenth century and was later lined with statues of saints. A walk across Charles Bridge provides by far the best views of Prague's medieval past. From the Moldau a bluish haze was rising, and down on Kampa Island, which the people of Prague call their little Venice, the shadows were already very dark. The city was no longer reflected in the water. Just ahead of me was Malá Strana Square, whose St. Nicholas Church many people—and not only in Prague—consider the finest baroque church in Europe. At its best, the Prague baroque is finer than either the Viennese or the Italian baroque—less flamboyant, more meditative. I stood there watching the last rays of the setting sun bathe the Gothic silhouette of Hradčany Castle, high above the river, in liquid gold, and then, suddenly, the whole thing went deep blue. It was incredibly beautiful.

FROM

THE EVENTS IN MAY:
A PARIS NOTEBOOK

Mavis Gallant

SEPTEMBER 14, 1968

MAY 3

PHOTOGRAPHS, IN NEWSPAPERS, of students in front of the Sorbonne. Members of Occident, an extreme right-wing student group, waiting in the street to beat up Nanterre *enragés*, start fighting with police when they see *enragés* arrested.

MAY 4

H. T. caught in traffic jam around Saint-Germain-Saint-Michel in midst of student disorders. Says this is "different"—they all seem very young. He sees a barricade made of parked cars they have moved away from the curb. Is very impatient—hates disorder.

Talk with M. B. She saw the police charge, outside the Balzar Brasserie. Says their apartment full of tear gas—they live on the fifth floor! Wouldn't let her daughter talk on telephone in sight of windows. Police think nothing of throwing grenades into houses. Doubt if they could throw one up to fifth floor. Says gas makes it impossible to sleep at night.

Crowds, traffic jams. See a crowd. I feel the mixture of tension and curiosity that is always the signal of something happening, and I hear shouting and see police cars. I duck into Saint-Germain Métro. I hate these things. See more pictures in papers, and accounts, surprising, of how the students, far from fleeing, "regroup and charge."

MAY 6

In the night, hear that familiar wave of sound, as during the crisis in 1958. Get dressed, go out as far as Carrefour Raspail. All confusion. Students do not run—it is not 1958, after all. Attack in a kind of frenzy that seems insane. The courage of these kids! Don't get too near. See what is obviously innocent bystander hit on the ear by a policeman. Decide not to tell anyone, as friends would have fit. All night, shouts, cries, harsh slogans chanted, police cars, ambulances, cars going up and down my one-way street, running feet. I open a shutter and see that I am the only person on the street at a window. Are they scared, or respectable, or what? Scared of police, or of students?

MAY 7

Dined at the B.s', Quai Saint-Michel. No one takes a car now—not safe to park in the area. Students are marching all over Paris: *"Libérez nos camarades!"*—meaning those who were sentenced by a monkey court on Sunday. From the B.s' living room you see Seine, sunset, expanse of quais, very few cars, scarcely any traffic, many police. Christine (fifteen) says, "But it is my *duty* to be out there with the students." Nothing doing. However, I notice she does not eat her dinner with us. Has it by herself in the kitchen. Almost seems like the heart of the matter—not with the adults, not with the kids. In Métro, find I have tears in my eyes. Astonished. Think: I must be tired—working too much? See everyone is dabbing and sniffling. It is tear gas that has seeped down. By Saint-Placide it is almost unbearable, prickling under the lids, but so funny to see us all weeping that I begin to laugh.

Out of the métro, Rue de Rennes a wall of people. The end of the student march. They have been all over Paris. Quiet, grave, in rows straight across the road, linking arms, holding hands. Boys and girls. I find their grave young faces extremely moving. Perfect discipline, a quiet crowd. They are packed all the way up the street to the ruined Montparnasse Station—I can't see the end of them. They hold the banners of the

C.N.R.S. (National Scientific Research Center) and a banner reading, "LES PROFESSEURS DE NANTERRE CONTRE LA RÉPRESSION." Behind a red flag, a tight cluster of non-identified, other than by the meaning of the flag. Ask if I can cross the street. Boy parts the rows so I can get through; girls begin chanting at me, *"Avec nous! Avec nous!"* Slogans start up, swell, recede as if the slogans themselves were tired: *"Li-bé-rez nos ca-ma-rades. Fi-ga-ro fa-sciste."* Marchers look exhausted. The police bar their route up near the Hôtel Lutetia. Sometimes the marchers have to move back, the word is passed along: *"Reculez doucement!"* A number of good citizens of our neighborhood watch without commenting and without letting their faces show how they feel. A little girl, about four feet nine, collects from everyone "for the wounded." Notice that the non-identified lot behind the red flag give freely, the watchers around me a little less. At midnight, the news; someone has parked a minute car on the edge of the crowd with a portable radio on the roof. Touching narcissism of the young; a silence, so that they can hear the radio talk about *them.* When the announcer describes where we are—the Rue de Rennes—and says that there are about fifteen thousand left out of the thirty thousand who were earlier on the Champs-Élysées, a satisfied little ripple is almost visible. Something to do with looks exchanged. But then he says, "The police are simply hoping they will, finally, be tired and go home," and a new slogan is shouted, quite indignantly: *"Nous sommes pas fatigués!"* This is a good one—three beats repeated twice—and goes on quite a long time. But they are tired. They have, in fact, been sitting down in the roadway. They remind me of children who keep insisting they are not sleepy when in reality they are virtually asleep on the carpet. This seems to me the end. Unlikely that they will press on for the release of their *camarades.*

MAY 10

Walked from Île Saint-Louis to top of Boul' Mich'. Light evening. The bridges are guarded by C.R.S. (Compagnies Républicaines de Sécurité)—riot police, under the Ministry of the Interior. Self-conscious as one walks by (they, not I). Middle-aged men, professionals. *"Laissez passer la dame,"* etc. They must know they are hated now. They may wonder why. One fastening the other's helmet chin strap, as if going to a party. I mistake their grenade-throwers for guns, and I think: If they have these guns, they must intend to use them. Place Saint-Michel. I am part of a stupid, respectable-looking small crowd staring—just dumbly staring—at the spectacle of massed power on the bridge. Up the Boul' Mich'. Crowds, feeling of tension. Street dirtier than usual, and it is never very clean. Still has that feeling of a Cairo bazaar. Side streets leading to Sorbonne and Latin Quarter blocked by more police, and I have that feeling of helpless anger I had earlier today. The Sorbonne is empty, and it is kept empty by a lot of ignorant gumshoes. The last stand of the illiterate. Difference between now and early afternoon is that the students are back from their mass meeting in Denfert-Rochereau and— shifting, excited, sullen, angry, determined—they want to get by those large, armed men and back to *their* Latin Quarter. Electric, uneasy, but oddly gay. Yes, it is like a holiday in a village, with the whole town out on the square.

Home, turn on news. Suddenly wonder about Anna, who was at Denfert-Rochereau. She turned up at her family's apartment between ten and eleven tonight with some hairy youth and said, *"Maman, je voudrais la permission de passer la nuit au Quartier Latin—il y a des barricades."* She is seventeen. Nice kid, came all the way home, knew they'd be worried. Parents handled it beautifully—said they hadn't eaten, took both kids to a restaurant. Anna, *pure et dure,* said, "How can I eat in a restaurant while my *camarades* are out there, etc.?" Call their apartment and am told that parents have persuaded boy to spend night at their place, and, without actually forbidding anything, have kept both kids out of it. Z. tells me this in low voice. Boy is sleeping in living room. Both kids worn out, upset.

MAY 11

Listened to nightmare news half the night. Around two o'clock, when the C.R.S. were "regrouped and ordered to charge," I said to no one, "Oh no! No!" I've never seen barricades "charged," but once you have seen any kind of police charge in Paris you never forget it. They charge on the double—they seem invincible. How brave these kids are now! Until now I'd never seen them do anything but run. Finally fell asleep, thought I had dreamed it, but on the eight-o'clock news (Europe I) the speaker said, "Have you slept well? Because this is what went on in your city last night," and told.

The ripped streets around the Luxembourg Station. People who live around here seem dazed. Stand there looking dazed. Paving torn up. The Rue Royer-Collard, where I used to live, looks bombed. Burned cars—ugly, gray-black. These are small cars, the kind you can lift and push around easily. Not the cars of the rich. It's said that even the car owners haven't complained, because they had watched the police charge from their windows. Armed men, and unarmed children. I used to think that the young in France were all little aged men. Oh! We all feel sick. Rumor of two deaths, one a student, one a C.R.S. Rumor that a student had his throat cut "against a window at 24 Rue Gay-Lussac"—so a tract (already!) informs. They say it was the police incendiary grenades, and not the students, that set the cars on fire, but it was probably both. A friend of H.'s who lost his car found tracts still stuffed in it, half charred, used as kindling. Rumor that police beat the wounded with clubs, that people hid them (the students) and looked after them, and that police went into private homes. When the police threw the first tear-gas bombs, everyone in the houses nearby threw out basins of water to keep the gas close to the ground.

Shopkeeper saying, "I sold nothing all day. I gave water away, without charge. That's all the business I did." Feeling of slight, unpleasant pressure. I don't like it. Shopkeepers "encouraged" (by whom?) to proclaim, with signs, publicly, their "solidarity" with the students. Well, they did have their shops wrecked, and shopkeepers have no solidarity with anyone. Anyway, I don't like it. Too much like post-Occupation.

Am told that a Belgian tourist bus stopped, a father and son descended, son stood on remains of barricade with a stone in each hand while father took his picture. Then they got back in the bus. Didn't see this, but saw plenty of people taking pictures. Last thing I'd want to photograph. Curious tendency—men and boys pick up these paving stones, weigh them, make as if to throw them. See themselves as heroes. Am embarrassed by elderly professors suddenly on the side of students. If they thought these reforms were essential, why the hell didn't they do something about it before the kids were driven to use paving stones? Maurice Duverger, professor of political science—gray crewcut on TV, romanticism of barricades. Wanted to say, "Come off it, *vieux père.*"

Voice of the people: Wife of a Garde Mobile (paramilitary police, the Gardes Mobiles belong to the Army) lives in my *quartier.* Much surrounded. Very simple, plain creature. Says, "When my husband came in this morning, he told me that the barricades were manned by North

Africans aged forty and fifty. That was why the police had to be so rough." This is *believed*. Indignant housewives. "Send them back to North Africa!" I have a queer feeling this is going to be blamed on foreigners—I mean the new proles, the Spanish and Portuguese. And, of course, the North Africans are good for everything.

Evening. The Boul' Mich' still smells of tear gas. Last night like a year ago. One's eyes sting and smart under the lids, the inner corners swell. Aimless youths wander up and down under the trees and street lights. No cars. It is a pleasant evening, and this aimless walking up and down (curious onlookers on the sidewalks, young people in the roadway) is like a *corso* in a Mediterranean town.

Gardes Mobiles and the C.R.S. here now are big, tough middle-aged men. Their black cars and their armored gray cars have brought them from Marseille and from Bordeaux—we recognize the license plates. Stout, oddly relaxed, they stand around and about the intersection of the Boul' Mich' and the Boulevard Saint-Germain, both of which are thronged with a holiday sort of sightseeing crowd. I can't believe these young people are students. I think the students were last night, on the barricades. These boys simply don't resemble the kids I saw last night. They look like suburban working-class boys on any Saturday night—like the boys we called *blousons noirs* in the nineteen-fifties. H. T. says I am mistaken. Anyway, they form an untidy knot, spread out, begin to walk up the Boulevard Saint-Germain. The police stand still, and those kids going up and down the road, restless, moving, more and more of them, remind me of waves on a rock. The police just in themselves seem to be a sort of provocation, and for the life of me I can't see why the police aren't taken right out of the Latin Quarter at once. Finally, a compact crowd crosses the Boulevard Saint-Germain singing the "Marseillaise" and giving the cops the Nazi salute. The police laugh. These are obviously a fresh lot. If they had been around last night, they wouldn't be laughing.

The police: The police involved in last night's debacle had been brought in from Brittany, where Breton nationalists had been staging a strike. They travelled all night. From the morning, when they arrived—from their breakfast time, say—they were given no more food. They stood from noon until two o'clock in the morning without one scrap of food—they stood, they didn't sit down—and they watched the barricades going up, knowing they were going to have to demolish them and the kids behind them. At around two in the morning, they were given the order to charge. They had been given clubs to hit with and gas bombs to throw. What were they supposed to do? Boy who lives in my building tells me a story that sounds like a dream. How the people who lived on those streets showered the students with *saucissons* and chocolate and brought them coffee (not the police!). How some of the students actually began to talk to the police. Not arguing—discussing. Talking (he says seriously) about their problems and, dear God, the structure of society. The C.R.S. were just people, and not all of them middle-aged, some of them only boys. At around two, their order came: Regroup, get back in your lines, put on your helmets, and charge. He says it was unreal, dreamlike—the tear gas, the armed men with those great round shields, the beatings, but they were the same men.

Talk with young Anna. "The German students are being deported," she tells me. "But we need them here—they are organized, they can tell us what to do. *Oui, nous avons besoin des allemands.*" Her mother, who spent the war years in a concentration camp, says nothing. I feel as if I were watching two screens simultaneously.

De Gaulle still invisible. Says nothing.

PART FIVE
NEW ARRIVALS

A NOTE BY MALCOLM GLADWELL

M Y FAVORITE PIECE in the section you have before you is A. J.
Liebling's encounter with the young Cassius Clay. Clay was
twenty at the time, still some years from his transformation
into an international celebrity, as Muhammad Ali. Liebling, of course,
was one of the greatest of *The New Yorker* old guard, who had been at the
magazine, by that point, for a quarter century. He had watched Clay in
the 1960 Rome Olympics, where Clay won the gold medal, and pronounced him "attractive but not probative." He thought the boxer had a
"skittering style, like a pebble scaled over water." Liebling listens to
Clay's poems—the little ditties that would later become such a key part
of his playful public persona—and seems a little baffled: "There are
trainers I know who, if they had a fighter who was a poet, would give up
on him, no matter how good he looked."

Liebling was a student of boxing. *The Sweet Science*, perhaps his masterpiece, had come out a few years earlier. He was ringside during boxing's golden age. But in Clay, he understands, he has come face-to-face
with an entirely new kind of athlete. "Now Cassius reappeared, a glass of
fashion in a snuff-colored suit and one of those lace-front shirts, which I
had never before known anybody with nerve enough to wear," Liebling
writes. "His tie was like two shoestring ends laid across each other, and
his smile was white and optimistic. He did not appear to know how
badly he was being brought up."

What follows is a snapshot of *The New Yorker*'s confrontation with the
1960s. The magazine came of age in the parochial confines of the 1930s,
when the nation was pinched by Depression. (It is worth remembering
that the round table at the Algonquin Hotel—the symbol of the magazine in those years—was *across the street*.) But fast-forward thirty years,
and suddenly that same institution was face-to-face with the *world*. It's
all here: the Beatles, the moon landing, Joan Baez, Ronald Reagan,
Simon and Garfunkel, touch-tone phones!

In one of its Talk of the Town pieces, the magazine pays a visit to Marshall McLuhan. He had come to New York to give a lecture at Spencer Memorial Church in Brooklyn: "Every new technology, according to the Professor, programs a new sensory human environment, and our computer technology has catapulted us right out of the specialist age and into a world of integral knowledge and synesthetic responses. 'The computer is not merely an extension of our eyes, like print, but an extension of our whole central nervous system,' he explains."

In less self-confident hands, that moment could have been played for laughs or, at least, an eye-roll. This was the 1960s! A computer was something the size of a garage that ran on punch cards. It was, to say the least, a stretch to think of it as our central nervous system. One wonders what *The New Yorker* of the 1930s would have made of McLuhan's grandiose imaginings. But Eustace Tilley, in his middle age, had the self-confidence to give the Professor the benefit of the doubt.

· · ·

On of the writers of that piece, Lillian Ross, later hears *Sgt. Pepper's Lonely Hearts Club Band,* by the Beatles, and ventures out to gauge its impact. She finds a New York D.J. named Joe O'Brien, who compares the Beatles to Picasso, calls the band's new work a "terribly intellectual album" and then adds: "My youngest son is a freshman at Yale. He tells me that the day the album was issued the entire student body of Yale went out and bought it. Exactly the same thing happened at Harvard."

The modern ear, trained by the snark of social media and the blogosphere, waits for the hint of contempt. It doesn't come. A piece on Simon and Garfunkel ends with the two of them doing a sound check before a concert in New Haven.

> He looked up at the rows and rows of empty seats, and then up toward the last row, where Garfunkel, silhouetted against the blustery sky, stood listening.

> > "And ev'ry stop is neatly planned
> > For a poet and a one-man band.
> > Homeward bound."

That could have run in the magazine last week. They could all have.

NEVER BEFORE
SEEN

PORTABLE ROBOT

F. S. Norman, Brendan Gill, and Thomas Meehan

MARCH 19, 1960

ORE NEWS FROM the spooky world of automation! The Monroe Calculating Machine Company has just unveiled a new all-purpose computer, called the Monrobot Mark XI (having given their machine the most inhuman name possible, and in the form of a pun at that, the Monroe people apparently hope to strike a note of humanity by listing successive models as if they were kings, not things), and of course we have been to see the machine, at the Monroe show-room, on Park Avenue, and have been almost instantaneously outwitted by it, in a not very fierce battle of ticktacktoe. Walter K. Clifford, vice-president in charge of marketing at Monroe, told us that the latest approach to computers is to make them compact and low-priced, both of which Mark XI is. Resembling, in length, breadth, and height, an ordinary steel desk surmounted by an ordinary typewriter, Mark XI struck us as much less forbidding than the truck-size computers we've grown used to. We weren't surprised when Clifford gave it a friendly pat. "Mark XI solves many of the technical problems that we in the computer game have been bucking for years," he said, with a passion that left us in no doubt about how he had come to be vice-presidential non-robot in charge of marketing. "Up to now, all-purpose computers have required a great amount of space to sit down in and couldn't be readily moved from place to place. Mark XI weighs only three hundred and seventy-five pounds and is therefore completely portable; you can use it wherever there's an electric outlet. Speaking of electricity, I might mention that most computers call for a good bit of rewiring, to handle the heavy load of current they consume, but the Mark XI plugs into a standard outlet and consumes about half as much electricity as a toaster does. Furthermore, computers have always been so delicate that they had to be operated in carefully air-conditioned rooms; the Mark XI can operate anywhere, without regard to temperature."

The Mark XI seemed to preen itself a little, and we half expected the visible knob of brains atop it to type out some politely modest comment. Before this could happen, Mr. Clifford was heaping further compliments on it. "The *real* news about Mark XI is its price," he said. "Just after the war, when the first all-purpose computers came on the market, they cost about a million dollars. Gradually, the price has come down— first to half a million, then to a quarter of a million, and last year to a hundred and eighty-five thousand. But Monroe has made the breakthrough that the small businessman has been waiting for. Hold your breath!" Obediently, we did so. "The Monrobot Mark XI will sell for the amazingly low price of twenty-four thousand five hundred dollars," Clifford said, his eyes rolling like marbles. "A giveaway price! And for an absolutely idiot-proof machine! When data is fed into it by punched tape or cards, the machine is capable of untended operation. It can do an average of five thousand arithmetical computations per minute. By itself, with only a monitor in the room, it can automatically compute the earnings—including all deductions, overtime payments, and so on—of a payroll of eight hundred people *and* print their pay checks for them. It can also be programmed to do sales analysis, inventory control, invoicing, brokerage accounting, differential equations, and probability analysis, to name a few of its applications."

We let out our breath, and Mr. Clifford urged us to try beating the Mark XI at a game of ticktacktoe. He pulled a switch, and the typewriter on Mark XI typed out "Your move." Clifford explained that the numbers 1 through 9 on the keyboard of the typewriter had been set to represent the squares in the game. Nervily, we pressed number 5. Mark XI chose number 3.

We got trimmed in five straight games, and the vice-president in charge of marketing seemed very much pleased.

TELSTAR

Lillian Ross and Thomas Whiteside

AUGUST 4, 1962

"THINK OF TRANSOCEANIC television," Sylvester L. Weaver, Jr., who was then vice-president of the National Broadcasting Company, urged a group of N.B.C. writers just about ten years ago. "You know Something happens in Athens. *Boing!* The guy pushes the button 'Athens' and the lights begin to blink all over the place as Athens starts pouring in." Well, the great day of transatlantic television is here, thanks to the American Telephone & Telegraph Co.'s orbiting Telstar communications satellite, and if Athens itself hasn't yet started pouring in, live, through viewers' sets in this country, a stream of shots from other capitals of the Old World—London, Paris, Geneva, Brussels, Vienna, Rome—did appear on their screens the other day, while in a similar manner European viewers received on *their* screens a series of shots from New York, San Francisco, Chicago, Washington, and a number of other points in this country, during the first formal exchange of live television programs between the United States and Europe. On this side, the exchange was made possible by the joint television-production efforts of the news departments of three networks here—the Columbia Broadcasting System, the National Broadcasting Company, and the American Broadcasting Company—with the cooperation of the Canadian Broadcasting Corporation, and, on the other side, the efforts of the television branch of the European Broadcasting Union (Eurovision) whose membership embraces the broadcasting systems of eighteen European countries. The American program was produced by a tri-network committee composed of Ted Fetter (A.B.C.), Fred Friendly (C.B.S.), and Gerald Green (N.B.C.), who worked on it for a month before air time; the whole production staff, we were proudly informed by a temporarily omni-network-minded press agent at N.B.C. a day or so before the broadcast, amounted to some two hundred people, including correspondents, cameramen, producers, directors, engineers, and technicians, from the three networks.

Attracted by the grandness of the occasion, we insinuated ourself, around midday of the day of the broadcast, into Studio 4 J in the R.C.A. Building, the coordinating control room for the American part of the Telstar program, to watch part of the dress rehearsal for the final show. The control room—a comparatively small one, although specially equipped to handle complex broadcast pickups—was dimly lit and crammed with technicians and production people, and what with voices that seemed to have no point of origin within the room issuing from various loudspeakers, and the urgent voices of people present, the place seemed to us to be in a tumult. The focus of attention was a semicircular array of monitoring screens, large and small, before which a row of technicians and assistant directors, some wearing headsets with microphones, sat at a long and elaborate control panel, while another row of network men, including Fetter, Friendly, and Green, were squeezed in behind the control-panel men in a space about a quarter the size of that behind the average lunch counter. The small monitoring screens were showing scenes being fed in from various parts of the country—one showed the Statue of Liberty; another showed the big dome of the A.T.&T. Telstar transmitting and receiving equipment at Andover, Maine; another was focussed on the carved face of George Washington at Mount Rushmore; yet another showed an incessantly zooming-in and zooming-out shot of the Capitol's dome in Washington—and as the scheduled time for each one arrived, it appeared on a large monitoring screen labelled "Program." We found the whole effect bewildering.

"Stand by, El Paso! Stand by!" Sid Smith, the director of the program, who sat at the center of the control panel, was saying as we found a niche in a wall to one side of the room.

In a few moments, after a shot from El Paso, we heard a cry, "Washington, you're on!" and Chet Huntley's image appeared on the big "Program" screen.

"Switch to Chicago!" said someone at the control panel. A shot of the Cubs-Phillies game at Wrigley Field leaped on. "You should be giving the baseball sound," the same man said sharply.

The sound of the ballpark came on. "Ladees and gennelmen," a voice called out from the ballpark, "we've just been informed that this baseball game is being shown on television to Europe by Telstar. Let's give all the baseball fans in Europe a big hello from Chicago." This being only the rehearsal, the voice wasn't carried over the ballpark loudspeaker, and consequently there was no big—or any—hello from the crowd.

"Hurray!" someone at the control panel said, perfunctorily, to indicate the lapse.

Next came a tape of a Presidential press conference, in lieu of the one that was to follow, at air time.

"Go, Canaveral!" Smith cried, and John Glenn came on, talking about space exploration.

"Stand by, St. Lawrence! Switch!" Smith said after a few minutes. The St. Lawrence River appeared on the screen.

"Stand by, Stratford!" Smith said. A scene from *Macbeth,* played at the Festival Theatre, in Stratford, Ontario, came on.

"Come in, Seattle!" said Smith. Various shots of the World's Fair at Seattle appeared, including one of a boy eating a large Danish waffle.

Half the people in the control room began chanting a countdown together—from ten to one. What they were counting down was a cue to a series of live shots at Mount Rushmore.

"Stand by for 'Mighty Fortress'!" someone called as three hundred and twelve members of the Mormon Tabernacle Choir came on the screen, accompanied by an audio-tape of the choir singing "A Mighty Fortress Is Our God."

Friendly got into a discussion with one of the production people, a young man named David Buksbaum, about communications with Mount Rushmore. "We've got to cue them on 'Mighty Fortress' well ahead of time," he said.

Howard K. Smith came onscreen, and talked about the United Nations and the late Dag Hammarskjöld.

"Five! Four! Three! Two! One!" a chorus in the control room cried.

"*And* cue," the director said. "Dissolve to the Golden Gate! Dissolve to Canada! Dissolve Seattle! Dissolve Canaveral! Dissolve Statue of Liberty! Dissolve Mount Rushmore! Dissolve Niagara Falls! Dissolve U.N.!"

Chet Huntley and Walter Cronkite, onscreen, began an ad-lib discussion of the still pictures of the preceding program as they would be received in Europe and radiophotographed back here for inspection. Friendly reached over the shoulder of a technician at the control panel, picked up a microphone, and, standing in for the chief announcer at the European Broadcasting Union control center, in Brussels, said into it, "This is Mr. Dimbleby, in Brussels. We hope you have been receiving our still pictures of your program satisfactorily."

"We did indeed, Mr. Dimbleby," Cronkite said.

"Thank you very much. Good night, Chet. Good night, Walter," Friendly said. He turned again to Buksbaum. "We've *got* to cue the choir on 'Mighty Fortress' *well* ahead of time."

The program moved to what the director referred to as the pre-show section, in which the American program would make contact with Brussels. At the moment, the communication was only aural.

"We're ready," a metallic voice, with a British accent, said over a small loudspeaker in the control room.

Walter Cronkite's image appeared on the screen. "Hello, Brussels," Cronkite said.

A telephone rang at the control panel. Buksbaum answered it. "It's Bill Monroe, in Washington," he told Friendly. "He says that Pierre Salinger wants to know when we intend coming in on the press conference."

"It depends on the orbit. We don't have a time yet," Friendly said.

The metallic voice said, over the loudspeaker, "I am speaking on the microphone that Richard Dimbleby [the B.B.C. announcer] will be using. Dimbleby says, 'Yes, I have the picture. Go, America, go.' As soon as he says, 'Go, America, go—'"

"Then we wipe to full screen," Cronkite said.

"It's starting to rain at Rushmore," the director announced.

"Chet, if the choir moves indoors, you'll have to ad-lib your way through," Friendly said.

A shot of a couple of buffalo grazing in the distance flashed onto the screen.

We asked Buksbaum where the shot originated.

"Custer State Park, in South Dakota. I went out West to work on that buffalo spot, among other things, but I had to come back here again," Buksbaum replied. "They have three hundred of them out on the range. They're being rounded up right now. At air time, we'll get them to run onscreen on cue."

Buksbaum turned to a production man nearby. "Three hundred buffalo," Buksbaum said. "I guaranteed that I'd deliver them, and I guarantee that you'll see them. Every nickel's worth."

. . .

Meanwhile, back at A.T.& T. headquarters, at 195 Broadway, we had a little talk with Mr. J. W. Cook, an executive vice-president who was minding the twenty-six-story building (1914), with its spacious, cool, marble-columned halls, bronze-inlaid marble floors, marble drinking fountains, marble friezes of winged cherubs over elevators operated by handsome and unmistakably human girls—the whole beautiful works carrying a modest slogan in its ground-floor windows: "Long Distance Telephone Conquers Time and Space."

"Pretty good building we've got here. Hard to replace," said Mr. Cook, who wore a fine sunburn and a neat blue suit. "We might gussy it up a bit—the lighting is a little old-fashioned—by cleaning the porcelain shades, but I wouldn't change anything in our surroundings. They're highly economical. They're chock-full of character. We overlook the graveyards of St. Paul's and Trinity. This place has substance. Space is sort of exotic. Telstar is a first. A great thrill. But our basic business is still the telephone call."

"Then what's Telstar?" we asked.

"Another string to our bow," Mr. Cook said. "We're a service business. The Princess telephone furnishes a service. Automatic dialling furnishes a service. Telstar gives us another way to make your telephone call. There's lots more going on around here besides that bird up there. The guidance system of the anti-missile missile—that's ours, too. Engineering, Marketing, Testing—all our departments are constantly working on new services. Our marketing people might be thinking of using Telstar for high-speed data machines. Machines talk to machines these days. Say you're a large corporation. You have branches in Italy, France, Belgium, West Germany, Spain, and you like to keep your finger on the pulse. Costs. Investments. Telstar may be useful in keeping your machines in touch with their machines. Like that!" Mr. Cook snapped his fingers. "Telstar supplements our use of cables for transoceanic telephone calls. Once you get a world system operating, with a lot of the birds up there going around, Brazil could use Telstar to call North Africa. Right now, however, the point is we made our calculations, declared ourselves, and brought it off. The whole ball of wax cost between forty-five and fifty million dollars."

"Any shareholders complain about spending all that money?" we asked.

"Not a one," Mr. Cook said. "I've owned a few shares myself for many years, and I go along with the way most of the shareholders feel—proud. I don't regard Telstar as just another supplementary piece of equipment—a new button to shut off the telephone with, or those chimes that ring in your house instead of an ordinary telephone bell, or the Rapidial. You can't beat the plain telephone, but you don't make character going downhill; you make character going uphill. Down here"—Mr. Cook pushed the bar on a Rapidial on his desk, and the machine (which dials numbers *for* you) whirred around, making do-it-itself noises—"I get a chance to fool with a lot of the different gadgets we come out with. Up there"—he waved both hands at Telstar—"you lose a large share of your collective control. Once you put it up there, you can never get it back."

"Which would you choose," we asked, "if you had to choose?"

"I beg the question," Mr. Cook said.

"Now," said a young assistant assigned to us by Mr. Cook, "we'll just look in on the chairman of the board."

"He's at a meeting," the secretary of the c. of the b. told us. "The past week, it's been one hectic meeting after another. Go take a rest in his office. It's very restful. It's very mellow."

We rested there for a few minutes, in one of several immense leather armchairs, looking at Oriental rugs and a white ceiling embossed with cherubs and figures of the zodiac. Set on a bookshelf was an old-fashioned mahogany radio, a Stromberg-Carlson of early-thirties vintage. "I polish that old radio myself," the c. of the b.'s secretary told us. "Everybody around here loves it."

THE BIG BANG

John Updike

JUNE 5, 1965 ("NOTES AND COMMENT")

WE CONFESS OURSELF pleased that the "big-bang" theory of cosmogony seems to have scored over its less flashy rival, the "steady-state" theory. The big-bang theory was proposed, you will recall, when it became apparent, in the 1920s, that the galaxies beyond our own galaxy, the Milky Way, were flying from us at speeds proportionate to their distances. Simple calculation indicated that all cosmic matter had therefore once been concentrated at one point, a gigantic, gigantically dense and hot "cosmic atom," which had in an instant exploded into fragments that settled, over the aeons, into stars, planets, oceans, minerals, amoebae, and the constituents of this page and of the eyes perusing it. Whence the aboriginal ball of matter, and wherefore, were permitted to remain mysterious. The steady-state theory, in protest, claims that the universe is eternal and constant, and therefore had no definite beginning. The observed fact of cosmic expansion is explained rather curiously; to wit, new matter, in the form of hydrogen atoms, is unceasingly being generated *out of nothing* in the empty spaces between galaxies, which are retreating to make room for the new matter. So an infinite number of microcosmic miracles are substituted for a single macrocosmic one. The slow garnering of tiny, colorless somethings from vast fields of vacuity has always struck us as a somewhat dreary harvest, and we are glad that our aesthetic preferences have recently been reinforced by the plunging researches of radio astronomy.

In brief, it is now thought that the flash of the initial explosion still exists in the air, in the form of radio waves. The expansion of the universe in the thirteen billion years or so since the blessed event has stretched the light waves into a low hum audible to a giant horn antenna in Homdel, New Jersey. The first emissions of creation, stretched out of visibility, still hover in the air; the command "Let there be light" is continuously arriving from the black gulf beyond the quasars. We find all this more comforting than not. Such simultaneity makes a haven of time, and satisfies that ancient man within us who likes a story to have a distinct beginning, middle, and end.

· · ·

We were present not long ago at a literary ceremonial (an occasion customarily as innocuous as a confluence of angels on the head of a pin) that began with a kind of bang—a stately, though startling, tirade against our government's present role in Vietnam—and the next day we witnessed a meeting of the United Nations Security Council at which, to our surprise, the representative from Cuba, predictably attacking our intercession in the Dominican Republic, frequently referred for support and corroboration to the editorial columns of the New York *Times*. We cannot remember any time in the last twenty years when United States foreign policy has received so much domestic criticism. Insofar as the present debate strengthens the democratic habit of debate, it is to the good. Insofar as it weakens the ties of respect and exchange between the intellectual community and the federal administration, it is to be regretted. The colleges seem to be fostering a self-righteous and rather idyllic pacifism, while the shadowy agencies of power perpetrate a self-righteous and rather grim activism.

Now, a nation utterly unwilling to use its power has abdicated reality. But in our own recent use of power there has been a change of tone that is unwelcome even to those willing to believe that the gambles taken were well calculated. Perhaps the change has been reflected back to us from the world. Communism no longer appears a monolithic menace, so our own position feels deprived of grandeur. In the headlines that report our ubiquitous self-assertions, there is something naked, something at once petty and reckless. A nation is a mass of intertwined selfishnesses that yet must seem selfless to itself. It is not enough to have national interests and to administer them; when Rome degenerated from an ideal to an administrative system, men had to be paid to risk death for it. There are no simple alternatives. The possibility of total destruction limits crusades; yet the United States, in adjusting to a pragmatic world of piecemeal decisions, may have overadjusted.

TOUCH-TONE

George W. S. Trow

APRIL 8, 1967 ("(YET ANOTHER) FIRST STEP")

Mr. A. T. Engkvist, a district manager of the New York Telephone Company, wrote the other day to tell us about a step he was taking—it was a "First Step"—to improve communications services. Mr. Engkvist is a polite man who addresses us, in formal fashion, as "Dear Customer," and he is very fond of issuing stirring announcements, all of which we have read with interest. This time, he brought news of an important achievement: the elimination of the old dial tone, which was getting in the way, in favor of a new—and presumably better—one, noticeably "lower in pitch." We remembered that Mr. Engkvist, or his predecessor, in previous "First Step"s, had eliminated the telephone operator and the telephone exchange, and we began to see that there were no lengths to which he and his company would not go to improve service.

Following a suggestion in Mr. Engkvist's letter, we dialled 759-5820 (this used to be PLaza 9-5820, in the days when there was a Third Avenue "L" and a Roxy Theatre) to hear a preview sample of the new tone. We heard, successively, a sound like an overloaded Waring Blendor, a nice recorded young lady telling us that the new tone would improve our communications services, and then the Waring Blendor sound again. This, though entertaining, and very neatly done, did not completely satisfy our curiosity, so we went downtown to the New York Telephone Company's Headquarters to talk to some people in the know.

We visited Mr. Al Smith, who is a tall man, and gray, and genial, in his office, on the tenth floor of 140 West Street. Mr. Smith (he is not related to the other Al Smith) told us that the new dial tone is a part of "The Touch-Tone Story," which is a phrase that telephone people use when they want to talk about improved communications services. Touch-tone telephones have small buttons (one for every number), which make strange little sounds when you touch them. Anyone with practice can play them very quickly, which is the whole point. "Now, on the rotary dial a ten-digit pull—number plus area code—will take you, on the average, about fourteen seconds," Mr. Smith said. "On the touch-tone unit it will take you about *four* seconds. If you have a rotary-dial phone, you see, and you have a lot of eights or nines or zeros in the number, you have to wait for the dial to come back. *That's* where the touch-tone makes the saving."

Mr. Smith introduced us by phone to an engineer called Ken, who explained why the old dial tone wouldn't do for touch-tone purposes. "We had to pick the touch-tone sounds very carefully, so our equipment wouldn't confuse them with other sounds—like music on the radio," Ken said. "The old dial tone was wrong for this system and *would* have confused the equipment. Also, the new tone is much more interesting musically. It is a chord, really—two pure, different frequencies. The old one was one tone modulated by another tone."

Mr. Smith said that touch-tone equipment could be installed (at a slight extra cost) only on lines that had been changed over to the new dial tone, that there weren't very many of those lines now, but that the Telephone Company hoped to have a hundred thousand available to customers by the end of the year. Then he showed us the most modern touch-tone telephone of all, a unit called the Touch-Tone Trimline, which is only a month old, and a unit known as the Card Dialler, which has been in use for five or six years. Mr. Smith told us that when a programmed card is inserted in a slot the Card Dialler will dial a number automatically. Mr. Smith looked through some cards, found one that was programmed for the New York weather number, and demonstrated. The unit dialled the number automatically in something over fourteen seconds. Mr. Smith said that he sometimes read the paper while the number was being dialled, and that struck us as a very sensible thing to do.

SGT. PEPPER

Lillian Ross

JUNE 24, 1967

Meet the Beatles, the first (January, 1964) record album in the United States of John, Paul, George, and Ringo, has sold five million three hundred thousand copies to date. Pictures of the faces of John, Paul, George, and Ringo appeared on its cover. The songs "I Want to Hold Your Hand," "I Saw Her Standing There," and "All My Loving," among others, were featured. *Sgt. Pepper's Lonely Hearts Club Band,* the thirteenth and latest (June, 1967) album of John, Paul, George, and Ringo, came out the week before last and has sold twelve hundred thousand copies to date, with ninety-five thousand more in back orders. On the cover, John, Paul, George, and Ringo are pictured, wearing old-timey satin-and-braid brass-band costumes, in the company of the faces of—to name just a few—Shirley Temple, H. G. Wells, Marilyn Monroe, Karl Marx, Lenny Bruce, Edgar Allan Poe, Lawrence of Arabia, Marlene Dietrich, Johnny Weissmuller, Dion, Carl Jung, Mae West, Fred Astaire, Tom Mix, W. C. Fields, Laurel and Hardy, Karlheinz Stockhausen, Bob Dylan, Oscar Wilde, and Madame Tussaud's wax figures of John, Paul, George, and Ringo. On this record, the Beatles (with Paul singing most of the solos) create the effect of a live show, starting with a number about *Sgt. Pepper* and going on, with no more than momentary interruptions, to numbers called, among others, "A Little Help from My Friends," "Lucy in the Sky with Diamonds," "Fixing a Hole," "She's Leaving Home," "When I'm Sixty-four," "Lovely Rita," and "A Day in the Life." (The other Beatles albums: No. 2, *The Beatles' Second Album*, was brought out in April, 1964. No. 3, *Something New*, was brought out in July, 1964. No. 4, *A Hard Day's Night*, September, 1964. No. 5, *The Beatles' Story*, November, 1964. No. 6, *Beatles '65*, December, 1964. No. 7, *The Early Beatles*, March, 1965. No. 8, *Beatles VI*, June, 1965. No. 9, *Help!*, the sound track of the movie of that name, August, 1965. No. 10, *Rubber Soul*, December, 1965. No. 11, *Yesterday and Today*, June, 1966. No. 12, *Revolver*, August, 1966.)

About a year ago, the screams of the Beatles' teen-age fans abated somewhat, and other voices began to be heard, saying that the Beatles were "going too far," or were "burned out," or were "getting too serious," or weren't "funny anymore." Now *Sgt. Pepper* is out, and it's a huge success, and we've been talking to some record people about it. "We were the first to play it on the air," a WMCA disc jockey named Joe O'Brien told us. "We played 'A Day in the Life' on April 18th, six weeks before the album came out. This to me is the first *album* that's ever been made by a popular group. All others, including all other Beatles albums, are a collection of singles. This one is a forty-minute-*long* single."

"How did the listeners react?" we asked.

"Not much," O'Brien said. "They're unprepared. Just as people were unprepared for Picasso. That's because this album is not a teen-age album. It's a terribly intellectual album. My youngest son is a freshman at Yale. He tells me that the day the album was issued the entire student body of Yale went out and bought it. Exactly the same thing happened at Harvard. The college students are now the hard-core Beatles fans. This album is really a cantata. Teen-agers don't want *that*."

"Proof positive of their musical maturity," was Murray the K's pronouncement to us. "The Beatles had the guts to go ahead and do something different from anything they've ever done before. There are very few commercial songs in this one, but it's a giant step forward. I've been playing the whole album, non-stop, on my show. I don't have to worry. My listeners are in the eighteen-to-twenty-five age group."

We went over to Sam Goody's West Forty-ninth Street record shop, and there we ran into a couple of young men who were picking up the album. "It's like a show!," a tieless, shoeless guitar carrier named Richard Mellerton told us. "It stones you." We elicited a more detailed response from a dark-suited young man wearing gold-rimmed spectacles, who told us he was an English Lit. major at C.C.N.Y. and is now a summer busboy at the Hotel Penn Garden Coffee House. The student, John Van Aalst, told us, "I'm really more interested in classical music, but this Beatles record goes beyond the sound of the record. It's technically interesting and imaginative. This is no longer computerized rock 'n' roll. This may have grown out of the hoodlum rock 'n' roll of the fifties, but it's an attempt to create music with meaning. It goes beyond making you feel good, although it does do that. It has aesthetic appeal. It conforms more to my conception of art."

One of Goody's staff men watched the parade of Beatles buyers with a friendly eye. The record, he told us, was big, very big, at Goody's. "We've sold thousands," he said. "It's selling like the first Horowitz Carnegie Hall return concert."

Up at the Colony Record Center, on Broadway at Fifty-second Street, we came across a spirited, professorial-looking man named Lawrence LeFevre, who was plucking the Beatles' new record from a bin that contained the works of the Jefferson Airplane, the Blues Project, the Mamas and the Papas, and the Lovin' Spoonful. Mr. LeFevre gave us a little lecture: "This is really a coming of age for the Beatles," he said. "In musical substance, *Sgt. Pepper* is a much bigger advance than *Revolver*, and *Revolver* was a tremendous advance, if you recall. There are many musical structures here that are both new and extremely interesting, as well as new combinations of rhythms, new chord progressions, new instrumentations, and a continuation of the great fresh flow of melody. The Beatles, as you know, have drawn upon everything musical that has been done in the past, including Romantic, baroque, liturgical, and all the popular genres of music, including blues, jazz, the English music hall, English folk, and, of course, rock 'n' roll. Many people have pointed out how eclectic the Beatles are. They've drawn on everything. But now this is *Beatles* music. Hundreds of people are imitating what they do, but no one even gets close. This record is a musical *event*, comparable to a notable new opera or symphonic work. However, there is more going on musically in this one record than has gone on lately almost anywhere else. 'A Day in the Life' is not only the most ambitious thing they ever wrote but possibly the best piece of music they've done up to now. One can't say just what it is—it fits into no category—but it's a complex and powerful number. Another number, 'When I'm Sixty-four,' has so much charm and taste. It's a parody, but, like the best parody, it is written with affection, and it has an excellence in its own right, independent of its value as parody. And 'Fixing a Hole' is right up there with the Beatles' nicest. The Beatles write to please themselves. Unlike many artists now, who get their kicks out of offending the public, they're having a great time with the stuff itself. It has enormous cheerfulness, along with the sadness that keeps turning up. It's buoyant. This album is a whole world created by the Beatles. It's a musical comedy. It's a film. Only, it's a record. There's no individual number that's as downright lovely as, say, 'Michelle' or 'Here, There, and Everywhere,' but you have to look at this album as an entity, and as such it has considerable beauty. Of course, you can't talk about the Beatles without mentioning the transcendent Duke Ellington. Just as he has never fit into the jazz scheme of things, the Beatles don't fit into the rock-'n'-roll scheme. They are off by themselves, doing their own thing, just as Ellington always has been. Like Ellington, they're unclassifiable musicians. And, again like Ellington, they are working in that special territory where entertainment slips over into art. I might add that in this record there isn't anything that is manufactured or contrived or synthetic. All of it is spontaneous, inspired music. There's a wry kind of sweetness in several of the numbers, some of which has to do with McCartney's—excuse me, I mean Paul's—way of singing. You never feel that the Beatles are writing themselves out. They have a lot in reserve. This is just a beginning for them. The high point of the high point for me is the delicate way, in 'A Day in the Life,' Lennon—John—sings the words 'oh boy.' Let me add one last thing. The Beatles have done more to brighten up the world in recent years than almost anything else in the arts."

APOLLO 11

Henry S. F. Cooper, Jr.

JULY 26, 1969 (FROM "LETTER FROM THE SPACE CENTER")

JULY 21

AFTER THE LAUNCH of Apollo 11 at Cape Kennedy last week, several thousand people who had been at the Cape checked into hotels in the vicinity of the Manned Spaceflight Center, in Houston. One of the arrivals was Dr. Harold C. Urey, the elder statesman among selenologists, who had gone from here to the Cape early last week. The launch, he said, had more than lived up to his expectations. "The V.I.P. bleachers were so far away that we didn't hear the noise until the base of the rocket had reached the top of the tower," he said on his return. "Then there was this enormous light, and the rocket goes up and up, and then it goes through the first skiff of clouds, and then through the second skiff of clouds, and then you see a puff of smoke—the first burn-out—and then the rocket disappears. The precision! The accuracy! If only a fraction of this precision and accuracy spins off into industry, it will pay for the whole space program." David Reed, the Flight Dynamics Officer, who for months had been practicing the flight in simulations, and who was sitting in the front row of the Mission Control Room in Houston after liftoff, said that the reason he knew the launch was the real thing and not another simulation was that everything was going so well. . . .

. . .

On Sunday afternoon, after the lunar module had touched down on the moon, the only way a visitor could tell that anything out of the ordinary was going on at the Space Center was that suddenly, at a little after three o'clock, many people started pinning buttons on their lapels that read "Lunar Contact." Outside the Public Affairs Building, a number of demonstrators sat around a full-size mockup of the LM displaying signs that read "Texas—Big on Hunger" and "Good Luck from the Hungry Children of Houston." The demonstrators refused to leave at five o'clock, when the Space Center closes to visitors, and they lingered on during a thunderstorm, from which a few of them took refuge beneath the LM. On the roof of a nearby building, a radio dish was aimed at the moon, which was behind a thundercloud, and as the evening progressed the dish tilted farther and farther to the west.

A little after eight, I joined Dr. Urey and his wife, a gray-haired lady in a blue dress, who had already turned on their television set and were waiting for Neil Armstrong to come out of the LM. Mrs. Urey set a bowl of green grapes on the table in front of the television set, and explained quickly that they came from Arizona, not California. Dr. Urey, who has had a number of ideas about what the moon is like, was obviously settling back to enjoy the evening; he said that he wasn't particularly anxious about any of his theories, because he had good reasons for them even if they should prove wrong. But he added that he hoped they were right. Dr. Urey has been one of the impact selenologists, who believe in a relatively cold moon, though one that may have had a certain amount of volcanic activity, and recently he has inclined toward the view that the flat *maria* such as the one the astronauts were on were sediments deposited by oceans long since dried up. Vulcanists, on the other hand, have believed that the same ground was made up of lava or ash flows. The astronauts lowered the pressure inside the LM, and as the television camera was turned on and Armstrong came down the ladder and stepped onto the moon, Dr. Urey sat forward in his chair and remained absolutely still. He seemed pleased when Armstrong described the moon's surface as primarily gray (a color Dr. Urey had opted for against brown), covered with fine particles, and sticky. Stickiness, he said in a hurried aside, was a characteristic of small particles in vacuums. Moments later, however, when Armstrong, gathering the contingency sample, said that he saw vesiculations—bubbles of a sort—in some rocks, Dr. Urey seemed downcast; vesiculations, he explained, are characteristic of pumice, and pumice is a lava—a relatively frothy one. When Colonel Aldrin came out of the LM and Armstrong took the television camera some thirty feet away in order to record a panoramic view of the countryside, Dr. Urey said that it was beautiful in the manner of an Arctic wasteland, and, indeed, the two astronauts, in their heavy suits, did look like old photographs of Admiral Peary at the North Pole. They moved as though the ground were slippery (as it would be at the Pole)—a characteristic that Dr. Urey and others had thought likely. In fact, except for the vesiculations, nothing surprised Dr. Urey. A minute later, he expressed surprise over a report of Armstrong's that many of the rocks littering the ground were standing on edge. This bothered Dr. Urey, because rocks that had been ejected from craters during their formation shouldn't be standing up on the surface but should be buried beneath it. He wondered aloud whether this phenomenon might not suggest some sort of erosion that had removed the fine particles from around the rocks. Dr. Urey quite evidently couldn't wait to get his hands on some of those rocks, and he expressed a particular desire for a large angular one in the foreground of the television screen, which he hoped the astronauts would bring back. (They didn't.) As Armstrong and Aldrin erected the American flag, jumped around to test their mobility, and photographed each other, Dr. Urey said impatiently, "Oh, hurry up and get the samples!" Shortly afterward, Armstrong, who had got back to business (as Dr. Urey saw it) and was again reporting on the ground beneath his feet, remarked that the rocks he had first described as vesiculated no longer appeared that way. Dr. Urey said almost gleefully, "No pumice! The astronauts haven't seen pumice after all! The astronauts know very well what pumice looks like, yet they're not reporting any pumice!" He beamed at Armstrong, who was now saying that he thought the little holes in the rocks might have been made by impacting micrometeorites. As time was running out and the astronauts were behind schedule, Dr. Urey began to worry that they wouldn't have time to take any underground core samples. He was anxious about the core samples because if there had once been oceans on the moon, they might show layers of sediment. As the astronauts were hurrying to pack up and get back into the LM, Dr. Urey said, "Don't forget Geiss's experiment!" (Dr. Johannes Geiss, whose solar-wind experiment with a silvery foil the astronauts were to bring back with them, was once a post-doctoral fellow of Dr. Urey's, and an old friend.) Dr. Urey sat on the edge of his chair during the last-minute scramble on the moon, though he leaned back again in evident dismay when Armstrong, who was gathering a final batch of rocks, suddenly used the word "vesiculation" again. Dr. Urey said that he was quite confused now about whether Armstrong had really seen vesiculations. "I'm inclined to think that he was in a hurry the two times he used the word," he said. "The time he corrected himself was probably his more considered opinion." After the astronauts were safely back in the LM, Dr. Urey—clearly impressed with the operation—said everything had gone so smoothly and predictably that he didn't know much more about the moon than he had known before. "When they come back with the samples, we'll have some real answers," he said.

BRIEF
ENCOUNTERS

ORNETTE COLEMAN

Donald Stewart and Whitney Balliett

JUNE 4, 1960 ("THE TRUE ESSENCE")

OR THE PAST six months, the built-in seismographs with which jazz admirers record every move of their idols have been writing right off the page, short-circuiting, or simply going dead. The cause of this impressive disturbance, which has been equalled in jazz only by the Louis Armstrong eruption in the early twenties, the Benny Goodman explosion in the late thirties, and the Charlie Parker–Dizzy Gillespie–Thelonious Monk upheaval in the mid-forties, is an unassuming and hitherto unknown thirty-year-old alto saxophonist from Fort Worth named Ornette Coleman, whose quartet has been performing off and on since last November before bulging houses at the Five Spot, a small Third Avenue–type bar on Cooper Square. (Suffice it to say that Coleman's playing, which is largely indescribable, involves a unique form of free improvisation, set forth in a flow of sounds that may resemble an automotive disorder in one measure and pure bird song in the next.) These houses have included every jazz critic in town; celebrated jazz musicians, like Miles Davis, Charlie Mingus, Percy Heath, and Lionel Hampton, all of whom have become so exercised by Coleman that they have asked, and been granted, permission to sit in with his quartet; and a host of the merely curious, among them Leonard Bernstein, Faye Emerson, Jule Styne, the Ambassador to the United Nations from Ghana, Marc Blitzstein, Sam Levenson, Virgil Thomson, Betty Comden, and the thirty-four members of the senior class of the Stockbridge School, who made a pilgrimage to the Five Spot all the way from Massachusetts. In an effort to find out a little more about this Wizard of Oz, we arranged to have dinner with Coleman one evening last week at a restaurant on West Eleventh Street. He arrived a moment or two after we did, carrying a compact instrument case, a large navel orange, and a tightly furled umbrella, which swung easily from his left arm. A slim, handsome colored man of medium height, dressed in an impeccable dark-green suit and a black tie, and wearing a beard, Coleman checked his case and umbrella, placed the orange carefully beside his butter plate, shook hands in the self-deprecating way that is often affected by the great, sat down opposite us, and, without hesitation, began a concentrated, non-stop, from-the-inside-looking-out monologue that had a lot in common with one of his instrumental solos: "I'm not very hungry. I just ate a little while ago, but I'll have a small Salisbury steak and a salad, maybe with some Thousand Island dressing. I haven't heard one person yet who can explain what I'm doing. People laugh at me, shake their heads. But I won't let any of that affect me. There's but one thing you can do—play the true essence of yourself. Talent and appearances have nothing to do with each other. Look at van Gogh. He cut off his ear; it didn't hurt his talent. Most people fail to hear what is being played at the *moment* it is played. They pay more attention to behavior and what they see than to what is happening musically. I know exactly what I'm doing. I'm beginning where Charlie Parker stopped. Parker's melodic lines were placed across ordinary chord progressions. My melodic approach is based on phrasing, and my phrasing is an extension of how I hear the intervals and pitch of the tunes I play. There is no end to pitch. You can play flat in tune and sharp in tune. It's a question of vibration. My phrasing is spontaneous, not a style. A style happens when your phrasing hardens. Jazz music is the only music in which the same note can be played night after night but differently each time. It's the hidden things, the subconscious that lies in the body and lets you know: you feel this, you play this. Do you understand that? After all, *music* is harmless. It all depends on which way a person is using it. I give my musicians one of my tunes and tell them, 'You play that your way. You add to it what you can. Enlarge it. Extend it.' But this isn't easy, I know. The other night, at a rehearsal for a concert I played in of Gunther Schuller's music at the Circle in the Square, Schuller made me play a little four-measure thing he'd written six or seven times before I got it right. I could read it, see the notes on the paper. But I heard those notes in my head, heard their pitch, and what I heard was different from what Schuller heard. Then I got it right. I got it his way. It was as simple as that."

Coleman paused abruptly, picked up the orange, hefted it, and rolled it around reflectively in his hands. We asked him to tell us about his early career. "I started playing the alto when I was about fourteen," he said, replacing the orange and attacking his Salisbury steak. "My family couldn't afford to give me lessons, so I bought an instruction book and taught myself, but I taught myself wrong. I thought the low C on my horn was the A in the book, and when I joined a church band the leader said, 'Look at this boy. Playing the instrument wrong for two years. He'll never be a saxophone player.' You can't live down your mistakes, but if you keep thinking about them you can't emerge from them, either. I hooked up with a carnival band, then a rhythm-and-blues group, which stranded me in California in 1950. They kept telling me in that band I was doing this wrong, doing that wrong. In the next six, seven years, I travelled back and forth between Fort Worth and California, playing once in a while but doing day work mostly—stockboy, houseboy, freight-elevator operator. By 1957, I had got very depressed in California, and I wired my ma would she send me a bus ticket home, and on the day the ticket arrived, Les Koenig, of Contemporary Records, asked me to audition some of my tunes for him. I did, and he gave me my first record session. I began playing around California, and in 1959 John Lewis heard me in Frisco and asked me to come to the School of Jazz, at Lenox, Massachusetts, that summer, and after that, since I felt I'd never got a chance to exist properly, to know what I truly am, I migrated to New York. Now I'm set. Or, anyway, set to be set. What I'd like most now is a vacation, but I've got three musicians depending on me. I'm tired. Six hours a night, six nights a week. Sometimes I go to the club and I can't understand what I feel. 'Am I here? How will I make it through tonight?' I say to myself. I'd like to play a couple of nights a week is all. I'd have more to say. I'd get closer to harnessing my feelings, to getting down to the true essence. Well, it's time to work."

Coleman yawned, picked up his orange, and tossed it into the air.

"What are you going to do with that orange?" we asked.

"Why, eat it, man," he said, laughing. "What else? An orange is very pleasant two o'clock in the morning."

CASSIUS CLAY

A. J. Liebling

MARCH 3, 1962 (FROM "POET AND PEDAGOGUE")

WHEN FLOYD PATTERSON regained the world heavyweight championship by knocking out Ingemar Johansson in June, 1960, he so excited a teen-ager named Cassius Marcellus Clay, in Louisville, Kentucky, that Clay, who was a good amateur light heavyweight, made up a ballad in honor of the victory. (The tradition of pugilistic poetry is old; according to Pierce Egan, the Polybius of the London Prize Ring, Bob Gregson, the Lancashire Giant, used "to recount the deeds of his Brethren of the Fist in heroic verse, like the Bards of Old." A sample Gregson couplet was "The British lads that's here / Quite strangers are to fear." He was not a very good fighter, either.) At the time, Clay was too busy training for the Olympic boxing tournament in Rome that summer to set his ode down on paper, but he memorized it, as Homer and Gregson must have done with their things, and then polished it up in his head. "It took me about three days to think it up," Clay told me a week or so ago, while he was training in the Department of Parks gymnasium, on West Twenty-eighth Street, for his New York début as a professional, against a heavyweight from Detroit named Sonny Banks. In between his composition of the poem and his appearance on Twenty-eighth Street, Clay had been to Rome and cleaned up his Olympic opposition with aplomb, which is his strongest characteristic. The other finalist had been a Pole with a name that it takes two rounds to pronounce, but Cassius had not tried. A book that I own called *Olympic Games: 1960*, translated from the German, says, "Clay fixes the Pole's punch-hand with an almost hypnotic stare and by nimble dodging renders his attacks quite harmless." He thus risked being disqualified for holding and hitting, but he got away with it. He had then turned professional under social and financial auspices sufficient to launch a bank, and had won ten tryout bouts on the road. Now he told me that Banks, whom he had never seen, would be no problem.

I had watched Clay's performance in Rome and had considered it attractive but not probative. Amateur boxing compares with professional boxing as college theatricals compare with stealing scenes from Margaret Rutherford. Clay had a skittering style, like a pebble scaled over water. He was good to watch, but he seemed to make only glancing contact. It is true that the Pole finished the three-round bout helpless and out on his feet, but I thought he had just run out of puff chasing Clay, who had then cut him to pieces. ("Pietrzykowski is done for," the Olympic book says. "He gazes helplessly into his corner of the ring; his legs grow heavier and he cannot escape his rival.") A boxer who uses his legs as much as Clay used his in Rome risks deceleration in a longer bout. I had been more impressed by Patterson when *he* was an Olympian, in 1952; he had knocked out his man in a round.

At the gym that day, Cassius was on a mat doing situps when Mr. Angelo Dundee, his trainer, brought up the subject of the ballad. "He is smart," Dundee said. "He made up a poem." Clay had his hands locked behind his neck, elbows straight out, as he bobbed up and down. He is a golden-brown young man, big-chested and long-legged, whose limbs have the smooth, rounded look that Joe Louis's used to have, and that frequently denotes fast muscles. He is twenty years old and six feet two inches tall, and he weighs a hundred and ninety-five pounds.

"I'll say it for you," the poet announced, without waiting to be wheedled or breaking cadence. He began on a rise:

> "You may talk about Sweden [down and up again], You may
> talk about Rome [down and up again],
> But Rockville Centre is Floyd Patterson's home [down]."

He is probably the only poet in America who can recite this way. I would like to see T. S. Eliot try.

Clay went on, continuing his ventriflexions:

> "A lot of people say that Floyd couldn't fight,
> But you should have seen him on that comeback night."

There were some lines that I fumbled; the tempo of situps and poetry grew concurrently faster as the bardic fury took hold. But I caught the climax as the poet's voice rose:

> "He cut up his eyes and mussed up his face.
> And that last left hook *knocked his head out of place!*"

Cassius smiled and said no more for several situps, as if waiting for Johansson to be carried to his corner. He resumed when the Swede's seconds had had time to slosh water in his pants and bring him around. The fight was done; the press took over:

> "A reporter asked: 'Ingo, will a rematch be put on?'
> Johansson said: 'Don't know. It might be postponed.'"

The poet did a few more silent strophes, and then said:

> "If he would have stayed in Sweden,
> He wouldn't have took that beatin'."

Here, overcome by admiration, he lay back and laughed. After a minute or two, he said, "That rhymes. I like it."

There are trainers I know who, if they had a fighter who was a poet, would give up on him, no matter how good he looked, but Mr. Dundee is of the permissive school. Dundee has been a leading Italian name in the prizefighting business in this country ever since about 1910, when a manager named Scotty Monteith had a boy named Giuseppe Carrora whom he rechristened Johnny Dundee. Johnny became the hottest lightweight around; in 1923, in the twilight of his career, he boiled down and won the featherweight championship of the world. Clay's trainer is a brother of John R. Stingo, an ancient connoisseur, who says, "Body-punching is capital investment," or the late Sam Langford, who, when asked why he punched so much for the body, said, "The head got eyes."

Now Cassius reappeared, a glass of fashion in a snuff-colored suit and one of those lace-front shirts, which I had never before known anybody with nerve enough to wear, although I had seen them in shirt-shop windows on Broadway. His tie was like two shoestring ends laid across each other, and his smile was white and optimistic. He did not appear to know how badly he was being brought up.

GLENN GOULD

Lillian Ross

M R. GLENN GOULD, the pianist, held a private showing one recent morning, for Mr. Yehudi Menuhin, the violinist, of a movie starring himself. The movie, which had been made from an hour-long video-tape recording, was entitled *The Anatomy of Fugue*. It was projected on a screen the size of a pillowcase, in a room the size of an average closet, in the local office of the Canadian Broadcasting Corporation, which had broadcast the tape. Mr. Gould, unslept and unbarbered, was in town for a couple of days from his home, in Toronto. He had on his usual baggy dark-blue suit with outmoded overpadded shoulders, a raggedy brown sweater, and a worn-out bluish necktie. A yellow pencil protruded, eraser end up, from his coat pocket. He was burdened with a baggy brown overcoat, a brown wool muffler, and a navy-blue cap. Mr. Menuhin, pink-cheeked, chubby, trim, and serene, had come to town from *his* home, in London, to start on a three-month, twenty eight-city recital tour that would include several benefit appearances and one appearance on the *Bell Telephone Hour*. He was neatly encased in well-tailored pin stripes and well-laundered supplementation. Mr. Gould sat on a straight-backed office chair, with his coat, cap, and muffler on his lap, and with his arms crossed and his hands tucked under his arms. Mr. Menuhin sat on a straight-backed office chair right behind him, his fingers intertwined over his midriff.

"I'm so glad you could come, I'm so glad you could really make it," Mr. Gould said, turning around, to Mr. Menuhin. "I want you to see this one. This one is a special pet."

"Such a nice thing to do in New York," Mr. Menuhin said, in a light, warm voice, and gave Mr. Gould a gentle, warm smile. "Seeing a movie, at eleven o'clock in the morning! I'm so happy you suggested it."

"I like making these films," Mr. Gould said. "I've always felt this terrible frustration in concerts—you do it and it's gone. Why not put it on film and have it? So that it will *be* there."

"Wonderful idea. Wonderful," Mr. Menuhin said, his smile broadening and a look of appreciation coming into his eyes.

Mr. Gould grinned.

"I did a television film on Bartók, covering the musical influences in his life, and playing some of his arrangements of Hungarian folk tunes and excerpts from the solo violin sonata he wrote for me, and speaking in between, and I did another one about Yoga," Mr. Menuhin said. "I find it rather difficult when they put you in front of the camera and say '*Do* something.'"

Mr. Gould bobbed his head in agreement. "We had a very good director for this one, and we even built a set, as you'll see," he said. "We shot the whole thing in two days. After two months of conferences, of course."

"Was it dreadfully expensive?" Mr. Menuhin asked. "These things do cost so much."

"Thirty thousand dollars, about," Mr. Gould said. "But I wanted to do it right. There's no point in doing it at all if you can't get what you want." He waved a hand at the projectionist, who was peeking out of a square hole in the back wall. "We're ready any time you want to start," Mr. Gould said.

Mr. Menuhin gave a little sigh and tightened his hands around his middle. "I hope this will be made available to television in this country," he said.

Mr. Gould grinned again. "Well, *they've* got Leonard Bernstein," he said. "I don't do it the way he does it. Not that I don't admire the way he does it. He has the ability to communicate on a great many levels at once. My way is different." He bobbed his head vigorously. "I don't know if my film is for the mass public. Sometimes I think they don't know what the hell I've said, but they feel elevated."

Mr. Menuhin's eyes twinkled.

"Roll it," Mr. Gould said to the projectionist behind the wall. He turned back toward the screen, and tossed his coat, muffler, and cap on the floor. The lights went out, and the movie started, showing Mr. Gould at the piano playing an improvisation based on "Do Re Mi," from Richard Rodgers' score for *The Sound of Music*. When he had finished it, he looked up, on the screen, and said to the camera, "For hundreds of years, musicians have been doing the sort of thing that I was attempting just now. They have been taking little bits of musical trivia, like that theme from *The Sound of Music*, and trying to find complicated equations into which, like a common denominator, these tidbits will fit. In fact, there is some part of almost every musician that longs to experiment with the mathematical quantities of music and to find forms in which these quantities can function most successfully. And perhaps the long-time favorite of such forms is that special musical mix we call the fugue. The fugue is normally conceived in a number of voices, a number of individual lines that, up to a certain point, may lead a life of their own. But they must have in common a responsibility to some special material that is examined in the course of the fugue, and consequently each of the voices is first heard announcing, in its most comfortable register, the same theme. . . ."

As Mr. Gould elaborated on the give-and-take between the voices in the fugue—each musical voice, he said, went off on "some pretty wacky tangents of its own"—Mr. Menuhin listened intently, and when Mr. Gould explained that the relation of the subject of a fugue to its counter-subject would be something like that of "God Save the Queen" to "The Star-Spangled Banner," Mr. Menuhin made a soft sound of concurrence. "They ought to combine and complement their personalities in a manner that, as Johann Sebastian Bach once said, suggests three or four civilized gentlemen conducting a reasonable conversation," Mr. Gould continued. "And the conversation that they carry on does not necessarily always deal with particularly imposing matters. . . . In fact, in certain cases the more ordinary the subject the better."

"Good," Mr. Menuhin said. "Very good."

The offscreen Mr. Gould got up and went right up to the pillowcase screen, shaking his head ruefully. "Can you get a slightly sharper focus?" he called back to the projectionist.

Nothing changed in the focus. Mr. Gould sat down again. Onscreen, he was saying, "When we hear a fugue like the one in E Flat from Volume II of Bach's *The Well-Tempered Clavier,* we hear a composition that not only disciplines four profoundly beautiful lines but makes them more compelling by having them work within a superbly disciplined harmonic regime." He then played the fugue on the piano.

"Lovely," Mr. Menuhin said when he had finished. "Lovely."

The offscreen Mr. Gould gave Mr. Menuhin a pleased look. Then he got up and went back to see the projectionist. When he returned, a moment later, the image on the screen was sharper. "Better?" he asked Mr. Menuhin.

"Much better, yes," Mr. Menuhin said.

Both men settled back more easily in their chairs. Mr. Gould crossed his legs. He hunched forward as he heard himself say, on the screen, that he was now going to play a much more intense fugue from Volume II of *The Well-Tempered Clavier*—the B Flat Minor, one of the finest of Bach's fugues.

"Wonderful," Mr. Menuhin said at the end of the fugue.

"It's a great piece," Mr. Gould said.

Mr. Menuhin commented on the lightness of the piano sound, and Mr. Gould said that this particular piano had almost no aftertouch.

At one point, when the camera zeroed in on Mr. Gould as he was playing, the watching Mr. Gould shuddered. "God, that's a nasty shot," he said. "It's like Cornel Wilde in *A Song to Remember*, with Merle Oberon leaning over the piano."

"Oh, no, it comes over beautifully!" Mr. Menuhin said.

Every time Mr. Gould finished playing something on the screen, Mr. Menuhin would lean forward slightly, Mr. Gould would turn around to him, and Mr. Menuhin would say, "Wonderful performance, wonderful performance." Near the end of the movie, Mr. Gould said, onscreen, "Paul Hindemith is one of the few composers of our own time who can undeniably be called a fuguist to the manner born. Hindemith has developed a very special language of his own, a language that is contemporary in the best sense of the word but in its attempt to provide harmonic logic uses what you might call a substitute tonality." Then he played the fugue from Hindemith's Third Piano Sonata, which Mr. Menuhin immediately said was a wonderful piece.

"And now!" the offscreen Mr. Gould said, standing up. "We come to what we've all been waiting for!" He adjusted a knob near the screen that turned the sound up. "We have to have *this* louder, that's for sure," Mr. Gould said, laughing and shaking with his laughter.

Mr. Menuhin smiled.

On the screen, a quartet—a baritone, a tenor, a soprano, and a contralto—started singing a composition in fugue style by Mr. Gould:

> "So, you want to write a fugue,
>   You've got the urge to write a fugue,
>   You've got the nerve to write a fugue.
>   The only way to write one is to plunge right in and write one.
>   So go ahead."

"Lovely, lovely," Mr. Menuhin commented.

The movie ended. The lights came on.

"Wonderful program!" Mr. Menuhin said. "Beautifully done!"

Mr. Gould suddenly looked shy. "Thank you," he said. "It was really quite fun to do. But it took a hell of a lot of work."

"I love your approach to the music and the completely unmechanical way you play," Mr. Menuhin said, beaming at Mr. Gould with admiration. "And you spoke throughout so *smoothly*. Was it impromptu?"

"I had it on the TelePrompTer," Mr. Gould said. "I looked at it often enough to pick up all the cues, but I forced myself to invent phrases as I went along, to keep it sounding natural and not too formal."

"Yes, wonderful," Mr. Menuhin said. "Especially if the words are your own."

Mr. Gould laughed shyly.

"For the one I did on Bartók, I had quite good dialogue, but not quite as good as yours," Mr. Menuhin said. He gave a little sigh. "Most enjoyable!" he said.

"Next year, if you're going to have some time, we might do one together," Mr. Gould said. "You ever done the Schoenberg Fantasia?"

"Oh!" Mr. Menuhin gave a little gasp. "What a splendid idea! I must look at the music."

"It's a dry work—one of his last things," Mr. Gould said.

"I have the music," Mr. Menuhin said. "You're not coming to England next summer? We might do it there."

"I'd love to come and visit you," Mr. Gould said. "But I'm finished with concerts. You know my feeling about concerts. I'm bored with them."

Mr. Menuhin smiled wistfully. "On the screen, it does gain dimensions," he said.

"Some people say that every performance is an experience, but it's not that for me in concerts," Mr. Gould said. "It's animal. It's all a circus. It's immoral."

"Yes, I do know what you mean," Mr. Menuhin said mildly.

"When I'm onstage, I can shut them out, but I don't like it," Mr. Gould said. "I won't do more than six concerts a year. My view of the future is the end of the concert experience and the revitalization of the home experience. I haven't gone to a concert in months. When I'm in the audience, I'm completely distracted, I'm acutely uncomfortable. I don't feel the therapy of private listening."

"You are recording, though?" Mr. Menuhin said, beginning to look alarmed.

Mr. Gould said of course, and laughed. "I want to send you the Six Bach Partitas that just came out," he said. "I'm rather proud of that record."

Mr. Menuhin appeared relieved. "Would you come to England in July?" he asked. "To make the film?"

Mr. Gould bobbed his head and grinned. "The Schoenberg," he said. "In July."

Mr. Menuhin got up to go, smiling and looking utterly at peace. He gave Mr. Gould his hand. "It will be lovely," he said. "We will do it, and then it will *be* there."

BRIAN EPSTEIN

D. Lowe and Thomas Whiteside

DECEMBER 28, 1963 ("BEATLE MAN")

NTIMATIONS HAVE LATELY been reaching us of a rapidly developing craze among young people in England for the music of, and public appearances by, a group of pop singers called the Beatles. The Beatles—the origin of the name is obscure—are four young men from Liverpool, all of whom were born during the blitz. Their appearance, to judge by the photographs of them in the English press, is distinctive, their getup including identical haircuts in dishmop—or, as one London newspaper put it, Ancient British—style, and lapelless suits patterned after a Pierre Cardin design. Their music is marked by a strong rhythm that has come to be known, variously, as the Liverpool Sound and the Mersey Beat, and, altogether, the effect on English teen-agers seems to be overwhelming. The Beatles put on a Royal Command performance at the Prince of Wales Theatre, in London, which was attended by the Queen Mother and Princess Margaret, and even the Queen Mother seemed to be impressed; she is reported to have conversed with the Beatles backstage after the performance longer than she normally does with the most distinguished artists. The English press has recently devoted almost as much effort and space to attempting to analyze the attraction of the Beatles as it has to discussing the political position of the new Prime Minister. In an article entitled "The Anatomy of Beatlemania," the London *Sunday Times* printed the opinions of a number of psychiatrists on the subject. One of them wrote, "In a sense, the open hero worship of the group is an indication of how fully emancipated adolescents have become, a sign that adolescence is now a proud experience rather than a shameful phase."

Whatever the nature of Beatlemania, this country is about to be exposed to its carriers. The other day, the Beatles' manager, a twenty-nine-year-old Englishman named Brian Epstein, flew in to New York to arrange for three appearances of the Beatles on *The Ed Sullivan Show* in February, and before he flew back to England, contract in pocket, we had a chat with him, in his suite at the Regency Hotel. He proved to be a polite, round-faced man, elegantly but conservatively dressed, and with a quite conventional haircut. "Most of my time here has been taken up with discussions with Ed Sullivan about the Beatles' appearances, so I haven't seen too much of New York, I'm afraid," Mr. Epstein told us. "I found Mr. Sullivan to be a charming man. He got his first glimpse of the impression the Beatles have been making in England one day a few weeks ago when he found himself at London Airport. At that time, it happened, the Prime Minister was supposed to fly out to Scotland, and the Queen Mother was supposed to land from a trip to Ireland. But everything was out of whack, because, you see, the *Beatles* were flying in from a tour of Sweden, and the whole airport was in an uproar because of the crowds that turned up to welcome them. Mr. Sullivan knew a good thing when he saw it. The Beatles have broken every conceivable entertainment record in England. They are the most worshipped, the most idolized boys in the country. They have tremendous style, and a great effervescence, which communicates itself in an extraordinary way. Their beat is something like rock 'n' roll but different from it. They are quite different from the big English rock 'n' rollers in that they are not phony. They have none of that mean hardness about them. They are genuine. They have life, humor, and strange, handsome looks. Their accents are Liverpudlian—of the Liverpool area—and they have been called a working-class phenomenon, but I disagree with the sometimes expressed notion that their appeal is merely to the working classes. The Beatles are classless. We get fan letters from public schools as well as from working-class people. Mummies like the Beatles, too—that's the extraordinary thing. They think they are rather sweet. They *approve*."

For all Epstein's single-mindedness about the Beatles, his account of their allure was delivered with an air that we associated more with an English drawing room than with Tin Pan Alley, and we asked him how he had happened to become manager of the group. "That came about two years ago, when I was working as a director of my family business, in Liverpool," he said. "We own five shops in the area, three of them specializing in radios, TV, and records. I had been working at that for several years, except for eighteen months that I spent as a student at the Royal Academy of Dramatic Art, in London, hoping to become an actor. I gave up that idea when I found I had become acclimatized as a businessman and couldn't really settle down to being a student. I went back into the family business and specialized in records; we became the biggest retailers of records in the North of England. Well, one afternoon in October of 1961 someone came into the shop and asked for a record made by a group called the Beatles—a new name to me—and, to please the customer, I tried to track the record down. I had no idea where it had been made, and I began writing all over for it. I finally tracked down the Beatles right in Liverpool, in a cellar place called The Cavern, about a hundred yards from my office. They were four singularly untidy young men who were beating out a very loud sound—vocal numbers accompanied by three electric guitars and a drum. They introduced their numbers with humorous patter; they have a certain Beatle way of talking. I was excited to find that they had an extraordinary quality and presence that wafted itself across the cellar. Not to bore you, I subsequently got together with the group and we entered into a management contract, and in no time I was divorced from my family business and was managing not only the Beatles but a number of other first-rate groups, too. I find the business enormously stimulating. So far, the Beatles have sold over five million records. They've put in some TV appearances in England, but we don't overdo that. The crowds at their personal-appearance dates have taxed the strength of the British police; wherever they make an appearance, police leaves are cancelled. Only the other day, in Birmingham, the police, to get the Beatles through the crowd to the theatre where they were appearing, had to smuggle them in dressed in blue police raincoats and helmets. Teen-age girls fall weeping on the streets when they find they cannot get tickets to hear the Beatles. Riotous scenes have occurred all over the country. Well, that's about it, really. I think that America is ready for the Beatles. When they come, they will hit this country for six."

ROY WILKINS

Andy Logan

MARCH 27, 1965 (FROM "MOMENT OF HISTORY")

NOT MANY HOURS after the President's address to Congress on voting rights, which Roy Wilkins, the executive secretary of the National Association for the Advancement of Colored People, described the next day as "a moment at the summit in the life of our nation," we stopped by to see Mr. Wilkins at the headquarters of the N.A.A.C.P., on West Fortieth Street. Everyone was going about his business there as if nothing had happened. It seemed to be quiet business. Young men in gray suits, many of them carrying briefcases, moved in and out of small offices opening off the waiting room. One of them stopped for a moment to take a closer look at a framed drawing, from an old newspaper, whose caption read, "Exciting Scene in the House of Representatives, January 31st, 1865, on the Passing of the Amendment to the Constitution Abolishing Slavery For Ever," and then moved on. A pretty girl in a turquoise wool dress, sitting under a cardboard sign that read "Keep Smiling," was efficiently doubling as receptionist and switchboard operator, repeating over and over into her mouthpiece, "National Association. I'll see if he's available," and plugging in wires with graceful hands. On a table just outside the switchboard enclosure was a gilded plaster statue about two feet high, labelled *The Fugitive's Story*. It showed a turbaned Negro woman, a baby on her shoulder and a bandana containing her belongings at her feet, standing in a beseeching pose before three men, identified at the base of the statue as John Greenleaf Whittier, Henry Ward Beecher, and William Lloyd Garrison. "Harriet Tubman," the receptionist told us politely, running her hands through her hair, and then she turned back to her mouthpiece to explain that Mr.

Moon was in conference and that Mr. Morsell was in the *same* conference. Through the open office doors sentences drifted out to us: "The
foundation is definitely interested." . . . "The N.L.R.B. gets it next
week." . . . "What's the chance for certiorari?"

A few minutes later, Roy Wilkins came out and escorted us into his
office, at the end of a short corridor. He is a slender, soft-spoken man in
his early sixties, and his eyes were shining. "If we seem very quiet for a
revolutionary headquarters, you must remember that this *is* only a headquarters," he told us, with a smile. "Some of the men you have seen—and,
of course, we have women representatives, too—have come here from all
over the country. We figure out what must be done, and then they go back
into the field to a very different life. One of them, you know, was Medgar
Evers." Mr. Wilkins stood for a moment by a window that looked out on
the Public Library, and then sat down in his chair. "I never doubted that
someday it would come," he told us. "But I also never dreamed that in my
lifetime a President of the United States would stand up before the world
and speak as Mr. Johnson did the other night. He didn't say 'Boys, you
know how I feel' behind his office door. He didn't say 'unless' or 'provided
that,' or engage in any other double-talk. He stood there before the people
and put his role in history on the line. The completeness and warmth of
his commitment! And in a Texas accent!" Wilkins shook his head, as if
he still couldn't believe his ears. "I have been hearing from individuals all
over the United States, and I believe that most American Negroes felt as
I did," he went on. "Oh, I know that a few leaders, when the words were
scarcely out of the President's mouth, were saying 'Deeds, not words,' or
'Wait and see,' and I understand this. We've been fooled, flummoxed, sold
down the river so often in the past. And then all Americans today live in
a climate of skepticism. How many times a day do we think, What's in it
for him? But it seems to me a sad thing that now, when we are given the
great affirmation we have sought so long, some people cannot bring
themselves to embrace it. To me, it was an exhilarating moment—the
homecoming of all our hopes, of all we believe in."

Mr. Wilkins paused for a second, and then went on, "A good many of
the newcomers to the civil-rights movement are very young. They are
energetic, imaginative, and fearless. In a crusty movement like this long
struggle for freedom, an invasion such as theirs is a good thing. They
have no use for the rituals, the traditional minuets of organizational behavior. They say only 'Now!,' just as Selma's Sheriff Clark says 'Never!,'
and they forge ahead. Most of the demonstrations they have led, with or

without support from the N.A.A.C.P., have been useful to the cause. I gladly admit it. They have dramatized it as no tedious arguments before any tribunal could do. It is a difficult thing to dramatize disenfranchisement, for example, but what happened at Selma did dramatize it, so that no literate American could misunderstand the problem: we are denied the right to vote; we are denied even the right to protest this denial without endangering our lives. When you come down to it, however, the civil-rights revolution has been a revolution in the law. The turning point—forty-three years after the N.A.A.C.P. filed its first case seeking equal justice before the law for a Negro citizen—was the 1954 Supreme Court decision in the Brown case, banning segregation in the schools. It defined, at last, the Negro's role in American society: separate but equal was not enough. I'm not surprised that these young people in the movement, like young people everywhere, are inclined to think that nothing worthwhile was done until they came along. But how can you understand the importance of this moment if you don't remember that in 1917 the N.A.A.C.P. was fighting desperately to persuade Woodrow Wilson, a good President and a good man, to say just one word against lynching? He would never say that word. Even Franklin Roosevelt, in 1940, wasn't ready to denounce lynching in so many words. It's been a long, bloody struggle, but now, extraordinarily, we find in the van of this citizens' army the President of the United States." He paused again. "Did you notice the date of his great speech?" he asked us. "The Ides of March! Beware, indeed! Rejoice!"

MARSHALL MCLUHAN

Lillian Ross and Jane Kramer

MAY 15, 1965 ("THE MCLUHAN METAPHOR")

WHEN THE WESTINGHOUSE people announced that at the end of the World's Fair they will again bury a Time Capsule filled with assorted cultural and technological mementos of twentieth-century man, a friend of ours suggested that they should re-place the codes and artifacts with Dr. Marshall McLuhan, who could be counted on to explain us vividly to anybody digging around in Flushing Meadow two thousand years from now. Dr. McLuhan, a professor of English at St. Michael's College of the University of Toronto, is also the director of the university's Center for Culture and Technology and the author of three startling books on Western civilization—*The Mechanical Bride, The Gutenberg Galaxy,* and, most recently, *Understanding Media,* in which he joyfully explores the tribal virtues of popular culture, casts a cynical eye on the "classification traditions" that came in with print, and sees near-mythic possibilities in our computer age. He has compared the Bomb to the doctoral dissertation; discussed the "depth-involving" qual-ities of sunglasses, textured stockings, discothèques, and comic books; reported on the iconic properties of Andy Warhol's signed soup cans; and predicted a happy day when everyone will have his own portable computer to cope with the dreary business of digesting information. In so doing, Dr. McLuhan has earned a reputation among the cognoscenti as the world's first Pop philosopher.

Last week, Dr. McLuhan flew to New York to deliver a lecture at Spencer Memorial Church (which has its *own* reputation, as the world's first far-out Presbyterian congregation), and we took the subway to Brooklyn Heights to hear him. At the church, an old, oak-beamed build-ing that was bustling with young McLuhan enthusiasts, we found the Professor sitting quietly in the pulpit while a young man in a green cor-duroy jacket and narrow trousers propped an enormous Rauschenberg painting against it. The young man, who turned out to be Spencer's minister, William Glenesk, explained to us that the poster was "left over from my Rauschenberg sermon." He then told the audience that he had been a fan of Dr. McLuhan's ever since 1951, when he attended the Pro-fessor's course on Eliot, Joyce, and the Symbolist movement at the Uni-versity of Toronto. Dr. McLuhan, a tall, steel-haired man given to twirling a pair of horn-rimmed glasses in appropriately professorial style, stood up, thanked Mr. Glenesk, and remarked that the warm May weather was certainly as depth-involving as a good Rauschenberg or a good elephant joke. The new art and the new jokes have no strict, literal content, no story line, he said, and continued, "They are the forms of an electronic age, in which fragmented, dictionary-defined data have been bypassed in favor of integral knowledge and an old tribal instinct for pat-terned response." Several members of the audience nodded ecstatically, and Dr. McLuhan went on to tackle practically every cultural phenomenon from the tribal encyclopedia to the shaggy-dog story, from Shakespeare to Fred Allen, from the wheel to the electromagnetic circuit. He good-naturedly blamed Plato for writing down Socrates' dialogues and thus inaugurating "codified culture," and he praised the singing commercial for reinstating the old tribal institution of memorized wisdom. Every new technology, according to the Professor, programs a new sensory human environment, and our computer technology has catapulted us right out of the specialist age and into a world of integral knowledge and synesthetic responses. "The computer is not merely an extension of our eyes, like print, but an extension of our whole central nervous system," he explained. He paused, twirled his glasses, and went on to say that every new environment uses as its content the old environment— "the way Plato used the old oral tradition of the dialogue for his books and the way television now uses the story form of the novel and the movies"—but that it is the technological nature of any new medium, and not its borrowed content, that conditions the new human response. Pop Art, he said, glancing affectionately at the Rauschenberg, is merely our old mechanical environment used as the content of our new electronic environment. "One environment seen through another becomes a metaphor," he continued. "Like Andy Warhol's *Liz Taylor*. Our new, non-literal response to the literal content of that blown-up and endlessly repeated photograph turns Liz into an icon. It takes a new technology like ours to turn an old environment like Liz into an art form."

Dr. McLuhan next suggested the possibility of a new technology that would extend consciousness itself into the environment. "A kind of computerized ESP," he called it, envisioning "consciousness as the corporate content of the environment—and eventually maybe even a small portable computer, about the size of a hearing aid, that would process our private experience through the corporate experience, the way dreams do now." Then he said, "Well, that's enough pretentious speculation for one night," and turned to Mr. Glenesk, who suggested that the audience have "an old Socratic go" at some questions and answers.

Mr. Glenesk thereupon introduced the Professor to some of the McLuhan disciples in the audience.

The first disciple told Dr. McLuhan that he had been amplifying several sounds in one room at the same time, to get the "depth-involving" sound that is part of Dr. McLuhan's brave new world.

"Must make one hell of a racket," Dr. McLuhan said approvingly.

A second disciple, a rather nervous woman from the neighborhood, announced that she could hardly wait to have an experience-processor of her own. "The way things are now, I never can remember anything," she said, and was immediately interrupted by a third disciple, a bearded student sitting next to her.

The student expressed equal eagerness for computerized ESP. "Gee, just think!" he continued. "I could go to sleep a painter and wake up a composer!"

"Terrifying," Dr. McLuhan said.

JOAN BAEZ

Kevin Wallace

OCTOBER 7, 1967 ("NON-VIOLENT SOLDIER")

S PORADIC NEWS DISPATCHES from California over the past couple of years have kept us posted on the ups and downs, in the sedate Carmel Valley, of Joan Baez's Institute for the Study of Non-Violence. We read, for instance, of the failure of a zoning challenge brought by a neighbor who regarded the Institute's afternoon sessions as "detrimental to the peace, morals, or general welfare of Monterey County." The sessions, so the items informed us, involved twenty-five students at a time in a six-week curriculum of picnic lunches, silent meditation, and discussions of points raised in the writings of such thinkers as Henry Thoreau, Mohandas Gandhi, and Jiddu Krishnamurti. The Institute is supported and regularly attended by Miss Baez, and it is directed by a man from St. Louis named Ira Sandperl, whom Miss Baez discovered when she was sixteen, ten years ago, at a Quaker meeting near Stanford University, where her father was on the physics faculty. Roving along the West Coast on a recent rainy Saturday, and finding ourself in the vicinity of Carmel with an hour on our hands, we arranged to drive up the Valley and have a talk with Miss Baez at the Institute.

The Institute's grounds occupy a grassy, oak-strewn expanse between road and river. Its plant is a former one-room public schoolhouse that has been stuccoed over, reroofed with red Spanish tile, cleared of school desks, and outfitted with lounging mats and a native chalk-rock fireplace; a small residential wing for Mr. Sandperl has been added. It was Mr. Sandperl, as it turned out, who was lounging in the schoolhouse doorway and greeting his arriving student body when we approached. The students, who included several couples trailing small children, looked and chatted with one another like young suburbanites getting together anywhere on a Saturday noon. Mr. Sandperl could have been their tennis pro. He is a sinewy man in his early forties, crew-cut, clean-shaven, very deeply tanned, alert of eye, and generally smiling, and he was wearing an open sports shirt, gray slacks, and clean green sneakers. He acknowledged the unusual weather wryly and added, "Joan's supposed to be giving a benefit concert outdoors at the Monterey County Fair Grounds this evening, but this rain puts the matter in doubt." He led us around a clump of chatting students toward the fireplace and a smaller group that included Miss Baez, who was wearing black pants and pullover sweater, and who struck us as startlingly more beautiful than any of her photographs suggest—features more delicately sculptured, expressions more luminously candid and humorous, hair only shoulder-length—and who, besides all that, was not behaving like a star whose concert was in imminent peril of being rained out.

"The dog is friendly, sweetheart—you can pat her," Miss Baez was explaining to an ambulatory infant who stood eye to eye with a cloud-gray shaggy dog at Miss Baez's feet.

Miss Baez invited us to follow her to Mr. Sandperl's quarters for our talk. The shaggy dog, whose name proved to be Anathea, came along, too. We took a chair while Miss Baez arranged herself on a couch in such a way that Anathea could doze comfortably on her knee. Then Miss Baez told us, "I used to avoid interviews, because I hadn't found out what I thought, or if I had anything to say, but not now. I'm interested in ending war. I'm not interested in gazing through a blue marble at Miss Baez. What I'm all about is that I'm a non-violent soldier. That's to be distinguished a little from being a pacifist. It's not just withdrawing and growing your own vegetables and not paying taxes. It means doing more than being nice to birds and small animals. I dislike the word 'goal,' but I suppose that's what we have here—we want to let out the news that the time has come when killing in the outside world is no more proper than killing within the national boundaries. Not that absolutely everybody agrees yet that even killing within the nation is no longer acceptable. There's still that cultural inertia left over from nearly three hundred years when it was the thing for us to carry guns, since there was always the chance we might have to shoot a neighbor. Today, there's certainly enough proof around that violence can't be appropriate anymore anywhere, but people want to hang on to that old feeling. You know—'It's a sunny day. Let's go kill something.' When the world was proved round, that news was evidently just as hard to accept. In spite of the disadvantages of a flat world—monsters at the edge, sailboats falling off—people hated giving it up. Right now, people hate to give up weapons. We've changed the War Department's name to the Defense Department, but weapons are still made for killing, and boys are still trained to run bayonets through people, and the word 'murder' still doesn't seem to ring a bell. I don't mean to say that there may not always be barroom brawls and things like that—though among the Hopi and Zuñi, if you slug someone, it's regarded as poor form and you're out of it—but brawling is on a different plane from organized mass killing. And non-violence is— well, totally misunderstood. It's not avoiding violence. It's the opposite of running. It means confronting violence and having to come up with something more intelligent in response. Perhaps the only response that can possibly be effective today is refusing to cooperate, and going to jail. But we don't go into tactics and techniques here. Dr. Martin Luther King's movement has problems because its emphasis is all on tactics. At the University of California, the kids' trouble was that they only had a technique: if the cops came in, they knew they were supposed to drop to the floor. However, if you're rooted in the understanding that the Ku Klux Klansman and the Negro garbageman are both your brothers, then there's a chance you'll know the right thing to do."

The door flew open, and Mr. Sandperl popped in, saying, "Please excuse me for breaking into my room, but can I ask just one question? What's my unlisted telephone number?"

"I'll write it down for you," Miss Baez said, producing a pencil and a slip of paper and writing. She handed over the paper and said, "You can give me mine later."

Mr. Sandperl left, and Miss Baez told us, "Unlisted numbers have a way of getting out, so we keep getting new ones. Anyway, about non-violence. There are certain pitfalls. There's a Fort Ord boy who comes here with the schizo idea that he's non-violent because he takes a supercilious view of the Army and can ridicule his job as a soldier. And I've been corresponding with a boy in Vietnam who thinks he's eased his conscience because he managed to exchange his gun for a camera, and now he writes about the bizarre beauty of war. It's so easy to kid yourself. Like believing that an Army ambulance driver's first duty isn't to get banged-up soldiers back to their guns as soon as possible. Not that one mustn't care for the hurt and dying—but for *all* the hurt and dying, on all sides. We don't always like to notice what we're doing. What people mainly do is to avoid boredom. We'd rather feel anything than boredom, and boredom is oneself. The meditation we try here means only that you stop doing the things you do all day long to avoid yourself—listening to the radio, making conversation, woolgathering—and after that it's hard to define. It's not concentrating on an idea. Krishnamurti gave a clue when he said, 'If the interest is there, that's a beginning.' The interest turns into paying attention—trying to listen as though you'd never heard before. We all grew up learning to try and then to expect a result from trying, but here it's not a result that's the point but simply the trying. Krishnamurti also said that, as far as he could see—No, he didn't say that; he's never that modest. He said, 'Creativity is when the mind is still.' As to effort—well, there's a kind of effort. For instance, I try to write, and if I sit at the typewriter and make the effort to start writing just a lot of 'x's, after a while something begins to happen. You know that song 'Be Not Too Hard'?"

We said we did. It leads off Miss Baez's 1967 Vanguard album ("Be not too hard, for life is short, and nothing is given to man. . . . / Be not too hard if he's sold or bought, for he must manage as best he can./ Be not too hard when he blindly dies, fighting for things he does not own. . . ."), and it reminded us to ask whether the neighbors were as hard on the Institute as the wire services had led us to think.

Miss Baez said, "No, the community is fine to us. At first, a few people imagined we were doing awful things—smoking pot, or making love—but we asked them to walk in and see. The worst trouble came from a lady across the street. She looked in and saw we were doing nothing—literally nothing, since it was meditation time—and that really got to her. She went into her house for a gun and fired it into the hillside. As you see, the kids here are mostly regular-looking college-age people. Flower children, thank God, aren't interested. They've divorced themselves completely from reality. They're so lost. I talked to one the other day who told me, 'Man, that non-violence thing, that's for me.' So I asked, 'Then how come you're still pushing acid?' The cyclists, too. I met a couple of the heads of Berkeley's Hell's Angels. They said they just loved my music. I looked down at their Iron Crosses. They simply don't know what's going on. Maybe Allen Ginsberg was helpful to them—getting them off skull-cracking and onto pot."

Miss Baez smiled radiantly, and we asked if she was always so composed on the afternoon of a concert in hazard.

"Oh, no," she said. "This just happens to be one of my good days."

Early that evening, as our plane lifted off Monterey Airport bound for San Francisco and our connection to New York, we were gratified to see the rain clouds blowing away eastward, in plenty of time to insure that the concert would go on.

TWIGGY

Thomas Whiteside

NOVEMBER 4, 1967 (FROM "A SUPER NEW THING")

THE FOLLOWING DAY, Twiggy went for the first of her photographic sessions with Richard Avedon, for *Vogue*. The sessions went on day after day. Shortly after they started, I asked Twiggy how she liked working with Avedon. "It's wonderful," Twiggy said. "Avedon makes you *feel* beautiful." I arranged to visit Avedon's studio while Twiggy was posing for him. His studio is on the top floor of a building on East Fifty-eighth Street, and when I arrived, I learned that Twiggy was already on the scene, and was getting herself ready in a dressing room. Avedon came out to greet me in a reception area—a slight, intense, alert-looking man who was wearing large horn-rimmed glasses and, over his shirt, a brown sweater. He led me from the reception area, the walls of which were adorned with blowups of Avedon candid shots of Charlie Chaplin and Rudolf Nureyev, along a corridor that was lined with an array of *Vogue*'s paraphernalia—shoes, bangles, spangles, stockings, gloves, all jumbled together on tables as on the counter of a bargain store—and into an alcove containing a desk and some filing cabinets. We sat down and talked briefly.

"One thing you have to realize about Twiggy is that, relatively speaking, she has hardly been photographed," Avedon said. "After all, Jean Shrimpton had considerable experience—she had been on perhaps fifty magazine covers before anyone took much notice of her. Twiggy has really only been modelling for less than a year. I didn't know what to expect of her. But I found that the moment she was under the lights she performed as all the finest models do. For her to have developed that amount of control is extraordinary. At our first sitting, we spent three-quarters of the day making preparations—working with makeup, and so on, and I was trying to get used to her face—and then she went in front of the camera and it was as though we'd been working together for months. Lots of models come to the studio and do things they think the photographer wants. Twiggy presented herself quite honestly to the camera. Not that she doesn't have some faults—the occasionally vacant stare, the dead eye. But she has a quality that is small and very special, in which it's the slightest nuance that counts. The best pictures I've taken of Twiggy have been those in which she did the least. The less she did, the truer the pictures seemed to be—truer to herself, truer to my work. That's representative of the period. Women move in certain ways that convey an air of the time they live in, and Twiggy, when she's in front of lights, is bringing her generation in front of the camera. I think what's involved is the stripping away of certain affectations about what is beautiful. Twiggy is made for that. As a photographer, I'm interested in young girls not because of knock-knees and tongues sticking out but because of what I can find about them that is beautiful. With Twiggy, I consider the shape of her head beautiful, and also the simplicity and gentleness of her gestures; even the narrowness of her leg is interesting." Avedon reached out to a pile of black-and-white contact prints and showed me a number of pictures he had taken of Twiggy, several of which he had circled with a red grease pencil. Some of the representations seemed pretty lush to me, considering the subject. However, in what I thought were the best, Twiggy's eyes had a more limpid and feminine quality than I had seen in any other pictures of her, and I noticed, too, that the excessive angularity I was used to in Twiggy's poses was absent. I was particularly struck by one photograph, showing Twiggy in profile from behind, in which the fashion photographer had concentrated on the contours of her arm and back in such a way as to accentuate a special manner in which her hand and wrist hung loosely—"almost African," Avedon called it.

From the dressing room I heard the sound of Twiggy's laughter—the kind of two-syllable rising shriek that might be heard any morning over the wall of a northwest-London back yard. Avedon excused himself and walked off to see whether Twiggy was ready for the sitting. While he was away, I noticed on his desk a folded piece of paper bearing the words:

OFFICE MEMORANDUM
to: Mrs. Mellen   from: Mrs. Vreeland
copy to: Mr. Avedon
RE: Twiggy

Having myself been in communication with Mrs. Vreeland on this subject a couple of days earlier, and having been impressed by her enthusiasm for Twiggy ("This little girl is not a Cockney phenomenon. For us at *Vogue,* she represents beauty, not Twiggery. We love her silky throat, her naturalness, her inner serenity"), I was interested in getting some more of her views on Twiggy, and when Avedon returned I asked him if I might have a look at the memorandum. Later, with Mrs. Vreeland's permission, he let me do so. It read:

Do not forget Twiggy is dreadfully swaybacked. . . . This form of weakness is easily righted by having her stand straight and sit up. She should be treated as a perfect flower with a straight stem and a bloom at the top and not like a half deformed teenager.

Also remember we do not want the hair to the side as it does nothing to bring out her beauty. Do remember her nose is beautiful and her hair back from her face straight-curved from forehead reveals this. Ask her to pull in her behind and shoot up her spine and you will have a glorious girl and not an ill fed adolescent.

Also she must smile with her eyes and be happy, as the "Elle" pix show her with sullen eyes and pouting lips and all this should not appear in *Vogue.* Let us handle her as a precious package. . . .

Shortly after Avedon returned, Twiggy emerged from the dressing room and Avedon led her onto the set. This consisted of a white paper backdrop, perhaps twelve feet wide, that was hanging from a long roll, in the manner of a huge paper towel, and that also curved to extend across the floor of the studio for some distance, concealing the line be-tween the wall and the floor. At its forward edge, the paper was fixed flat to the floor by pieces of masking tape. On the paper, to one side and near the edge, there stood a single strobe light in a silvery umbrellalike reflector; it was mounted about six feet above the floor, and was pointed down toward a high, plain black stool that stood on the paper. Facing the backdrop was a camera tripod, and behind the tripod was a small wooden cabinet on casters, its sides painted white and its top covered with some sort of shiny black plastic, on which three Rolleiflexes were lined up, their chrome metalwork reflected in the shiny material. Be-hind the Rolleiflexes, perhaps a couple of dozen up-ended rolls of un-used film were ranged, like columns. On the sides of the cabinet, various rolls of masking tape and cloth tape were neatly hung. Beside the left wall of the studio, there stood a phonograph. Twiggy had brought her own records for the session—numbers by the Supremes (*A Bit of Liver-pool*), the Kinks (*The Kinks' Greatest Hits*), Wilson Pickett (*The Wicked Pickett*), and Tim Hardin (*Hang On to a Dream*)—and now Avedon asked her what she wanted to hear while she worked. Twiggy chose the Kinks for a starter, and an assistant put the record on. Then, while an-other assistant mounted one of the Rolleiflexes on the empty tripod, Twiggy was asked by Avedon just to stand for a few moments so that he could look at her, and, when the few moments were up, took her place, at his request, on the plain black stool. Twiggy was wearing a simple black dress and black net stockings, and on her feet she had a pair of men's lamb's-wool slippers, belonging to Avedon, which he had lent her; they were going to be out of camera range. The strobe was switched on to what is known among photographers as a "viewing light"; that is, a steady, non-flashing light that enables the photographer to view his subject under lighting conditions comparable to the ones that his cam-era will record when the stroboscopic flash is activated by the camera shutter.

Avedon went to work. The process was quite unlike that of any other photographer I had seen at work with Twiggy. Whereas in other studios I had seen Twiggy in a "leading" role, with the photographer pretty much content to record this or that split-second phase of a large variety of poses she freely adopted, Avedon exercised meticulous control over his model, almost as though he were working from a blueprint. Nearly half an hour of the time Twiggy spent sitting on the stool was devoted to adjusting a band of silvery material around her hair. Polly Mellen, who was the *Vogue* editor assigned to the sitting, assisted with that, while Avedon knelt over his Rolleiflex, its tripod having been shortened for a low viewing angle, and gave instructions for minute changes in the position of the band. Twiggy responded to the instructions patiently and with interest. "All right, now, very straight," Avedon would tell Twiggy, and she would sit up straight and gaze directly into the camera with very small variations of expression. Her face looked more elegant and more serious than I had seen it look in any other studio. Her lips were slightly parted, and that clarity of glance which I had noticed in the better pictures of her by other photographers seemed heightened. Detailed though Avedon's instructions were on the poses that Twiggy should adopt, he did not give her any specific instructions about her expression. But neither did he leave that entirely to Twiggy. When her expression was one that he wasn't interested in photographing, nothing would happen, but when a shift of pose or expression produced something that interested him, the strobe light would flash—with a peculiar dulled gonglike sound accompanying each high-voltage discharge—in a rapid series of three, four, five, six brilliant bursts. These bursts of strobe light seemed to serve as a sort of beat, so that photographer and model appeared to be in communication essentially through this wordless staccato rhythm. The expert fashion photographer smiles upon his model with bolts of synthetic lightning.

RONALD REAGAN

James Stevenson

JANUARY 27, 1968 ("REAGAN")

Governor RONALD REAGAN made a quick trip to New York one day last week to address a banquet of the Economic Club, and late that afternoon we learned that photographers and television cameramen had been invited to photograph the Governor just before the dinner, so we put our Kodak Instamatic in our raincoat pocket and hurried over to the Waldorf.

In the Jade Room, on the third floor, a young man who seemed to know what was going on greeted us, offered us some coffee, and told us about the Economic Club while cameras were being set up at the far end of the room. "All the people who belong to this outfit are at *least* vice-presidents," he said. "It's not the P.-T.A. They have banquets four times a year, and they've had some goodies—Khrushchev, Prime Minister Wilson. Reagan was invited a year ago."

We were early, so we strolled down the hall to the Grand Ballroom. It was a glittering, awesome sight. Waiters in red coats were hustling around among the tables (red tablecloths), dropping ice into glasses. A man in a dark suit was standing on the three-tiered dais and directing the waiters through a public-address system. "Gentlemen!" he implored, his voice filling the vast room. "I ask you again! Please have your ice and water in the water glasses *before* the program goes on!" Around him, men were piling white roses on the dais, and behind it a huge American flag was stretched across the wall, filling it completely. We sniffed a rose, and it was real; there were about three thousand roses, we estimated. A man from the florist's, wearing a black ski jacket, was picking up leaves from the floor. We asked him what kind of leaves they were.

"We call 'em green," he said.

We tried to elicit a political opinion from the man, asking him if he favored Reagan for President.

"Maybe yes, maybe no," he said guardedly.

"Hey!" a waiter near us called to another waiter. "Who is it tonight?"

"Ronald Reagan," came the reply.

The first waiter nodded sagely. "No wonder everyone's so hotsy-totsy," he commented.

We quickly turned to him and asked *him* about Reagan.

"I'll tell you the truth," he said. "I wouldn't vote for him. He's not so hot. He has a nice personality, but I wouldn't go for the personality. I don't like his platform. Let him come out straight." He clasped his hands behind his back and ran through a critique of the other potential candidates—none of them were so hot, he felt—and then he branched out into international affairs. "Our State Department don't say boo," he was declaring, waving one finger angrily, when we realized that we might be late for the Governor's arrival in the Jade Room. We excused ourself and hurried down the hall.

There were about twenty photographers in the Jade Room by now, and lots of lights, and suddenly Reagan was walking into the room, chatting with another man. Reagan was in a tuxedo. He seemed completely at ease, unassuming, well combed; his face was less lined than we'd expected, and he was a bit taller.

A reporter moved in, asked him a question, and said, on receiving a reply, "You're just being modest, Governor."

"I've got a lot to be modest about," replied Reagan, with a twinkly smile.

Reagan then placed himself at the disposal of the photographers, and they asked him to stand behind a group of microphones and appear to be giving his speech. He did so, and they kept asking him to smile.

"If I keep on smiling, it looks like I have a very lighthearted speech," Reagan said, but he smiled some more.

"Will you gesture, Governor?" someone asked.

"I don't gesture very much when I talk," Reagan said, but he made a few mild gestures anyway.

The cameras clicked on and on. "Now, you *will* get all these published?" Reagan said, grinning.

A TV man asked him to read some of his speech.

"Oh dear!" Reagan said, but he reached into his pocket and pulled out a stack of large white cards, held together by a rubber band. Removing the band, he glanced through them. The words were in half-inch type, with some underlined in red. He leafed through them. "My notes are sort of messed up," he said. "Wait'll I find the part . . ." Presently he was ready to begin, but one of the TV cameras was not. There was a pause. "Ready when you are, C.B.," Reagan murmured patiently.

At last, he read some excerpts from his speech, in a quite formal and forceful manner: "The relentless inch-by-inch erosion . . . rights of the people . . . aims and credibility . . . divided people . . . sharp reduction in private American investment abroad . . . brought inflation back . . ." He paused. "Enough?" he asked.

Next, he agreed to answer questions, and was asked about Vietnam negotiations. He said that no one could speak with real authority from the outside, then added, "I think we should be very cautious . . . when we remember what happened in Korea. . . . More Americans died during the negotiations than died before. . . . The final solution has to be military. . . . Convince them. . . . Then they will come to the conference table simply because it hurts too much not to. . . . The enemy [must know] once and for all not only that he cannot succeed but if he continues it will lead to a complete military defeat." He quoted Dean Acheson, and then was asked about his choice for Republican Presidential candidate. "I'm in no position . . ." he began, and explained that he was a favorite son. "The purpose of a favorite son is for your delegation to use its strength at the right time to gain some mileage for your state."

Reagan was asked about Rockefeller's intentions.

"You're asking the wrong non-candidate," Reagan said. "Ask him."

"The Gallup poll shows that your popularity as a potential candidate is slipping," a reporter declared. "How do you explain that?"

"I regard that as a tribute to my efforts to convince people I'm not a candidate," Reagan said easily.

Reagan's speech that evening would conflict with the President's State of the Union address on television, a reporter pointed out. Did he feel bad about this?

"Well, you know what they say about preachers," said Reagan. "There's no worse audience for a preacher than another preacher."

After several more questions, he was asked to say what the No. 1 issue in the campaign would be.

"I'd like to have a dead heat," Reagan said, and explained that there were two issues of equal importance. "One has to do with a kind of morality issue—eroding moral standards," he said. "And the second has to do with economics. . . . Inflation has eroded people's savings . . . the stability of our currency. . . . Put these together. . . ."

A moment later, Reagan was finished. He took time on his way out to sign an autograph and exchange a few words with people. Someone mentioned *Death Valley Days* and a Borax commercial that Reagan had made. He said, "I miss *Death Valley Days* once in a while." There was a short discussion of the commercial, and Reagan exclaimed, "You know, I made 'em prove it to me before I'd say the ad, and it works!" Then, with a last handshake, and a smile, Reagan was gone.

TOM STOPPARD

Geoffrey T. Hellman

MAY 4, 1968 ("PLAYWRIGHT-NOVELIST")

Tom Stoppard, the author of *Rosencrantz and Guildenstern Are Dead*, which last week won the Tony Award as the best play of the season, and a few days later was named best play of the year by the New York Drama Critics Circle, was born in 1937 in Zlín, Czechoslovakia, a town that is the center of the Czech shoe industry, which was founded in 1913 by Tomáš Bata. Zlín was renamed Gottwaldov in 1948, after Klement Gottwald, the first Communist President of Czechoslovakia, and the Bata industries were nationalized around that time and renamed Svit. Bata had factories all over the world, and in 1939, when Mr. Stoppard was not quite two and the Germans were about to take over the country, his father, a company doctor, was transferred to a Bata branch in Singapore. In 1942, when the Japanese were about to take over that naval base from the British, Mrs. Stoppard and her two sons were evacuated to India; Dr. Stoppard was killed shortly thereafter. The boys went to an American school in Darjeeling for a couple of years, and in 1946 their mother, who had married an Englishman, took them to Bristol, England. "I went to prep school in Nottinghamshire and to public school in Yorkshire," Mr. Stoppard told us when we called on him at the Algonquin shortly before the Tony Awards were announced. "I became a reporter on the *Western Daily Press*, in Bristol, when I was seventeen, and after four years I moved over to the Bristol *Evening World*, which is now defunct. I was interested in life more than in literature. My ambitions were exclusively journalistic. I wanted to end up as God knows what—a correspondent under fire in some foreign field, perhaps."

We asked Mr. Stoppard how he got into the theatre, and he said, "I wrote a lot about the Bristol theatre, which was flourishing, and I knew the people in it. I became quite hooked on it. I wrote a play, *A Walk on the Water*, that was produced on television in England in 1963. The next year, I spent five months in Berlin, on a Ford Foundation grant. I lived in a large house on the edge of the city with twenty other Ford-grantee writers—German, English, and American. It was part of the battle to keep Berlin culturally alive. There I wrote a one-act verse burlesque called 'Rosencrantz and Guildenstern,' and I subsequently wrote *Rosencrantz and Guildenstern Are Dead,* which has no connection with the other. It was well received at the 1966 Edinburgh Festival and has been in the National Theatre's repertory since last April. My first play has just been produced in London under the title *Enter a Free Man.* It has been badly received."

Mr. Stoppard handed us a New York *Times* report on it by Charles Marowitz, who characterized it as "about as weighty as a feather boa and as substantial as a blancmange left out in the sun." "I'm inclined to agree," Stoppard said. "It was produced in Hamburg, in German, in 1964, and I went to see it. I guess I should have left it at that. I don't understand any German, so I couldn't really judge that production. It was Charles Marowitz who recommended me for the Ford grant, by the way." The telephone rang, and he said to someone, "A tuxedo? I don't have one. . . . I don't *have* a white shirt. . . . I don't *have* a dark coat. I just don't have the right kind of clothes, do I?" Mr. Stoppard, who was wearing a bright-colored flowered shirt, a flowing black silk tie, and light-brown tweed trousers, hung up, smiled engagingly, and said, "Alexander Cohen's office. They want me to tape an acceptance of the Tony Awards thing, which will be announced on television on a day when I won't be here. They're going to lend me a white shirt and a dark coat. All the candidates who won't be here then have to tape acceptances. Of course, I have no idea whether I'll get an award or not. It's rather ghostly, isn't it, talking to a nonexistent audience about a nonexistent award?"

Stoppard had come to New York for a week to look in on his play, "do a little fiddling with the actors," and be on hand for the Knopf publication of a novel, *Lord Malquist and Mr. Moon,* which was published in London in 1966. We asked him how it was received there. "It was not received at all," he said. "It got very few reviews. It just sort of slunk in. It stopped dead in its tracks. I liked it enormously when I wrote it—I worked on it for months, all day and half the night, while my wife and I were living in a flat in London, and she read the new pages out loud in bed every night—and I thought that it would be a great success and that *Rosencrantz,* which I'd just finished, would simply be an interesting episode. The action of the novel takes place within twenty-four hours in contemporary London. The characters have a sort of eccentricity that moves them into a Surrealistic context, but the book isn't in the least

Surrealistic. Nothing in it is unreal or distorted, although some of it is heightened to a degree of absurdity. I think that realism has room for absurdity. It's sort of a funny book. I wrote it to be funny. Writing it was a very nice period of my life. Things you write tend to go off, like fruit. There are very few things I've written that haven't tended to decompose, later on, before my startled gaze—that is perfectly natural, since literary material isn't mineral but organic, and nature changes—but *Malquist* wears well, at least for me."

SIMON & GARFUNKEL

James Stevenson

SEPTEMBER 2, 1967

P AUL SIMON AND Art Garfunkel are both twenty-five years old. Paul Simon is short and black-haired. Art Garfunkel is tall and thin and has curly blond hair. When we met them, at a hotel in New Haven late one afternoon not long ago, both were wearing jerseys, Levi's, and low boots. The records of Simon and Garfunkel (including the albums *Parsley, Sage, Rosemary and Thyme* and *Wednesday Morning, 3 a.m.*) have sold over six million copies. Their songs—written by Simon, arranged by Garfunkel, and sung by both, with guitar by Simon—form one of the most original and moving bodies of pop music in America. Both Simon and Garfunkel were raised in Kew Gardens Hills and attended Forest Hills High School. Simon graduated from Queens College, and Garfunkel graduated from Columbia, where he is now working toward a Ph.D. in mathematical education.

One of Simon's songs, "A Simple Desultory Philippic (Or How I Was Robert McNamara'd into Submission)," goes:

> I been Norman Mailer'd, Maxwell Taylor'd,
> I been John O'Hara'd, McNamara'd,
> I been Rolling Stone'd and Beatle'd

Till I'm blind.
I been Ayn Rand'd, nearly branded
Communist, 'cause I'm left-handed.

GARFUNKEL: People who have gone through our kind of experience in pop music are baffled by the role they're in. Only two years earlier, they were fans. The "in" person is not a different cat, but there's a fantastic bombardment of stimuli thrown at you. If you go to work and try to digest them right away, though, the effect will be a kind of growth.

SIMON: Our name is honest. I think if we ever lie, they're going to catch us. I always thought it was a big shock to people when Bob Dylan's name turned out to be Bob Zimmerman. It was so important to people that he should be true. You have to be vulnerable. Then people can see you laid out, and they don't hit, and they know you won't hit them. Every time you drop a defense, you feel so much lighter. There have been times when I've had no defenses, and I felt like I was flying.

Another of Simon's songs, "The Sounds of Silence," goes:

The words of the prophets are written on subway walls
And tenement halls
And whisper in the sounds of silence.

GARFUNKEL: I care that what we do is good. A lot of people in pop music are influenced by the fact you don't have to be good, but I can't do that; I can't help but take it seriously.

SIMON: I think a lot of the praise we've had is really not warranted. If people's standards were higher . . . A lot of the things we've done have been hack. I don't take the title of "poet." It would be a slap in the face of Wallace Stevens to do that. But I see the possibility now that I *could* be one, and that pop music *could* be an art form.

GARFUNKEL: When we were teen-agers, we didn't care so much about being good as about being popular. We were real fans of rock 'n' roll. We recorded our first song in one of those booths at Coney

Island for twenty-five cents. It was early Alan Freed. We laughed a lot. I used to dig the idea of lists. I'd keep charts of the top forty songs on big sheets of graph paper. Each record was a colored dot on a vertical line. The records became very personal to me; I'd watch a song fall off from No. 2 to No. 7 and then strain to get back up to No. 4. I wish I still had those graphs. I have a real love of facts. Paul and I have different disciplines. I follow the use of logic to an end, rather than the play of ideas. I have very few beliefs. Paul is the opposite—what I call a "divergent thinker." He loves the idea of going off in different directions. The "convergent thinker" takes the facts and thinks the world should make sense. Even as you know it's a dead end, there's a stirring to know: "Is this really right?" The fact that people have so much trouble understanding each other drives me crazy. All I want to do is understand the world. I wonder "How accurately am I reading it?" We had a small hit record in 1956; it was just rock 'n' roll. Then, in 1963, Paul started writing songs—songs that were different. Bob Dylan had opened it up. I thought Paul's songs were really nice. We made an album for Columbia called *Wednesday Morning, 3 a.m.* It had been out for a year, and it wasn't doing anything, so Columbia took one of the cuts, "The Sounds of Silence," and overdubbed some background—bass, electric guitar, drums—and released it as a single. In three months, it was an established hit. The music business has taken over now, but teaching is an experience I'd still like to include in my life. Like a trip to Japan. I've been at Columbia for eight years, and I've always been teaching on the side, in my neighborhood. What really excites me is the scientific side of teaching—the lab aspect. Two people's brains, and the psychological interaction.

SIMON: After "The Sounds of Silence," the Simon-and-Garfunkel thing just kept going. There was no time to get off. Finally, I said, "This is what I want to do, and I want to do it as well as I possibly can." I'm stimulated to go forward. If I fail, I've got so many ego points I'll never be as paranoid as I was. So—straight ahead, and work! When you find you're in control of your destiny, it's fun. You do things you want to do.

GARFUNKEL: For a long time, I had a real dislike for all aspects of the recording business. The trappings held nothing for me—the fan structure, all that.

SIMON: Interviews are a big danger. An interview is a real ego trip. You have to remember that your opinion is not *important*—it's merely of interest.

GARFUNKEL: I didn't take very well to the stage. To be out, and involved, is not my natural state. When I was in high school, I withdrew a lot. My friends were reduced to one or two. I read a lot, and I played the game of "doing well in school"—maybe by default. My parents never pushed me, or were overly proud, though. I could never accept myself as "one of the gang." Everything I did was cast in the image and perspective of the outsider. I became a sociologist in spirit, an incessant observer. I've got more relaxed onstage, though. It's the impetus of Paul. And singing for large groups increases one's sense of power.

SIMON: I always like to perform, given the proper circumstances—a full house and good sound. I'm in complete control, and I get the pleasure of making music with someone else. When I'm on the stage, I'm up, and happy. I feel like laughing. I'm continually surprised at the response. I never thought we would affect people so much. It's not so much the epiphany for them as the relief. People fear that they're alone. They listen, and they feel what I feel, and they say, "I'm not alone!" The basic approach on the stage is to exaggerate things and make them larger than life. But we're in a time when so much is larger than life. So we take an uncommon approach. I feel you can be effective by being the same size as life, or smaller.

Another of Simon's songs, "The Dangling Conversation," goes:

> It's a still-life watercolor
> Of a now-late afternoon
> As the sun shines through the curtain lace
> And shadows wash the room
> And we sit and drink our coffee
> Couched in our indifference
> Like shells upon the shore.
> You can hear the ocean roar
> In the dangling conversation

And the superficial sighs
The borders of our lives . . .

SIMON: Writing is often an excruciating process. I've been working on one song for three months now. In the past, I could go
faster, but I wouldn't accept those songs now. Now I say, "No. It's
got to be framed right," and I spend months. Every time I pick up
the guitar, I start on the song. When I go to sleep, I spend half
an hour thinking about it. Songs get stagnant, and they turn on
me. Lines that were good you begin to discard. I use the guitar. I
grab a chord, and then I'm into something. My early songs were
derivative. I was influenced by so many people. Elvis Presley influenced me to play the guitar; the Everly Brothers influenced our
singing; Bob Dylan . . . Later, these merge with your personality.
I use less imagery now, less metaphor. I give you the picture,
stretch it, and let you feel it. When your mind is about to turn
off, I try and get a word or a line that's different, so you snap
back. If I lose the guy, I don't get him back. I want to make the
words rich and yet plain—tasteful without being prissy or too
delicate. One word can throw it off. It's not poetry. I'm writing
sounds that must be sung, and heard sung. I'm conscious of the
medium I'm working in. What should be said in a song? What
would be better said in an essay? A song is an impression when
it's heard only once. Of course, sometimes I make a song purely
an impression, like "Feelin' Groovy." I think: Yellow . . . pink . . .
blue . . . bubbles . . . gurgle . . . happy. The line "I'm dappled and
drowsy"—it doesn't make sense. I just *felt* dappled. Sleepy, con-
tented. The song only runs one minute and twenty-nine seconds,
with a long fadeout. When you've made your impression, stop. I
don't want the audience to have time to think. It's a happy song,
and that's what it was. There's the other kind of song, like "The
Dangling Conversation." It's intricately worked out. Every word
is picked on purpose. Maybe it's English-major stuff, but if you
haven't caught the symbolism, you haven't missed anything,
really. You've got to keep people moving. The attention span is
very limited. People don't listen carefully. Unless you jolt 'em, it's
going to be down the drain. You've got to get the right mixture
of sound and words. I write about the things I know and observe.

I can look into people and see scars in them. These are the people I grew up with. For the most part, older people. These people are sensitive, and there's a desperate quality to them—everything is beating them down, and they become more aware of it as they become older. I get a sense they're thirty-three, with an awareness that "Here I am thirty-three!" and they probably spend a lot of afternoons wondering how they got there so fast. They're educated, but they're losing, very gradually. Not realizing, except for just an occasional glimpse. They're successful, but not happy, and I feel that pain. They've got me hooked because they are people in pain. I'm drawn to these people, and driven to write about them. In this country, it's painful for people to grow old. When sexual attractiveness is focussed on a seventeen-year-old girl, you must feel it slipping away if you're a thirty-three-year-old woman. So you say, "I'm going to stop smoking. I'm going to get a suntan. I'm going on a diet. I'm going to play tennis." What's intriguing is that they are just not *quite* in control of their destiny. Nobody is paying any attention to these people, because they're not crying very loud. I feel a strong affinity with the flower scene. I always think about beautiful people and beautiful fields, and I think about floating through them. People say, "Why don't you split?"— I'm sitting here making a quarter of a million dollars—and "Why live in it?" But I'm really strung out over people. I'm drawn to people; they all know what pain is. I give my money away. I give it in chunks. I'm always trying to run around and patch things up. The ghettos. It's not human to live like that. I met a Puerto Rican acid-head by the Park one day, and he said, "You're Paul Simon," and we talked, and I took him to my apartment. It must have looked like Shea Stadium to him. I said, "I want to lay the Beatles album on him," so I put the earphones on him, and he's flipping out, and I think: Everybody should have what I have. I used to think I was much sharper than everyone else— very aware, perceptive, seeing things. Then, recently, I realized it wasn't true. Everyone's perceptive. Everyone is sensitive and perceptive, and they all know what pain is. I have compassion for that. There's a gentleness and understanding in young people today, and there's only one choice: the human race *must* come to the aid of the human race.

It was now seven o'clock. The evening was cloudy and threatening. Simon and Garfunkel, who were on a concert tour, drove from their New Haven hotel out to the Yale Bowl, where they were scheduled to perform at eight-fifteen. They went out early because Simon wanted to make sure the sound system was right. After parking their car, they walked down a ramp under the Bowl and out onto the football field, near the fifty-yard line. The grass was a brilliant, eerie green under the dark, rainy sky. Carrying Simon's guitars, they walked downfield to one of the end zones, where a stage had been set up. Except for some concert officials and a number of policemen who had gathered at the portals, ready to cope with the huge crowd that was anticipated, the vast stadium was empty. Ten minutes later, Simon climbed onto the stage to test the sound. He stood alone, a slight figure, holding a twelve-string guitar in front of the microphones. He struck the first notes of a song of his called "Homeward Bound," and the sound seemed to leap out and fill the stadium. He began to sing:

> "I'm sittin' in the railway station,
> Got a ticket for my destination.
> On a tour of one-night stands
> My suitcase and guitar in hand."

He looked up at the rows and rows of empty seats, and then up toward the last row, where Garfunkel, silhouetted against the blustery sky, stood listening.

> "And ev'ry stop is neatly planned
> For a poet and a one-man band.
> Homeward bound."

Then Garfunkel waved with both arms to Simon, signalling that the sound was fine, and Simon finished the song as Garfunkel came bounding down the concrete steps.

An hour later, the stands had filled with fifteen thousand people, and the concert began.

MAHARISHI MAHESH YOGI

Ved Mehta

JUNE 1, 1968 (FROM "INDIAN JOURNAL PART III")

HAVE JUST SPENT some time at Jhusi, which is one vast stretch of saffron tents interrupted by straw huts, by sheds roofed with sheets of corrugated iron, by bamboo towers, and by bamboo poles flying the flags or signs of every imaginable sect of *sadhus*. And though I am not clear yet about what those dreams are that come true here, at times I did feel as though I were sleepwalking through some celestial bazaar. . . .

. . .

One large colony of tents is marked by a sign that reads "Spiritual Regeneration Movement Foundation of India." This is the headquarters of Maharishi Mahesh Yogi. I know of him, or know the few available facts about him (all uncorroborated): that he was born around 1910; that his father was a revenue inspector; that he attended Allahabad University; that he worked in a factory for a time; that for some years he studied in the Himalayas with the *jagadguru* (Sanskrit for "universal teacher") Shankaracharya of Badri ka Ashram; and that, unlike most Indian sages, who use one religious title, he prefers to use two—Maharishi, which is Sanskrit for "great seer," and Yogi, which is from the Sanskrit *"yoga,"* meaning "effort." Inside the first tent, which is packed with such items as tomato sauce, cornflakes, soap, toothpaste, and chewing gum—all imports, to judge from the labels—a man in a brown lounge suit and with a vermilion mark on his forehead comes up to me. He tells me his name and continues, in English, "I am America-returned. I am M.A. and Ph.D. in public administration from the States. Guruji has fifty-four *chelas* from distant foreign lands here at Kumbha. I myself am going to be initiated on this Amavasya, when Guruji will recite some *mantras* to me by the side of Mother Ganga, and I will recite them back. I met the Guruji only a month ago. After I set my eyes on Guruji, I left my five children to follow him."

He takes me to an open area among the tents, where many Westerners, some in Indian dress, are standing around a serving table finishing a meal of macaroni and custard. I accept a small dish of custard from a girl in Western dress. She has very long eyelashes and the slightly bored expression of a fashion model.

"Where are you from?" I ask her.

"From Canada," the girl replies. "Guruji is a fact, and, like a fact, he manifested himself to me in Canada."

When I ask her to tell me something about the Spiritual Regeneration Movement, she says tersely, "You must address any questions you have to Guruji himself."

An Englishwoman joins us. "Guruji has been around the world six times, and now we have a half-dozen Spiritual Regeneration Movement Centers in Britain," she says. "They teach Guruji's simple technique of meditation."

The members of the group start moving into a tent. They arrange themselves as best they can on the floor in front of Maharishi Mahesh Yogi, a merry-looking little man with smooth skin, blunt features, and long, well-oiled hair. He is dressed in a flowing cream-colored silk robe. Three tape recorders stand near him on the floor, as sacred books might surround another *guru*.

Maharishi Mahesh Yogi urges the audience to ask questions, and I ask a general question about the nature of his movement.

He asks me to identify myself, and when I do, he says, in English, in a soft, rich, bemused voice, "All I teach is a simple method of meditation. We are all conscious on a mundane level, but beneath that consciousness, in each one of us, there is an ocean vaster than any in the world. It's there that most new thoughts originate. The bridge between the mundane level of consciousness and the ocean is meditation—not reading, because if you read you can have only second-hand thoughts. Meditation expands the consciousness and leads to the greatest production of goods and services. The ultimate test of my method of meditation is therefore its utility—the measure of the usefulness of people to society. Through my method of meditation, the poor can become as rich as the rich, and the rich can become richer. I taught my simple method of meditation to a German cement manufacturer. He taught the method to all his employees and thereby quadrupled the production of cement. As I said when addressing a meeting in the Albert Hall, in London, my technique does not involve withdrawal from normal material life. It enhances the material values of life by the inner spiritual light. My method is, in my London example, 'like the inner juice of the orange, which can be enjoyed without destroying the outer beauty of the fruit. This is done simply by pricking the orange with a pin again and again, and extracting the juice little by little, so that the inner juice is drawn out on the surface, and both are enjoyed simultaneously.'"

During the rest of the session, which goes on for a few hours, with the tape recorders running, Maharishi Mahesh Yogi expounds on his simple method of meditation. He has a way of dismissing everything. Not only does he rule out at the start all questions concerning morality, theology, and philosophy—implying at one point that men are free to do anything in their personal lives, to themselves or to others, as long as, by the technique of meditation, they experience the bliss that is within themselves—but he seems to remove himself from the whole process of intellectual discourse by giggling at every question put to him and then at his own answer to the question, so one feels that no matter how long one talked to him one would come away with, at worst, chagrin at having been ridiculed and, at best, vague excitement at having been tantalized.

THE WHO

Hendrik Hertzberg

NOVEMBER 15, 1969

S EVERAL AFTERNOONS AGO, we found ourself in the Grand Ballroom of the Holiday Inn on West Fifty-seventh Street, where the Who were to receive gold records for having sold a million dollars' worth of albums of the rock opera *Tommy*. The Who are the third most important of the English rock bands (after the Rolling Stones and the Beatles), having first attracted public attention through their custom, since abandoned, of smashing their instruments to bits onstage. *Tommy* is their opera—the first rock opera ever written, in fact—and they were in town performing it for a week at the Fillmore East.

At first, we thought we had come to the wrong ballroom, since it was empty except for a little knot of perhaps a dozen people in one corner, and nothing especially ceremonial seemed to be going on. Then the four members of the Who separated themselves out, and, holding their gold records, which were mounted and framed, lined up to be photographed. They were dressed in a variety of imaginative costumes, and, of course, they all had long hair. A well-barbered man whose black hair was going gray, and who was wearing a blue suit, a blue shirt, and a blue tie, lined up with them.

"Who's that?" we asked a handy public-relations man.

"That's the executive vice-president of Decca Records," he whispered back.

The well-barbered man stepped to one side, and another well-barbered man, also with black hair going gray and also wearing a blue suit, a blue shirt, and a blue tie, took his place.

"Who's that?" we asked.

"That's the executive vice-president of the Music Corporation of America," the P.R. man said.

A third man moved up to be photographed with the Who. He was like his two predecessors in every respect except that his well-barbered sideburns (which were going gray) were half an inch longer and his blue suit was double-breasted.

"Who's *that*?" we asked.

"That is the director of creative services of Decca Records," the P.R. man said, a bit edgily.

The photographer left, thus putting an end to the ceremony, and the Who went upstairs to relax for a couple of hours before going downtown for their performance. When we joined them, a few minutes later, they were talking about the Woodstock rock festival.

"That was the worst gig we ever played," Roger Daltrey, the lead singer, was saying, in a gravelly voice. He was wearing suède bell-bottoms and a ski sweater, and a halo of dark-blond curls surrounded his bony face. "We waited in a field of mud for fourteen hours, sitting on some boards, doing nothing, and doing nothing is the most exhausting thing in the world. As a result, we gave one of the worst shows we've ever done."

"From a human point of view, it was great," said John Entwhistle, the bass guitarist—a hulking, broad-shouldered man wearing, among other things, a pair of snakeskin boots. "Three people died and two people were born and half a million people managed to get on together. But musically it was awful. The only good thing was when the sun came up just as we were getting to the end of *Tommy*. That was marvellous. It felt like a blessing from God."

There was a soft knock at the door. Keith Moon, the drummer, who had on an electric-blue suit that matched the chair he was sitting in, called out "Come in!" and then added "Better still, get out!"

"The girl from last night is here," said a man's voice outside.

Moon raised his eyebrows and lowered them.

"I don't think we'll be playing gigs like Woodstock in the future," said Peter Townshend, who is the leader of the Who and the composer and librettist of *Tommy*. He is thin, with large hands and wrists, a small chin, and an oversized nose. "A festival is essentially a public occasion, and the music is just background. We haven't seen the worst yet. One promoter I've heard about is trying to organize a festival in Wyoming next summer. Not any particular part of Wyoming—the whole state."

There was another knock, and the same voice said, "The girl from the third row is here. She said you'd know."

No one seemed to know.

Townshend continued, "Whether or not you participate in something like that depends on whether you regard rock as a commodity or as something more—recognizing, fair enough, that it's something that can make a lot of money. But it's not going to stop tomorrow, it's not going to die, and so there's no need to wring it dry today. For example, we could have played Madison Square Garden instead of the Fillmore and made more money in one night than we'll get for the whole week. But we've become so serious and so obsessed with keeping happy and performing that we're willing to turn down huge offers for the chance to reach an audience. The problem with a place like the Garden is that the audience can't see you wince. They can't see you smile. And that's important to us, because to us a rock concert is as much a theatrical performance as a musical one."

We asked the Who if anything in particular had struck them about America during their visit, and Roger Daltrey said, "The generation gap. It's about fifty times worse here than it is at home."

"In England, I'm a respected member of the community," Entwistle said. "Here, right here in the lobby downstairs, somebody came up to me yesterday and called me a dirty hippie. Why is everybody with long hair automatically considered dirty? If you don't have hair that's so short you can see the scalp through it, you're not quite human. In England, even the politicians have long hair—to keep the draft off their necks. It's a cold country."

"Our parents spent six years in air-raid shelters while their houses were being blown up over their heads," Daltrey said. "They built up a sense of humor. We respect them, and they respect us."

The group broke up to get ready for the show, and we went along with Townshend to his room. While he changed his shirt, he talked about *Tommy*, which, properly speaking, is not an opera but an oratorio. It is about a boy, born during the First World War, who goes blind, deaf, and dumb after seeing his father kill his mother's lover. He becomes a pinball champion, operating the machine solely through his sense of touch, and then is miraculously cured. He becomes the leader of a religious movement and acquires millions of followers, who finally reject him when he tells them that to achieve enlightenment they must tape up their eyes, ears, and mouths, and play pinball. All in all, not a particularly outlandish plot for an opera.

We said that we had been impressed the night before by the Who's energetic stage performance, which is full of leaps and grand gestures, and Townshend said, "Yes, the Who are very athletic. You have to be fit, and keeping fit is a serious problem on a tour like this. I've never been able to do anything athletic in the sense of sports or games, but onstage I can pour incredible energy out of nowhere, just by drawing on the resources that I think every human being has. I wish I could jump sixty feet in the air, land, and play a guitar note."

It was time to move on to the Fillmore, and as we left we asked Townshend if he thought rock was one of the causes of the cultural changes that have affected young people everywhere.

"I don't think rock causes change," he said. "Rock doesn't cause change; it's there because changes have taken place. It's a reflection of changes in ideas. If rock really is a reflection of the current mood, I can only be optimistic, and not just because I'm a part of it. I can't pinpoint the changes; if I could, I'd be in government instead of playing the guitar. But rock is going in a certain direction, and I think it's a good direction. I'm not worried."

PART SIX

ARTISTS & ATHLETES

A NOTE BY LARISSA MACFARQUHAR

ONCE A DECADE becomes an adjective, it's transformed into a cartoon version of itself, and it becomes very difficult to remember what living through it was actually like. This is the reason to read journalism long after its moment has passed: because it doesn't know what's coming. Historians know what's going to happen, but journalists don't, any more than their subjects do, and this ignorance can convey better than hindsight the peculiar temper of the time.

It seemed, for instance, to Nat Hentoff, in 1964, as though the up-and-coming folksinger Bob Dylan might be around for a while, but who knew for sure? He was only twenty-three; maybe he was just a flash in the pan. When Allen Ginsberg told Jane Kramer, in 1968, that he had just met with Robert Kennedy in Washington to talk about the war, and was planning to go to Chicago for the Democratic Convention in August and stage "a mass manifestation of gaiety," neither one of them had the faintest idea how vastly different America would be by the end of the summer. The only thing that anybody knew for sure was that the New York Mets would lose and keep on losing, but then, in 1969, they didn't. They actually beat the Orioles in five games and won the World Series, and after that impossible event a great gray fog descended over the perceptible future, and all bets were off.

As is often the case with decades, the sixties took a while to become the sixties. It was still the fifties for the first few years. The American military had been involved in Vietnam since 1950, but the real escalation didn't begin until Lyndon Johnson took office. The Beatles didn't appear on *The Ed Sullivan Show* until 1964. At the beginning of the sixties, Jimi Hendrix was in the Army, at Fort Campbell, Janis Joplin was a transfer student at the University of Texas, and Jerry Garcia was in East Palo Alto living in his car. Muhammad Ali was still Cassius Clay. Certain things were still surprising, in those early years, that wouldn't be for long. It was still worthy of note in 1961 that some comedians (notably Elaine May and her partner, Mike Nichols) regarded their fellow-humans with outsider hostility rather than glad-handing bonhomie. It was worthy of note in 1964 that Bob Dylan didn't wear a tie.

In the second half of the decade, the sixties proper began. *The New Yorker* was, in the Summer of Love, forty-two years old. It was born funny, and it was still funny, but it was wry in a zany age. By 1967, it had lived through the Depression, Hiroshima, three regular wars, and a cold one. Just because a bunch of kids were taking their tops off and getting high in public parks, it didn't believe either that civilization as we knew it was ending or that the glorious revolution had finally arrived. But something was happening, no question, and it wanted to figure out what.

The magazine did not aspire to become part of the counterculture, like *Esquire* or *Rolling Stone*. It was not going to leap wildly about, throwing great fistfuls of exclamation points around like ripped-up money or flowers at a Be-In. It was not going to tear pages out of *Webster's* and roll joints with them. But neither was it stodgily aloof. It kept its eye on developments in the Haight and upstate New York. No matter how crazy things got, it tended to remain deadpan, relying on sheer accumulation of detail—the tambourines, Sanskrit chanting, Yoruba beads, amulets, parachutes, jerkins, batik, wheat germ, conch horns, electric Tibet—to set the mood. It permitted itself, every now and then, a raised eyebrow—Jane Kramer referring, for instance, in a piece about Allen Ginsberg, to "a neighborhood guru with the *nom de psychedélie* of Buddha," that *nom de psychedélie* being one of just a very few cracks in ten thousand words of otherwise resolutely straight-faced exposition and repressed commentary. But, for the most part, it let the decade speak for itself, in long, meandering scenes that allowed the electric-rainbow-jerkin-tambourine bizarritude to unspool according to its own rhythms.

This straight tone, this disciplined-seeming neutrality, could be devastating. "Negroes are getting more confidence," Arthur Ashe's opponent, Clark Graebner, observed to John McPhee around the time of the first U.S. Open in 1968. "They are asking for more and more, and they are getting more and more. They are looser. They're liberal. In a way, 'liberal' is a synonym for 'loose.' And that's exactly the way Arthur plays. I've always kidded him, saying, 'If the Negroes take over, please make me a lieutenant. Not a general or a colonel. Just a lieutenant.'" The *New Yorker* storytelling style put on display an ordinary racism less dramatic and savage but more pervasive than the headline events of the civil-rights movement. A tale of post–Voting Rights Act race relations came in sideways, while McPhee and his readers faced forward and watched the match. "Even though Arthur is well accepted in a place like Philip Morris, he's never going beyond that level," Graebner says. "I accept Arthur any way, but many people don't. He's accepted only because he's a tennis player. . . . I think he's too smart to marry a white girl. That's a headache. If he marries a white girl, who's going to house him? He'll live in a very lovely residence somewhere, but I don't know where. I don't know where a Negro executive lives in New York. I don't even know."

Nobody knew how Arthur Ashe's life would turn out, not even Ashe himself—he did not know that he would die at forty-nine—and that was the point. The sixties had set many things in motion that would take much of the seventies to play out: five more years of Vietnam, four of Nixon, ten before bell-bottoms would be replaced by shoulder pads and John Lennon was shot. But nobody knew what was temporary, what would turn out to be merely part of the cartoon sixties, and what would become a permanent feature of American life. As Roger Angell wrote while incredulously contemplating the Mets' victory at the end of the decade, which proved, in case further proof was needed, that even though civilization had not ended and the revolution had not arrived, still a lot had happened in the past ten years: "I had no answer for the question posed by that youngster in the infield who held up—amid the crazily leaping crowds, the showers of noise and paper, the vermillion smoke-bomb clouds, and the vanishing lawns—a sign that said 'WHAT NEXT?'"

A TILTED INSIGHT

Robert Rice

APRIL 15, 1961 (MIKE NICHOLS & ELAINE MAY)

ONE SURPRISING DEVELOPMENT in the entertainment business during the last half-dozen years has been the ascent of a generation of young comedians whose public attitude is indignation and whose subject matter is man's inhumanity to man—of which, if their work is a reflection of their state of mind, they consider themselves to be outstanding victims. Gone is the time when being jocose about Bing Crosby's toupee, Jayne Mansfield's structure, or the outcome of the daily double at Hialeah was fashionable; the new comedy covers a bleak political-psychological-sociological-cultural range that reaches from the way public affairs are conducted in Washington to the way private ones are conducted in Westchester. Of the members of the group of suffering entertainers—though it may be disrespectful to use the word "group" to describe people who spend much of their time being disrespectful to groups—the two who have devised the most striking way of making their pain laughable are the team of Mike Nichols and Elaine May. Nichols and May use the Stanislavski method of acting to perform comedy sketches in classic blackout form. The result is a wholly original technique that allows them, at one and the same time, to make funny faces and wear funny hats and to deal accurately and candidly with what one man who has worked with them calls "the secrets of the family"—the appalling (to them, at least) relationships that habitually exist between mothers and sons, fathers and daughters, brothers and sisters, husbands and wives, or, in short, males and females. As depicted by Nichols and May, mothers tend to whine, grown-up sons to snivel, adolescents to pant or prattle, unfaithful wives to simper, little boys to bluster, and husbands to drone. Their attitude toward the people they have invented is rigorously unsentimental but by no means unemotional; as well they might, they often seem to be enraged by the way their characters are behaving. A comment that both of them feel is a just description of what they do and how they do it was recently made by the critic Walter Kerr, who wrote, "It's a good thing Mike Nichols and Elaine May are partners. How would either of them ever find anyone else he'd distrust so much?" One thing most Nichols and May characters are addicted to is clichés, spoken in tones of embarrassed and embarrassing sincerity. "I can't stand to see you this way," one of them, horrified by the agonies the other one is going through in an effort to give up smoking, will say, to the accompaniment of those circumstantial spasms of the larynx, the nostrils, and the jawline that are characteristic equally of a congenital clown and of a Method actor. Or "I wouldn't respect you and I wouldn't respect myself," or "Darling, I'm so ashamed." Not only is the acting of Nichols and May so substantial that they can construct believable characters out of literary rubble like that, but their literary discipline is substantial enough for them to know when a character is so solidly built that he can deliver a punch line. In view of the fact that family secrets, even when they are handled in a resolutely anti-soap-opera manner, are an inexhaustible source of best-selling copy, no one need be flabbergasted to learn that Nichols and May, neither of whom has yet reached thirty, have been deriving from their work in night clubs, television, and radio, and on Broadway, where their show *An Evening with Mike Nichols and Elaine May* is in its seventh month, gross annual receipts of nearly half a million dollars.

Nichols is light-haired, light-eyed, and light-skinned. He is not only the male lead but the master of ceremonies, and in the latter role he is debonair and self-assured enough. Once he plunges into a scene, though, it becomes apparent that he is a doomed man. His full-lipped and rather fleshy face is peculiarly suited to expressing the nuances of frustration, from the compressed mouth and round eyes of helpless resignation, through a whole gamut of pouts, to the expanded nostrils and knitted brows of ineffectual anger. His somewhat nasal voice can ring just about all the changes on querulousness. As the doomed man, he is flimflammed by telephone operators, browbeaten by his mother, and terrified when his girl friend submits to his amorous advances. Sometimes he tries to be satanically dominant—with his little sister, say, or with an audience of women gathered to hear him lecture on the drama—but his masterfulness and malevolence are usually feeble. Nichols' characterizations are ably conceived and executed, but there is no more doubt in his mind than in anyone else's that Miss May is the team's virtuoso actor. She is a short, buxom young woman, as uncompromisingly brunette as Nichols is blond, with an enormous amount of crazy hair and crazy energy. She can arrange her features and tune her voice in so many different ways that it is impossible to say what she really looks or sounds like. As a movie starlet with wide eyes, a dazzling smile, and a husky voice, she is clearly one of the most alluring women in America; as a mother with sagging shoulders and jowls, twitching hands, and a whine, she is one of the most repellent; as an Englishwoman with protruding teeth, a rigid spine, and clipped diction, or as a clubwoman with unmanageable eyebrows, aimless gestures, and a shrill cackle, she is one of the most absurd.

However, describing Nichols and May as solo performers is beside the point, for the essence of the act is that it is a duet. If there is a difference in kind between the contributions of the two, it is that Nichols, as the one less likely to lose himself in what he is doing, is the one more likely to know when the moment has come to change the direction of a scene or to end it. Certainly it is Nichols who has taken day-by-day command of the team's career. Alexander H. Cohen, the producer of *An Evening with Mike Nichols and Elaine May*, estimates that he has a telephone conversation about business with Miss May every ten or twelve days and that he has one with Nichols three or four times every day. "Mike's middle name is Emergency," Cohen, who has limitless affection for the eccentricities of actors in general and for those of Nichols and May in particular, said not long ago. "He may call me at home from his dressing room during intermission to tell me the theatre is 'in total darkness,' and when I check with the stage manager I'll find that one bulb burned out up on the bridge and has already been replaced." The sort of thing that exasperates Miss May professionally is of a different order, which she recently summarized by imagining a situation in which the team appears on a television show with Dinah Shore. The hypothetical script calls for Miss Shore and Miss May to exchange the customary inconsequences before the team goes into its act, with Miss Shore beginning by saying, "Why, Elaine, you're wearing the same dress I am." Miss May finds it psychologically impossible to make any reply but "Certainly, didn't you see it at dress rehearsal?," and her part of the badinage is suppressed. Because Miss May's imagination teems with mortifying predicaments like that, Nichols handles most of the public chitchat for the pair.

In most respects, though, Nichols and May are a team that carries teamwork to extraordinary lengths. As trained and convinced Method actors—Nichols took lessons from Lee Strasberg, the theoretician-in-chief of the Actors' Studio, and Miss May studied under the late Maria Ouspenskaya, an alumna of the Moscow Art Theatre—they both insist that establishing and maintaining a believable personal relationship on-stage is the foundation of good acting, and therefore of good comedy, and that any effects, however showy, that are irrelevant to such a relationship are inartistic, and therefore unfunny. The way they compose their pieces is an even more impressive demonstration of teamwork than the way they perform them. The characters Nichols plays and the words Nichols speaks were invented by Nichols, and the characters Miss May plays and the words Miss May speaks were invented by Miss May. Everything they do started as an improvisation and was gradually hardened and polished in the course of performance without ever having been written down or even discussed much. "We've killed some promising things with too much talk, so we've learned to talk very carefully," Miss May said recently. Miss May tends to use words in a special way. There is little carefulness in the accepted sense in the way they talk to each other privately during practically every intermission. In fact, these colloquies are often conducted in such injurious terms that the team sounds much like a married couple on the way home from a particularly disorderly cocktail party; how-dare-you-treat-me-this-way is a recurrent theme. The sense in which they can be said to exercise care after the curtain comes down is that they confine themselves to discussing their general attitude toward each other while the curtain was up, and avoid all mention of details of inflection, gesture, or grimace. They cherish the spontaneous nature of their work so fiercely that they have a calculated policy of remaining as ignorant as they can of such minutiae. Their instinctive reflex when one of the scenes is analyzed in their presence is not to listen, and when one of them is written down, not to look. In order to be able to cue *Evening*'s backstage crew properly, the show's stage manager, shortly after it opened, obtained a script by the use of a tape recorder and a typist. One day, Miss May injudiciously read what she had been saying in a solo scene as a Parent-Teacher Association chairlady. She was amazed to find that, in her words, "there isn't a joke in it." The discovery made her so self-conscious that she wasn't satisfied with the way she performed the scene for a couple of weeks, which was how long it took her to stop listening to herself telling all those non-jokes and to regain her confidence that her acting was funny enough to compensate for the absence of verbal wit. Since Miss May and Nichols have more respect than any audience for their mysterious ability to mesh their separate notions into a coherent piece ad lib, it is improbable that they have ever studied the script of one of their joint numbers. They are able to account for their rapport only in the most general way. A recent manful, if not altogether lucid, attempt by Nichols to explain it was, "Neither of us is capable of having a different kind of idea from the other." As for Miss May, she defines the element that binds their work together as "a tilted insight."

. . .

Although it is clear from what Nichols and May do that their insight tilts in the direction of being aggrieved, they seldom make their grievances explicit. Their method of voicing an opinion is to embed it in an ostensibly factual report rather than to proclaim it in an editorial. They make known their suspicion of mother love, for example, by enacting a seven-and-a-half-minute telephone conversation between a young man and his mother, who has phoned him because for weeks he has neglected to phone her. The sketch, one of their most renowned, reaches its climax when Nichols says, "I feel awful," and Miss May replies, "Arthur, if I could only believe that, I'd be the happiest mother in the world." They have a forthright attitude toward adultery, which, in essence, seems to be that committing it and not committing it are equally pointless; it takes them ten and a half minutes to expound this theory by way of a series of three scenes in the lobby of a hotel. The first is between a conscience-stricken American couple. (NICHOLS: "You want to know how bad *I* feel? If I hadn't rented that room already, I'd say forget it.") The second is between a tight-lipped English couple. (MISS MAY: "I'm early." NICHOLS [*not moving*]: "Nice to have the extra time." MISS MAY [*sitting down*]: "Yes.") The third is between a preposterously exuberant French couple. (NICHOLS: "Where's George?" MISS MAY: "My husband? . . . But, darling, I don't know. Didn't *you* bring him?") In much the same deprecatory manner, they deal at length with female civic-mindedness, industrial bureaucracy, modern child-rearing, radio journalism, the cult of Southern squalor, and adolescent courtship. In addition, they have made dozens of summary, but no less disenchanted, comments on subjects they evidently regard as not complicated enough to merit exhaustive treatment, like space travel, Christmas, police corruption, summer camps, the Presidential election, psychiatry, and almost anyone's literary output. Their evaluation of the novels of Fëdor Dostoevski takes just ten seconds; Miss May laughs hilariously for nine and a half seconds, Nichols says, "Unhappy woman!" and the lights go out. The painstakingly documentary nature of almost any Nichols and May scene that runs much longer than ten seconds tends to provoke a kind of laughter that, while voluminous, is distinctly uneasy. At a midweek matinée, there is generally a tinge of hysteria in the obbligato of soprano giggles that accompanies Miss May's impersonation of the P.-T.A. chairlady, and few audiences are able to keep their mirth from sounding shrill as they watch "Teen-agers," a detailed examination of what a high-school boy and a high-school girl on their first date say and do in the back seat of a parked car. Some people even find Nichols and May too precise to be funny at all, among them a number of ardent admirers who look upon the team less as entertainers than as important social critics, or even leaders of a crusade for a more decent world. One such devotee, a social critic himself, recently asserted that he remembers being moved by just three broadcasts: the radio announcement of the Japanese attack on Pearl Harbor, the radio announcement of the death of Franklin D. Roosevelt, and the first television performance of "Teen-agers." Few comedians, surely, have ever received such an accolade—and still fewer, not including Nichols and May, have ever sought one.

Perhaps the most complete, and certainly the most complex, statement given by Nichols and May of their distrust of each other and everything else is an eighteen-and-a-half-minute scene they call "Pirandello." It uses that skeptical Italian playwright's system of questioning the integrity of all human relationships to demonstrate that two small children who play at being their parents and apparently become their parents really are two actors playing a scene in which children become their parents—or, rather, *really* are Mike Nichols and Elaine May playing two actors playing a scene in which children become their parents. It is a piece that gives Nichols and May a chance to be leery of each other from, so to speak, the cradle to the grave, and it provides a splendid setting for the disclosure of family secrets as well. It lets them express in detail what is conceivably a chief ingredient of their common view of life—that people, whether they are children, adults, actors, or Nichols and May, treat each other in much the same way: abominably. It lets them disparage in passing, to name just a few of the objects of their scorn, *Zorro* comic books, cocktail parties, the theatrical temperament, profane language, witty women, and skeptical Italian playwrights who question the integrity of all human relationships. It lets them display their profound sense of theatre, since they have worked the material so that it yields suspense and a number of frightening climaxes as well as laughter. And it lets them act their heads off—particularly Miss May. Her portrayal of a solemn, inarticulate little girl is one of the most meticulously observed, most heartfelt, and funniest characterizations on Broadway. Nichols and May use "Pirandello" to close the first half of *Evening*, presumably so that an audience can smoke off its shock in the lobby. As a matter of fact, though "Pirandello" may be their definitive statement, it is the only thing of its kind they do. The ways they unburden themselves most naturally and most often are by turning everyday events into melodramas, by turning melodramas into everyday events, and by enacting Most Embarrassing Moments, a category of human experience they seem to be inordinately, not to say painfully, well acquainted with. The dialogue about giving up smoking and the telephone conversation between the mother and son are fair examples of the first method. Typical of the second are a pair of radio skits, one a version of *Oedipus Rex* that has Oedipus saying plaintively to Jocasta, "Look, sweetheart, you're my mother," the other a domestic contretemps that has the husband saying cheerily to his wife when she tells him she has been chosen to be the first woman into space, "I'll manage the house somehow." As for Most Embarrassing Moments, perhaps the funniest radio skit they ever did was about a psychiatrist with the hiccups, and another effective one concerned a traffic policeman trying to elicit a bribe from a woman driver too obtuse to understand his hints. They also operate quite often in the area of humor that is currently known as "sick." False teeth, falling hair, protruding ears, and gross overweight crop up a good deal in their work. "Sweetie, have you ever thought of bleaching your mustache?" is a fairly characteristic thing for Nichols to say to Miss May when they are groping for new material.

Nichols and May do a good deal of groping in the course of discovering what they want to say. Since they shoot from the hip, they necessarily score a great many partial hits and total misses. For the last year or so, they have been recording a series of one- to five-minute improvised comedy spots that are inserted, at the average rate of five times a weekend, into N.B.C. radio's weekend program called *Monitor*. By now they must have attempted more than six hundred taped spots. Perhaps three hundred have been considered usable by the *Monitor* people, many of them after considerable cutting and splicing, and of those not more than a dozen or so represent Nichols and May at the top of their form. They have also been improvising regularly for the last year as the voices in a series of cartoon television tributes—for which they receive no billing, only a great deal of money—to Jax Beer, a New Orleans beverage that both of them now stock in their iceboxes. Their percentage of successes for Jax has been higher than for *Monitor*, but the percentage of real triumphs almost certainly much smaller. In a night club or a theatre, they do only their high-gloss set pieces, except for one improvisation, toward the end of each show, based on a suggestion from the audience, and they themselves say that the improvisation is seldom on a par with the rest of the pieces. When it does come off, though, it shakes an audience more than any set piece ever can. It also shakes Nichols and May. Things they are quite unable to explain happen to them when they are carried away by an improvisation. Once, in a night club, they held a couple of hundred semi-sober delegates to a sales convention spellbound for fifteen or twenty minutes with an improvisation inspired by Plato's "Dialogues," a work that they had no reason to believe any member of their audience except the one who suggested it was familiar with, and, moreover, one that they themselves had had no idea they felt any passion about. On another occasion, Nichols suddenly became aware, with a feeling much like terror, that he was speaking fluent Yiddish—a language he didn't know he knew.

· · ·

Nichols and May began their life together with an improvisation. It was a performance designed solely for their private entertainment, though it may well have also entertained, or astounded, a number of loiterers in the waiting room of the Randolph Street station of the Illinois Central in Chicago, which is where it took place. One evening in the spring of 1954, Nichols was walking through the waiting room on his way to a train and Miss May was sitting on a bench reading a magazine. They knew each other by sight, both having for a time hung around the University of Chicago and been associated with various little-theatre groups that originated on or around its campus. As Nichols remembers it, he had avoided becoming acquainted with Miss May, because he was sure she was sneering at him. He still speaks of "the look of utter contempt" that he believes was on her face as she watched him playing a part in Strindberg's *Miss Julie*—the first time he recalls seeing her. Miss May denies that she ever regarded Nichols with contempt. "I didn't regard him at all," she said recently. In any case, that day in the waiting room Nichols resolved to face up to Miss May. He sat down beside her and, talking out of the corner of his mouth, assumed the character of a secret agent making contact with a colleague. She responded in a heavy Russian accent, and they went into a long scene that Nichols recalls as "half spy, half pickup." They no longer remember just what they said, of course, but if by any chance the scene foreshadowed a spy spot they did a few months ago for *Monitor*, it may have begun something like this:

NICHOLS: I beg your pardon. Do you have a light?

MISS MAY: Yes, certainly.

NICHOLS: I had a lighter, but (*pause*) *I lost it on Fifty-seventh Street!*

MISS MAY: Oh. Then you're Agent X-9?

They both enjoyed their performance immensely. "It took the place of a lot of chitchat and coffee cups," Miss May said not long ago. In subsequent weeks, they had further meetings and conversations, and evidently discovered how much they had in common. Both of them were, as an old Chicago acquaintance of theirs has put it, "on the lam from their childhoods," which in Nichols' case had been spent largely in New York and in Miss May's largely in Los Angeles. Both of them had found the University of Chicago campus an asylum for insurgent spirits like theirs. Both of them were fascinated by the sort of theatre—Strindberg, Pirandello, Brecht—that is a good deal more likely to fascinate insurgent spirits in Chicago than commercial managers in New York or Los Angeles. Both of them had sharp tongues. And both of them were broke. Nichols recalls that one evening in Chicago he was so hungry, and so reluctant to cadge either another meal from friends or another package of bologna from a grocery store, that he dined on a jar of mustard, the only eatable in his room. He also recalls that when Miss May asked him to eat with her, in a cellar she was then occupying, the dish she was most likely to serve was a delight consisting of a small amount of hamburger, a small amount of cream cheese, and a large amount of ketchup. He says it was delicious. It is possible that he really thought so, since not long ago a friend who was sitting with him in the living room of his East Side penthouse watched him sup, with every evidence of pleasure, on a glass of butterscotch Metrecal and a can of corn, eaten cold out of the can.

The trail that led Nichols to the Illinois Central waiting room began in Berlin, where he was born in November, 1931, to parents who qualified in almost every possible respect as objects of Nazi persecution. His father was a Russian-born Jewish doctor, Paul Peschkowsky, who, after the revolution, had settled in Germany. His mother's family was prominently identified with the German Social Democratic Party; in fact, her father was an early victim of Nazi assassins. Hitler became Chancellor when Nichols was two. Nichols' chief memories of his personal life in the Germany of the thirties are of attending a segregated school for Jewish children and of being taunted and jostled sometimes on his way to and from school by boys with respectable ancestors. He was able to leave the country at an early enough age to have been spared experiences more devastating than those. In 1938, his father acquired the papers that were needed to effect his own departure from Germany and admission to the United States, and sailed for New York, with the idea of sending for his family when he had qualified to practice medicine here and was able to earn a living. Upon his arrival, he took the name of Nichols. A year later, Michael arrived, accompanied only by his younger brother—now an interne in San Francisco. Their mother was ill, and had been unable to make the trip with them, as she had planned. She came in 1941, only a few weeks before the United States entered the war. Dr. Nichols rapidly built up a good enough practice to maintain the family comfortably in the West Seventies, near Central Park. For the first three or four years here, Michael was bandied about from school to school; finally, he was installed, for his high-school years, in the Walden School, an institution of the kind known as progressive. It is possible that his attitude as an adolescent toward the adult world is recapitulated in the last line of a summer-camp spot that he and Miss May did for *Monitor*. The camp director says, "If I didn't hate kids so much, I'd close this camp." In 1944, Dr. Nichols was stricken with leukemia, and died. Since he had not been working long enough in this country to accumulate much of a reserve, the family had to reduce its standard of living sharply, but Michael was able to continue at Walden as a scholarship student. However, organized education was one of many things he had little use for. Once he had squeezed through Walden, with a minimum of effort, he had no idea of undertaking any further formal studies, except, perhaps, those connected with the theatre, a vocation to which he felt called but for which he was certain he would never be chosen. "I knew I was bright, but I didn't think I had any talent," he said recently. "I simply couldn't imagine a part anyone would cast me for." He did make a halfhearted investigation of the Department of Dramatic Arts of New York University, but when he discovered that one thing N.Y.U. students were expected to master was the words and melody of the school anthem ("Oh grim, grey Palisades . . ."), he left indignantly and got a job as a shipping clerk in a company that made costume jewelry. After a year there, it occurred to him that if it came to choosing between rhinestones and alma-mater songs, there was probably something to be said for alma-mater songs. He therefore enrolled in an academic course at the University of Chicago, but he made a point of seldom attending classes or taking examinations. The intellectual and artistic ferment on the Chicago campus did stimulate him, though, and he began to come to grips with his destiny when he joined practically every theatre group in sight. One of his first appearances was in the production of *Miss Julie* that was the occasion of Miss May's giving him the alleged fisheye. Presently, he was able to free himself partly from a mustard-eating economy by getting a job as an announcer for an FM radio station that concentrated on classical music, which he admires and knows a good deal about. He was on his way from the radio station to his lodgings, on the South Side, when he encountered Miss May in the waiting room.

Miss May arrived at Nichols by just as rocky a road. She was born in 1932 in Philadelphia, though it might as well have been any other large city in the United States, Canada, or Mexico, because her father, Jack Berlin, was the director of, the writer for, and the principal actor in a travelling Jewish theatrical company. She herself began appearing onstage at an early age, playing little boys, who, to the best of her recollection, were all named Benny. When she was ten, her father died and her mother went into partnership with one of Miss May's uncles, who operated a Chicago establishment called Fogarty's Grill. A couple of years later, the family moved to Los Angeles. Miss May's schooling was brief indeed. Because she was on the road, she didn't start it until she was eight, and because her resistance to education was monumental, even by comparison with Nichols', she stopped it when she was fourteen. The only thing she ever liked to do in school, she has said, was diagram sentences. Mathematics she found impenetrable and history inconceivable. She has too hard a time remembering what year anything happened to *her* to be able to say what year something happened to Pepin the Short.

While still in her teens, she was married to a young man named Marvin May, and something more than a year later she had a daughter, who, to show how circular life can be, is now attending the Walden School. (The Mays' marriage was ended by divorce some seven years ago.) Miss May looks back with distaste on her years in Los Angeles, a city she abhorred and abhors. "I feel in opposition to almost everything anyway, but it comes to its height in Los Angeles," she recently explained. Though she says she felt no specific urge then, and feels none now, to be an actress— or, in her words, "be anything"—the theatre was evidently her destiny, just as it was Nichols', because soon after her marriage she drifted into Mme. Ouspenskaya's acting classes. She acquired a good deal of useful training there, she thinks, though she had a difficult time at first, particularly with a standard Method exercise in which the actor is expected to portray a seed that gradually sprouts from the ground, grows into a tree, buds, and bursts into leaf. Miss May has always been strict about living the part she is playing. "They all had to wait for me. I couldn't bud to save my life. I knew I wasn't a tree," she recalled not long ago. She also drifted into association with various theatre enthusiasts in Los Angeles, and when some of them moved to Chicago to pursue their work, she followed, and found herself in the circle in which Nichols had been moving.

. . .

The friendship that developed between Nichols and Miss May after the scene in the station was only a prologue to their professional association. When about six months had passed, Nichols resolved that the time had come for him to plunge, and he returned to New York to study under Strasberg. At first, he tried living in the city and paying his way by working. He got a job as a waiter in a Howard Johnson's restaurant, for example, but it ended abruptly after two weeks, when, upon being asked for the fortieth time in one day, what kind of ice cream the establishment served, he grinned maniacally—he has one of the best maniacal grins in the business—and answered, "Chicken." There were other on-the-job crises, and so he moved to Philadelphia (life is circular), where his mother, who had remarried, was living, and still lives. He got a job with a Philadelphia radio station and commuted to New York twice a week for his lessons with Strasberg. Meanwhile, back in Chicago, Miss May joined one of the theatre companies that Nichols had been in. She acted in an assortment of plays that included *Peer Gynt*, *Red Gloves*, *Murder in the Cathedral*, and *A Midsummer Night's Dream*, and both she and the company scored such smashing successes that when she had been with it for only a few months her salary was raised from twelve dollars a week to twenty-five. Then, in the spring of 1955, the Fire Department closed the company's theatre, and one of its producers, David Shepherd, who was a theatre buff with a little money and a lot of admiration for what went on in European cabarets, said, as Miss May recalls it, "The hell with all the forms," and organized Compass Theatre—not a theatre but a night club, in which half a dozen actors (four male and two female), using brief scenarios based on ideas they either thought up themselves or elicited from the spectators, improvised scenes. Compass, of which Miss May was a charter member, proved sufficiently attractive to the drinking public to pay its performers fifty-five dollars a week. Late in 1955, a vacancy occurred at Compass, and Nichols, in Philadelphia, was asked by Shepherd to come to Chicago and fill it. Nichols had not maintained any contact with Miss May during the time they were apart—"Neither of us ever maintains any contact with anybody," he remarked a few weeks ago—but they had no difficulty in resuming their friendship at the point where they had suspended it, and they found working with each other, and at Compass, exhilarating. Most of the major pieces they do today had their origin at Compass. (Compass cheated about improvising in one respect; if a scene worked out well, it was kept in the repertory, though it changed from one performance to the next.) As a matter of fact, one of their scenes, a series of hysterical dialogues between a man who has lost his last dime in a coin telephone and a procession of operators, was first performed by Miss May and Shelley Berman, a contemporary of theirs at Compass who has also graduated from the fifty-five-dollar-a-week class. It is the only big Nichols and May number that involves no family secret. Considerably more representative of what they used to do together was a scene, evidently containing the first inklings of "Pirandello," that covered the history, from childhood to old age, of a couple who spent their lives playing games with each other. (A Compass improvisation could go on for an hour, if that was the way the actors felt about it.) The scene started with their playing Monopoly, proceeded through gin rummy, and finally arrived at chess. Nichols always lost. At last, when they were doddering and palsied, he was able to cry "Checkmate!" Miss May dropped dead. Nichols paid her no attention. "I won! I won!" he shouted, jumping with glee. End of scene.

Nichols and Miss May spent a couple of years exchanging joyous thoughts like that with each other and with their colleagues. Then Compass suffered a complex of business ailments, and in the fall of 1957 it had to be disbanded. Shepherd reconstituted the company in St. Louis, with the idea of taking it on to New York, and a new Compass, with Nichols and May as its cadre, did enjoy a four-month run in St. Louis, in what Miss May has graphically described as "a tiny place called the Crystal Palace." The move to New York did not come about, though. The only insurance that the team had taken out against such an emergency was to get, from a friend of Nichols', the name, address, and telephone number of Jack Rollins, a New York manager who was presumably looking for new acts to manage. Since both Nichols and May were in New York, participating in the abortive negotiations for Compass to appear here, they called on Rollins and, over lunch at the Russian Tea Room, gave him an idea of what they did. He was struck by the excerpts they offered between mouthfuls of beef Stroganoff, and asked them to return a day or two later for a more formal audition, in his office. On the basis of that performance, he undertook to represent them. They returned to St. Louis, where Compass had three or four weeks to run before making its next-to-last disappearance from any stage. (It was revived for about six months in 1958.) Meanwhile, Rollins arranged for them to have an audition at the Blue Angel when they got back to town. In discussing the audition, Rollins uses such inescapable managerial adjectives as "unique," "exciting," and, of course, "great," but for once they seem to be approximately accurate. (He has also said of the audition, "They're so unshowbusiness they didn't know to be scared.") The audience at the Blue Angel cheered them, and the club's owner immediately offered them a booking in ten days, when he would be changing shows. He was so carried away, in fact, that when they looked forlorn at the idea of having to wait so long to work—they had just forty dollars between them at the time—he put them at once into another of his clubs, the Village Vanguard, to serve as a curtain-raiser for Mort Sahl until the vacancy at the Blue Angel occurred.

• • •

Since then, Nichols and May have coasted rapidly uphill. At the moment, any night club in the country would be glad to get them; the two records they have made are selling well; *Evening* does close to capacity business on West Forty-fifth Street; *Monitor* is pleased with them; they have won a couple of scrolls for excellence in making commercials; and not long ago Rollins informed an acquaintance, in a hushed voice, that offers for television spectaculars had been coming in at such a rate that he had had to reject eight of them that very week. The abrupt transition from the obscurity and penury of Compass to the luxuries of stardom has left Nichols puzzled and Miss May rather breathless. Nichols, who, of course, spent much of his childhood in the neighborhood of Central Park West, has had no trouble adjusting to taxicabs, Brooks Brothers shirts, and a penthouse. He says, though, that success has made no inward impression on him, whatever it has done outwardly. "My ambitions are not connected with success," he told a friend not long ago. "I perceive nothing operationally different in my life." Miss May, on the other hand, speaks of having money as "an enormous kind of adventure." When she arrived in New York, she had seldom worn high heels, had sometimes worn second-hand clothes, and had had her hair set only twice. Climbing out of her black stockings and tennis shoes and making the acquaintance of Lord & Taylor salesladies, interior decorators, and an eminent hairdresser named Mr. Kenneth has been a process that has alternately entertained and repelled her. "My dresser at the theatre is a nice lady," she told a friend shortly after the show opened. "She lets me dress myself, mostly." Miss May says that while she was having a decorator do the apartment—a roomy one on Riverside Drive—where she lives with her daughter, Jeannie, she couldn't resist occasionally saying to an antique dealer who was becoming particularly rhapsodic over a cobbler's bench or a dry sink, "You mean it's second hand?"

The way Miss May organizes her life would distress any employer less purposefully tolerant than Alexander H. Cohen. He says, "Elaine relates to things that are important, and she knows what's important. She may be late for half-hour call at the theatre, or forget to comb her hair, but she never misses a dinner with Jeannie." Some months ago, he tried to reshape Miss May into the model of efficiency that he thought at first she should be, but he soon gave up. The occasion of his change of heart was a strong lecture that he delivered to her in his office one afternoon. In the course of it, he laid out a complete daily schedule for her, reproved her for neglecting a number of chores she had undertaken to do, and gave her various pieces of avuncular advice about how to live her life. She sat speechless through the whole thing, he remembers, her eyes cast down and her hands in her lap, and when he had run out of things to say, she left quietly and with every evidence of contrition. It was closing time by then, and Cohen started clearing the top of his desk—a task he faithfully performs every day, since he *is* a model of efficiency. Concealed in the mass of papers he found a page from a small memorandum pad. It was covered with Miss May's handwriting, and read:

Wake up (open eyes), get out of bed.
Get hair fixed.
Take bath (get towel, soap, washcloth; undress; fill tub).
Dry self.
Dress (put on underwear, dress and/or skirt & blouse, shoes).
Comb hair.
Do other things (as thou wouldst have them, etc.).
Correct Alex's souvenir program.
Look for hat.
Give insurance policies to Ronnie at 6:00.
BUY STAMPS.
Avoid answering phone in case it is Michael (or answer in disguise).
Avoid door in case it is neighbor (or answer in disguise).
BE AT ALEX'S AT 4:00!

Cohen never attempted to lecture Miss May again. He simply gave her the use of a limousine and chauffeur for the run of the show.

In the years since Compass expired, Nichols and May, despite their voluminous improvising, have developed few new full-scale pieces. And since by now they have exposed a good part of their repertory—a fragment at a time on television and almost *in toto* in the theatre—they do not have the material to do eight spectaculars in a week, or in a year, even if Rollins wanted them to. What's more, they are not at all sure that working up a new *Evening's* worth of numbers—presumably from those *Monitor* spots—is what they want to do. Both of them apparently have the feeling that if they aren't careful, their career as entertainers will develop a sinister force of its own that will compel them to keep on doing the same thing long after they have ceased to get any satisfaction from it. Miss May recently quoted with approval something that Nichols said to her soon after they became rich and famous: "You do your work and you have your career, and the two are diametrically opposed." On her own, she added, "The funniest thing that has happened to us is that we make our living this way—but nobody laughs." What their career is is made clear to them every day, in a seemingly endless series of interviews with newspapermen, luncheons with advertising-agency executives, conferences with Rollins, and long-distance telephone conversations with movie producers—not to mention the laughter and applause of their audiences and the pay checks that are sent to Rollins every week. They wish they could be equally clear about their work.

Miss May has written a play—a comedy about family secrets, of course—which she hopes will be produced next season. Nichols would like to write a play, too, but he hasn't yet been able to build up enough resolution to sit down to it. He has been in what he considers a state of torpor ever since *Evening* settled down to its run. "I can't think of the show as a full-time job," he said plaintively not long ago. "There are twenty-two other hours in the day." As to whether or not, separately or together, they have a message worth delivering, Miss May is a good deal more positive than Nichols, who recently said, with vehemence, "I have no sense of mission about our work. I have nothing I want to tell people." Miss May has things she wants to tell people. "Remember Swift and the Irish babies?" she asked a friend a few weeks ago. "That's the way you have to go." That's the way she does go, too. "The nice thing is to make an audience laugh and laugh and laugh, and shudder later," she says. Note the word "nice."

THE CRACKIN', SHAKIN', BREAKIN' SOUNDS

Nat Hentoff

OCOTBER 24, 1964 (BOB DYLAN)

THE WORD "folk" in the term "folk music" used to connote a rural, homogeneous community that carried on a tradition of anonymously created music. No one person composed a piece; it evolved through generations of communal care. In recent years, however, folk music has increasingly become the quite personal—and copyrighted— product of specific creators. More and more of them, in fact, are neither rural nor representative of centuries-old family and regional traditions. They are often city-bred converts to the folk style; and, after an apprenticeship during which they try to imitate rural models from the older approach to folk music, they write and perform their own songs out of their own concerns and preoccupations. The restless young, who have been the primary support of the rise of this kind of folk music over the past five years, regard two performers as their preeminent spokesmen. One is the twenty-three-year-old Joan Baez. She does not write her own material and she includes a considerable proportion of traditional, communally created songs in her programs. But Miss Baez does speak out explicitly against racial prejudice and militarism, and she does sing some of the best of the new topical songs. Moreover, her pure, penetrating voice and her open, honest manner symbolize for her admirers a cool island of integrity in a society that the folk-song writer Malvina Reynolds has characterized in one of her songs as consisting of "little boxes." ("And the boys go into business / And marry and raise a family / In boxes made of ticky tacky / And they all look the same.") The second—and more influential—demiurge of the folk-music microcosm is Bob Dylan, who is also twenty-three. Dylan's impact has been the greater because he *is* a writer of songs as well as a performer. Such compositions of his as "Blowin' in the Wind," "Masters of War," "Don't Think Twice, It's All Right," and "Only a Pawn in Their Game" have become part of the repertoire of many other performers, including Miss Baez, who has explained, "Bobby is expressing what I—and many other young people—feel, what we want to say. Most of the 'protest' songs about the bomb and race prejudice and conformity are stupid. They have no beauty. But Bobby's songs are powerful as poetry and powerful as music. And, oh, my God, how that boy can sing!" Another reason for Dylan's impact is the singular force of his personality. Wiry, tense, and boyish, Dylan looks and acts like a fusion of Huck Finn and a young Woody Guthrie. Both onstage and off, he appears to be just barely able to contain his prodigious energy. Pete Seeger, who, at forty-five, is one of the elders of American folk music, recently observed, "Dylan may well become the country's most creative troubadour—if he doesn't explode."

Dylan is always dressed informally—the possibility that he will ever be seen in a tie is as remote as the possibility that Miss Baez will perform in an evening gown—and his possessions are few, the weightiest of them being a motorcycle. A wanderer, Dylan is often on the road in search of more experience. "You can find out a lot about a small town by hanging around its poolroom," he says. Like Miss Baez, he prefers to keep most of his time for himself. He works only occasionally, and during the rest of the year he travels or briefly stays in a house owned by his manager, Albert Grossman, in Bearsville, New York—a small town adjacent to Woodstock and about a hundred miles north of New York City. There Dylan writes songs, works on poetry, plays, and novels, rides his motorcycle, and talks with his friends. From time to time, he comes to New York to record for Columbia Records.

A few weeks ago, Dylan invited me to a recording session that was to begin at seven in the evening in a Columbia studio on Seventh Avenue near Fifty-second Street. Before he arrived, a tall, lean, relaxed man in his early thirties came in and introduced himself to me as Tom Wilson, Dylan's recording producer. He was joined by two engineers, and we all went into the control room. Wilson took up a post at a long, broad table, between the engineers, from which he looked out into a spacious studio with a tall thicket of microphones to the left and, directly in front, an enclave containing a music stand, two microphones, and an upright piano, and set off by a large screen, which would partly shield Dylan as he sang, for the purpose of improving the quality of the sound. "I have no idea what he's going to record tonight," Wilson told me. "It's all to be stuff he's written in the last couple of months."

I asked if Dylan presented any particular problems to a recording director.

"My main difficulty has been pounding mike technique into him," Wilson said. "He used to get excited and move around a lot and then lean in too far, so that the mike popped. Aside from that, my basic problem with him has been to create the kind of setting in which he's relaxed. For instance, if that screen should bother him, I'd take it away, even if we have to lose a little quality in the sound." Wilson looked toward the door. "I'm somewhat concerned about tonight. We're going to do a whole album in one session. Usually, we're not in such a rush, but this album has to be ready for Columbia's fall sales convention. Except for special occasions like this, Bob has no set schedule of recording dates. We think he's important enough to record whenever he wants to come to the studio."

Five minutes after seven, Dylan walked into the studio, carrying a battered guitar case. He had on dark glasses, and his hair, dark-blond and curly, had obviously not been cut for some weeks; he was dressed in blue jeans, a black jersey, and desert boots. With him were half a dozen friends, among them Jack Elliott, a folk singer in the Woody Guthrie tradition, who was also dressed in blue jeans and desert boots, plus a brown corduroy shirt and a jaunty cowboy hat. Elliott had been carrying two bottles of Beaujolais, which he now handed to Dylan, who carefully put them on a table near the screen. Dylan opened the guitar case, took out a looped-wire harmonica holder, hung it around his neck, and then walked over to the piano and began to play in a rolling, honky-tonk style.

"He's got a wider range of talents than he shows," Wilson told me. "He kind of hoards them. You go back to his three albums. Each time, there's a big leap from one to the next—in material, in performance, in everything."

Dylan came into the control room, smiling. Although he is fiercely accusatory toward society at large while he is performing, his most marked offstage characteristic is gentleness. He speaks swiftly but softly, and appears persistently anxious to make himself clear. "We're going to make a good one tonight," he said to Wilson. "I promise." He turned to me and continued, "There aren't any finger-pointing songs in here, either. Those records I've already made, I'll stand behind them, but some of that was jumping into the scene to be heard and a lot of it was because I didn't see anybody else doing that kind of thing. Now a lot of people are doing finger-pointing songs. You know—pointing to all the things that are wrong. Me, I don't want to write *for* people anymore. You know—be a spokesman. Like I once wrote about Emmett Till in the first person, pretending I was him. From now on, I want to write from inside me, and to do that I'm going to have to get back to writing like I used to when I was ten—having everything come out naturally. The way I like to write is for it to come out the way I walk or talk." Dylan frowned. "Not that I even walk or talk yet like I'd like to. I don't carry myself yet the way Woody, Big Joe Williams, and Lightnin' Hopkins have carried themselves. I hope to someday, but they're older. They got to where music was a tool for them, a way to live more, a way to make themselves feel better. Sometimes I can make myself feel better with music, but other times it's still hard to go to sleep at night."

A friend strolled in, and Dylan began to grumble about an interview that had been arranged for him later in the week. "I hate to say no, because, after all, these guys have a job to do," he said, shaking his head impatiently. "But it bugs me that the first question usually turns out to be 'Are you going down South to take part in any of the civil-rights projects?' They try to fit you into things. Now, I've been down there, but I'm not going down just to hold a picket sign so they can shoot a picture of me. I know a lot of the kids in S.N.C.C.—you know, the Student Nonviolent Coordinating Committee. That's the only organization I feel a part of spiritually. The N.A.A.C.P. is a bunch of old guys. I found that out by coming directly in contact with some of the people in it. They didn't understand me. They were looking to use me for something. Man, everybody's hung up. You sometimes don't know if somebody wants you to do something because he's hung up or because he really digs who you are. It's awful complicated, and the best thing you can do is admit it."

Returning to the studio, Dylan stood in front of the piano and pounded out an accompaniment as he sang from one of his own new songs:

"Are you for real, baby, or are you just on the shelf?
I'm looking deep into your eyes, but all I can see is myself.

If you're trying to throw me, I've already been tossed.
If you're trying to lose me, I've already been lost. . . ."

Another friend of Dylan's arrived, with three children, ranging in age from four to ten. The children raced around the studio until Wilson insisted that they be relatively confined to the control room. By ten minutes to eight, Wilson had checked out the sound balance to his satisfaction, Dylan's friends had found seats along the studio walls, and Dylan had expressed his readiness—in fact, eagerness—to begin. Wilson, in the control room, leaned forward, a stopwatch in his hand. Dylan took a deep breath, threw his head back, and plunged into a song in which he accompanied himself on guitar and harmonica. The first take was ragged; the second was both more relaxed and more vivid. At that point, Dylan, smiling, clearly appeared to be confident of his ability to do an entire album in one night. As he moved into succeeding numbers, he relied principally on the guitar for support, except for exclamatory punctuations on the harmonica.

Having glanced through a copy of Dylan's new lyrics that he had handed to Wilson, I observed to Wilson that there were indeed hardly any songs of social protest in the collection.

"Those early albums gave people the wrong idea," Wilson said. "Basically, he's in the tradition of all lasting folk music. I mean, he's not a singer of protest so much as he is a singer of *concern* about people. He doesn't have to be talking about Medgar Evers all the time to be effective. He can just tell a simple little story of a guy who ran off from a woman."

After three takes of one number, one of the engineers said to Wilson, "If you want to try another, we can get a better take."

"No." Wilson shook his head. "With Dylan, you have to take what you can get."

Out in the studio, Dylan, his slight form bent forward, was standing just outside the screen and listening to a playback through earphones. He began to take the earphones off during an instrumental passage, but then his voice came on, and he grinned and replaced them.

The engineer muttered again that he might get a better take if Dylan ran through the number once more.

"Forget it," Wilson said. "You don't think in terms of orthodox recording techniques when you're dealing with Dylan. You have to learn to be as free on this side of the glass as he is out there."

Dylan went on to record a song about a man leaving a girl because he was not prepared to be the kind of invincible hero and all-encompassing provider she wanted. "It ain't me you're looking for, babe," he sang, with finality.

During the playback, I joined Dylan in the studio. "The songs so far sound as if there were real people in them," I said.

Dylan seemed surprised that I had considered it necessary to make the comment. "There are. That's what makes them so scary. If I haven't been through what I write about, the songs aren't worth anything." He went on, via one of his songs, to offer a complicated account of a turbulent love affair in Spanish Harlem, and at the end asked a friend, "Did you understand it?" The friend nodded enthusiastically. "Well, I didn't," Dylan said, with a laugh, and then became sombre. "It's hard being free in a song—getting it all in. Songs are so confining. Woody Guthrie told me once that songs don't have to rhyme—that they don't have to do anything like that. But it's not true. A song has to have some kind of form to fit into the music. You can bend the words and the metre, but it still has to fit somehow. I've been getting freer in the songs I write, but I still feel confined. That's why I write a lot of poetry—if that's the word. Poetry can make its own form."

As Wilson signalled for the start of the next number, Dylan put up his hand. "I just want to light a cigarette, so I can see it there while I'm singing," he said, and grinned. "I'm very neurotic. I need to be secure."

By ten-thirty, seven songs had been recorded.

"This is the fastest Dylan date yet," Wilson said. "He used to be all hung up with the microphones. Now he's a pro."

Several more friends of Dylan's had arrived during the recording of the seven songs, and at this point four of them were seated in the control room behind Wilson and the engineers. The others were scattered around the studio, using the table that held the bottles of Beaujolais as their base. They opened the bottles, and every once in a while poured out a drink in a paper cup. The three children were still irrepressibly present, and once the smallest burst suddenly into the studio, ruining a take. Dylan turned on the youngster in mock anger. "I'm gonna rub you out," he said. "I'll track you down and turn you to dust." The boy giggled and ran back into the control room.

As the evening went on, Dylan's voice became more acrid. The dynamics of his singing grew more pronounced, soft, intimate passages being abruptly followed by fierce surges in volume. The relentless, driving beat of his guitar was more often supplemented by the whooping thrusts of the harmonica.

"Intensity, that's what he's got," Wilson said, apparently to himself. "By now, this kid is outselling Thelonious Monk and Miles Davis," he went on, to me. "He's speaking to a whole new generation. And not only here. He's just been in England. He had standing room only in Royal Festival Hall."

Dylan had begun a song called "Chimes of Freedom." One of his four friends in the control room—a lean, bearded man—proclaimed, "Bobby's talking for every hung-up person in the whole wide universe." His three companions nodded gravely.

The next composition, "Motorpsycho Nitemare," was a mordantly satirical version of the vintage tale of the farmer, his daughter, and the travelling salesman. There were several false starts, apparently because Dylan was having trouble reading the lyrics.

"Man, dim the lights," the bearded friend counselled Wilson. "He'll get more relaxed."

"Atmosphere is not what we need," Wilson answered, without turning around. "Legibility is what we need."

During the playback, Dylan listened intently, his lips moving, and a cigarette cocked in his right hand. A short break followed, during which Dylan shouted, "Hey, we're gonna need some more wine!" Two of his friends in the studio nodded and left.

After the recording session resumed, Dylan continued to work hard and conscientiously. When he was preparing for a take or listening to a playback, he seemed able to cut himself off completely from the eddies of conversation and humorous byplay stirred up by his friends in the studio. Occasionally, when a line particularly pleased him, he burst into laughter, but he swiftly got back to business.

Dylan started a talking blues—a wry narrative in a sardonic recitative style, which had been developed by Woody Guthrie. "Now I'm liberal, but to a degree," Dylan was drawling halfway through the song. "I want everybody to be free. But if you think I'll let Barry Goldwater move in next door and marry my daughter, you must think I'm crazy. I wouldn't let him do it for all the farms in Cuba." He was smiling broadly, and Wilson and the engineers were laughing. It was a long song, and toward the end Dylan faltered. He tried it twice more, and each time he stumbled before the close.

"Let me do another song," he said to Wilson. "I'll come back to this."

"No," Wilson said. "Finish up this one. You'll hang us up on the order, and if I'm not here to edit, the other cat will get mixed up. Just do an insert of the last part."

"Let him start from the beginning, man," said one of the four friends sitting behind Wilson.

Wilson turned around, looking annoyed. "Why, man?"

"You don't start telling a story with Chapter Eight, man," the friend said.

"Oh, man," said Wilson. "What kind of philosophy is that? We're recording, not writing a biography."

As an obbligato of protest continued behind Wilson, Dylan, accepting Wilson's advice, sang the insert. His bearded friend rose silently and drew a square in the air behind Wilson's head.

Other songs, mostly of love lost or misunderstood, followed. Dylan was now tired, but he retained his good humor. "This last one is called 'My Back Pages,'" he announced to Wilson. It appeared to express his current desire to get away from "finger-pointing" and write more acutely personal material. "Oh, but I was so much older then," he sang as a refrain, "I'm younger than that now."

By one-thirty, the session was over. Dylan had recorded fourteen new songs. He agreed to meet me again in a week or so and fill me in on his background. "My background's not all that important, though," he said as we left the studio. "It's what I am now that counts."

. . .

Dylan was born in Duluth, on May 24, 1941, and grew up in Hibbing, Minnesota, a mining town near the Canadian border. He does not discuss his parents, preferring to let his songs tell whatever he wants to say about his personal history. "You can stand at one end of Hibbing on the main drag an' see clear past the city limits on the other end," Dylan once noted in a poem, "My Life in a Stolen Moment," printed in the program of a 1963 Town Hall concert he gave. Like Dylan's parents, it appears, the town was neither rich nor poor, but it was, Dylan has said, "a dyin' town." He ran away from home seven times—at ten, at twelve, at thirteen, at fifteen, at fifteen and a half, at seventeen, and at eighteen. His travels included South Dakota, New Mexico, Kansas, and California. In between flights, he taught himself the guitar, which he had begun playing at the age of ten. At fifteen, he was also playing the harmonica and the autoharp, and, in addition, had written his first song, a ballad dedicated to Brigitte Bardot. In the spring of 1960, Dylan entered the University of Minnesota, in Minneapolis, which he attended for something under six months. In "My Life in a Stolen Moment," Dylan has summarized his college career dourly: "I sat in science class an' flunked out for refusin' to watch a rabbit die. I got expelled from English class for using four-letter words in a paper describing the English teacher. I also failed out of communication class for callin' up every day and sayin' I couldn't come. . . . I was kept around for kicks at a fraternity house. They let me live there, an' I did until they wanted me to join." Paul Nelson and Jon Pankake, who edit the *Little Sandy Review*, a quarterly magazine, published in Minneapolis, that is devoted to critical articles on folk music and performers, remember meeting Dylan at the University of Minnesota in the summer of 1960, while he was part of a group of singers who performed at The Scholar, a coffeehouse near the university. The editors, who were students at the university then, have since noted in their publication: "We recall Bob as a soft-spoken, rather unprepossessing youngster . . . well-groomed and neat in the standard campus costume of slacks, sweater, white oxford sneakers, poplin raincoat, and dark glasses."

Before Dylan arrived at the university, his singing had been strongly influenced by such Negro folk interpreters as Leadbelly and Big Joe Williams. He had met Williams in Evanston, Illinois, during his break from home at the age of twelve. Dylan had also been attracted to several urban-style rhythm-and-blues performers, notably Bo Diddley and Chuck Berry. Other shaping forces were white country-music figures— particularly Hank Williams, Hank Snow, and Jimmie Rodgers. During his brief stay at the university, Dylan became especially absorbed in the recordings of Woody Guthrie, the Oklahoma-born traveller who had created the most distinctive body of American topical folk material to come to light in this century. Since 1954, Guthrie, ill with Huntington's chorea, a progressive disease of the nervous system, had not been able to perform, but he was allowed to receive visitors. In the autumn of 1960, Dylan quit the University of Minnesota and decided to visit Guthrie at Greystone Hospital, in New Jersey. Dylan returned briefly to Minnesota the following May, to sing at a university hootenanny, and Nelson and Pankake saw him again on that occasion. "In a mere half year," they have recalled in the *Little Sandy Review*, "he had learned to churn up exciting, bluesy, hard-driving harmonica-and-guitar music, and had absorbed during his visits with Guthrie not only the great Okie musician's unpredictable syntax but his very vocal color, diction, and inflection. Dylan's performance that spring evening of a selection of Guthrie . . . songs was hectic and shaky, but it contained all the elements of the now-perfected performing style that has made him the most original newcomer to folk music."

The winter Dylan visited Guthrie was otherwise bleak. He spent most of it in New York, where he found it difficult to get steady work singing. In "Talkin' New York," a caustic song describing his first months in the city, Dylan tells of having been turned away by a coffeehouse owner, who told him scornfully, "You sound like a hillbilly. We want folk singers here." There were nights when he slept in the subway, but eventually he found friends and a place to stay on the Lower East Side, and after he had returned from the spring hootenanny, he began getting more frequent engagements in New York. John Hammond, Director of Talent Acquisition at Columbia Records, who has discovered a sizable number of important jazz and folk performers during the past thirty years, heard Dylan that summer while attending a rehearsal of another folk singer, whom Hammond was about to record for Columbia Records. Impressed by the young man's raw force and by the vivid lyrics of his songs, Hammond auditioned him and immediately signed him to a recording contract. Then, in September, 1961, while Dylan was appearing at Gerde's Folk City, a casual refuge for "citybillies" (as the young city singers and musicians are now called in the trade), on West Fourth Street, in Greenwich Village, he was heard by Robert Shelton, the folk-music critic for the *Times,* who wrote of him enthusiastically.

Dylan began to prosper. He enlarged his following by appearing at the Newport and Monterey Folk Festivals and giving concerts throughout the country. There have been a few snags, as when he walked off the Ed Sullivan television show in the spring of 1963 because the Columbia Broadcasting System would not permit him to sing a tart appraisal of the John Birch Society, but on the whole he has experienced accelerating success. His first three Columbia albums—*Bob Dylan, The Freewheelin' Bob Dylan,* and *The Times They Are A-Changin'*—have by now reached a cumulative sales figure of nearly four hundred thousand. In addition, he has received large royalties as a composer of songs that have become hits through recordings by Peter, Paul, and Mary, the Kingston Trio, and other performers. At present, Dylan's fees for a concert appearance range from two thousand to three thousand dollars a night. He has sometimes agreed to sing at a nominal fee for new, nonprofit folk societies, however, and he has often performed without charge at civil-rights rallies.

. . .

Musically, Dylan has transcended most of his early influences and developed an incisively personal style. His vocal sound is most often characterized by flaying harshness. Mitch Jayne, a member of the Dillards, a folk group from Missouri, has described Dylan's sound as "very much like a dog with his leg caught in barbed wire." Yet Dylan's admirers come to accept and even delight in the harshness, because of the vitality and wit at its core. And they point out that in intimate ballads he is capable of a fragile lyricism that does not slip into bathos. It is Dylan's work as a composer, however, that has won him a wider audience than his singing alone might have. Whether concerned with cosmic spectres or personal conundrums, Dylan's lyrics are pungently idiomatic. He has a superb ear for speech rhythms, a generally astute sense of selective detail, and a natural storyteller's command of narrative pacing. His songs sound as if they were being created out of oral street history rather than carefully written in tranquillity. On a stage, Dylan performs his songs as if he had an urgent story to tell. In his work there is little of the polished grace of such carefully trained contemporary minstrels as Richard Dyer-Bennet. Nor, on the other hand, do Dylan's performances reflect the calculated showmanship of a Harry Belafonte or of Peter, Paul, and Mary. Dylan off the stage is very much the same as Dylan the performer—restless, insatiably hungry for experience, idealistic, but skeptical of neatly defined causes.

In the past year, as his renown has increased, Dylan has become more elusive. He felt so strongly threatened by his initial fame that he welcomed the chance to use the Bearsville home of his manager as a refuge between concerts, and he still spends most of his time there when he's not travelling. A week after the recording session, he telephoned me from Bearsville, and we agreed to meet the next evening at the Keneret, a restaurant on lower Seventh Avenue, in the Village. It specializes in Middle Eastern food, which is one of Dylan's preferences, but it does not have a liquor license. Upon keeping our rendezvous therefore, we went next door for a few bottles of Beaujolais and then returned to the Keneret. Dylan was as restless as usual, and as he talked, his hands moved constantly and his voice sounded as if he were never quite able to catch his breath.

I asked him what he had meant, exactly, when he spoke at the recording session of abandoning "finger-pointing" songs, and he took a sip of wine, leaned forward, and said, "I looked around and saw all these people pointing fingers at the bomb. But the bomb is getting boring, because what's wrong goes much deeper than the bomb. What's wrong is how few people are free. Most people walking around are tied down to something that doesn't let them really *speak,* so they just add their confusion to the mess. I mean, they have some kind of vested interest in the way things are now. Me, I'm cool." He smiled. "You know, Joanie—Joanie Baez—worries about me. She worries about whether people will get control over me and exploit me. But I'm cool. I'm in control, because I don't care about money, and all that. And I'm cool in myself, because I've gone through enough changes so that I know what's real to me and what isn't. Like this fame. It's done something to me. It's O.K. in the Village here. People don't pay attention to me. But in other towns it's funny knowing that people you don't know figure they know *you.* I mean, they think they know everything about you. One thing is groovy, though. I got birthday cards this year from people I'd never heard of. It's weird, isn't it? There are people I've really touched whom I'll never know." He lit a cigarette. "But in other ways being noticed can be a weight. So I disappear a lot. I go to places where I'm not going to be noticed. And I *can.*" He laughed. "I have no work to do. I have no job. I'm not committed to anything except making a few records and playing a few concerts. I'm weird that way. Most people, when they get up in the morning, have to do what they *have* to do. I could pretend there were all kinds of things I *had* to do every day. But why? So I do whatever I feel like. I might make movies of my friends around Woodstock one day. I write a lot. I get involved in scenes with people. A lot of scenes are going on with me all the time—here in the Village, in Paris during my trips to Europe, in lots of places."

I asked Dylan how far ahead he planned.

"I don't look past right now," he said. "Now there's this fame business. I know it's going to go away. It has to. This so-called mass fame comes from people who get caught up in a thing for a while and buy the records. Then they stop. And when they stop, I won't be famous anymore."

We became aware that a young waitress was standing by diffidently.

Dylan turned to her, and she asked him for his autograph. He signed his name with gusto, and signed again when she asked if he would give her an autograph for a friend. "I'm sorry to have interrupted your dinner," she said, smiling. "But I'm really not."

"I get letters from people—young people—all the time," Dylan continued when she had left us. "I wonder if they write letters like those to other people they don't know. They just want to tell me things, and sometimes they go into their personal hangups. Some send poetry. I like getting them—read them all and answer some. But I don't mean I give any of the people who write to me any *answers* to their problems." He leaned forward and talked more rapidly. "It's like when somebody wants to tell me what the 'moral' thing is to do, I want them to *show* me. If they have anything to say about morals, I want to know what it is they *do*. Same with me. All I can do is show the people who ask me questions how I live. All I can do is be me. I can't tell them how to change things, because there's only one way to change things, and that's to cut yourself off from all the chains. That's hard for most people to do."

I had Dylan's *The Times They Are A-Changin'* album with me, and I pointed out to him a section of his notes on the cover in which he spoke of how he had always been running when he was a boy—running away from Hibbing and from his parents.

Dylan took a sip of wine. "I kept running because I wasn't free," he said. "I was constantly on guard. Somehow, way back then, I already knew that parents do what they do because they're up tight. They're concerned with their kids in relation to *themselves*. I mean, they want their kids to please them, not to embarrass them—so they can be proud of them. They want you to be what *they* want you to be. So I started running when I was ten. But always I'd get picked up and sent home. When I was thirteen, I was travelling with a carnival through upper Minnesota and North and South Dakota, and I got picked up again. I tried again and again, and when I was eighteen, I cut out for good. I was still running when I came to New York. Just because you're free to move doesn't mean you're free. Finally, I got so far out I was cut off from everybody and everything. It was then I decided there was no sense in running so far and so fast when there was no longer anybody there. It was fake. It was running for the sake of running. So I stopped. I've got no place to run from. I don't have to be anyplace I don't want to be. But I am by no means an example for any kid wanting to strike out. I mean, I wouldn't want a young kid to leave home because I did it, and then have to go through a lot of the things I went through. Everybody has to find his *own* way to be free. There isn't anybody who can help you in that sense. Nobody was able to help me. Like seeing Woody Guthrie was one of the main reasons I came East. He was an idol to me. A couple of years ago, after I'd gotten to know him, I was going through some very bad changes, and I went to see Woody, like I'd go to somebody to confess to. But I couldn't confess to him. It was silly. I did go and talk with him—as much as he could talk—and the talking helped. But basically he wasn't able to help me at all. I finally realized that. So Woody was my last idol."

There was a pause.

"I've learned a lot in these past few years," Dylan said softly. "Like about beauty."

I reminded him of what he had said about his changing criteria of beauty in some notes he did for a Joan Baez album. There he had written that when he first heard her voice, before he knew her, his reaction had been:

> "I hate that kind a sound," said I
> "The only beauty's ugly, man
> The crackin', shakin', breakin' sounds're
> The only beauty I understand."

Dylan laughed. "Yeah," he said. "I was wrong. My hangup was that I used to try to *define* beauty. Now I take it as it is, however it is. That's why I like Hemingway. I don't read much. Usually I read what people put in my hands. But I do read Hemingway. He didn't have to use adjectives. He didn't really have to define what he was saying. He just said it. I can't do that yet, but that's what I want to be able to do."

A young actor from Julian Beck's and Judith Malina's Living Theatre troupe stopped by the table, and Dylan shook hands with him enthusiastically. "We're leaving for Europe soon," the actor said. "But when we come back, we're going out on the street. We're going to put on plays right on the street, for anyone who wants to watch."

"Hey!" said Dylan, bouncing in his seat. "Tell Julian and Judith that I want to be in on that."

The actor said he would, and took Dylan's telephone number. Then he said, "Bob, are you doing only your own songs now—none of the old folk songs at all?"

"Have to," Dylan answered. "When I'm up tight and it's raining out-

side and nobody's around and somebody I want is a long way from me—
and with someone else besides—I can't sing 'Ain't Got No Use for Your
Red Apple Juice.' I don't care how great an old song it is or what its tradition is. I have to make a new song out of what *I* know and out of what
I'm feeling."

The conversation turned to civil rights, and the actor used the term
"the Movement" to signify the work of the civil-rights activists. Dylan
looked at him quizzically. "I agree with everything that's happening," he
said, "but I'm not part of no Movement. If I was, I wouldn't be able to do
anything else but be in 'the Movement.' I just can't have people sit around
and make rules for me. I do a lot of things no Movement would allow."
He took a long drink of Beaujolais. "It's like politics," he went on. "I just
can't make it with *any* organization. I fell into a trap once—last
December—when I agreed to accept the Tom Paine Award from the
Emergency Civil Liberties Committee. At the Americana Hotel! In the
Grand Ballroom! As soon as I got there, I felt up tight. First of all,
the people with me couldn't get in. They looked even funkier than I did,
I guess. They weren't dressed right, or something. Inside the ballroom, I
really got up tight. I began to drink. I looked down from the platform
and saw a bunch of people who had nothing to do with my kind of politics. I looked down and I got scared. They were supposed to be on my
side, but I didn't feel any connection with them. Here were these people
who'd been all involved with the left in the thirties, and now they were
supporting civil-rights drives. That's groovy, but they also had minks
and jewels, and it was like they were giving the money out of guilt. I got
up to leave, and they followed me and caught me. They told me I had to
accept the award. When I got up to make my speech, I couldn't say anything by that time but what was passing through my mind. They'd been
talking about Kennedy being killed, and Bill Moore and Medgar Evers
and the Buddhist monks in Vietnam being killed. I had to say something about Lee Oswald. I told them I'd read a lot of his feelings in the
papers, and I knew he was up tight. Said I'd been up tight, too, so I'd got
a lot of his feelings. I saw a lot of myself in Oswald, I said, and I saw in
him a lot of the times we're all living in. And, you know, they started
booing. They looked at me like I was an animal. They actually thought
I was saying it was a good thing Kennedy had been killed. That's how far
out they are. I was talking about Oswald. And then I started talking
about friends of mine in Harlem—some of them junkies, all of them
poor. And I said they need freedom as much as anybody else, and what's

anybody doing for *them*? The chairman was kicking my leg under the table, and I told him, 'Get out of here.' Now, what I was supposed to be was a nice cat. I was supposed to say, 'I appreciate your award and I'm a great singer and I'm a great believer in liberals, and you buy my records and I'll support your cause.' But I didn't, and so I wasn't accepted that night. That's the cause of a lot of those chains I was talking about—people wanting to be accepted, people not wanting to be alone. But, after all, what is it to be alone? I've been alone sometimes in front of three thousand people. I was alone that night."

The actor nodded sympathetically.

Dylan snapped his fingers. "I almost forgot," he said. "You know, they were talking about Freedom Fighters that night. I've been in Mississippi, man. I know those people on another level besides civil-rights campaigns. I know them as friends. Like Jim Forman, one of the heads of S.N.C.C. I'll stand on his side any time. But those people that night were actually getting me to look at colored people as colored people. I tell you, I'm never going to have anything to do with any political organization again in my life. Oh, I might help a friend if he was campaigning for office. But I'm not going to be part of any organization. Those people at that dinner were the same as everybody else. They're doing their time. They're chained to what they're doing. The only thing is, they're trying to put morals and great deeds on their chains, but basically they don't want to jeopardize their positions. They got their jobs to keep. There's nothing there for me, and there's nothing there for the kind of people I hang around with. The only thing I'm sorry about is that I guess I hurt the collection at the dinner. I didn't know they were going to try to collect money after my speech. I guess I lost them a lot of money. Well, I offered to pay them whatever it was they figured they'd lost because of the way I talked. I told them I didn't care how much it was. I hate debts, especially moral debts. They're worse than money debts."

Exhausted by his monologue, Dylan sank back and poured more Beaujolais. "People talk about trying to change society," he said. "All I know is that so long as people stay so concerned about protecting their status and protecting what they have, ain't nothing going to be done. Oh, there may be some change of levels inside the circle, but nobody's going to learn anything."

The actor left, and it was time for Dylan to head back upstate. "Come up and visit next week," he said to me, "and I'll give you a ride on my motorcycle." He hunched his shoulders and walked off quickly.

PATERFAMILIAS—1

Jane Kramer

AUGUST 17, 1968 (ALLEN GINSBERG)

"You're such an *experimenter*, Allen."
—*Louis Ginsberg to his son Allen, Paterson, New Jersey, March 18, 1967*

I N JANUARY OF 1967, on the night before the first evangelical picnic anywhere to be called a Gathering of the Tribes for a Human Be-In, Allen Ginsberg, the poet, took off his shoes and sat down cross-legged on the living-room floor of an apartment in the Haight-Ashbury, in San Francisco, to preside over what was very likely the oddest planning-committee meeting in the city's crazy and indulgent history. There were eight people in a circle on the floor with Ginsberg. It was their last chance to arrive at some sort of schedule for the next day's program of poetry readings, sacred Sanskrit chanting, psychedelic-rock concerts, and communal love, and they worked together smoothly for about an hour. Then, when they were down to the last item on the agenda—determining whether the LSD enthusiast Timothy Leary, who was coming to the be-in all the way from New York, was to be considered a poet, and therefore allotted seven minutes on the bandstand, or a bona-fide prophet, and therefore entitled to a full half hour—the committee members found that they could not agree. Philosophically baffled by the fine line between poetry and prophecy, they took a break, at Ginsberg's suggestion, to think things over and wait for guidance. Gary Snyder, a red-bearded Zen monk from the state of Washington, who is a poet himself, immediately stripped for meditation down to the earring in his left ear and went to work displacing his rib cage with violent yogi machinations. Near him, a chubby Hasidic book reviewer named Leland Meyerzove started bouncing up and down with his eyes shut tight and was soon transported, wailing softly in tongues. Lenore Kandel, a local love priestess and poet, began belly-dancing in front of an attentive, tweedy English professor from Berkeley, who sucked contemplatively on his pipe, and Michael McClure, the poet and playwright, who lived in the apartment, picked up his autoharp from a coffee table and, accompanying himself, cherubically crooned a song that he had just composed, called "Come On, God, Buy Me a Mercedes-Benz." The official master of ceremonies for the be-in, a neighborhood guru with the *nom de psychedélie* of Buddha, wandered around the room in a radiant array of pink, orange, green, and purple silks and velvets, kissing everybody until he was faint with affection and sank down on the floor next to a pretty young photographer, who was stretched out on her back taking pictures of the ceiling. The last committee member was Freewheelin' Frank, the secretary of the San Francisco Hell's Angels and the commandant of a be-in honor guard of motorcycle outlaws, who were going to protect the celebrants and their electronic paraphernalia from saboteurs. Freewheelin', who had been leaning against a wall nodding noncommittally from time to time, took stock of the available opportunities for spiritual refreshment, shrugged, and began pacing Mr. Meyerzove's bounces with a tambourine that was fastened to one of the cartridge rings on his leather belt.

Ginsberg himself—forty years old, getting bald and a little myopic—stayed in the middle of the floor, his horn-rimmed glasses on and his shoes off, staring at a pair of unmatched socks. He made a comfortable, avuncular presence—a rumpled, friendly-looking man with a nice, toothy face, big brown owl eyes behind the glasses, and a rather affecting weary slouch. Without his beads, and the bushy tangle of full beard, droopy mustache, and long black ringlets, hanging like a thatch corona from his bald spot, that has become as emblematic as the Beatles' bangs or Albert Einstein's mop of wild white hair, Ginsberg might have passed for the market researcher he once was, for a few years in the fifties. Tonight, he was dressed in chinos, a worn white button-down shirt, and an old striped Shetland pullover. He had put on two necklaces for the meeting—a string of blue Hopi stones and some Yoruba beads, from Cuba, in the seven colors of the seven Yoruba gods—and also had a Mexican Indian metal god's-eye dangling from a piece of rope around his neck, and he was wearing a Tibetan oracle's ring on the forefinger of his right hand. On the floor in front of him were two brass finger cymbals from Times Square and a purple woollen shopping bag from Greece. The bag contained a large address book, an appointment pad, one of the School Time composition books in which he likes to jot down thoughts, and a tattered copy of *Prajna Paramita Sutra*, a sacred Buddhist text concerning the ultimate nature of the universe.

"Man, I'd just as soon no one says a word tomorrow," Buddha said to Ginsberg half an hour later, when the thinking was over and the committee had formed a new circle on the floor. "Just beautiful silence. Just everybody sitting around smiling and digging everybody else."

"What we really should have is a sunset celebration on the beach," Ginsberg said.

"Yeah, naked," Snyder said, getting up and stepping back into his pants. "That would spook the city of San Francisco."

Ginsberg banged his cymbals. "And maybe, at the end, a groovy naked swim-in," Ginsberg said.

"Tim Leary's a professor—he's not going to want to smile and walk off, or swim," Meyerzove broke in, panting a little and pushing back a peaked astrakhan hat, which had slipped over his forehead during his trance.

"Well, how much time *do* we allow Leary?" Ginsberg asked, laughing. "*I* say he gets the same time as the poets."

"Is Leary a prima donna?" the photographer, Beth Bagby, asked. She was still lying on her back.

"Man, I don't think so. After all, he's taken acid," Buddha replied.

"Leary just needs a little of the responsibility taken off him," Ginsberg said firmly. "Seven minutes, and, anyway, if he gets up tight and starts to preach, Lenore can always belly-dance."

Seven minutes was set aside for Leary's speech, and Ginsberg, who had been eying his cymbals, announced that now, if no one minded, he was going to chant. Looking extremely happy, he closed his eyes. He rocked for a while to the high, clattering counterpoint of the cymbals, and then he began a mantra to Siva, the Hindu god of destruction, preservation, and cannabis. The words of the mantra were *"Hari om namo Sivaye,"* and he chanted them slowly at first, in a kind of low, plaintive wail. His voice was deep, sweet, throbbing, and full of melody ("He sounds more like a rabbi than a swami," Meyerzove whispered to Mc-Clure), and soon most of his friends were up and dancing around him.

Miss Kandel began to whirl, her arms kneading the air and her stomach rippling to the mantra sounds. Meyerzove shook, groaning ecstatically. Snyder bounded around, samurai-like. Buddha hopped, waving a nursery rattle. And Freewheelin' swayed, shaking his tambourine. Ginsberg chanted faster and faster, until he was sobbing, singing, and laughing at the same time. His head pitched forward with each beat of the cymbals. He seemed on the edge of consciousness, and then, for a minute, he seemed beyond consciousness and part of the strange, hypnotic rhythm of the chant. Suddenly, he was exhausted. He slumped forward, with a shudder. One by one, the others dropped onto the floor.

"Wow!" Freewheelin' Frank said.

"We should be doing this tomorrow, in the park, with like five hundred thousand people," Ginsberg said. His eyes were shining.

"Yeah, but for a minute there we were really on our way to the delicatessen!" Buddha cried, shaking his head.

Ginsberg jumped up, and started laughing. "Hey, I'm hungry," he said. "Who wants to hit the doughnut shop?"

. . .

In a country that has never been very comfortable in the presence of poetic heroes and prophetic poets, Ginsberg is a poet, a hero, a prophet, and a man who was largely responsible for the love-happy condition of a multitude of children. He has been revered by thousands of flower wielding boys and girls as a combination guru and paterfamilias, and by a generation of students—who consider him a natural ally, if for no other reason than that he terrifies their parents with his elaborate and passionate friendliness—as a kind of ultimate faculty adviser. Flower Power began in the fall of 1965, when he presented a rally of beleaguered and embittered Berkeley peace marchers with a set of instructions for turning political demonstrations into "exemplary spectacle . . . outside the war psychology": "Masses of flowers—a visual spectacle—especially concentrated in the front lines. Can be used to set up barricades, to present to Hell's Angels, police, politicians, and press & spectators, whenever needed or at parade's end. . . ." Later, preaching and colonizing a brave new never-never world of bearded, beaded, marijuana-smoking, mantra-chanting euphoria, Ginsberg set the tone of the countless be-ins, love-ins, kiss-ins, chant-ins, sacred orgies, and demon-dispelling exorcisms of local draft boards, all of which began with the San Francisco Gathering of the Tribes.

A year and a half has passed since the Gathering and the first epidemic of hippie celebrations. Although there are still many hippies around—this summer particular attention has been given to those on Boston Common—they have begun to drop back into history. In the youth movement, the emphasis has shifted from love to political activism. The Haight-Ashbury has outlived its short, exemplary season and has deteriorated into a bizarre and shadowy nighttown, feeding on some of the hippie culture's more grotesque innovations, but it has been replaced as a Utopia by hundreds of hippie enclaves in cities and towns, and on campuses, across the country. Two hundred thousand children are estimated to have left home to try anything from a weekend to a life of sackcloth and marijuana ashes, and, from all reports, a few million others have spent a good deal of time wistfully thinking about following them. Over the past year and a half, while stern city councilmen debated hippie-curbing legislation (in Dallas, where an ordinance was passed last summer barring hippies from the downtown business section of the city, one impeccably bearded young pediatrician threatened a lawsuit against the municipality when policemen began rerouting his car as he hurried back and forth across town on house calls), the love people held their ground and, in fact, took over the landscape. They began calling press conferences to announce their metaphysical conclusions, and the media, in reply, took to carrying hippie news as a matter of national concern. Nearly every national magazine ran off a hippie issue, complete with on-the-spot coverage of the most alarming sort of LSD hallucinating and, invariably, an earnest, thoughtful "I Was a Hippie for Two Weeks" essay by one of its younger reporters. The San Francisco press boomed on fillers from the Haight-Ashbury, and toward last summer the minutiae of life in the East Village were recorded on an almost daily basis in the *Times*. The television networks, for their part, were busy dispatching camera crews to neo-Buddhist festivals and to teen-age "seed-power" collectives, where crops were tended on advice from the Ouija and the I Ching. The hippies, who were alternately worshipped, wooed, and taken over, soon became too fashionable to be altogether apocalyptic. By the time a group of fledgling hippie economists had torn up all their money and floated it down from the visitors' gallery onto the floor of the New York Stock Exchange, chanting "Make Love Not Profits" and ringing bells, several of upper Fifth Avenue's specialty shops were showing their first psychedelic collections and at least one brokerage house in San Francisco was offering the auxiliary services of a securities astrologer.

Underwear was out and bare feet were de rigueur, according to the women's magazines, which scoured the underground for signs of chic, and the barber business was trailing far behind the national growth rate, according to the International *Herald Tribune*'s recap of the financial year. Yoga replaced the Canadian Air Force exercises as the latest antidote to overeating; the Jefferson Airplane was being piped into office elevators, Greyhound waiting rooms, and Chinese restaurants; suburban couples started taking off their clothes at parties and painting each other to resemble Day-Glo Apaches; and a cheerful living-room poster of Ginsberg, whose name was once synonymous with the word "Beat" in all its connotations, became tantamount to an instant full-blown hippie ambience.

Ten years, a religious revival, a cold war, a hot war, and lysergic acid diethylamide, or LSD, separated the Beat scene from the first hippie season. The Beats had been, originally, a literary event—a scattered pack of writers who had broken through, in print and in person, what Ginsberg once called "the syndrome of shutdown." Almost all of them were born into the Depression, and they grew up during the Second World War to take up their pens under the long shadow of McCarthyism and the grim prosperity that supported it. Somebody once described them as Hugh Selwyn Mauberleys in sweatshirts. Their holy men were all the pariahs of American life, and they practiced, in print, a metre and a diction drawn from their own extravagant and often desperate experiences. In person, they practiced a sort of sociological hit-and-run, rattling people who were too close to the shutdown and too new to the riches to listen to them. As it turned out, the best thing about the Beat credo was the writers who invented it. Its disciples were conspicuous mainly for the thoroughness of their rejections, and they were left behind when the Beat literati eventually moved on to explore new ground. Ginsberg spent most of the early sixties travelling around the world, and came home to a generation of postwar babies who were ready to shed the stigma of real or imagined complicity in the spiritual lag. The coincidence of Ginsberg's homecoming, the Beatles' inauguration of a new sound-sensibility, and Timothy Leary's LSD crusade marked the beginnings of a mystique for them. Somebody has described these little hippies as champions of the pretty. Their style was somewhat limited by an aesthetic based largely upon the forms of the East as interpreted by novelties manufacturers and appraised, through crystal beads, under the influence of hallucinogens, but they worshipped good intentions, and this in itself was something of a religious leap. (It is difficult to imagine Jack Kerouac or Norman Mailer arriving at the Stock Exchange with flowers in his hair.) *Their* holy men were holy men, and they invited everybody to join them in a loving universe of family sacraments, group trips, and total rapport.

Ginsberg himself was too political to settle down with the hippies for very long. Given the priorities as he saw them, he was content to leave the details of a loving universe to his friends while he went back to work trying to preserve the universe at hand. Last summer, he flew to London for a long symposium called the Dialectics of Liberation, with Ronald Laing, Paul Goodman, Gregory Bateson, Stokely Carmichael, and Herbert Marcuse, and then, in the fall, he took a room in a *pensione* in Venice, next door to Ezra Pound, to start putting together three new books of journals and poems. From Europe, he plotted what was very likely the first American rite of exorcism since the Navajo Enemy Way, whipped up a fine Pentagon mantra as an accompaniment, and by these and other appropriate means directed *in absentia* the mass circumambulation of the Defense Department by several thousand demonstrators on October 21st. The anniversary of the San Francisco Gathering of the Tribes for a Human Be-In found him in court in New York, accused of having blocked the entrance to the Whitehall Street induction center during End the Draft Week. (He pleaded guilty to a misdemeanor and was given an unconditional discharge. It was his first conviction, and his East Village neighbors, who wanted him to run for President, were very unhappy about it.) A week or so later, he turned up at a rally at Town Hall protesting the indictment of Dr. Benjamin Spock for encouraging resistance to the draft. He spent the rest of January digging up information on the sins of the American military-industrial complex, and in February, armed with statistics, he left for a tour of thirty or forty colleges. In March, he was in Washington, talking with Robert Kennedy about the war. When the Democrats meet in Chicago, he will be there with his bells on, for "a mass manifestation of gaiety" by a few hundred thousand of his friends.

Out in the world, Ginsberg has proved to be so irreproachably immune to the rewards held out to tractable, commercially exploitable, or socially decorative bohemians that over the past year he has become something of a symbol of the profound and often comic incompatibility between the values of the Establishment and the values of the amalgamated hippie-pacifist-activist-visionary-orgiastic-anarchist-Orientalist-psychedelic underground whose various causes and commitments he has managed to espouse. He has been the subject of more argument between the generations than any other American poet since Whitman, whom he admires, and his impact has perhaps been stronger than Whitman's, for, whether enthusiastic about Ginsberg or enraged by him (possibly, Ginsberg says, because of "the unjust equation of *my* long hair with *their* nightmare visions of some monster beatnik"), people who know him, or know about him, seem to put a great deal of energy into reacting to him. Much of Ginsberg's mail, which is voluminous, comes from strangers: "Dear Allen, This letter was written due to a line where you stated 'Communicate with me.' Do you realize that you would not be you if not for me? Please acknowledge my presence," and "Dear Mr. Ginsberg, Occasional escape from reality is good, but it seems to me that you are too real . . . and your 'ultra' reality in which you blot out the unreal shows you're not really where it's at and probably just an exhibitionist." Some of the writers need advice: "Dear Allen, How do I become a poet? Could you just tell me *something* about it?" and "Dear Allen, I am very sad and want to ask you whether or not you believe that an innate capacity for opening the mind and loosening the heart exists in all, however angry, afraid, submerged they may be?" and "Dear Allen, Being a student and, at the same time, being a *person*, I am searching for reconciliation through art and the self. . . . I am 20 years old and do not expect magical solutions. Merely insight, and a new view. Would you correspond with me?" Others want information: "Dear Allen Ginsberg, I plan on heading toward northern India and Nepal and on to Japan, if necessary, in search of a guru. . . . I was wondering what my chances would be of finding one that spoke English. If you happen to know of certain individuals who might instruct me on my search for the realization of the truth, I would appreciate it very much if you would let me know," and "Dear Mr. Ginsberg, In my English course we are required to write ten short papers on various topics. You are my first topic. . . ." In one day's batch of mail a few months ago, Ginsberg received requests for a character reference and a guarantee of financial support from a Japanese poet who wanted a permanent visa with which to enter the country; for a piece of his beard (which he immediately clipped and mailed) as a contribution to the annual fund-raising sale of a high-school literary club in Bakersfield, California; for a manuscript (which he sent) to be auctioned off at a benefit in London for the relief of South African political prisoners; for a manuscript (which he also sent) to be auctioned off at a benefit in France for a new committee to end the Vietnam war; and for a love potion of his own choosing, from a petitioner who wrote, "If you are whimsical or have time, send something to the boy I love. He has had acid already. I wish it worked" (which he did nothing about). In addition, there was a note from an Albuquerque jail, which went, "Mr. Ginsberg: I am also a poet. . . . I was arrested in Albuquerque, New Mexico, late last year for the possession of the herb; three dollars' worth. I am now awaiting trial. . . . May I, Mr. Ginsberg, with your permission, read your statement on marijuana from the *Atlantic Monthly* at my trial? . . . I saw you once from afar and said, 'Hello, Mr. Soul.'"

Ginsberg also gets a great many letters from friends. They write to let him know where they are: "Dear Allen, Another day in the bug house!" and "I am on my way to India and the India beyond India but I will see you before and there, of course. You were right. Siva really dances!" And they keep him up to date on what is happening there: "Dear Allen, Things really seem to be in a state of chaos here in London. The news. First, 12 policemen visited the bookstore on Thursday last week. . . . They seized *all* back issues of the *International Times* (about 10,000 copies), including all the reference copies, they didn't leave us one . . . and from the shop they seized all the copies we had of: *Naked Lunch, I, Jan Cremer, Memoirs of a Shy Pornographer,* by Patchen, *The Sonnets* by Ted Berrigan . . ." and "Hello Allen, The students at the London School of Economics are 'doing a Berkeley.' They have been holding sit-downs, fasts, marches with flowers, etc., and recently declared the formation of an 'open university' within the school. . . . But everyone—poets, pop stars, students, intellectuals, kids—is moving together into a united force in reaction to the official heavy hand."

Ginsberg answers all his letters. He puts them first into a big, worn manila envelope with "Unanswered" scribbled over an old address. Then they go into a second worn manila envelope—this one marked "Answered"—which, when it is full, is stuffed into one of many bulging cartons, labelled "Letters," that are stacked in vaguely chronological order on the floor of a five-room apartment he lives in on East Tenth Street, in New York. Important mail, such as communiqués about drug laws and obscenity trials, is clipped, underlined, and stowed away in the appropriate folder in a cross-referenced file cabinet in his dining room.

One of Ginsberg's friends has called him the central casting office of the underground. He enters in the address book that he always carries in his purple bag the name, address, and phone number of anyone he meets who plays, or is apt to play, a part in what he thinks of as the new order, or has information that might be useful to it, and he goes to considerable trouble to put people he likes in touch with each other and with sympathetic and influential Establishment characters who might be helpful to them. In this way, he has managed to create a network of the like-minded around the world. Any one of his friends who goes to a city that Ginsberg has ever visited knows in advance where to stay, whom to see, and what local statutes to avoid breaking, not to mention who the local shamans are, what politicians are friendly, who has bail money, who sells pot, the temperament of the chief of police, the sympathies of the editors of all the newspapers, the phone numbers of the local activists, and where the best sex and the best conversation can be found.

Ginsberg's passion for an entirely communicado underground has made him the most practically effective dropout around. He has contacts in Washington and most of the big city halls, and also in law firms, Civil Liberties Union offices, and universities scattered across the country. Since most of the information that he needs is at his fingertips, Ginsberg can accomplish with a phone call what many of his friends would take months to plow through. He will direct a friend with a problem to a United States senator's office—"Call. They owe me a favor"—or, with the aplomb of a bank president, ring up the Mayor of San Francisco for a hippie in distress, and he can recommend a lawyer by offering a complete rundown of pertinent cases undertaken and a conclusive "Use him. He's good. He turns on." Ginsberg's friend Gregory Corso, the poet, once complained that Ginsberg was operating like a businessman, but all of Ginsberg's friends—including Corso—agree that as an operator he is invaluable. Few of them have either his talent for coping with the tangly protocol and bewildering façades of the square world or his tolerance and affection for its unregenerate inhabitants. He likes most people, and, consequently, he does not share the compulsion of many of his companions to dismiss them, avoid them, or put them down. He tries his best to be soothing rather than startling. He will scold a friend for frightening a fellow-being on the other side of the Establishment fence by "coming on like some spooky super-exclusive angry beatnik egomaniac madman," and he works hard to assure everybody that nothing human—not even Ginsberg—is really terribly alarming.

"I hope that whatever prejudgment you may have of me or my bearded image you can suspend so that we can talk together as fellow-beings in the same room of Now, trying to come to some harmony and peacefulness between us" was the way he introduced himself to Senators Quentin

Burdick and Jacob Javits at a special Judiciary Subcommittee hearing on narcotics legislation in the spring of 1966. "I am a little frightened to present myself—the fear of your rejection of me, the fear of not being tranquil enough to reassure you that we can talk together, make sense, and perhaps even *like* each other, enough to want not to offend, or speak in a way which is abrupt or hard to understand." Senator Javits, who was a little jittery at being in a room of Now with Ginsberg, interrupted the poet to tell him not to worry so much about his bearded image, but Ginsberg went along calmly, talking to the senators about his peyote visions, about learning to love better under the good influence of ayahuasco, and about praying for Lyndon Johnson's "tranquil health" after taking LSD on a cliff cove at Big Sur on the day of the President's gallbladder operation. He told the senators to try to think of LSD as "a useful educational tool" and (this was long before any records that could be considered reliable had been compiled on the psychological and genetic dangers of LSD) to consider the possibility that the terror preceding most of the acid breakdowns that had been reported was an effect less of the drug itself than of threatening laws and unfriendly social circumstances. Then he said that to *really* discourage the use of LSD the senators should supply the kind of society in which "nobody will need it to break through to common sympathy." The senators were no more unnerved by this piece of advice than Timothy Leary was when Ginsberg told *him*, one night last winter, that in a "groovy" society drugs like LSD would be irrelevant. Leary had just invited Ginsberg to join him on "an LSD march around the world." Ginsberg replied that in his opinion it would be far more sensible for everybody to stay home and help the government figure out how to stop the war. "All I'm trying to do, really," Ginsberg said later, "is get the people who smoke pot and take acid talking to the people who don't, and clear up some of the paranoia around."

The people who don't are apt to have learned about Ginsberg's mission—Senator Burdick introduced Ginsberg to his colleagues as the Pied Piper of the drug movement—from newspaper pictures of the poet chanting *"Hare Krishna"* at one of Leary's sell-out psychedelic celebrations or marching across Sheridan Square with a big grin on his face and with a homemade sign saying "POT IS FUN!" pinned to his overcoat. Actually, Ginsberg has spent years doing research on the ins and outs of the marijuana laws and compiling historical, scientific, and religious arguments against them. Marijuana, known in its various incarnations as hemp, hashish, ganga, kef, and *Cannabis sativa,* is smoked, chewed, baked into cakes, or brewed into tea and enjoyed as a daily pick-me-up in a good part of the world, by Africans, Latin Americans, Hindus, and Moslems, many of whom regard the ingestion of alcohol as a sin; the official panic about the herb in the United States has therefore always been something of a mystery to travellers like Ginsberg, who has shared it by the pipeful with Arab Sufis and sipped it in milk with professors in Indian faculty clubs. In fact, it was legal in this country until a onetime Prohibition officer by the name of Harry Anslinger became commissioner of the newly created Federal Bureau of Narcotics, around the time of Repeal. Anslinger steered through Congress the country's first marijuana-control bill, the Marijuana Tax Act of 1937, and within a few years he had managed to convert the Bureau from a tiny Treasury Department offshoot concerned with the collection of taxes on opiates into a massive watchdog operation, with a staff of agents, that enjoyed near autonomy within the government. Under Anslinger and, more recently, under Henry Giordano, the Bureau, which is empowered to prefer federal "possession" charges carrying high mandatory minimum sentences, has been embroiled in a running war of wits with Ginsberg and his friends. The war involves match-point propaganda—once, in 1961, Ginsberg attacked the Bureau on a Saturday-night television panel show, and the Bureau demanded, and received, equal time—and a good deal of tactical one-upmanship. The Bureau, which used to train agents as beatniks, now has a crack corps of hippies and "students" circulating in the universities and through the underground. Ginsberg, for his part, keeps a volunteer "marijuana secretary" busy cataloguing the clippings, documents, and correspondence that accumulate in his apartment, and his marijuana file is one of the most complete and accurate private records of its kind anywhere. (His favorite among the articles about marijuana he has turned out, a long piece for the *Atlantic Monthly* called "The Great Marijuana Hoax," was sprinkled with footnotes and citations from such ponderous and unlikely authorities as the 1925 Panama Canal Zone Governor's Committee's report on marijuana and the *Report of the British India Hemp Commission, 1893–1894*.) Reporters use the file, and so do the students and scholars of the marijuana movement who live around New York. Lawyers preparing marijuana cases refer to Ginsberg's papers, and the papers are the basis of the poet's own latest marijuana project—the sponsorship and support of a brief to the effect that the existing marijuana statutes violate the legal right of artists to the necessary materials of their trade. Ginsberg would like to use the brief in Washington, eventually, in a test case in the Supreme Court. He estimates that the costs will come to some fifty thousand dollars.

Ginsberg likes to call his own well-known experiments with marijuana and the hallucinogens "pious investigations." He often compares himself in this respect to the French Symbolist poets, and, like them, he has kept a faithful record of his investigations in poems and journals written over the years and under a variety of influences—ranging, in his case, from psilocybin mushrooms to his dentist's laughing gas. The first of these records, a journal, covered the day he took peyote for the first time. Ginsberg, then twenty-four, was at his father's house, in Paterson, New Jersey, and after gagging down the last of the peyote, which is terrible-tasting stuff, he sat down to a phantasmagoric Sunday dinner with a crowd of bickering, unsuspecting relatives. His published letters from Peru to William Burroughs (and Burroughs' letters to him from a visit that Burroughs had made earlier) were written under and about yage, which is a hallucinogenic brew distilled by local *curanderos* from a vine called *Banisteriopsis cappi*. Part II of Ginsberg's poem "Howl" was inspired by a peyote vision that he had in San Francisco, staring out of his window one night at the tower of the Sir Francis Drake Hotel and being reminded of Moloch by the tower's grinning, mask-like façade; the long elegy to his mother, "Kaddish," was the product of forty-odd hours awake on a combination of amphetamines; and the recent "Wales Visitation," which he calls his "first great big Wordsworthian nature poem," was written under LSD.

In the course of more eclectic pious investigations, Ginsberg has also meditated toward satori with a Zen roshi in Kyoto, made fire magic with a North African witch doctor, shared hemp and nakedness with the burning-ghat saddhus in Calcutta, explored the spiritual transports of yogic breathing and "chant turn-on" with Swami A. C. Bhaktivedanta, circumambulated sacred Indian mountains in California, burned butter to Siva with a teacher of Sanskrit at Columbia, and communed with the Oakland Hell's Angels through a split sacrament of the "Prajna Paramita Sutra" and LSD. Lately, he has been writing poems with titles such as "Consulting 'I Ching' Smoking Pot Listening to the Fugs Sing Blake," "Wichita Vortex Sutra," and "Holy Ghost on the Nod Over the Body of Bliss," and he has been waving goodbye, on the way out of his apartment, to a little private shrine on a bookshelf above his television set. The shrine consists of his Tibetan oracle's ring, an Islamic amulet, a small bronze laughing Ho Te Buddha, a miniature of Krishna and Radha, a

Maltese cross, a zodiac poster, some holy cards depicting his favorite Christian martyrs, a package of cigarette papers, and a photograph of his roommate of thirteen years, Peter Orlovsky, posing as a Jain saint.

One night at the hot springs of the Esalen Institute in Big Sur, Ginsberg, who was looking forward to a panel discussion on religion with Gary Snyder, Bishop James Pike, and Dr. Harvey Cox, of the Harvard Divinity School, found himself sharing a bathtub with a group of visiting Episcopal ministers and their wives. After a long talk about Christianity, punctuated by sulphurous splashings on all sides, one of the ministers asked Ginsberg what, exactly, his religion was. Ginsberg slid deep into the water and began thinking about this. After a while, he said that he was probably a Buddhist Jew with attachments to Krishna, Siva, Allah, Coyote, and the Sacred Heart. Then he said no—he was simply on a sort of pilgrimage, "shopping around." In a minute, he corrected himself again, saying that he really thought *all* the gods were "groovy," and so, in fact, he was more of a Buddhist Jewish *pantheist*. Climbing out of the steaming yellow water, he pointed to Orlovsky, who was perched on a railing by the ocean conversing in loud braying noises with the full moon. "I figure one sacrament's as good as the next one, if it works," Ginsberg said.

. . .

The day of the first Gathering of the Tribes for a Human Be-In was hot and splendidly sunny, and the twenty thousand people who came to the Polo Field in San Francisco's Golden Gate Park were able to Be in their brightest, barest psychedelic costumes, without the dreary camouflage of overcoats and boots. In fact, according to an announcement that morning by Michael Bowen, a young Haight-Ashbury painter with an inspirational tale of having been rescued from an amphetamine habit by love, Tantric Buddhism, and LSD, Mexico had generously exchanged climates with northern California, at the intercession of his Mexican guru, in the interests of a thoroughly successful day. (Bowen said that it had snowed hard in Mexico.) Ginsberg himself came to the park in a pair of blue rubber bathing thongs, which he had picked up at a Japanese stall on the way over to the park, and a hospital orderly's white uniform, which he likes to wear for ceremonial events. Seven hours later, with his dress whites muddy, sweaty, and stained by flowers, he was to be found hunting for his new sandals under piles of electronic-rock equipment on a deserted bandstand at one end of the field. It was a calm pink twilight.

People were moving in slow, sleepy coveys toward the road. Ginsberg, who had just led them in silent meditation on the setting sun and in a closing mantra—"*Om Sri Maitreya*"—to the Buddha of the Future, stopped to watch some of them disappear over the crest of a hill bordering the field. He looked elated, exhausted, and a little sick to his stomach, from fruit, cookies, candy bars, cigarettes, Cokes, and peanut-butter sandwiches that had been pressed on him by his admirers, and he was covered from head to toe with gifts of beads, bells, amulets, buttons, and one enormous, dazzling flowered tie.

It had been a beautiful day, Ginsberg told a boy who climbed up onto the bandstand to say good night and to admire the tie, which the poet held out proudly, saying, "Hey, look! Someone laid this groovy tie on me today." He had arrived at the park at eleven, before the crowds, in order to chant some Buddhist dharanis, or short prayers, for removing whatever disasters might be hovering in the vicinity, and to circumambulate the field—a purification ritual that he had learned from the Hindus, who always circumambulate *their* fields before a mela, which is a similarly gala Indian gathering of seekers and holy men. The Hell's Angels had pulled up on their Harley-Davidsons a little white later, as they had promised, to guard the generators and trunk lines for the rock groups who were going to play. Unfortunately, Freewheelin' had presently fallen off a sound truck onto a ketchup bottle and cut his face in several places, but he had been the only casualty of the day. Someone *had* slashed one of the feed lines to a sound truck belonging to the Grateful Dead, but it had been repaired quickly, and one of the Dead musicians, who wanted to make a citizen's arrest of a heckler "for destroying my sanity," had been quietly persuaded by his colleagues that the destruction of sanity was a Constitutional prerogative. Timothy Leary and Jerry Rubin, a young Berkeley activist who had been bailed out of jail that morning expressly for the be-in, had both made short, loving speeches, to the relief of the planning committee. (Leary had spent most of the day on the bandstand playing pat-a-cake with a steady succession of stray children.) A young man in a black mask had floated down from the sky, attached to a Paisley parachute, and landed in the middle of the field, frightening a few picnickers but giving rise to considerable speculation among the others as to whether the Buddha of the Future had not appeared at last. A sulphur bomb, planted by a nonbeliever, had exploded under the bandstand at three in the afternoon, but the celebrants in the immediate area had been so euphoric by that time that they took it for a new brand of incense and applauded enthusiastically. Shortly before the bomb went off, Roshi Shunryu Suzuki, the master of the Soto Zen Center, in San Francisco, had arrived unexpectedly, carrying a wreath of flowers and followed by a human chain of brown-robed disciples, and had smiled his blessing on the vast, frolicking manifestation of illuminated consciousness. The costumes had been beautiful. There had been Colonial petticoats, buckskins and war paint, Arabian desert robes, Paisley body stockings on girls and Paisley diapers on babies, Hopi tops and Hindu bottoms, mistletoe escutcheons, bedspreads, capes, togas, and ancestral velvets. Roughly one-fortieth of the population of the city of San Francisco had spent the afternoon in the park together, and the keynote had been sounded by the poets: "Peace in your heart dear / Peace in the park here" (Ginsberg), "Let it go, whatever you do is beautiful" (Kandel), and "This is really it, and it is all perfect" (McClure).

Looking at the boy on the bandstand, Ginsberg grinned. The boy was wearing a suit of armor, which he had draped with rosebuds, daisies, and daffodils. He was a peace warrior, he said. "I guess you can tell by the way I'm dressed," he added. "I kind of dig freedom."

"I wish I had a camera," Ginsberg said. Then he jumped off the bandstand and ran up the hill to catch his friends.

Ginsberg was due at Bowen's place on Haight Street for a macrobiotic supper and some chanting, and half an hour later he was standing in front of one of the fancy, battered Victorian buildings that lined the street and managed to give it a somewhat less belligerently shabby face than the hippie enclaves in Chicago and New York. He was with a girl called Maretta, a gaunt, shy sibyl of twenty-four with long, blond hair who had been travelling with him ever since she returned that fall from India, where she had spent two years in a relentless search for her sadhana, or true path. Maretta had hitchhiked from Europe to India, and had eventually been converted to Tibetan Buddhism, which was the favorite Buddhism of visionary people then. At the moment, Maretta was talking to Ginsberg about her sadhana, which she believed to be hashish this time around in her cycle of rebirth. They had been watching the street for Peter Orlovsky and Peter's older brother Julius, both of whom they had lost track of during the afternoon. Peter Orlovsky, who has described himself as a loony lyric poet of manic compassions, was in the habit of wandering off with a rag and a big bottle of Lysol to scrub down cars, stoops, windows, and sidewalks, in line with his own sadhana, which was keeping the universe clean. His brother also had a habit of disappearing. Julius had once spent twelve years of his life in silence, and even now, with Ginsberg and Peter looking after him, he rarely said a word. Ginsberg told Maretta that he suspected Julius of having taken off at the be-in to have a talk.

Ginsberg and Maretta waited on the sidewalk for five minutes, and then left messages for the Orlovskys with an assortment of hippie pedestrians and climbed a flight of stairs to Bowen's apartment, where the post-celebration celebration was already under way. Bowen greeted them at the door—a big, gangly young man with a mop of fuzzy brown hair, rosy cheeks, and a boyish gap between his two front teeth. He had thrown off his dress shirt—an elaborate purple jerkin—at some point during the be-in, but he still wore several strands of beads and a pair of expensive-looking brown suède pants. Maretta admired them, and Bowen complimented her on her own costume—she had on flowing houndstooth culottes, red on one leg and green on the other, an orange middy blouse, and a red fringed head shawl, and she was trailing a length of gauzy purple sari cloth. Then he announced that, according to a calculation by Gavin Arthur, a grandson of Chester A. Arthur who was a local clairvoyant, the population of the earth at that particular moment in time was equal to the total of all the dead in human history. "That means we're all back, we're all together," Bowen said.

"Beautiful," Maretta murmured.

"Groovy," Ginsberg said. "Are we too late for dinner?"

Bowen pointed down the hall to a brightly lit kitchen, where a young woman in a long green corduroy skirt was standing over a stove dishing out brown rice to a line of wan and softly chanting hippie girls. The young woman, who will here be called Lavinia, had abandoned her own last name—she felt that it did not express the "real" her—when she first left home for San Francisco, and now, at twenty-one, she was a veteran hippie householder. She had settled down with Bowen in the fall, after several months of purifying meditation alone in a tent at Big Sur, and her experience in the woods as a hunter-gatherer-meditator had made her a heroine to the newer arrivals in the Haight-Ashbury, who regarded her retreat as a kind of ultimate gesture. Whereas Bowen was admired for the aphorisms of hippie life that he regularly loosed on visiting reporters from the news weeklies—"The psychedelic baby eats the cybernetic monster in San Francisco" and "We are building an electric Tibet in California" were two of his favorites—Lavinia was famous locally as an expert on nonpoisonous berries, outdoor mantra chanting, latrine digging, and all-weather dressmaking. Ginsberg had known her since the fall of 1966, when they had gone, with Snyder, on a five-week camping and climbing trip through the Northern Cascades, and he greeted her warmly while helping himself to a slice of damp, leaden homemade wheat-germ bread that was lying on the kitchen table. Then he introduced her to Maretta, who said, "Got any hashish, man?"

"My yoga at the moment is cooking," Lavinia answered dryly. "Feeding everybody with natural breads and oats and corn. Seeing that the people here get wholesome, vegetarian food."

"*My* yoga is giving up smoking—that is, until this week it was," Ginsberg said, laughing. He reached into his jacket pocket for a Pall Mall. "In New York, I met this really groovy swami named Satchidananda. At a party Christmas Eve, I think it was. And I was complaining about smoking too much, and like he said that giving up smoking could be interpreted as a valid form of yoga. Like it involves all the yogic disciplines—control of temper, concentration, devotion, the happy concurrence of body and mind. So like I vowed then and there to stop, and I was doing all right till I hit San Francisco." Ginsberg shrugged, looking ashamed of himself.

Lavinia handed Ginsberg a plateful of steaming rice, and he stayed in the kitchen for a while, eating and gossiping. Then, with Maretta in tow, he wandered down the hall, following the sounds of voices, bells, and cymbals, and the sharp mingled smells of incense and tobacco, to a small, square room that was dimly lit by a set of fat black dripping candles. The room, which was Bowen's meditation room, was hung with the batik bedspreads that served in psychedelic circles as everything from wallpaper to evening gowns. Thin mattresses had been laid out, side by side, around the walls, and in the middle of the room, on a worn Oriental rug, there was a low, scrolled wooden table holding a candelabra, a saucer of burning incense, a tiny bronze Buddha, and a scattering of flowers. The remains of a light fixture on the ceiling were draped with bells, god's-eyes, and long strands of crystal beads, which dipped down almost to the floor and swung, tinkling, whenever anybody touched them. One of Bowen's paintings, an LSD vision of eyes, hearts, broad squiggly lines, and strange Coptic-looking configurations, was tacked to one of the bedspreads, next to an aquatint of Mary and Jesus at an angel party of some sort, and across the room, taking up most of a wall, was a large and extremely rare Tibetan tanka, or silk-scroll painting, of the Maitreya. (Snyder had discovered the scroll in Kyoto, Ginsberg had paid for it, and they had entrusted it to Bowen to be used as an altarpiece, probably for an "indigenous American ashram" in the Haight-Ashbury.)

About eighteen people, in their be-in costumes, were snuggled in companionable heaps on the mattresses. Some of them were talking or chanting quietly to themselves. The others were staring amiably into space. They were all in the process of sharing a peace pipe when Ginsberg and Maretta, tripping over a pile of people on the threshold, stumbled in. Maretta headed for a dark corner, where she staked out a few feet of mattress, curled up into a ball of culottes and fringe, and almost instantly fell asleep. Ginsberg located Snyder on a mattress behind the candelabra and sat down next to him. Snyder was wearing clothes—a pair of green corduroy jeans and a green blouse blocked with big mauve leaves and flowers—and waving a gallon jug of California Bordeaux around. Just as Ginsberg reached for the jug, a light went on, and two television men, dragging kliegs and cables, began maneuvering toward him. They said that Bowen had invited them. Ginsberg groaned.

"I don't know why, but this whole day strikes me as absolutely sane and right and beautiful," one of the men said cheerfully, holding a light meter up to Ginsberg's nose. "Mike must have put something in my tea last night."

"What's so *in*sane about a little peace and harmony?" Ginsberg asked him, inching over on the mattress to make room for Maretta, who had been awakened by the light. Maretta nodded sleepily.

"It was beautiful, man," she said.

"Like *thousands* of people would like to come to the park on a day like today," Ginsberg went on. "So they can relate to each other as—as dharma beings. All sorts of people. Poets, children, even Hell's Angels. People are lonesome. *I'm* lonesome. It's strange to be in a body. So what I'm doing—what we're all doing—on a day like today is saying, 'Touch me, *talk* to me.'"

"People are groovy," Snyder said.

"Zap!" Ginsberg said, and snapped his fingers. "You know how Reagan said, 'Once you've seen one redwood tree you've seen them all.'"

"That's an incredible mentality to us," Snyder broke in.

"Actually, I used to be in love with Reagan in the thirties—I used to see all of his movies," Ginsberg said, smiling ingenuously. "So Ronald Reagan and I are one. Ronald Reagan, you and I are *one*!"

Bowen came running into the room with a telephone in his hand and called to Ginsberg that he had Santa Barbara on the line. "In Santa Barbara, they meditated with us for six whole hours while we were at the be-in," Bowen shouted as he leaped over a mattress, dropped down on his hands and knees, and began tossing pillows aside to find an extension socket in the wall.

"You mean to say you have a phone in your meditation room?" Ginsberg said, and he burst out laughing.

"Electric Tibet, baby," Bowen said, flipping Ginsberg the phone. "Say something, will you, Allen?"

"Hello. What's your name?" Ginsberg said, sticking a finger in his free ear. "Bright? Hey, that's a groovy name." Ginsberg turned to Snyder. "His name is Bright. That's nice." And then back to Santa Barbara. "We're just saying that Ronald Reagan should prove his good faith by turning on."

"In the middle of the redwood forest, tell him!" Snyder shouted.

Bowen reached for the phone. "It's really far out here, man," Bowen said.

Ginsberg peered at the television man, who was crawling around him with a long microphone cord in one hand.

"Take the phone call, for example," Ginsberg told the television man. "It's like we've bridged the gap between all sorts of people with this—this kind of community festival. I thought it was very Edenlike today, actually. Kind of like Blake's vision of Eden. Music. Babies. People just sort of floating around having a good time and everybody happy and smiling and touching and turning each other on and a lot of groovy chicks dressed up in their best clothes and . . ."

"But will it *last*?" the television man asked.

Ginsberg shrugged. "How do *I* know if it will last?" he said. "And if it doesn't turn out, who cares?"

"I met a policeman at the park who really dug the consciousness today," a boy in a plaid blanket whispered from across the room. "He told me that he thought today was beautiful."

"Even the Hell's Angels dug the consciousness," Ginsberg added, nodding. "Like they were all turned into big, happy, benevolent beings."

The television man wanted to know how important LSD was to this new benevolence.

"Come on, there are other yogas besides LSD, you know," Ginsberg said. "Chanting, for one. Sex. Love. Giving up smoking. And running laps—that's also yoga." Ginsberg stopped to pat a baby who had crawled into the meditation room and was reaching for his beard, gurgling with curiosity.

"Acid just happened to turn up as the product of this particular society, to correct its own excesses," Snyder said.

The television man signaled to his partner, who had moved back to the door and was standing there with a hand-held camera, to start shooting. They worked for half an hour, and just as they ran out of film, Timothy Leary, in a bright-red Aran Islands sweater, rushed into the room. Leary was a little out of breath, and so was his Los Angeles lawyer, a man in a pink shirt and a tweed Eisenhower jacket, who ran in after him.

"Out there, on the street!" the lawyer, whose name was Seymour Lazar, called to the meditators. "Five paddy wagons! At least five. And they're arresting kids right and left."

"What for *now*?" Ginsberg asked them.

"Non-dispersal, or something," Leary said. "All I know is that we were taking a walk up Haight Street and heard a group of kids singing outside the Psychedelic Shop, and then suddenly the police arrived, out of nowhere, and started busting everybody."

"Well, they're not busting *us*," Snyder said.

"But they're grabbing hostages, and for a reason," Bowen, who was pulling on his jerkin, said. "Terror's the reason, man."

Most of the people in the room nodded.

"Oh, come on," Ginsberg said, getting up and heading for the stairs. "The police are people. They're just a little paranoid. Something must have scared them. Anyway, I'm going down and have a look around."

Ginsberg left with Leary, Lazar, and perhaps ten people from the party. He returned about ten minutes later, stuck his head into the meditation room to say "Someone threw a bottle, or something," and then went into a huddle with Lazar and Leary on the kitchen table. He told Lazar that the Haight needed to organize and hire a lawyer to handle its troubles with the police.

"You see, if you've got trouble—LSD, marijuana, prostitution—just talk to Seymour," Leary told some boys and girls who had followed the men to the kitchen and were standing at the door, listening.

"Well, there's nothing we can do about the busts tonight," Ginsberg said, finally. He was perched on the table, in between several loaves of fresh natural bread.

"Tell me something, Allen," Lazar, who had been watching Ginsberg, said suddenly. "You must have a little money now. You can *afford* things. Tell me why you stay in such funky places."

"How do *you* know?" Ginsberg demanded. "You ever been to one of our funky places?" He began chanting, cheerfully, at the lawyer.

"And all this chanting," Lazar said.

Ginsberg shrugged. "It's kicks," he said. "*Hare Krishna,* Seymour."

Ginsberg hopped off the table and, still chanting, padded barefoot back into the meditation room and sat down on a mattress. Snyder welcomed him with a blast from a conch horn that he had blown to the four winds at the be-in that afternoon. The conch horn was wrapped in blue net and garlanded with wild flowers, and Ginsberg said that he thought it looked very magical. Then he began talking to it. "Tell me, O Conch, will I have to give up love at the fourth level of enlightenment?" He held the conch to his ear and waited for an answer.

Everyone giggled but a young man in a turn-of-the-century merchant-marine dress uniform, who had been staring sullenly at Ginsberg from a mattress across the room. "Here you are, the great Ginsberg, sitting there talking like this was *your* scene," the boy said.

"We had some of this scene going ten years ago," Ginsberg told him. "At least some of us were accomplishing *something* like this then."

"Yeah, but then there were ten years when you had nothing to say to the world," the boy said.

"You're right." Ginsberg nodded agreeably.

The boy glared, and added, "Anyway, I didn't mean *this* scene, like here tonight. I meant the *communal* scene."

"But we had a communal thing going, too," Ginsberg said, chuckling. "The trouble was that less people wanted to commune."

Snyder spoke up, looking at the boy. "I'd say the big difference between our old scene and now is *this*. We had a friend then—a poet—who killed himself, and he took a lot of bad karma, magically speaking, with him when he died. We knew we didn't need or want that kind of self-defeating scene anymore."

"Anyway, we *did* have a big, friendly, family scene," Ginsberg said. "It's recorded literary history. Anybody who wants to can look it up." He glanced around the room. "Like we even took off our clothes at parties."

"Well, why not now, or on the street, man?" Bowen said enthusiastically.

The boy shrugged. "I take it that you—the older generation—are responsible for *this*, for the way we live, for—"

"Sure, why not?" Ginsberg said, and, leaning toward the boy, he put his fingertips together and touched them to his forehead, to signify that he recognized and respected the presence of another sentient being in the meditation room.

"The great Ginsberg won't even let me finish," the boy complained.

Bowen jumped up. "Hey, man, we don't get nasty here," he said.

"What do you want to hurt my feelings for, anyway?" Ginsberg asked the boy. He sounded curious.

Snyder started laughing. "Don't take it all out on Allen," he said. "This has been going on since the Stone Age. Why, there's a chain of us going back to the late Paleolithic. Like Jeffers, and Whitman. *They* had good scenes going."

"The only thing is that more people love and kiss and touch now," Ginsberg said.

"And more people kill and bomb—that's the *other* side of Kali," Bowen broke in. He sounded astonished at his insight.

"But the other side of Kali is Parvati, and she's beautiful, and dances!" a girl in orange feathers called out from the bottom of a pile of people.

"It's all one, baby," Bowen philosophized.

Ginsberg stood up, stretching. Leary had just walked in with the early edition of the next day's *Chronicle,* and he handed it to Ginsberg. On the front page, over a picture of the be-in, was the headline "HIPPIES RUN WILD."

"That's ridiculous," Ginsberg said when he had finished reading their reviews. "Like it was an aesthetically very good scene. They should have sent an art critic."

"It's a bad bag, reporting," Snyder mused. "Somehow, I don't think it's possible to be in that bag and get anywhere, spiritually speaking."

Ginsberg said that, nevertheless, he had "better straighten things out." He left the meditators debating the spiritual pitfalls of journalism, and, down the hall in Bowen's studio, where there was another telephone, he dialled the *Chronicle* and asked for the night editor. Maretta trailed in after him holding a cigarette. He took a long, weary puff.

"What is this nonsense about hippies running wild?" Ginsberg said, scolding the night editor. "Your story has the kind of inaccuracy of tone and language that's *poisoning* the community. Is *that* what you want to do?" He proceeded to dissect the story, word by word. "What do you mean nobody *told* you that?" he said. "What kind of reporting is *that?*"

"We sent our hippiest reporter," the night editor said.

"I don't know what kind of hippies you've got over there at *your* place," Ginsberg said, chuckling. "Besides, what is this hippie business? What does 'hippie' mean, anyway? These kids aren't hippies—they're *seekers*. Today was a serious religious occasion."

Maretta nodded vigorously.

Ginsberg gave her a hug. He told the night editor to expect him early Monday morning for a talk with the reporter about an accurate followup.

The editor agreed.

"Well, peace," Ginsberg said, and he hung up.

FROM

LEVELS OF THE GAME—1

John McPhee

JUNE 14, 1969 (ARTHUR ASHE, CLARK GRAEBNER)

T HE MIND OF ARTHUR ASHE is wandering. It wanders sometimes at crucial moments, such as now—in the second set of the semifinals of the first United States Open Championships, at Forest Hills. Games are six—all. Ashe and Clark Graebner have long since entered the danger zone where any major mistake can mean the loss of the set—and for Ashe, who is down one set already, the probable loss of the match. Ashe has just won three service games while losing only two points. Graebner, in his turn, has just served three games, losing no points at all. Ashe lifts the ball and hits to Graebner's forehand. Graebner answers down the line. With the premium now maximum on every shot, Ashe is nonetheless thinking of what he considers the ideal dinner— fried chicken, rice, and baked beans. During matches, the ideal dinner is sometimes uppermost in Ashe's mind. Graebner, like other tennis players, knows this and counts on it. "He'll always daydream. That's one of his big hangups. That's why he escapes to the movies so much. But in a match he won't dream long enough. I wish he would do it longer."

At these moments, Ashe thinks primarily of food, but also of parties, places he has been, things he has done, and girls, whom he dates in three colors. "This is my way of relaxing. Other people call it lack of concentration. Which is true. But I do it by habit, instinctively." Moving up with his racquet low, he picks up Graebner's forehand drive with a half volley and sends the ball, perhaps irretrievably, to Graebner's backhand corner.

There is a personally signed photograph of Richard Nixon on Graebner's desk in his apartment. Watching Nixon on television, Graebner will say, "Doesn't that make sense? How could *anyone* be more right? How could *anyone* fail to be *for* the guy?"

"Graebner is a straight, true Republican," Ashe will say. "He seems to tend that way. You think of a person, when you first meet him, in reference points. Clark is tall, strong, white, Protestant, middle-class, conservative. After a while, the adjectives fall away and he's just Clark. As far as most Negroes are concerned, whites are categorically bad until proved otherwise. My upbringing leads me to think the same way. But Clark is just Clark to me now. I don't think about it. It's just Clark over there, not a white man. I don't think he is a liberal. He's tight with his money, and he wants to see the poor work for their money. I don't entirely disagree with him, but he probably doesn't see all the ramifications. He probably doesn't care what's happening in Spanish Harlem. . . . The guy was spoiled rotten when he was a kid. All of us are spoiled to a large degree. Clark played with Charlie Pasarell, doubles. If they lost, Clark's mother said it was Charlie's fault. Clark is an only child. He's high-strung, and he can be very demanding. His speaking style sometimes sounds abrasive, staccatolike, but he doesn't mean it that way. It sounds pushy. If I'm in a bad mood, it bugs me. But I wouldn't say he's ill-tempered. There is no way you could say he is not a nice guy if you had just met him, with no preconceived notions. With his kids, he is like any father—eager to show them off. He's a nice guy, but he has been accustomed to instant gratification. As soon as he wanted something, he got it. Put all this on a tennis court, and the high-strung part, the conservative, and the need for instant gratification become predominant."

Running flat out, Graebner hits a superb hard backhand that surprises Ashe and slants past him to win the point. Ashe has been thinking of food, among other things, and did not keep his eye on the ball. Love-fifteen. Graebner feels the surge of possibilities, and tells himself, "I have a chance in this game. I'm ahead now, and Arthur is sleeping."

Ashe hits a twist to Graebner's backhand, and Graebner, instead of hitting out, chips the ball back—the cautious thing to do.

"There is not much variety in Clark's game. It is steady, accurate, and conservative. He makes few errors. He plays stiff, compact, Republican tennis. He's a damned smart player, a good thinker, but not a limber and flexible thinker. His game is predictable, but he has a sounder volley than I have, and a better forehand—more touch, more power. His forehand is a hell of a weapon. His moves are mediocre. His backhand is underspin, which means he can't hit it hard. He just can't hit a heavily top-spun backhand. He hasn't much flair or finesse, except in the lob. He has the best lob of any of the Americans. He's solid and consistent. He tries to let you beat yourself."

Ashe, on his way to the net, picks up the chip and hits it without exceptional force or placement to Graebner's forehand. Graebner could now probably explode one. He has what is almost a setup on his power side. But instead he tries a careful, hang-in-there, soft crosscourt topspin dink, and it is Ashe who explodes. The orthodox way to hit a volley is to punch it, with a backswing so short that it begins in front of the player's body. Ashe now—characteristically—draws his racquet back as far as he can reach and volleys the ball with a full, driving swing. The impact is perfect, and the ball goes past Graebner's feet like a bullet fired to make him dance. "I hit too soft and short," Graebner tells himself. "That's the difference between playing on one level and playing on another. You've got to hit it *authoritatively*." Fifteen-all.

Ashe hits a big serve. He is not daydreaming now. Graebner blocks back a good return. Ashe, moving in, must half-volley. The shot should be deep—to protect his position, his approach to the net. Instead, he tries one of the most difficult shots in tennis. Basically, it is a foolhardy shot. It is not a percentage shot, and is easier to miss than to make. Players call it a half-volley drop shot. Ashe reaches down, lightly touches the rising ball, and sends it on a slow, sharply angled flight toward the net. The risk is triple—hitting the net, missing the placement, and leaving a sitter for Graebner to put away if he should be able to get to the ball. The ball settles down to a landing in Graebner's forecourt. Graebner is headed for it at top speed, and he almost gets there in time. He drives the ball into the umpire's chair, and straightens up with a disgusted look on his face. Ashe's half-volley drop shot was the sort of thing a person should try once a match, if at all, and hardly in the most vital moments of the second set, when—already losing—he is in imminent peril of falling almost hopelessly behind. It was a loose flick shot, requiring tremendous ball control, and Ashe, in Graebner's view, was very lucky to succeed with it. "How can he do it?" Graebner asks himself. His shoulders droop as he walks back to the baseline. Thirty-fifteen.

"I've never been a flashy stylist, like Arthur. I'm a fundamentalist. Arthur is a bachelor. I am married and conservative. I'm interested in business, in the market, in children's clothes. It affects the way you play the game. He's not a steady player. He's a wristy slapper. Sometimes he doesn't even know where the ball is going. He's carefree, lacksadaisical, forgetful. His mind wanders. I've never seen Arthur really discipline himself. He plays the game with the lacksadaisical, haphazard mannerisms of a liberal. He's an underprivileged type who worked his way up. His family are fine people. He's an average Negro from Richmond, Virginia. There's something about him that is swashbuckling, loose. He plays the way he thinks. My style is playmaking—consistent, percentage tennis—and his style is shotmaking. He won't grub around. He doesn't gut out a lot of points where he has to work real hard, probably because he is concerned about his image. He doesn't want to appear to be a grubber. He comes out on the court and he's tight for a while, then he hits a few good shots and he feels the power to surge ahead. He gets looser and more liberal with the shots he tries, and pretty soon he is hitting shots everywhere. He does not play percentage tennis. Nobody in his right mind, really, would try those little dink shots he tries as often as he does. When he hits out, he just slaps. He plays to shoot his wad. He hits the ball so hard that it's an outright winner or he misses the shot. When he misses, he just shrugs his shoulders. If he were more consistent, he might be easier to play. Negroes are getting more confidence. They are asking for more and more, and they are getting more and more. They are looser. They're liberal. In a way, 'liberal' is a synonym for 'loose.' And that's exactly the way Arthur plays. I've always kidded him, saying, 'If the Negroes take over, please make me a lieutenant. Not a general or a colonel. Just a lieutenant.'"

Lieutenant Ashe, USA (stationed at West Point), professes to enjoy the irony of this request, and promises to do what he can. He endorses Graebner's analysis of his game, and says, "To put it simply, I just blast the ball back and the point's over. Of course, I miss a lot. Tennis is a means to an end, that's all. If I could really be what I wanted to be, I would love to be a pro quarterback." He lifts the ball and hits another hard first serve at Graebner. Almost an ace, it jerks Graebner far off balance, but he hits it back solidly, up the middle. Ashe, moving up, is again confronted with the need to half-volley. For the second time in a row, instead of hitting the deep, correct ball, he tries to pull a drop shot off the grass, and for the second time in a row he succeeds. *"Another* half-volley drop shot!" Donald Dell comments. "How loose can you get?" Dell is captain of the United States Davis Cup Team, of which Ashe and Graebner are members. Graebner, sprinting, gets to this one, barely, and more or less pushes it down the line—a remarkable effort—but Ashe, standing straight up and not even bothering to stroke with form, flips a slow, looping crosscourt wood-shot forehand into Graebner's court and just beyond his reach—a stroke that might have been made with a broom handle. Forty-fifteen.

Graebner slams his racquet down onto the turf. He shouts, "God damn it, Arthur, you're so lucky!" To anyone who can halfway read lips, the sentiment goes out over national TV. Ashe stands quietly. He does not show the pleasure he must feel. He bounces the ball six times with his racquet, and he shoves his glasses back up his nose. "Graebner is now completely infuriated," Dell continues. "Look at him—the Greek tragic hero always getting pushed around by the gods. He really sees himself that way, and it's his greatest weakness." Graebner has been known to do a great deal more than slam his racquet down, spit sour grapes, and take the Prime Mover's name in vain. He has been a behavioral case study in a game in which—at least among Americans—brattishness seems to be generic. Apparently, he feels that he can accurately assign blame outside himself for almost every shot he misses, every point he loses. He glowers at his wife. He mutters at other people in the crowd. Airplanes drive him crazy. Bad bounces are personal affronts. He glares at linesmen. He carps at linesmen. He intimidates ball boys. He throws his racquet from time to time, and now and then he takes hold of the fence around a court and shakes it violently, his lips curling. He seems to be caged. The display of misery that he can put on is too convincing not to be genuine. If his opponent makes a great shot, Graebner is likely to mutter a bitter aside, then turn and say "Good shot" with mechanical magnanimity. He has shouted four-letter obscenities at people in the grandstands, and in the Australian National Championships one year he told an umpire to shut up. At Longwood in 1966, he swatted a ball at a linesman about twenty feet away from him. The ball didn't harm the man, perhaps because it didn't hit him.

Ashe is detached about Graebner in a way that some tennis players are not when they talk about him. "When things go wrong, Clark can't seem to resist saying or doing something that shows dissatisfaction, to put it mildly," Ashe says. "I think it has sunk in that he sometimes offends people, and I can see him fighting it, trying to correct it." Tennis players frequently compare Graebner to Dr. Jekyll and Mr. Hyde, the essence of what they say being that he is a completely different, friendly, smiling person away from a tennis court, and that off the court of late he has obviously made a particular effort to be nice. Graebner's friend Warren

Danne has always enjoyed his company off the court, but says that "Clark has behaved like an ass on the court since he was eighteen." Dr. Paul Graebner, Clark's father, argues that Clark is merely ignoring an irrational ethic. "Just because someone once wrote that this is a gentleman's game, you have no right to blow up like any full-blooded desirous person," Dr. Graebner says. "Tennis is a business. Tennis isn't fun. The opportunities tennis gives are tremendous, but not at no cost to the individual."

"He has gone out of his way to be a good boy," his mother says. "Basically, I don't know of any better boy all around than Clark has been. He was never a problem, never a bad teen-ager."

"He has always tried to be what we have wanted him to be, what he felt he should be, what he felt we would have liked him to be," his father says. "He makes friends wherever he goes. He has more friends than you can shake a stick at."

"Someone should have sat on him when he was young," Clark's wife, Carole, says. "Officials threatened him but did not act. No one blocked him."

"He's very German," Warren Danne goes on. "I don't think I've met anyone in this country who's more German than Graebner—clean, positive, always moving forward. I don't think he debates alternatives. He sees things one way and acts."

There is perhaps something Germanic about Graebner on a tennis court. His kills are clean, but when he kills he tends to overkill. His overhead is hit with his whole arm—no mere flick of the wrist. The arm comes down like the moving part of a paper cutter. "One fell swoop of the arm and the ball is gone," Ashe says. "And I think he enjoys hitting his forehands as hard as he can. He can hit them harder than anyone else playing, I think." Graebner likes to hit drop shots, and when other players race to them and make desperate gets he stands at the net and crunches their feeble returns—a standard thing to do, except that other players sometimes believe that the direction the ball takes indicates that Graebner is trying to kill them. They have stopped in the middle of matches to ask Graebner what he thinks he is doing. "Graebner will sometimes literally hit the ball through you," Ashe will say. "If you don't get out of the way, he'll hurt you with it."

Graebner has won cups for sportsmanship. At crucial moments in crucial matches, he has stepped to the umpire's chair to say that a point apparently his should be credited to his opponent, because his racquet ticked the ball. After hitting the ball at the linesman in 1966, he was suspended from the United States Davis Cup Team. The team—Ashe was on it—went to Pôrto Alegre without Graebner, and the United States lost miserably to Brazil. "Clark felt that this was a way that God was looking out for him," his wife reveals. "Instead of being away when we had our first baby, he was at home and he was not in on the disgrace of losing in Brazil. He has always been very religious." The day he was suspended happened to be Clark Graebner Day in Beachwood, Ohio, his home town.

"Arthur's manners have always been quiet and restrained on the tennis court," Graebner says. "What I wonder is: Would he have been that way if he had been white? For me, there was always the spoiled-brat thing. I probably *was* a brat, to some extent. People have called me—and a lot of others spoiled brats. Would it have been the same for Arthur? He has had to master the restraint of his emotions on the court. In fact, I think he works too hard at trying to keep his cool. He comes off the court after winning a title and gives it the cool play. It's not human to be that cool. He is penned in. Feelings need an outlet. I hope he is not going to lose his cool by trying to keep his cool."

Ashe was trained, in large part, by Dr. Robert Walter Johnson, of Lynchburg, Virginia, who has given much of his life to the development of young black tennis players. For many years, within the strict dimensions of Dr. Johnson's approach to white tennis, Ashe played under the disadvantage of stifling his reactions, of never complaining, of calling close ones against himself. Now the training is paying off. When things get tough, he has control. His latent confidence—his cool—works in his favor. Even in very tight moments, other players think he is toying with them. They rarely know what he is thinking. They can't tell if he's angry. It is maddening, sometimes, to play against him. He has said that what he likes best about himself on a tennis court is his demeanor. "I strive to cultivate it. It's a conversation point. It's a selling point. 'He's icy and he's elegant. Imperturbable.' What it is is controlled cool, in a way. Always have the situation under control, even if losing. Never betray an inward sense of defeat." He once lost in the finals of the Australian National Championship when a foot fault was called against him on the last point of the match. Almost any other American player would have instantly turned into flaming gasoline. Ashe came very close to it, but he kept control. "You must expect four or five bad calls a match," he says. "A match can be won or lost on a bad call." About as close as he will come to complaining is to stare evenly for a moment at a linesman. In an extreme case, he may walk to the point just outside the line where he believes his opponent's shot landed and draw a little circle around the spot with the handle of his racquet.

"I used to have a hang-loose attitude," he will say. "That suggests a don't-care attitude. If I won, fine; if I didn't win, too bad. But you just *have* to care—about anything you have to do. You appreciate excellence for excellence's sake." It is part of his cool that he almost never lets himself say or show how much he loves the game he plays, but one has only to watch him on the courts at West Point, playing with the cadet varsity tennis players, to see the extent of his athletic generosity and his affection for what he is doing. He gives away points when he knows that the cadets will not suspect him. He plays at a minor pace with a spectacular suggestion of high effort. He mixes encouragement with instruction and humor in an unending stream of words across the net. "When you run for a ball that's real wide, you run as if you were going to take one more step when you get there. One more step and you would have had it," he will say. Or, "One of the best shots against a man at the net is to hit it right at him. If he's standing there and you hit it hard right at him, what the hell is he going to do?"

As a cadet's good shot goes past him, he shouts, "That's just too tough!" But, of course, he is realistic with the cadets. He doesn't want to hurt them, or waste his own effort. So he always wins. "I am really happy in this game sometimes," he will admit. "One time I am really happy is when the last point is over in a tournament and I have won. Five minutes later, however, it's all gone."

He lifts the ball and hits a deep, flat serve at Graebner down the middle—too deep. Fault. He goes up to serve again, deciding, "I might try to fool him by hitting to the other side, even if I waste a point." He hits a slice so hard and with such sharp placement, close to the sideline, that the ball jumps cleanly past Graebner's racquet for a service ace. "Way to go, Art, baby," Ashe says to himself, and he walks to the umpire's chair and reaches for a cool, damp towel. Game to Lieutenant Ashe. He leads, seven games to six, second set.

"I don't know how deeply rooted Arthur's feelings are. I would guess they are getting deeper at the moment. He's going to be very wrapped up in civil rights. He's got to come through that first. The question is: Is he going to make a business out of civil rights, or is he going to be a businessman and give time to civil rights? Is he going to be a devotee of a belief, or is he going to attend to a business career? He works now, part time, for Philip Morris International—a job he got as a result of tennis. I got my job with Hobson Miller through tennis, but even without tennis I would have had a good job, through my background and social contacts. With his poor, liberal, Democratic background, he has to be always striving to get ahead, striving for recognition, and he is achieving something daily through his tennis conquests. I think he'll stay with Philip Morris. I think he's too selfish not to want to *be* somebody at the age of thirty-five. Of course, he's never going to be chairman of the board, or president. He'll be a brand manager, or a vice-president in charge of marketing, making fifty or sixty thousand a year. That's an easy way to go. It's a lot easier to make half a fortune than a whole fortune. Even though Arthur is well accepted in a place like Philip Morris, he's never going beyond that level. I accept Arthur any way, but many people don't. He's accepted only because he's a tennis player. If the West Side Tennis Club rejected Dr. Bunche, they're going to reject him. Meanwhile, he'll get married around age twenty-eight and have three kids. I think he's too smart to marry a white girl. That's a headache. If he marries a white girl, who's going to house him? He'll live in a very lovely residence somewhere, but I don't know where. I don't know where a Negro executive lives in New York. I don't even know. I don't know where they live. I just don't know."

"I think I might live in Europe for a while. In Spain or Sweden. I go out now and then with a Swedish tennis player. Her name is Ingrid. She really enjoys life. It's unbelievable. If two people are in love, they're cowards not to get married. In general, though, I lean toward a Negro girl. It's easier. I haven't the slightest idea what I am going to be doing twenty years from now. Graebner will still be in New York. His daughter and his son will have gone to the best private schools. His son will be at Princeton or Yale. Clark will be a member of the Knickerbocker Club, or one of those. He'll just be living the quiet, middle-class life. He'll be the president of that paper company if he tends to his knitting. I'll probably be something like Jackie Robinson, involved in business and politics. I'd like to be in business for myself. I have my hopes—for financial security, for three or four children. What else is there to life besides a family and financial security?"

"If I could, right now, I would join the Racquet Club or the River Club, but these things take time and can't be hurried. I don't want to be just a fifty-to-sixty-thousand-a-year man. I don't know if I'm shrewd, but if I see an opportunity I'll try to take advantage of it. If I had to bet on it, I would say I have a good opportunity to be a millionaire by forty, or perhaps even somewhere on the thirty-five-to-forty plateau. I'll be living in Manhattan, Greenwich, or Scarsdale then. My kids will have gone to Chapin, Spence, Trinity—the best schools—and on to Lawrenceville, Williams, Vassar, Northwestern. Carole will be active in the Junior League—that type of circle. I'll be the president of Hobson Miller and on the board of Saxon Industries, the mother company. I'll play tennis a little, and, hopefully, belong to the Racquet Club and the River Club. Hopefully, I will have made a lot of money. One thing I'll always try to do is keep religion in the forefront of the children's minds. That I regard as very, very important. If you lead the type of life that the Lord wants you to lead, He'll give to you. Things come to those who profess and believe."

Graebner, standing with Ashe by the umpire's chair while exchanging ends, rubs sawdust on his racquet handle to dry it and keep it from slipping in his grip. "Thank God I never have trouble with my handle," Ashe remarks, and returns to the court. Graebner eventually follows, and serves. The ball is too fast to be playable. Ashe gets his racquet on it but deflects it low, into the net. Fifteen-love.

Graebner serves wide. Ashe stretches to hit a crosscourt backhand. Graebner volleys from his own backhand—a deep, heavy ball. Ashe flips a lob into the air. Both players now make tactical errors. Graebner decides that the ball is on its way out, and fails to pick the overhead out of the air. The ball drops safely within the baseline, and Graebner desperately sprints around it and drives it with his backhand. Ashe, meanwhile, has watched all this in fascination and has forgotten to go to the net to position himself to destroy what has to be a vulnerable return. As it happens, though, Graebner's shot lands several inches out of bounds. "I'm one of the luckiest guys around," Ashe tells himself. Fifteen-all.

Graebner rocks and hits, and Ashe lets the serve go by. He thinks it ticked the cord and is a let. He waits for official confirmation of this, but none comes. The serve is an official ace. Thirty-fifteen.

Ashe says nothing, and walks to the other side of the court to await Graebner's next one. He sends it back down the line. Graebner, coming to the ball about a foot behind the service line, volleys it on his forehand— into the net. "Can you imagine *me* hitting a shot like that?" Graebner asks himself. "Lazy. Lazy. Bad volley. I was too far back. I should have been in another two feet." The set itself is now hanging on one or two threads. Graebner has the commanding advantage of the serve. Ashe has the unnerving advantage of being within two points of winning. The pressure is total in both directions. Graebner glances at his wife, Carole, who is sitting in the Marquee, a covered grandstand at the east end of the lawn. She is holding her fists up—a signal that means "Come on, now. This is a big point." Thirty-all.

Graebner rocks. Hits. Fault. He serves again, safely, in the middle of the box, and Ashe, who has not moved in on the serve, hits a backhand up the middle—so far so conservative on both sides of the net. Graebner half-volleys to Ashe, on the baseline, in the middle. Ashe loosens. He drives the ball to Graebner's forehand. Graebner punches back hard a volley down the line. Ashe is on it with speed, his racquet back. He hits a flippy backhand, acutely angled crosscourt, with lots of top spin and lots of risk. There is no possibility of Graebner's getting near it but every possibility that the shot will go out. It's a liner. It leaves chalk dust in the air. Ashe turns, in the cascade of applause for his sensationally incautious shot, and walks away from the court. He withdraws into himself, his back to the court and to Graebner. Thirty-forty. Set point.

"Look at him going away from the court, away from the situation," says Donald Dell. "Believe me, he never does that. He's nervous. Think of the pressure on him. And still he hits a shot like that one. That's why he's a great tennis player. It's like a pro quarterback when he is down six points, third and twenty on his own forty, forty-two seconds to go, and he throws a pass into the end zone. The big play at the right time. He not only tries it, he makes it."

Graebner hits his big serve to Ashe's forehand, and Ashe drives the ball into the umpire's chair. But the serve was a couple of inches out. Graebner serves again, and Ashe's low, underspun return drops in the service box. Graebner moves up and hits to Ashe's backhand. Ashe gets set to hit. He can do anything out of his backhand backswing, and now he seems to be preparing for a dink or a drop shot. But he is faking, to draw Graebner in. Graebner runs for the net. Ashe lobs. Graebner is moving one way and the ball, above him, is moving the other way. It drops fifteen inches inside the line. The set is over. The match is even.

"He fooled me completely. I had no idea," Graebner says to himself.

Ashe is saying to himself, "I think I'm going to win it all."

"A set apiece. I'm still in there," Graebner thinks. He looks worried.

Ashe bounces the ball ten times, while applause subsides, and then he pushes his glasses into place, lifts the ball, and hits an uncomplicated ace that splits the court. He hits another ace. And with four additional shots he wins the first game of the third set.

. . .

When Ashe's alarm clock sounds, he gets out of bed and, sleepily, invariably, says, "What's happening?" Sometimes he stumbles as he crosses the room, because any number of objects may be on the floor. There is always an open, half-filled suitcase somewhere. Tennis clothes fan out of it like laundry spread to dry. Racquets are all over the place, strung and unstrung—on the floor, on bookshelves, under the bed. "I hate orderliness," he will say. There are piles of unanswered letters. His conscience tells him to answer them all. Ripped envelopes are so numerous that they should probably be removed with a rake. There is a stack of copies of the Richmond *Afro-American*. Tennis trophies are here and there like unwashed dishes—West of England Lawn Tennis Championships; U.S. National Clay Court Men's Singles Winner 1967. His books are more or less concentrated on bookshelves, but some can also be found on or under every other piece of furniture in the room. They have accumulated during the time—fourteen months—he has been living in the Bachelor Officers' Quarters at the United States Military Academy. Under his bed is *Report of the National Advisory Commission on Civil Disorders*. On a chair near his pillow are *Fundamentals of Marketing* and *The Autobiography of Malcolm X*. Along the shelves go *Human Sexual Response*, *Black Power*, *Emily Post's Etiquette*, *Contract Bridge for Beginners*, *Ulysses*, *The Rise and Fall of the Third Reich*, *The Confessions of Nat Turner*, *The Human Factor in Changing Africa*, *Paper Lion*, *Mata Hari*, *Dynamic Speed Reading*, *The Naked Ape*, *The New York Times Guide to Personal Finance*, *Marketing Management, Analysis and Planning*, *A Short History of Religions*, *Elementary French*, *Spanish in Three Months*, *Aussie English*, and *U.S. Equal Employment Opportunity Commission Hearings—N.Y., N.Y. 1968*.

The Graebners' apartment, on East Eighty-sixth Street, is trim and orderly, with comfortable new, non-period furniture and a TV set that rolls on wheels. The apartment is a module many floors up in a modern concrete hive. The hall outside is narrow, and all the doors along it are made of hollow steel and have peepholes. Graebner has been reading *The Arrangement* ("just for trash"), *The Effective Executive* (because that is exactly what he would like to be), a biography of Richard Nixon, *The Rich and the Super-Rich*, *Airport* ("for more trash"), and *The Pro Quarterback*. Graebner is less verbal than Ashe. Graebner's language is casual and idiomatic. A word like "phraseology" will come out of him in four syllables, and if Ashe happens to hear it he is likely to call Graebner's attention to the error, for Ashe is meticulous about some things, and language is one. Ashe is very literal. In restaurants, for example, the Davis Cup Team trainer is forever asking waitresses for "diet sugar," and Ashe will say, "Diet *sugar?* Diet sweetener, maybe." He says he would like to write. Meanwhile, he does the *Times* crossword puzzle every day and drives himself crazy until he has it complete and correct. He calls up friends long distance to ask for help if he needs it. When they ask him why he does the crossword with such energy, he will say something like "I'm not sure. It may give me a false sense of intellectual security."

The door of Ashe's clothes closet is always open, and the light in there has been on for fourteen months. Love beads hang on a hook on the door. Ashe looks extremely contemporary when he goes off to New York for a date wearing the beads, a yellow turtleneck, and what he calls his "ru" jacket. More often, he just looks trim and conventional, like Graebner, in a business suit. In uniform, he is the model soldier—salutes and does all the things an officer is supposed to do. He seems to get pleasure out of it. It would probably be an exaggeration to say that he enjoys the West Point life, but he plays the game. He works hard when he is on the post. He gets up at seven and is at his desk by eight. Graebner works even harder. A million dollars must seem a long way off when you can't even get an American Express credit card. Graebner applied and was turned down, apparently on the ground of insufficient visible income—to the limitless amusement of all the other players on the Davis Cup Team. Ashe and Graebner are both extraordinarily conscious of the stock market, and each thinks he is a shrewd investor. An amateur tennis player at their level can have something to invest, since he can collect in expenses and sundry compensations as much as twenty thousand dollars a year. Ashe never misses the *Times'* stock-market quotations, and as his eye runs through them he says, "Too tough. . . . Fantastic. . . . Unbelievable." Graebner has three brokers. He describes them as "a conservative, a middle-of-the-roader, and a flier." The conservative is his mother's broker, in Cleveland. The middle-of-the-roader is a man in Richmond whom Graebner met on the tennis circuit. The flier was a friend of Graebner's at Northwestern and now works in New York for Smith, Barney & Co. When tennis takes Graebner to a place like Las Vegas or San Juan, he goes to the gaming tables and hangs on every roll of the dice as if he were in the semifinals of the United States Open Championships. Ashe is a few feet up the velvet, behaving the same way.

New balls come into the match. Graebner hits three unmanageable serves. He quickly raises the score to one–all, third set.

As amateurs, Ashe and Graebner qualify for none of the prize money that is available to professionals in this tournament. Noting this, an anonymous woman feels such pity for Ashe that she sends him a hundred shares of General Motors common. One evening, Graebner learns about it from Ashe.

"A *hundred* shares of General *Mo*tors!" Graebner says, and his vocal cords seem tight.

"That's right," Ashe tells him. "From an anonymous donor."

"White or Negro?"

"I don't know. She saw me play and felt sorry for me."

"How much is it a share—forty dollars?"

"Hell, no. Ninety-five."

"She gave you *nine thousand five hundred dollars?*"

"You better believe it."

"That's too tough. Why didn't she give it to me? I deserve it as much as you. You son of a bitch, you owe me four thousand seven hundred and fifty dollars."

Graebner appears to be somewhat tense under the pressure of not being able to do much against Ashe's serve, which is becoming perceptibly stronger. In the last ten games that Ashe has served, Graebner has won only nine scattered points. Ashe double-faults. Graebner looks happy. Ashe takes four straight points, including one on a loose, liberal, infuriating touch shot. Graebner mutters, "Arthur, you lucky bastard. How can you hit that shot?" Game to Lieutenant Ashe. He leads, two games to one. . . .

. . .

By the umpire's chair, Graebner unfolds a fresh towel, puts it in his pocket, rubs sawdust all over his racquet handle, returns to the court, and slams back Ashe's first two serves of the fourth set. Love-thirty. It is an inaccurately auspicious beginning, for Ashe now begins to hit shots as if God Himself had given them a written guarantee. He plays full, free, wind-milling tennis. He hits untouchable forty-five-degree volleys. He hits overheads that skid through no man's land and ricochet off the stadium wall. His backhands win everywhere—crosscourt, down the line—and one of them, a return of a second serve, is almost an exact repetition of the extraordinary shot that finished the third set. "When you're confident, you can do anything," Ashe tells himself. Both he and Graebner are, for the most part, hitting the ball even harder than they have been previously, and the average number of shots per point, which rose slightly in the second and third sets, is down again, to 2.5. Graebner is not in any sense out of the match. His serve seems stronger. His volleys are decisive. Ashe sends a big, flat serve down the middle, and Graebner, standing on the center mark, hits the ball off his forehand so hard that Ashe cannot get near it—an all but impossible shot from that position, requiring phenomenal power. Ashe serves again to Graebner's forehand. Graebner drives another hard return, and runs for the net. Ashe is now playing almost consistently on the level he stepped up to in the last three shots of the third set. Moving fast, he intercepts, and sends a light and graceful putaway past Graebner, down the line.

There are very few places in the world where Ashe feels at ease or at home. One, of course, is around his family's place in Gum Spring, Virginia, where the milieu he moves in is entirely black. His defenses are alert everywhere else he goes, with only four exceptions—Australia, the islands of the South Pacific, Sweden, and Spain. "A Negro draws stares in Australia, but you can pretty much tell they're not malicious. They only mean 'What the hell is *he* doing here?' I don't look like an aborigine. When I first played in Spain, I could tell by the way the Spanish tennis players acted that I had nothing to worry about. The Spaniards would just as soon hustle my sister, if I had one. They don't care. It's a great feeling to get away from all this crap in the United States. Mentally and spiritually, it's like taking a vacation. It's like going from New York to the black world of Richmond and Gum Spring. Your guard goes down. Everywhere else I go, my sensors are out. Everywhere. It's a waste of energy, but maybe I can do two things at one time—think about something else and have my sensors out, too."

In 1960, Arthur was sent to St. Louis for his senior year of high school, and it is generally assumed that this arrangement was made (by Dr. Johnson) because Arthur was not allowed to compete with white tennis players in Richmond. This was true but not relevant. By that time, there was no tennis player of any color in or near Richmond who could play points with him. Tennis is a game of levels, and it is practically impossible for a player who is on one level to play successfully with a player on any other. Arthur needed high-level competition the year around, and St. Louis was full of McKinleys and Buchholzes and indoor courts. There were a few problems. One young St. Louis tennis player took Arthur to a private tennis club one day that spring, and as Arthur was beginning to hit, a voice called out to him, "Hey, you! Get off there. We don't allow colored in this club." Arthur left. He was graduated from Sumner High School with the highest grades in his class. On the summer tennis circuit, he went to every length to attract no attention, to cause no difficulty. Moving in and out of expensive white atmospheres, he used the manners that his father and Dr. Johnson had taught him, and he noticed that the manners of the white players, and much of their general behavior, tended to suggest a lower standard. "When an experience is new, you're not sure of yourself mentally, but basic politeness got me through." Meanwhile, he would look down at his plate and find two steaks there. He knew what was happening. A message had come from the kitchen, on the Afro-American telegraph.

While he was at U.C.L.A., the level of his game became so high that he was made an honorary member of the Beverly Hills Tennis Club, where he played with people like Hank Greenberg and Charlton Heston. Of Heston he says, "He's not that coordinated. He plays tennis like he drives a chariot." Of Greenberg he says, "He's a tennis buff. He covers the court well. He's a big guy. A big, big guy. Jesus!" On a street in the Bronx, Ashe once played tennis with John Lindsay ("Good forehand"), and in the Washington ghetto he played with Bobby Kennedy ("Another good forehand"). In tennis, the nearest black was light-years below him now, and he became, in his own words, "a sociological phenomenon." He has been kept extremely busy on the U-Rent-a-Negro circuit. He has been invited to the White House four times. Only two years ago, he was very hesitant about walking into the dining room of the West Side Tennis Club, in Forest Hills. Sometimes when his phone rings in his rooms at West Point, he picks it up and an anonymous voice says to him, for instance, "You have your God-damned black nerve running around the country playing tennis while my son is fighting in Vietnam."

Ashe leads two games to one in the fourth set. He moves in on Graebner's second serve and tries one more backhand crosscourt megablast. Out. By inches. Fifteen-love.

Graebner's next serve is wide to Ashe's backhand. Ashe drives the ball down the line to Graebner's forehand, following to the net. Ashe admits to himself, "In effect, I'm saying to him, 'O.K., Clark, I can beat you on your forehand.' I'm being a little arrogant." Graebner catches the ball at the limit of his reach and sends back an unforceful volley. Ashe wipes the point away with his backhand. Fifteen-all.

Graebner's big serve goes down the middle. Ashe leaps for it and blocks it back. Graebner hits a low, underspun crosscourt backhand. Ashe runs to it and answers with a backhand even more acutely angled. Graebner has to dive for it, but he gets it, hitting a slow deep volley. Ashe, on the backhand again, drives the ball—much too fast to be contested—down the line. "Get in there!" he shouts, and the ball gets in there. Fifteen-thirty. Graebner thinks, "If I had his backhand and he had my forehand, we'd be invincible."

Ashe's forehand is something to see as it is. Graebner rocks, goes up, and—to Ashe's forehand—smashes the ball. Ashe slams it back through the service box and out the side of the court. "Most players hit a shot like that once in a lifetime," says Donald Dell. Fifteen-forty.

Ashe now has two chances to break Graebner. He looses a heavy backhand return, but Graebner stops it and hits it to the baseline. Ashe lobs. At the service line, Graebner moves in under the overhead and brings down the paper cutter. The shot goes within four feet of Ashe but is too powerful to be as much as touched. Thirty-forty.

Break point No. 2. Graebner rocks, and lifts the ball. Crunch. Unmanageable. Right down the middle. Deuce.

Graebner serves. Fault. Again. Double fault. Advantage Ashe.

Graebner faults once more, then hits a wide slice to Ashe's backhand. Ashe moves to it and explodes another all-time winner down the line. Game to Ashe. Games are three–one, fourth set. Graebner is broken.

Because Ashe is black, many people expect him to be something more than a tennis player—in fact, demand that he be a leader in a general way. The more he wins, the more people look to him for words and acts beyond the court. The black press has criticized him for not doing enough for the cause. He has repeatedly been asked to march and picket, and he has refused. Militant blacks have urged him to resign from the Davis Cup Team. Inevitably, they have called him an Uncle Tom. Once, in Milwaukee, he was asked to march with Stokely Carmichael but said no, and on the same day he visited a number of Milwaukee playgrounds, showing black children and white children how to play tennis. The demands of others have never moved him to do anything out of character. He will say what he thinks, though, if someone asks him. "Intrinsically, I disapprove of what black militants do. Human nature being what it is,

I can understand why they have such a strong following. If you had nothing going for you and you were just a black kid in a ghetto, you'd have historical momentum behind you and it would be chic to be a black militant—easy to do, very fashionable. You'd have your picture and name in the paper because you'd be screaming your head off. They sound like fire-and-brimstone preachers in Holy Roller churches. But you must listen to them. You can't completely ignore them. Their appeal is to the here and now. If I were a penniless junkie, I'd go for it, too. I'd have nothing to lose, nowhere to go but up. But you can't change people overnight. If you took a demographic survey of blacks, you'd find, I think, that the farther up the socio-economic scale you got, the fewer people would be behind Stokely. I'm not a marcher. I'm not a sign carrier. I'm a tennis player. If you are a leader in any field, and black, you are a hero to all blacks, and you are expected to be a leader in other fields. It's beautiful. People in Richmond look upon me as a leader whether I like it or not. That's the beautiful part of it. The other side of the coin is that they expect the same of some light-heavyweight boxer that they do of me. But he doesn't have my brain. *He* tries to get into politics, and we lose some leverage.

"Guerrilla warfare is going to start. Businesses will burn. There will be more riots. More nationally known political figures may be killed. But eventually more middle-class blacks will become involved in human rights. Extreme militants will lose their power and influence. So I am cautiously optimistic. I define the cause as the most good for the most people in the least amount of time, and that has absolutely nothing to do, specifically, with color. Anything I can do to help the cause is good. Nobody listens to a loser. If I put myself in a position where I can't compete, I am merely a martyr. We don't need any more martyrs right now. One must separate the emotional from the practical. Don't bite off more than you can chew. A little bit is better than nothing, no matter how you may feel. Progress and improvement do not come in big hunks, they come in little pieces, and the sooner people accept this the better off they'll be. I wouldn't tell my son to content himself that things will come gradually. You've got to push. You've got to act as though you expect it to come tomorrow. But when you know it's not going to come, don't give up. We're outnumbered ten to one. We'll advance by quiet negotiation and slow infiltration—and by objective, well-planned education, not an education in which you're brainwashed. Education reflects a culture's values. If that culture is warped, you get a warped education, with white

Janes and Dicks in the schoolbooks and white pale-faced guys who made history. There are so many insidious ways you can get brainwashed to think white equals good—white Howdy-Doody, white Captain Kangaroo. I didn't feel like a crusader once. I do now. I've always been fair with all people. I always wanted to be a solid citizen. I went to college. I graduated. I have put in time in the armed services. I treat all people equally—rich, poor, black, white. I am fairly generous. Nobody can find fault with that. But in the spirit of the times—in some people's eyes—I'm an Uncle Tom. The phrase is empty."

"His racquet is his bag," Ronald Charity's wife, Ruth, says. "Arthur has to fight in his own way." Arthur's sensors are still extremely active. He boils within when he hears a white man call him "boy" or "son." He says, "Do I look like your son?" He also can't stand blacks who tell him not to trust whites, and he says he feels sorry for Negroes who become upset when they see a Negro woman with a white man. At U.C.L.A., he was fond of a white girl, and he saw her with some frequency until her mother saw *him* on TV. He laughs out loud when he tells the story. "It's funny now," he says. "It stung then." He uses "black" and "Negro" interchangeably. In hotels, somewhat inconsistently, he often asks, "Where's the boy for the bag?" He thinks there is a certain inherent motor superiority in black athletes. "At an early age, we seem to be a little looser, a little more athletic than white kids. You go through Harlem and you'll see kids less than five feet tall with pretty good jump shots and hook shots. White kids that age don't have those shots." He is suspicious of Greek standards in art. He wonders where all the other races were when Polyclitus was shaping his canon. He urges white American friends to refresh their perspectives by living in Asia, he pays his annual dues to the National Association for the Advancement of Colored People, and he is not at all troubled by men like Alabama's George Wallace. "Wallace is beautiful. He's doing his own thing. He's actually got a little bit of soul. What I worry about is people who say one thing and do another. Wallace is in his bag, and he enjoys it." Ashe's particular hero is Jackie Robinson—"because of what he went through, the self-control, the perseverance." Asked if he has any white heroes, he says, "Yes, I have. John F. Kennedy, Robert Kennedy, Benjamin Franklin, and Pancho Gonzales."

Tilting forward, looking up, Ashe whips his racquet over the ball and aces Graebner with a sharp-angled serve. "I stood as far over as I possibly could and still he aced me," Graebner mumbles. Ashe misses his next first serve, then follows an American twist recklessly to the net. Graebner chips. Ashe hits the world's most unorthodox volley, on the dead run, drawing his racquet back all the way and smashing the ball out of the air, out of sight, with a full roundhouse swing. "He just pulls his racquet back and slaps," Clark's father comments, but there is only mild disparagement in the remark, for he adds, "That's what Laver does." (Before the year is out, Laver and Ashe will be ranked first and second in the world.) Ashe hits another wide serve—unmanageable. Donald Dell says, "Arthur is knocking the hell out of the ball." Graebner thinks, "He's smashing every God-damned first serve, and they're all going in." Ashe leads four games to one, fourth set. His game is so big now that it is beyond containment. There is something about it that suggests a very large aircraft beginning its descent for Kennedy. In Graebner remain sporadic aces.

Twenty-six hours hence, beside the Marquee, Dell, Pasarell, and Graebner will meet spontaneously, from separate parts of the stadium, and go to press-section seats, close to one end of the court. Their teammate will be in the fifth set of the finals, against the Dutch player Tom Okker, and they will help draw him through it—"Move your feet, Arthur." . . . "Bend your knees." . . . "Spin it." . . . "Chip the returns, Arthur." . . . "Get your first serve in." Graebner, Pasarell, and Dell will shout these things in moments when the crowd is clapping, because coaching from the grandstand is not strictly approved. When Ashe breaks through Okker's serve, in the fifth game, he will look up at the Davis Cup group and close his fist, and when the match is over he will turn, point up to them with the handle of his racquet, and bow to them, giving them something of his moment as the winner of the first United States Open Championship. "Subdued disbelief," in his words, is what he will feel, but he will speak with nonchalant clarity into microphones and he will put an arm around his weeping father. When he returns to the United States Military Academy, he will have dinner with the cadet corps, and all the cadets will stand up and cheer for him for three and a half minutes while he pushes his glasses into place and affectionately looks them over.

Meanwhile, he aces Graebner for the last time. Graebner looks at the ball as it goes by, watches it hit the stadium wall, shakes his head, then looks again at the empty air beside him where the ball was and thinks, "I can't believe he can hit it that hard. I didn't even *see* the ball. Arthur is just playing too well. He's forcing me into errors." Games are five–two, fourth set.

Graebner serves to Ashe's forehand. Ashe drives the ball up the middle. Graebner hits hard for Ashe's backhand corner, and misses. Love-fifteen.

Ashe chips a return into the net. Fifteen-all.

Ashe blocks another return into Graebner's forehand service court, and Graebner, rushing in, tries a drop half volley, the extraordinarily difficult shot that has almost been Ashe's signature in this match—that Ashe has scored with time after time. Graebner fails to make it good. He whips himself. "An unbelievable shot for me to try—difficult in the first place, and under this pressure ridiculous. Stupid." Fifteen-thirty.

Graebner now sends his farewell ace past Ashe. Crunch. Right down the middle. Thirty-all.

Graebner rocks, swings, hits. Fault. He lifts the ball again. Double fault. Thirty-forty.

"Match point," Ashe tells himself. "Now I'll definitely play it safe." But Graebner hits the big serve into the net, then hits his second serve to Ashe's backhand. The ball and the match are spinning into perfect range. Ashe's racquet is back. The temptation is just too great, and caution fades. He hits for it all. Game, set, match to Lieutenant Ashe. When the stroke is finished, he is standing on his toes, his arms flung open, wide, and high.

DAYS AND NIGHTS WITH THE UNBORED

Roger Angell

NOVEMBER 1, 1969 (WORLD SERIES 1969)

THE SERIES AND the season are over—four days done at this writing—and the Mets are still Champions of the World. Below midtown office windows, scraps and streamers of torn paper still litter the surrounding rooftops, sometimes rising and rearranging themselves in an autumn breeze. I just looked out, and they're still there. It's still true. The Mets won the National League's Eastern divisional title, and won it easily; they won the playoffs, beating the Atlanta Braves in three straight; they took the World Series—one of the finest Series of all time—beating the Orioles in five games. The Mets. The New York Mets? . . . This kind of disbelief, this surrendering to the idea of a plain miracle, is tempting but derogatory. If in the end we remember only a marvellous, game-saving outfield catch, a key hit dropped in, an enemy batter fanned in the clutch, and then the ridiculous, exalting joy of it all—the smoke bombs going off in the infield, the paper storm coming down and the turf coming up, and the clubhouse baptisms—we will have belittled the makers of this astonishment. To understand the achievement of these Mets, it is necessary to mount an expedition that will push beyond the games themselves, beyond the skill and the luck. The journey will end in failure, for no victorious team is entirely understandable, even to itself, but the attempt must always be made, for winning is the ultimate mystery that gives all sport its meaning. On the night of September 24th, when the Mets clinched their divisional title,

Manager Gil Hodges sat in his clubhouse office after the game and tried to explain the season. He mentioned good pitching, fine defense, self-reliance, momentum, and a sense of team confidence. The reporters around his desk nodded and made notes, but they all waited for something more. From the locker room next door came a sharp, heady whiff of sloshed champagne and the cries of exultant young athletes. Then someone said, "Gil, how did it all happen? Tell us what it all *proves*."

Hodges leaned back in his chair, looked at the ceiling, and then spread his large hands wide. "Can't be done," he said, and he laughed.

Disbelief persists, then, and one can see now that disbelief itself was one of the Mets' most powerful assets all through the season. Again and again this summer, fans or friends sitting next to me in the stands at Shea Stadium would fill out their scorecards just before game time and then turn and shake their heads and say, "There is no way—just *no* way—the Mets can take this team tonight." I would compare the two lineups and agree. And then, later in the evening or at breakfast the next morning, I would think back on the game—another game won by the Mets, and perhaps another series swept—and find it hard to recall just how they *had* won it, for there was still no way, *no* way, it could have happened. Finally, it began to occur to me that if my friends and I, partisans all, felt like this, then how much more profoundly those other National League teams, deeper in talent and power and reputation than the Mets, must have felt it. For these were still the Mets—the famous and comical losers, ninth-place finishers last year, a team that had built a fortune and a following out of defeat and perversity, a team that had lost seven hundred and thirty-seven games in seven years and had finished a total of two hundred and eighty-eight and a half games away from first place. No way, and yet it happened and went on happening. . . .

. . .

The playoffs—the television-enriching new autumn adjunct known officially as the Championship Series—matched up the Orioles and the Minnesota Twins, and the Mets and the Atlanta Braves, who had barely escaped the horrid possibility of three-way or four-way pre-playoff play-offs with the Dodgers, Giants, and Cincinnati Reds in the National League West. Atlanta filled its handsome white stadium to capacity for its two weekend games against New York, but to judge from the local headlines, the transistor-holders in the stands, the television interviews with Georgia coaches, and the high-school band and majorettes that performed each morning in the lobby of the Regency Hyatt House hotel, autumn baseball was merely a side attraction to another good old Deep South football weekend. Georgia beat South Carolina, 41–16; Clemson beat Georgia Tech, 21–10; the Colts beat the Falcons, 21–14; and the Mets beat the Braves, 9–5 and 11–6. The cover of the official program for the baseball games displayed a photograph of the uniformed leg of an Atlanta Brave descending from an LM onto a home plate resting on the moon, with the legend "One Step for the Braves, One Giant Leap for the Southeast," but Manager Hodges saw to it that the astronaut never got his other foot off the ladder. Not wanting to lose his ace in the significant first game, he kept Tom Seaver on the mound for seven innings, while Seaver absorbed an uncharacteristic eight-hit, five-run pounding. Tom plugged away, giving up homers and doubles, and resolutely insisting in the dugout that the Mets were going to win it. The lead changed hands three times before this finally happened, in the eighth, when the Mets scored five times off Phil Niekro on three successive hits, a gift stolen base, a fearful throwing error by Orlando Cepeda, and a three-run pinch single by J. C. Martin. The next day's match was just as sloppy. The Braves scored five runs with two out in the fifth, all off Koosman and all too late, since the Mets had already run up a 9–1 lead. Hank Aaron hit his second homer in two days, Agee and Jones and Boswell hit homers for the Mets, and the Braves left for Shea Stadium with the almost occult accomplishment of having scored eleven runs off Seaver and Koosman without winning either game.

Hodges, having demonstrated slow managing in the first game, showed how to manage fast in the last one. His starter, Gary Gentry, who had given up a two-run homer to the unquenchable Aaron in the first inning, surrendered a single and a double (this also by Aaron) in the third, and then threw a pitch to Rico Carty that the Atlanta outfielder bombed off the left-field wall on a line but about two feet foul. Hodges, instantly taking the new ball away from Gentry, gave it to Nolan Ryan, in from the bullpen, who thereupon struck out Carty with one pitch, walked Cepeda intentionally, fanned Clete Boyer, and retired Bob Didier on a fly. Agee responded in obligatory fashion, smashing the first pitch to him in the same inning for a homer, and Ken Boswell came through with a two-run job in the fourth, to give the Mets the lead. Cepeda, who so far had spent the series lunging slowly and unhappily at Met singles and doubles buzzing past him at first, then hit a home run well beyond the temporary stands behind the left-center-field fence, making it 4–3, Braves. Even he must have sensed by then what would happen next: Ryan, a .103 hitter, singled to lead off the home half; Garrett, who had hit but one home run all year, hit another into the right-field loges, for two runs; Jones and Boswell and Grote and Harrelson and Agee combined to fashion two insurance runs; Ryan fanned seven Braves in all, and won by 7–4. Just about everybody got into the act in the end—the turf-moles onto the field again, Nolan Ryan and Garrett under the kliegs, and Mayor Lindsay under the champagne. Forehandedly, he had worn a drip-dry.

. . .

After a season of such length and so many surprises, reason suggested that we would now be given a flat and perhaps one-sided World Series, won by the Orioles, who had swept their three playoff games with the Minnesota Twins, and whom reporters were calling the finest club of the decade. There would be honor enough for the Mets if they managed only to keep it close. None of this happened, of course, and the best news— the one *true* miracle—was not the Mets' victory but the quality of those five games. They added up to a baseball drama I have not seen surpassed in thirty-seven years of watching—an assemblage of brilliant parables illustrating every varied aspect of the beautiful game.

The Baltimore fans expected neither of these possibilities, for there were still plenty of tickets on sale before the opener at Memorial Stadium, and the first two Series games were played to less than capacity crowds. This is explicable only when one recalls that two other league champions from Baltimore—the football Colts and the basketball Bullets—had been humiliated by New York teams in post-season championships this year. Baltimore, in fact, is a city that no longer expects *any* good news. In the press box, however, the announcement of the opening lineups was received in predictable fashion ("Just *no* way . . ."), and I could only agree. The Orioles, who had won a hundred and nine games in the regular season, finishing nineteen games ahead of the next team and clinching their divisional title on September 13th, were a poised and powerful veteran team that topped the Mets in every statistic and, man for man, at almost every position. Their three sluggers—Frank Robinson, Boog Powell, and Paul Blair—had hit a total of ninety-five homers, as against the Mets' *team* total of a hundred and nine. Their pitching staff owned a lower earned-run average than the Mets' sterling corps. Their ace, screwballer Mike Cuellar, had won twenty-three games and led the staff in strikeouts; their second starter, Dave McNally, had won

ven games in a row this year; the third man, Jim Palmer, had a record
-4, including a no-hitter. Since Cuellar and McNally are left-
, Hodges was forced to start his righty specialists (Clendenon,
Swoboda, and Weis) and bench the hot left-handed hitters
, Garrett, Shamsky, and Boswell) who had so badly damaged
st *no* way.

n seemed instantaneous when Don Buford, the minia-
ft fielder, hit Seaver's second pitch of the game over the
st above Swoboda's leap. (Swoboda said later that his
ball "at my apogee.") For a while after that, Seaver
much more strongly than he had in Atlanta, in
n the Baltimore fourth the steam suddenly went

in
came
It was

but ab-
with a
his year.
, was in
with his
He was
o Orioles,
ly, cross-
ding with
ll the way
bing of his
try walked
. Paul Blair
ok wing for
idding dive
. The entire
outing trib-
, more accu-
ommie Agee.
in deep trou-

time the early
to the visitors'
in two weeks,
eaver, trying to
had scored only
ejected from the

Orioles racked up three more runs. The game,
3uford, or to the other Oriole hitters, or to
son, the perennial All-Star Baltimore third
ll a continuous lesson in how the position
e beginning, I became aware of the pres
d batter with his aggressive stance (the
der his chin), his closeness to the plate,
is almost supernaturally quick reactions
mbidextrous; he bats and throws right-
-pong, and fields blue darters with his
s on a tough, deep chance that leaped
after the Mets had scored once on a
he rally when he sprinted in toward
it up barehanded, and got off the
hy yards. The Orioles won, 4–1,
hem.

Frank Robinson had baited them
ence in their dugout), and they
oks Robinson went on making
v—an extraordinary catch and
rtstop Mark Belanger, a base-
. (The tensions of the season
ed and sixty-eight to a hun-
1–0, on Donn Clendenon's
, and Baltimore had no hits
venth, when Paul Blair led
ond on a change-up curve,

and Brooks Robinson scored him with a single up the mi
seemed only to make the crowd more apprehensive, and t
partisans seemed unamused when a large "LET'S GO, METS
peared in the aisle behind home plate; it was carried by four
Mesdames Pfeil, Dyer, Ryan, and Seaver, smashers all, wh
the night before out of a Sheraton bed-sheet. There were t
top of the ninth before the Mets could act on this R.S.V.P.
game on successive singles by Charles and Grote, and a fir
left by the .215 terror, Al Weis. Koosman, throwing mostly
late going, walked two Orioles in the bottom half, but Ror
in to get the last out and save Jerry's two-hit, 2–1, essential
a game that would have delighted John McGraw.

Back at Shea Stadium, before an uncharacteristically el
solutely jam-packed audience, Tommie Agee rocked Jim
lead-off first-inning homer—Agee's fifth such discouragen
Gary Gentry, who had taken such a pounding from the
fine form this time, challenging the big Baltimore slug
hummer and comforted by a 3–0 lead after the second in
further comforted in the fourth, when Tommie Agee, wit
aboard, ran for several minutes toward deep left and
handed, pulled down Elrod Hendricks' drive just before
the fence. Agee held on to the ball, though, and carried
back to the infield like a trophy, still stuck in the topmost
glove. It was 4–0 for the home side by the seventh, when
the bases full with two out and was succeeded by Nolan Ry
hit his 0–2 pitch on a line to distant right. Three Orioles
the plate, but Agee, running to his left this time, made a
just at the warning track and again came up with the ba
crowd—all 56,335 of us—jumped to its feet in astonished,
ute as he trotted off the field. The final score was 5–0,
rately, 5–5—five runs for the Mets, five runs saved by
Almost incidentally, it seemed, the Orioles were suddenly
ble in the Series.

It was Cuellar and Seaver again the next day, and this
homer was provided by Donn Clendenon—a lead-off sho
bullpen in the second. Seaver, who had not pitched wel
was at last back in form, and Baltimore manager Earl W
rattle him and to arouse his own dormant warriors, who
one run in the past twenty-four innings, got himself

fifteen games in a row this year; the third man, Jim Palmer, had a record of 16–4, including a no-hitter. Since Cuellar and McNally are left-handers, Hodges was forced to start his righty specialists (Clendenon, Charles, Swoboda, and Weis) and bench the hot left-handed hitters (Kranepool, Garrett, Shamsky, and Boswell) who had so badly damaged the Braves. Just *no* way.

Confirmation seemed instantaneous when Don Buford, the miniature Baltimore left fielder, hit Seaver's second pitch of the game over the right-field fence, just above Swoboda's leap. (Swoboda said later that his glove just ticked the ball "at my apogee.") For a while after that, Seaver did better—pitched much more strongly than he had in Atlanta, in fact—but with two out in the Baltimore fourth the steam suddenly went out of his fastball, and the Orioles racked up three more runs. The game, however, belonged not to Buford, or to the other Oriole hitters, or to Cuellar, but to Brooks Robinson, the perennial All-Star Baltimore third baseman, who was giving us all a continuous lesson in how the position can be played. Almost from the beginning, I became aware of the pressure he puts on a right-handed batter with his aggressive stance (the hands are cocked up almost under his chin), his closeness to the plate, his eager appetite for the ball. His almost supernaturally quick reactions are helped by the fact that he is ambidextrous; he bats and throws right-handed, but eats, writes, plays ping-pong, and fields blue darters with his left. In the fifth, he retired Al Weis on a tough, deep chance that leaped up and into his ribs. In the seventh, after the Mets had scored once on a pair of singles and a fly, he crushed the rally when he sprinted in toward Rod Gaspar's topped roller, snatched it up barehanded, and got off the throw, overhand, that retired Gaspar by yards. The Orioles won, 4–1, and Brooks had made it look easy for them.

The Mets were grim the next day (Frank Robinson had baited them after their loss, commenting on the silence in their dugout), and they played a grim, taut, riveting game. Brooks Robinson went on making fine plays, but he had plenty of company—an extraordinary catch and falling throw to second by Baltimore shortstop Mark Belanger, a base-robbing grab by gaunt little Bud Harrelson. (The tensions of the season had burned Harrelson down from a hundred and sixty-eight to a hundred and forty-five pounds.) The Mets led, 1–0, on Donn Clendenon's wrong-field homer off McNally in the fourth, and Baltimore had no hits at all off Koosman until the bottom of the seventh, when Paul Blair led off with a single. Two outs later, Blair stole second on a change-up curve, and Brooks Robinson scored him with a single up the middle. The tie seemed only to make the crowd more apprehensive, and the Baltimore partisans seemed unamused when a large "LET'S GO, METS!" banner appeared in the aisle behind home plate; it was carried by four Met wives—Mesdames Pfeil, Dyer, Ryan, and Seaver, smashers all, who had made it the night before out of a Sheraton bed-sheet. There were two out in the top of the ninth before the Mets could act on this R.S.V.P., winning the game on successive singles by Charles and Grote, and a first-pitch hit to left by the .215 terror, Al Weis. Koosman, throwing mostly curves in the late going, walked two Orioles in the bottom half, but Ron Taylor came in to get the last out and save Jerry's two-hit, 2–1, essential victory. It was a game that would have delighted John McGraw.

Back at Shea Stadium, before an uncharacteristically elegant but absolutely jam-packed audience, Tommie Agee rocked Jim Palmer with a lead-off first-inning homer—Agee's fifth such discouragement this year. Gary Gentry, who had taken such a pounding from the Braves, was in fine form this time, challenging the big Baltimore sluggers with his hummer and comforted by a 3–0 lead after the second inning. He was further comforted in the fourth, when Tommie Agee, with two Orioles aboard, ran for several minutes toward deep left and finally, cross-handed, pulled down Elrod Hendricks' drive just before colliding with the fence. Agee held on to the ball, though, and carried it all the way back to the infield like a trophy, still stuck in the topmost webbing of his glove. It was 4–0 for the home side by the seventh, when Gentry walked the bases full with two out and was succeeded by Nolan Ryan. Paul Blair hit his 0–2 pitch on a line to distant right. Three Orioles took wing for the plate, but Agee, running to his left this time, made a skidding dive just at the warning track and again came up with the ball. The entire crowd—all 56,335 of us—jumped to its feet in astonished, shouting tribute as he trotted off the field. The final score was 5–0, or, more accurately, 5–5—five runs for the Mets, five runs saved by Tommie Agee. Almost incidentally, it seemed, the Orioles were suddenly in deep trouble in the Series.

It was Cuellar and Seaver again the next day, and this time the early homer was provided by Donn Clendenon—a lead-off shot to the visitors' bullpen in the second. Seaver, who had not pitched well in two weeks, was at last back in form, and Baltimore manager Earl Weaver, trying to rattle him and to arouse his own dormant warriors, who had scored only one run in the past twenty-four innings, got himself ejected from the game in the third for coming onto the field to protest a called strike. Weaver had a longish wait in his office before his sacrifice took effect, but in the top of the ninth, with the score still 1–0 and the tension at Shea nearly insupportable, Frank Robinson and Boog Powell singled in succession. Brooks Robinson then lined into an out that tied the game but simultaneously won the World Series for the Mets. It was a low, sinking drive, apparently hit cleanly through between Agee and right fielder Ron Swoboda. Ron, who was playing in close, hoping for a play at the plate, took three or four lunging steps to his right, dived onto his chest, stuck out his glove, caught the ball, and then skidded on his face and rolled completely over; Robinson scored, but that was all. This marvel settled a lengthy discussion held in Gil Hodges' office the day before, when Gil and several writers had tried to decide whether Agee's first or second feat was the finest Series catch of all time. Swoboda's was. Oh, yes—the Mets won the game in the tenth, 2–1, when Grote doubled and his runner, Rod Gaspar, scored all the way from second on J. C. Martin's perfect pinch bunt, which relief pitcher Pete Richert picked up and threw on a collision course with Martin's left wrist. My wife, sitting in the upper left-field stands, could not see the ball roll free in the glazy, late-afternoon dimness and thought that Martin's leaping dance of joy on the base path meant that he had suddenly lost his mind.

So, at last, we came to the final game, and I don't suppose many of us who had watched the Mets through this long and memorable season much doubted that they would win it, even when they fell behind, 0–3, on home runs hit by Dave McNally and Frank Robinson off Koosman in the third inning. Jerry steadied instantly, allowing only one single the rest of the way, and the Orioles' badly frayed nerves began to show when they protested long and ineffectually about a pitch in the top of the sixth that they claimed had hit Frank Robinson on the leg, and just as long and as ineffectually about a pitch in the bottom of the sixth that they claimed had *not* hit Cleon Jones on the foot. Hodges produced this second ball from his dugout and invited plate umpire Lou DiMuro to inspect a black scuff on it. DiMuro examined the mark with the air of a Maigret and proclaimed it the true Shinola, and a minute later Donn Clendenon damaged another ball by hitting it against the left-field façade for a two-run homer. Al Weis, again displaying his gift for modest but perfect contingency, hit his very first Shea Stadium homer to lead off the seventh and tie up the game, and the Mets won it in the eighth on doubles by Jones and Swoboda and a despairing but perfectly understandable Oriole double error at first base, all good for two runs and the famous 5–3 final victory.

. . .

I had no answer for the question posed by that youngster in the infield who held up—amid the crazily leaping crowds, the showers of noise and paper, the vermillion smoke-bomb clouds, and the vanishing lawns—a sign that said "WHAT NEXT?" What was past was good enough, and on my way down to the clubhouses it occurred to me that the Mets had won this great Series with just the same weapons they had employed all summer—with the Irregulars (Weis, Clendenon, and Swoboda had combined for four homers, eight runs batted in, and an average of .400); with fine pitching (Frank Robinson, Powell, and Paul Blair had been held to one homer, one RBI, and an average of .163); with defensive plays that some of us would remember for the rest of our lives; and with the very evident conviction that the year should not be permitted to end in boredom. Nothing was lost on this team, not even an awareness of the accompanying sadness of the victory—the knowledge that adulation and money and the winter disbanding of this true club would mean that the young Mets were now gone forever. In the clubhouse (Moët et Chandon this time), Ron Swoboda said it precisely for the TV cameras: "This is the first time. Nothing can ever be as sweet again."

Later, in his quiet office, Earl Weaver was asked by a reporter if he hadn't thought that the Orioles would hold on to their late lead in the last game and thus bring the Series back to Baltimore and maybe win it there. Weaver took a sip of beer and smiled and said, "No, that's what you can never do in baseball. You can't sit on a lead and run a few plays into the line and just kill the clock. You've got to throw the ball over the goddam plate and give the other man his chance. That's why baseball is the greatest game of them all."

PART SEVEN

CRITICS

A NOTE BY ADAM GOPNIK

Two arcs of ambition, both still very much in motion today, arrived in *New Yorker* criticism in the 1960s. First, its brow got pushed ever higher, taking in erudite and even academic voices and manners. What twenty years earlier would have been seen as material for *The Partisan Review* became, in the sixties, material for the one-time "comic weekly," as a Harold Rosenberg or a Hannah Arendt found a home in the magazine's pages.

The other phenomenon, one set seemingly at right angles, though in truth part of the same process, was that the magazine became ever more attentive to pop culture, its pleasures and its discontents. If the "middle-brow" was the great problem of the fifties—how to respond to the spread of high art previously limited to a self-approving, educated audience—the "pop" question had the same force in the sixties: how could you talk intelligently about television and the movies and, above all, the new rock music? The question wasn't treating them with seriousness. The trick was finding the right kind of seriousness to treat them with.

And so the tone of our shared sentences—most of what really matters in criticism—became oddly both more polemical and more personal. It became more polemical because there were now arguments to make rather than just attitudes to register; more personal because the only way to give those arguments the shapeliness and grace demanded by a magazine always meant to be read for pleasure in the first instance was to find ways to fill them with "voice," personal address. Both new sounds captured a sense that the stakes mattered more than before. So we found passionate polemics, making the case against passionate polemics, or both sides of the case for sex onstage made by competing critics, with our own Brendan Gill taking on our own Kenneth Tynan over *Oh! Calcutta!*

The newly arrived movie critic Pauline Kael brought the most influential and distinctive voice to emerge in that decade, and her work, re-

read, continues to prove that a great critic can be interesting about anything while being wrong about everything. Though she went after *Butch Cassidy and the Sundance Kid* with a hatchet, it remains a legendary entertainment even today. Still, her tone taught a generation a new way to argue over such things: passionately, intelligently, unfairly, at length.

Rock music was the great event of the time, but it was not the only event: we can read both Whitney Balliett's matchlessly precise registry of the sounds of jazz at sunset—a vibraphone that "suggests a bedspring swinging in the wind"—and Ellen Willis's hyper-astute analysis of the coming of age of rock music, a piece whose first sentence includes, significantly, the word "sociology." (Rock was not all sociology, but the social life of rock, she knew, was a huge part of its artistic presence.)

In the midst of it all, John Updike kept his almost unreal charm and almost Shakespearean serenity of tone. Yet the charm and serenity did not conceal his increasing seriousness of purpose. The light poet who had written in the fifties of usherettes and Harry Truman here began to take on, one by one, the austere masters of modernism and what was only becoming to be known as postmodernism, where "literature—that European empire augmented with translations from remote kingdoms—is now the only world capable of housing and sustaining new literature." If literature were to be locked forever in that hall of mirrors, what might happen to criticism? Well, the best of it reminds us that criticism remained in the sixties, as before, just writing, with the same difficulties, and the same delights.

THE CURRENT CINEMA

ROGER ANGELL

ALL HOMAGE

FEBRUARY 11, 1961 (*BREATHLESS*)

I N AN ART medium whose potentials appear to be almost continuously beyond the reach of its practitioners, a masterwork is likely to be handicapped by excessive praise. Since there is no help for this that I can see, I must risk injuring a French film called *Breathless* (created by the New Wave director Jean-Luc Godard) by saying quickly that it is far and away the most brilliant, most intelligent, and most exciting movie I have encountered this season. Its virtues are so numerous and so manifest that I am confident not only that it will survive the small burden of my superlatives but that it will be revisited almost instantly by many of its viewers, that it will be imitated endlessly, and probably ineptly, by dozens of filmmakers, and that it may even threaten the Kennedys as the warmest topic of local conversation for weeks to come.

The adventurous, almost inconsequential story of *Breathless* deals with a Parisian cool cat who steals cars for a living. In the short time span of the movie, he murders a policeman and begins a casual, painfully erratic flight from the authorities, in the course of which he attempts to collect a shady debt, offhandedly commits a mugging and two or three car thefts, and recommences a love affair with a pretty but equally unadmirable American girl, who betrays him to the police. Lacking even the tiny moral energy to attempt escape, he is shot down, and the film ends. This, of course, sounds like a routine *policier,* but it is immediately evident that M. Godard and his associates have something vastly more fascinating in mind, which is nothing less than to make comprehensible, and therefore touching and serious, the lives of two disorderly, disconnected, nihilistic young moderns—and to do so, moreover, by seeing and hearing their unlovely world with exactly the same nervous glances and flighty inattentiveness that they themselves must rely on. To say that the film almost entirely succeeds in this awesome undertaking may explain why, in my estimation, it achieves the heights and confirms the men of the New Wave as the makers of a powerful new tradition in the art of the film.

The camera in *Breathless,* which was wielded by Raoul Coutard, is jumpy, fluid, irritable, and comic—alive with glimpses, sudden turns, rude stares, and angry changes of mood. It moves in and about the boulevards and side streets and bars and bedrooms of Paris, pausing to glance at every distraction and ridiculous detail with which city people fill their days. The microphone is equally irresponsible, picking up horns, sirens, scraps of music, and fragments of conversation that add marvellously to the tone and excitement of the movie. It must not be surmised from this that the film depends on the kind of artificial rapid-fire action and cutting that sustain most contemporary screen adventures. The most important and astonishing passage in *Breathless* is a slow, incredibly protracted bedroom scene between the two lovers that is built out of pauses, non sequiturs, cigarettes, heart-breakingly intimate games, tiny cruelties, revelations, and small talk about death, automobiles, childhood, books, phonograph records, sex, and loneliness. At the end of this, we have not simply "understood" the murderer and his girl for the self-destructive, attractive, and frightening narcissists that they are; we have, to a large degree, *become* them, because the scene has been allowed to continue so long that it has taken us into its own time and pace, and we can no more believe of the film than we can of life itself that it is moving toward some known, prearranged ending.

The risk this kind of movie runs is that of succumbing to mere flashiness, and *Breathless* avoids this only by the skin of its teeth. What saves it is the sensitivity and perception of its script (written by M. Godard), particularly in the closing moments, when the girl reports her lover to the police for no intelligible reason, and he, instead of taking to his heels, bemusedly announces that prison might be an experience as valid as any other, and so awaits his destruction with a detached, chilling curiosity. Here and in the conversation that follows—an overlapping double monologue in which the two of them can only talk about their own feelings—we comprehend the egotism of their sexual attraction and the extent of their unconscious commitment to any violent emotion for its own sake. I cannot conceive of a clearer, more intuitive delineation of the kind of icy animalism that apparently infects so many of our young and terrifies so many of the rest of us.

M. Godard, who is thirty, is the newest of the *nouvelle-vague* directors, and *Breathless* is his first full-length film. His genius was recognized by two better-known members of the group—François Truffaut, who made the estimable *The 400 Blows,* and Claude Chabrol—after they had seen several short films he had made, and they offered their own services (Truffaut by writing the original story and Chabrol by supervising the production) in order to lure him into attempting *Breathless.* It would be presumptuous of me to congratulate any of these gentlemen for this dedicated collaboration, but it is pleasant to be able to report that *À Bout de Souffle* (as the movie was called in its native tongue) has been a financial as well as an artistic triumph in France, and that M. Godard is now the most discussed and sought-after director in Europe.

Another new celebrity created by this movie is Jean-Paul Belmondo, who plays the unhappy thief in this, his first film role. A former prizefighter, with a thick, wonderfully battered face, he is a born actor who manages, without drawing a visible deep breath, all the lightning changes—from arrogance to humor to insouciant stupidity to childlike innocence—that his huge part demands. The American is played by Jean Seberg, and I must report that I am unable to decide whether she acts beautifully or not at all. Her role requires her to be pretty, wooden, and apparently entranced by her own confusions, and Miss Seberg is all of these and no more. In any case, both of these young people and their hopeless plight are now so permanently fixed in my mind that they must be accepted as full partners in this masterpiece, and to them and to M. Godard I offer my distinguished homages.

PENELOPE GILLIATT

AFTER MAN

APRIL 13, 1968 (*2001: A SPACE ODYSSEY*)

I THINK STANLEY KUBRICK'S *2001: A Space Odyssey* is some sort of great film, and an unforgettable endeavor. Technically and imaginatively, what he put into it is staggering: five years of his life; his novel and screenplay, with Arthur C. Clarke; his production, his direction, his special effects; his humor and stamina and particular disquiet. The film is not only hideously funny—like *Dr. Strangelove*—about human speech and response at a point where they have begun to seem computerized, and where more and more people sound like recordings left on while the soul is out. It is also a uniquely poetic piece of sci-fi, made by a man who truly possesses the drives of both science and fiction.

Kubrick's tale of quest in the year 2001, which eventually takes us to the moon and Jupiter, begins on prehistoric Earth. Tapirs snuffle over the Valhalla landscape, and a leopard with broken-glass eyes guards the carcass of a zebra in the moonlight. Crowds of apes, scratching and ganging up, are disturbingly represented not by real animals, like the others, but by actors in costume. They are on the brink of evolving into men, and the overlap is horrible. Their stalking movements are already exactly ours: an old tramp's, drunk, at the end of his tether and fighting mad. Brute fear has been refined into the infinitely more painful human capacity for dread. The creatures are so nearly human that they have religious impulses. A slab that they suddenly come upon sends them into panicked reverence as they touch it, and the film emits a colossal sacred din of chanting. The shock of faith boots them forward a few thousand years, and one of the apes, squatting in front of a bed of bones, picks up his first weapon. In slow motion, the hairy arm swings up into an empty frame and then down again, and the smashed bones bounce into the air. What makes him do it? Curiosity? What makes people destroy anything, or throw away the known, or set off in spaceships? To see what Nothing feels like, driven by some bedrock instinct that it is time for something else? The last bone thrown in the air is matched, in the next cut, to a spaceship at the same angle. It is now 2001. The race has survived thirty-three years more without extinction, though not with any growth of spirit. There are no Negroes in this vision of America's space program; conversation with Russian scientists is brittle with mannerly terror, and the Chinese can still be dealt with only by pretending they're not there. But technological man has advanced no end. A space way station shaped like a Ferris wheel and housing a hotel called the Orbiter Hilton hangs off the pocked old cheek of Earth. The sound track, bless its sour heart, meanwhile thumps out "The Blue Danube," to confer a little of the courtliness of bygone years on space. The civilization that Kubrick sees coming has the brains of a nuclear physicist and the sensibility of an airline hostess smiling through an oxygen-mask demonstration.

Kubrick is a clever man. The grim joke is that life in 2001 is only faintly more gruesome in its details of sophisticated affluence than it is now. When we first meet William Sylvester as a space scientist, for instance, he is in transit to the moon, via the Orbiter Hilton, to investigate another of the mysterious slabs. The heroic man of intellect is given a nice meal on the way—a row of spacecraft foods to suck through straws out of little plastic cartons, each decorated with a picture of sweet corn, or whatever, to tell him that sweet corn is what he is sucking. He is really going through very much the same ersatz form of the experience of being well looked after as the foreigner who arrives at an airport now with a couple of babies, reads in five or six languages on luggage carts that he is welcome, and then finds that he has to manage his luggage and the babies without actual help from a porter. The scientist of 2001 is only more inured. He takes the inanities of space personnel on the chin. "Did you have a pleasant flight?" Smile, smile. Another smile, possibly pre-filmed, from a girl on a television monitor handling voice-print identification at Immigration. The Orbiter Hilton is decorated in fresh plumbing-white, with magenta armchairs shaped like pelvic bones scattered through it. Artificial gravity is provided by centrifugal force; inside the rotating Ferris wheel people have weight. The architecture gives the white floor of the Orbiter Hilton's conversation area quite a gradient, but no one lets slip a sign of humor about the slant. The citizens of 2001 have forgotten how to joke and resist, just as they have forgotten how to chat, speculate, grow intimate, or interest one another. But otherwise everything is splendid. They lack the mind for acknowledging that they have managed to diminish outer space into the ultimate in humdrum, or for dealing with the fact that they are spent and insufficient, like the apes.

The film is hypnotically entertaining, and it is funny without once being gaggy, but it is also rather harrowing. It is as eloquent about what is missing from the people of 2001 as about what is there. The characters seem isolated almost beyond endurance. Even in the most absurd scenes, there is often a fugitive melancholy—as astronauts solemnly watch themselves on homey B.B.C. interviews seen millions of miles from Earth, for instance, or as they burn their fingers on their space meals, prepared with the utmost scientific care but a shade too hot to touch, or as they plod around a centrifuge to get some exercise, shadowboxing alone past white coffins where the rest of the crew hibernates in deep freeze. Separation from other people is total and unmentioned. Kubrick has no characters in the film who are sexually related, nor any close friends. Communication is stuffy and guarded, made at the level of men together on committees or of someone being interviewed. The space scientist telephones his daughter by television for her birthday, but he has nothing to say, and his wife is out; an astronaut on the nine-month mission to Jupiter gets a pre-recorded TV birthday message from his parents. That's the sum of intimacy. No enjoyment—only the mechanical celebration of the anniversaries of days when the race perpetuated itself. Again, another astronaut, played by Keir Dullea, takes a considerable risk to try to save a fellow-spaceman, but you feel it hasn't anything to do with affection or with courage. He has simply been trained to save an expensive colleague by a society that has slaughtered instinct. Fortitude is a matter of programming, and companionship seems lost. There remains only longing, and this is buried under banality, for English has finally been booted to death. Even informally, people say "Will that suffice?" for "Will that do?" The computer on the Jupiter spaceship—a chatty, fussy genius called Hal, which has nice manners and a rather querulous need for reassurance about being wanted—talks more like a human being than any human being does in the picture. Hal runs the craft, watches over the rotating quota of men in deep freeze, and plays chess. He gives a lot of thought to how he strikes others, and sometimes carries on about himself like a mother fussing on the telephone to keep a bored grown child hanging on. At a low ebb and growing paranoid, he tells a hysterical lie about a faulty piece of equipment to recover the crew's respect, but a less emotional twin computer on Earth coolly picks him up on the judgment and degradingly defines it as a mistake. Hal, his mimic humanness perfected, detests the witnesses of his humiliation and restores his ego by vengeance. He manages to kill all the astronauts but Keir Dullea, including the hibernating crew members, who die in the most chillingly modern death scene imaginable: warning lights simply signal "Computer Malfunction," and sets of electrophysiological needles above the sleepers run amok on the graphs and then record the straight lines of extinction. The survivor of Hal's marauding self-justification, alone on the craft, has to battle his way into the computer's red-flashing brain, which is the size of your living room, to unscrew the high cerebral functions. Hal's sophisticated voice gradually slows and he loses his grip. All he can remember in the end is how to sing "Daisy"—which he was taught at the start of his training long ago—grinding down like an old phonograph. It is an upsetting image of human decay from command into senility. Kubrick makes it seem a lot worse than a berserk computer being controlled with a screwdriver.

The startling metaphysics of the picture are symbolized in the slabs. It is curious that we should all still be so subconsciously trained in apparently distant imagery. Even to atheists, the slabs wouldn't look simply like girders. They immediately have to do with Mosaic tablets or druidical stones. Four million years ago, says the story, an extraterrestrial intelligence existed. The slabs are its manifest sentinels. The one we first saw on prehistoric earth is like the one discovered in 2001 on the moon. The lunar finding sends out an upper-harmonic shriek to Jupiter and puts the scientists on the trail of the forces of creation. The surviving astronaut goes on alone and Jupiter's influence pulls him into a world where time and space are relative in ways beyond Einstein. Physically almost pulped, seeing visions of the planet's surface that are like chloroform nightmares and that sometimes turn into closeups of his own agonized eyeball and eardrum, he then suddenly lands, and he is in a tranquilly furnished repro Louis XVI room. The shot of it through the window of his space pod is one of the most heavily charged things in the whole picture, though its effect and its logic are hard to explain.

In the strange, fake room, which is movingly conventional, as if the most that the ill man's imagination can manage in conceiving a better world beyond the infinite is to recollect something he has once been taught to see as beautiful in a grand decorating magazine, time jumps and things disappear. The barely surviving astronaut sees an old grandee from the back, dining on the one decent meal in the film; and when the man turns around it is the astronaut himself in old age. The noise of the chair moving on the white marble in the silence is typical of the brilliantly selective sound track. The old man drops his wineglass, and then sees himself bald and dying on the bed, twenty or thirty years older still, with his hand up to another of the slabs, which has appeared in the room and stands more clearly than ever for the forces of change. Destruction and creation coexist in them. They are like Siva. The last shot of the man is totally transcendental, but in spite of my resistance to mysticism I found it stirring. It shows an X-raylike image of the dead man's skull recreated as a baby, and approaching Earth. His eyes are enormous. He looks like a mutant. Perhaps he is the first of the needed new species.

It might seem a risky notion to drive sci-fi into magic. But, as with *Strangelove,* Kubrick has gone too far and made it the poetically just place to go. He and his collaborator have found a powerful idea to impel space conquerors whom puny times have robbed of much curiosity. The hunt for the remnant of a civilization that has been signalling the existence of its intelligence to the future for four million years, tirelessly stating the fact that it occurred, turns the shots of emptied, comic, ludicrously dehumanized men into something more poignant. There is a hidden parallel to the shot of the ape's arm swinging up into the empty frame with its first weapon, enthralled by the liberation of something new to do; I keep remembering the shot of the space scientist asleep in a craft with the "Weightless Conditions" sign turned on, his body fixed down by his safety belt while one arm floats free in the air.

PAULINE KAEL

THE BOTTOM OF THE PIT

SEPTEMBER 27, 1969 (*BUTCH CASSIDY AND THE SUNDANCE KID*)

A COLLEGE-PROFESSOR FRIEND OF mine in San Francisco who has always tried to stay in tune with his students looked at his class recently and realized it was time to take off his beads. There he was, a superannuated flower child wearing last year's talismans, and the young had become austere, even puritanical. Movies and, even more, movie audiences have been changing in the six months that I've been away. The art houses are now (for the first time) dominated by American movies, and the young audiences waiting outside, sitting on the sidewalk or standing in line, are no longer waiting just for entertainment. The waiting together may itself be part of the feeling of community, and they go inside almost for sacramental purposes. For all the talk (and fear) of ritual participation in the "new" theatre, it is really taking place on a national scale in the movie houses, at certain American films that might be called cult films, though they have probably become cult films because they are the most interesting films around. What is new about *Easy Rider* is not necessarily that one finds its attitudes appealing but that the movie conveys the mood of the drug culture with such skill and in such full belief that these simplicities are the truth that one can understand why these attitudes are appealing to others. *Easy Rider* is an expression and a confirmation of how this audience feels; the movie attracts a new kind of "inside" audience, whose members enjoy tuning in together to a whole complex of shared signals and attitudes. And although one may be uneasy over the satisfaction the audience seems to receive from responding to the general masochism and to the murder of Captain America, the movie obviously rings true to the audience's vision. It's cool to feel that you can't win, that it's all rigged and hopeless. It's even cool to believe in purity and sacrifice. Those of us who reject the heroic central character and the statements of *Easy Rider* may still be caught by something edgy and ominous in it—the acceptance of the constant danger of sudden violence. We're not sure how much of this paranoia isn't paranoia.

Some of the other cult films *try* to frighten us but are too clumsy to, though they succeed in doing something else. One has only to talk with some of the people who have seen *Midnight Cowboy*, for example, to be aware that what they care about is not the camera and editing pyrotechnics; they are indifferent to all that by now routine filler. John Schlesinger in *Midnight Cowboy* and, at a less skillful level, Larry Peerce in *Goodbye, Columbus* hedge their bets by using cutting and camera techniques to provide a satirical background as a kind of enrichment of the narrative and theme. But it really cheapens and impoverishes their themes. Peerce's satire is just cheesy, like his lyricism, and Schlesinger's (like Tony Richardson's in *The Loved One* and Richard Lester's in *Petulia*) is offensively inhuman and inaccurate. If Schlesinger could extend the same sympathy to the other Americans that he extends to Joe Buck and Ratso, the picture might make better sense; the point of the picture must surely be to give us some insight into these derelicts—two of the many kinds of dreamers and failures in the city. Schlesinger keeps pounding away at America, determined to expose how horrible the people are, to dehumanize the people these two are part of. The spray of venom in these pictures is so obviously the directors' way of showing off that we begin to discount it. To varying degrees, these films share the paranoid view of America of *Easy Rider*—and they certainly reinforce it for the audience— but what the audience really reacts to in *Midnight Cowboy* is the two lost, lonely men finding friendship. The actors save the picture, as the actors almost saved parts of *Petulia;* the leading actors become more important because the flamboyantly "visual" exhibitionism doesn't hold one's interest. Despite the recurrent assertions that the star system is dead, the audience is probably more interested than ever in the human material on the screen (though the new stars don't always resemble the old ones). At *Midnight Cowboy,* in the midst of all the grotesque shock effects and the brutality of the hysterical, superficial satire of America, the audiences, wiser, perhaps, than the director, are looking for the human feelings— the simple, *Of Mice and Men* kind of relationship at the heart of it. Maybe they wouldn't accept the simple theme so readily in a simpler setting, because it might look square, but it's what they're taking from the movie. They're looking for "truth"—for some signs of emotion, some evidence of what keeps people together. The difference between the old audiences and the new ones is that the old audiences wanted immediate gratification and used to get restless and bored when a picture didn't click along; these new pictures don't all click along, yet the young audiences stay attentive. They're eager to respond, to love it—eager to *feel.*

Although young movie audiences are far more sentimental now than they were a few years ago (Frank Capra, whose softheaded populism was hooted at in college film societies in the fifties, has become a new favorite at U.C.L.A.), there is this new and good side to the sentimentality. They are going to movies looking for feelings that will help synthesize their experience, and they appear to be willing to feel their way along with a movie like Arthur Penn's *Alice's Restaurant,* which is also trying to feel its way. I think we (from this point I include myself, because I share these attitudes) are desperate for some sensibility in movies, and that's why we're so moved by the struggle toward discovery in *Alice's Restaurant,* despite how badly done the film is. I think one would have to lie to say *Alice's Restaurant* is formally superior to the big new Western *Butch Cassidy and the Sundance Kid.* In formal terms, neither is very good. But

Alice's Restaurant is a groping attempt to express something, and *Butch Cassidy* is a glorified vacuum. Movies can be enjoyed for the *quality* of their confusions and failures, and that's the only way you can enjoy some of them now. Emotionally, I stayed with Penn during the movie, even though I thought that many of the scenes in it were inept or awful, and that several of the big set pieces were expendable (to put it delicately). But we're *for* him, and that's what carries the movie. Conceptually, it's unformed, with the director trying to discover his subject as well as its meaning and his own attitudes. And, maybe for the first time, there's an audience for American pictures which is willing to accept this.

Not every movie has to *matter;* generally we go hoping just to be relaxed and refreshed. But because most of the time we come out slugged and depressed, I think we care far more now about the reach for something. We've simply spent too much time at movies made by people who didn't enjoy themselves and who didn't respect themselves or us, and we rarely enjoy ourselves at their movies anymore. They're big catered affairs, and we're humiliated to be there among the guests. I look at the list of movies playing, and most of them I genuinely just can't face, because the odds are so strong that they're going to be the same old insulting failed entertainment, and, even though I may have had more of a bellyful than most people, I'm sure this isn't just my own reaction. Practically everybody I know feels the same way. This may seem an awfully moral approach, but it comes out of surfeit and aesthetic disgust. There's something vital to enjoyment which we haven't been getting much of. Playfulness? Joy? Perhaps even honest cynicism? What's missing isn't anything as simple as talent; there's lots of talent, even on TV. But the business conditions of moviemaking have soured the spirit of most big movies. That's why we may be willing to go along with something as strained and self-conscious as *Alice's Restaurant*. And it's an immensely hopeful sign that the audience isn't derisive, that it wishes the movie well.

· · ·

All this is, in a way, part of the background of why, after a few minutes of *Butch Cassidy and the Sundance Kid,* I began to get that depressed feeling, and, after a half hour, felt rather offended. We all know how the industry men think: they're going to try to make "now" movies when now is already then, they're going to give us orgy movies and plush skin-flicks, and they'll be trying to feed youth's paranoia when youth will, one hopes, have cast it off like last year's beads. This Western is a spinoff from *Bonnie and Clyde;* it's about two badmen (Paul Newman and Robert Redford) at the turn of the century, and the script, by William Goldman, which has been published, has the prefatory note "Not that it matters, but most of what follows is true." Yet everything that follows rings false, as that note does.

It's a facetious Western, and everybody in it talks comical. The director, George Roy Hill, doesn't have the style for it. (He doesn't really seem to have the style for anything, yet there is a basic decency and intelligence in his work.) The tone becomes embarrassing. Maybe we're supposed to be charmed when this affable, loquacious outlaw Butch and his silent, "dangerous" buddy Sundance blow up trains, but how are we supposed to feel when they go off to Bolivia, sneer at the country, and start shooting up poor Bolivians? George Roy Hill is a "sincere" director, but Goldman's script is jocose; though it reads as if it might play, it doesn't, and probably this isn't just Hill's fault. What can one do with dialogue like Paul Newman's Butch saying, "Boy, I got vision. The rest of the world wears bifocals"? It must be meant to be sportive, because it isn't witty and it isn't dramatic. The dialogue is all banter, all throwaways, and that's how it's delivered; each line comes out of nowhere, coyly, in a murmur, in the dead sound of the studio. (There is scarcely even an effort to supply plausible outdoor resonances or to use sound to evoke a sense of place.) It's impossible to tell whose consciousness the characters are supposed to have. Here's a key passage from the script—the big scene when Sundance's girl, the schoolteacher Etta (Katharine Ross), decides to go to Bolivia with the outlaws:

ETTA (*For a moment, she says nothing. Then, starting soft, building as she goes*): I'm twenty-six, and I'm single, and I teach school, and that's the bottom of the pit. And the only excitement I've ever known is sitting in the room with me now. So I'll go with you, and I won't whine, and I'll sew your socks and stitch you when you're wounded, and anything you ask of me I'll do, except one thing: I won't watch you die. I'll miss that scene if you don't mind . . .
(*Hold on Etta's lovely face a moment—*)

It's clear who is at the bottom of the pit, and it isn't those frontier schoolteachers, whose work was honest.

Being interested in good movies doesn't preclude enjoying many kinds of crummy movies, but maybe it does preclude acceptance of this enervated, sophisticated business venture—a movie made by those whose talents are a little high for mere commercial movies but who don't break out of the mold. They're trying for something more clever than is attempted in most commercial jobs, and it's all so archly empty—Conrad Hall's virtuoso cinematography providing constant in-and-out-of-focus distraction, Goldman's decorative little conceits passing for dialogue. It's all posh and josh, without any redeeming energy or crudeness. Much as I dislike the smugness of puritanism in the arts, after watching a put-on rape and Conrad Hall's "Elvira Madigan" lyric interlude (and to our own Mozart—Burt Bacharach) I began to long for something simple and halfway *felt*. If you can't manage genuine sophistication, you may be better off simple. And when you're as talented as these fellows, perhaps it's necessary to descend into yourself sometime and try to find out what you're doing—maybe, even, to risk banality, which is less objectionable than this damned waggishness.

Butch Cassidy will probably be a hit; it has a great title, and it has star appeal for a wide audience. Redford, who is personable and can act, is overdue for stardom, though it will be rather a joke if he gets it out of this non-acting role. Newman throws the ball to him often—that's really exactly what one feels he's doing—and is content to be his infectiously good-humored (one assumes) self. He plays the public image of himself (as an aging good guy), just as Arlo Guthrie plays himself as a moonchild. Yet, hit or no, I think what this picture represents is finished. Butch and Sundance will probably be fine for a TV series, which is what I mean by finished.

. . .

One can't just take the new cult movies head on and relax, because they're too confused. Intentions stick out, as in the thirties message movies, and you may be so aware of what's wrong with the movies while you're seeing them that you're pulled in different directions, but if you reject them because of the confusions, you're rejecting the most hopeful symptoms of change. Just when there are audiences who may be ready for something, the studios seem to be backing away, because they don't understand what these audiences want. The audiences themselves don't know, but they're looking for *something* at the movies. This transition into the seventies is maybe the most interesting as well as the most confusing period in

American movie history, yet there's a real possibility that, because the tastes of the young audience are changing so fast, the already tottering studios will decide to minimize risks and gear production straight to the square audience and the networks. That square audience is far more alienated than the young one—so alienated that it isn't looking for *anything* at the movies.

ART &
ARCHITECTURE

LEWIS MUMFORD

FALSE FRONT OR
COLD-WAR CONCEPT

OCTOBER 20, 1962

T HESE LAST FEW years, the United States government has been erecting new embassy buildings all over the world, on a scale that rivals the number of Air Force bases we constructed a little earlier. In some of these embassies the spirit of the airbases seems to have affected the program of our less warlike missions, and in the design of one of the most important of these structures we have gratuitously awakened no little local resentment. This embassy is in London, the last place one would think a misinterpretation of our purposes—indeed, a literal misconstruction—could have taken place. In certain cities the new embassies have added to the prestige of American architecture, for, by a happy reversal of the usual official procedures, the panel of architects who competed for the job included many of the best of our older exponents of modern architecture. There were no inhibiting provisions that these buildings should be Georgian, Early Republican, or plaster-cast Classic in outward form, so they stand on their own as exemplars of the contemporary American mode, touched with what our architects have recently learned from other lands.

In Edward Stone's adaptation of the Indian screen wall for our embassy in New Delhi, he made a graceful bow to regional tradition. Its practical outcome, by all reports, has not, though, been on the level of its aesthetic success, for he unhappily forgot how difficult it is to translate ancient forms into modern materials. For Stone overlooked the fact, as did Le Corbusier and his associates at about the same time in designing the new Indian city of Chandigarh, that a concrete or stone grille, unlike its wooden counterpart, absorbs enough heat during the day to counteract even the cooling night air. Architects in America who have been copying Stone's innovation even in places where our summers are almost as torrid as India's may eventually regret their eagerness to take over this seemingly foolproof device for masking the familiar dullness of repetitive windows or for avoiding the imbecility of compensating for acres of exposed glass by using tightly drawn Venetian blinds. Employed judiciously, for a rational purpose, on a single wall, the grille may be a blessing, but, applied wholesale, it is both aesthetically depressing and functionally absurd.

The architect of the London embassy, the late Eero Saarinen, counts, like his father before him, as one of the most distinguished exponents of current American architecture. He was the one-man equivalent of the gigantic architectural corporation known as Skidmore, Owings & Merrill, and his buildings can be found on almost every great campus in the country—recreation halls, dormitories, auditoriums, hockey rinks, to say nothing of such a structure as the General Motors Research Laboratories near Detroit, which forms almost a super-campus of its own. Unlike the S. O. & M. brand, Mr. Saarinen's trademark was a disinclination to repeat himself, yet it happens that in planning the London embassy he borrowed a façade he had already created for the American embassy in Oslo. If this design were a happy one, there would be nothing against such repetition, for a well-seasoned architect, dealing for the second time with a building of a particular sort, should not be afraid to refine and perfect an earlier form, as Frank Lloyd Wright, despite his boundless powers of invention, did with his basic "prairie house" to the end of his life. For in official buildings abroad expressive design is now a matter of great importance. Our embassies are no longer simply places of official residence with an attached office; they are, rather, a complex of governmental, economic, and cultural functions, with offices, an exhibition hall, a library, and an auditorium—places in which our government not merely does business with its own citizens but attempts to make a good impression upon the country in which, for all its extra-territoriality, it is domiciled. The problem in creating such a building is not unlike the problem an American lecturer faces in addressing a foreign audience: of retaining his individuality and his national idiom without making any blatant assertion of his Americanism—being, in fact, a better representative of our many-faceted national tradition by showing his ability to find common ground with his hosts. The ambassador who has not the tact to do this should be kept at home; the embassy that cannot create a likable concept of our country has not fulfilled a main purpose.

· · ·

The London embassy occupies the major share of one side of Grosvenor Square—a large eighteenth-century square with long evidence of American occupation, first by our earlier embassy, then by the postwar memorial to Franklin D. Roosevelt that the grateful English erected there. The plot runs along the South Audley Street side of the square, from Upper Grosvenor Street north to Upper Brook Street, providing an all too imposing frontage on the square of some three hundred and fifty feet and a depth of some two hundred feet. Unlike the more formal squares of Bloomsbury and Belgravia, Grosvenor Square offers a considerable variety of form and color in its façades, though the buildings are mainly of the traditional, limited height. By the doubtful expedient of placing one floor half a story below the street level, and the tall ground floor half a story above that level, Saarinen respected this height limitation (the embassy shows only five stories aboveground), and when the trees are in leaf in the square the foliage mercifully hides the embassy's massive uniform façade from the spectator until it hits him full in the face. In any event, the square is so large that each side is a unit by itself, with little aesthetic relationship to the other sides, except at the corner meetings. Yet, as several British architectural critics have pointed out, the device of setting the embassy building back from the sidewalks, to get light for the below-street floor, created openings that disrupt the unity of the square far more than an additional story aboveground would. Not only that, but the building is further separated from the sidewalks by a formidable sloping stone-faced embankment, topped by a straw-colored metal fence.

A retaining wall backs up the embankment, and between this wall and the building lies a deep if waterless moat—a drop capable of daunting any invader who dared to scale the outer barrier. From a military standpoint, the building is vulnerable only at the entrances, but for the purposes of friendly diplomacy this sidewalk barricade, which rises above the eye level, has the effect of a calculated insult—and has been so regarded by many not unduly sensitive Britons. Both the building and the barricade say, "Keep your distance! Do not enter!," though this is the precise opposite of our program for introducing the British to our educational and cultural achievements while performing the other necessary offices of an embassy. To provide sufficient space for these cultural functions, the first two floors cover the entire plot, save for the setback; the four stories above form a rectangular U—with its base on Grosvenor Square—around a central light court. This upper mass juts out several feet to overhang the lower floors and is supported by a series of boldly expressed beams. Offices of both stenographers and officials, all with outside windows, are ranged along the sides of the U. There are three entrances to the building—the central embassy entrance on the square, with a double bank of elevators right at hand to give access to the whole building; a consular entrance on the south flank; a United States Information Service entrance on the north flank.

On the principle that the positive virtues of a building should be presented first, let me dwell on the interior public spaces, which give the ground floor a monumental scale that properly contrasts with that of the upper office floors and so provides the façade with what formal distinction it has. The tall, oblong windows on this level, which reach from floor to ceiling, have some justification for their existence, for though the exhibition hall, which is in the center of the building, is not served by them, they at least provide daylight for the library, which occupies one whole corner of the Information side of the building. This serene library, "all beautified with omissions," as Henry James said of The Great Good Place, is just what a library should be—the readers' tables close to the windows, and the stacks, holding some twenty-five thousand volumes of Americana, easily accessible. To give the authentic American touch, there is even an American Bible, but no King James Version! I cannot say as much in praise of the furniture. The clumsy, armless, almost immovable chairs were obviously chosen by someone with little experience in sitting or reading, much less in note-taking; they achieve a maximum of cushioned discomfort with a minimum of efficiency, and, compared with the not altogether adequate but still commodious oak armchairs of the reading rooms in the New York Public Library at Forty-second Street, they are singularly inept. There are today, incidentally, five badly designed "contemporary" chairs on the market for one that is even tolerably good, and the meekness with which the fashion-minded public accepts these incompetent pieces of furniture is second only to its eagerness to pay good money for the more infantile forms of modern painting. Here was a place for a dexterous innovation in modern library furniture, to match the high standard we have achieved in the conduct, if not always the design, of lending libraries. A room that vies in excellence with the library is the auditorium, for it is done with a quiet perfection that happily recalls Saarinen's smaller theatre in the Kresge Auditorium at M.I.T. Whether such a single-purpose room, for intermittent use, is justified in the embassy is another question; the Beveridge Room in the University of London, so arranged that it can accommodate as little as twenty people at a seminar or two or three hundred at a concert or a lecture, seems to me a far more adroit solution.

The fact that the exhibition hall serves frequently as an art gallery—like the lesser space at the Information entrance—is an excellent feature of the plan, since until recently America's contributions to painting and sculpture have been overlooked in other countries, a situation for which we have been partly to blame. Unfortunately, the hall is little more than a corridor, and space that might have been used to provide temporary alcoves, for a show of prints, perhaps, is sacrificed to a singularly irrelevant architectural device—a long, lengthwise trough of water, split by a wedge-shaped bank of stone that is punctuated by spouts, presumably to serve as a fountain. This trough cuts the gallery space in two without adding to its charm or usefulness. Possibly no one has yet backed into this watering trough, but it remains a clear and present danger, and, what is worse, it prevents one from going back and forth between pictures on opposite sides of the hall, as one often wishes to do when viewing a single artist's work.

The upper-floor corridors and offices are a smooth miracle of cold anonymity, as violently antiseptic as an operating room in a hospital, and even on the hot day in summer when I inspected them the absence of color and contrast was far from ingratiating. One of Conan Doyle's early villains tries to drive his girl victim insane by putting her in a white room with no hangings or decorations of any sort. This once seemed to me merely a quaint commentary on the Victorian conception of decoration, but after also looking at the endless array of white cubicles in the inner row of offices on the ground floor of the embassy I began to wonder whether there mightn't be something in the notion, and I shuddered at the thought of coming into this building not out of the summer sun but out of the dark, dank fog of a London November or the cold rain that one may encounter at any London season. Under such conditions it would take more than central heating to make the embassy seem anything but bleak and forbidding. Only a distinguished architect could carry through his original errors with such consistency—and with so little misgiving about his basic premises.

. . .

On the exterior, Saarinen attempted a more positive note in the four upper stories—in the bold fashion of Le Corbusier when he was modelling his Unity House in Marseille—by alternating oblong windows in broad, forward-thrusting stone frames and in narrow fluted frames that are not merely recessed into the walls but divided vertically by a bar. This pattern of alternation is carried through in the placing of the windows one above the other, so that a recessed window frame sits over a projecting window frame, and this scheme prevails through the entire façade. Such a strong modelling restores to us an almost forgotten part of the architectural curriculum—the traditional course on Lights and Shadows—and the contrasts hereby achieved will be strikingly accentuated, unless London's smoke nuisance abates further, when the Portland stone Saarinen wisely employed weathers, in standard London fashion, into streaks and patches of charcoal and gray, set off against gleaming white. Then the alternation of the flat stone surfaces of the broader window frames with the fluted units that border the other windows may become far more effective than it is now. All in all, Saarinen used his best talents to give this façade the character of an old-fashioned masonry structure, and if one of the youngest leaders of the "Brutalist" school has complained that the embassy is too monumental, the fact is that at least its masculine strength compares most favorably with the slickly neuter glass walls that have dominated the buildings of the past decade. With the admirable structural consistency that was so marked in Frank Lloyd Wright's work, Saarinen even carried the heavy beams of the lowest projecting floor out to the exterior, not alone to support the overhanging stories but to create a bold, serrated edge that sets off the recessed windows of the set-back ground floor as effectively as an old-fashioned cornice. Aesthetically, this is a far sounder feature of the façade than the overeffortful window frames, but the architect, alas, softened the effect by covering his beams with straw-colored anodized aluminum sheathing. The use of this feeble color throughout the building wherever a metallic covering is needed is an unfortunate lapse; it not merely looks fatally cheap, like imitation gold, but offers insufficient contrast with the diluted cream of the unweathered exterior stone.

What the architect sought here is obvious—he made a desperate attempt to conceal the incurable monotony of his façade by breaking away from the glib modern curtain wall, yet without going back to the simple repeating pattern of window and masonry wall that marked the buildings on the decently unobtrusive eighteenth-century London squares. In the older order of London, architects concentrated their efforts at individuality and distinction on the entrances of the houses, with their delicate fanlights and inviting classic porticoes; at most, they gave the special dignity of column and pediment to the building at the center of a row of houses, just because of its position. Saarinen sought to overcome the dull uniformity of a long, unbroken façade by making every other window stand out, but the power of his forms only increases the building's obsessive, repetitive beat. In contriving this form of aesthetic escape, he chose a solution that was not quite so arbitrary as that in his elevation for the new girls' dormitory at the University of Pennsylvania, in which, for no reason except superficial decoration, quite inadequate horizontal windows alternate with equally meaningless vertical ones. The truth of the matter is that if the functions within a building are themselves unduly repetitive, one cannot save the situation by overemphasizing that embarrassment.

In point of fact, Saarinen embraced the bureaucratic functions of the embassy too eagerly, and neglected to express the cultural functions that could have given life to this unnecessarily monotonous and sterile building. One would hardly guess from this façade that the embassy is not a mere office building. The library, the exhibition hall, the auditorium, the more public features of the building were all at the architect's call, waiting for appropriate architectural expression—indeed, demanding it—to dramatize the building's special ties to the great city and to those many

Englishmen who are eager to come closer to our country's culture. That culture, in all its brief historic exuberance, is in contrast to the conformities and standardizations of our more recent affluent, bellicose, and bureaucratized society, and this vitality and variety should not be hidden behind a uniform façade. On his own confession, Saarinen knew that the administrators of the Grosvenor estate planned to rebuild the other sides of the square to a height of nine stories, so, quite apart from the embassy's privilege of extraterritoriality, there were no spatial limits to his handling of the varied functions of the embassy. By rejecting any formal expression of the cultural functions of his building, Saarinen repeated in his own fashion the mistakes of the United Nations headquarters in both New York and Paris—he gave precedence and eminence only to the bureaucratic function, thus bowing too complaisantly to the ruling force of our age and simply overlooking, or bluntly denying, our not inconsiderable cultural advantages.

. . .

When the plans for the embassy were made public, it appeared that a dominant feature of a purely decorative order, trite but overwhelming, had indeed been provided, in the form of a seemingly huge golden eagle with outspread wings perched high above the main entrance, and a great deal of criticism was aroused in London, even in usually friendly circles, over this flaunting of our national bird. But when this pale eagle finally materialized it had shrunk into tame inoffensiveness, and now blends quite innocuously into the anodized aluminum of the rest of the decoration. What still causes resentment among many Britons—justifiably, it may as well be said—is the embankment of concrete. For this feature, I have been told, the State Department is responsible, unbelievable as that may seem. This device is a far remove from the Renaissance habit of placing a free-standing building on a plinth or base whose bold intervention between the ground and the structure not merely raised the building but set it off without violating its aesthetic composure. Many far less offensive barriers were available, even under the conditions Saarinen faced. One that instantly suggests itself is the cheerful London fashion of a bastion of flower boxes, which offers at most seasons the touch of color and organic form that is now lacking at every point in this building. Even for an embassy in Moscow, this quasi-military design would have been an unfriendly, if perhaps prudent, gesture; among our British friends and allies it is much worse. At the moment the State Department is urging people to smile in their passport photographs, our London embassy presents a cold, unsmiling face, a face unfortunately suggesting national arrogance and irresponsive power. We should amend this concept even if this demands that we take a long look at ourselves, to find out why the official Face of America and the Voice of America today so often contradict our historic character and our present professions of idealism.

No architect can solve that problem singlehanded.

. . .

I do not wish to leave this discussion of the work of a dead man, who cannot defend himself, without citing a quite different appraisal, from a contemporary English architect who is full of admiration for this building. Though dubious about the pallid metal trim, he praises the use of the Portland stone and the effort to achieve a strong, characterful façade. He feels that the decorative treatment of the interior is exquisitely chaste—read "hospital coldness" in my report—and he regards the detailing of the structure and the craftsmanship as setting a standard well above most contemporary work in his country. He is charitably willing to overlook the sidewalk barricade—though he winces at it—and he thinks that the building will settle down into the townscape of Grosvenor Square as a happy addition, full of character, if not charm. Since he is one of the most English of Englishmen, this is a most objective judgment, if not a representative one. I wish I could share his sentiments. But to me the whole style and message of the building seem as ominous as the depersonalized sort of thinking that comes out of our Air Force research centers. By the very perfection of its technique and the emptiness of its performance, it seems to say—as, indeed, our newer technologies often seem to say—that, quite apart from possible nuclear catastrophes, our civilization has come close to a dead end. At this juncture, we shall have to surrender what is left of our more humane values or retrace our steps to the point where we took the wrong road. One is not as yet easily persuaded that this blank, bureaucratic-military mask is the true face of America; certainly it does not represent the America we love, the America that other countries once found both enviable and lovable.

HAROLD ROSENBERG

THE NINETEEN-SIXTIES: TIME IN THE MUSEUM

JUNE 29, 1967

T
HE EXHIBITION AT the Museum of Modern Art entitled "The 1960s" avoids making any overt critical or philosophical assertion about the decade or the art produced in it. Possible disagreement regarding the selections is turned aside by the subtitle of the show, "Painting and Sculpture from the Museum Collections," which suggests an institution's summer inventory of its acquisitions of recent works. In contrast to such aggressive critical sorties of the past few years as the "Responsive Eye" show at the Museum of Modern Art, the "Primary Structures" show at the Jewish Museum, the "Post-Painterly Abstraction" show at the Los Angeles County Museum, the "Systemic Painting" show at the Guggenheim, "The 1960s" is in the passive mood. It is offered without catalogue or preface, and all the exhibitions just mentioned, together with others that have been much discussed, are reflected in it. Two-fifths of its hundred and twenty-seven paintings and sculptures emanate from two sources—Philip Johnson and the Larry Aldrich Foundation—so the concept of the decade presented by the show owes much to their judgment; only a handful of the works were bought by the Museum itself. Faced by this built-in disclaimer, I was curious to know whether the omission of artists who seem to me of current importance— they range from Gottlieb and de Kooning, through Alex Katz and Lester Johnson, to Saul Steinberg and Fairfield Porter—is to be attributed to the circumstance that no works done by them in the 1960s had been acquired by the Museum. On inquiry, I learned that paintings done in the sixties by most of these artists were available, as were sixties paintings by Rothko, Hofmann, Motherwell, and others, but that the "1960s" exhibition was selected, as a Museum release put it, "to illustrate the contemporary movements, styles, and the forms of expression which seem most characteristic of the current decade," and that therefore these artists were all left out. Evidently some contemporary "styles and forms of expression" are (or seem) not "characteristic" of the decade, while others are.

Artists like Gottlieb or de Kooning, it was explained, were typical of the 1950s rather than of the sixties, and their work was on display in another part of the building. This all seemed well intentioned, yet when I heard it I felt that all modesty had departed from the exhibition, since verdicts of the utmost gravity were being delivered. That living artists were being expelled from the present and relegated to the Museum proper—that is, to the past—was hardly to be taken lightly, however lightly intended. Not so long ago these painters stood large in the sunlight, but though they continue to produce works and exhibit them, they—like spirits in Hades—no longer cast a shadow. Nor is it the relentless stream of time that has brought them to this pass, for other artists, of the same age group and even older—Reinhardt, Calder, Nevelson, Fontana—are represented in the exhibition. It is their affiliation with the "styles and forms of expression" that the Museum now judges to be obsolete that deprives them of relevance to the living.

I noted, too, the names of some who, never prominent in the past, were also denied access to the present and were conveyed directly into the limbo of the Museum's general collection—artists such as Lester Johnson and Fairfield Porter, who have come into the foreground only in the past few years yet have apparently failed to be characteristic of the 1960s. And what of Nakian and Saul Steinberg, who have been well known for three decades yet have not been characteristic of any? By the measure of the "1960s" exhibition, none of these belong in the present. A concept of time different from that of the calendar has obviously been at work in the Museum, though no one there seems to be aware of it. For all its reticence, the Museum has, by its acts of choice, proclaimed a theory about the Now in art. Inasmuch as some artists have been dropped from the decade and others denied admission, the decade itself as a living span of time has been redefined as consisting of a set of characteristic traits. As described in the Museum's release, these consist of "assemblage technique; 'stain' or 'color field' painting; systemic painting; hard-edge abstraction and the shaped canvas; optical and kinetic art; 'primary' sculpture; and various forms of realism and 'pop.'" In sum, the decade has been stretched over a conceptual framework. When necessary, it has even been pulled over the edge into the fifties; for example, two paintings and a collage by Jasper Johns, one dated 1954 and two 1955, are included, obviously to make the point that Johns' flags, targets, and objects in wooden frames assimilate themselves into the stripes and boxes prominent in Optical and systemic painting and assemblage. There are also a

1959 Ellsworth Kelly, a 1957 Yves Klein, a 1958 Jean Tinguely, and 1959 paintings by Morris Louis and Frank Stella, all of whom are considered 1960s personalities. But the Museum's 1962 Hofmann, 1963 Tworkov, 1958 Sam Francis, 1959 Porter, 1962 Johnson, and similar nonconforming items have been placed outside the "1960s" compound. Albers, Newman, and Cornell are also among the missing, and in a room where Frankenthaler, Louis, and Olitski are gathered, one misses their inevitable companion, Noland. Yet the presence of each of these is invoked in the appropriate chamber—Albers by the hard-edge, Newman and Noland by the color field, Cornell by the assemblage. They are present in their absence. But the absence of the Abstract Expressionists, and of landscape and figure painters, no matter how unorthodox, is an absolute absence. In the outdoor sculpture court a bit of air is, appropriately, let in between the categories by the inclusion of Calder and Ipousteguy. On the whole, however, "The 1960s" is as strict a survey of our ongoing history-making as one would expect to find in a freshman outline. Whatever the works started out to mean, here they are embodiments of the formulas and phrases by which the collective opinions of the art world have been shaped in this decade. Time in the Museum is a grocery list of the most actively publicized names, labels, and events.

. . .

It is precisely the collective thinking represented in "The 1960s" that makes it (and its exclusions) significant as a reflection of current trends in the public life of art. Between the 1959 junk sculpture of Richard Stankiewicz or the 1960 kitchen-litter assemblage of Daniel Spoerri and the glass-and-chromium cube of Larry Bell or the painted-aluminum sections of Ronald Bladen, drastic changes have taken place in the selection and handling of materials, as well as in prevalent feeling, attitudes, and ideas. Most obviously, painting has been steadily deemphasized in favor of sculpture, craft, and technological constructions. The paintings in the exhibition are sandwiched between rooms of early-sixties assemblages and sculptures (among them a Rauschenberg, an Ossorio, a Bontecou, an Arman, a Dine, and a genuine slum artifact by Ortiz—a burnt mattress) and rooms of current kinetic inventions and light displays. Compared to the all-out associations of the assemblages with Happenings and of the motorized and electrified constructions with science and industry, painting itself here takes on a middle-of-the-road quality, which is enhanced by the fact that all the canvases on display are not only familiar but thickly overlaid with art-historical justifications. In terms of number and variety, the paintings are a skimpy collection, arranged according to their ideological and technical affinities. After an overture of two blown-up silk-screened Warhol Art Nouveau Campbell Soup labels in luscious lavender, cherry, and orange, and the three Johns, comes a group that might be labelled the Bennington acrylics—Frankenthaler, Louis, Olitski, Feeley—all of whom paint, or painted, with synthetics on unsized canvas. They are followed by painters of reiterated elements (Poons, Stella, Reinhardt, and Agnes Martin), then by Optical painters and a few assorted borderline cases (Dorazio, Kawashima); in one of the last rooms there is a swing back to some Pop and pre-Pop painters— Rivers, Lichtenstein, Wesselmann. As colored images, the canvases of Frankenthaler, Louis, and Olitski are arresting, especially as one comes upon them after two or three roomfuls of assemblages. Miss Frankenthaler's abstract shapes have become more definite and emphatic than they used to be, and the Olitski and the larger Louis (I find his stripe paintings tiresome) are fairly daring, though in conventional terms. The weakness of these paintings is in the quality of their absorbed color, which they all share on a didactic basis. While the soaked-in paint produces a uniform transparency, it results in a thinness that diffuses the eye instantaneously across the entire surface of the picture. As a result, the image in these paintings is all there is to them. Their quality is akin to that of the photograph or color reproduction; they could be cast on a screen without much loss. Perhaps this is what endears the work of these artists to art-historian curators, who are habituated to thinking of paintings as they appear in slides and reproductions.

Paul Jenkins, a pioneer in rolling luminous pigment on tilted canvases, is, to the credit of the Museum, given a place among the thin-paint contingent, though his metaphysical sensibility differentiates his work from their art-for-art's-sake purposefulness. Among the other "pure" painters, Poons and Stella are the most interesting. In completely different ways, both raise the traditional problem of the expressive scope of an art built entirely on the placement, reiteration, and variation of uniform elements. Musical-mathematical experimentation is a continuing strain in abstract art, and Poons is one of its most gifted younger practitioners. His two paintings in the "1960s" exhibition are not of his eye-jumping phase, and their carefully bunched ovals, though they are all equal in size, brought to my mind the object-spotting on a bright one-color ground of certain Mirós. In the jutting angles of his shaped stretchers, Stella achieves a drama, essentially structural, that is lacking in his parallel-line exercises.

In all aspects of the recent art, materials assume priority in determining effects. The inherent luminosity of synthetic pigments parallels the qualities gained by the electrification and motorization of sculptural constructions. The complex mechanism of Pol Bury's slow-motion *31 Rods Each with a Ball* is an invisible element that projects the elegant aura of nineteenth-century music boxes. By contrast, the use of pencil and oil paint by Agnes Martin supplies in itself a traditionalist overtone that tempers the extremist reductionism of her graphlike compositions. That aluminum, chromium, stainless steel, and plastics are replacing older art materials, including junk and battered found objects—Louise Nevelson exemplifies the trend in her recent switch from wood to aluminum—represents an alteration in the social and psychological content of art as well as in its tonality and visual organization. The spread of new industrial products into the studios and workshops has brought with it the habits and moral outlook of the model manufacturing plant. An aesthetic of neatness, of clean edges, smooth surfaces, efficient construction, supervenes above the various styles to blend together color-field painting, hard-edge, shaped canvases, Optical and minimal art—in fact, all of the modes identified with the latter part of the still incomplete 1960s. From Stankiewicz's sinister 1959 *Natural History,* a package consisting of iron pipes and a boiler barely visible through a wrapping of rusty iron mesh, to the aseptic chromium-plated bronze effigies of Ernest Trova's continuing *Falling Man* series, a stride has been taken much longer than the one from Rauschenberg's *First Landing Jump* to an absent de Kooning like *Gotham News.* Works of the early sixties composed of materials from the street and the junk yard participate in the city spirit of Abstract Expressionist painting; as the decade wears on, bohemia and the slums give way to the laboratory, and the measure of its span is from Oldenburg's plaster hamburgers to Flavin's fluorescent tube.

Unfortunately, change refuses to take place in an orderly succession of phases, and some artists did in 1960 what others are emphasizing now. But if decades are to be denominated in terms of qualities, the Museum of Modern Art's hunt for the currently characteristic should have led it to start the decade around 1962. By deleting from "The 1960s" all that junky stuff of Arman, Bontecou, César, Chamberlain, Latham, Gentils, Lindner, Mallary, Ortiz, Ossorio, Spoerri, Tinguely, and half a dozen "soft" (i.e., psychologically or technically tentative) paintings, those by

Rivers, Copley, Kitaj, Rosenquist, Dine, Oldenburg, a much more unified—hence forceful—statement of the new taste and the values that support it could have been presented. Neatness is a physical manifestation of intellectual and social order; anarchists, bohemians, hipsters, tramps are presumed to be slovenly. The immaculate sculptures of Bell, Trova, Bladen, Morris, Flavin, Schöffer, and the equally tidy paintings of the Bennington acrylics (Frankenthaler et al.), the Op painters, and Reinhardt, Kelly, D'Arcangelo not only immerse the spectator in a sheath of prophylaxis but reassure him of the operation in art of a rationale of conception, practice, and utility. The aesthetic of cleanliness has a political dimension; the fuss about thick paint, or "painterliness," banned from "The 1960s," derives from the wish to affirm middle-class tidiness and security produced by washes of color upon stretched fabric. In contrast, an artist like di Suvero, who continues to build sculptures out of stained, broken beams and twisted iron, identifies himself with social intransigence and resistance to the war in Vietnam. It is consistent with 1960s orderliness that sculptures should not be made "by hand" in the sculptor's studio but fabricated for him in a machine or carpentry shop, and that paintings should be blown up and manufactured for the artist in plastic and silk-screen. The gesture of Barnett Newman in covering with a patina of rust a sculpture made for him in a machine shop may be regarded as a protest against both the shiny surfaces and the rationalism of the kind of art with which he is usually identified. Critical catch phrases such as "color field," "hard edge," "primary," "systemic," though they are used to describe different modes of painting and sculpture, overlap to denominate a general movement in art in which sensibility is subordinated to aesthetic and technical systems. The art of the sixties is not worked   it is done according to plan.

Perceptual neatness and rationalized execution accommodate the art of the sixties to the new status of painting and sculpture as professions and as subjects of study and training in the universities. The typical smooth-surfaced, color-rationed, mechanically contrived, historically authenticated objects favored by dealers, museum officials, and advanced art reviewers look back to the craft-oriented procedures and house-beautiful objectives of the Bauhaus. As against the bohemian eccentric of earlier American art, the prosperous or institutionally connected personage of the new art leadership enters into direct dialogue with the middle class and its cultural programmers.

Optical and "minimal" art have introduced group formations and ideologies different in character from the older art movements. From Impressionism to Pop, the relation of the artist to his "school" consisted of a loose exchange of ideas and practices, often below the verbal level, in which each painter developed the implications suggested by his sensibility. In the new art, communication among individuals has often been superseded by individuals' working together in teams. In Europe, the concept of creation has been repudiated in favor of collective research by artists functioning in disciplined groups under a pledge of anonymity; the project has been opposed to the creative act. The assumptions on which most of the art in "The 1960s" is based seem to lead inevitably to this conclusion of impersonality. The visual researches of Julio le Parc have proved astonishingly fertile in variety, and would gain nothing by repeating a single image in order to establish a signature.

Group exhibitions cut across personalities by their very nature, in order to present works that illustrate the ideas of their organizers. If the selection consists of masterpieces, each work also stands by itself as a summation of the artist's vision. In our time, masterpieces are no longer created; at any rate, they do not manifest themselves on the spot. Thus, for works to convey their full vitality they must be seen in the context of the artist's intellectual and emotional "system"—for example, in a retrospective. There is a depressing flavor about the "1960s" exhibition that is in part attributable to the surface drift of art in the past few years. But the depression is also owing to the curtailment of individuals in favor of objects made in styles that have become familiar. A lesson-plan art-history survey like "The 1960s" not only excludes important figures for the sake of an ideological pattern but omits the developmental dimension of the artists whom it does present—that is to say, their subjective time. The self-transformation of artists through their work is, however, the most interesting thing in art today. To think of the modifications during the past few years in the creations of artists of such diverse temperaments as Oldenburg, Nevelson, Liberman, Lindner, Poons, D'Arcangelo, Segal—to name a few in the show—is to shake off the enervating mood induced by the Museum exhibition. Besides the examples of home industry displayed as characteristic of the sixties, the actual sixties in art is constituted by the presences of artists like these—together with those disorderly presences whose Happenings and public manifestations, as by the "Provos" of Los Angeles, have gone beyond the encompassment of art by museums and perhaps past the borders of art itself.

TELEVISION

MICHAEL J. ARLEN

TELEVISION'S WAR

MAY 27, 1967

SUMMERTIME NOW, OR very nearly. Kids already gabbling about the last day of school. Women walking down East Eighty-sixth Street in those jouncy cotton dresses. Connecticut suntans. Air-conditioning in Schrafft's. *Daktari* reruns on the television. *Lassie* reruns. *Gilligan's Island* reruns. *Star Trek* reruns. Lots of baseball. (Not much doing on television in the good old, mythic old American summertime.) The other Saturday, just back from a trip, and for some reason conscious more pointlessly than ever of that miserable war, I made a mental note to watch, at five o'clock that afternoon, an N.B.C. program called *Vietnam Weekly Review* for whatever it might have to offer, and went outside (it was a nice day—warm, sunny, full of the first hints of summer's dust and laziness, of all those hammocks one will never swing in), toward Fifth Avenue and the Park, past which close to one hundred thousand men, women, and children were marching as part of a "Support Our Boys in Vietnam" parade. Lots of people in the streets. Lots of American Legion posts. Lots of those Catholic high-school bands. A flatbed truck went by full of teamsters, many of them holding aloft placards reading, "It's Your Country! Love It Or Leave It!" The Putnam County John Birch Society went by singing "America the Beautiful." An American Legionnaire went by in a wheelchair, carrying a placard reading, "Victory over Atheistic Communism." The crowd applauded. Somewhere up toward Ninety-sixth Street a band was playing "The Yellow Rose of Texas." Children all around me clutched American flags and looked the way children usually do, with or without flags.

I went back home at ten to five, got out a beer, turned on the TV set. There was a baseball game in progress on N.B.C. (No *Vietnam Review* that week.) Not a bad game, either. Clendenon hit a long ball in the tenth and wrapped it up for Pittsburgh. I forget who Pittsburgh was playing, but you could look it up. From Fifth Avenue, two blocks away (you could hear it through the open window), a band was finishing up "The Marine Corps Hymn," then started "Sister Kate." Sometimes I wonder what it is that the people who run television think about the war. I'm sure they think about it. Everybody thinks about it. I'm sure they care a lot. (At times, I even picture them sitting around in the Communications Club after hours, brows furrowed in meditation, their tumblers of brandy and Perrier water barely sipped at. Finally, a voice is raised. "Well, hang it, Fred. I think Tom Hayden speaks for all of us.") Perhaps one is unfair. Perhaps not. In any case, there are good men who work for television trying to tell us about the war. For example, the other Monday night, a little after seven, Walter Cronkite peered out at us pleasantly from the TV screen, said, "Today's Vietnam story in a moment," and then there we were, via film that had been taken twenty-six hours earlier, eighteen miles south of the DMZ, watching a Marine scout detail that had been sent out to look for North Vietnamese encampments. The film began routinely, with the C.O. briefing his patrol leaders (a sequence that always seems to be staged, although it probably isn't), and then we were watching a small group of men on their way up a thickly wooded hill ("They went up to investigate the distant voices," said the on-the-scene correspondent), and heard the sound of faraway small-arms fire, and suddenly men were running here and there in front of the camera, the small-arms fire became louder and more intense, and once again—in our living room, or was it at the Yale Club bar, or lying on the deck of the grand yacht Fatima with a Sony portable TV upon our belly?—we were watching, a bit numbly perhaps (we have watched it so often), real men get shot at, real men (our surrogates, in fact) get killed and wounded. At one point in the film, a mortar round fell near the cameraman, and for a couple of seconds the film spun crazily until it (and he) got straightened out again, and then we were looking, through the camera, at a young man—a boy, surely no more than nineteen or twenty—square-jawed, handsome, All-American, poised there on the side of the hill, rifle held in close to him, waiting on the side of the hill for the signal to move up to where the shooting was, and afraid. In the background, you could hear machine guns firing and the voice of the platoon sergeant, a deep-voiced Negro, calling, "Git on up there! Git! Git!" And the boy stayed there for several moments in the camera's eye, his own eyes staring straight ahead, his face so full of youth, fear, bravery, whatever else, until he finally moved up. One thinks of how one's memories of those other wars (wars one didn't fight in) exist for the most part frozen in the still photographs of the great war photographers—Robert Capa's picture of the Spanish Loyalist falling on the Catalonian hillside, Eugene Smith's Marine face-down on the beach at Tarawa, Margaret Bourke-White's St. Paul's Cathedral against the blitz, David Duncan's Marines advancing through the Korean mud. Vietnam is different, to be sure. Not quite so "exciting." Not quite so photogenic. But it seems to me that Kurt Volkert, the man who held and worked that camera, who caught the meaning of that face, is one of the best journalists of the war, and one could probably say the same for many of the other cameramen covering Vietnam for the American networks.

Another afternoon not long ago, I watched a routine film clip, this one taken by Vo Huynh, a Vietnamese who works for N.B.C., about a military engagement in the South: scenes of men moving in to attack, and attacking—scenes, in fact, of men living close to death and killing—with one heartrending sequence of a young soldier being carried out, his leg apparently smashed, screaming to his comrades, "It hurts! It hurts!" The special qualities of courage, energy, and strange, tough sensitivity that made men like Robert Capa so good at what they did—so good because so useful, so useful because they went in there (Capa's great pictures of the second wave at Omaha Beach were so blurred that you could barely make out the faces) and tried to show us what it was really like—are qualities that don't exist to any lesser degree in men like Kurt Volkert and Vo Huynh. They, too, seem to be trying to show us what it's like—at least, what the small, small corner allotted to them is like—and Lord knows there are mighty few other people on television who seem to be trying.

Vietnam is often referred to as "television's war," in the sense that this is the first war that has been brought to the people preponderantly by television. People indeed look at television. They really look at it. They look at Dick Van Dyke and become his friend. They look at a new Pontiac in a commercial and go out and buy it. They look at thoughtful Chet Huntley and find him thoughtful, and at witty David Brinkley and find him witty. They look at Vietnam. They look at Vietnam, it seems, as a child kneeling in the corridor, his eye to the keyhole, looks at two grown-ups arguing in a locked room—the aperture of the keyhole small; the figures shadowy, mostly out of sight; the voices indistinct, isolated threats without meaning; isolated glimpses, part of an elbow, a man's jacket (who is the man?), part of a face, a woman's face. Ah, she is crying. One sees the tears. (The voices continue indistinctly.) One counts the tears. Two tears. Three tears. Two bombing raids. Four seek-and-destroy missions. Six Administration pronouncements. Such a fine-looking woman. One searches in vain for the other grownup, but, ah, the keyhole is so small, he is somehow never in the line of sight. Look! There is General Ky. Look! There are some planes returning safely to the Ticonderoga. I wonder (sometimes) what it is that the people who run television think about the war, because *they* have given us this keyhole view; we have given them the airwaves, and now, at this critical time, they have given back to us this keyhole view—and I wonder if they truly think that those isolated glimpses of elbow, face, a swirl of dress (who *is* that other person, anyway?) are all we children can really stand to see of what is going on inside that room. Vo Huynh, admittedly, will show us as much of the larger truth of a small battle and of a wounded soldier as he is able to, and C.B.S., as it did some nights ago, will show us a half-hour special interview with Marine Corps General Walt, which is nice of C.B.S., but there are other things, it seems, that make up the Vietnam war, that intelligent men *know* make up the Vietnam war—factors of doubt, politics, propaganda, truth, untruth, of what we actually do and actually don't do, that aren't in most ways tangible, or certifiably right or wrong, or easily reducible to simple mathematics, but that, even so (and even now), exist as parts of this equation that we're all supposedly trying so hard to solve—and almost none of them get mentioned. It seems almost never to get mentioned, for example, that there's considerable doubt as to the effectiveness of the search-and-destroy missions we watch so frequently on television. (The enemy casualty figures seem to be arbitrarily rigged, and the ground we take isn't anything we usually plan to keep.) It seems almost never to get mentioned, for example, that there's considerable doubt as to the actual efficacy of many of the highly publicized (on TV, as elsewhere) sweeps into territory that, if you read the fine print, you realize the enemy has often already left, and presumably will come back to when we, in turn, have gone. It seems rarely to get mentioned that there has been considerable doubt as to the effectiveness of our bombing, or that an air force that can't always hit the right village certainly can't avoid killing civilians when it bombs power plants in Hanoi. It doesn't seem to get mentioned, for example, that we are using "anti-personnel" weapons such as the Guava and the Pineapple more than the military appears to want to admit, or that any people who drop their tortures from planes flying at five thousand feet are likely to be regarded as no less accomplices than if they had stood in person in some village square and driven little slivers of metal, at high velocity, into the flesh of other human beings. It doesn't seem to get mentioned, for example, that "anti-personnel," "delivering hardware," "pacification mission," and "nation building" are phrases, along with "better dead than Red," that only a people out of touch with the meaning of language could use with any seriousness. It doesn't seem to get mentioned, for example, that when a senior member of the Administration states that he sees no reason for thinking we will have to send more troops to Vietnam this year he is probably not telling the truth, and that the fact of his probably not telling the truth is now more important than the fact of the troops. It doesn't seem to get mentioned—Well, enough of that. It is summertime now, or nearly. My kids were squabbling over bathing suits this morning, and who will learn to sail and who to ride. In summertime, we cook outdoors a lot, play coronary tennis, drink, watch pretty sunsets out across the water. This summer, I will almost certainly perfect my backhand, write something beautiful (or very nearly), read *Finnegans Wake*, or something like it. This summer—already the streets outside seem quieter, more humane. A car rolls softly over a manhole cover—a small clank. All those quiet streets, all those brave middle-class apartments—and what lies beneath those manhole covers? Wires? Cables? Dying soldiers? Dying children? Sounds of gunfire? Screaming? Madness? My television set plays on, talking to itself—another baseball game, in fact. Juan Marichal is pitching to Ron Hunt. Hunt shifts his stance. Marichal winds up. The count is three and two.

THE BOMBS BELOW GO
POP-POP-POP

MARCH 4, 1967

I T SEEMS HARD to believe that in mid-winter of 1967, at a time when this country is conducting an air campaign against North Vietnam in an almost unparalleled context of national unease and international distress, a major television network could undertake an allegedly serious examination of this campaign and then come up with as childish and unaware and fundamentally chicken a piece of journalism as C.B.S. did recently in *Vietnam Perspective: Air War in the North*. By "chicken" I mean that C.B.S. knowingly (they're not a bunch of kids over there) ducked out on something it shouldn't have ducked out on. I mean if you are in favor of the air attacks against the North, then come out and say so, and be intelligent about it. Or if you are against the air attacks in the North, then say that, and be intelligent about it. Or if, as a journalist, you want to say something about the whole situation, both sides, then do that— always a difficult matter—or, with honesty and skill, at least *try* to do it. C.B.S. did none of these things. C.B.S. took one of the most controversial and important political-emotional issues of the moment, made a few brief stammers at journalistic "objectivity," presented government propaganda for fifty minutes, then gave us some hurried, underweighted glimpses of the "opposition" for a final five minutes, and that was it.

The principal part of the program—a good three-quarters of it, in fact—consisted of a face-value, and therefore implicitly deferential and pro-military, "documentary" of the Air Force and Navy pilots who fly the missions against the North, with occasional Defense Department footage of specific bombing raids. The point of view of C.B.S. "reporter" Bill Stout seemed at all times to be unquestioning, and glowing with the kind of military-technological "tough-mindedness" that is presumably useful among military officers but is maybe not such a hot thing to have in a reporter who is supposedly telling us how things are. "A few days ago, these five-hundred-pound bombs were part of the flight-line inventory at Danang Air Base, South Vietnam" is the way the program opens, Bill Stout standing tall behind a neatly arranged lineup of bombs and missiles. "Goods on the shelf, ready for delivery to North Vietnam. By the time this report goes on the air in the United States, delivery will have been made. . . . All of it . . . designed to kill and destroy. All of it, according to the United States government, intended to shorten the war in Vietnam." Well, come on, now, Bill Stout. We know that's what the United States government intends. What one needs a news service for is to tell us how things actually are—and when a reporter gives us a sentence like that and then drops the subject, that, by implication, is how things are.

We were then shown the preparation and flying of bombing missions by Air Force and Navy pilots, with lots of *Twelve O'Clock High* sequences on weather briefings ("The weather in the Red River Delta, running four thousand broken, tops at seven thousand") and Intelligence briefings ("Good morning, gentlemen. Your target for this afternoon, as advertised, is . . ."), a long sequence in which the flight leader instructs his men on how to avoid a SAM attack ("I understand some of you have not seen a SAM attack before—"), and then some fine I-love-a-parade stuff, with planes whooshing off the runways and in the air (mountains, sky, clouds) and then down below the bombs making little unnoisy, faraway, almost pretty splashes (*pop-pop-pop*) of white and red on the dark green of the forest. Now, the last thing in the world I'd want to do is question the bravery or competence of these pilots, who, after all, have the job of fighting this miserable war for all of us; but to devote the principal part of what's supposed to be a serious study of a mighty complicated situation to the above-described our-brave-men-at-war type of coverage is, intentional or not, plain propaganda. Yes, of course, pilots like Air Force Colonel Sam Hill (whom we saw quite a bit of) are brave men, and there's no reason not to say so at some point. But if you present merely admiring sequences of this same Colonel Hill, brave, professional, old-pro-just-doing-his-job, for most of your program, you're in fact doing quite a number of other things as well. In choosing to spend your time this way, and thereby refusing to spend it in taking a hard, fair look at the disagreement over the consequences of the bombing—the military, political, and diplomatic consequences—you imply that a disagreement doesn't really exist, or that the causes for the disagreement are insubstantial, neither of which is true. In picturing the actuality of bombing as a remote, technological act (a "delivery" of "goods on the shelf"), when to at least 50 percent of the people involved—namely, the deliverees—it is a near-mythic, deeply human experience, you make it that much more difficult, at a critical time, for your human audience to grasp in human terms the human enemy's sometimes complicated responses to what Colonel Hill is doing. And, worse still, you're leading people to *approve* of what he's doing (which is one kind of fact, and which deserves to be examined on its own merits) for the simple, specious reason that he's such a brave, professional, etc., man (which is quite another).

After the bombing mission, the men come back to the base. Here are reporter Bill Stout and one of the pilots chatting about it afterward:

STOUT: Well, Colonel, what was it like?

COLONEL: Real good mission. The weather was real good. We got good bombs on the target, and we had an excellent road cut by Otter Four. He got his bombs real well on the road.

STOUT: Was it a road that you were after?

COLONEL: We had a road and a truck park, and we got our bombs all on the truck park, and Otter Four got his bombs on the truck park plus the road going through it.

STOUT (*concluding sequence*): Their exuberance is genuine—partly pride in the job they've done, partly relief. It's been a good day. No one was hit; they all came back.

Reporter Stout then interviewed the pilots on what they thought of the merits of bombing the North. Said Lieutenant Colonel Gast, an undoubtedly brave man, "I think it's shortening the war." Said Lieutenant Colonel Tanguy, an undoubtedly brave man, "I think we're going to have to apply more pressure." Said Colonel Hill, "I agree with you." Said Colonel Stanfield, "I think the North Vietnamese are as much a part of this war as the Vietcong, and to grant them any sort of sanctuary would tend to encourage them more than discourage them." At no point in the above did reporter Stout or C.B.S. detach himself or itself from these views, or attempt to comment on them, or, more important still, attempt to put them in a more useful perspective, alongside equally weighted interviews with other, non-military people. In fact, from the cheery, earnest way Stout put the whole question of the bombing campaign into the laps of the people who were doing the bombing (otherwise known as the "Ask the Man Who Owns One" theory of reporting), you'd think there wasn't anyone else around whose opinion on the subject carried quite so much weight—and maybe he's right. "It is," as Stout explained things for us (referring to the bombing campaign), "in the opinion of Americans, from the President to the pilots flying North, a critically important part of the Vietnam effort."

When, a few moments later, assuming an expression of high serious-ness, Stout informed us that we were finally going to take "a look at the effectiveness of that bombing campaign," it seemed only natural that he first asked an admiral. The admiral hedged a bit at the beginning, but, under Stout's careful investigative prodding ("Do you think, Admi-ral, that the cost of what we're doing is worth the return?"), he informed us, "Yes, I do think that the cost is definitely worth it." Then Stout asked a general, who sat before a map, wearing lots of medals and looking very splendid. The general happened to be the general who is in charge of the Air Force planes that do the bombing, and the essence of his views, which were couched in a longish speech full of military and business-military-English phrases about "continuing interdiction activities," was "I think we've had a major effect on the lines of communication." Then he asked General Curtis LeMay—That's right. Then he asked General Curtis LeMay, who was in civilian dress but very grand— actually, you had to look fairly closely to realize that he was in civilian dress—and who contributed to the general clarification as follows: "I would tell the North Vietnamese that we are going to start hitting their expensive and vital targets . . . and start out by eliminating Haiphong There are many ways of doing it. . . . Then I'd start right out with what industry they have, their power plants . . . the transportation system . . . warning the people to get away. . . . If they want everything in the country destroyed, tell them we're going to destroy everything." Then back to the Navy and another admiral—Admiral Sharp, as it happens, who is in charge of all the Navy in the Pacific—who was a little sulky at first on the subject ("We, as military men, would like to see these restrictions removed, of course, but, as the unified commander, I recognize that in Washing-ton . . ."), but was able to brighten up at least to the extent of advising us, "Well, I think the bombing is shortening the war, and surely if we stop bombing I think that would automatically prolong the war."

By now, you probably think that C.B.S. is another branch of the gov-ernment, or of the military, or of both. Not a bit of it. After all, there are bound to be two sides to the bombing controversy, aren't there? If there *is* a bombing controversy, which C.B.S. seemed just a little reluctant to face up to. Fifty-three minutes after the hour, with five minutes to go (not counting commercials), C.B.S. unleashed the opposition, which consisted of a minute-long extract of testimony by Harrison Salisbury, very tweedy, unmedalled, his face only one among many faces, at a Senate hearing (at which no one on camera seemed to be paying him any attention) on the relative advantages and drawbacks of the bombing ("To my way of thinking, the one cancels out the other . . ."), and a short, prim little interview with the inevitable Senator Fulbright, who remarked that Secretary McNamara had said that the bombing hadn't appreciably cut down on the infiltration of men and supplies—an idea that the C.B.S. audience was now hearing, fleetingly, for the first time that evening—and that "I don't think it's accomplished its purpose."

After a commercial, Stout reappeared briefly, referred in passing to the matter of civilians' having been killed by bombing ("Civilians always are killed in war"), and then attempted to truthify—a word I just made up and now present to C.B.S. for the duration—the previous fifty-eight minutes of propaganda by admitting, without much conviction, that the bombing had only "partly" succeeded. Well, swell. One points out that C.B.S., along with N.B.C., is the major source of news and opinion for most of the people in this country. One points out that, at a rough guess, nine million people watched *Vietnam Perspective* that evening. One points out that we elect our government—so we say—on the basis of what we know and are given to know. One points out that one deserves a damned lot better.

THE THEATRE

KENNETH TYNAN

SWEET BIRDIE OF YOUTH

APRIL 23, 1960 (*BYE BYE BIRDIE*)

THE FIRST HALF of *Bye Bye Birdie,* at the Martin Beck, contains a dream ballet wherein a jealous young woman vengefully imagines her fiancé being put to death by a variety of means, including the firing squad, the guillotine, the sword, and the axe. It is a phrenetic and repetitive piece of horseplay, and I wish it could be done away with. Moreover, the girl's jealousy, which not only inspires the ballet but sets in motion the events of the second act, is brought about by a device of singular fragility—the arrival, out of left field, of a billowing blonde who ogles the fiancé, gets herself a job as his assistant, and exits immediately afterward, never to be seen again. To add to the list of complaints, I am not exactly wild about the title of the show, which derives its alliteration from the fact that the plot has to do with a rock-'n'-roll singer named Conrad Birdie and his departure from civilian life to undergo military training. Furthermore, I didn't like the picture on the cover of the program, and the theatre struck me as being overheated. And that about does it; as far as derogation is concerned, I have shot my bolt. Everything else about *Bye Bye Birdie* seemed to me completely enchanting, and filled with a kind of affectionate freshness that we have seldom encountered since Mr. Rodgers collaborated with Mr. Hart on *Babes in Arms.* In saying this, I don't think I have been unduly swayed by the boisterous enthusiasm of the first-night audience. Nobody knows better than I that ecstatic applause early in the evening is infectious and self-perpetuating. Those who start it feel in honor bound to sustain it, and the rest join in out of a mystical desire to be brushed by the wings of success. In the present case, at least half the clamor was justified, and that is saying a great deal.

What impressed me most about the production was the unanimity of its teamwork, and I hope I won't be charged with invidiousness if I begin by praising the actors. The hero, Birdie's bedevilled manager, is played by Dick Van Dyke with the casual, lantern-jawed grace of Astaire, and there are hints of Gene Kelly in the dance he shares with a glum little girl (Sharon Lerit) who, alone among the members of Birdie's fan club in Sweet Apple, Ohio, cannot bring herself to crack a welcoming smile when her idol visits the town. Mr. Van Dyke's lanky vagueness contrasts splendidly with the purposeful compactness of Chita Rivera, as his secretary and fiancée. Miss Rivera, who looks like a cross between Marlene Dietrich and a Latin-American soubrette, performs smartly throughout, but her high point is a number called "Spanish Rose," in which she parodies Hispanophilia in all its aspects, from *cante hondo* to "La Cucaracha." Her worst enemy is Mr. Van Dyke's self-pitying mother. The latter role is played by the incomparable Kay Medford, traipsing about in a mink coat at all hours of the day and night and uttering every syllable in a tone of reproachful resignation that is expressly intended to make her son squirm with guilt. (At one point, stung by a filial rebuff, Miss Medford sinks to her knees, mink and all, and carefully inserts her head in a gas oven. The practiced ease with which she carries out the maneuver is indelibly funny.) Then, there is Susan Watson, as an eager adolescent who has been chosen to receive Birdie's last kiss before the Army swallows him up. "How lovely to be a woman!" she sings, pulling on her Argyle socks and zipping up her jeans, and such is Miss Watson's charm that we readily overlook the subsequent lapse whereby she identifies Ingrid Bergman's ex-husband as Benito Mussolini. Her bashful boy friend is engagingly played by Michael J. Pollard, who, disillusioned by her defection to Birdie, hesitantly swaggers into a bar and demands "a double rocks on the Scotch." Nor have I anything but admiration for Paul Lynde, as Miss Watson's father—an edgy, enfeebled male, capable at times of startling his family with fits of pettish exasperation but totally incapable of repressing a broad, meaningless grin when he finds himself facing a television camera. (Among other things, he worries about his age. "I'm not an old man," he snarls at his daughter. "I was eighteen in World War Two.") A nimble horde of ruddy-cheeked juniors is on hand to sing Birdie's praises, and Dick Gautier plays the god of their idolatry with resplendent sideburns, a surly mien, a built-in slouch, and a wardrobe full of leopard-skin dressing gowns and gold lamé tights.

The book, by Michael Stewart, is shiny with metropolitan, upper-bohemian wit, and its references to Ruby Keeler and Margo suggest to me that Mr. Stewart, like several other authors in the musical-comedy dodge, is enthralled by the early history of talking pictures. My favorite line, which has nothing to do with Hollywood, is delivered by Mr. Lynde. "Who's the head of the F.B.I.?" he asks. "Is it Pat Nixon yet?" This may be as good a time as any to remind ourselves of the fact that *Bye Bye Birdie* is what the trade calls an original; apart from *The Music Man*, it is the only musical play on Broadway that is not based on something else. Charles Strouse wrote the tunes, and Lee Adams the lyrics; by my count, the score includes eight memorable numbers, chief among them a gentle tribute, entitled "One Boy," to the pleasure of going steady, and an ironic full-throated hymn dedicated to the greater glory of Ed Sullivan. The molding hand, however, and the supervising intelligence unquestionably belong to Gower Champion, who directed the show and took care of the choreography. I attribute to him the filmed prologue, in which shots of Birdie brandishing his pelvis are alternated with glimpses of Khrushchev, Eisenhower, and Frank Sinatra, all looking extremely dubious; to him, too, I ascribe the beguiling first-act routine wherein dozens of teen-agers—each occupying a section of what resembles a Gargantuan jungle gym—exchange telephone calls in polyphonous song; nor have I yet mentioned the extraordinary ballet, featuring Miss Rivera and a group of lecherous Shriners, that takes place at, away from, and under (mostly under) a long conference table. I congratulate Mr. Champion, and I urge you to see and hear what he and his colleagues have wrought.

THE THEATRE ABROAD:
LONDON

NOVEMBER 9, 1968

O RSON WELLES, WHO hasn't touched the theatre with a barge
pole of late (though he flung a harpoon at it in 1955, playing
Ahab in his own production of *Moby Dick*), once said to me,
"London is the actor's city, Paris is the playwright's city, and New York
is the director's city." At the time—some seven years ago—that was just
about true, but Welles, never a man to be caught with a dated generaliza-
tion, has since revised his opinions. He now believes that New York is
David Merrick's city and that Paris is no longer of any theatrical interest
whatever but that "London is still the great place for actors." The old
whaler is right again. To be more precise, in stage performers under
thirty and over fifty (most of the best of the rest are busy paying for the
country house, the Bentley, and the unostentatious yacht by working in
movies and television) London leads Europe and probably the Western
world. The town is full of flexible, classless actors, predominantly young,
who are equally at home in Elizabethan blank verse and in the blank
prose of authors like Harold Pinter. It is much less full of playwrights. In
this category, nearly everyone of mature years—Terence Rattigan and
Christopher Fry are salient examples—has been driven out to pasture in
the cinema, and the theatrical field is occupied by an amorphous group
of younger talents, numbering not more than a dozen. As for directors,
Britain has only a handful who are of international stature. Even so, it
wouldn't be difficult to make a persuasive case for London as a directo-
rial stronghold, since the top-ranking few—men like Peter Hall, Peter
Brook, and John Dexter—wield a tremendous amount of power. Quite
as much as the playwrights and the actors, they are the molders of taste,
because the plays of their choice get not only the best staging but the
most distinguished casts.

What follows is a hindsight survey of the London theatre as it revealed itself in 1967. The first thing to be said is that its private sector has
changed hardly at all in the past decade. Thrillers, farces, and musicals
have still been hopefully crowding the playbills, eked out with safe classical revivals and the odd adventurous novelty. But the scene as a whole

has been transformed—and the theatre of commerce has been dwarfed—by the advent of two state-subsidized titans: the Royal Shakespeare Company, which branched out from its Stratford headquarters in 1960 to take over the Aldwych Theatre in London, and the National Theatre, which set up shop at the Old Vic in 1963. Faced with these enormous competitors, the West End producers—who never planned ahead, naïvely supposing that their middle-class, middle-aged, undiscriminating audience would be perpetually self-renewing—are hanging on to the ropes. Some of them are even demanding that their box-office gambles be safeguarded against loss by government aid. Implicit in this proposal is a self-incriminating admission: that the commercial theatre has ceased, for the most part, to be commercial.

It used to be, at least, somewhere to go for a laugh. Great comics don't readily fit into repertory companies, where their anarchic gusto tends to burst the seams of any production in which they appear; it's hard, for example, to imagine Phil Silvers as the porter in *Macbeth*. (Great tragedians are much easier to accommodate. Most of the longest parts in the classical repertoire belong either to tragedy or to its house-trained, bourgeois cousin high comedy. There is room in Congreve for the genius of an Olivier but not for that of a Silvers.) The commercial stage has traditionally been the spawning ground and the stamping ground of comic talent. Latterly, however, the guffaws have been less than deafening. Brian Rix, a hardworking actor-manager who made a fortune for many years out of the kind of formula farce in which meanings, takes, and beds are invariably double, moved into the Garrick Theatre over a year ago and advertised his new home as "The Theatre of Laughter." Thus far, he hasn't found farces plausible enough or actors outrageous enough (or vice versa) to justify that hubristic subtitle. The right people for this genre, authors and performers alike, seem either to have died out or to have gone over, tamed and domesticated, to situation comedy on TV. What we've seen at the Garrick to date has been curiously academic—conventional farce as it might be re-created a century hence by a keen group of archeology students. The results have been about as jolly as the Christmas long-jumping contests in Lapland. I can't say much more for Alan Ayckbourn's *Relatively Speaking*, the official laugh smash of 1967, which is an atavistic country-house comedy written with the sort of smirking cuteness that often accompanies a punning title. It's all about misconstrued relationships—a husband mistakes his mistress's boyfriend for his wife's lover, and the boyfriend mistakes the mistress's lover for her father. If any of them were to ask a couple of obvious questions, the whole uninsurable structure would collapse, and the curtain would fall inside thirty minutes. The setting was pure nostalgia: wickerwork furniture on a terrace in burning sunlight, with a willow casting its shadow on a heavily creased backcloth. The company was led by Celia Johnson and Michael Hordern, who rowed away furiously like stoical scullers trapped in a waterlogged skiff. Meanwhile, at the East End theatre where she made (and consolidated) her name with such productions as *A Taste of Honey, The Hostage,* and *Oh, What a Lovely War!,* Joan Littlewood directed a bonhomous little crowd pleaser called *Mrs. Wilson's Diary.* Her admirers hid their chagrin under gallant smiles, but it wasn't easy: a cozier, more rubber-fanged piece of political lampooning you could scarcely conceive. It's based on a popular column that the authors, Richard Ingrams and John Wells, contribute to the satirical fortnightly *Private Eye.* Life with the Prime Minister is seen from the viewpoint of his awed but adoring wife, in whose chatty journal Downing Street becomes the epitome of chintzy suburbia, ruled by a plump, Pooterish figure with a bad case of *folie de grandeur.* The joke is sharper on the page—where it deftly mirrors the suffocating banality of the Wilson regime—than it is on the stage. Having gone through the Littlewood treatment, it emerged as featherweight gossip, distinguished by three clever acts of impersonation: Myvanwy Jenn was a winningly gauche first lady, Bob Grant struck the right note of apologetic bluster as George Brown, and Bill Wallis was a chubby young ringer for the ringmaster himself. Clad as Batman when he made his first entrance, Mr. Wallis later changed into Churchillian garb and sonorously declared, "I am now going into the garden to paint a brick wall with my bare hands." From time to time, members of the cast indulged in typical Cockney ad libs, all of them robustly unfunny. The production's failure as satire was proved by the fact that nobody either loved it or hated it.

"*Le mieux est l'ennemi du bien.*" True, but Voltaire might have added that the worse is the friend of the bad. Compared with most of what was going on around it, *Wise Child*—a bizarre first play by Simon Gray— seemed almost tolerable. "At least," I heard someone say in the intermission, "it's fairly *pretentious.*" The theme is sexual ambiguity, exemplified by a trio of social outcasts: a robber on the run, disguised as a middle-aged matron and holed up in a provincial hotel; his accomplice, a willowy lad with an Oedipal fixation, who is posing as his son; and the Scottish hotelier, a deeply religious homosexual named Simon ("after Simon called Peter, the fisher of men"), who sets his cap at the pseudo son. This triangle is extended by an ingenuous West Indian chambermaid to whom the robber, an impenitent hetero, takes a passing shine. After two hours of sour and only occasionally penetrating banter, matters rise to a climax of gratuitous violence—that obligatory hallmark of black comedy. The passionate Scot is clubbed to death by the junior Oedipus. But the play has not earned its right to that kind of seriousness. What we have here is a farce that has tried to get above itself and failed for want of emotional propulsion. The best acting, in the sense of psychological identification, came from Gordon Jackson as the prim, devoutly effusive Scottish queer. The best performance, in the sense of technical virtuosity, was that of Alec Guinness, who played the enforced transvestite. He skated rings round the part, his voice changing—often within a sentence, sometimes within a phrase—from a tight-lipped Kensington twitter to a beery Cockney growl. No sooner did you catch yourself peering inquisitively at his stocking tops than he recalled you to sanity with a baritone jeer. This was a marvellous display of external skills, and it fully confirmed what a shrewd critic of acting once told me: "Alec has no center. He works best on the outer edges of his personality. At the periphery of himself, he is a master."

Wise Child was no isolated oddity but part of a pattern to which many of the younger British playwrights are at present conforming. Their characteristic mode is comic menace couched in enigmatic non sequiturs and finally erupting in arbitrary brutality; their watchword is moral noncommitment; and their martyred saint is Joe Orton—the author of *Entertaining Mr. Sloane* and *Loot*—whose short life (he was thirty-four) ended dreadfully last year, when he was battered to death by his roommate. Orton wrote shapely, deadpan comedies about the grimier aspects of human behavior, on which he cast a cool but not censorious eye. His style was often jejune, and he died before it could properly mature, but at its best it had a laconic, unshockable grace that contrasted superbly with the squalor of his subject matter. In diluted form, the Orton manner survives in his imitators. No harm in that, but they have also inherited his complete lack of interest in social and political change. The work they produce is entirely unprotesting. Calm acceptance of the evitable as well as the inevitable—such is the attitude they reflect and, by implication, recommend. (And the setting need not be modern. Witness the flamboyant fatalism of Tom Stoppard's *Rosencrantz and Guildenstern Are Dead*—a worm's-eye view of *Hamlet* with the doomed worms humbly acquiescing in their own extinction.) The mutinous energies that were released in 1956 by the première of John Osborne's *Look Back in Anger* seem now to be temporarily exhausted. According to Hilary Spurling, the drama critic of the *Spectator*, we ought to have expected that "the primitives of the fifties would be followed by a wave of more sophisticated playwrights." Miss Spurling then refers to the famous British revue *Beyond the Fringe*, in which Alan Bennett preached a comic sermon on the text "Behold, Esau my brother is an hairy man, and I am a smooth man." Using this as her springboard, she claims that the hairy age of British theatre is over, and that "just as John Osborne provided a battle cry for an earlier generation, so Mr. Bennett's is the text of our own." I won't pretend to share Miss Spurling's delight in this development. With smoothness has come detachment—a civilized virtue, to be sure, but one that tends to drive out passion.

In the work of Harold Pinter, however, though he is the prophet of the smooth school, an apparent detachment conceals strong and complex feelings. They freeze when they are exposed to the Arctic climate of mutual mistrust in which his characters (and, by implication, most people) habitually communicate with one another, but passion is always there, just under the quick-frozen surface, and this pressure of emotion is what distinguishes his world from that of his followers. Getting him to write a play is like begging a glacier to hurry, and nothing new from his pen arrived on the London stage in 1967. He was, however, responsible for the gelid direction of *The Man in the Glass Booth*, the *drame à thèse* by the actor-novelist-playwright Robert Shaw that has now moved to Broadway. This fashionably applauded piece, in transposing the Eichmann trial into fictional terms, sets out to shock us into a fresh awareness of the meaning of guilt, but it plays like a pompous detective thriller. The author's aim is to show us a new Christ figure, willing to take upon himself all the sins of the world, Jewish and Gentile alike. The thesis is fascinating, but the characters are vinyl cutouts. Donald Pleasence, who plays the principal role, resembles a parody of the late Lenny Bruce impersonating Louis B. Mayer—or so, at least, it seemed in London. Playgoers in New York, always notorious for their anglophilia, may have other views of Mr. Pleasence's performance.

The best new British play to hit the commercial sector of the London theatre in 1967 was Peter Nichols' *A Day in the Death of Joe Egg*, known on Broadway as *Joe Egg tout court*. It began its career, significantly, with a state-subsidized repertory company in Glasgow. From there it was transferred to the West End, with the original cast substantially intact. The London opening was one of those occasions that mark a seismographic shift in public taste: something theretofore taboo entered the realm of theatrical acceptance. How can a young provincial schoolteacher and his wife cope with reality when their child turns out to be a spastic? Only (according to Mr. Nichols, himself the father of a handicapped daughter) by treating the agony as a grotesque cosmic joke—by laughing at what would otherwise be unbearable. Cruelty cauterizes, and if you are the parents of a "human vegetable" it's saner to invent vaudeville routines about your predicament than to spend your time in floods of self-pity. The first half of the play is faultless, a model of desperate hilarity, and the London production had movingly funny performances by Joe Melia and Zena Walker as Dad and Mum. Part II doesn't walk the tightrope with quite the same aplomb. Mr. Nichols trumps up a melodramatic dénoucment in which the husband leaves his wife after trying to freeze their daughter to death by exposing her to the nocturnal blasts of an English winter. This makes a strong ending, but the crux of the situation is that it cannot end. It is tragic precisely because it is permanent. In seeking to solve an insoluble problem, Mr. Nichols fails, but he fails at a very high level. When he slips, it is off a mountain, not a molehill. It takes great talent to steer a work of art to a position in which such mistakes are possible. I don't think it's irrelevant to harp on the fact that the play had its first showing at the hands of a state-aided company. How many commercial producers would have risked their money on a comedy about a spastic? Moreover, the play is an essentially theatrical experience, in that many of its best effects occur when one of the actors steps out of a scene and directly addresses the audience. This is a trick that never really works in movies or in television drama, where we know that the actors are addressing a single, impassive, robot spectator—the camera.

BRENDAN GILL

OFF BROADWAY

JUNE 28, 1969 (*OH! CALCUTTA!*)

ITH ALL MY heart, I recommend staying away from the slick and repulsive come-on called *Oh! Calcutta!*, the very title of which—a pun in English on a ribald French slang phrase—hints at the abject schoolboy level of wit to which this "entertainment with music" laboriously aspires. The drama critic and impresario Kenneth Tynan is billed as having "devised" the show, and I am at a loss to understand how he has managed to plunge so unnimbly far below the standards that he has always set for others. I am also at a loss to know why Jacques Levy should wish it to be known that the "entire production was conceived and directed by Jacques Levy." In Mr. Levy's shoes, I would have given it out that the director's name was Millard Fillmore, or maybe Gyp the Blood. The authors of the tasteless and talentless skits that make up the bulk of the show are mercifully denied individual credit for their handiwork; writhing together like snakes in a pail under the heading "Contributors" are Samuel Beckett, Jules Feiffer, Dan Greenburg, John Lennon, Jacques Levy, Leonard Melfi, Sam Shepard, Kenneth Tynan, Sherman Yellen, and the team of David Newman and Robert Benton. Even the least of this uneven assortment of names is diminished by its association with *Oh! Calcutta!* As for the attractive young actors and actresses who people the stage of the inappropriately renamed Eden Theatre, what can they have been thinking of when they consented to appear in roles that in most cases require little more of them than that they shuck off their clothes, talk dirty, and manipulate themselves and each other sexually in a dreary succession of conventional burlesque blackouts? I suppose the question answers itself: actors prefer working to thinking, and for them any stage is better than none.

Of the many gifts of the many people associated with *Oh! Calcutta!*, the one that has served the show best is Mr. Tynan's Barnum-like capacity for lining up suckers by dint of skillful advance publicity. In a number of pronunciamentos handed down to the press before the opening, he indicated that his intention was to give the public what it richly deserves and rarely gets—a demonstration in a theatre of the joyful nature of sex.

To this end, it was archly promised that all of the members of the cast would be, from time to time, totally naked (and how beautiful their bodies are, in the pride and disciplined suppleness of their youth!), but obviously there is more to sex than nudity, and it is perversely Victorian of Mr. Tynan to have put so much emphasis upon it. But the chief indictment to be made of *Oh! Calcutta!* is that, a couple of dance numbers aside, there is not a single joyful thing about it; it is a radically anti-erotic enterprise, whose gloomy and preposterous message is that women are objects, either dangerous or funny, and, in any case, deserving to be abased and defiled. An audience that sits and listens to such a message is also abased and defiled.

MUSIC

WHITNEY BALLIETT

NEWPORT NOTES

JULY 22, 1967

RIDAY. TONIGHT, WHICH was promisingly cool and clear, was touted as a history of jazz and the "Schlitz Salute to Jazz in 1967" (the beer people plunked down a manly twenty-five-thousand-dollar subsidy for the evening), but it turned out to be an astonishing parade of pianists made up of Willie the Lion Smith, Earl Hines, Count Basie, Thelonious Monk, and John Lewis. (The concert also turned out to be in the classic horn-of-plenty Newport Jazz Festival tradition; there were no fewer than ten groups, and the concert lasted over five hours. The departing crowd, bent and shuffling, resembled a mass of Stepin Fechits and Groucho Marxes.) Hines was the guidon. After a good solo rendition of "You Can Depend on Me," he was joined by Ruby Braff for a couple of surprisingly successful duets. The two men, both fearless, self-preoccupied ornamentalists, had never played together before, but they got off a graceful "These Foolish Things" and a fast, intent "Rosetta." Hines' solos were full of his arrhythmic whirlpools and upper-register, single-note jubilations, and Braff managed to move in apposite parallels. Willie the Lion, got up in his summer uniform (straw skimmer, white jacket, and cigar), played a vigorous if brief "Carolina Shout" and then teamed up for three numbers with Don Ewell, a hardy disciple of Jelly

Roll Morton and Fats Waller. Smith, who gives the deceptive impression when he plays that he is stretched out on a chaise longue casually dictating his memoirs, is almost always unpredictable, and tonight was no exception. He produced booming, irregular chord patterns and rifle-shot single notes, while Ewell, a correct but swinging pianist, was an admirable foil. Basie backed Buddy Tate and Buck Clayton in two sensuous numbers (Tate and Clayton are not only the two best-looking men in the world but the most luxurious-sounding) and then headed up his own cartel, but he was, lamentably, visible only in short solos and behind soloists. (When will someone march Basie into a recording studio with a first-rate rhythm section and let him loose—an event that hasn't taken place for over twenty years?) An impossible all-star reunion of former bebop kings—Dizzy Gillespie, James Moody, Milt Jackson, Thelonious Monk, Percy Heath, and Max Roach—was indeed impossible, save for Monk. Gillespie seemed inhibited, Moody was uncertain, Jackson was mechanical, and Roach, as is his custom, was on Cloud 9. But Monk, stewing enjoyably in his own inexhaustible juices, was imperturbable, particularly in "How High the Moon," in which he took an excellent solo and supplied Gillespie with a stream of sudden, jarring chords that suggested a sheriff shooting up the ground around a sluggish outlaw. John Lewis brought up the rear with the Modern Jazz Quartet, demonstrating again that there are few pianists—tonight's diamonds included—who put as much grace and thought and intensity into each chorus. In his quiet, deliberate way, he took the blue ribbon.

The evening had other pleasures. The Newport Jazz Festival All Stars (Ruby Braff, Pee Wee Russell, Bud Freeman, George Wein, Jack Lesberg, and Don Lamond) offered, among other numbers, a slow "Sugar," in which Russell, more sotto-voce than usual, fashioned—or perhaps was fashioned by—a four-bar phrase made up of incredibly juggled notes, and a slow "Summertime," in which Budd Johnson, sitting in on soprano saxophone, wailed and pirouetted à la Sidney Bechet. The concert was closed by the Albert Ayler Quintet, a "new-thing" group that includes Ayler (a saxophonist), his brother (a trumpeter), and the drummer Milford Graves. Most of their efforts were expended on an occasionally funny parody of what sounded like a Salvation Army hymn and of fragments of "There's No Place Like Home" and "Eeny-Meeny-Miney-Mo." After a small sampling, the audience began packing up and leaving, causing my companion to observe that "Ayler is really breaking it up."

. . .

Saturday. The weather is getting restless. It is still cool, but fog has been doing the mazurka up and down Narragansett Bay all afternoon, and tonight it circled once about the town and fell asleep. So did much of tonight's concert. The John Handy Quintet (vibraphone, guitar, bass, drums, and the leader's alto saxophone) punched and plodded through two endless numbers, one a musical attempt at "what it took to get James Meredith into the University of Mississippi" and the other a Spanish-tinged new-thing number called "Señor Nancy." Nina Simone, a Juilliard-trained pianist and singer who relishes a mean country blues, got hung up in a couple of interminable laments about loose men and fast women, and Dizzy Gillespie, appearing with his quintet, did four by-rote numbers. But the oddest disappointment was the new and revolutionary Gary Burton Quartet, which has Larry Coryell on guitar, Steve Swallow on bass, Stu Martin on drums, and the leader on vibraphone. Burton's group, like that of Jeremy Steig, is working toward a distillate compounded of rock and roll and jazz, but these important explorations were only fitfully apparent. Coryell and Burton played an intricate duet, using a variety of rhythms, and in a slow blues Coryell, who is the first great hope on his instrument since Charlie Christian and Django Reinhardt, hit on one of those seemingly stumbling but perfectly executed phrases—several barely audible behind-the-beat single notes followed by silence and a leaping, brilliant run—that Charlie Parker coined. Earl Hines, accompanied by Bill Pemberton (bass), Oliver Jackson (drums), and Budd Johnson, just about matched his Friday-night performance, and in a slow ballad he indulged in a bit of cheerful vaudeville; he played an introduction and then gave way to Johnson, who, though nowhere in sight, could be heard thunderously from the loudspeakers. It was the Lord calling from backstage. At twelve o'clock, Buddy Rich appeared with his big band, and the pumpkin turned into a golden coach. Rich started with a medium blues, soared through Bill Holman's ingenious arrangement of the McCartney-Lennon "Norwegian Wood," and went on to his display number, the "Bugle Call Rag." His solo was a wonder. It incorporated a section in which his left hand moved at a thousand r.p.m.s on his snare while his right hand floated casually back and forth between his tomtoms, a long, diminuendo roll that sank to barely audible knitting-needle clicking on his snare rims, and a zowie Big Bertha climax. No sooner was the number over than Rich, bowing and sweating, launched into what appeared to be an introductory twelve-bar solo in medium tempo, reared back, and said, "What'll we play?" It was a throwaway gag, but it was also an incredible little solo, a perfect solo. Gillespie then ambled onstage and blew a dozen choruses of blues with the band, and for the final number, an eleven-minute version of "West Side Story," he climbed into the trumpet section, whispered to the other trumpeters, yawned, peered elaborately at the sheet music, and ogled and shouted at Rich, who, his hands two windmills in a high wind, never batted an eye.

The afternoon concert was a genteel bust. Labelled "The Five Faces of Jazz," it was devoted to Middle Eastern music, pseudo-ragas, Afro-Cuban funk, the bossa nova, and "Norwegian Wood." The participants included Herbie Mann, the Hungarian guitarist Gabor Szabo, Luis Enrique of Brazil, and such ringers as Gillespie and the German trombonist Albert Mangelsdorff. It all sounded like a ho-hum day at the U.N.

. . .

Sunday. More fog, accompanied by snappy winds and low, pressing clouds. The afternoon concert began with half a dozen not at all surprising selections by Nobuo Hara and his Sharps and Flats, an eighteen piece Japanese band. Swathed in smiles, the group was a formidable cross between late Jimmie Lunceford and early Stan Kenton (it used a shuffle rhythm at one point that had the audience bobbing like a rooster), and its soloists suggested J. J. Johnson, Art Farmer, and Clifford Brown, plus Gene Krupa laced with Louis Bellson. In three numbers, the band accompanied Housan Yamamoto, who played a large wooden flute called the shakuhachi. He gets a husky, pleasing tone on his instrument and a direct, lyrical quality not unlike that of Joe Marsala. He should stay behind when the Sharps and Flats go home. The main event was a vibraphone workshop—Bobby Hutcherson, Gary Burton, Red Norvo, Milt Jackson, and Lionel Hampton. The vibraphone has never struck me as being a true instrument. It suggests a bedspring swinging in the wind, the sound of neon. But there were moments. Burton sent up a ghostly unaccompanied ballad that was all willows and Debussy and moonshafts; Norvo produced a creditable "I Love You" (Cole Porter's) and then went into his old anthem, "I Surrender, Dear." He switched to the xylophone after the first chorus, achieving a delicate, piping flow, mostly in the high register, and, returning to the vibraphone, made it clear that he is the only vibraphonist who miraculously transmits emotion through his non-instrument. He ended with a funny "Ida," for which he turned off his resonator and, using heavy mallets, clumped around the keyboard like a slow-motion tap-dancer. At odd intervals, he shot out his right elbow—clearly a prearranged signal for Roy Haynes, his drummer, to play a rim-shot. Haynes misfired as often as not, and it was good hamming. The rest was predictable. Hampton unloaded his customary two-by-fours, Hutcherson jammed a hundred notes into each measure, and Jackson kept his lyric cool. All five vibraphonists got together for a closing blues; then the rain, floating around the rafters for the past twenty-four hours, came, blending its sound perfectly with the heavy work onstage.

The rain was still needling in low and hard and cold at eight, when the evening began. Festival Field was tented with umbrellas and preventive do-me-good was plentiful. As it turned out, we could have all gone home and curled up before the telly. Marilyn Maye, a modern nasal Hildegarde, sag and sag and sag; Bill Evans, along with Eddie Gomez (bass) and Philly Joe Jones, swam steadily toward the surface but never reached it; Max Roach and his quintet struck off hard-bop clichés; Woody Herman's big band dipped into the gospel bag, the blues bag, and the flag-waver bag; Miles Davis, wearing a dinner jacket and an untied bow tie, spent more time offstage than on. The Blues Project, a heavily amplified five-piece group that has been moving from rock and roll toward jazz, opened the evening but was allowed just two numbers before being unplugged to make way for Miss Maye. Its amplifiers were barely warm.

The various m.c.s, however, have been warming up all weekend. We have had Billy Taylor, Father Norman O'Connor, Del Shields, and George Wein, and when they have not been babbling about the music they have been engaging in mutual admiration ("And now I would like to introduce one of the nicest . . ."). A printed program (there is one) and a curtain (there is none) dropped at the end of each act would effortlessly put them out of business.

. . .

Monday. With a couple of exceptions, tonight was a continuation of last night. (The rain, coming in tropical explosions, continued all morning and then subsided into fog.) The Dave Brubeck Quartet showed more candlepower than has been its wont in recent years, and Sarah Vaughan wandered through eight follow-me-if-you-can numbers. The evening and the festival were closed by Lionel Hampton and a big band made up largely of Hampton alumni, among them Milt Buckner, Joe Newman, Frank Foster, Benny Powell, Jerome Richardson, and Snooky Young. The alumni, however, spent most of the dozen numbers sitting on their instruments while Hampton labored at the vibraphone, the drums, and the piano. In "Flying Home," though, Illinois Jacquet, who had played well earlier in the evening, went through his celebrated calisthenics, and it was like hearing Francis Scott Key sing "The Star-Spangled Banner." The other successful numbers in the concert were done by Red Norvo, Ruby Braff, and the Wein-Lesberg-Lamond rhythm section. Norvo floated earnestly over his vibraphone, playing excellent tag in his exchanges with Braff and Lamond, and looked—with his bearded, benign, expectant way of continually lifting his head from his instrument and searching the audience—like God watching out for the Devil.

The afternoon was given over almost wholly to big bands. Don Ellis's nineteen-piece group, outfitted with an eight-man rhythm section (three bassists, four drummers, and a pianist) and a mass of electronic equipment, played five completely absorbing numbers. There were fugues and passacaglias, raga-like passages, time signatures of five/four, three-and-a-half/four, and seven/four, a sterling parody of "Bill Bailey, Won't You Please Come Home?," and electronic effects that sounded like enormous, windy caves. For all these doodads, the band swings steadily and plays with remarkable precision. The concert ended with an extravaganza called the Milford (Massachusetts) Youth Band. It is, as far as I know, the largest jazz band in history, for it boasts sixteen saxophones, eleven clarinets, five trombones, twelve trumpets, a bass, four woodwinds, a French horn, drums, and three percussion. The band ranges in age from eleven to eighteen and includes nine girls. It played a recent Basie number, Benny Goodman and Artie Shaw, a blues, a Kentonish avant-garde number, a ballad, and a Near Eastern number, and played them almost as well as any current big band. The soloists were nearly as good. Best of all were the passages in which the brass section, eighteen strong, opened up. It was glory materialized.

ELLEN WILLIS

ROCK, ETC.

JULY 6, 1968 (PACKAGING ROCK AND POST-ROCK)

THE SOCIOLOGY OF rock and post-rock has been based on three concepts: the star, the sound, and the scene. That sociology, like most, is firmly rooted in economics. Since the simplicity that gave rock its mass appeal also made it relatively easy to create, performers and the businessmen behind them faced a problem familiar to the makers of cigarettes and cars: How do you outsell a horde of competitors whose products are as good as yours? The solution was equally familiar: attractive packaging. The crucial elements in the package were charisma and sound—the artist's trademark, the gimmick that unified his work and set it apart (Little Richard's scream, the Everly Brothers' close harmonies, the Beatles' falsetto). If a performer or group did not have a unique sound, it helped to identify with a collective sound—usually that of a subculture (rockabilly, the Mersey sound) or of a creative producer (Phil Spector, Berry Gordy). I do not mean to conjure up the spectre of hucksters sitting around the Brill Building cold-bloodedly inventing salable gimmicks. Sometimes it worked that way. But mostly the process was unconscious: performers whose personal style was naturally gimmicky, or whose managers understood intuitively how to get attention, survived and bred imitators. Actually, before rock and roll became self-conscious, commercial and aesthetic considerations were almost indistinguishable; the geniuses of that period, from Chuck Berry to the early Beatles and Stones, owed their greatness to the same qualities that made them bestsellers. (Presley was an exception, and he ended up in Hollywood singing ballads.)

The Beatles were transitional figures. For one thing, their charisma was much more interesting than that of any previous rock-and-roll stars. Their image—that androgynous, childlike insouciance, the way they revelled in their fame and wealth without ever taking it or themselves seriously—sold records, which is what Brian Epstein had in mind when he made them wear mop tops and Edwardian suits. But it was also a comment on success, an embodiment of ingenuous youth in the affluent society—and "comments" and "embodiments" are, after all, aesthetic categories. Similarly, the Beatles' sound—a deliberate attempt *not* to sound black, contrary to custom—was at once a commercial novelty and an artistic self-assertion. These developments fascinated Pop artists and others for whom the aesthetic significance of commercial phenomena was a major preoccupation—enter the first self-conscious rock fans. The Beatles were also responsible for the bohemianization of rock. The concept of the rock "scene"—a term borrowed from jazz and implying an élite In group as much as a place—originated in Mod London and spread to San Francisco. Rock became identified less with particular superstars or sounds than with a whole life-style; "psychedelic" music was not so much a sound as a spirit. In 1965, the average person, asked to associate to the phrase "rock and roll," would probably have said "Beatles"; by 1967 the answer would more likely have been "hippies," "drugs," or "long hair." When American bohemians took up rock, they brought along their very un-Beatlish distinctions between art and Mammon, and for the first time people talked about "serious," as opposed to merely commercial, rock. Yet if such talk was possible, it was only because the Beatles (with a lot of help from Bob Dylan) had paced a miraculous escalation in the quality of pop songs. Since *Sgt. Pepper*, few people deny that "serious" pop is serious art. And though there is still some overlap, the split between the AM-radio-singles-teenie market and the FM-L.P.-student-hippie-intellectual audience is a fact of life.

With this evolution has come a shift in the way the music is perceived. There is, for example, an unprecedented demand for technical virtuosity. Good musicianship was once as irrelevant to rock as it was rare; the whole point of electric guitars and dubbing and echo chambers was that kids with no special talent could make nice noises. But now the music has enough scope to attract excellent instrumentalists, as well as an audience interested in traditional criteria of quality. Not that this audience's taste necessarily lives up to its pretensions; often flash is mistaken for skill. Still, a few years ago it would have been impossible for an Eric Clapton or a Mike Bloomfield to make it in pop music on the strength of fine guitar playing. The new audience also favors complex music and lyrics—a trend that threatened to get totally out of hand until Dylan's *John Wesley Harding* provided some timely propaganda for simplicity. What all this adds up to is an increasing tendency to judge pop music intrinsically, the way poetry or jazz is judged. Social context is still important, as it is for most art. But although social and economic factors were once an integral part of the rock aesthetic—indeed, defined that aesthetic—they are now subordinate to the "music itself."

On balance, in spite of all the good music that would never have happened otherwise, I think this tendency is regrettable. What it means is that rock has been co-opted by high culture, forced to adopt its standards—chief of which is the integrity of the art object. It means the end of rock as a radical experiment in creating mass culture on its own terms, ignoring élite definitions of what is or is not intrinsic to aesthetic experience. The reason the Beatles, the Stones, and Dylan are the unchallenged—and probably unchallengeable—giants of pop is that through and beyond their work their personalities have a continuing impact on the public consciousness that, if it is not aesthetic, is something just as good. (This is especially true of Dylan, an indifferent musician who never bothered to become a studio expert.) The new standards are bound to inhibit further exploration in this area. In addition, lack of a compelling image puts the new performer at an almost insuperable disadvantage in trying to make an impression on a public whose imagination is deeply involved with established artists. At best, new performers are taking longer to be recognized, and fewer and fewer will attain that special relationship to the public psyche that is so often uncomprehendingly dismissed as "mere celebrity." I'm thinking, for example, of the Sweet Inspirations, a Gospel-oriented quartet whose first album came out a while ago. They're great, and by all rights should take over the position of preeminent girl group last held by the Supremes and before that by the Shirelles. But though they have a hit single ("Sweet Inspiration"), I doubt that they will make that pinnacle. So what? Well, part of the fun of listening to the Supremes was that they were the *Supremes*.

A related problem is the loss of the mass audience. Whether the upgrading of the music is in itself responsible for that loss is questionable. The Beatles held the loyalty of their original teen-age fans long after they had stopped making simple, happy dance music; when the kids finally turned off, it was less because the Beatles were esoteric than because they were old hat. More recently, the Doors and Jefferson Airplane have done very well outside the coterie. Jimi Hendrix, on the other hand, has not, though he has all the accoutrements of the superstar—a distinctive personality (he's the only expatriate black hippie around), a distinctive sound (achieved by choke-neck playing on the electric guitar), and a spectacular live act (he plucks his guitar with his teeth, sets fire to it, and breaks it up). What *is* certain is that the new music has thoroughly confused the record industry; no one can figure out how to promote it. Since the beginning of this year, the sheer quantity of serious pop, as well as its immense variety, has defied sloganeering. Most of the new musicians are not interested in gimmickry or image-making; they just want to make music. It's no longer possible to attract notice with a fancy album cover and a way-out name. And the scenes are dying. The Small Faces are the only interesting British group to break since Cream. The best first albums of this year's San Francisco crop come from two of the original underground groups, the Loading Zone and Quicksilver Messenger Service; except for a little-known group called Serpent Power, and Blue Cheer, which has a certain crude energy going for it (what I mean is, it's loud), the "second generation" San Francisco groups are a disaster. Early this year, MGM Records, out of naïveté or desperation, tried to invent a new scene, and a few other companies went along. It was called the Boston Sound (though there was no special sound involved) and was promoted as anti-drug and anti-exotic—rather negative premises on which to build a scene. The groups themselves were a dreary lot, ranging from the competently frenetic Beacon Street Union to the sublimely ridiculous Earth Opera. (By the time the E.O. album was released, the vibrations were pretty bad, so the group was billed as a *Cambridge* product. It didn't help.) Moral: scenes may be made, but they have to be born first.

For the sake of completeness, I ought to note that there are two areas of pop music in which sociology still dominates. First, *negative* charisma is very potent. A group that is thought of as a teenybopper band won't be accepted by most serious rock fans no matter how good it is. Ask someone in the audience at the Fillmore East what he thinks of the Hollies or the Young Rascals. Second, there is a minor cult of sensitive adolescent folkies like Tim Buckley and Steve Noonan, for no reason I can discern except that they are probably just like the kids who idolize them. In the case of Richie Havens, the attraction must be that he is black and friendly—an irresistible combination these days.

ROCK, ETC.

SEPTEMBER 6, 1969 (WOODSTOCK)

YOU HAVE TO give the producers of the Woodstock Music and Art Fair this much credit: they are pulling off a great public-relations coup. They have apparently succeeded in creating the impression that the crisis in Bethel was a capricious natural disaster rather than a product of human incompetence, that the huge turnout was completely unexpected (and, in fact, could not have been foreseen by reasonable men), and that they have lost more than a million dollars in the process of being good guys who did everything possible to transform an incipient fiasco into a groovy weekend. Incredibly, instead of hiding from the wrath of disappointed ticket-buyers and creditors they are bragging that the festival was a landmark in the development of youth culture and have announced that they plan to hold it again next year. But before history is completely rewritten, a few facts, semi-facts, and strong inferences are in order.

For at least a month before the festival, it was obvious to everyone involved in the music scene—industry people, writers for both the straight and the underground press, radicals, and hippies—and also to the city fathers of Wallkill, New York, that the crowd was going to be enormous and the facilities inadequate. The four under-thirty backers of Woodstock Ventures seemed to be motivated less by greed than by sheer hubris: the ambitiousness of the project was meant to establish them as *the* pop producers, kingpins of the youth market. Their promotion was pervasive. On July 18th, a month before the festival, the *Times* reported that the management expected as many as two hundred thousand people and had already sold fifty thousand tickets. At that time, they were planning to hold the festival in Wallkill, on a three-hundred-acre site—half the size of the grounds in Bethel—linked to civilization by three country roads. When a Concerned Citizens Committee warned that Wallkill's water supply could not accommodate the anticipated influx and that festival officials had not made realistic plans to cope with traffic, health, or security, the producers vowed to fight the town's attempt to exclude them and implied that the opposition came from anti-youth rednecks. When the change of site was announced, just twenty-four days before the scheduled opening of the Fair, there was a lot of speculation that it would never come off at all. An experienced promoter told me, "It'll happen, but only because they've got so much money tied up in it. They can't afford to back out. But they'll never finish their preparations in three weeks. Monterey took three months. It's going to be complete chaos." Alfred G. Aronowitz, of the *Post*, one of the few journalists to cast a consistently cold eye on the four young entrepreneurs, wrote witty on-location reports giving them the needle and adding to the general pessimism. Meanwhile, back on St. Marks Place, Woodstock was rapidly evolving into this year's thing to do. A "Woodstock Special" issue of the underground weekly *Rat*, published the week of the festival, featured a page of survival advice that began, "The call has been put out across the country for hundreds of thousands to attend a three-day orgy of music and dope and communal experience." I left for Bethel in much the same spirit that I had gone to Chicago at the time of the Democratic Convention. I was emotionally prepared for a breakdown in services and a major riot. If I enjoyed the festival, that would be incidental to participating in a historic event. The actual number of people who showed up was a surprise. The only other real surprise was that there was no riot. The extra numbers could not excuse the flimsiness of the water pipes (they broke down almost immediately), the paucity of latrines (about eight hundred for an expected two hundred thousand people) and garbage cans, or the makeshift medical facilities (the press tent had to be converted into a hospital). One kid reportedly died of a burst appendix—an incident that in 1969 should at least inspire some questions.

Although it is possible that the Fair lost money, many knowledgeable people are inclined to doubt that the loss was anywhere near the one and a half million dollars Woodstock Ventures is claiming. The corporation should open its books to the public. The thousands of ticket-holders who were turned away from the site because of traffic jams (while other thousands of contributors to the traffic jams got in free) deserve some consideration. So far, the management has said nothing about refunds, and there has been talk of setting up a group suit to demand the money. One complication is that since no tickets were collected there is no way of distinguishing those who made it from those who didn't, but rumor has it that the state may sidestep this problem by suing the producers on the ground that they had no serious intention of taking tickets at the fairgrounds.

If the festival succeeded in spite of the gross ineptitude of its masterminds, it was mostly because three hundred thousand or more young people were determined to have a good time no matter what. The accounts of the peacefulness and generosity of the participants are all true, but they have tended to miss the point. The cooperative spirit did not stem from solidarity in an emergency—the "we all forgot our differences and helped each other" phenomenon that attends power blackouts and hurricanes—so much as from a general refusal to adopt any sort of emergency psychology. The widespread conviction that the Lord (or the Hog Farm, or the people of Monticello, or someone) would provide removed any incentive to fight or to hoard food, and the pilgrims simply proceeded to do what they had come to do: dig the music and the woods, make friends, reaffirm their life style in freedom from hostile straights and cops, swim naked, and get high. Drug dealing was completely open; kids stood on Hurd Road, the main thoroughfare of the festival site, hawking mescaline and acid. But the most exhilarating intoxicants were the warmth and fellow-feeling that allowed us to abandon our chronic defenses against other people. As for the music, though rock was the only thing that could have drawn such a crowd, it was not the focal point of the festival but, rather, a pleasant background to the mass presence of the hip community. Few of us got close enough to see anything, and as the music continued for seventeen hours at a stretch our adrenalin output naturally decreased. (On Sunday, a boy who had driven in from California commented, "Wow, I can't believe all the groups here, and I'm not even listening to them." "It's not the music," said another. "It's—all this!") The sound system was excellent, and thousands listened from camps in the woods, dozing and waking while the music went on till dawn. Everyone was so quiet you felt almost alone in the dark, but you couldn't move very far without stepping on someone's hand or brushing against a leg.

. . .

The festival site was like the eye of a storm—virtually undisturbed by the frantic activity behind the scenes. Once the nuisance of getting there was over with (I eventually got a ride in a performers' police-escorted caravan) and the Lord had provided (I just happened to bump into some friends with a leakproof tent and plenty of food), I found the inconveniences trivial compared to the pleasures. But then I did not have to sleep out in the mud for two nights, and by Sunday I couldn't help suspecting that some of the beautiful, transcendent acceptance going around was just plain old passivity. It was a bit creepy that there was such a total lack of resentment at the Fair's mismanagement, especially among those who had paid from seven to eighteen dollars. People either made excuses for Woodstock Ventures ("They couldn't help it, man; it was just too big for them") or thought of the festival as a noble social experiment to which crass concepts like responsible planning were irrelevant. For the most part, they took for granted not only the discomforts but the tremendous efforts made by the state, the local communities, and unpaid volunteers to distribute cheap or free food and establish minimum standards of health and safety. No one seemed to comprehend what the tasks of mobilizing and transporting emergency food, water, and medical personnel, clearing the roads, and removing garbage meant in terms of labor and money. Ecstatic heads even proclaimed that the festival proved the viability of a new culture in which no one worked and everything was free. And in the aftermath anyone who has dared to complain has been put down as a crank. It should be possible to admit that the people created a memorable gathering without embracing those who botched things up. (A letter writer in the *Village Voice* went as far as to say, "Woodstock Ventures should be congratulated and not chastised for giving us smiles, peace, music, and good vibrations." All those paying customers might disagree about being "given" music; personally, I don't see why Woodstock Ventures should get credit for my smiles.) But maybe it isn't. And maybe there is a lesson here about the political significance of youth culture. From the start, the cultural-revolutionary wing of the radical movement saw Woodstock as a political issue. The underground papers made a lot of noise about businessmen profiting from music that belonged to the community, and some movement people demanded and received money to bring political groups to the festival and set up an enclave called Movement City as a center for radical activity. If the festival staff had been foolish enough to try to restrict the audience to paid admissions, the movement might have had something to do. As it was, Movement City was both physically and spiritually isolated from the bulk of the crowd. It was not the activists but a hundred-odd members of the Hog Farm, a Santa Fe–based pacifistic commune, who were the most visible community presence, operating a free kitchen, helping people recover from bad acid trips, and setting up a rudimentary communication system of oral and written survival bulletins. A few radicals talked hopefully of liberating the concessions or the stage area. Abbie Hoffman interrupted the Who's set on Saturday night to berate the crowd for listening to music when John Sinclair, a Michigan activist, had just been sentenced to a long prison term for giving some marijuana to a cop. Peter Townshend hit Hoffman with his guitar, and that is more of a commentary on the relation of rock to politics than all of *Rat*'s fuzzy moralizing.

What cultural revolutionaries do not seem to grasp is that, far from being a grass-roots art form that has been taken over by businessmen, rock itself comes from the commercial exploitation of blues. It is bourgeois at its core, a mass-produced commodity, dependent on advanced technology and therefore on the money controlled by those in power. Its rebelliousness does not imply specific political content; it can be—and has been—criminal, Fascistic, and coolly individualistic as well as revolutionary. Nor is the hip life style inherently radical. It can simply be a more pleasurable way of surviving within the system, which is what the Pop sensibility has always been about. Certainly that was what Woodstock was about: ignore the bad, groove on the good, hang loose, and let things happen. The truth is that there can't be a revolutionary culture until there is a revolution. In the meantime, we should at least insist that the capitalists who produce rock concerts charge reasonable prices for reasonable service.

WINTHROP SARGEANT

WHITHER?

SEPTEMBER 21, 1968

A S A DEMONSTRATION of the bankruptcy of the musical avant-garde, the concert given in Carnegie Hall by Lukas Foss and the Buffalo Philharmonic on Wednesday evening of last week was pretty convincing. It started off with a piece called "Re-ak" for Large Orchestra, by the Korean serialist composer Isang Yun, which contained a few moderately interesting sound effects but nothing more. Then came Charles Ives' "Calcium Light Night," which, of course, has nothing to do with the avant-garde, and is one of those compositions in which Ives sought to convey the impression of several bands or orchestras playing at the same time. It is, however, very short and, to my mind, does not exemplify Ives at his best. After that, we had Mr. Foss's own "Baroque Variations"—an example of his Mona Lisa's–mustache music, in which a movement from Handel's Concerto Grosso No. 12, Scarlatti's Sonata No. 23, and the prelude to Bach's Partita in E for Solo Violin were subjected to various distortions, including slowing down, speeding up, making the music come in and out of focus, a lot of soundless bowing by violins, and the interpolation of some wrong notes and sounds from bells and cymbals. The Bach item had been heard here before, though Mr. Foss had added some things to it—some of that soundless bowing, for one thing. If all this was supposed to be funny, I think it missed its mark. (The revived Bach item sounded like a stale joke.) I am happy to report that many in the audience booed loudly, though some applauded. I suspect that the applauders were applauding the discernible fragments of Handel, Scarlatti, and Bach, rather than what Mr. Foss had done to them. After the intermission came something terribly tedious called "Correspondences for Strings and Tape," by the Princeton mathematician and musicologian Milton Babbitt. This was written for string orchestra plus electronic sounds recorded on tape. I could find nothing of the slightest interest in it. Mr. Babbitt has recently become famous for an article entitled "Who Cares If You Listen?" I, for one, don't—at least as far as Mr. Babbitt's music is concerned. The evening closed with a Capriccio for Violin and Orchestra by the Pole Krzysztof Penderecki. I *can* say that the violin part, played expertly by Paul Zukofsky, was well conceived for that instrument. Otherwise, I found the work a total bore.

. . .

It was a pleasure on the previous evening (Tuesday) to attend a concert of music by the California composer Harry Partch at the Whitney Museum. Mr. Partch, as is pretty well known, is a complete individualist, who not only creates his own kind of music but also builds the instruments it is played on. I arrived at the Museum to find a long line of hopeful auditors waiting to get in (most of them didn't), and it was only by explaining that I was a critic and *had* to get in that I gained admittance. Inside the room allotted to this concert there were already hundreds of people sitting on the floor or standing at the back. I took up my position among the latter. A lot of tuning was going on. Mr. Partch is very particular about pitch, which is something that the serialists, with their inaccurate, piano-keyboard ears, have long since forgotten. Mr. Partch is, in fact, so particular about pitch that he has divided the octave into forty-three intervals, as opposed to the twelve intervals of the keyboard. This arrangement enables him to attain a purity of intonation that one is seldom privileged to hear. He does not, of course, use all forty-three intervals at once. Most of his music is diatonic. The forty-three are there just to provide the possibility of an exact sort of intonation that derives from the theories of the great Greek mathematician and musical theoretician Pythagoras.

The instruments on which Mr. Partch's music is played look rather bizarre at first glance. There are a couple of organs specially tuned to the forty-three intervals. There are a number of xylophone- or gamelan-like instruments made of bottles, light bulbs, and redwood planks, some of the last-named emitting very low tones. There are various instruments of the zither type, a system of glass bells made from old laboratory equipment, and many other things. The sounds drawn from these instruments by Mr. Partch and a group of six or eight disciples are somewhat Oriental in character. The first number on the program, "Olympos' Pentatonic," was, in fact, based on a scale—C, D, E flat, G, A flat—that is rather common in Japanese music today, as it was among the ancient Greeks. There was a great variety of timbre, or instrumental color, ranging from low thumps to tinkles; the music was melodious as well as colorful, and everywhere it was evocative and charming. It is a pity that the size and fragility of Mr. Partch's instruments prevent them from being transported easily. It is also a pity, in a way, that his art is absolutely unique. Unlike more traditional forms of music, it will probably die with its creator, never to be heard again.

• • •

Ravi Shankar, whose first name is Sanskrit for "The Sun," had been shining most of the week at Philharmonic Hall, and I went to bask in his particular variety of Indian music on Thursday night. A fair-sized audience, made up mostly of young people, was present, and the greater part of the program, which was participated in by thirteen musicians besides Mr. Shankar, was quite delightful. Mr. Shankar himself is, of course, a prodigious virtuoso on the sitar, and to me the most memorable event of the evening was a *gath* performed by him, with tabla (drum) accompaniment by Alla Rakha—this even though he broke off his *alap* (or rhythmless introductory section) in order to bow to applause before beginning the *gath* proper, which is something that would not happen in India. There were, as a matter of fact, a number of things on this program that would not have happened in India, among them a *gath* for the combination of sitar and sarod—instruments that were played either in unison or alternately, in an arrangement that made one doubt whether pure improvisation was taking place. And the program ended, rather monstrously, with a nine-piece big-band ensemble, which Mr. Shankar conducted as if he were Zubin Mehta. This was something so foreign to the spirit of Indian music that it aroused doubts as to whether or not Shankar the showman was taking precedence over Shankar the musician. However, there were many moments of pleasure—some agile singing by Lakshmi Shankar, and a percussion duet (almost a duel) between Alla Rakha, who played the banya and the tabla, and Palghat Raghu, who played the mridangam. This was Indian rhythm at its purest, and the mathematical complexity of syncopation with which Mr. Rakha and Mr. Raghu assaulted each other made one reflect that it was not for nothing that the Indians invented both the concept of zero and the algebraic x.

. . .

The occurrences of the week—all of them rather out of the ordinary—made me give a thought or two to the current state of music. It is obvious that the grand eighteenth- and nineteenth-century tradition of symphonic music is in its death throes, and that it has been succeeded by a rather foolish school of modern composition whose exponents would be more at home as mathematicians than as musicians. It is also obvious that the music of India, through such musicians as Mr. Shankar, is becoming more and more influential in the West. What has the immediate future got in store for us? In my opinion, new musical traditions do not descend from above through the ideas of educated composers. They are more apt to rise from below—from the music of the people. I need not present the well-known historical precedents for this theory. The music of the people is now rock. I confess that though I originally found rock merely annoying, I have since come to find it an exceedingly interesting type of music—or perhaps "interesting" is not the word; "hypnotic" is better. Forget the enormous loudness that its youthful followers seem to regard as its most important characteristic. Loudness—or softness, for that matter—is not integral to the structure of music, and any music worthy of the name exerts a hypnotic spell. Rock, in the wide spectrum of style that reaches from the Beatles to its wilder manifestations, includes an enormous variety of musical language, reaching back even to baroque and Renaissance idioms. It has preserved the regular pulse (usually referred to as "beat") that underlies nearly all great music from the Gregorian chant on and has been left out only in some music of our century. It is more "integrated"—that is to say, slightly less "African"—than jazz, and much freer in matters of rhythm. Its chord structure, which is agreeably simple, is of the do-mi-sol variety, and hence is in the mainstream of music. Most important, it is capable of inducing a wider range of emotional responses than jazz. I could never imagine a jazz *Tristan and Isolde* (if you don't like Tristan, pick your own great myth), but I can imagine a rock *Tristan*. To be sure, what I am writing about is at present regarded as a kind of folk music. But I think that it sometimes approaches art music. Perhaps this is where the future of music lies.

B◯◯KS

DWIGHT MACDONALD

FROM

OUR INVISIBLE POOR

JANUARY 19, 1963 (MICHAEL HARRINGTON'S *THE OTHER AMERICA*)

N HIS SIGNIFICANTLY titled *The Affluent Society* (1958) Professor J. K. Galbraith states that poverty in this country is no longer "a massive affliction [but] more nearly an afterthought." Dr. Galbraith is a humane critic of the American capitalist system, and he is generously indignant about the continued existence of even this nonmassive and afterthoughtish poverty. But the interesting thing about his pronouncement, aside from the fact that it is inaccurate, is that it was generally accepted as obvious. For a long time now, almost everybody has assumed that, because of the New Deal's social legislation and—more important—the prosperity we have enjoyed since 1940, mass poverty no longer exists in this country.

Dr. Galbraith states that our poor have dwindled to two hard-core categories. One is the "insular poverty" of those who live in the rural South or in depressed areas like West Virginia. The other category is "case poverty," which he says is "commonly and properly related to [such] characteristics of the individuals so afflicted [as] mental deficiency, bad health, inability to adapt to the discipline of modern economic life, excessive procreation, alcohol, insufficient education." He reasons that such poverty must be due to individual defects, since "nearly everyone else has mastered his environment; this proves that it is not intractable." Without pressing the similarity of this concept to the "Social Darwinism" whose fallacies Dr. Galbraith easily disposes of elsewhere in his book, one may observe that most of these characteristics are as much the result of poverty as its cause.

Dr. Galbraith's error is understandable, and common. Last April the newspapers reported some exhilarating statistics in a Department of Commerce study: the average family income increased from $2,340 in 1929 to $7,020 in 1961. (These figures are calculated in current dollars, as are all the others I shall cite.) But the papers did not report the fine type, so to speak, which showed that almost all the recent gain was made by families with incomes of over $7,500, and that the rate at which poverty is being eliminated has slowed down alarmingly since 1953. Only the specialists and the statisticians read the fine type, which is why illusions continue to exist about American poverty.

Now Michael Harrington, an alumnus of the *Catholic Worker* and the Fund for the Republic who is at present a contributing editor of *Dissent* and the chief editor of the Socialist Party biweekly, *New America*, has written *The Other America: Poverty in the United States* (Macmillan). In the admirably short space of under two hundred pages, he outlines the problem, describes in imaginative detail what it means to be poor in this country today, summarizes the findings of recent studies by economists and sociologists, and analyzes the reasons for the persistence of mass poverty in the midst of general prosperity. It is an excellent book—and a most important one. . . .

. . .

In the last year we seem to have suddenly awakened, rubbing our eyes like Rip van Winkle, to the fact that mass poverty persists, and that it is one of our two gravest social problems. (The other is related: While only 11 percent of our population is non-white, 25 percent of our poor are.) Two other current books confirm Mr. Harrington's thesis: *Wealth and Power in America* (Praeger), by Dr. Gabriel Kolko, a social historian who has recently been at Harvard and the University of Melbourne, Australia, and *Income and Welfare in the United States* (McGraw-Hill), compiled by an imposing battery of four socio-economists headed by Dr. James N. Morgan, who rejoices in the title of Program Director of the Survey Research Center of the Institute for Social Research at the University of Michigan.

Dr. Kolko's book resembles Mr. Harrington's in several ways: It is short, it is based on earlier studies, and it is liberally inclined. It is less readable, because it is written in an academic jargon that is merely a vehicle for the clinching Statistic. Although it is impossible to write seriously about poverty without a copious use of statistics—as this review will demonstrate—it is possible to bring thought and feeling to bear on such raw material. Mr. Harrington does this more successfully than Dr. Kolko, whose prose is afflicted not only with academic blight but also with creeping ideology. Dr. Kolko leans so far to the socialist side that he sometimes falls on his nose, as when he clinches the inequality of wealth in the United States with a statistic: "In 1959, 23% of those earning less than $1,000 [a year] owned a car, compared to 95% of those earning more than $10,000." The real point is just the opposite, as any citizen of Iran, Ghana, Yemen, or the U.S.S.R. would appreciate—not that the rich have cars but that almost a quarter of the extremely poor do. Similarly, although Dr. Kolko has two chapters on poverty that confirm Mr. Harrington's argument, his main point is a different and more vulnerable one: "The basic distribution of income and wealth in the United States is essentially the same now as it was in 1939, or even 1910." This is a half fact. The rich are almost as rich as ever and the poor are even poorer, in the percentage of the national income they receive. Yet, as will become apparent later, there have been major changes in the distribution of wealth, and there has been a general improvement in living standards, so that the poor are much fewer today than they were in 1939. "Most low-income groups live substantially better today," Dr. Kolko admits. "But even though their real wages have mounted, their percentage of the national income has not changed." That in the last half century the rich have kept their riches and the poor their poverty is indeed a scandal. But it is theoretically possible, assuming enough general increase in wealth, that the relatively poor might by now have achieved a decent standard of living, no matter how inferior to that of the rich. As the books under consideration show, however, this theoretical possibility has not been realized. Inequality of wealth is not necessarily a major social problem per se. Poverty is. The late French philosopher Charles Peguy remarks, in his classic essay on poverty, "The duty of tearing the destitute from their destitution and the duty of distributing goods equitably are not of the same order. The first is an urgent duty, the second is a duty of convenience. . . . When all men are provided with the necessities what do we care about the distribution of luxury?" What indeed? Envy and emulation are the motives—and not very good ones—for the equalization of wealth. The problem of poverty goes much deeper. . . .

. . .

The most obvious citizens of the Other America are those whose skins are the wrong color. The folk slogans are realistic: "Last to be hired, first to be fired" and "If you're black, stay back." There has been some progress. In 1939, the non-white worker's wage averaged 41.4 percent of the white worker's; by 1958 it had climbed to 58 percent. A famous victory, but the non-whites still average only slightly more than half as much as the whites. Even this modest gain was due not to any Rooseveltian or Trumanian social reform but merely to the fact that for some years there was a war on and workers were in demand, whether black, white, or violet. By 1947, the non-whites had achieved most of their advance—to 54 percent of white earnings, which means they have gained, in the last fifteen years, just 4 percent.

The least obvious poverty affects our "senior citizens"—those over sixty-five. Mr. Harrington estimates that half of them—8,000,000—live in poverty, and he thinks they are even more atomized and politically helpless than the rest of the Other America. He estimates that one-fourth of the "unrelated individuals" among them, or a million persons, have less than $580 a year, which is about what is allotted *for food alone* in the Department of Agriculture's minimum-subsistence budget. (The average American family now spends only 20 percent of its income for food—an indication of the remarkable prosperity we are all enjoying, except for one-quarter of us.) One can imagine, or perhaps one can't, what it would be like to live on $580 a year, or $11 a week. It is only fair to note that most of our senior citizens do better: The average per-capita income of those over sixty-five is now estimated to be slightly over $20 a week. That is, about $1,000 a year.

The aged poor have two sources of income besides their earnings or savings. One is contributions by relatives. A 1961 White House Conference Report put this at 10 percent of income, which works out to $8 a week for an income of $4,000—and the 8,000,000 aged poor all have less than that. The other is Social Security, whose benefits in 1959 averaged $18 a week. Even this modest sum is more than any of the under-$4,000 got, since payments are proportionate to earnings and the poor, of course, earned less than the rest. A quarter of them, and those in general the neediest, are not covered by Social Security. The last resort is relief, and Mr. Harrington describes most vividly the humiliations the poor often have to put up with to get that.

The problem of the aged poor is aggravated by the fact that, unlike the Italians or the English, we seem to have little respect for or interest in our "senior citizens," beyond giving them that honorific title, and we don't include them in family life. If we can afford it, we are likely to send them to nursing homes—"a storage-bin philosophy," a Senate report calls it—and if we can't, which is the case with the poor, they must make do with the resources noted above. The Michigan study has a depressing chapter on "The Economics of Living with Relatives." Nearly two-thirds of the heads of families queried were opposed to having their aged parents live with their children. "The old do not understand the young, and the young do not understand the old or the young," observed one respondent, who must have had a sense of humor. Other replies were "Old people are pretty hard to get along with" and "The parents and the children try to boss each other and when they live with you there's always fighting." The minority in favor gave practical reasons, like "It's a good thing to have them with you so you can see after them" and "The old folks might get a pension or something, so they could help you out." Hardly anyone expressed any particular respect for the old, or a feeling that their experience might enrich family life. The most depressing finding was "People most able to provide support for relatives are most opposed to it. Older people with some college education are eleven to one against it." The most favorable toward including older people in the home were Negroes, and even they were mostly against it.

The whole problem of poverty and the aged is especially serious today because Americans are living longer. In the first half of this century, life expectancy increased 17.6 years for men and 20.3 years for women. And between 1950 and 1960 the over-sixty-five group increased twice as fast as the population as a whole.

The worst part of being old and poor in this country is the loneliness. Mr. Harrington notes that we have not only racial ghettos but geriatric ones, in the cheap rooming-house districts of large cities. He gives one peculiarly disturbing statistic: "One-third of the aged in the United States, some 5,000,000 or more human beings, have no phone in their place of residence. They are literally cut off from the rest of America."

Ernest Hemingway's celebrated deflation of Scott Fitzgerald's romantic notion that the rich are "different" somehow—"Yes, they have money"—doesn't apply to the poor. They are different in more important ways than their lack of money, as Mr. Harrington demonstrates:

Emotional upset is one of the main forms of the vicious circle of impoverishment. The structure of the society is hostile to these people. The poor tend to become pessimistic and depressed; they seek immediate gratification instead of saving; they act out.

Once this mood, this unarticulated philosophy becomes a fact, society can change, the recession can end, and yet there is no motive for movement. The depression has become internalized. The middle class looks upon this process and sees "lazy" people who "just don't want to get ahead." People who are much too sensitive to demand of cripples that they run races ask of the poor that they get up and act just like everyone else in the society.

The poor are not like everyone else. . . . They think and feel differently; they look upon a different America than the middle class looks upon.

The poor are also different in a physical sense: they are much less healthy. According to *Poverty and Deprivation*, the proportion of those "disabled or limited in their major activity by chronic ill health" rises sharply as income sinks. In reasonably well-off families ($7,000 and up), 4.3 percent are so disabled; in reasonably poor families ($2,000 to $3,999), the proportion doubles, to 8 percent; and in unreasonably poor families (under $2,000), it doubles again, to 16.5 percent. An obvious cause, among others, for the very poor being four times as much disabled by "chronic ill health" as the well-to-do is that they have much less money to spend for medical care—in fact, almost nothing. This weighs with special heaviness on the aged poor. During the fifties, Mr. Harrington notes, "all costs on the Consumer Price Index went up by 12 per cent. But medical costs, that terrible staple of the aged, went up by 36 per cent, hospitalization rose by 65 per cent, and group hospitalization costs (Blue Cross premiums) were up by 83 per cent."

This last figure is particularly interesting, since Blue Cross and such plans are the A.M.A.'s alternative to socialized medicine, or, rather, to the timid fumblings toward it that even our most liberal politicians have dared to propose. Such figures throw an unpleasant light on the Senate's rejection of Medicare. The defeat was all the more bitter because, in the usual effort to appease the conservatives (with the usual lack of success—only five Republicans and only four Southern Democrats voted pro), the bill was watered down in advance. Not until he had spent $90 of his own money—which is 10 percent of the annual income of some 3,000,000 aged poor—would a patient have been eligible. And the original program included only people already covered by Social Security or Railroad Retirement pensions and excluded the neediest of all the 2,500,000 aged poor who are left out of both these systems. These untouchables were finally included in order to placate five liberal Republican senators, led by Javits of New York. They did vote for Medicare, but they were the only Republicans who did.

Mental as well as physical illness is much greater among the poor, even though our complacent cliché is that nervous breakdowns are a prerogative of the rich because the poor "can't afford" them. (They can't, but they have them anyway.) This bit of middle-class folklore should be laid to rest by a study made in New Haven: *Social Class and Mental Illness*, by August B. Hollingshead and Frederick C. Redlich (Wiley). They found that the rate of "treated psychiatric illness" is about the same from the rich down through decently paid workers—an average of 573 per 100,000. But in the bottom fifth it shoots up to 1,659 per 100,000. There is an even more striking difference in the *kind* of mental illness. Of those in the four top income groups who had undergone psychiatric treatment, 65 percent had been treated for neurotic problems and 35 percent for psychotic disturbances. In the bottom fifth, the treated illnesses were almost all psychotic (90 percent). This shows there is something to the notion that the poor "can't afford" nervous breakdowns—the milder kind, that is—since the reason the proportion of *treated* neuroses among the poor is only 10 percent is that a neurotic can keep going, after a fashion. But the argument cuts deeper the other way. The poor go to a psychiatrist (or, more commonly, are committed to a mental institution) only when they are completely unable to function because of psychotic symptoms. Therefore, even that nearly threefold increase in mental disorders among the poor is probably an underestimate.

The poor are different, then, both physically and psychologically. During the fifties, a team of psychiatrists from Cornell studied "Midtown," a residential area in this city that contained 170,000 people, of all social classes. The area was 99 percent white, so the findings may be presumed to understate the problem of poverty. The description of the poor—the "low social economic status individual"—is blunt: "[They are] rigid, suspicious, and have a fatalistic outlook on life. They do not plan ahead. . . . They are prone to depression, have feelings of futility, lack of belongingness, friendliness, and a lack of trust in others." Only a Dr. Pangloss would expect anything else. As Mr. Harrington points out, such characteristics are "a realistic adaptation to a socially perverse situation."

As for the isolation that is the lot of the American poor, that is a point on which Mr. Harrington is very good:

> America has a self-image of itself as a nation of joiners and doers. There are social clubs, charities, community drives, 'and the like. [One might add organizations like the Elks and Masons, Rotary and Kiwanis, cultural groups like our women's clubs, also alumni associations and professional organizations.] And yet this entire structure is a phenomenon of the middle class. Some time ago, a study in Franklin, Indiana [this vagueness of reference is all too typical of *The Other America*], reported that the percentage of people in the bottom class who were without affiliations of any kind was eight times as great as the percentage in the high-income class.
>
> Paradoxically, one of the factors that intensifies the social isolation of the poor is that America thinks of itself as a nation without social classes. As a result, there are few social or civic organizations that are separated on the basis of income and class. The "working-class culture" that sociologists have described in a country like England does not exist here. . . . The poor person who might want to join an organization is afraid. Because he or she will have less education, less money, less competence to articulate ideas than anyone else in the group, they stay away.

One reason our society is a comparatively violent one is that the French and Italian and British poor have a communal life and culture that the American poor lack. As one reads *The Other America*, one wonders why there is not even more violence than there is. . . .

. . .

The poor actually pay more taxes, in proportion to their income, than the rich. A recent study by the Tax Foundation estimates that 28 percent of incomes under $2,000 goes for taxes, as against 24 percent of the incomes of families earning five to seven times as much. Sales and other excise taxes are largely responsible for this curious statistic. It is true that such taxes fall impartially on all, like the blessed rain from heaven, but it is a form of egalitarianism that perhaps only Senator Goldwater can fully appreciate.

The final irony is that the Welfare State, which Roosevelt erected and which Eisenhower, no matter how strongly he felt about it, didn't attempt to pull down, is not for the poor, either. Agricultural workers are not covered by Social Security, nor are many of the desperately poor among the aged, such as "unrelated individuals" with incomes of less than $1,000, of whom only 37 percent are covered, which is just half the percentage of coverage among the aged in general. Of the Welfare State, Mr. Harrington says, "Its creation had been stimulated by mass impoverishment and misery, yet it helped the poor least of all. Laws like unemployment compensation, the Wagner Act, the various farm programs, all these were designed for the middle third in the cities, for the organized workers, and for the . . . big market farmers. . . . [It] benefits those least who need help most." The industrial workers, led by John L. Lewis, mobilized enough political force to put through Section 7(a) of the National Industrial Recovery Act, which, with the Wagner Act, made the C.I.O. possible. The big farmers put enough pressure on Henry Wallace, Roosevelt's first Secretary of Agriculture—who talked a good fight for liberal principles but was a Hamlet when it came to action—to establish the two basic propositions of Welfare State agriculture: subsidies that now cost $3 billion a year and that chiefly benefit the big farmers; and the exclusion of sharecroppers, tenant farmers, and migratory workers from the protection of minimum-wage and Social Security laws. . . .

· · ·

In short, one reaches the unstartling conclusion that rewards in class societies, including Communist ones, are according to power rather than need. A recent illustration is the campaign of an obscure organization called Veterans of World War I of the U.S.A. to get a bill through Congress for pensions of about $25 a week. It was formed by older men who think other veterans' organizations (such as the American Legion, which claims 2,500,000 members to their 200,000) are dominated by the relatively young. It asks for pensions for veterans of the First World War with incomes of under $2,400 (if single) or $3,600 (if married)—that is, only for *poor* veterans. The editorials have been violent: "STOP THIS VETERANS' GRAB," implored the *Herald Tribune;* "WORLD WAR I PENSION GRAB," echoed the *Saturday Evening Post.* Their objection was, in part, that many of the beneficiaries would not be bona-fide poor, since pensions, annuities, and Social Security benefits were excluded from the maximum income needed to qualify. Considering that the average Social Security payment is about $1,000 a year, this would not put any potential beneficiary into the rich or even the comfortably-off class, even if one assumes another $1,000, which is surely too high, from annuities and pensions. It's all very confusing. The one clear aspect is that the minuscule Veterans of World War I of the U.S.A. came very near to bringing it off. Although their bill was opposed by both the White House and by the chairman of the House Committee on Veterans' Affairs, two hundred and one members of the House signed a petition to bring the measure to a vote, only eighteen less than needed "to accomplish this unusual parliamentary strategy," as the *Times* put it. These congressmen were motivated by politics rather than charity, one may assume. Many were up for reelection last November, and the two hundred thousand Veterans of World War I had two advantages over the fifty million poor: They were organized, and they had a patriotic appeal only a wink away from the demagogic. Their "unusual parliamentary strategy" failed by eighteen votes in the Congress. But there will be another Congress.

· · ·

It seems likely that mass poverty will continue in this country for a long time. The more it is reduced, the harder it is to keep on reducing it. The poor, having dwindled from two-thirds of the population in 1936 to one-quarter today, no longer are a significant political force, as is shown by the Senate's rejection of Medicare and by the Democrats' dropping it as an issue in the elections last year. Also, as poverty decreases, those left behind tend more and more to be the ones who have for so long accepted poverty as their destiny that they need outside help to climb out of it. This new minority mass poverty, so much more isolated and hopeless than the old majority poverty, shows signs of becoming chronic. . . .

Children born into poor families today have less chance of "improving themselves" than the children of the pre-1940 poor. Rags to riches is now more likely to be rags to rags. "Indeed," the Michigan surveyors conclude, "it appears that a number of the heads of poor families have moved into less skilled jobs than their fathers had." Over a third of the children of the poor, according to the survey, don't go beyond the eighth grade and "will probably perpetuate the poverty of their parents." There are a great many of these children. In an important study of poverty, made for a Congressional committee in 1959, Dr. Robert J. Lampman estimated that eleven million of the poor were under eighteen. "A considerable number of younger persons are starting life in a condition of 'inherited poverty,'" he observed. To which Mr. Harrington adds, "The character of poverty has changed, and it has become more deadly for the young. It is no longer associated with immigrant groups with high aspirations; it is now identified with those whose social existence makes it more and more difficult to break out into the larger society." Even when children from poor families show intellectual promise, there is nothing in the values of their friends or families to encourage them to make use of it. Dr. Kolko, citing impressive sources, states that of the top 16 percent of high-school students—those scoring 120 and over in I.Q. tests—only half go on to college. The explanation for this amazing—and alarming—situation is as much cultural as economic. The children of the poor now tend to lack what the sociologists call "motivation." At least one foundation is working on the problem of why so many bright children from poor families don't ever try to go beyond high school. . . .

The problem of educating the poor has changed since 1900. Then it was the language and cultural difficulties of immigrants from foreign countries; now it is the subtler but more intractable problems of internal migration from backward regions, mostly in the South. The old immigrants wanted to Better Themselves and to Get Ahead. The new migrants are less ambitious, and they come into a less ambitious atmosphere. "When they arrive in the city," wrote Christopher Jencks in an excellent two-part survey, "Slums and Schools," in the *New Republic* last fall, "they join others equally unprepared for urban life in the slums—a milieu which is in many ways utterly dissociated from the rest of America. Often this milieu is self-perpetuating. I have been unable to find any statistics on how many of these migrants' children and grandchildren have become middle-class, but it is probably not too inaccurate to estimate that about 30,000,000 people live in urban slums, and that about half are second-generation residents." The immigrants of 1890–1910 also arrived in a milieu that was "in many ways utterly dissociated from the rest of America," yet they had a vision—a rather materialistic one, but still a vision—of what life in America could be if they worked hard enough; and they did work, and they did aspire to something more than they had; and they did get out of the slums. The disturbing thing about the poor today is that so many of them seem to lack any such vision. Mr. Jencks remarks:

> While the economy is changing in a way which makes the eventual liquidation of the slums at least conceivable, young people are not seizing the opportunities this change presents. Too many are dropping out of school before graduation (more than half in many slums); too few are going to college. . . . As a result there are serious

shortages of teachers, nurses, doctors, technicians, and scientifically trained executives, but 4,500,000 unemployables.

. . .

"Poverty is the parent of revolution and crime," Aristotle wrote. This is now a half truth—the last half. Our poor are alienated; they don't consider themselves part of society. But precisely because they don't they are not politically dangerous. It is people with "a stake in the country" who make revolutions. The best—though by no means the only—reason for worrying about the Other America is that its existence should make us feel uncomfortable.

The federal government is the only purposeful force—I assume wars are not purposeful—that can reduce the numbers of the poor and make their lives more bearable. The authors of *Poverty and Deprivation* take a dim view of the Kennedy administration's efforts to date:

> The Federal Budget is the most important single instrument available to us as a free people to induce satisfactory economic performance, and to reduce poverty and deprivation. . . .
> Projected Federal outlays in the fiscal 1963 Budget are too small. The items in this Budget covering programs directly related to human improvement and the reduction of mass poverty and deprivation allocate far too small a portion of our total national production to these great purposes.

The effect of government policy on poverty has two quite distinct aspects. One is the indirect effect of the stimulation of the economy by federal spending. Such stimulation—though by wartime demands rather than government policy—has in the past produced a prosperity that did cut down American poverty by almost two-thirds. But I am inclined to agree with Dr. Galbraith that it would not have a comparable effect on present-day poverty:

> It is assumed that with increasing output poverty must disappear [he writes]. Increased output eliminated the general poverty of all who worked. Accordingly it must, sooner or later, eliminate the special poverty that still remains. . . . Yet just as the arithmetic of modern politics makes it tempting to overlook the very poor, so the

supposition that increasing output will remedy their case has made it easy to do so too.

He underestimates the massiveness of American poverty, but he is right when he says there is now a hard core of the specially disadvantaged—because of age, race, environment, physical or mental defects, etc.—that would not be significantly reduced by general prosperity. (Although I think the majority of our present poor *would* benefit, if only by a reduction in the present high rate of unemployment.)

To do something about this hard core, a second line of government policy would be required; namely, direct intervention to help the poor. We have had this since the New Deal, but it has always been grudging and miserly, and we have never accepted the principle that every citizen should be provided, at state expense, with a reasonable minimum standard of living regardless of any other considerations. It should not depend on earnings, as does Social Security, which continues the inequalities and inequities and so tends to keep the poor forever poor. Nor should it exclude millions of our poorest citizens because they lack the political pressure to force their way into the Welfare State. The governmental obligation to provide, out of taxes, such a minimum living standard for all who need it should be taken as much for granted as free public schools have always been in our history.

It may be objected that the economy cannot bear the cost, and certainly costs must be calculated. But the point is not the calculation but the principle. Statistics—and especially statistical forecasts—can be pushed one way or the other. Who can determine in advance to what extent the extra expense of giving our 40,000,000 poor enough income to rise above the poverty line would be offset by the lift to the economy from their increased purchasing power? We really don't know. Nor did we know what the budgetary effects would be when we established the principle of free public education. The rationale then was that all citizens should have an equal chance of competing for a better status. The rationale now is different: that every citizen has a right to become or remain part of our society because if this right is denied, as it is in the case of at least one-fourth of our citizens, it impoverishes us all. Since 1932, "the government"—local, state, and federal—has recognized a responsibility to provide its citizens with a subsistence living. Apples will never again be sold on the street by jobless accountants, it seems safe to predict, nor will any serious political leader ever again suggest that share-the-work and local charity can solve the problem of unemployment. "Nobody starves" in this country any more, but, like every social statistic, this is a tricky business. Nobody starves, but who can measure the starvation, not to be calculated by daily intake of proteins and calories, that reduces life for many of our poor to a long vestibule to death? Nobody starves, but every fourth citizen rubs along on a standard of living that is below what Mr. Harrington defines as "the minimal levels of health, housing, food, and education that our present stage of scientific knowledge specifies as necessary for life as it is now lived in the United States." Nobody starves, but a fourth of us are excluded from the common social existence. Not to be able to afford a movie or a glass of beer is a kind of starvation—if everybody else can.

The problem is obvious: the persistence of mass poverty in a prosperous country. The solution is also obvious: to provide, out of taxes, the kind of subsidies that have always been given to the public schools (not to mention the police and fire departments and the post office)— subsidies that would raise incomes above the poverty level, so that every citizen could feel he is indeed such. *"Civis Romanus sum!"* cried St. Paul when he was threatened with flogging—and he was not flogged. Until our poor can be proud to say *"Civis Romanus sum!,"* until the act of justice that would make this possible has been performed by the three-quarters of Americans who are not poor—until then the shame of the Other America will continue.

RENATA ADLER

POLEMIC AND THE NEW REVIEWERS

JULY 4, 1964

IN LITERARY CRITICISM, polemic is short-lived, and no other essay form becomes as quickly obsolete as an unfavorable review. If the work under attack is valuable, it survives adverse comment. If it is not, the polemic dies with its target. A critic is therefore measured not by the books he prosecutes but by the ones he praises (we turn to Edmund Wilson for Proust, Joyce, Eliot, and Hemingway, not for Kafka), and it is surprising that among a younger generation of critics polemic should be so widely regarded as the most viable and rewarding kind of criticism. Three recent works—*The Sense of Life in the Modern Novel,* by Arthur Mizener (Riverside); *A World More Attractive,* by Irving Howe (Horizon); and *Doings and Undoings,* by Norman Podhoretz (Farrar, Straus)—may provide an explanation.

Arthur Mizener is the most affirmative critic of the three, the least polemical, and the least interesting. His book is little more than a splicing together of enthusiasms. He recounts plots (from Trollope to Updike), lists dates, quotes and compares passages (good ones, from many sources); he seems tempted to pick up the novels whole and deliver them to the reader. His critical sympathies, in short, are strong; his critical intelligence, however, is weak or self-effacing. Mr. Mizener seldom explains or analyzes, and whenever he does, his prose neatly strangles whatever his thought may have been:

> The problem for writers like Dreiser is apparently how to release from deep beneath the viscous and muddy surface of their conscious minds their imaginative apprehension of their experience, and the only way they seem able to do so is, paradoxically, by a slow roiling of the muddy surface.
>
> What criticism of the novel needs is a theory that will put at the center of our attention the world envisioned by the novel, which will then serve to limit and discipline the exercise of our metaphysics upon it. Our lot would very much like to circumambulate the novel's charms for the nearly exclusive purpose of keeping our metaphysics warm. The only valid source of discipline for this corrupting impulse to metaphysical speculation is the unique object that is the novel itself.

What the second of these paragraphs seems to recommend is that the critic leave theories alone and let literature speak for itself. And Mr. Mizener, for one, is clearly well advised to do so. The effect, however, of his constant citing of excerpts from the works themselves is to make his book almost a scrap album. Or a whirlwind tour of the sights. ("And on your left, ladies and gentlemen, the beautiful opening passage of *Across the River and Into the Trees.* . . . And, on your right, the historic scene from E. M. Forster. . . . Notice, in particular, the portico . . .") The effect is also, on a slightly higher plane, that of a benign, unanalytic book column in a reviewing section of the Sunday newspapers, to which Mr. Mizener is a frequent contributor.

· · ·

While Mr. Mizener subordinates himself so completely to the works he admires that his intelligence becomes invisible, Irving Howe does the reverse; he dominates a book and wrenches it to suit his concern of the moment. And his concern is nearly always extra-literary—sociological or political. The title of his new book, *A World More Attractive,* suggests a utopian outlook, and even in his literary essays he is primarily concerned with social action—"images of war and revolution, experiment and disaster, apocalypse and skepticism; images of rebellion, disenchantment, and nothingness." When a writer—Wallace Stevens, for example—seems less preoccupied with these "images" than Mr. Howe himself, Mr. Howe discerns them as a "premise," or a "background," or a "pressure upon all subjects":

> Stevens does not examine society closely or even notice it directly for any length of time; he simply absorbs "the idea" of it. . . . A perspective upon history is brilliantly maintained; history as it filters through his consciousness of living and writing at a given time.

This line of argument can, of course, be used to demonstrate that anyone is really writing about anything whatever—"as it filters through his consciousness of living and writing at a given time"—and the author of *A World More Attractive* makes frequent and imaginative use of what we might call the ascribed, or foisted, premise: "Dostoevsky had not read Max Weber. But the anticipation is there." For Mr. Howe seeks, above all, to establish a *position,* and he uses his intelligence to force that position upon the literary work. (If the work resists, so much the worse for it; Mr. Howe will find it lacking in "moral style.") Yet it need not be supposed that this exercise of intelligence gives Mr. Howe an advantage in clarity over Mr. Mizener:

> The ideal of socialism has become a problematic one, but the problem of socialism remains an abiding ideal.

But if one turns from the immediate political struggle to a kind of socio-cultural speculation by means of which certain trends are projected into an indefinite future, there may be some reason for anticipating a society ruled by benevolent Grand Inquisitors, a society of non-terroristic and bureaucratic authoritarianism, on top of which will flourish an efficient political-technical elite—a society, in short, that makes Huxley's prophecy seem more accurate than Orwell's, except insofar, perhaps, as Orwell's passion and eloquence helped invalidate his own prophecy.

Whatever these two sentences may mean, their vocabulary, at least, suggests that we are in the presence of an intellectual—a radical intellectual, of the sort that was identified in the thirties with such "little journals" as *Partisan Review*. And as an intellectual of the thirties Irving Howe has become, if not an interesting critic, at least an interesting criticism of the predicament of letters in the sixties—particularly in the little journals, to which *he* is a frequent contributor. Most of these journals were born of the depression and defended underdogs, who seemed at the time to fall into two broad categories—the artists and the poor. After the Second World War, old issues began to cloud, old protégés made good, and expository writers with a low tolerance for complexities were at a loss. A good part of the thirties' poor had become the fifties' bourgeoisie; most genuine depression artists had become the culture heroes of an age of affluence. Whom to defend? A stalwart revolutionary, Mr Howe seemed to find himself without a cause, a comrade, or an enemy. He soon started a magazine of vaguely Socialist persuasion, called *Dissent*, and the dissenting position he has taken is a paradoxical one. He has turned upon old protégés to begrudge them the successes that time has brought. He now assails the former underdog, now part of the post-depression middle class, for everything—its new comforts, its tastes, and its morals. He now wishes to bar from "the raids of mass culture," and from the "contamination" of the "middle-brow," the "serious culture" that the radicals sought in the thirties to bring to the people. At the same time, he wants to bar to the artists and intellectuals the success—"this rise in social status"—that he sought in the thirties to help them achieve. If only, he seems to be saying, the middle class and the artists might become befriendably poor again:

Today, in a sense, the danger is that the serious artists are not scorned enough.

Suppose, then, that the goal of moderate material satisfaction is reached. . . . What would the intellectuals say? . . . [They would be like Christ, facing the Grand Inquisitor.] He has nothing to say. . . . [His] kiss is a kiss of despair, and He retreats, forever, in silence.

In short, now that the revolution of the thirties has begun to bear fruit, Mr. Howe has come to distrust the notion of progress, and he seeks in literature (or imposes upon literature) that aversion to the modern which he himself feels. Lacking a new direction for his liberalism, he dissents; he seems to bear his banner proudly backward toward the thirties and the "world more attractive" those years represent for him.

. . .

An editor of *Commentary* and a regular reviewer for *Show*, Norman Podhoretz inhabits a middle ground between the tame Sunday newspapers of Arthur Mizener and the radical little journals of Irving Howe. He is, in fact, one of those writers for little journals who have of late been assimilated almost en bloc into the magazines of broader circulation, and his adjustment, as a thirties liberal, to the sixties is a highly pragmatic, even a classic one. The rebel whose cause has succeeded traditionally develops a concern with personal power, and the title of Mr. Podhoretz's collection of critical essays, *Doings and Undoings,* implies a faith in the power of the critic to affect, or even determine, the fate of authors and literary works—"to correct," in Mr. Podhoretz's phrase, "what he considers to be an egregious error in the prevailing estimate of a book or a literary reputation."

Doings and Undoings is not, Mr. Podhoretz points out, a unified collection. "How many people wrote it, then? Two, I think, or possibly three." The first estimate seems accurate; there are two distinct personalities at work in this book—one a literary critic far more canny than Mr. Mizener, the other a post-revolutionary, extra-literary polemicist far more effective than Mr. Howe. Essays on Faulkner, Edmund Wilson, and Nathanael West seem to reflect the first personality; essays on Norman Mailer, Mary McCarthy, Hannah Arendt, and John Updike, among others, seem to reflect the second. Since the second personality—the author, one supposes, of "Undoings"—is the more recent chronologically, and since his work clearly dominates the collection, it might be well to begin with his position, as Mr. Podhoretz defines it in the piece entitled "Book Reviewing and Everyone I Know." In praise of contributors to a new periodical, *The New York Review of Books*, Mr. Podhoretz remarks:

> All these reviewers inhabit much the same intellectual milieu, and what they have in common, apart from talent and intelligence, is an attitude toward books and an idea about the proper way to discuss them. This attitude might be characterized as one of great suspiciousness: a book is assumed to be guilty until it proves itself innocent—and not many do. . . . The major premise behind such suspiciousness is that books are enormously important events, far too important to be confronted lightly, and certainly too important to permit of charitable indulgence.

The argument that a sign of a book's importance is that it should be "assumed to be guilty until it proves itself innocent" is a curious one, since our whole legal system rests upon the opposite premise—that the sign of an individual's importance is that he should be assumed innocent until he is proved guilty. But Mr. Podhoretz conceives of this position of "great suspiciousness" as an antidote to the "bland and uncritical" reviewing columns of the Sundays newspapers (so much for Mr. Mizener) and as a solution (here he agrees with Mr. Howe) to "the problems of mass culture . . . and . . . the need for an embattled struggle against the deterioration of literary and intellectual standards." Finally, he pinpoints what he considers the salient quality of *The New York Review* reviewers: "A book for them is, quite simply, an occasion to do some writing of their own." And he adds that if only "*The New York Review*" were to succeed in establishing itself on a permanent footing . . . everyone I know would certainly be happy."

There are several remarkable things about this essay and the point of view it represents. First, "everyone I know" occurs fourteen times (aside from its appearance in the title), and "someone I know," "no one I know," "someone I *don't* know," and "everyone they know" make one appearance each. Although it must be admitted that repetition is a rhetorical device of which, in any case, Mr. Podhoretz has always been inordinately fond ("what really happened in the thirties" occurs nine times in another essay, and "tells us nothing about the nature of totalitarianism" several times in a third), it seems quite safe to say that "Book Reviewing and Everyone I Know" is pervaded by a sense of comradeship and solidarity; Mr. Podhoretz clearly does not consider himself a speaker in isolation.

On the other hand, such terms as "embattled," "struggle," and "suspiciousness" seem to indicate, on behalf of the group, a feeling of beleaguered hostility. Moreover, such unembarrassed statements as "Among our most talented literary intellectuals (including just about everyone I know) reviewing is regarded as a job for young men on the make" and "A book for them is, quite simply, an occasion to do some writing of their own" imply that the New Reviewers regard criticism less as a sympathetic response to literature than as an opportunity for an assertion of personality. (One conclusion is inescapable here: A book is going to have an exceedingly difficult time "proving itself innocent" if the reviewer "assumes" it "guilty" and then uses it, "quite simply," as "an occasion to do some writing of [his] own.") Finally, a glowing nostalgic reference to "the back files of magazines like *Partisan Review* and *Commentary*," combined with an expression of despair over the present ("But except for Dwight Macdonald and one or two others, everyone I know—indeed, everyone who writes—is often afflicted with the feeling that all he is doing is dropping stone after stone down the bottomless well of American culture. Who listens? Who cares?"), seems to complete a picture, a philosophical adjustment, an answer to the predicament of Mr. Howe. The radical child of the thirties, the contributor to the back files of little journals, finding himself at present directionless, embattled, and perhaps even unheeded, achieves a solidarity in numbers in the security of "everyone I know." The political fervor of the ex-revolutionary is not lost; it is simply redirected into literary channels, where it appears as a certain hostility toward books ("assumed guilty"), a pronounced defensiveness toward presumptive readers ("the bottomless well of American culture"), and an attitude toward the job at hand—reviewing—as an opportunity to assert personal ambition ("young men on the make . . . do some writing of their own"). In short, the rebellion has succeeded, the junta is in power, and it is now the era of the purge.

To interpret a whole collection on the basis of a single essay would be, of course, to oversimplify, and Mr. Podhoretz is a more complicated and interesting writer than this single essay might suggest. But "Book Reviewing and Everyone I Know" does announce a group, a program, and perhaps even the emergence of a new critical school, and since Mr. Podhoretz is a singularly articulate spokesman for that school, it might be well to explore his program as it recurs in some of the other essays in *Doings and Undoings,* and in the work of other New Reviewers—those who share what Mr. Podhoretz calls "the same intellectual milieu."

. . .

Mr. Podhoretz, to begin with, clearly regards reviewing as a continuous dialogue, and he devotes, in his reviews, considerable attention to the opinions of previous reviewers. In the essay "In Defense of James Baldwin," he writes:

> With few exceptions, the major reviewing media were very hard on *Another Country*. It was patronized by Paul Goodman in *The New York Times Book Review*, ridiculed by Stanley Edgar Hyman in *The New Leader*, worried over . . . by Elizabeth Hardwick in *Harper's*, summarily dismissed by *Time*'s anonymous critic, loftily pitied by Whitney Balliett in *The New Yorker*, and indignantly attacked by Saul Maloff in *The Nation*.

And in "A Dissent on Updike" he cites not only written opinions but spoken ones as well:

> When his first novel, *The Poorhouse Fair*, came out in 1958, I remember arguing about it at great length with Mary McCarthy. . . .
> I cannot for the life of me understand what there is about him that so impresses people like Mary McCarthy, Arthur Mizener, and Stanley Edgar Hyman—to mention only three critics who . . .

The "Defense" in one case and the "Dissent" in the other might seem to require such a roll call, but it is Mr. Podhoretz's method throughout the collection to orient his point of view in terms of what he calls "the prevailing estimate of a book or a literary reputation." And he is not the only one to do so. There is a kind of reciprocity along the reviewing circuit that, while it occasionally imparts a pleasing continuity to critical discussion (the reader who suspects that the reviewer does not do justice to the book under consideration may be consoled by the knowledge that the reviewer has read at least all previous reviews of it), more often resembles nothing so much as a ticker-tape compendium or a caucus in an airless convention hall. "Irving Howe and I discussed this tendency some time ago, and wrote . . ." says Lewis Coser in *Partisan Review*. "The last time I remember talking about the novel was a year ago last June or July," Norman Mailer writes in *Esquire*, "and it was in a conversation with Gore Vidal." "Even Norman Mailer," Alfred Chester writes in a review of William Burroughs' *Naked Lunch*, "unpredictably mislaid himself long enough to write: 'Burroughs is the only American novelist living today who may conceivably be possessed by genius.'" "It was from Sartre that I first heard of Jean Genet," Lionel Abel writes in *The New York Review*; and "These have been duly underscored by her critics," says another contributor to the same periodical, "notably Lionel Abel, in a long and trenchant essay in . . ." "I have only once had the privilege of meeting Paul Goodman," George Steiner remarks in *Commentary*. "I stress 'privilege.' There is no one whose encounter flatters in a more exacting way."

This elaborate system of cross-references is one to which Mr. Podhoretz—at least in *Undoings*—subscribes, and when he feels he must disagree with what he frequently calls "the serious critics," he does so warily. His essay on James Baldwin continues:

> Three of these reviewers—Goodman, Hardwick, and Hyman— are first-rate critics, and I therefore find it hard to believe that their wrongheaded appraisals of *Another Country* can be ascribed to a simple lapse of literary judgment. How could anyone as sensible and knowledgeable as Elizabeth Hardwick have been led so astray . . . ? How could a man of Stanley Edgar Hyman's sophistication have been so fooled . . . ? How could Paul Goodman, who most assuredly knows better, have taken . . .

Mr. Podhoretz is not, of course, the only reviewer to feel so bewildered by his own divergence from the mainstream of critical opinion that he must temper his remarks with "sensitive," "sophistication," and "knows better." Occasionally, such differences are bridged with the elaborate courtesy of a junior executive introducing his immediate superior at a Rotary banquet. "This collection of essays . . . reflects the amazing catholicity of Mr. Schlesinger's tastes and interests," Lewis Coser begins his attack on Arthur Schlesinger, Jr. "His range is wide indeed." And Frank Kermode, concluding an ambivalent review of Mary McCarthy's essays, concedes himself "aware that one is incomparably less honest, as well as less clever, than she," and adds, "I can think of no writer whose silence would be more damaging to our moral and intellectual hygiene." A more relaxed approach, along the reviewing circuit, to the moment of painful dissent is manifest in the use of first names: Norman Mailer, in attacking Nelson Algren, calls him "Nelson"; Alfred Chester, in disparaging Henry Miller, calls him "Henry"; Paul Goodman, in disagreeing with Harold Rosenberg, calls him "Harold"; and Lionel Abel, in discussing the misdeeds of the ghetto leader Chaim Rumkowski, refers to him familiarly as "Chaim." Mr. Podhoretz is more formal. "On the other hand, Macdonald, Rahv, and Kazin," he concludes his summary dismissal of their essays, "even in their perfunctory moments, have more to say than most of us when we are trying hard." The apparent source of such affectionate concern with the opinions of other reviewers is a conviction that the value of an opinion can be defined by the admiration one feels for the holder of that opinion. "Not *which* idea but *whose*?" the reviewer seems to ask himself. The original judgments of respected critics quickly acquire an aura not only of self-evidence but of finality (*they* at least are assumed innocent until they are proved guilty): "I admire [Edmund] Wilson greatly," Lionel Abel writes, in an essay on Alfred Kazin, "from which it will be seen that I do not . . ." And, says another reviewer, "As a conscious artist, O'Neill was stiff and crude, as Mary McCarthy has established." The New Reviewers hastily stand up to be counted, and reviewing becomes not merely a circuit but a cartel.

Apart from the group orientation of *Doings and Undoings*, the book is interesting primarily for its arguments. In his introduction, Mr. Podhoretz establishes the premises on which his critical arguments are based:

> Most often the event [that produced these essays] was the appearance of a new book that seemed to me to raise important issues . . . and almost always it was the issues rather than the book itself that I really cared about. Is that a damaging admission for a literary critic to make? . . . We may be looking in the wrong place for the achievements of the creative literary imagination when we look for them only where they were last seen—in novels and poems and plays. . . . These may all be of great interest to me as a student of literature, and they may be of some interest to me as an habitual reader. But they are of no interest to me as a man living in a particular place at a particular time and beset by problems of a particular kind.

This position is a consistent and audacious one, and Mr. Podhoretz adopts it with full awareness of its implications. But, again, particularly in his lapse of faith in pure fiction, he does not speak entirely in isolation. "I wonder, who reads short stories?" writes John Thompson in *Partisan*

Review. "When you pick up a magazine, do you turn to the short story? What is it doing there, anyway? It looks as boring as a poem, and probably it is. Maybe if you yourself write short stories, yes, you take a quick slice at it, to see who's doing it now, is he one up on you or not, what's he copying . . ." "The novel is having a hard time," Alfred Chester remarks in *Commentary;* and in *Show* Kenneth Lamott observes, "People who care about such things have agreed for as long as I can remember that the novel is in a bad way." "Her book is memorable to me," Julian Moynahan writes of Brigid Brophy in *The New York Review,* "only because halfway through reading it I was seized by a cramping suspicion that the novel as a viable literary form might after three hundred years of life be ready for burial." And, referring to a statement made by Paul Goodman, a reviewer writes, "Such an observation calls into question the validity of fiction itself."

Mr. Podhoretz, however, does not go quite so far; he does not discount fiction altogether. He has simply, in his words, "lost my piety toward the form in its own right, which means that I do not feel an automatic sympathy for the enterprise of novel-writing," and he continues:

> A large class of readers . . . has found itself responding more enthusiastically to . . . non-fiction (and especially to magazine articles and even book reviews) than to current fiction. . . . And what the novel has abdicated has been taken over by discursive writers. Imagination has not died (how could it?) but it has gone into other channels. . . . What I have in mind—and I cheerfully admit that the suggestion sounds preposterous—is *magazine articles.*

The suggestion does not sound preposterous at all, particularly in a passage pointing out the literary takeover by "discursive writers." (It explains, for one thing, why reviewers pay so much attention to other reviewers, and it attempts to explain, for another, why Mr. Podhoretz's magazine articles should have been published in book form.) One result, however, of a conviction that imagination has been diverted from fiction into expository writing is that the expository writer, particularly the reviewer, is often tempted to press his *own* imagination upon the work of fiction, to prescribe for the novelist the kind of work that the reviewer thinks he ought to have written. Thus, Mr. Podhoretz berates John Updike for having written about old age, and not having written a reminiscence of childhood, in *The Poorhouse Fair:*

. . . In any case there was something that gave me the creeps about the way he had deliberately set out to reverse the usual portrait-of-the-artist-as-a-young-man pattern of the first novel.

And he further instructs the novelist (as though Mr. Podhoretz's pains necessarily resembled Updike's, and as though Mr. Podhoretz himself were writing a novel including a description of them):

Severe pain in one part of the body does not travel through the system, either on wet wings or dry; on the contrary, after the first flash of burning sensation, its effect is actually to focus one's entire consciousness on the hurt spot . . . Consequently the appropriate images for rendering such an experience . . . would be . . .

He reproaches Saul Bellow for the ending of a novel ("If, however, Bellow had been ruthless in following out the emotional logic of *Seize the Day*, it would almost certainly have been murder—and *Seize the Day* would almost certainly have been a great book"), and he suggests his own ending for Joseph Heller's *Catch-22*. He even rebukes Harry Truman for not "admitting" in his autobiography that he was the "ambitious, perhaps lonely boy who dreamed of greatness" that Mr. Podhoretz thinks he must have been. In his conviction that it is the business of criticism to prescribe for literature, Mr. Podhoretz is again not quite alone. "It is the Orestes-Iphigenia story, we see here, that Salinger all along had been trying to rewrite," Leslie Fiedler (himself much occupied with myth) prescribes for Salinger, "the account of a Fury-haunted brother redeemed by his priestess-sister." "He could become the best of our literary novelists," Norman Mailer prescribes for another author (as opposed, one wonders, to our *non*-literary novelists?), "if he could forget about style and go deeper into the literature of sex." (A "forgetting" and a "going deeper" that, *bien entendu*, Mailer himself has managed to achieve.)

A difficulty, however, in pitting the reviewer's imagination against the author's, in assuming that critics have an obligation to correct not merely, in Mr. Podhoretz's words, "the prevailing estimate of a book or a literary reputation" but the book itself, is that the relationship between writer and reviewer soon becomes a contest—and a contest, occasionally, of a highly personal sort. The book under review is not written as the reviewer would have written it; he begins to speculate as to what personal deficiency in the author could possibly account for this lapse. If the author has received widespread public recognition, the line of personal attack is clear: he has been corrupted by success in the mass media—and New Reviewers will go to enormous lengths to ferret out references to the author in *Life, Time, Newsweek,* best-seller lists, and so on, in order to establish some kind of guilt by non-obscurity. More commonly, however, the reviewer's attack upon an author is quite direct—an allegation that his personality, particularly in its sexual and moral attitudes, must be somehow diseased. Alfred Chester, for example, confidently impugns Henry Miller's sexual prowess: "Miller, in fact, never makes his reader raise more than a blush and, more often than not, the blush is for Henry's delusions of grandeur." Leslie Fiedler, on the other hand, attempts psychoanalysis: "Finally, like his characters, Salinger is reconciled with everything but sex. . . ." And Edzia Weisberg impugns the personal competence not of the author but of previous reviewers: "Except for Middleton Murry, who for reasons all too transparent found *Aaron's Rod* 'the greatest of Lawrence's novels,' and F. R. Leavis, who for reasons almost as transparent is extremely indulgent toward the novel, no one has ever considered either *Aaron's Rod* or *Kangaroo* successful." (To Miss Weisberg, perhaps, the reasons are transparent; the reader scarcely dares admit that he finds them opaque.) The reviewer hastens, however, to assure the reader that his *own* house is sexually and morally in order. "I just don't want to give up my skin," a reviewer informs us, in a rather tangential comment on a book under review. "It feels so good, especially in the sun or in the woods or in the sea or against another." And Mr. Podhoretz himself, in the essay "My Negro Problem—And Ours," while he admits that his own moral stand is not irreproachable, excludes the possibility that most other right-thinking people can be better off. Having outlined the violent and unhappy childhood that left him, to his dismay, with a residual fear and envy of Negroes, he begins to claim for his feelings a certain universality:

This, then, is where I am; it is not exactly where I think all other white liberals are, but it cannot be so very far away either.

The pervasiveness, assurance, and self-congratulation of that "I" in *Doings and Undoings* and in the works of other New Reviewers lead occasionally to a highhandedness that is almost grotesque. Alfred Chester writes:

I think I am precisely the man for whom serious modern novels *are* written, since I am one of the men they are written about. Look at four of the most influential novelists of the last twenty years. . . . By influential I mean, of course, that which has impact on the thinking of those capable of thinking, and this, at least in France, is without reference to sales or to the behavior patterns of beatniks and college students.

Having excluded "sales" (i.e., the buyers of books) and "college students" (i.e., some of the most avid readers of them) from the category of "those capable of thinking," Mr. Chester is naturally left with himself, the reviewer, as the man for and about whom "serious modern novels" are written. But one danger in the assumption that it is the reviewer who occupies the center of the literary universe is that he begins to regard everything about himself, however tangential to the book under review, as of universal interest and importance. "Nearly everyone I know would rather see a movie than read a book . . ." Mr. Chester writes. "And I count among my friends . . ." (And he counts among his friends, we may safely assume, Leslie Fiedler, whom Podhoretz notes as having said that "the sight of a group of new novels stimulates in *him* 'a desperate desire to sneak out to a movie.'") Despite this tendency to express in criticism all the reviewer's little feelings and preferences —his delight in movies, the predilections of his friends, the situations in which his skin feels good—New Reviewing personalities are not, in general, so idiosyncratic that a reader cannot find one quality they have in common:

> Yet the truth is that the great national "debates" that the New York *Times* daily calls upon us to consider are invariably puerile from an intellectual point of view and far beneath the consideration of any sophisticated mind.

Showing up their weaknesses is child's play for a sophisticated critic.

Granted that painters and actors need not—indeed should not—be capable of discussing their respective arts with genuine sophistication, is it really necessary . . .

He is in the presence of a writer who is very sophisticated indeed and who therefore cannot possibly be as callow and sentimental . . .

Now, this black-and-white account, with the traditional symbolisms reversed, is not the kind of picture that seems persuasive to the sophisticated modern sensibility—the sensibility that has been trained by Dostoyevski and Freud, by Nietzsche and Kierkegaard, by Eliot and Yeats, to see moral ambiguity everywhere, to be bored by melodrama, to distrust the idea of innocence.

On the other hand, of course, there are equally sophisticated critics like Robert Brustein and Kenneth Tynan who have arrived at opposite conclusions, finding [Lenny] Bruce not . . .

Those who find Bergman profound and sophisticated (as if the artist who could move them deeply had to be a deep thinker) are very likely to find Satyajit Ray rather too simple.

Apart from its truth, I find this very refreshing indeed, because most of us are too sophisticated to have written it or thought it. . . . We all believe and know these things, but we fear that to say them out loud would be to evoke the superior smile.

What these passages (the first five by Mr. Podhoretz, the remaining three by assorted contributors to *Partisan Review* and *Commentary*) have in common is a keynote of sophistication—or, at any rate, the mention of the word. Sophistication, one gathers, is a quality lacking in *Times* editorial writers, illusory in Bergman films, absent in artists and actors talking about their work, present in Robert Brustein and Kenneth Tynan, and conditioned by Dostoevski, Freud, Nietzsche, Kierkegaard, Eliot, and Yeats (although in what sense Dostoevski can be said to train the modern sensibility to be bored by melodrama, or Nietzsche to see moral ambiguity everywhere, or Yeats to distrust the idea of innocence, is something that Mr. Podhoretz is too sophisticated to explain). Richard Chase points out the sophisticate's fear of evoking "the superior smile." The definite article is puzzling. *The* smile? Whose smile? Why, the communal smile of Norman Podhoretz, Alfred Chester, Lionel Abel, and the rest—the collective smile of the New Reviewing school.

And the stimulus for that sophisticated, perhaps not altogether winning smile is, when it is not the author of a literary work, none other than the reader, who is allowed occasionally to believe that he is in on an exclusive circuit secret but more often is reminded that he is hopelessly out—a child permitted to eavesdrop on the nocturnal conversation of his elders. No opportunity is lost to cast aspersions on the mind and the behavior of that child. "Who listens? Who cares?" Mr. Podhoretz inquires rhetorically, and he deplores the dwindling of "a reading public literate enough to understand a complicated exposition." Concern, in fact, about the mental calibre of a hypothetical reader slurred as middle-class, middle-brow—indeed, middle-everything—is so widespread that Fiedler professes himself disappointed because he cannot find a novel "which might have caught once and for all the pathos and silliness of middle-class, middle-brow intellectual aspiration"; and even the publisher of *Esquire* feels impelled to announce in his column that "'The mindless dictatorship of the audience' was the most provocative single sentence uttered at Princeton during the entire *Response Weekend.*" (Calling "the mindless dictatorship of the audience" a "sentence" is but one indication of the publisher's concern. In his anxiety over mindlessness, he neglects to parse.) "Is it really so difficult to tell a good action from a bad one?" Frank Kermode inquires in *Partisan Review,* and he answers with a ringing New Reviewing anti-Everyman cliché: "It would seem so, since most people appear to be wrong most of the time." "People like to think Eichmann mediocre," says Lionel Abel. "I think they also like the idea of Miss Arendt, implied by her subtitle, that evil can be banal. Perhaps they are flattered to believe that in the ordinary and dulling conduct of their lives they are at the very least doing something wrong." Here Mr. Abel delivers a threefold vote of no confidence in readers: with the carelessness of his grammar ("Miss Arendt" for "Miss Arendt's"); with the shakiness of his assumption (that the reader's conduct is any more "ordinary and dulling" than Mr. Abel's own); and with the injustice of his insinuation (that the reader would accept the invalid-conversion fallacy—evil is banal, therefore banality is evil, as one might say all dogs are animals, therefore all animals are dogs—which Mr. Abel permits himself). Not merely readers, however—*everything* is on the wane. A New Reviewing Cassandra seems to have issued an encyclical announcing that the sky is falling—a conclusion that has travelled ever since, in slightly diluted form (as in the childhood game of "Whisper"), around the whole reviewing circle. "Is 'the sickness of our time' a literary hoax?" Benjamin DeMott inquires in *Harper's.* "Are the writers who call the present age a cesspool mistaking personal whiffiness for objective truth?" The questions are purely rhetorical; Mr. DeMott's answer, needless to say, is No.

> The multiplication of commodities and the false standard of living, on the one hand, the complication of the economic and technical structure in which one can work at a job, on the other hand, and the lack of direct relationship between the two have by now made a great part of external life morally meaningless.

Thus, knotting unintelligibly together a few strands of defeatist cliché, George Steiner exemplifies both a prose style and a world view: Everything is bad, science and technology advance, moral values are in permanent eclipse, and there is no hope. (There is no syntax, either— only jargon to express the futility of it all.) "I . . . suppose, they talk about plot and character, style and setting," John Thompson speculates mournfully of the universities. "Maybe it is just too late."

This generalized cultural alarmism has created among the New Reviewers a forensic device that we might call not name- but catastrophe-dropping. Whenever a reviewer's exposition is in danger of disintegration, he simply mentions a calamity to distract the reader's attention (much as a member of a debating society might cry "Fire!" in a crowded auditorium when his argument is going badly). In his discussion of his Negro problem Mr. Podhoretz makes repeated reference to the *violence* of his feelings, as if in evidence of their universality. And Norman Mailer, inveighing querulously against modern architecture, has a comparable inspiration:

> That rough beast is a shapeless force, an obdurate emptiness, an annihilation of possibilities. It is totalitarianism: that totalitarianism which has haunted the twentieth century, haunted the efforts of intellectuals to define it, of politicians to withstand it, and of rebels to find a field of war where it could be given battle.

Totalitarianism. Haunted. Annihilation. Beast. The reader gasps. What has the analogy to do with modern architecture? Nothing. But Mr. Mailer is ready with another gambit: "Our modern architecture reminds me a little of cancer cells. Because the healthy cells of the lung have one appearance and those in the liver another. But if both are cancerous they tend to look a little more alike." What has cancer to do with architecture? What "sameness" is there between, say, Edward Stone and Le Corbusier? None. But the reader is meant to agree, in a state of typographical shock.

"I write the sentence, *six million innocent people were slaughtered*," Irving Howe writes in *Commentary*, "and for a person of adequate sensibilities may it not be as affecting as an embodiment in a conventional narrative?" Well, no, Mr. Howe, but it may give the illusion of shoring up a sickly argument. "It is dead. It is evil, like racial prejudice," Alfred Chester writes of the comedy of Vladimir Nabokov. "Less evil . . . were the Eichmann jokes making the rounds last year which mocked and trivialized the death of six million Jews—and which, nonetheless, even I and other Jews could laugh at." Racial prejudice. Dead. Evil. Eichmann. What relevance have they to the comedy of Vladimir Nabokov? None. They are simply a reviewer's form of literary demagoguery. Other devices on the same order are the frequent use of obscenity and a kind of strident excremental prose that masquerades as a perpetual assertion of manliness. Norman Mailer, for example, writes in a review, "A bad maggoty novel. Four or five half-great short stories were buried like pullulating organs in a corpse of fecal matter"; and Alfred Chester, addressing the author of a book on homosexuality, barks, "Better cut out all that ceaseless groping, Jack, and get down to work!"

Mr. Podhoretz, however, is seldom coarse or shrill. On the contrary, he seeks, by his own account, "a language in which it is possible to talk sensibly and with due proportion about new books." Here is Mr. Podhoretz arguing "sensibly and with due proportion" about the works of John Updike:

His short stories—which I usually find myself throwing away in disgust before I can get to the end—strike me as all windup and no delivery.

How Mr. Podhoretz can detect the "delivery" if he throws stories away "before I can get to the end" is a problem that he seems not to have posed himself. Nor need he bother to pose it, for although there may be considerable discussion among those in the milieu, there is little dialectic, and arguments of extraordinary inventiveness are permitted to flourish unchallenged. The warm, permissive climate of the New Reviewing is sealed protectively against all intellectual discipline, and it has managed to foster in comfort a whole new genre of fallacy. Lionel Abel, for example, in disagreeing with Hannah Arendt about Adolf Eichmann, takes an argument of Miss Arendt's own, treats it as his, and arrives at a new form of argument altogether, a kind of preemptive bid—agreement-as-refutation: "Is there any contradiction between being morally monstrous and also comical?" he asks. "I am inclined to think that there is none, that anyone who considers the comical traits of Iago and Richard III must be of my opinion." Precisely, and of Miss Arendt's as well—but one must concede Mr. Abel the novelty of his argument; he simply restates, in less subtle terms, what Miss Arendt has said, and expects her to cry *"Touchée!"*

"On the subject of Trotsky," Lionel Abel writes, in another article, "Mr. Kazin exhibits a harshness, intemperateness, and insensitivity which he does not show at all in responding to Herman Melville's Captain Ahab. And this is all the more striking to me since everything Mr. Kazin has to say against Trotsky could be said with equal or greater force against Melville's hero." This appears to be some sort of art/reality interchange, whereby everything that can be said against Mr. Abel can probably be said with equal or greater force against Dogberry. We might call it, perhaps, the argument-from-socio-critical-ineptitude.

Alfred Chester, on the other hand, touches all the forensic bases, and doffs his cap at every one:

> So *Tropic of Cancer*, says I, isn't a great book. So? There is a consolation prize, however, think of what pleasure it is to disagree with Karl Shapiro. And what pleasure it is to disagree with that long and laudatory list of eminent names that appears on the dust jacket like a list of vitamins and minerals: Eliot, Pound, Durrell, Anaïs Nin, Orwell, etc. And what pleasure to disagree also with the whole of the beat generation and their sycophants who have learned from Miller . . . to posture at revolutions that even *Time* Magazine approves of.

This passage, despite its strange, uncertain irony, calls into being the argument-from-the-stature-of-the-people-with-whom-one-disagrees.

"The sum effect is that *The Glass Bees* puzzles," writes Theodore Solotaroff, "by its technique of steadily delimiting and generalizing its particulars, to the point of turning them into abstractions that could mean this or could mean that, and producing eventually a type of moral sensationalism and sentimentalism." "Delimiting . . . particulars to the point of . . . abstractions . . . producing . . . moral sensationalism"—the sum effect is that this argument puzzles by its technique of steadily ensnarling and obfuscating its terms that could mean this and could mean that, and producing eventually a kind of logical surrealism and vertigo.

And, finally, Mr. Podhoretz himself has argued in *Show* that if two authors "had really wanted to give us a profile of the art of acting, rather than a profile of the practitioners themselves, they would have tried to induce these people to talk candidly about each other's work instead of about their own lives and careers." The argument that a book is improved when its subjects "talk candidly about each other's work" is—"for reasons," as Miss Weisberg would say, "all too transparent"—a characteristically New Reviewing prescription. "Hamlet," Mr. Podhoretz says in the same piece, "would exist without John Gielgud to play him, but would the heroine of *Sweet Bird of Youth* have existed without Geraldine Page? For me, the fact that I can't remember her name is answer enough." Answer enough, perhaps, for Mr. Podhoretz. The reader may detect the birth of the argument-from-personal-amnesia.

It is hardly necessary to go on citing instances of the inexhaustible variety of argument along the reviewing circuit. There are signs, in any case, that the cloud (catastrophe-droppers might say "the *mushroom* cloud") is passing. Or, in purely mechanical terms, there are beginning to be some short circuits in the New Reviewing system. Steven Marcus, in *The New York Review*, crosses three wires (anti-Everyman cliché, reviewer centrality, and catastrophe-dropping), with this result:

It is almost as if for three hundred years the literature of Western culture had not, so to speak, conducted a campaign to demonstrate that the middle class family is about as close as we have come to achieving hell on earth.

"The literature of Western culture," as represented by Henry James, Thomas Mann, and Jane Austen—to name authors of but three nationalities—has conducted no such "campaign." Mr. Marcus has confused "the literature of Western culture" with the expository writing of

Norman Podhoretz, Leslie Fiedler, Lionel Abel, and the rest of the New Reviewing school.

. . .

One can view Mr. Podhoretz as an exponent of a group program only because, in his polemic, or "Undoings," he insistently invites one to do so, and because (aside from an ill-informed and poorly reasoned piece on Hannah Arendt and his well-intentioned but poorly reasoned essay on the Negro problem, both of which have a kind of negative fascination) the "Undoings" have no interest *except* as examples of a school of critical writing. And the principles that unite the New Reviewing school are—if it is possible to call them "principles" at all—an elaborate system of cross-references that amounts to mutual coattail-hanging; a stale liberalism gone reactionary in anti-Everyman snobbery and defeatist cliché; a false intellectualism that is astonishingly shabby in its arguments; a hostile imperiousness toward fiction that results in near megalomania on the part of expository writers; and a withering condescension toward authors and readers that finds expression in a strident tendency to shout the opposition down. The New Reviewing is, more generally, a pastiche of attitudes and techniques vying to divert the attention of the reader from the book ostensibly under review to the personality of the reviewer, striving intrusively and valiantly to hold the line against the arts. And the "Undoings" in this collection are, for the most part, models of New Reviewing principle.

In the essays, however, in which Mr. Podhoretz is least interesting as a member of, or spokesman for, something—in his "Doings," in short—Mr. Podhoretz does manage to assert himself as a genuine critic. Most of these "Doings" are included in a section called "Traditions"— non-topical, non-polemical, even non-controversial essays—and they are the considered, sympathetic works of a young man more interested in interpreting books than in pitting himself against them. There are not enough of them to constitute a volume of three hundred and seventy-one pages, but they are evidence that the critical writings of Norman Podhoretz may yet result in a worthwhile collection.

JOHN UPDIKE

FROM

THE AUTHOR AS LIBRARIAN

OCTOBER 30, 1965 (J. L. BORGES)

T HE BELATED NORTH American acknowledgment of the genius of Jorge Luis Borges proceeds apace. In 1964, the University of Texas Press published two volumes by this Argentine fantasist, critic, poet, and librarian: *Dreamtigers* (translated from the Spanish by Mildred Boyer and Harold Morland) and *Other Inquisitions, 1937–1952* (translated by Ruth L. C. Simms). These translations, together with Grove Press's *Ficciones,* bring to three the number of complete books by Borges available in English. There is also New Directions' *Labyrinths*, an excellent selection, translated by various hands. And in 1965 the New York University Press published a book *about* Borges: *Borges the Labyrinth Maker,* by Ana Maria Barrenechea (translated from the Spanish by Robert Lima).

Four years ago, when Borges shared with Samuel Beckett the Prix International des Éditeurs, he was known here to few but Hispanic specialists. A handful of poems and short stories had appeared in scattered anthologies and magazines. I myself had read only "The Garden of the Forking Paths," originally published in *Ellery Queen's Mystery Magazine* and subsequently a favorite of detective-story anthologies. Though vivid and intellectual beyond the requirements of its genre, the story can be read without awareness that its creator is a giant of world literature. I was prompted to read Borges seriously by a remark made—internationally enough—in Rumania, where, after a blanket disparagement of contemporary French and German fiction, Borges was praised by a young critic in a tone he had previously reserved for Kafka. An analogy with Kafka is inevitable, but I wonder if Borges' abrupt projection, by the university and avant-garde presses, into the bookstores will prove as momentous as Kafka's publication, by the commercial firm of Knopf, in the thirties. It is not a question of Borges' excellence. His driest paragraph is somehow compelling. His fables are written from a height of intelligence less rare in philosophy and physics than in fiction. Furthermore, he is, at least for anyone whose taste runs to puzzles or pure speculation, delightfully entertaining. The question is, I think, whether or not Borges' lifework, arriving in a lump now (he was born in 1899 and since his youth has been an active and honored figure in Argentine literature), can serve, in its gravely considered oddity, as any kind of clue to the way out of the dead-end narcissism and downright trashiness of present American fiction.

Borges' narrative innovations spring from a clear sense of technical crisis. For all his modesty and reasonableness of tone, he proposes some sort of essential revision in literature itself. The absolute conciseness of his style and the eerie comprehensiveness of his career (in addition to writing poems, essays, and stories, he has collaborated on detective novels, translated from many tongues, edited, taught, and even executed film scripts) produce a strangely terminal impression: he seems to be the man for whom literature has no future. I am haunted by knowing that this insatiable reader is now virtually blind. . . .

. . .

The great achievement of his art is his short stories. In an attempt to round off this review of accessory volumes, I will describe two of my favorites.

"The Waiting" is from his second major collection, *El Aleph,* and is found, translated by James E. Irby, in *Labyrinths.* It is a rarity in Borges' *œuvre*—a story in which nothing incredible occurs. A gangster fleeing from the vengeance of another gangster seeks anonymity in a northwest part of Buenos Aires. After some weeks of solitary existence, he is discovered and killed. These events are assigned a detailed and mundane setting. The very number of the boarding house where he lives is given (4004: a Borgian formula for immensity) and the neighborhood is flatly described: "The man noted with approval the spotted plane trees, the square plot of earth at the foot of each, the respectable houses with their little balconies, the pharmacy alongside, the dull lozenges of the paint and hardware store. A long windowless hospital wall backed the sidewalk on the other side of the street; the sun reverberated, farther down, from some greenhouses." Yet much information is withheld. "The man" mistakenly gives a cabdriver a Uruguayan coin, which "had been in his pocket since that night in the hotel at Melo." What had happened that night in Melo and the nature of his offense against his enemy are not disclosed. And when the landlady—herself unnamed, and specified as having "a distracted or tired air"—asks the man his name, he gives the name, Villari, of the man hunting him! He does this, Borges explains, "not as a secret challenge, not to mitigate the humiliation which actually he did not feel, but because that name troubled him, because it was impossible for him to think of any other. Certainly he was not seduced by the literary error of thinking that assumption of the enemy's name might be an astute maneuver."

Villari—Villari the hunted—is consistently prosaic, even stupid. He ventures out to the movies and, though he sees stories of the underworld that contain images of his old life, takes no notice of them, "because the idea of a coincidence between art and reality was alien to him." Reading of another underworld in Dante, "he did not judge the punishments of hell to be unbelievable or excessive." He has a toothache and is compelled to have the tooth pulled. "In this ordeal he was neither more cowardly nor more tranquil than other people." His very will to live is couched negatively: "It only wanted to endure, not to come to an end." The next sentence, grounding the abhorrence of death upon the simplest and mildest things, recalls Unamuno. "The taste of the maté, the taste of black tobacco, the growing line of shadows gradually covering the patio—these were sufficient incentives."

Unobtrusively, the reader comes to love Villari, to respect his dull humility and to share his animal fear. Each brush with the outer world is a touch of terror. The toothache—"an intimate discharge of pain in the back of his mouth"—has the force of a "horrible miracle." Returning from the movies, he feels pushed, and, turning "with anger, with indignation, with secret relief," he spits out "a coarse insult." The passerby and the reader are alike startled by this glimpse into the savage criminal that Villari has been. Each night, at dawn, he dreams of Villari—Villari the hunter—and his accomplices overtaking him, and of shooting them with the revolver he keeps in the drawer of the bedside table. At last—whether betrayed by the trip to the dentist, the visits to the movie house, or the assumption of the other's name we do not know—he is awakened one July dawn by his pursuers:

> Tall in the shadows of the room, curiously simplified by those shadows (in the fearful dreams they had always been clearer), vigilant, motionless and patient, their eyes lowered as if weighted down by the heaviness of their weapons, Alejandro Villari and a stranger had overtaken him at last. With a gesture, he asked them to wait and turned his face to the wall, as if to resume his sleep. Did he do it to arouse the pity of those who killed him, or because it is less difficult to endure a frightful happening than to imagine it and

endlessly await it, or—and this is perhaps most likely—so that the murderers would be a dream, as they had already been so many times, in the same place, at the same hour?

So the inner action of the narrative has been to turn the utterly unimaginative hero into a magician. In retrospect, this conversion has been scrupulously foreshadowed. The story, indeed, is a beautiful cinematic succession of shadows; the most beautiful are those above, which simplify the assassins—"(in the fearful dreams they had always been clearer)." The parenthesis of course makes a philosophic point: it opposes the ambiguity of reality to the relative clarity and simplicity of what our minds conceive. It functions as well in the realistic level of the story, bodying forth all at once the climate, the moment of dawn, the atmosphere of the room, the sleeper's state of vision, the menace and matter-of-factness of the men, "their eyes lowered as if weighted down by the heaviness of their weapons." Working from the artificial reality of films and gangster novels, and weaving his hypersubtle sensations of unreality into the furniture of his plot, Borges has created an episode of criminal brutality in some ways more convincing than those in Hemingway. One remembers that in *The Killers* Ole Andreson also turns his face to the wall. It is barely possible that Borges had in mind a kind of gloss of Hemingway's classic. If that is so, with superior compassion and keener attention to peripheral phenomena he has enriched the theme. In his essay on Hawthorne, Borges speaks of the Argentine literary aptitude for realism; his own florid fantasy is grafted onto that native stock.

"The Library of Babel," which appears in *Ficciones,* is wholly fantastic, yet refers to the librarian's experience of books. Anyone who has been in the stacks of a great library will recognize the emotional aura, the wearying impression of an inexhaustible and mechanically ordered chaos, that suffuses Borges' mythical universe, "composed of an indefinite, perhaps an infinite, number of hexagonal galleries, with enormous ventilation shafts in the middle, encircled by very low railings." Each hexagon contains twenty shelves, each shelf thirty-two books, each book four hundred and ten pages, each page forty lines, each line eighty letters. The arrangement of these letters is almost uniformly chaotic and formless. The nameless narrator of "The Library of Babel" sets forward, pedantically, the history of philosophical speculation by the human beings who inhabit this inflexible and inscrutable cosmos, which is equipped, apparently for their convenience, with spiral stairs, mirrors, toilets, and lamps ("The light they emit is insufficient, incessant").

This monstrous and comic model of the universe contains a full range of philosophical schools—idealism, mysticism, nihilism:

> The idealists argue that the hexagonal halls are a necessary form of absolute space or, at least, of our intuition of space. They contend that a triangular or pentagonal hall is inconceivable.

> The mystics claim that to them ecstasy reveals a round chamber containing a great book with a continuous back circling the walls of the room. . . . That cyclical book is God.

> I know of a wild region whose librarians repudiate the vain superstitious custom of seeking any sense in books and compare it to looking for meaning in dreams or in the chaotic lines of one's hands. . . . They speak (I know) of "the febrile Library, whose hazardous volumes run the constant risk of being changed into others and in which everything is affirmed, denied, and confused as by a divinity in delirium."

Though the Library appears to be eternal, the men within it are not, and they have a history punctuated by certain discoveries and certain directions now considered axiomatic. Five hundred years ago, in an upper hexagon, two pages of homogeneous lines were discovered that within a century were identified as "a Samoyed-Lithuanian dialect of Guaraní, with classical Arabic inflections" and translated. The contents of these two pages—"notions of combinational analysis"—led to the deduction that the Library is total; that is, its shelves contain all possible combinations of the orthographic symbols:

> Everything is there: the minute history of the future, the autobiographies of the archangels, the faithful catalogue of the Library, thousands and thousands of false catalogues, a demonstration of the fallacy of these catalogues, a demonstration of the fallacy of the true catalogue, the Gnostic gospel of Basilides, the commentary on this gospel, the commentary on the commentary on this gospel, the veridical account of your death, a version of each book in all languages, the interpolations of every book in all books.

Men greeted this revelation with joy; "the universe suddenly expanded to the limitless dimensions of hope." They surged onto the stairs, searching for Vindications—books that would vindicate and explain his life to each man. Sects sprang up. One used dice and metal letters in an attempt to "mimic the divine disorder" and compose by chance the canonical volumes. Another, the Purifiers, destroyed millions of books, hurling them down the air shafts. They believed in "the Crimson Hexagon: books of a smaller than ordinary format, omnipotent, illustrated, magical." A third sect worshipped the Man of the Book—a hypothetical librarian who, in some remote hexagon, must have perused a book "which is a cipher and perfect compendium of *all the rest*." This librarian is a god. "Many pilgrimages have sought Him out."

The analogies with Christianity are pursued inventively and without the tedium of satire. The narrator himself confides, "To me, it does not seem unlikely that on some shelf of the universe there lies a total book. I pray the unknown gods that some man—even if only one man, and though it have been thousands of years ago!—may have examined and read it." But in his own person he has only the "elegant hope" that the Library, if traversed far enough, would repeat itself in the same disorder, which then would constitute an order. At hand, in this illegible chaos, are only the tiny rays of momentary sense, conglomerations of letters spelling *O Time your pyramids, Combed Clap of Thunder,* or *The Plaster Cramp.*

This kind of comedy and desperation, these themes of vindication and unattainability, suggest Kafka. But *The Castle* is a more human work, more personal and neurotic; the fantastic realities of Kafka's fiction are projections of the narrator-hero's anxieties, and have no communion, no interlocking structure, without him. The Library of Babel instead has an adamant solidity. Built of mathematics and science, it will certainly survive the weary voice describing it, and outlast all its librarians, already decimated, we learn in a footnote, by "suicide and pulmonary disease." We move, with Borges, beyond psychology, beyond the human, and confront, in his work, the world atomized and vacant. Perhaps not since Lucretius has a poet so definitely felt men as incidents in space.

What are we to make of him? The economy of his prose, the tact of his imagery, the courage of his thought are there to be admired and emulated. In resounding the note of the marvellous last struck in English by Wells and Chesterton, in permitting infinity to enter and distort his imagination, he has lifted fiction away from the flat earth where most of our novels and short stories still take place. Yet discouragingly large areas of truth seem excluded from his vision. Though the population of the Library somehow replenishes itself, and "fecal necessities" are provided for, neither food nor fornication is mentioned—and in truth they are not generally seen in libraries. I feel in Borges a curious implication: the unrealities of physical science and the senseless repetitions of history have made the world outside the library an uninhabitable vacuum. Literature—that European empire augmented with translations from remote kingdoms—is now the only world capable of housing and sustaining new literature. Is this too curious? Did not Eliot recommend forty years ago, in reviewing *Ulysses,* that new novels be retellings of old myths? Is not the greatest of modern novels, *Remembrance of Things Past,* about the writing of itself? Have not many books already been written from within Homer and the Bible? Did not Cervantes write from within Ariosto and Shakespeare from within Holinshed? Borges, by predilection and by program, carries these inklings toward a logical extreme: the view of books as, in sum, an alternate creation, vast, accessible, highly colored, rich in arcana, possibly sacred. Just as physical man, in his cities, has manufactured an environment whose scope and challenge and hostility eclipse that of the natural world, so literate man has heaped up a counterfeit universe capable of supporting life. Certainly the traditional novel as a transparent imitation of human circumstance has "a distracted or tired air." Ironic and blasphemous as Borges' hidden message may seem, the texture and method of his creations, though strictly inimitable, answer to a deep need in contemporary literary art—the need to confess the fact of artifice.

GEORGE STEINER

THE FIRE LAST TIME

NOVEMBER 25, 1967 (WILLIAM STYRON'S *CONFESSIONS OF NAT TURNER*)

A s BY NOW almost everyone knows, William Styron's *The Confessions of Nat Turner* (Random House) deals with a brief slave revolt that took place in the late summer of 1831 in Southampton

County, a remote corner of southeastern Virginia. The uprising was a ragged affair, doomed from the start. It involved seventy-five Negroes and resulted in the killing of fifty-five whites; most of the insurgent slaves were hacked down or executed. The body of Nat Turner, begetter and ringleader, was taken from the gallows, its flesh was boiled into grease, and small leather keepsakes were made of the skin. In Richmond, in 1832, T. R. Gray issued a pamphlet entitled "The Confessions of Nat Turner." Several other accounts of the mutiny were written, among them William Sidney Drewry's "The Southampton Insurrection." Though strategically puerile, the revolt of Nat Turner sent a shock of fury and baffled alarm through the South comparable to the one occasioned a generation later by John Brown's raid. It was the only organized rebellion, however short-lived, in the annals of American Negro slavery.

Mr. Styron grew up not far from Southampton County and thought to make of Nat Turner the subject of his first novel. Instead, he produced *Lie Down in Darkness*, a marvellously dense and vehement statement of what it is like to come of age Southern and haunted. This was followed by *The Long March* and that much criticized but revealing tale of Europe and America in their postwar, post–Thomas Wolfe interaction—*Set This House on Fire*. After which Mr. Styron embarked on a long silence and the theme that had from the first been ripening in his consciousness. *The Confessions of Nat Turner* is a return home, a falconlike gyring toward the point of departure which is characteristic of a number of American novelists (among Hemingway's last projects was a novel set in the Michigan of his boyhood). Is it merely fanciful to note how clear and symbolic a design lurks in Mr. Styron's earlier titles? Nat Turner lies in a great darkness, seeks to make the long march to the local and celestial Jerusalem, and leaves houses burning in his wake. But two forces more recent than Mr. Styron's initial impulse have acted on the book. It is difficult to listen to Nat Turner's canny, self-baring, or impassioned tone without hearing at the same time the voice of Mr. James Baldwin. The other modifier is, of course, recent history—the coming of the storm that now blows across American life. The crisis of civil rights, the new relationships to each other and to their own individual sensibilities that this crisis has forced on both whites and Negroes (as yet, we capitalize the one but not the other) give Mr. Styron's fable a special relevance. This is a book about a small fire last time in the light, at once revelatory and magnifying, of the great blaze now.

The narrative is set in a flashback older than Victor Hugo's *Last Days of a Condemned Man*, older even than the monitory thieves' pamphlets of the seventeenth century. During the five days preceding his execution, Nat Turner reviews the confession he has dictated to T. R. Gray, his inquisitor, spokesman before the court, and final intimate. Gray is not seeking to rack his doomed client. He is baffled by the fact that Turner has himself killed only one white person—the flower of genteel Virginian girlhood, Margaret Whitehead—and that he feels no remorse for the general butchery: "You mean to tell me that now, after all these here months, your heart ain't touched by the agony of an event like that?" Seeking to answer these queries, not to Mr. Gray so much as to himself, Nat lets his memory play over the past. On the verge of a mean death, he settles accounts inwardly. We eavesdrop on this long dialogue of spirit and self as we do on the actual exchanges—garrulous, pungent, broken by long silences—between the white man and the black.

A blackness heavier than the lost African past or the drowsy, storm-brooding Virginian nights has gone into the forging of Nat Turner. It is more than the inevitable posture of bondage, with its "unspeakable boot-licking Sambo, all giggles and smirks and oily, snivelling servility." It is more than the shock of seeing a mother acquiescent in partial rape or fellow-slaves chastised in petty or savage ways. It is an inner night accepted by both master and slave: to his owners the Negro is by God's definition a creature "who cannot spell *cat*," whom molasses and the lash keep in a condition just short of humanity. The Negro accepts this devaluation, not consciously but because the very words through which he forms his needs and croons his content are borrowed; the image he finds in his mirror has been put there by the white man. To a Negro slave, narcissism is subjection. But little Nathaniel is fortunate. Samuel Turner, his master, rejoices in his nascent powers, in his learning to read—a wonder of stealth and illumination finely rendered by Mr. Styron. Nat's study of Scripture and reveries of eloquence are fostered. At Turner's Mill, the child becomes "a grinning elf in a starched jumper who gazed at himself in mirrors, witlessly preoccupied with his own ability to charm." Plans are laid for his further training and, ultimately, for his emancipation. Nat passes into the mulatto zone of the half-free, into that sweet and cruel place of special acceptance where white masters have often cajoled and unmanned their more talented colonial subjects. But the South is visited by economic blight, and Nat finds himself thrown suddenly into the pit of common hell. First with the Reverend Eppes, who, his homosexual advances thwarted, reduces Nat to a worn chattel; then with Thomas Moore, an illiterate brute of a farmer. "I had never felt a whip before, and the pain of it when it came, coiling around the side of my neck like a firesnake, blossomed throughout the hollow of my skull in an explosion of light." By that searing light, Nat Turner lets his "exquisitely sharpened hatred for the white man" ripen to a purpose. He resolves to capture the armory in Jerusalem, the all too suitably named county seat, and transform a handful of tormented menials, cowering in a barbecue pit on Sunday afternoons and conspiring in dim, apocalyptic hatred, into the "majestic black army of the Lord!"

Mr. Styron has set himself the obviously formidable task of representing—no, of finding a credible poetic counterpart to—the mentality of an inspired Negro slave who lived briefly and died grimly a hundred and thirty-six years ago. "I have allowed myself the utmost freedom of imagination in reconstructing events," says Mr. Styron. What he means by "events" are necessarily the feelings, surges of memory, and introspective musings of Nat Turner. Here the reality available to the novelist, the sole means whereby he can convey his re-creative authority to the reader, is that of style. In few other recent novels has idiom borne so large a weight. We believe in Nat Turner's modes of speech, in the world of his words, or we do not believe in him at all. Mr. Styron has not attempted to offer a facsimile of the diction of a Tidewater Negro of the 1830s, though flashes of dialect and subliterate parlance do come through when minor characters speak. He has tackled the problem that always confronts the serious writer of historical fiction, be he Thackeray or Robert Graves: the working out of a credible linguistic convention, of a cadence and turn of phrase remote from yet susceptible to the undertones and pressures of the modern. It is fascinating to watch Mr. Styron at work. Several strands are visible. There is Mr. Styron's ability, salient in everything he writes, to make violent feeling pictorial, to accumulate words toward a graphic crescendo. There is a level of formal Latinity, of Miltonic sonorities, eroded by time and provincial usage, that governed the speech of high feeling in the Old Dominion. Principally, we find a constant echo of the Authorized Version and Book of Common Prayer. Nat Turner's conceptions, the timber of which he builds an apocalyptic world inside himself in order to ignite others with something of its visionary flame, are Biblical throughout. Job and Ezekiel possess his tongue. This is historically plausible and is, indeed, reflected in what we have of Nat Turner's own speech. But it proves effective at a deeper level as well. It relates the novel to other moments in American consciousness and prose in which the syntax of the Jacobean Bible, compressed by Puritan intensity or loosened and made florid by political rhetoric, served to define the new world. From Cotton Mather to Faulkner and James Baldwin, Biblical speech has set a core of vision and public ornament inside the American language.

One of the subtlest things in the book is Nat's feverish recollection of a buggy ride through the countryside with young Margaret Whitehead. She is brimming with unrealized, teasing sensuality. Nat Turner's nerves are tautened to near madness:

> On she prattled in her whispery voice, love-obsessed, Christ-crazed, babbling away in an echo of all the self-serving platitudes and stale insipid unfelt blather uttered by every pious capon and priestly spinster she had listened to since she was able to sit upright, misty-eyed and rapt and with her little pantalettes damp with devotion, in a pew of her brother's church. She filled me with boredom and lust—and now, to still at least the latter emotion, once and for all, I let her constant rush of words float uncaptured through my mind, and with my eyes on the horse's bright undulating rump, concentrated on a minor but thorny problem that was facing me at the very outset of my campaign.

His killing of the girl at the climax of the revolt is an enactment both literal and symbolic of the crazed yearnings that assail him in the "ferny coolness" of the woods. As she leans against him, Nat Turner feels the electric passage across his cheek of Margaret's chestnut-colored hair: "During that moment I heard her breathing and our eyes met in a wayward glint of light that seemed to last much longer than any mere glance exchanged between two strangers journeying of a summer afternoon to some drowsy dwelling far off in the country." The whole episode recalls a nocturnal dog-cart ride, tense with unfulfilled desire and stifled sensuality, in *Parade's End*. The echo of Ford Madox Ford is probably relevant. The ceremonious intensity of Ford's style seems to have influenced both William Styron and Allen Tate. And it is precisely beside Tate's great novel of the broken South, *The Fathers*, that we can most fairly set *The Confessions of Nat Turner*.

The question now is this: Would a Negro recognize Nat Turner for one of his own, would he find Mr. Styron's fiction authentic to his own experience? The literate Negro of today, one gathers, finds little save embarrassment and *mauvaise foi* in the masks devised for him by Faulkner. Whatever the answer, the question does not infirm the intelligence, the imaginative generosity of Mr. Styron's novel. He has every artistic right to make of his Nat Turner less an anatomy of the Negro mind than a fiction of complex relationship, of the relationship between a present-day white man of deep Southern roots and the Negro in today's whirlwind. The essential imaginative need in this beautiful, honest book arises from a white sensibility exploring its own social, racial future by dramatizing, necessarily in its own terms, the Negro past. It is something like this Styron may have in mind when he says that he wished "to produce a work that is less an 'historical novel' in conventional terms than a meditation on history."

Nevertheless, the question nags. Nor would a review by Mr. Baldwin give a representative reply (a great gift is like leprosy; it isolates a man or makes him a member of a special community). How many Negro "common readers," in Virginia Woolf's positive sense of the phrase, will this novel reach, how many will tell us of their response? What will they make of Mr. Styron's use of a white man—the brilliantly drawn Jeremiah Cobb—as the agent of Nat's awakening, as the goad to Nat Turner's vision of a possible revolt? Or of Mr. Styron's insistence, tactful and ironic as it is, on the role played by loyal Negro slaves in the crushing of Turner's insurrection? ("I had caught sight for the first time of Negroes in great numbers with rifles and muskets at the barricaded veranda, firing back at us with as much passion and fury and even skill as their white owners and overseers who had gathered there to block our passage into Jerusalem.") As one asks them, such questions seem to carry their own charge of relevant sadness. A few years ago, the hope of a natural dialogue between white and Negro, engaging such values as are implicit in Mr. Styron's narrative, seemed in closer reach than it does today. Now, at moments, the intimation of a gap across which sudden violence or hysterical intimacy offers the only bridge is as vivid as it was to Nat Turner. Nat's decision to root out of his mind forever the one white man to whom he stood in a relationship of love is all too suggestive of those spurts of harsh mockery or curtains of silence that so many Negroes now interpose between themselves and those who would be friends, allies, travellers down the same long road. "1831," writes Mr. Styron, "was, simultaneously, a long time ago and only yesterday." Or only tomorrow.

BRENDAN GILL

THE UNFINISHED MAN

MARCH 8, 1969 (PHILIP ROTH'S *PORTNOY'S COMPLAINT*)

PHILIP ROTH'S LATEST novel, *Portnoy's Complaint* (Random House), is one of the dirtiest books ever published. It is also one of the funniest. From first to last, it is unremittingly revolting and hilarious—a single, hysterical howl of excrementitious anguish, at which, uncannily, we are invited to laugh. What is more uncanny is that we actually do laugh, that we cannot avoid laughing, it being often wrung from us against our will, if not by the shock of an obscenity we recognize then by the shock of one we don't. Mr. Roth, in the person of his hero and counterpart, Alexander Portnoy, has expanded enormously the range of Pope's "What oft was thought but ne'er so well expressed." Portnoy is an irresistibly eloquent, foul-mouthed showoff/wisecracker/victim/windbag. "Look, you guys, you goyim," he seems to cry, "I'm dying, I'm as good as dead! What am I saying—as *good* as dead? Isn't that wild? And you know what's killing me? My mother's love. My father's love. My Jewishness. My gorgeous libido. All the great things, ripping the guts out of me. Poor Portnoy!" He holds up a copy of *Portnoy's Complaint*, on his sweating face the parody of a pitchman's ingratiating smirk. "Read all about me!" he begs. "Get the lowdown on poor A.P.'s horrible hangups! Read the filthy memoirs of a smart kid too big for his breeches!"

A hooknosed, Brillo-haired Punchinello, Roth's Portnoy reels in frantic high spirits about the spotlighted center ring, and from where we sit watching him in the shadows it is impossible to tell whether the liquid that gushes out of that painted, smiling clown's muzzle is blood or ketchup, his or Heinz. Nor does he wish us to be able to tell. He falls on his knees in the sawdust, writhing. For a moment, we fear that he may be in his death agony; a moment later, we suspect a hoax. The only thing we can be sure of is that Portnoy is having the time of his life. Never has anyone been so radiantly miserable, never has greater pleasure been squeezed from pain. Roth has taken Whitman's austerely noble "I am the man, I suffered, I was there" and transformed it into a whining and superbly comic "I am the boy, I ache all over, I am here." For Portnoy, still swaddled in polymorphous perversity at thirty-three, it is plain that there *is* no place but here; his bounds are the bounds of his mother-haunted, desire-tormented, guilt-ridden body. "I touch and sin, therefore I am." His heart is not the only organ he wears upon his sleeve, and it is certainly not the most conspicuous, but all of Portnoy's organs are equally precious to him and equally importunate in their need to be exhibited. Well, and no wonder; it turns out that they are the sum not only of what he is but also of what he knows. Beyond his troubled, panting, incessantly swelling and subsiding flesh lies terra incognita, inhabited by fire-eating and fire-breathing dragons that are, in fact, only other desperate people leading desperate lives. Most of these dragons are Gentiles, Portnoy's natural foe, and he strives to keep them at bay by cravenly abasing himself before their imaginary fierceness. Pratfalling into cataracts of scatological hyperbole, he becomes the biggest Jewish joke that ever was, and so, he hopes, the most harmless of creatures.

Roth insists again and again on our seeing Portnoy as a joke—one that, for his quaking hero, is a nightmare he is unlikely ever to waken from. The form of the joke is a series of psychoanalytical sessions, during which Portnoy pours out in exuberant disarray a rich sampling of lubricious recollections. His ever-silent, ever-receptive listener is Dr. Spielvogel, whose first utterance is also the last sentence of the novel: "So. Now vee may perhaps to begin. Yes?" This vaudeville take-off of a German accent strikes an unwelcomely gaglike note; best to forgive it as the author's revenge on the obviousness of the literary device he has employed to frame and sustain his novel. (And the "Yes" with its question mark is surely a prankish tribute to the most celebrated final word in the history of the novel—a "yes" that is content to be followed by a full stop.) One sees the advantages of the device: among other things, it permits the author to juggle chronology in a fashion so vivid that it almost succeeds in taking the place of the conventional suspense provided by a plot, which *Portnoy's Complaint* flagrantly omits. It can also permit the author to practice an indetectable carelessness of composition; it must be far easier to write a book higgledy-piggledy, in purported imitation of the tendentiousness of the unconscious mind, than to impose the calculated order of a "story" on it. Advantages allowed for, there remains something irritatingly old-fashioned about this particular device. For decades now, it has often been our lot to discover that the narrator of a novel is the inmate of a sanitarium, prison, or what you will, and is addressing his remarks—the body of the novel—not to us but to someone having a professional relationship to him; we readers are only eavesdroppers, presumably all the more ready to accept the validity of what is being said because we have no right to overhear it. Why, this late in the day and this late in the novel, cannot a work of fiction speak in its own voice, unaccounted-for? Wallace Stevens wrote that "The poem is the cry of its occasion, part of the res itself," and so should a novel be; the trappings of a laborious verisimilitude (Dr. Spielvogel, say, or the pretense that Portnoy is the Assistant Commissioner of Human Opportunity in the Lindsay administration) are but archaic nuisances.

Be all that as it may, Portnoy lives—lives with an intensity of comic force that reminds us at first of the opening chapters of Lenny Bruce's autobiography and of the Norman Mailer of *Why Are We in Vietnam?* and then, much more closely and more interestingly, of Mark Twain. How Twain in Heaven, vexed as usual and still having trouble with his "goddamns," must envy Roth his freedom to write as he pleases! Roth's exhilarating power of invention, his fearless upward spirals of exaggeration are obviously akin to Twain's and to the whole nineteenth-century pioneer tradition of humor. Roth's robust curiosity and coprophilous earthiness are also to be discerned in Twain, sometimes under astonishingly demure disguises. Obscenity is a notable enhancer of life and is suppressed at grave peril to the arts; if Twain had enjoyed today's wise permissiveness in respect to what one may write and publish, his career would probably not have been plagued by so long and sorry a sequence of false starts. No doubt he passes his time in Heaven pleasantly enough, swapping dirty limericks with Tennyson (who is said to have developed a fondness for them in old age), but he would have preferred joining the company of the great pornographers and scatologists—Rabelais, Restif de la Bretonne, Shakespeare, Rochester, Joyce, Céline. With this one short novel, easily raced through at a single sitting, Roth has edged into the outskirts of that company. It is an enviable place for a young writer to be.

At the start, Roth prints a mock dictionary definition of his hero's affliction:

Portnoy's Complaint (pôrt´-noiz kəm-plānt´) *n*. [after Alexander Portnoy (1933–   )] A disorder in which strongly-felt ethical and altruistic impulses are perpetually warring with extreme sexual longings, often of a perverse nature. Spielvogel says: "Acts of exhibitionism, voyeurism, fetishism, auto-eroticism and oral coitus are plentiful; as a consequence of the patient's 'morality,' however, neither fantasy nor act issues in genuine sexual gratification, but rather in overriding feelings of shame and the dread of retribution, particularly in the form of castration." (Spielvogel, O. "The Puzzled Penis," *Internationale Zeitschrift für Psychoanalyse*, Vol. XXIV p. 909.) It is believed by Spielvogel that many of the symptoms can be traced to the bonds obtaining in the mother-child relationship.

This definition is characteristic of Roth in being both funny and exact, as far as it goes, but one would do more justice to the novel if one were to summarize it with the help of a single verse out of Yeats' "A Dialogue of Self and Soul":

> A living man is blind and drinks his drop.
> What matter if the ditches are impure?
> What matter if I live it all once more?
> Endure that toil of growing up;
> The ignominy of boyhood; the distress
> Of boyhood changing into man;
> The unfinished man and his pain
> Brought face to face with his own clumsiness?

As the novel ends, there is no assurance that Portnoy's ignominy and distress can be mitigated; he may never become that worthy thing "the finished man among his enemies." But back of Portnoy and his perhaps incurable complaint looms the figure of his creator—the confident artist, rejoicing in the maturity of an exceptional talent and an exceptional intelligence. Roth has come into himself and into the world. He is a finished man, and if he finds himself among enemies they are almost certain to be of his own choosing. Patrick Kavanagh said of the Irish peasantry from which he sprang, "They live in the dark cave of the unconscious, and they scream when they see the light." *Portnoy's Complaint* is Roth's scream, and from now on, whenever he screams, it will have the sound of song.

L. E. SISSMAN

THE WHOLE TRUTH

DECEMBER 6, 1969 (JOYCE CAROL OATES'S *THEM*)

W E IN THIS country have a bad habit of overpraising or over-damning our young writers; if they are not tarred and feathered and ridden out of town on a rail, they are paraded through our book reviews with a motorcycle escort and a cloud of ticker tape. Joyce Carol Oates is too good, and too serious, a writer to deserve the parade, which she seems in danger of. What she *does* deserve is a constructive and dispassionate appraisal of her strengths and shortcomings, both of which are quite in evidence in *them* (Vanguard), her latest book.

them (a plague on titles with a lower-case initial, however significant; I'm calling it *Them* from here on), *Them*, then, is a five-hundred-page "work of history in fictional form," according to Miss Oates's preface, and it is based on the recollections of a former student of hers—recollections that cover thirty years of a family's life in the slums of a Midwestern city that is perhaps Toledo and of Detroit. From 1937 to 1967, Miss Oates traces the moral and emotional history of Loretta Wendall and of two of her children, Maureen (the former student) and Jules.

Let me say right now that I think this book is mainly a work of fiction and not of history at all; a good deal of internal evidence, which I'll get to later, suggests that Miss Oates, starting with a few factual clues, designed and constructed most of the fabric of events herself, and with considerable coherence and skill. Almost all the way, it succeeds in reproducing the psychological tenor of poverty—a series of stultifying routines interrupted irregularly and arbitrarily by radical change and blinding violence—and its stunting effect on the emotional scope of the poor. It does, though (at least for me), fail to bond the foreground characters to the background of their time and place, especially in the first half of the novel. While I sympathize with Miss Oates's desire to avoid the cluttered, too explicit stage sets of the old-time naturalistic novel and her determination to view the world through the minds and reactions of her people, I think that in discarding circumstantiality she has also discarded an essential key to their character. The city and the country slums of the thirties and forties—profusely detailed and profoundly interesting, too, like so many backgrounds to despair—cannot merely be assumed if we are to understand the people who lived in them. It is not a mass of detail but the significant detail that can illumine a character and his actions. In *Them*, backgrounds are scanted, glossed over, seen as in a dream, without weight or definition, without place names or map references. Thus, Loretta Wendall, the main figure in the first part of the book, is never in sharp relief—in her person, her actions, or her speech—as an individual. Though it is the author's intention to show the submergence of her people's personalities in the crushing numbness of poverty, it is also her intention—stated in her preface—to write a novel "which is truly about a specific 'them' and not just a literary technique of pointing to us all." For her first two hundred pages, she points mainly to us all, or, at any rate, to all the poorer ones. Miss Oates, we feel, cannot successfully isolate and identify with Loretta Wendall and her time and place.

Fortunately, the opposite is true of Loretta's daughter, Maureen. When she assumes the center of the stage—as a sixteen-year-old who seeks dignity, power, and freedom by sleeping with a picked-up married man for money—the novel springs jarringly and truthfully to life. Somewhere in Salinger, Seymour Glass criticizes the triviality of his brother Buddy's fiction by saying, "I want your *loot*." In Maureen, we get Miss Oates's loot—the whole double armload of truth of character she has swiped for her book. The whole truth of the book, in fact, resides in Maureen, and in her despairing, hopeful attempts to escape the cage of her life—and the cage of her person—as she grows older. Beaten by her stepfather for possession of her inexplicable money, she retreats into a kind of catatonia and grows grossly fat in her slatternly bedroom; after a year, she awakens and resumes her faceless losing battle of a life, this time as a night-school student. She accepts a nothing job, she goes on taking courses, she eventually sets her cap for a poor, seedy English instructor—a married man with children—choosing him as the escape mechanism to deliver her from her past and present, from herself. All this rings true.

At this point, Maureen writes two letters to Miss Oates. The first probably is a genuine letter from a troubled girl to her former teacher. The second is something else entirely: an extended emotional autobiography, written with such literary craft, sustained at such a high and skillful pitch that we cannot quite accept it as the work of a failed night-school composition student. Maureen has revealed herself so well in dialogue and action that this letter seems gratuitous; it does not, however, destroy the development of her story or deter her final flight into a life of illusory acceptability. Maureen remains the crown of this book and its reason for being; she is one of the enduring women of contemporary American fiction.

Her brother, Jules, falls short of this distinction. A fitfully realized character, he tumbles through a series of arbitrary and often unbelievable adventures. After a few years as a petty tough, he is employed by a mad financial manipulator, who is immediately murdered. Having fallen in love with Nadine, the financier's niece, Jules uses his new job of delivering flowers to track her down to her Grosse Pointe house. Leaving his truck in the driveway, he talks his way into the house and up to her bedroom, where they spend the afternoon and evening. Her mother returns; cocktail guests arrive and leave; incredibly, nobody notices the truck in the drive. Finally, at one in the morning, they slip out, steal a neighbor's car, and set off for the Southwest, where, after a nightmare tour of small-town motels, Jules, down with the flu and fever, is abandoned by Nadine. His progress through the South is traced by a series of funny and affecting letters to his mother and Maureen. When he comes home, he sees Nadine, now a suburban wife, in a restaurant. They consummate their affair in a rented apartment. The ferocious love scenes, meant, like Jules's whole odyssey, to illuminate some versions of the lower-class American dream, succeed brilliantly on their own terms, but only by distorting and betraying the character of Jules. He becomes, like Nadine, a sort of upper-middle-class demon lover; his talk is not that of a recent dropout, a former slum kid, but of the other man in a worldly triangle. Nadine asks, "Don't you want to know about me?" He answers, "As conversation, yes. For the next thirty years. But it isn't essential. I can't concentrate on it. I can't even ask you whether you've had any lovers since your marriage, or before, because that isn't any of my business." The affair ends when Nadine, who can neither accept him nor reject him, shoots and nearly kills him. Eventually, he drifts, aimlessly, into a circle of student militants in Detroit. He takes part, aimlessly, in the 1967 Detroit riots; aimlessly, he murders a policeman. Without motive, he escapes. In the household she has set up with her captured English instructor, he visits Maureen, but they part without comprehension of what they have become, and Jules goes to California, in his new air-conditioned car, for his new job with a fraudulent anti-poverty program.

In the end, we can just manage to accept Jules as a protean mirror that reflects a dozen states of modern American consciousness; we cannot accept him at all as a character who ever was. As I've suggested, it's difficult, too, to regard *Them* as a genuine history—difficult because the characters vary so radically in their definition and intensity; difficult because so many incidents, especially Jules's love affair and the climactic race riots, seem introduced to round out a picture or make a point without having an organic part in the story; difficult because, on legal grounds alone, it is hard to believe that any writer would write or any publisher publish an account of a presumably unsolved 1967 murder committed by a real, only thinly disguised person. All that aside, Miss Oates is a writer of daring, discipline, and talent. Her taste is almost unerring; few writers have her gift for handling sexual scenes with masterly tact and suggestion, avoiding the wrenchingly explicit and the bathetically lyrical. Her skill in realizing character is rare and growing. *Them* is a novel to be read for its virtues.

PART EIGHT
POETRY

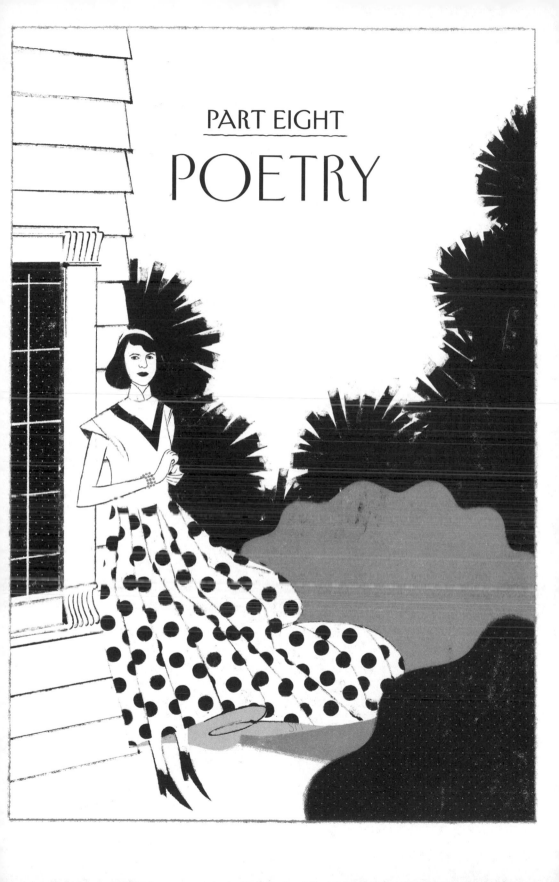

A NOTE BY DANA GOODYEAR

Poetry's subversions are subtle, deep, and methodical, and can catch you unawares, as when the bough breaks in the nursery rhyme and you are left to wonder what befell the sleeping babe. In the 1960s, while the known shapes of the world were exploding at time-lapse speed, many of the poets published in *The New Yorker* clung to form, building scaffolds around the shocking, unruly, difficult narratives they felt emboldened to design. Their poems are more disturbing for these soothing surfaces, and full of exquisite, excruciating tensions and turns.

James Merrill, in the seven dazzling sonnets of "The Broken Home," conjures his childhood as in a séance, examining its myths to see if, at thirty-six, his only offspring avocado seeds grown in a jar, he is as "real" as the large-looming, gold-lit figures of his memory. His parents—one a warrior of boardroom and bedroom, the many-times-married founder of Merrill Lynch; the other named only "whom we sought," iconic and doomed—he wittily casts as "Father Time and Mother Earth, / A marriage on the rocks." The ornate patterning suggests a dutiful working over of the problem, and the poet's resurgent hope that some new form will resolve the played-on-repeat drama of his past.

Some of these writers, because they revealed themselves unsparingly and allowed the details of the poems to track to their biographies, were referred to as "confessional poets." But these are not so much poems of revelation as poems of inquiry. What place should the self occupy in a world where the bonds of family and society are coming unglued? Sylvia Plath's "Tulips," published in the year before her suicide, chronicles a patient convalescing in a hospital. She has given up her history to the anesthetist and her body to the surgeons, and wishes to rid herself of her remaining "baggage," including her husband and her child. The white room represents radical detachment—stillness, peace, effacement, death—but for the dozen red tulips someone has delivered, which, in their insistent, troubling vitality, call her to attend, to think, to write, and, for the time being, to stay alive.

Plath is considered a feminist because she was a woman who wrote brilliantly about her cultivation of and rebellion against domestic life; Merrill was openly gay at a time when being out in public represented considerable social and legal risk. Yet neither poet was remotely political: in "The Broken Home," Merrill admits that he barely reads the newspaper or votes. As the decade progressed and the Vietnam War intensified, subversion surfaced from the underground and went pop. Poetry in the magazine became a site of protest. Writing in 1966, under the pointed title "The Asians Dying," W. S. Merwin assailed American nihilism, racism, and environmental carelessness: "The dead go away like bruises / The blood vanishes into the poisoned farmlands / Pain the horizon / Remains." The poem is unpunctuated—it describes all-encompassing, open-ended devastation, history obliterated, tomorrow in flames. The following year, Muriel Rukeyser's "Endless" mournfully addressed a victim of the war, whose body is turned to dirt. "I look down at the one earth under me, / through to you and all the fallen / the broken and their children born and unborn / of the endless war."

Mid-century poetry was a clubby affair: Sylvia Plath and Ted Hughes were married; W. S. Merwin knew them well; Anne Sexton and Plath studied with Robert Lowell (not represented here), who was friends with Randall Jarrell, who is. James Merrill and May Swenson were both close to Elizabeth Bishop, who published in the magazine for decades. Howard Nemerov and Muriel Rukeyser, New Yorkers like Merrill, both went to Ethical Culture; James Dickey and Jarrell were rivals. But the poets did not form a school. What they had in common was that they spoke in a voice that was personal rather than rhetorical; idiomatic, not ideological. The poems were rigorous, carefully crafted, and risky; they had one foot in a past of commonly held values and one foot in an unknowable future.

THE HEAVEN OF ANIMALS

Here they are. The soft eyes open.
If they have lived in a wood
It is a wood.
If they have lived on plains
It is grass rolling
Under their feet forever.

Having no souls, they have come
Anyway, beyond their knowing.
Their instincts wholly bloom,
And they rise.
The soft eyes open.

To match them, the landscape flowers,
Outdoing, desperately
Outdoing what is required:
The richest wood,
The deepest field.

For some of these,
It could not be the place
It is, without blood.
These hunt, as they have done,
But with teeth and claws grown perfect,

More deadly than they can believe.
They stalk more silently,
And crouch on the limbs of trees,
And their descent
Upon the bright backs of their prey

May take years
In a sovereign floating of joy.
And those that are hunted
Know this as their life,
Their reward: to walk

Under such trees in full knowledge
Of what is in glory above them,
And to feel no fear,
But acceptance, compliance.
Fulfilling themselves without pain

At the cycle's center,
They tremble, they walk
Under the tree,
They fall, they are torn,
They rise, they walk again.

—James Dickey
November 18, 1961

TULIPS

The tulips are too excitable; it is winter here.
Look how white everything is, how quiet, how snowed-in!
I am learning peacefulness, lying by myself quietly
As the light lies on these white walls, this bed, these hands.
I am nobody; I have nothing to do with explosions.
I have given my name and my day-clothes up to the nurses
And my history to the anesthetist and my body to surgeons.

They have propped my head between the pillow and the
    sheet-cuff
Like an eye between two white lids that will not shut.
Stupid pupil, it has to take everything in.
The nurses pass and pass; they are no trouble;
They pass the way gulls pass inland in their white caps,
Doing things with their hands, one just the same as another,
So it is impossible to tell how many there are.

My body is a pebble to them; they tend it as water
Tends to the pebbles it must run over, smoothing them gently.
They bring me numbness in their bright needles, they bring me
    sleep.

Now I have lost myself, I am sick of baggage—
My patent-leather overnight case like a black pillbox,
My husband and child smiling out of the family photo.
Their smiles catch onto my skin, little smiling hooks.

I have let things slip, a thirty-year-old cargo boat
Stubbornly hanging onto my name and address.
They have swabbed me clear of my loving associations.
Scared and bare on the green plastic-pillowed trolley,
I watched my tea set, my bureaus of linen, my books
Sink out of sight, and the water went over my head.
I am a nun now; I have never been so pure.

I didn't want any flowers, I only wanted
To lie with my hands turned up and be utterly empty.
How free it is, you have no idea how free!
The peacefulness is so big it dazes you,
And it asks nothing—a name tag, a few trinkets.
It is what the dead close on, finally; I imagine them
Shutting their mouths on it, like a Communion tablet.

The tulips are too red in the first place; they hurt me.
Even through the gift paper I could hear them breathe
Lightly, through their white swaddlings, like an awful baby.
Their redness talks to my wound, it corresponds.
They are subtle: they seem to float, though they weigh me
     down,
Upsetting me with their sudden tongues and their color,
A dozen red lead sinkers round my neck.

Nobody watched me before; now I am watched.
The tulips turn to me and the window behind me,
Where, once a day, the light slowly widens and slowly thins,
And I see myself, flat, ridiculous, a cut-paper shadow
Between the eye of the sun and the eyes of the tulips,
And I have no face. I have wanted to efface myself.
The vivid tulips eat my oxygen.

Before they came, the air was calm enough,
Coming and going, breath by breath, without any fuss.
Then the tulips filled it up like a loud noise.
Now the air snags and eddies round them the way a river
Snags and eddies round a sunken rust-red engine.
They concentrate my attention that was happy
Playing and resting without committing itself.

The walls, also, seem to be warming themselves.
The tulips should be behind bars, like dangerous animals;
They are opening like the mouth of some great African cat,
And I am aware of my heart: it opens and closes
Its bowl of red blooms out of sheer love of me.
The water I taste is warm and salt, like the sea,
And comes from a country far away as health.

—*Sylvia Plath*
April 7, 1962

NEXT DAY

Moving from Cheer to Joy, from Joy to All,
I take a box
And add it to my wild rice, my Cornish game hens.
The slacked or shorted, basketed, identical
Food-gathering flocks
Are selves I overlook. Wisdom, said William James,

Is learning what to overlook. And I am wise
If that is wisdom.
Yet somehow, as I buy All from these shelves
And the boy takes it to my station wagon,
What I've become
Troubles me even if I shut my eyes.

When I was young and miserable and pretty
And poor, I'd wish
What all girls wish: to have a husband,

A house and children. Now that I'm old, my wish
Is womanish:
That the boy putting groceries in my car

See me. It bewilders me he doesn't see me.
For so many years
I was good enough to eat: the world looked at me
And its mouth watered. How often they have undressed me,
The eyes of strangers!
And, holding their flesh within my flesh, their vile

Imaginings within my imagining,
I too have taken
The chance of life. Now the boy pats my dog
And we start home. Now I am good.
The last mistaken,
Ecstatic, accidental bliss, the blind

Happiness that, bursting, leaves upon the palm
Some soap and water—
It was so long ago, back in some Gay
Twenties, Nineties, I don't know. . . . Today I miss
My lovely daughter
Away at school, my sons away at school,

My husband away at work—I wish for them.
The dog, the maid,
And I go through the sure unvarying days
At home in them. As I look at my life,
I am afraid
Only that it will change, as I am changing:

I am afraid, this morning, of my face.
It looks at me
From the rearview mirror with the eyes I hate,
The smile I hate. Its plain, lined look
Of gray discovery
Repeats to me, "You're old." That's all, I'm old.

And yet I'm afraid, as I was at the funeral
I went to yesterday.
My friend's cold made-up face, granite among its flowers,
Her undressed, operated-on, dressed body
Were my face and body.
As I think of her I hear her telling me

How young I seem; I *am* exceptional;
I think of all I have.
But really no one is exceptional,
No one has anything, I'm anybody,
I stand beside my grave
Confused with my life, that is commonplace and solitary.

—Randall Jarrell
December 14, 1963

THE BROKEN HOME

Crossing the street,
I saw the parents and the child
At their window, gleaming like fruit
With evening's mild gold leaf.

In a room on the floor below,
Sunless, cooler—a brimming
Saucer of wax, marbly and dim—
I have lit what's left of my life.

I have thrown out yesterday's milk
And opened a book of maxims.
The flame quickens. The word stirs.

Tell me, tongue of fire,
That you and I are as real
At least as the people upstairs.

My father, who had flown in World War I,
Might have continued to invest his life
In cloud banks well above Wall Street and wife.
But the race was run below, and the point was to win.

Too late now, I make out in his blue gaze
(Through the smoked glass of being thirty-six)
The soul eclipsed by twin black pupils, sex
And business; time was money in those days.

Each thirteenth year he married. When he died
There were already several chilled wives
In sable orbit—rings, cars, permanent waves.
We'd felt him warming up for a green bride.

He could afford it. He was "in his prime"
At three score ten. But money was not time.

When my parents were younger this was a popular act:
A veiled woman would leap from an electric, wine-dark car
To the steps of no matter what—the Senate or the Ritz Bar—
And bodily, at newsreel speed, attack

No matter whom—Al Smith or José Maria Sert
Or Clemenceau—veins standing out on her throat
As she yelled *War mongerer! Pig! Give us the vote!*,
And would have to be hauled away in her hobble skirt.

What had the man done? Oh, made history.
Her business (he had implied) was giving birth,
Tending the house, mending the socks.

Always that same old story—
Father Time and Mother Earth,
A marriage on the rocks.

One afternoon, red, satyr-thighed
Michael, the Irish setter, head

Passionately lowered, led
The child I was to a shut door. Inside,

Blinds beat sun from the bed.
The green-gold room throbbed like a bruise.
Under a sheet, clad in taboos,
Lay whom we sought, her hair undone, outspread,

And of a blackness found, if ever now, in old
Engravings where the acid bit.
I must have needed to touch it
Or the whiteness—was she dead?
Her eyes flew open, startled strange and cold.
The dog slumped to the floor. She reached for me. I fled.

Tonight they have stepped out onto the gravel.
The party is over. It's the fall
Of 1931. They love each other still.

SHE: Charlie, I can't stand the pace.
HE: Come on, honey—why, you'll bury us all!

A lead soldier guards my windowsill:
Khaki rifle, uniform, and face.
Something in me grows heavy, silvery, pliable.

How intensely people used to feel!
Like metal poured at the close of a proletarian novel,
Refined and glowing from the crucible,
I see those two hearts, I'm afraid,
Still. Cool here in the graveyard of good and evil,
They are even so to be honored and obeyed.

. . . Obeyed, at least, inversely. Thus
I rarely buy a newspaper, or vote.
To do so, I have learned, is to invite
The tread of a stone guest within my house.

Shooting this rusted bolt, though, against him,
I trust I am no less time's child than some
Who on the heath impersonate Poor Tom
Or on the barricades risk life and limb.

Nor do I try to keep a garden, only
An avocado in a glass of water—
Roots pallid, gemmed with air. And later,

When the small gilt leaves have grown
Fleshy and green, I let them die, yes, yes,
And start another. I am earth's no less.

A child, a red dog roam the corridors,
Still, of the broken home. No sound. The brilliant
Rag runners halt before wide-open doors.
My old room! Its wallpaper—cream, medallioned
With pink and brown—brings back the first nightmares,
Long summer colds, and Emma, sepia-faced,
Perspiring over broth carried upstairs
Aswim with golden fats I could not taste.

The real house became a boarding school.
Under the ballroom ceiling's allegory,
Someone at last may actually be allowed
To learn something; or, from my window, cool
With the unstiflement of the entire story,
Watch a red setter stretch and sink in cloud.

—James Merrill
October 30, 1965

THE ASIANS DYING

When the forests have been destroyed their darkness remains
The ash the great walker follows the possessors
Forever
Nothing they will come to is real

Nor for long
Over the watercourses
Like ducks in the time of the ducks
The ghosts of the villages trail in the sky
Making a new twilight

Rain falls into the open eyes of the dead
Again again with its pointless sounds
When the moon finds them they are the color of everything

The nights disappear like bruises but nothing is healed
The dead go away like bruises
The blood vanishes into the poisoned farmlands
Pain the horizon
Remains
Overhead the seasons rock
They are paper bells
Calling to nothing living

The possessors move everywhere under Death their star
Like columns of smoke they advance into the shadows
Like thin flames with no light
They with no past
And fire their only future

—W. S. Merwin
August 13, 1966

AT THE AIRPORT

Through the gate, where nowhere and night begin,
A hundred suddenly appear and lose
Themselves in the hot and crowded waiting room.
A hundred others herd up toward the gate,
Patiently waiting that the way be opened
To nowhere and night, while a voice recites
The intermittent litany of numbers
And the holy names of distant destinations.

None going out can be certain of getting there.
None getting there can be certain of being loved
Enough. But they are sealed in the silver tube
And lifted up to be fed and cosseted,
While their upholstered cell of warmth and light
Shatters the darkness, neither here nor there.

—*Howard Nemerov*
November 12, 1966

SECOND GLANCE AT A JAGUAR

Skinful of bowls, he bowls them,
The hip going in and out of joint, dropping the spine
With the urgency of his hurry
Like a cat going along under thrown stones, under cover,
Glancing sideways, running
Under his spine. A terrible, stump-legged waddle,
Like a thick Aztec disemboweller
Club-swinging, trying to grind some square
Socket between his hind legs round,
Carrying his head like a brazier of spilling embers,
And the black bit of his teeth   he takes it
Between his back teeth, he has to wear his skin out,
He swipes a lap at the water trough as he turns,
Swivelling the ball of his heel on the polished spot,
Showing his belly like a butterfly,
At every stride he has to turn a corner
In himself and correct it. His head
Is like the worn-down stump of another whole jaguar,
His body is just the engine shoving it forward,
Lifting the air up and shoving on under,
The weight of the fangs hanging the mouth open,
Bottom jaw combing the ground. A gorged look,
Gangster, club tail lumped along behind gracelessly,
He's wearing himself to heavy ovals,
Muttering some mantra, some drum song of murder
To keep his rage brightening, making his skin

Intolerable, spurred by the rosettes, the Cain brands,
Wearing the spots off from the inside,
Rounding some revenge. Going like a prayer wheel,
The head dragging forward, the body keeping up,
The hind legs lagging. He coils, he flourishes
The blackjack tail as if looking for a target,
Hurrying through the underworld, soundless.

—Ted Hughes
March 25, 1967

ENDLESS

Under the tall black sky you look out of your body
lit by a white flare of the time between us
your body with its touch its weight smelling of new wood
as on the day the news of battle reached us
falls beside the endless river
flowing to the endless sea
whose waves come to this shore a world away.

Your body of new wood your eyes alive barkbrown of
    treetrunks
the leaves and flowers of trees stars all caught in crowns of trees
your life gone down, broken into endless earth
no longer a world away but under my feet and everywhere
I look down at the one earth under me,
through to you and all the fallen
the broken and their children born and unborn
of the endless war.

—Muriel Rukeyser
October 7, 1967

MOON SONG

I am alive at night.
I am dead in the morning—
an old vessel who used up her oil,
bleak and pale-boned.
No miracle. No dazzle.
I'm out of repair,
but you are tall in your battle dress
and I must arrange for your journey.
I was always a virgin,
old and pitted.
Before the world was, I was.

I have been oranging and fat,
carrot-colored, gaped at,
allowing my cracked O's to drop on the sea
near Venice and Mombasa.
Over Maine I have rested.
I have fallen like a jet into the Pacific.
I have committed perjury over Japan.
I have dangled my pendulum,
my fat bag, my gold, gold,
blinkedy light
over you all.

So if you must inquire, do so.
After all, I am not artificial.
I looked long upon you,
love-bellied and empty,
flipping my endless display
for you, my cold, cold
coverall man.
You need only request
and I will grant it.
It is virtually guaranteed
that you will walk into me like a barracks.
So come cruising, come cruising,
you of the blastoff,

you of the bastion,
you of the scheme.
I will shut my fat eye down,
headquarters of an area,
house of a dream.

—*Anne Sexton*
September 7, 1968

FEEL ME

"Feel me to do right," our father said
on his death bed. We did not quite
know—in fact, not at all—what he meant.
His last whisper was spent as through a slot in a wall.
He left us a key, but how did it
fit? "Feel me
to do right." Did it mean

that, though he died, he would be felt
through some aperture, or by some unseen instrument
our dad just then had come
to know? So, to do right always, we need but feel his
spirit? Or was it merely
his apology for dying? "Feel that I
do right in not trying, as you insist, to stay

on your side. There is the wide
gateway and the splendid tower,
and you implore me to wait here, with the worms!"
Had he defined his terms, and could we discriminate
among his motives, we might
have found out how to "do right" before *we* died—supposing
he felt he suddenly knew

what dying was.
"You do wrong because you do not feel
as I do now" was maybe the sense. "Feel me, and emulate

my state, for I am becoming less dense—
I am feeling right, for the first
time." And then the vessel burst, and we were kneeling
around an emptiness.

We cannot feel our
father now. His power courses through us, yes, but *he*—
the chest and cheek, the foot and palm,
the mouth of oracle—is calm. And we still seek
his meaning. "*Feel* me," he said,
and emphasized that word.
Should we have heard it as a plea

for a caress—A constant caress,
since flesh to flesh was all that we could do right
if we would bless him? The dying must feel
the pressure of that
question—lying flat, turning cold
from brow to heel—the hot
cowards there above

protesting their love, and saying,
"What can we do? Are you all
right?"—While the wall opens
and the blue night pours through. "What
can we do? We want to do what's right."
"Lie down with me, and hold me, tight. Touch me. Be
with me. Feel with me. *Feel* me, to do right."

—*May Swenson*
October 12, 1968

PART NINE

FICTION

A NOTE BY JENNIFER EGAN

I N THE SIXTIES we discovered, as a culture, the thrill of watching ourselves. It was love at first sight. The televising of the Vietnam War in
1965 marked the birth of mass media as we know it: a ubiquitous,
image-generating machine that purports to display raw human experience. Media coverage played a pivotal role in the student antiwar protests, as Todd Gitlin, president of Students for a Democratic Society in
the early sixties, now a cultural critic, has argued persuasively. According
to Gitlin, media coverage of S.D.S. protests altered the perceptions of
the protesters themselves, creating tensions and distortions within the
movement that ultimately undermined it. In a decade that was, for many
young people, about altering consciousness, the most mind-bending new
drug in town had nothing to do with hallucinogens. We've yet to begin
our return from the trip it launched

We're savvier now, of course. Today, students forming a national
movement would anticipate the need for a P.R. strategy—might well
have taken classes on it in college. Everyone knows that media imagery
obscures as much as it reveals, that reality TV is no less engineered than
situation comedy. Yet the great irony of our technological age is that the
phoniness of mediated experience leaves us craving authenticity that
only more media can seem to satisfy. The historian Daniel Boorstin
identified this paradox in his 1962 manifesto, *The Image: A Guide to
Pseudo-Events in America:* "The pseudo-events which flood our consciousness are neither true nor false in the old familiar senses. The very
same advances which have made them possible have also made the
images—however planned, contrived, or distorted—more vivid, more
attractive, more impressive, and more persuasive than reality itself. . . .
Our progress poisons the sources of our experience. And the poison
tastes so sweet that it spoils our appetite for plain fact."

It can also spoil our appetite for serious fiction. More mediation leads naturally to fetishization of the "real" as we sense that we're getting less of it. And entertainment-oriented reportage—celebrity gossip, for example—can satisfy a desire for human drama while masquerading as news. The role of fiction as a source of cultural self-knowledge has been squeezed from both sides for decades. Some of the most celebrated novels of the sixties, like Claude Brown's *Manchild in the Promised Land* and Truman Capote's *In Cold Blood*, were exciting, in part, precisely because they were *true*. New Journalists made a canny bid for relevance by applying novelistic techniques (many of them were fiction writers) to national and world events that seemed more urgent and extreme for having been thrust into millions of American living rooms.

We read nonfiction to find answers, fiction to find questions. Judging by the short stories gathered in this volume, the questions an era produces do very well at laying bare its preoccupations. Period anthologies are biased, of course, toward work that seems to tell the story we've settled on. Muriel Spark's 1960 "The Ormolu Clock," set in postwar Austria, dramatizes the tension between a fading aristocracy and industrial capitalism. John Updike's 1961 "A & P" reads like an anthem of a generation moved to flout its parents' expectations. The generational chasm makes an appearance in Mavis Gallant's 1962 "The Hunter's Waking Thoughts," in which a woman remarks to her extramarital lover, nine years her junior, "You're too young to remember the war." That simple fact divides them.

Common to all of the stories is the tingling prospect of upheaval. In "The Indian Uprising" (1965), by Donald Barthelme, whose experimental works *The New Yorker* championed from early in his career, narrative unruliness storms the story's surface, refusing to let it resolve into any one plot or set of characters. In John Cheever's "The Swimmer," a man's affluent suburban life appears, at first, as serenely untouchable as his self-confidence. In the course of an afternoon's caprice, that life collapses into figments of a delusion. "At what point had this prank, this joke, this piece of horseplay become serious?" he wonders, a question that might caption any number of hopes that soured toward the end of the sixties. And equally, "He had covered a distance that made his return impossible."

Cheever's story, published in 1964, seems to expose the dread and unease percolating under the surface of nineteen-fifties suburban complacency. It might also manifest the anxieties of one suburban family man—John Cheever—whose bisexuality was a source of personal anguish. Both readings are plausible, even compatible, along with any number of others we (an evolving entity, of course) are compelled by. Readings change over time; the casual misogyny of Sammy, the nineteen-year-old narrator of "A & P," was probably funnier in 1961 than it is today. Muriel Spark's story, which includes voyeurism with binoculars and communication via the placement of a Baroque clock, reads to me now as a meditation on privacy and telecommunications. I'm tempted to lay out that argument right here, right now, but I'll spare you.

Like artifacts of a collective dream life, the best fiction diverts every-day trappings into the service of a mystery. The stronger the work, the more inexhaustible—and receptive to readers' own preoccupations (all right, *I'm* obsessed with voyeurism and telecommunications). Isaac Bashevis Singer's 1969 "The Key" is set in New York City—which, in the view of the story's irascible widowed protagonist, has been reduced to rubble and flames by a predatory, anarchic, and racially mixed populace. Hers is the lament of a generation overthrown, consigned to urban solitude: "God in Heaven, since Sam died, New York, America—perhaps the whole world—was falling apart."

Yet the source of her misery turns out to be largely her own paranoia; awakened by a spiritual epiphany, she finds the world renewed. The story is both a portrait of a certain kind of New York life at a particular moment, and a timeless parable of redemption. Doubtless there are other readings, too. That richness is what makes fiction unique among cultural documents, able both to embody the time in which it was made and to long outlast it.

THE ORMOLU CLOCK

Muriel Spark

SEPTEMBER 17, 1960

THE HOTEL STROH stood side by side with the Guesthouse Lublonitsch, separated by a narrow path that led up the mountain, on the Austrian side, to the Yugoslavian border. Perhaps the old place had once been a great hunting tavern. These days, though, the Hotel Stroh was plainly a disappointment to its few drooping tenants. They huddled together like birds in a storm; their flesh sagged over the unscrubbed tables on the dark back veranda, which looked over Herr Stroh's untended fields. Usually, Herr Stroh sat somewhat apart, in a mist of cognac, his lower chin resting on his red neck, and his shirt open for air. Those visitors who had come not for the climbing but simply for the view sat and admired the mountain and were sloppily waited upon until the weekly bus should come and carry them away. If they had cars, they rarely stayed long—they departed, as a rule, within two hours of arrival, like a comic act. This much was entertainingly visible from the other side of the path, at the Guesthouse Lublonitsch.

I had come to this little town because it was cheap; I was waiting for friends to come and pick me up on their way to Venice. Frau Lublonitsch welcomed all her guests in person. When I arrived I was hardly aware of the honor, she seemed so merely a local woman—undefined and dumpy as she emerged from the kitchen wiping her hands on her brown apron, with her gray hair drawn back tight, her sleeves rolled up, her dingy dress, black stockings, and boots. It was only gradually that her importance was permitted to dawn upon strangers.

I climbed the lower slopes of the mountains while the experts in their boots did the thing earnestly up on the sheer crags above the clouds. When it rained, they came back and reported, "Tito is sending the bad weather." The maids were bored with the joke, but they obliged with smiles every time, and served them up along with the interminable veal.

The higher mountain reaches were beyond me except by bus. I was anxious, however, to scale the peaks of Frau Lublonitsch's nature.

. . .

One morning, when everything was glittering madly after a nervous stormy night, I came down early to look for coffee. I had heard voices in the yard some moments before, but by the time I appeared they had gone indoors. I followed the voices into the dark stone kitchen and peered in the doorway. Beyond the chattering girls, I caught sight of a further doorway, which usually remained closed. Now it was open.

Within it was a bedroom reaching far back into the house. It was imperially magnificent. It was done in red and gold. I saw a canopied bed, built high, splendidly covered with a scarlet quilt. The pillows were piled up at the head—about four of them, very white. The bed head was deep dark wood, touched with gilt. A golden fringe hung from the canopy. In some ways this bed reminded me of the glowing bed by which van Eyck ennobled the portrait of Jan Arnolfini and his wife. All the rest of the Lublonitsch establishment was scrubbed and polished local wood, but this was a very poetic bed.

The floor of the bedroom was covered with a carpet of red that was probably crimson but that, against the scarlet of the bed, looked purple. On the walls on either side of the bed hung Turkish carpets whose background was an opulently dull, more ancient red—almost black where the canopy cast its shade.

I was moved by the sight.

The girl called Mitzi was observing me as I stood in the kitchen doorway. "Coffee?" she said.

"Whose room is that?"

"It's Frau Chef's room. She sleeps there."

Now another girl, tall, lanky Gertha, with her humorous face and slightly comic answer to everything, skipped over to the bedroom door and said, "We are instructed to keep the door closed," and for a moment before closing it she drew open the door quite wide for me to see some more of the room. I caught sight of a tiled stove constructed of mosaic tiles that were not a local type; they were lustrous—ochre and green—resembling the tiles on the floors of Byzantine ruins. The stove looked like a temple. I saw a black lacquered cabinet inlaid with mother-of-pearl, and just before Gertha closed the door, I noticed, standing upon the cabinet, a large ornamental clock, its case enamelled rosily with miniature inset pastel paintings; each curve and twirl in the case of this clock was overlaid with the gilded-bronze alloy that is known as ormolu. The clock twinkled in the early sunlight, which slanted between the window hangings.

I went into the polished dining room, and Mitzi brought my coffee there. From the window I could see Frau Lublonitsch in her dark dress, her black boots, and wool stockings. She was plucking a chicken over a bucketful of feathers. Beyond her I could see the sulky figure of Herr Stroh standing collarless, fat and unshaven, in the open door of his hotel across the path. He seemed to be meditating upon Frau Lublonitsch.

. . .

It was that very day that the nuisance occurred. The double windows of my bedroom were directly opposite the bedroom windows of the Hotel Stroh, with no more than twenty feet between—the width of the narrow path that led up to the frontier.

It was a cool but sunny day. I sat in my room writing letters. I glanced out of the window. In the window directly opposite me stood Herr Stroh, gazing blatantly upon me. I was annoyed at his interest. I pulled down the blind and switched on the light to continue my writing. I wondered if Herr Stroh had seen me doing anything peculiar before I had noticed him, such as tapping my head with the end of my pen or scratching my nose or pulling faces—any of the things one might do while writing a letter. The drawn blind and the artificial light irritated me, and suddenly I didn't see why I shouldn't write my letters by daylight without being stared at. I switched off the light and released the blind. Herr Stroh had gone. I concluded that he had taken my action as a signal of disapproval, and I settled back to write.

I looked up a few moments later, and this time Herr Stroh was seated on a chair a little way back from the window. He was facing me squarely and holding to his eyes a pair of field glasses.

I left my room and went down to complain to Frau Lublonitsch.

"She's gone to the market," Gertha said. "She'll be back in half an hour."

So I lodged my complaint with Gertha.

"I shall tell Frau Chef," she said.

Something in her manner made me ask, "Has this ever happened before?"

"Once or twice this year," she said. "I'll speak to Frau Chef." And she added, with her music-hall grimace, "He was probably counting your eyelashes."

I returned to my room. Herr Stroh still sat in position, the field glasses in his hands resting on his knees. As soon as I came within view, he raised the glasses to his eyes. I decided to stare him out until such time as Frau Lublonitsch should return and take the matter in hand.

For nearly an hour, I sat patiently at the window. Herr Stroh rested his arms now and again, but he did not leave his seat. I could see him clearly, although I think I imagined the grin on his face as, from time to time, he raised the glasses to his eyes. There was no doubt that he could see, as if it were within an inch of his face, the fury on mine. It was too late now for one of us to give in, and I kept glancing down at the entrances to the Hotel Stroh, expecting to see Frau Lublonitsch or perhaps one of her sons or the yard hands going across to deliver a protest. But no one from our side approached the Stroh premises, from either the front or the back of the house. I continued to stare, and Herr Stroh continued to goggle through his glasses.

Then he dropped them. It was as if they had been jerked out of his hand by an invisible nudge. He approached close to the window and gazed, but now he was gazing at a point above and slightly to the left of my room. After about two minutes, he turned and disappeared.

Just then Gertha knocked at my door. "Frau Chef has protested, and you won't have any more trouble," she said.

"Did she telephone to him?"

"No, Frau Chef doesn't use the phone; it mixes her up."

"Who protested, then?"

"Frau Chef."

"But she hasn't been across to see him. I've been watching the house."

"No, Frau Chef doesn't visit with him. But don't worry, he knows all right that he mustn't annoy our guests."

When I looked out of the window again, I saw that the blind of Herr Stroh's room had been pulled down, and so it remained for the rest of my stay.

Meantime, I went out to post my letters in the box opposite our hotel, across the path. The sun had come out more strongly, and Herr Stroh stood in his doorway blinking up at the roof of the Guesthouse Lublonitsch. He was engrossed; he did not notice me at all.

I didn't want to draw his attention by following the line of his gaze, but I was curious as to what held him staring so trancelike up at our roof. On my way back from the postbox, I saw what it was.

Like most of the roofs in that province, the Lublonitsch roof had a railed ledge running several inches above the eaves, for the purpose of preventing the snow from falling in heavy thumps during the winter. On this ledge, just below an attic window, stood the gold-and-rose ormolu clock that I had seen in Frau Lublonitsch's splendid bedroom.

I turned the corner just as Herr Stroh gave up his gazing; he went indoors, sullen and bent. Two carloads of people who had moved into the hotel that morning were now moving out, shifting their baggage with speed and the signs of a glad departure. I knew that his house was nearly empty.

Before supper, I walked past the Hotel Stroh and down across the bridge to the café. There were no other customers in the place. The proprietor brought the harsh gin that was the local specialty over to my usual table and I sipped it while I waited for someone to come. I did not have to wait long, for two local women came in and ordered ices, as many of them did on their way home from work in the village. Mostly, they were shop assistants. They held the long spoons in their rough, knobbly hands and talked, while the owner of the café came and sat with them to exchange the news of the day.

"Herr Stroh has been defying Frau Lublonitsch," one of the women said.

"Not again?"

"He's been offending her tourists."

"Dirty old Peeping Tom."

"He only does it to annoy Frau Lublonitsch."

"I saw the clock on the roof. I saw—"

"Stroh is finished, he—"

"Which clock?"

"What she bought from him last winter when he was hard up. All red and gold, like an altarpiece. A beautiful clock—it was his grandfather's when things were different."

"Stroh is finished. She'll have his hotel. She'll have—"

"She'll have the pants off him."

"He'll have to go. She'll get the place at her price. Then she'll build down to the bridge. I've always said so, just wait and see. Next winter, she'll have the Hotel Stroh. Last winter, she had the clock. It's two years ago since she gave him the mortgage."

"It's only Stroh's old place that's standing in her way. She'll pull it down."

The faces of the two women and the man nearly met across the café table, self-hypnotized by the central idea of their talk. The women's spoons rose to their mouths and returned to their ices while the man clasped his hands on the table in front of him. Their voices went on like a litany.

"She'll expand down to the bridge."

"Perhaps beyond the bridge."

"No, no, the bridge will be enough. She's not so young."

"Poor old Stroh!"

"Why doesn't she expand in the other direction?"

"Because there isn't so much trade in the other direction."

"The business is down here, this side of the river."

"Old Stroh is upset."

"She'll build down to the bridge. She'll pull down his place and build."

"Beyond the bridge."

"Old Stroh. His clock stuck up there for everyone to see."

"What does he expect, the lazy old pig?"

"What does he expect to see with his field glasses?"

"The tourists."

"I wish him joy of the tourists."

They giggled, then noticed me sitting within earshot, and came out of their trance.

How delicately Frau Lublonitsch had sent her deadly message! The ormolu clock was still there on the roof ledge when I returned. It was thus she had told him that time was passing and the end of summer was near, and that his hotel, like his clock, would soon be hers. As I passed, Herr Stroh shuffled out to his front door, rather drunk. He did not see me. He was looking at the clock, where it hung in the sunset; he looked up at it as the quaking enemies of the Lord must have looked upon the head of Holofernes. I wondered if the poor man would even live another winter; certainly he had taken his last feeble stand against Frau Lublonitsch.

As for her, she would probably live till she was ninety—perhaps more.

The general estimate of her age was fifty-three, fifty-four, five, six: a healthy woman.

. . .

Next day, the clock was gone. Enough was enough. It had gone back to that glamorous room behind the kitchen, to which Frau Lublonitsch retired in the early hours of the morning to think up her high conceptions, not lying supine like a defeated creature but propped up on the white pillows, surrounded by her crimson, her scarlet, her gold-and-rosy tints, which, like a religious discipline, disturbed her spirit out of its sloth. It was here she must have got the inspiration to plant the palm tree and build the shops.

When, next morning, I saw her scouring the pots in the yard and plodding about in her boots among the vegetables, I was somewhat terrified. She could have adorned her own person in scarlet and gold; she could have lived in a turreted mansion rivalling that of the apothecary in the village. But like one averting the evil eye, or like one practicing a pure, disinterested art, she had stuck to her brown apron and her boots. And she would, without a doubt, have her reward. She would take the Hotel Stroh. She would march on the bridge, and beyond it. The café would be hers, the swimming pool, the cinema—all the market place would be hers before she died in the scarlet bed under the gold-fringed canopy, facing her ormolu clock, her deed boxes, and her ineffectual bottle of medicine.

Almost as if they knew it, the three tourists remaining in the Hotel Stroh came over that very afternoon to inquire of Frau Lublonitsch if there were any rooms available and what her terms were. Her terms were modest, and she found room for two of them. The third left on his motorcycle that night.

Everyone likes to be on the winning side. I saw the two new arrivals from the Hotel Stroh sitting secure under the Lublonitsch chestnut trees, taking breakfast, next morning. Herr Stroh, more sober than before, stood watching the scene from his doorway. I thought, Why doesn't he spit on us—he's got nothing to lose. I saw again, in my mind's eye, the ormolu clock set high in the sunset. But I had not yet got over my fury with him for spying into my room, and was moved, all in one stroke, with high contempt and deep pity, feverish triumph and chilly fear.

A & P

John Updike

JULY 22, 1961

I N WALKS THESE three girls in nothing but bathing suits. I'm in the third checkout slot, with my back to the door, so I don't see them until they're over by the bread. The one that caught my eye first was the one in the plaid green two-piece. She was a chunky kid, with a good tan and a sweet broad backside with those two crescents of white just under it, where the sun never seems to hit, at the top of the backs of her legs. I stood there with my hand on a box of HiHo crackers trying to remember if I rang it up or not. I ring it up again and the customer starts giving me hell. She's one of these cash-register-watchers, a witch about fifty with rouge on her cheekbones and no eyebrows, and I know it made her day to trip me up. She'd been watching cash registers for fifty years and probably never seen a mistake before.

By the time I got her feathers smoothed and her goodies into a bag— she gives me a little snort in passing, if she'd been born at the right time they would have burned her over in Salem—by the time I get her on her way the girls had circled around the bread and were coming back, without a pushcart, back my way along the counters, in the aisle between the checkouts and the Special bins. They didn't even have shoes on. There was this chunky one, with the two-piece—it was bright green and the seams on the bra were still sharp and her belly was still pretty pale so I guessed she just got it (the suit)—there was this one, with one of those chubby berry-faces, the lips all bunched together under her nose, this one, and a tall one, with black hair that hadn't quite frizzed right, and one of these sunburns right across under the eyes, and a chin that was too long—you know, the kind of girl other girls think is very "striking" and "attractive" but never quite makes it, as they very well know, which is why they like her so much—and then the third one, that wasn't quite so tall. She was the queen. She kind of led them, the other two peeking around and making their shoulders round. She didn't look around, not this queen, she just walked straight on slowly, on these long white prima-donna legs. She came down a little hard on her heels, as if she didn't walk in her bare feet that much, putting down her heels and then letting the weight move along to her toes as if she was testing the floor with every step, putting a little deliberate extra action into it. You never know for sure how girls' minds work (do you really think it's a mind in there or just a little buzz like a bee in a glass jar?) but you got the idea she had talked the other two into coming in here with her, and now she was showing them how to do it, walk slow and hold yourself straight.

She had on a kind of dirty-pink—beige maybe, I don't know—bathing suit with a little nubble all over it and, what got me, the straps were down. They were off her shoulders looped loose around the cool tops of her arms, and I guess as a result the suit had slipped a little on her, so all around the top of the cloth there was this shining rim. If it hadn't been there you wouldn't have known there could have been anything whiter than those shoulders. With the straps pushed off, there was nothing between the top of the suit and the top of her head except just *her*, this clean bare plane of the top of her chest down from the shoulder bones like a dented sheet of metal hanging in the light. I mean, it was more than pretty.

She had sort of oaky hair that the sun and salt had bleached, done up in a bun that was unravelling, and a kind of prim face. Walking into the A & P with your straps down, I suppose it's the only kind of face you *can* have. She held her head so high her neck, coming up out of those white shoulders, looked kind of stretched, but I didn't mind. The longer her neck was, the more of her there was.

She must have felt in the corner of her eye me and over my shoulder Stokesie in the second slot watching, but she didn't tip. Not this queen. She kept her eyes moving across the racks, and stopped, and turned so slow it made my stomach rub the inside of my apron, and buzzed to the other two, who kind of huddled against her for relief, and then they all three of them went up the cat-and-dog-food-breakfast-cereal-maca-roni-rice-raisins-seasonings-spreads-spaghetti-soft-drinks-crackers-and-cookies aisle. From the third slot I look straight up this aisle to the meat counter, and I watched them all the way. The fat one with the tan sort of fumbled with the cookies, but on second thought she put the package back. The sheep pushing their carts down the aisle—the girls were walking against the usual traffic (not that we have one-way signs or anything)—were pretty hilarious. You could see them, when Queenie's white shoulders dawned on them, kind of jerk, or hop, or hiccup, but their eyes snapped back to their own baskets and on they pushed. I bet you could set off dynamite in an A & P and the people would by and large keep reaching and checking oatmeal off their lists and muttering "Let me see, there was a third thing, began with A, asparagus, no, ah, yes, applesauce!" or whatever it is they do mutter. But there was no doubt, this jiggled them. A few houseslaves in pin curlers even looked around after pushing their carts past to make sure what they had seen was correct.

You know, it's one thing to have a girl in a bathing suit down on the beach, where what with the glare nobody can look at each other much anyway, and another thing in the cool of the A & P, under the fluorescent lights, against all those stacked packages, with her feet paddling along naked over our checkerboard green-and-cream rubbertile floor.

"Oh, Daddy," Stokesie said beside me. "I feel so faint."

"Darling," I said. "Hold me tight." Stokesie's married, with two babies chalked up on his fuselage already, but as far as I can tell that's the only difference. He's twenty-two, and I was nineteen this April.

"Is it done?" he asks, the responsible married man finding his voice. I forgot to say he thinks he's going to be manager some sunny day, maybe in 1990 when it's called the Great Alexandrov and Petrooshki Tea Company or something.

What he meant was, our town is five miles from a beach, with a big summer colony out on the Point, but we're right in the middle of town, and the women generally put on a shirt or shorts or something before they get out of the car into the street. And anyway these are usually women with six children and varicose veins mapping their legs and nobody, including them, could care less. As I say, we're right in the middle of town, and if you stand at our front doors you can see two banks and the Congregational Church and the newspaper store and three real-estate offices and about twenty-seven old freeloaders tearing up the main street because the sewer broke again. It's not as if we're on the Cape; we're north of Boston and there's people in this town haven't seen the ocean for twenty years.

The girls had reached the meat counter and were asking McMahon something. He pointed, they pointed, and they shuffled out of sight behind a pyramid of Diet Delight peaches. All that was left for us to see was old McMahon patting his mouth and looking after them sizing up their joints. Poor kids, I began to feel sorry for them, they couldn't help it.

. . .

Now here comes the sad part of the story, at least my family says it's sad, but I don't think it's so sad myself. The store's pretty empty, it being Thursday afternoon, so there was nothing much to do except lean on the register and wait for the girls to show up again. The whole store was like a pinball machine and I didn't know which tunnel they'd come out of. After a while they come around out of the far aisle, around the light bulbs, records at discount of the Caribbean Six or Tony Martin Sings or some such gunk you wonder they waste the wax on, sixpacks of candy bars, and plastic toys done up in cellophane that fall apart when a kid looks at them anyway. Around they come, Queenie still leading the way, and holding a little gray jar in her hand. Slots Three through Seven are unmanned and I could see her wondering between Stokes and me, but Stokesie with his usual luck draws an old party in baggy gray pants who stumbles up with four giant cans of pineapple juice (what do these bums *do* with all that pineapple juice? I've often asked myself) so the girls come to me. Queenie puts down the jar and I take it into my fingers icy cold. Kingfish Fancy Herring Snacks in Pure Sour Cream: 49¢. Now her hands are empty, not a ring or a bracelet, bare as God made them, and I wonder where the money's coming from. Still with that prim look she lifts a folded dollar bill out of the hollow at the center of her nubbled pink top. The jar went heavy in my hand. Really, I thought that was so cute.

Then everybody's luck begins to run out. Lengel comes in from haggling with a truck full of cabbages on the lot and is about to scuttle into that door marked manager behind which he hides all day, when the girls touch his eye. Lengel's pretty dreary, teaches Sunday school and the rest, but he doesn't miss that much. He comes over and says, "Girls, this isn't the beach."

Queenie blushes, though maybe it's just a brush of sunburn I was noticing for the first time, now that she was so close. "My mother asked me to pick up a jar of herring snacks." Her voice kind of startled me, the way voices do when you see the people first, coming out so flat and dumb yet kind of toney, too, the way it ticked over "pick up" and "snacks." All of a sudden I slid right down her voice into her living room. Her father and the other men were standing around in ice-cream coats and bow ties and the women were in sandals picking up herring snacks on toothpicks off a big glass plate and they were all holding drinks the color of water with olives and sprigs of mint in them. When my parents have somebody over they get lemonade and if it's a real racy affair Schlitz in tall glasses with "They'll Do It Every Time" cartoons stencilled on.

"That's all right," Lengel said. "But this isn't the beach." His repeating this struck me as funny, as if it had just occurred to him, and he had been thinking all these years the A & P was a great big dune and he was the head lifeguard. He didn't like my smiling—as I say, he doesn't miss much—but he concentrates on giving the girls that sad Sunday-school-superintendent stare.

Queenie's blush is no sunburn now, and the plump one in plaid, that I liked better from the back—a really sweet backside—pipes up, "We weren't doing any shopping. We just came in for the one thing."

"That makes no difference," Lengel tells her, and I could see from the way his eyes went that he hadn't noticed she was wearing a two-piece before. "We want you decently dressed when you come in here."

"We *are* decent," Queenie says suddenly, her lower lip pushing, getting sore now that she remembers her place, a place from which the crowd that runs the A & P must look pretty crummy. Fancy Herring Snacks flashed in her very blue eyes.

"Girls, I don't want to argue with you. After this come in here with your shoulders covered. It's our policy." He turns his back. That's policy for you. Policy is what the kingpins want. What the others want is juvenile delinquency.

All this while, the customers had been showing up with their carts but, you know, sheep, seeing a scene, they had all bunched up on Stokesie, who shook open a paper bag as gently as peeling a peach, not wanting to miss a word. I could feel in the silence everybody getting nervous, most of all Lengel, who asks me, "Sammy, have you rung up their purchase?"

I thought and said "No" but it wasn't about that I was thinking. I go through the punches, 4, 9, GROC, TOT—it's more complicated than you think, and after you do it often enough, it begins to make a little song, that you hear words to, in my case "Hello (*bing*) there, you (*gung*) hap-py pee-pul (*splat*)!" the *splat* being the drawer flying out. I uncrease the bill, tenderly as you may imagine, it just having come from between the two smoothest scoops of vanilla I had ever known were there, and pass a half and a penny into her narrow pink palm, and nestle the herrings in a bag and twist its neck and hand it over, all the time thinking.

The girls, and who'd blame them, are in a hurry to get out, so I say "I quit" to Lengel quick enough for them to hear, hoping they'll stop and watch me, their unsuspected hero. They keep right on going, into the electric eye; the door flies open and they flicker across the lot to their car, Queenie and Plaid and Big Tall Goony-Goony (not that as raw material she was so bad), leaving me with Lengel and a kink in his eyebrow.

"Did you say something, Sammy?"

"I said I quit."

"I thought you did."

"You didn't have to embarrass them."

"It was they who were embarrassing us."

I started to say something that came out "Fiddle-de-doo." It's a saying of my grandmother's, and I know she would have been pleased.

"I don't think you know what you're saying," Lengel said.

"I know you don't," I said. "But I do." I pull the bow at the back of my apron and start shrugging it off my shoulders. A couple customers that had been heading for my slot begin to knock against each other, like scared pigs in a chute.

Lengel sighs and begins to look very patient and old and gray. He's been a friend of my parents for years. "Sammy, you don't want to do this to your Mom and Dad," he tells me. It's true, I don't. But it seems to me that once you begin a gesture it's fatal not to go through with it. I fold the apron, "Sammy" stitched in red on the pocket, and put it on the counter, and drop the bow tie on it. "You'll feel this for the rest of your life," Lengel says, and I know that's true, too, but remembering how he made that pretty girl blush makes me so scrunchy inside I punch the No Sale tab and the machine whirs "pee-pul" and the drawer splats out. One advantage to this scene taking place in summer, I can follow this up with a clean exit, there's no fumbling around getting your coat and ear muffs, I just saunter into the electric eye in my white shirt that my mother ironed the night before, and the door heaves itself open, and outside the sunshine is skating around on the asphalt.

I look around for my girls, but they're gone, of course. There wasn't anybody but some young married screaming with her children about some candy they didn't get by the door of a powder-blue Falcon station wagon. Looking back in the big windows, over the bags of peat moss and aluminum furniture stacked on the pavement, I could see Lengel in my place in the slot, checking the sheep through. His face was dark gray and his back stiff, as if he'd just had an injection of iron, and my stomach kind of fell as I felt how hard the world was going to be to me hereafter.

THE HUNTER'S WAKING THOUGHTS

Mavis Gallant

SEPTEMBER 29, 1962

ETWEEN FRIDAY NIGHT and Saturday noon, the courtyard filled with cars and station wagons, lined up like animals feeding along the wall of the hunting lodge. The license plates were mostly 75s, from Paris, but some of the numbers meant Lyon and one was as far away from Sologne as Avignon. Across the court, under the oak trees, the dogs, each chained to his kennel, barked insanely. Only two of the shooting party had brought dogs; the twelve chained dogs belonged to M. Maitrepierre, who had let the shooting rights to his estate for the season. Walking under the oak trees to have a better look at the dogs, the men in their boots trod on acorns and snails. The men were stout and middle-aged but dressed like the slimmer, handsomer models in *Adam*. A recent issue of *Adam*, advising a wardrobe for the hunting season, was on the windowsill of the dining room reserved for the party. There was also *Entreprise*, a business journal, and several copies of *Tintin*.

The hunters slammed doors the whole morning and carried bushels of equipment from the cars to the lodge. M. Scapa, a repatriated *pied-noir* from Algiers, had brought a chauffeur to look after his guns, his own case of whiskey, and his plaid-covered ice bucket. The lodge was ugly and awkward and had been built two hundred years after the other buildings on the estate. The big house was sold. M. Maitrepierre reserved for himself, his wife, and his married daughter and her family a cottage separated from the lodge by a locked gate and a wall. The shooting rights, which were high, were not his only source of income; he ran a sheep farm and half a dozen of the secret French economic tangles that come to light during family squabbles or taxation lawsuits. He built blocks of flats in Paris, sold a hotel in Normandy, bought part of a clothing factory in Lille. He kept his family tamed by the threat that they were doomed and bankrupt and on the verge of singing for their supper on some rainy street.

The shooting season had been open for over a month, but game was still so plentiful here in Sologne that pheasants, with their suicidal curiosity about automobiles, stood along the roads. Small hunter-colored couples, they were parodies of hunters. Anyone gathering mushrooms or chestnuts raised pheasant and quail. In pastures the hind legs of hares were glimpsed in the long grass. Saturdays and Sundays the farmers tied their dogs and kept the children inside, for the men who arrived in the big cars with the smart equipment shot without aiming; they shot at anything. A man wearing a suède jacket had been mistaken for a deer and wounded in the shoulder. There were any number of shot cats, turkeys, and ducks. Every season someone told of a punctured sheep. Casual poachers who left their cars drawn up on the edge of the highway came back to find a hole in the windshield and a web of cracked glass.

This was flat country in a season of rich colors—brown, dark red, gold.

. . .

Philip Graves, who was in love with M. Maitrepierre's married daughter, Jeanne, and younger than she was by nine years, had been put in the lodge. The lodge smelled like a school. Philip had not come to shoot but to be near Jeanne. Now that he was here, and saw that he was to sleep in the lodge, and that Jeanne's husband had arrived, he wondered if there had been a mistake—if he had turned up on the wrong weekend. The hunters strode and stamped, carrying whiskey glasses. The wooden stairs shook under their boots. Some went out on Saturday afternoon, but most of the party waited for Sunday morning. They ate enormous meals. They neither washed nor shaved. It was part of the ritual of being away from their women.

Philip had been given a room with a camp bed and a lamp and a ewer of cold water, and a bucket with an enamel cover. Jeanne showed him the room and let him start to undress her on the bed before changing her mind. She worried about what the family would think—so she said—

and she left him there, furious and demented. Was it because of the husband? No, she swore the husband had nothing to do with it. She talked rapidly, fastening her cardigan. Nothing went on between Jeanne and the husband. It had gone wrong years ago. Well, one year ago, at least. The husband's room in the lodge was next to Philip's. Jeanne was to spend the night in her own girlhood bed, in her father's house. What other evidence did Philip want?

He was the only foreigner here. He was a bad shot, and loathed killing. He supposed that everyone looked at him and guessed his situation. Why was he here? She had invited him; but she had not told him her husband was coming, too, or that she would be sleeping in another house. They were an odd couple. Philip was slight and fair. He was in Paris, translating Jules Renard's letters. He had met Jeanne because it was through one of her father's multitudinous enterprises he had found a place to live. Jeanne was Spanish-looking, and rather fat since the birth of her second daughter. Philip loved her beyond reason and cherished dreams in which the husband, the two little girls, and Jeanne's own common sense about money were somehow mislaid.

. . .

On Sunday morning, he walked with a party of women. There were three: Jeanne, her mother, and Jeanne's closest woman friend. If he included Jeanne's little girls, he had five females in all. The lover trailed behind the women, peevish as a child. They were walking far from the shooting party, on the shore of a shallow pond. Along the path he saw a snail and trod on it, afterward wiping his shoe on fallen leaves. Most galling to him was the way the women admired Jeanne; there was no mistaking the admiration in their eyes. She was bringing off a situation they could only applaud; she was getting away with murder. She had put her husband and her lover in adjacent rooms while she slept in calm privacy in her father's house. Now here she was, fat and placid, with the lover tagging like a spaniel. What was the good of keeping slim, starving oneself, paying out fortunes to be smart, when fat Jeanne could keep two men on the string without half trying? Philip saw this in the other women's eyes.

He knew they thought she was his mother; but the maternal part of her life disgusted him. The idea of her having ever been a mother—the confirmation, the two girls, ran along before the women (Philip was like one of the women now!)—made him sick. Early that morning, Jeanne's father had taken Philip on a tour of the sheep farm, and at the sight of a lambing chart on the wall of a pen—a pen called *le nursery*—Philip had been puzzled by the diagram of a lamb blind and doubled up in a kind of labyrinth. His mind first told him, "Surrealistic drawing"; then he realized what it was and was revolted. The thought of Jeanne on a level with animals—ewes, bitches, mares—was unbearable. He could not decide if he wanted her as a woman or a goddess. When he returned from the sheep pens, he found that Jeanne, meanwhile, had been attending to her husband—unpacking for him, and giving him breakfast.

The children, the women, and Philip walked along the edge of the pond, and separated the strands of barbed wire that marked someone else's property. Before them, at the end of a long terrace, among oak and acacia trees, rose a shuttered house. It was an ugly and pretentious house, built fifty years ago, imitating without grace a deeper past. He saw the women admiring it, and Jeanne yearning for it—for a large, shuttered, empty, pretentious house. Jeanne was already seeing what she would "do" to the place. She described the tubs of hydrangeas along the façade and the wrought-iron baskets dripping with geraniums. He pressed her arm as if afraid. What will become of us? What will happen if we quarrel?

The two women, Jeanne's mother and Jeanne's best friend, were as kind to Philip as if he were a dog. He felt the justice of it. He had the dog's fear of being left behind. He was like the dog shut up in the automobile who has no means of knowing his owner will ever return. He had seen dogs' eyes yellow with anxiety. . . . The most abject of lovers can be saved by pride. He dropped her arm, made her sense he was moving away. It was no accident he had chosen as a subject of work conceited Jules Renard. The hideous house belonged to a broker who had fumbled or gone crooked on a speculation, but (explained Jeanne) luckily had this place to fall back on. He seldom lived in the house, but he *owned* it. It was his; it was real. He knew it was there. Jeanne could admire storybook castles, but she never wanted them. Storybook castles were what Philip wanted her to want, because they were all he could give her. He hadn't a penny. She was waiting for an inheritance from her father, and another from her mother. Her husband hadn't quite gone through her marriage settlement; not yet.

Jeanne stuffed her pockets with acorns and cracked them with her teeth. She was always making motions of eating, of biting. She bit acorns, chestnuts, twigs. She was solid as this house, and solidity was what she wanted: something safe, something she could fall back on. She spat a chewed acorn out of her mouth into her palm. "You're too young to re-member the war, Philip," she said, smiling at him. "We used to make coffee out of these filthy things."

· · ·

Sunday night the bag was divided, the courtyard slowly rid of its cars. Philip, earlier, had walked around the *tableau de chasse,* the still-life spread on the ground, pretending admiration. He saw hares so riddled they would never be clean of shot. He was sick for the larks. He was to spend Sunday night at the cottage, with Jeanne's father and mother. Her father would drive him up to Paris on Monday morning. He was to sleep in Jeanne's girlhood bed. His sheets had been thriftily moved from the lodge and carried the smell of the unwashed house. Jeanne's husband all at once wanted to be in Paris. He wanted to pack the car and leave now. The weekend was over; there was no reason to remain another second. Fat and placid Jeanne screamed at him, "You have imposed a dinner party on me for tomorrow night. Now, take your choice. We leave now, this minute, and you take tomorrow's guests to a restaurant. Or you wait until the game is divided and we have a hare." The family were not en-titled to any of the game, except by courtesy. Jeanne's husband had gone out with the shooting party, but he had not paid his share of the shooting rights on his father-in-law's property; he had no claim to so much as a dead thrush.

"You can't cook a freshly killed hare," said Jeanne's mother.

Everyone else kept out of it.

"He knows the butchers are closed on Mondays, and he knows I have an incompetent Spanish maid, and thrusts a Monday-night dinner party on me," cried Jeanne. The husband, black with temper, read *Tintin.* The little girls played dominoes on a corner of a table. Philip watched Jeanne without being noticed. If he had laid a hand on her now, she might have hit him.

She left, at last, with the token hare in a basket. Jeanne's mother's voice wailed after the car, "Jeanne! Jeanne! The hare should marinate at least twelve days!" She returned to the cottage and saw her daughter's guest, the lover, standing in the middle of the room. "My son-in-law is indescribable," she said. "My daughter is a saint. Have you enjoyed the weekend, Philip? Do you like the country, or do you like cities better? Would you like a drink?"

Her husband, Jeanne's father, had gone, flashlight in hand, to the hunting lodge, to recover anything left by the party: dregs of whiskey in open bottles, half-crumbled chocolate bars.

"How sensible you are not to marry," said Jeanne's mother, sitting down. "The world would be simpler if women lived with women and men with men. I don't mean anything perverse. But look at how peaceful we were without the men today." They had their drinks, and Philip crawled into his sheets, in his mistress's girlhood bed. It was then he started to wonder if he shouldn't look for someone to marry after all.

THE SWIMMER

John Cheever

JULY 18, 1964

IT WAS ONE of those midsummer Sundays when everyone sits around saying, "I *drank* too much last night." You might have heard it whispered by the parishioners leaving church, heard it from the lips of the priest himself, struggling with his cassock in the *vestiarium*, heard it on the golf links and the tennis courts, heard it in the wildlife preserve, where the leader of the Audubon group was suffering from a terrible hangover

"I *drank* too much," said Donald Westerhazy, at the edge of the Westerhazys' pool.

"We all *drank* too much," said Lucinda Merrill.

"It must have been the wine," said Helen Westerhazy. "I *drank* too much of that claret."

The pool, fed by an artesian well with a high iron content, was a pale shade of green. It was a fine day. In the west there was a massive stand of cumulus cloud, so like a city seen from a distance—from the bow of an approaching ship—that it might have had a name. Lisbon. Hackensack. The sun was hot. Neddy Merrill sat by the green water, one hand in it, one around a glass of gin. He was a slender man—he seemed to have the special slenderness of youth—and while he was far from young, he had slid down his banister that morning and given the bronze backside of Aphrodite on the hall table a smack, as he jogged toward the smell of coffee in his dining room. He might have been compared to a summer's day, particularly the last hours of one, and while he lacked a tennis racket or a sail bag, the impression was definitely one of youth, sport, and clement weather. He had been swimming, and now he was breathing deeply, stertorously, as if he could gulp into his lungs the components of that moment, the heat of the sun, the intenseness of his pleasure. It all seemed to flow into his chest. His own house stood in Bullet Park, eight miles to the south, where his four beautiful daughters would have had their lunch and might be playing tennis. Then it occurred to him that, by taking a dog-leg to the southwest, he could reach his home by water.

His life was not confining, and the delight he took in this thought could not be explained by its suggestion of escape. In his mind he saw, with a cartographer's eye, a string of swimming pools, a quasi-subterranean stream that curved across the county. He had made a discovery, a contribution to modern geography; he would name the stream Lucinda, after his wife. He was not a practical joker, nor was he a fool, but he was determinedly original, and had a vague and modest idea of himself as a legendary figure. The day was beautiful, and it seemed to him that a long swim might enlarge and celebrate its beauty.

He took off a sweater that was hung over his shoulders and dove in. He had a simple contempt for men who did not hurl themselves into pools. He swam a choppy crawl, breathing either with every other stroke or every fourth stroke, and counting somewhere well in the back of his mind the one-two one-two of a flutter kick. It was not a serviceable stroke for long distance, but the domestication of swimming had saddled the sport with some customs, and in his part of the world a crawl was customary. Being embraced and sustained by the light-green water seemed not as much a pleasure as the resumption of a natural condition, and he would have liked to swim without trunks, but this was not possible, considering his project. He hoisted himself up on the far curb—he never used the ladder—and started across the law. When Lucinda asked where he was going, he said he was going to swim home.

The only maps and charts he had to go by were remembered or imaginary, but these were clear enough. First there were the Grahams', the Hammers', the Lears', the Howlands', and the Crosscups'. He would cross Ditmar Street to the Bunkers' and come, after a short portage, to the Levys', the Welchers', and the public pool in Lancaster. Then there were the Hallorans', the Sachs', the Biswangers', the Shirley Abbott's, the Gilmartins', and the Clydes'. The day was lovely, and that he lived in a world so generously supplied with water seemed like a clemency, a beneficence. His heart was high, and he ran across the grass. Making his way home by an uncommon route gave him the feeling that he was a pilgrim, an explorer, a man with a destiny, and he knew that he would find friends all along the way; friends would line the banks of the Lucinda River.

He went through a hedge that separated the Westerhazys' land from the Grahams', walked under some flowering apple trees, passed the shed that housed their pump and filter, and came out at the Grahams' pool. "Why, Neddy," Mrs. Graham said, "what a marvellous surprise. I've been trying to get you on the phone all morning. Here, let me get you a drink." He saw then, like any explorer, that the hospitable customs and traditions of the natives would have to be handled with diplomacy if he was ever going to reach his destination. He did not want to mystify or seem rude to the Grahams, nor did he have time to linger there. He swam the length of their pool and joined them in the sun. A few minutes later, two carloads of friends arrived from Connecticut. During the uproarious reunions he was able to slip away. He went down by the front of the Grahams' house, stepped over a thorny hedge, and crossed a vacant lot to the Hammers'. Mrs. Hammer, looking up from her roses, saw him swim by, although she wasn't quite sure who it was. The Lears heard him splashing past the open windows of their living room. The Howlands and the Crosscups were away. After leaving the Crosscups', he crossed Ditmar Street and started for the Bunkers', where he could hear, even at that distance, the noise of a party.

The water refracted the sound of voices and laughter and seemed to suspend it in midair. The Bunkers' pool was on a rise, and he climbed some stairs to a terrace where twenty-five or thirty men and women were drinking. The only person in the water was Rusty Towers, who floated there on a rubber raft. Oh, how bonny and lush were the banks of the Lucinda River! Prosperous men and women gathered by the sapphire-colored waters while caterer's men in white coats passed them cold gin. Overhead, a red de Havilland trainer was circling around and around and around in the sky, with something like the glee of a child in a swing. Ned felt a passing affection for the scene, a tenderness for the gathering, as if it was something he might touch. In the distance he heard thunder.

As soon as Enid Bunker saw him, she began to scream, "Oh, look who's here! What a marvellous surprise! When Lucinda said that you couldn't come, I thought I'd *die*. . . ." She made her way to him through the crowd, and when they had finished kissing, she led him to the bar, a progress that was slowed by the fact that he stopped to kiss eight or ten other women and shake the hands of as many men. A smiling bartender he had seen at a hundred parties gave him a gin-and-tonic, and Ned stood by the bar for a moment, anxious not to get stuck in any conversation that would delay his voyage. When he seemed about to be surrounded, he dove in and swam close to the side, to avoid colliding with Rusty's raft. He climbed out at the far end of the pool, bypassed the Tomlinsons with a broad smile, and jogged up the garden path. The gravel cut his feet, but this was the only unpleasantness.

The party was confined to the pool, and as he went toward the house he heard the brilliant, watery sound of voices fade, heard the noise of a radio from the Bunkers' kitchen, where someone was listening to a ball game. Sunday afternoon. He made his way through the parked cars and down the grassy border of their driveway to Alewives' Lane. He did not want to be seen on the road in his bathing trunks, but there was no traffic, and he made the short distance to the Levys' driveway, marked with a "Private Property" sign and a green tube for the *Times*. All the doors and windows of the big house were open, but there were no signs of life, not even a barking dog. He went around the side of the house to the pool and saw that the Levys had only recently left. Glasses and bottles and dishes of nuts were on a table at the deep end, where there was a bathhouse or gazebo, hung with Japanese lanterns. After swimming the pool, he got himself a glass and poured a drink. It was his fourth or fifth drink, and he had swum nearly half the length of the Lucinda River. He felt tired, clean, and pleased at that moment to be alone, pleased with everything.

It would storm. The stand of cumulus cloud—that city—had risen and darkened, and while he sat there, he heard thunder. The de Havilland trainer was still circling overhead, and it seemed to Ned that he could almost hear the pilot laugh with pleasure in the afternoon; but when there was another peal of thunder, he took off for home. A train whistle blew, and he wondered what time it had gotten to be. Four? Five? He thought of the station where, at that hour, a waiter, his tuxedo concealed by a raincoat, a dwarf with some flowers wrapped in newspaper, and a woman who had been crying would be waiting for the local. It was suddenly growing dark—it was that moment when the pinheaded birds seem to organize their song into some acute and knowledgeable recognition of the storm's approach. From the crown of an oak at his back, there was a fine noise of rushing water, as if a spigot there had been turned on. Then the noise of fountains came from the crowns of all the tall trees. Why did he love storms? What was the meaning of his excitement when the front door sprang open and the rain wind fled rudely up the stairs? Why had the simple task of shutting the windows of an old house seemed fitting and urgent? Why did the first watery notes of a storm wind have for him the unmistakable sound of good news, cheer, glad tidings? There was an explosion, a smell of cordite, and rain lashed the Japanese lanterns that Mrs. Levy had bought in Kyoto the year before last, or was it the year before that?

. . .

He stayed in the Levys' gazebo until the storm had passed. The rain had cooled the air and he shivered. The force of the wind had stripped a maple of its red and yellow leaves and scattered them over the grass and the water. Since it was midsummer, the tree must be blighted, and yet he felt a sadness at this sign of autumn. He braced his shoulders, emptied his glass, and started for the Welchers' pool. This meant crossing the Pasterns' riding ring, and he was surprised to find it overgrown with grass and all the jumps dismantled. Had the Pasterns sold their horses or gone away for the summer and put them out to board? He seemed to remember having heard something about the Pasterns and their horses, but the memory was unclear. On he went, barefoot, through the wet grass to the Welchers', where he found that their pool was dry.

This breach in his chain of water disappointed him absurdly, and he felt like an explorer who is seeking a torrential headwater and finds a dead stream. He was disappointed and mystified. It was common enough to go away for the summer, but people never drained their pools. The Welchers had definitely gone away. The pool furniture was folded, stacked, and covered with a tarpaulin. The bathhouse was locked. All the windows of the house were shut, and when he went around to the driveway in front, he saw a "For Sale" sign nailed to a tree. When had he last heard from the Welchers—when, that is, had he and Lucinda last regretted an invitation to dine with them? It seemed only a week or so ago. Was his memory failing, or had he so disciplined it in the repression of unpleasant facts that he had damaged his sense of the truth? In the distance he heard the sound of a tennis game. This cheered him, cleared away all his apprehensions, and let him regard the overcast sky and the cold air with indifference. This was the day that Neddy Merrill swam across the county. That was the day! He started off then for his most difficult portage.

. . .

Had you gone for a Sunday-afternoon ride that day, you might have seen him, close to naked, standing on the shoulder of Route 424, waiting for a chance to cross. You might have wondered if he was the victim of foul play, or had his car broken down, or was he merely a fool? Standing barefoot in the deposits of the highway—beer cans, rags, and blowout patches—exposed to all kinds of ridicule, he seemed pitiful. He had known when he started that this was a part of his journey—it had been on his imaginary maps—but, confronted with the lines of traffic worming through the summery light, he found himself unprepared. He was laughed at, jeered at, a beer can was thrown at him, and he had no dignity or humor to bring to the situation. He could have gone back, back to the Westerhazys', where Lucinda would still be sitting in the sun. He had signed nothing, vowed nothing, pledged nothing—not even to himself. Why, believing as he did that all human obduracy was susceptible to common sense, was he unable to turn back? Why was he determined to complete his journey, even if it meant putting his life in danger? At what point had this prank, this joke, this piece of horseplay become serious? He could not go back, he could not even recall with any clearness the green water at the Westerhazys', the sense of inhaling the day's components, the friendly and relaxed voices saying that they had *drunk* too much. In the space of an hour, more or less, he had covered a distance that made his return impossible.

An old man, tooling down the highway at fifteen miles an hour, let him get to the middle of the road, where there was a grass divider. Here he was exposed to the ridicule of the northbound traffic, but after ten or fifteen minutes he was able to cross. From here he had only a short walk to the Recreation Center at the edge of the village of Lancaster, where there were some handball courts and a public pool.

The effect of water on voices, the illusion of brilliance and suspense, was the same here as it had been at the Bunkers', but the sounds here were louder, harsher, and more shrill, and as soon as he entered the crowd enclosure he was confronted with regimentation. "ALL SWIMMERS MUST TAKE A SHOWER BEFORE USING THE POOL. ALL SWIMMERS MUST USE THE FOOT-BATH. ALL SWIMMERS MUST WEAR THEIR IDENTIFICATION DISCS." He took a shower, washed his feet in a cloudy and bitter solution, and made his way to the edge of the water. It stank of chlorine and looked to him like a sink. A pair of lifeguards in a pair of towers blew police whistles at what seemed to be regular intervals, and abused the swimmers through a public-address system. Neddy remembered the sapphire water at the Bunkers' with longing, and thought that he might contaminate himself—damage his own prosperousness and charm—by swimming in this murk, but he reminded himself that he was an explorer, a pilgrim, and that this was merely a stagnant bend in the Lucinda River. He dove, scowling with distaste, into the chlorine, and had to swim with his head above water to avoid collisions, but even so he was bumped into, splashed, and jostled. When he got to the shallow end, both lifeguards were shouting at him: "Hey, you, you without the identification disc, get outa the water!" He did. They had no way of pursuing him, and he went through the reek of sun-tan oil and chlorine, out through the hurricane fence and past the handball courts. Crossing the road, he entered the wooded part of the Halloran estate. The woods were not cleared, and the footing was treacherous and difficult, until he reached the lawn and the clipped beech hedge that encircled the pool.

The Hallorans were friends, an elderly couple of enormous wealth who seemed to bask in the suspicion that they might be Communists. They were zealous reformers, but they were not Communists, and yet when they were accused, as they sometimes were, of subversion, it seemed to gratify and excite them. Their beech hedge was yellow, and he guessed it was suffering from a blight, like the Levys' maple. He called "Hullo, hullo," to warn the Hallorans of his approach. The Hallorans, for reasons that had never been explained to him, did not wear bathing suits. No explanations were in order, really. Their nakedness was a detail in their uncompromising zeal for reform, and he stepped politely out of his trunks before he went through the opening in the hedge.

Mrs. Halloran, a stout woman with white hair and a serene face, was reading the *Times*. Mr. Halloran was taking beech leaves out of the water with a scoop. They seemed neither surprised nor displeased to see him. Their pool was perhaps the oldest in the neighborhood, a fieldstone rectangle fed by a brook. It had no filter or pump, and its waters were the opaque gold of the stream.

"I'm swimming across the county," Ned said.

"Why, I didn't know one could!" exclaimed Mrs. Halloran.

"Well, I've made it from the Westerhazys'," Ned said. "That must be about four miles."

He left his trunks at the deep end, walked to the shallow end, and swam back. As he was pulling himself out of the water, he heard Mrs.

Halloran say, "We've been *terribly* sorry to hear about all your misfortunes, Neddy."

"My misfortunes?" Ned asked. "I don't know what you mean."

"Why, we heard that you'd sold the house, and that your poor children . . ."

"I don't recall having sold the house," Ned said, "and the girls are at home."

"Yes," Mrs. Halloran sighed. "Yes . . ."

Her voice filled the air with an unseasonable melancholy, and Ned said briskly, "Thank you for the swim."

"Well, have a nice trip," said Mrs. Halloran.

Beyond the hedge, he pulled on his trunks and fastened them. They were loose, and he wondered if during the space of an afternoon he could have lost some weight. He was cold, and he was tired, and the naked Hallorans and their dark water had depressed him. The swim was too much for his strength, but how could he have guessed this, sliding down the banister that morning and sitting in the Westerhazys' sun? His arms were lame. His legs felt rubbery and ached at the joints. The worst of it was the cold in his bones, and the feeling that he might never be warm again. Leaves were falling around him and he smelled woodsmoke on the wind. Who would be burning wood in the fireplace at this time of year?

He needed a drink. Whiskey would warm him, pick him up, carry him through the last of his journey, refresh his feeling that it was original and valorous to swim across the county. Channel swimmers took brandy. He needed a stimulant. He crossed the lawn in front of the Hallorans' house and went down a little path to where they had built a house for their only daughter, Helen, and her husband, Eric Sachs' pool was small, and he found Helen and her husband there.

"Oh, *Neddy*!" Helen said. "Did you lunch at Mother's?"

"Not *really*," Ned said. "I *did* stop to see your parents." This seemed to be explanation enough. "I'm terribly sorry to break in on you like this, but I've taken a chill, and I wonder if you'd give me a drink."

"Why, I'd *love* to," Helen said, "but there hasn't been anything in this house to drink since Eric's operation. That was three years ago."

Was he losing his memory, had his gift for concealing painful facts let him forget that he had sold his house, that his children were in trouble, and that his friend had been ill? Ned's eyes slipped from Eric's face to his abdomen, where he saw three pale, sutured scars, two of them at least a foot long. Gone was his navel, and what, Neddy thought, would the roving hand, bed-checking one's gifts at 3 A.M., make of a belly with no navel, no link to birth, this breach in the succession?

"I'm sure you can get a drink at the Biswangers'," Helen said. "They're having an enormous do. You can hear it from here. Listen!"

She raised her head, and from across the road, the lawns, the gardens, the woods, the fields he heard again the brilliant noise of voices over water. "Well, I'll get wet," he said, still feeling that he had no freedom of choice about his means of travel. He dove into the Sachs' cold water, and, gasping, close to drowning, made his way from one end of the pool to the other. "Lucinda and I want *terribly* to see you," he said over his shoulder, his face set toward the Biswangers'. "We're sorry it's been so long, and we'll call you *very* soon."

He crossed some fields to the Biswangers' and the sounds of revelry there. They would be honored to give him a drink, they would be happy to give him a drink, they would, in fact, be lucky to give him a drink. The Biswangers invited him and Lucinda for dinner four times a year, six weeks in advance. They were always rebuffed, and yet they continued to send out their invitations, unwilling to comprehend the rigid and undemocratic realities of their society. They were the sort of people who discussed the price of things at cocktails, exchanged market tips during dinner, and after dinner told dirty stories to mixed company. They did not belong to Neddy's set—they were not even on Lucinda's Christmas-card list. He went toward their pool with feelings of indifference, charity, and some unease, since it seemed to be getting dark and these were the longest days of the year. The party when he joined it was noisy and large. Grace Biswanger was the kind of hostess who asked the ophthalmologist, the veterinarian, the real-estate dealer, and the dentist. No one was swimming, and the twilight, reflected on the water of the pool, had a wintery gleam. There was a bar, and he started for it. When Grace Biswanger saw him, she came toward him, not affectionately, as he had every right to expect, but bellicosely.

"Why, this party has everything," she said loudly, "including a gate-crasher."

She could not deal him a social blow—there was no question about this—and he did not flinch. "As a gate-crasher," he asked politely, "do I rate a drink?"

"Suit yourself," she said.

She turned her back on him and joined some guests, and he went to the bar and ordered a whiskey. The bartender served him, but rudely. His was a world in which the caterer's men kept the social score, and to be rebuffed by a part-time barkeep meant that he had suffered some loss of social esteem. Or perhaps the man was new and uninformed. Then at his back he heard Grace say, "They went broke overnight—nothing but income—and he showed up drunk one Sunday and asked us to loan him five thousand dollars. . . ." She was always talking about money. It was worse than eating your peas off a knife. He dove into the pool, swam its length, and went away.

. . .

The next pool on his list, the last but two, belonged to his old mistress, Shirley Abbott. If he had suffered any injuries at the Biswangers', they would be cured here. Love—sexual roughhouse, in fact—was the supreme elixir, the painkiller, the brightly colored pill that would put the spring back into his step, the joy of life in his heart. They had had an affair last week, last month, last year. He couldn't remember. It was he who had broken it off, his was the upper hand, and as he stepped through the gate of the wall that surrounded her pool it seemed to be his pool, since the lover, particularly the illicit lover, enjoys the possessions of his mistress with an authority unknown to holy matrimony. She was there, her hair the color of brass, but her figure, at the edge of the lighted, cerulean water, excited in him no profound memories. It had been, he thought, a lighthearted affair, although she wept when he broke it off. She seemed confused to see him. If she was still wounded, would she, God forbid, weep again?

"What do you want?" she asked.

"I'm swimming across the county."

"Good Christ. Will you ever grow up?"

"What's the matter?"

"If you've come here for money," she said, "I won't give you another cent."

"You could give me a drink."

"I could, but I won't. I'm not alone."

"Well, I'm on my way."

He dove in and swam the pool, but when he tried to haul himself up onto the curb, he found that the strength in his arms and his shoulders had gone, and he paddled to the ladder and climbed out. Looking over his shoulder, he saw, in the lighted bathhouse, a young man. Going out

But it is you I want now, here in the middle of this Uprising, with the streets yellow and threatening, short, ugly lances with fur at the throat and inexplicable shell money lying in the grass. It is when I am with you that I am happiest, and it is for you that I am making this hollow-core door table with black wrought-iron legs. I held Sylvia by her bear-claw necklace. "Call off your braves," I said. "We have many years left to live." There was a sort of muck running in the gutters, yellowish, filthy stream suggesting excrement, or nervousness, a city that does not know what it has done to deserve baldness, errors, infidelity. "With luck you will survive until matins," Sylvia said. She ran off down the Rue Chester Nimitz, uttering shrill cries.

Then it was learned that they had infiltrated our ghetto and that the people of the ghetto instead of offering resistance had joined the smooth, well-coordinated attack with zipguns, telegrams, lockets, causing that portion of the line held by the I.R.A. to swell and collapse. We sent more heroin into the ghetto, and hyacinths, ordering another hundred thousand of the pale, delicate flowers. On the map we considered the situation with its strung-out inhabitants and merely personal emotions. Our parts were blue and their parts were green. I showed the blue-and-green map to Sylvia. "Your parts are green," I said. "You gave me heroin first a year ago," Sylvia said. She ran off down George C. Marshall Allée, uttering shrill cries. Miss R. pushed me into a large room painted white (jolting and dancing in the soft light, and I was excited! and there were people watching!) in which there were two chairs. I sat in one chair and Miss R. sat in the other. She wore a blue dress containing a red figure. There was nothing exceptional about her. I was disappointed by her plainness, by the bareness of the room, by the absence of books.

. . .

The girls of my quarter wore long blue mufflers that reached to their knees. Sometimes the girls hid Comanches in their rooms, the blue mufflers together in a room creating a great blue fog. Block opened the door. He was carrying weapons, flowers, loaves of bread. And he was friendly, kind, enthusiastic, so I related a little of the history of torture, reviewing the technical literature quoting the best modern sources, French, German, and American, and pointing out the flies which had gathered in anticipation of some new, cool color.

"What is the situation?" I asked.

onto the dark lawn, he smelled chrysanthemums or marigolds—some stubborn autumnal fragrance on the night air, strong as gas. Looking overhead, he saw that the stars had come out, but why should he seem to see Andromeda, Cepheus, and Cassiopeia? What had become of the constellations of midsummer? He began to cry.

It was probably the first time in his adult life that he had ever cried— certainly the first time in his life that he had ever felt so miserable, cold, tired, and bewildered. He could not understand the rudeness of the caterer's barkeep, or the rudeness of a mistress who had once come to him on her knees and showered his trousers with tears. He had swum too long, he had been immersed too long, and his nose and his throat were sore from the water. What he needed then was a drink, some company, and some clean dry clothes, and while he could have cut directly across the road to his home, he went on, instead, to the Gilmartins' pool. Here, for the first time in his life, he did not dive but went down the steps into the icy water and swam a hobbled sidestroke that he might have learned as a child. He staggered with fatigue on his way to the Clydes', and paddled the length of their pool, stopping again and again, with his hand on the curb, to rest. He climbed up the ladder and wondered if he had the strength to get home. He had done what he wanted—he had swum the county—but he was so stupefied with exhaustion that his triumph seemed vague. Stooped, holding onto the gateposts for support, he turned up the driveway of his own house.

The place was dark. Had Lucinda stayed at the Westerhazys' for supper? Had the girls joined her there, or gone someplace else? Hadn't they agreed, as they usually did on Sunday, to regret all their invitations and stay at home?

He tried the garage doors, to see what cars were in, but the doors were locked and rust came off the handles. Going toward the house, he saw that the force of the thunderstorm had knocked one of the rain gutters loose. It hung down over the front door like an umbrella rib, but it could be fixed in the morning. The house was locked, and he thought that the stupid cook or the stupid maid must have locked the place up, until he remembered that it had been some time since they had employed a maid or a cook. He shouted, pounded on the door, tried to force it with his shoulder, and then, looking in at the windows, saw that the place was empty.

THE INDIAN UPRISING

Donald Barthelme

MARCH 6, 1965

WE DEFENDED THE city as best we could. The arrows of the Comanches came in clouds. The war clubs of the Comanches clattered on the soft, yellow pavements. There were earthworks along the Boulevard Mark Clark and the hedges had been laced with sparkling wire. People were trying to understand. I spoke to Sylvia. "Do you think this is a good life?" The table held apples, books, long-playing records. She looked up. "No."

Patrols of paras and volunteers with armbands guarded the tall, flat buildings. We interrogated the captured Comanche. Two of us forced his head back while another poured water into his nostrils. His body jerked, he choked and wept. Not believing a hurried, careless, and exaggerated report of the number of casualties in the outer districts where trees, lamps, swans had been reduced to clear fields of fire we issued entrenching tools to those who seemed trustworthy and turned the heavy-weapons companies so that we could not be surprised from that direction. And I sat there getting drunker and drunker and more in love and more in love. We talked.

"Do you know Fauré's 'Dolly'?"

"Would that be Gabriel Fauré?"

"It would."

"Then I know it," she said. "May I say that I play it myself at certain times, when I am sad, or happy, although it requires four hands."

"How is that managed?"

"I accelerate," she said, "ignoring the time signature."

And when they shot the scene in the bed I wondered how you felt under the eyes of the cameramen, grips, juicers, men in the mixing booth: excited? stimulated? And when they shot the scene in the shower I sanded a hollow-core door working carefully against the illustrations in texts and whispered instructions from one who had already solved the problem. I had made after all other tables, one while living with Nancy, one while living with Alice, one while living with Eunice, one while living with Marianne.

Red men in waves like people scattering in a square startled by something tragic or a sudden, loud noise accumulated against the barricades we had made of window dummies, silk, thoughtfully planned job descriptions (including scales for the orderly progress of other colors), wine in demi-johns, and robes. I analyzed the composition of the barricade nearest me and found two ashtrays, ceramic, one dark brown and one dark brown with an orange blur at the lip; a tin frying pan; two-litre bottles of red wine; three-quarter-litre bottles of Black & White, aquavit, cognac, vodka, gin, Fad #6 sherry; a hollow-core door in birch veneer on black wrought-iron legs; a blanket, red-orange with faint blue stripes; a red pillow and a blue pillow; a woven straw wastebasket; two glass jars for flowers; corkscrews and can openers; two plates and two cups, ceramic, dark brown; a yellow-and-purple poster; a Yugoslavian carved flute, wood, dark brown; and other items. I decided I knew nothing.

The hospitals dusted wounds with powders the worth of which wa not quite established, other supplies having been exhausted early in tl first day. I decided I knew nothing. Friends put me in touch with a M R., a teacher, unorthodox they said, excellent they said, successful w difficult cases, steel shutters on the windows made her house safe. I just learned via an International Distress Coupon that Jane had l beaten up by a dwarf in a bar in Tenerife but Miss R. did not allov to speak of it. "You know nothing," she said, "you feel nothing, yo locked in a most savage and terrible ignorance, I despise you, m mon cher, my heart. You may attend but you must not attend no must attend later, a day or a week or an hour, you are making me i I nonevaluated these remarks as Korzybski instructed. But it wa cult. Then they pulled back in a feint near the river and we rusl that sector with a reinforced battalion hastily formed among the and cabdrivers. This unit was crushed in the afternoon of a began with spoons and letters in hallways and under windo men tasted the history of the heart, cone-shaped muscular c maintains *circulation of the blood*.

"The situation is liquid," he said. "We hold the south quarter and they hold the north quarter. The rest is silence."

"And Kenneth?"

"That girl is not in love with Kenneth," Block said frankly. "She is in love with his coat. When she is not wearing it she is huddling under it. Once I caught it going down the stairs by itself. I looked inside. Sylvia."

Once I caught Kenneth's coat going down the stairs by itself but the coat was a trap and inside a Comanche who made a thrust with his short, ugly knife at my leg which buckled and tossed me over the balustrade through a window and into another situation. Not believing that your body brilliant as it was and your fat, liquid spirit distinguished and angry as it was were stable quantities to which one could return on wires more than once, twice, or another number of times I said: "See the table?"

In Skinny Wainwright Square the forces of green and blue swayed and struggled. The referees ran out on the field trailing chains. And then the blue part would be enlarged, the green diminished. Miss R. began to speak. "A former king of Spain, a Bonaparte, lived for a time in Borden-town, New Jersey. But that's no good." She paused. "The ardor aroused in men by the beauty of women can only be satisfied by God. That is *very* good (it is Valéry) but it is not what I have to teach you, goat, muck, filth, heart of my heart." I showed the table to Nancy. "See the table?" She stuck out her tongue red as a cardinal's hat. "I made such a table once," Block said frankly. "People all over America have made such tables. I doubt very much whether one can enter an American home without finding at least one such table, or traces of its having been there, such as faded places in the carpet." And afterward in the garden the men of the 7th Cavalry played Gabrieli, Albinoni, Marcello, Vivaldi, Boccherini. I saw Sylvia. She wore a yellow ribbon, under a long blue muffler. "Which side are you on," I cried, "after all?"

"The only form of discourse of which I approve," Miss R. said in her dry, sack voice, "is the litany. I believe our masters and teachers as well as plain citizens should confine themselves to what can safely be said. Thus when I hear the words *pewter, snake, tea, Fad #6 sherry, serviette, fenestra-tion, crown, blue* coming from the mouth of some public official, or some raw youth, I am not disappointed. Vertical organization is also possible," Miss R. said, "as in

pewter

snake

tea
Fad #6 sherry
serviette
fenestration
crown
blue.

I run to liquids and colors," she said, "but you, you may run to something else, my virgin, my darling, my thistle, my poppet, my own. Young people," Miss R. said, "run to more and more unpleasant combinations as they sense the nature of our society. Some people," Miss R. said, "run to conceits or wisdom but I hold to the hard, brown, nut-like word. I might point out that there is enough aesthetic excitement here to satisfy anyone but a damned fool." I sat in solemn silence.

. . .

Fire arrows lit my way to the post office in Patton Place where members of the Abraham Lincoln Brigade offered their last, exhausted letters, postcards, calendars. I opened a letter but inside was a Comanche flint arrowhead played by Frank Wedekind in an elegant gold chain and congratulations. Your earring rattled against my spectacles when I leaned forward to touch the soft, ruined place where the hearing aid had been. "Pack it up! Pack it up!" I urged, but the men in charge of the Uprising refused to listen to reason or to understand that it was real and that our water supply had evaporated and that our credit was no longer what it had been, once.

We attached wires to the testicles of the captured Comanche. And I sat there getting drunker and drunker and more in love and more in love. When we threw the switch he spoke. His name, he said, was Gustave Aschenbach. He was born at L—, a country town in the province of Silesia. He was the son of an upper official in the judicature, and his forebears had all been officers, judges, departmental functionaries. . . . And you can never touch a girl in the same way more than once, twice, or another number of times however much you may wish to hold, wrap, or otherwise fix her hand, or look, or some other quality, or incident, known to you previously. In Sweden the little Swedish children cheered when we managed nothing more remarkable than getting off a bus burdened with packages, bread and liver-paste and beer. We went to an old church and sat in the royal box. The organist was practicing. And then into the graveyard next to the church. *Here lies Anna Pedersen, a good woman.* I threw a mushroom on the grave. The officer commanding the garbage dump reported by radio that the garbage had begun to move.

Jane! I heard via an International Distress Coupon that you were beaten up by a dwarf in a bar in Tenerife. That doesn't sound like you, Jane. Mostly you kick the dwarf in his little dwarf groin before he can get his teeth into your tasty and nice-looking leg, don't you, Jane? Your affair with Harold is reprehensible, you know that, don't you, Jane? Harold is married to Nancy. And there is Paula to think about (Harold's kid), and Billy (Harold's other kid). I think your values are peculiar, Jane! Strings of language extend in every direction to bind the world into a rushing, seamless whole.

And you can never return to felicities in the same way, the brilliant body, the distinguished spirit recapitulating moments that occur once, twice, or another number of times in rebellions, or water. The rolling consensus of the Comanche nation smashed our inner defenses on three sides. Block was firing a greasegun from the upper floor of a building designed by Emery Roth & Sons. "See the table?" "Oh, pack it up with your bloody table!" The city officials were tied to trees. Dusky warriors padded with their forest tread into the mouth of the mayor "Who do you want to be?" I asked Kenneth and he said he wanted to be Jean-Luc Godard but later when time permitted conversations in large, lighted rooms, whispering galleries with black-and-white Spanish rugs and problematic sculptures on calm, red catafalques. The sickness of the quarrel lay thick in the bed. I touched your back, the white, raised scars.

We killed a great many in the south suddenly with helicopters and rockets but we found that those we had killed were children and more came from the north and from the east and from other places where there are children preparing to live. "Skin," Miss R. said softly in the white, yellow room. "This is the Clemency Committee. And would you remove your belt and shoelaces." I removed my belt and shoelaces and looked (rain shattering from a great height the prospects of silence and clear, neat rows of houses in the subdivisions) into their savage black eyes, paint, feathers, beads.

THE KEY

Isaac Bashevis Singer

DECEMBER 6, 1969

T ABOUT THREE o'clock in the afternoon, Bessie Popkin began to
prepare to go down to the street. Going out was connected with
many difficulties, especially on a hot summer day: first, forcing
her fat body into a corset, squeezing her swollen feet into shoes, and
combing her hair, which Bessie dyed at home and which grew wild and
was streaked in all colors—yellow, black, gray, red; then making sure
that while she was out her neighbors would not break into her apartment
and steal linen, clothes, documents, or just disarrange things and make
them disappear.

Besides human tormentors, Bessie suffered from demons, imps, Evil
Powers. She hid her eyeglasses in the night table and found them in a
slipper. She placed her bottle of hair dye in the medicine chest; days later
she discovered it under the pillow. Once, she left a pot of borsch in the
refrigerator, but the Unseen took it from there and after long searching
Bessie came upon it in her clothes closet. On its surface was a thick layer
of fat that gave off the smell of rancid tallow.

What she went through, how many tricks were played on her and how
much she had to wrangle in order not to perish or fall into insanity, only
God knew. She had given up the telephone because racketeers and de-
generates called her day and night, trying to get secrets out of her. The
Puerto Rican milkman once tried to rape her. The errand boy from the
grocery store attempted to burn her belongings with a cigarette. To evict
her from the rent-controlled apartment where she had lived for thirty-
five years, the company and the superintendent infested her rooms with
rats, mice, cockroaches.

Bessie had long ago realized that no means were adequate against those determined to be spiteful—not the metal door, the special lock, her letters to the police, the mayor, the F.B.I., and even the President in Washington. But while one breathed one had to eat. It all took time: checking the windows, the gas vents, securing the drawers. Her paper money she kept in volumes of the encyclopedia, in back copies of the *National Geographic,* and in Sam Popkin's old ledgers. Her stocks and bonds Bessie had hidden among the logs in the fireplace, which was never used, as well as under the seats of the easy chairs. Her jewels she had sewn into the mattress. There was a time when Bessie had safe-deposit boxes at the bank, but she long ago convinced herself that the guards there had passkeys.

At about five o'clock, Bessie was ready to go out. She gave a last look at herself in the mirror—small, broad, with a narrow forehead, a flat nose, and eyes slanting and half closed, like a Chinaman's. Her chin sprouted a little white beard. She wore a faded dress in a flowered print, a misshapen straw hat trimmed with wooden cherries and grapes, and shabby shoes. Before she left, she made a final inspection of the three rooms and the kitchen. Everywhere there were clothes, shoes, and piles of letters that Bessie had not opened. Her husband, Sam Popkin, who had died almost twenty years ago, had liquidated his real-estate business before his death, because he was about to retire to Florida. He left her stocks, bonds, and a number of passbooks from savings banks, as well as some mortgages. To this day, firms wrote to Bessie, sent her reports, checks. The Internal Revenue Service claimed taxes from her. Every few weeks she received announcements from a funeral company that sold plots in an "airy ceme-tery." In former years, Bessie used to answer letters, deposit her checks, keep track of her income and expenses. Lately she had neglected it all. She even stopped buying the newspaper and reading the financial section.

In the corridor, Bessie tucked cards with signs on them that only she could recognize between the door and the door frame. The keyhole she stuffed with putty. What else could she do—a widow without children, relatives, or friends? There was a time when the neighbors used to open their doors, look out, and laugh at her exaggerated care; others teased her. That had long passed. Bessie spoke to no one. She didn't see well, either. The glasses she had worn for years were of no use. To go to an eye doctor and be fitted for new ones was too much of an effort. Everything was difficult—even entering and leaving the elevator, whose door always closed with a slam.

Bessie seldom went farther than two blocks from her building. The street between Broadway and Riverside Drive became noisier and filthier from day to day. Hordes of urchins ran around half naked. Dark men with curly hair and wild eyes quarrelled in Spanish with little women whose bellies were always swollen in pregnancy. They talked back in rattling voices. Dogs barked, cats meowed. Fires broke out and fire engines, ambulances, and police cars drove up. On Broadway, the old groceries had been replaced by supermarkets, where food must be picked out and put in a wagon and one had to stand in line before the cashier.

God in Heaven, since Sam died, New York, America—perhaps the whole world—was falling apart. All the decent people had left the neighborhood and it was overrun by a mob of thieves, robbers, whores. Three times Bessie's pocketbook had been stolen. When she reported it to the police, they just laughed. Every time one crossed the street, one risked one's life. Bessie took a step and stopped. Someone had advised her to use a cane, but she was far from considering herself an old woman or a cripple. Every few weeks she painted her nails red. At times, when the rheumatism left her in peace, she took clothes she used to wear from the closets, tried them on, and studied herself in the mirror.

Opening the door of the supermarket was impossible. She had to wait till someone held it for her. The supermarket itself was a place that only the Devil could have invented. The lamps burned with a glaring light. People pushing wagons were likely to knock down anyone in their path. The shelves were either too high or too low. The noise was deafening, and the contrast between the heat outside and the freezing temperature inside! It was a miracle that she didn't get pneumonia. More than anything else, Bessie was tortured by indecision. She picked up each item with a trembling hand and read the label. This was not the greed of youth but the uncertainty of age. According to Bessie's figuring, today's shopping should not have taken longer than three-quarters of an hour, but two hours passed and Bessie was still not finished. When she finally brought the wagon to the cashier, it occurred to her that she had forgotten the box of oatmeal. She went back and a woman took her place in line. Later, when she paid, there was new trouble. Bessie had put the bill in the right side of her bag, but it was not there. After long rummaging, she found it in a small change purse on the opposite side. Yes, who could believe that such things were possible? If she told someone, he would think she was ready for the madhouse.

. . .

When Bessie went into the supermarket, the day was still bright; now it was drawing to a close. The sun, yellow and golden, was sinking toward the Hudson, to the hazy hills of New Jersey. The buildings on Broadway radiated the heat they had absorbed. From under gratings where the subway trains rumbled, evil-smelling fumes arose. Bessie held the heavy bag of food in one hand, and in the other she grasped her pocketbook tightly. Never had Broadway seemed to her so wild, so dirty. It stank of softened asphalt, gasoline, rotten fruit, the excrement of dogs. On the sidewalk, among torn newspapers and the butts of cigarettes, pigeons hopped about. It was difficult to understand how these creatures avoided being stepped on in the crush of passersby. From the blazing sky a golden dust was falling. Before a storefront hung with artificial grass, men in sweated shirts poured papaya juice and pineapple juice into themselves with haste, as if trying to extinguish a fire that consumed their insides. Above their heads hung coconuts carved in the shapes of Indians. On a side street, black and white children had opened a hydrant and were splashing naked in the gutter. In the midst of that heat wave, a truck with microphones drove around blaring out shrill songs and deafening blasts about a candidate for political office. From the rear of the truck, a girl with hair that stood up like wires threw out leaflets.

It was all beyond Bessie's strength—crossing the street, waiting for the elevator, and then getting out on the fifth floor before the door slammed. Bessie put the groceries down at the threshold and searched for her keys. She used her nail file to dig the putty out of the keyhole. She put in the key and turned it. But woe, the key broke. Only the handle remained in her hand. Bessie fully grasped the catastrophe. The other people in the building had copies of their keys hanging in the superintendent's apartment, but she trusted no one—some time ago, she had ordered a new combination lock, which she was sure no master key could open. She had a duplicate key somewhere in a drawer, but with her she carried only this one. "Well, this is the end," Bessie said aloud.

There was nobody to turn to for help. The neighbors were her blood enemies. The super only waited for her downfall. Bessie's throat was so constricted that she could not even cry. She looked around, expecting to see the fiend who had delivered this latest blow. Bessie had long since made peace with death, but to die on the steps or in the streets was too harsh. And who knows how long such agony could last? She began to ponder. Was there still open somewhere a store where they fitted keys? Even if there were, what could the locksmith copy from? He would have to come up here with his tools. For that, one needed a mechanic associated with the firm which produced these special locks. If at least she had money with her. But she never carried more than she needed to spend. The cashier in the supermarket had given her back only some twenty-odd cents. "O dear Momma, I don't want to live anymore!" Bessie spoke Yiddish, amazed that she suddenly reverted to that half-forgotten tongue.

After many hesitations, Bessie decided to go back down to the street. Perhaps a hardware store or one of those tiny shops that specialize in keys was still open. She remembered that there used to be such a key stand in the neighborhood. After all, other people's keys must get broken. But what should she do with the food? It was too heavy to carry with her. There was no choice. She would have to leave the bag at the door. "They steal anyhow," Bessie said to herself. Who knows, perhaps the neighbors intentionally manipulated her lock so that she would not be able to enter the apartment while they robbed her or vandalized her belongings.

Before Bessie went down to the street, she put her ear to the door. She heard nothing except a murmur that never stopped, the cause and origin of which Bessie could not figure out. Sometimes it ticked like a clock; other times it buzzed, or groaned—an entity imprisoned in the walls or the water pipes. In her mind Bessie said goodbye to the food, which should have been in the refrigerator, not standing here in the heat. The butter would melt, the milk would turn sour. "It's a punishment! I am cursed, cursed," Bessie muttered. A neighbor was about to go down in the elevator and Bessie signalled to him to hold the door for her. Perhaps he was one of the thieves. He might try to hold her up, assault her. The elevator went down and the man opened the door for her. She wanted to thank him, but remained silent. Why thank her enemies? These were all sly tricks.

When Bessie stepped out into the street, night had fallen. The gutter was flooded with water. The street lamps were reflected in the black pool as in a lake. Again there was a fire in the neighborhood. She heard the wailing of a siren, the clang of fire engines. Her shoes were wet. She came out on Broadway, and the heat slapped her like a sheet of tin. She had difficulty seeing in daytime; at night she was almost blind. There was light in the stores, but what they displayed Bessie could not make out. Passersby bumped into her, and Bessie regretted that she didn't have a cane. Nevertheless, she began to walk along, close to the windows. She passed a drugstore, a bakery, a shop of rugs, a funeral parlor, but nowhere was there a sign of a hardware store. Bessie continued on her way. Her strength was ebbing, but she was determined not to give up. What should a person do when her key has broken off—die? Perhaps apply to the police. There might be some institution that took care of such cases. But where?

There must have been an accident. The sidewalk was crowded with spectators. Police cars and an ambulance blocked the street. Someone sprayed the asphalt with a hose, probably cleaning away the blood. It occurred to Bessie that the eyes of the onlookers gleamed with an uncanny satisfaction. They enjoy other people's misfortunes, she thought. It is their only comfort in this miserable city. No, she wouldn't find anybody to help her.

She had come to a church. A few steps led to the closed door, which was protected by an overhang and darkened by shadows. Bessie was barely able to sit down. Her knees wobbled. Her shoes had begun to pinch in the toes and above the heels. A bone in her corset broke and cut into her flesh. "Well, all the Powers of Evil are upon me tonight." Hunger mixed with nausea gnawed at her. An acid fluid came up to her mouth. "Father in Heaven, it's my end." She remembered the Yiddish proverb "If one lives without a reckoning, one dies without confession." She had even neglected to write her will.

Bessie must have dozed off, because when she opened her eyes there was a late-night stillness, the street half empty and darkened. Store windows were no longer lit. The heat had evaporated and she felt chilly under her dress. For a moment she thought that her pocketbook had been stolen, but it lay on a step below her, where it had probably slipped. Bessie tried to stretch out her hand for it; her arm was numb. Her head, which rested against the wall, felt as heavy as a stone. Her legs had become wooden. Her ears seemed to be filled with water. She lifted one of her eyelids and saw the moon. It hovered low in the sky over a flat roof, and near it twinkled a greenish star. Bessie gaped. She had almost forgotten that there was a sky, a moon, stars. Years had passed and she never looked up—always down. Her windows were hung with draperies so that the spies across the street could not see her. Well, if there was a sky, perhaps there was also a God, angels, Paradise. Where else did the souls of her parents rest? And where was Sam now? She, Bessie, had abandoned all her duties. She never visited Sam's grave in the cemetery. She didn't even light a candle on the anniversary of his death. She was so steeped in wrangling with the lower powers that she did not remember the higher ones. For the first time in years, Bessie felt the need to recite a prayer. The Almighty would have mercy on her even though she did not deserve it. Father and Mother might intercede for her on high. Some Hebrew words hung on the tip of her tongue, but she could not recall them. Then she remembered. "Hear, O Israel." But what followed? "God forgive me," Bessie said. "I deserve everything that falls on me."

It became even quieter and cooler. Traffic lights changed from red to green, but a car rarely passed. From somewhere a Negro appeared. He staggered. He stopped not far from Bessie and turned his eyes to her. Then he walked on. Bessie knew that her bag was full of important documents, but for the first time she did not care about her property. Sam had left a fortune; it all had gone for naught. She continued to save for her old age as if she were still young. "How old am I?" Bessie asked herself. "What have I accomplished in all these years? Why didn't I go somewhere, enjoy my money, help somebody?" Something in her laughed. "I was possessed, completely not myself. How else can it be explained?" Bessie was astounded. She felt as if she had awakened from a long sleep. The broken key had opened a door in her brain that had shut when Sam died.

The moon had shifted to the other side of the roof—unusually large, red, its face obliterated. It was almost cold now. Bessie shivered. She realized that she could easily get pneumonia, but the fear of death was gone, along with her fear of being homeless. Fresh breezes drifted from the Hudson River. New stars appeared in the sky. A black cat approached from the other side of the street. For a while, it stood on the edge of the sidewalk and its green eyes looked straight at Bessie. Then slowly and cautiously it drew near. For years Bessie had hated all animals—dogs, cats, pigeons, even sparrows. They carried sicknesses. They made everything filthy. Bessie believed that there was a demon in every cat. She especially dreaded an encounter with a black cat, which was always an omen of evil. But now Bessie felt love for this creature that had no home, no possessions, no doors or keys, and lived on God's bounty. Before the cat neared Bessie, it smelled her bag. Then it began to rub its back on her leg, lifting up its tail and meowing. The poor thing is hungry. I wish I could give her something. How can one hate a creature like this, Bessie wondered. O Mother of mine, I was bewitched, bewitched. I'll begin a new life. A treacherous thought ran through her mind: perhaps remarry?

The night did not pass without adventure. Once, Bessie saw a white butterfly in the air. It hovered for a while over a parked car and then took off. Bessie knew it was a soul of a newborn baby, since real butterflies do not fly after dark. Another time, she wakened to see a ball of fire, a kind of lit-up soap bubble, soar from one roof to another and sink behind it. She was aware that what she saw was the spirit of someone who had just died.

. . .

Bessie had fallen asleep. She woke up with a start. It was daybreak. From the side of Central Park the sun rose. Bessie could not see it from here, but on Broadway the sky became pink and reddish. On the building to the left, flames kindled in the windows; the panes ran and blinked like the portholes of a ship. A pigeon landed nearby. It hopped on its little red feet and pecked into something that might have been a dirty piece of stale bread or dried mud. Bessie was baffled. How do these birds live? Where do they sleep at night? And how can they survive the rains, the cold, the snow? I will go home, Bessie decided. People will not leave me in the streets.

Getting up was a torment. Her body seemed glued to the step on which she sat. Her back ached and her legs tingled. Nevertheless, she began to walk slowly toward home. She inhaled the moist morning air. It smelled of grass and coffee. She was no longer alone. From the side streets men and women emerged. They were going to work. They bought newspapers at the stand and went down into the subway. They were silent and strangely peaceful, as if they, too, had gone through a night of soul-searching and come out of it cleansed. When do they get up if they are already on their way to work now, Bessie marvelled. No, not all in this neighborhood were gangsters and murderers. One young man even nodded good morning to Bessie. She tried to smile at him, realizing she had forgotten that feminine gesture she knew so well in her youth; it was almost the first lesson her mother had taught her.

She reached her building, and outside stood the Irish super, her deadly enemy. He was talking to the garbage collectors. He was a giant of a man, with a short nose, a long upper lip, sunken cheeks, and a pointed chin. His yellow hair covered a bald spot. He gave Bessie a startled look. "What's the matter, Grandma?"

Stuttering, Bessie told him what had happened to her. She showed him the handle of the key she had clutched in her hand all night.

"Mother of God!" he called out.

"What shall I do?" Bessie asked.

"I will open your door."

"But you don't have a passkey."

"We have to be able to open all doors in case of fire."

The super disappeared into his own apartment for a few minutes, then he came out with some tools and a bunch of keys on a large ring. He went up in the elevator with Bessie. The bag of food still stood on the threshold, but it looked depleted. The super busied himself at the lock. He asked, "What are these cards?"

Bessie did not answer.

"Why didn't you come to me and tell me what happened? To be roaming around all night at your age—my God!" As he poked with his tools, a door opened and a little woman in a housecoat and slippers, her hair bleached and done up in curlers, came out. She said, "What happened to you? Everytime I opened the door, I saw this bag. I took out your butter and milk and put them in my refrigerator."

Bessie could barely restrain her tears. "O my good people," she said. "I didn't know that . . ."

The super pulled out the other half of Bessie's key. He worked a little longer. He turned a key and the door opened. The cards fell down. He entered the hallway with Bessie and she sensed the musty odor of an apartment that has not been lived in for a long time. The super said, "Next time, if something like this happens call me. That's what I'm here for."

Bessie wanted to give him a tip, but her hands were too weak to open her bag. The neighbor woman brought in the milk and butter. Bessie went into her bedroom and lay down on the bed. There was a pressure on her breast and she felt like vomiting. Something heavy vibrated up from her feet to her chest. Bessie listened to it without alarm, only curious about the whims of the body; the super and the neighbor talked, and Bessie could not make out what they were saying. The same thing had happened to her over thirty years ago when she had been given anesthesia in the hospital before an operation—the doctor and the nurse were talking but their voices seemed to come from far away and in a strange language.

Soon there was silence, and Sam appeared. It was neither day nor night—a strange twilight. In her dream, Bessie knew that Sam was dead but that in some clandestine way he had managed to get away from the grave and visit her. He was feeble and embarrassed. He could not speak. They wandered through a space without a sky, without earth, a tunnel full of debris—the wreckage of a nameless structure—a corridor dark and winding, yet somehow familiar. They came to a region where two mountains met, and the passage between shone like sunset or sunrise. They stood there hesitating and even a little ashamed. It was like that night of their honeymoon when they went to Ellenville in the Catskills and were let by the hotel owner into their bridal suite. She heard the same words he had said to them then, in the same voice and intonation: "You don't need no key here. Just enter—and *mazel tov*."

ACKNOWLEDGI

Special thanks—this is in contrast to the plain-va
we usually try to fob off on people—go to Pame
monoff, Fabio Bertoni, Erin Overbey, Joshua R
Chris Curry, Ann Goldstein, Eleanor Martin,
Hawthorne, Rozina Ali, Nimal Eames-Scott,
Hitchens, Tammy Kim, David Kortava, Sean L
Mendes, and Nicolas Niarchos; and to all the
bylined in the book. At Random House, we be
of Noah Eaker, the vigilant eye of Vincent La
Nina Arazoza and Emma Caruso, and the desi
livan. Love beads are owed to Alexandra Sch
The sixties were a long time ago. All these pe

CONTRIBUTORS

RENATA ADLER joined *The New Yorker* as a staff writer in 1962, and contributed reportage, fiction, criticism, and Talk of the Town pieces to the magazine over the next twenty-five years. A graduate of Bryn Mawr, the Sorbonne, and Yale Law School, she is the author of two novels, *Speedboat* (1976) and *Pitch Dark* (1983).

ROGER ANGELL, a senior editor and staff writer, has contributed to *The New Yorker* since 1944, and became a fiction editor in 1956. Since 1962, he has written more than a hundred Sporting Scene pieces for the magazine, along with film reviews, stories, casuals, and Comments. His writing has appeared in many anthologies, including *The Best American Sports Writing, The Best American Essays,* and *The Best American Magazine Writing,* and he is the author of several books on baseball. In 2015, he won the National Magazine Award for essays and criticism.

HANNAH ARENDT (1906–1975) was a writer and political theorist. Her reporting on the 1961 trial of Adolf Eichmann, excerpted here, coined the phrase "banality of evil," and was later published as a book, *Eichmann in Jerusalem.* After escaping Europe during the Holocaust and settling in America, she taught at Princeton University, the University of Chicago, and the New School. She is the author of several books, including *The Origins of Totalitarianism* (1951), *The Human Condition* (1958), *On Revolution* (1963), and *On Violence* (1970).

MICHAEL J. ARLEN joined *The New Yorker* in 1958, and served as the magazine's TV critic throughout the 1960s. He also contributed fiction and Comments to the magazine, and his 1975 book, *Passage to Ararat,* won a National Book Award for Contemporary Affairs.

JAMES BALDWIN (1924–1987) was a novelist, critic, activist, and essayist, whose work often explored the racial and sexual tensions of mid-twentieth-century America. After leaving the U.S. in his twenties, Baldwin spent most of the rest of his life in France. He is the author of several novels, including *Go Tell It on the Mountain* (1953), *Giovanni's Room* (1956), and *Another Country* (1962), as well as many essay collections, among them *Notes of a Native Son* (1955) and *The Fire Next Time* (1963), much of which was first published in *The New Yorker*.

WHITNEY BALLIETT (1926–2007) began writing for *The New Yorker* in 1952, and was the magazine's jazz critic from 1957 to 2001. He is the author of *Such Sweet Thunder* (1966), *Improvising* (1977), *American Musicians* (1986), and *Collected Works: A Journal of Jazz 1954–2000* (2000), among other books.

DONALD BARTHELME (1931–1989) published "L'Lapse," his first story for *The New Yorker*, in 1963, and was a regular contributor of fiction to the magazine until his death. The bulk of his work first appeared in *The New Yorker*, and much of it was later published in his eleven short story collections. He also co-founded the Creative Writing Program at the University of Houston, where he was on faculty from 1980 to 1989.

JACOB BRACKMAN is a journalist, screenwriter, and musical lyricist. Between 1966 and 1968, he wrote more than a dozen pieces for *The New Yorker*, including Comments and Talk of the Town stories. He later served as a film critic for *Esquire*, wrote the screenplays for *The King of Marvin Gardens* and *Times Square*, and co-wrote dozens of songs for the singer Carly Simon.

TRUMAN CAPOTE (1924–1984) published his first article for *The New Yorker*, a Talk of the Town piece, in 1944. His books include *Breakfast at Tiffany's* (1958) and *In Cold Blood* (1966), which originated as a series of *New Yorker* articles published the previous year.

RACHEL CARSON (1907–1964) was an American writer, conservationist, and marine biologist. Her 1962 book, *Silent Spring*, was first published in *The New Yorker*, and is widely acknowledged to have launched the modern environmental movement. She is also the author of *The Sea Around Us* (1951), which won a National Book Award, and *The Edge of the Sea* (1955). Both were first serialized in the magazine.

JOHN CHEEVER (1912–1982) sold his first story to *The New Yorker* in 1935, and was a regular contributor of fiction to the magazine until his death. His books include *The Wapshot Chronicle* (1957), *The Wapshot Scandal* (1964), and *Falconer* (1977).

HENRY S. F. COOPER, JR. (1933–2016) was a journalist and environmentalist who wrote for *The New Yorker* for thirty-five years. Known for his reporting on space travel, he was also the author of eight books, including *Apollo on the Moon* (1969) and *Thirteen: The Apollo Flight That Failed* (2013).

JAMES DICKEY (1923–1997) was an American poet and novelist who, starting with "Orpheus Before Hades," in 1959, published several dozen poems in *The New Yorker*. He is the author of numerous collections of poetry, including *Buckdancer's Choice*, which won a National Book Award in 1966. He taught, and was poet-in-residence, at the University of South Carolina from 1969 until his death.

JENNIFER EGAN has contributed fiction and commentary to *The New Yorker* since 1989, when she published "The Stylist," her first story in the magazine. She is the author of four novels, *The Invisible Circus* (1995), *Look at Me* (2001), *The Keep* (2006), and *A Visit from the Goon Squad* (2010), which won a Pulitzer Prize and National Book Critics Circle Award.

MAVIS GALLANT (1922–2014) was a Canadian-born writer. Between 1951 and 1996, she published 116 stories in *The New Yorker*. Her books include *Green Water, Green Sky* (1959), *The End of the World and Other Stories* (1974), and *Paris Stories* (2002).

BRENDAN GILL (1914–1997) joined *The New Yorker* in 1936 and wrote more than twelve hundred pieces for the magazine. He was the magazine's theatre critic from 1968 to 1987, and the main architecture critic from 1987 to 1996. His books include *Tallulah* (1972), *Here at The New Yorker* (1975), and *Late Bloomers* (1996).

PENELOPE GILLIATT (1932–1993) wrote film criticism for *The New Yorker* from 1968 to 1979, alternating reviewing duties with Pauline Kael. She wrote five novels, including *A State of Change* (1967) and *The Cutting Edge* (1978), and contributed several short stories to the magazine. She also wrote the screenplay for 1971's *Sunday Bloody Sunday*, which won best screenplay awards from the New York Film Critics Circle and the Writers Guild of America.

MALCOLM GLADWELL has been a staff writer at *The New Yorker* since 1996. In 2001, he was awarded the National Magazine Award for profiles. He is the author of *The Tipping Point* (2000), *Blink* (2005), *Outliers* (2008), *What the Dog Saw* (2009), and *David and Goliath* (2013).

DANA GOODYEAR, a staff writer, was on the editorial staff of *The New Yorker* from 1999 to 2007, when she began writing full time for the magazine. She is the author of two collections of poems, *Honey and Junk* (2005) and *The Oracle of Hollywood Boulevard* (2013). She teaches at the University of Southern California, and her book about foodie culture, *Anything That Moves*, was published in 2013.

ADAM GOPNIK began writing for *The New Yorker* in 1986. He is the recipient of three National Magazine Awards, for essays and for criticism, and the George Polk Award for magazine reporting. His books include *Paris to the Moon* (2000), *The King in the Window* (2005), *Through the Children's Gate* (2006), *Angels and Ages* (2009), and *The Table Comes First: Family, France, and the Meaning of Food* (2011).

EMILY HAHN (1905–1997) began writing for *The New Yorker* in 1928, and became the magazine's China correspondent in 1935. She contributed reportage, poems, and short stories to the magazine until her death. Her more than fifty books include *Chiang Kai-shek* (1955) and *Romantic Rebels* (1967).

GEOFFREY T. HELLMAN (1907–1977) began reporting for The Talk of the Town section in 1929. His books include *How to Disappear for an Hour* (1947), *Mrs. De Peyster's Parties* (1963), *The Smithsonian: Octopus on the Mall* (1967), and *Bankers, Bones, and Beetles* (1969).

NAT HENTOFF is an American historian, novelist, and critic. He has contributed book reviews and Profiles to *The New Yorker* since the sixties, and is known for his work in *The Village Voice,* for which he wrote criticism for fifty years, until 2009. He was named a Guggenheim Fellow in 1972, and in 2009 joined the Cato Institute as a senior fellow.

HENDRIK HERTZBERG originally joined *The New Yorker* as a reporter in 1969, and left in 1977 for the White House, where he was a speechwriter for President Jimmy Carter. In 1992, he returned to the magazine as executive editor, and later became a full-time staff writer. He is the author of *Politics: Observations & Arguments* (2004), *¡Obámanos!: The Birth of a New Political Era* (2009), and *One Million* (1970).

TED HUGHES (1930–1998) was an English poet who contributed poetry to *The New Yorker* from 1957 until his death. He wrote over a dozen collections of poetry, including *Crow: From the Life and Songs of the Crow* (1970) and *Birthday Letters* (1998), several children's books, and a prose study of Shakespeare, *Shakespeare and the Goddess of Complete Being* (1992). He also served as Britain's poet laureate from 1984 until his death.

CHARLAYNE HUNTER-GAULT is an American journalist. As one of the first two black students to attend the University of Georgia, she was profiled in Calvin Trillin's "An Education in Georgia," excerpted here. In 1963, she was hired by *The New Yorker* as an editorial assistant, and went on to become the magazine's first black regular contributor. She later reported for the *New York Times,* and served as National Public Radio's chief correspondent in Africa from 1997 to 1999. She won two Emmys and a Peabody Award for her work on PBS's *NewsHour.*

RANDALL JARRELL (1914–1965) was a poet and novelist who served as the United States poet laureate from 1956 to 1958. His books include *Pictures from an Institution* (1954) and *The Woman at the Washington Zoo* (1960), which won a National Book Award.

PAULINE KAEL (1919–2001) wrote for *The New Yorker* from 1967 until her retirement in 1991. In 1968, shortly after the publication of her review of *Bonnie and Clyde,* she became the magazine's film critic, and went on to write hundreds of Current Cinema columns. She was the author of thirteen books, including *I Lost It at the Movies* (1965), *Kiss Kiss Bang Bang* (1973), *5001 Nights at the Movies* (1982), and *Deeper into Movies* (1973), which won the 1974 National Book Award.

E. J. KAHN, JR. (1916–1994) became a staff writer at *The New Yorker* in 1937 and remained at the magazine for five decades. He wrote twenty-seven books, including *The Separated People* (1968), *The American People* (1974), and *About The New Yorker and Me* (1979).

KATHARINE T. KINKEAD (1910–2001) contributed to *The New Yorker* from 1939 until 1964. She is the author of *Walk Together, Talk Together: The American Field Service Student Exchange Program* (1962).

HANS KONINGSBERGER (1921–2007), who later changed his name to Hans Koning, was a writer and journalist. He is the author of more than forty books of fiction, reportage, and history, including *Columbus: His Enterprise—Exploding the Myth* (1976).

JANE KRAMER has been a staff writer for *The New Yorker* since 1964, and has written the Letter from Europe since 1981. Since 1970, most of her work has covered aspects of European culture, politics, and social history. Many of these pieces have been collected in books, including *Unsettling Europe* (1980) and *Europeans* (1988), which was nominated for the National Book Critics Circle Award for nonfiction. Her piece on multiculturalism and political correctness, "Whose Art Is It?," won the 1993 National Magazine Award for feature writing and was published as a book in 1994.

DANIEL LANG (1913–1981) was a war correspondent at *The New Yorker* and a contributor from 1941 until his death. His books include *Early Tales of the Atomic Age* (1948) and *Casualties of War* (1969).

JILL LEPORE is the David Woods Kemper '41 Professor of American History at Harvard University and a staff writer at *The New Yorker*, where she has contributed reviews and essays since 2005. Her books include *The Name of War* (1998), *New York Burning* (2005), *The Story of America* (2012), *Book of Ages* (2013), *The Secret History of Wonder Woman* (2014), and *Joe Gould's Teeth* (2016).

FLORA LEWIS (1922–2002) was an American journalist who covered international politics for over five decades. After beginning her career at the Associated Press, she reported from Europe and Latin America for *The Washington Post*, *Newsday*, and the *New York Post*. From 1980 to 1990, she was a foreign affairs columnist for the *New York Times*. She is the author of four books, including *Europe: A Tapestry of Nations* (1987).

A. J. LIEBLING (1904–1963) joined the staff of *The New Yorker* in 1935 and wrote the magazine's Wayward Press column for many years. His books include *The Sweet Science* (1956), *The Earl of Louisiana* (1961), and *Between Meals* (1962).

ANDY LOGAN (1920–2000) joined *The New Yorker* in 1942, and was the first woman to be hired as a Talk of the Town reporter. In over five decades at the magazine, she contributed hundreds of Talk pieces, Profiles, and Letters from Nuremberg. She was most known for her About City Hall column, first published in 1969, which dissected New York City politics and ran for twenty-five years.

DWIGHT MACDONALD (1906–1982) began writing for *The New Yorker* in 1933, and contributed several Profiles, essays, and book reviews to the magazine. His books include *The Memoirs of a Revolutionist* (1957), *Against the American Grain* (1962), and *Discriminations* (1974).

LARISSA MACFARQUHAR has been a staff writer for *The New Yorker* since 1998, and has written Profiles on John Ashbery, Barack Obama, Noam Chomsky, Aaron Swartz, and Hilary Mantel, among others. She has received two Front Page Awards from the Newswomen's Club of New York, and is the author of *Strangers Drowning: Grappling with Impossible Idealism, Drastic Choices, and the Overpowering Urge to Help* (2015).

DONALD MALCOLM (1932–1975) joined the staff of *The New Yorker* in 1957, and in 1958 became the magazine's first Off Broadway drama critic. He later contributed dozens of book reviews and Comments to the magazine.

TERRENCE MALICK is an American film director. Malick went to Harvard, then to Oxford, as a Rhodes Scholar, before working briefly for *The New Yorker* and *Life*. He has directed eight feature films in four decades, including *Days of Heaven*, which won the Best Director Award at the Cannes Film Festival, and *The Thin Red Line*, *The Tree of Life*, and *The New World*, which were all nominated for Academy Awards.

FAITH MCNULTY (1918–2005) joined *The New Yorker* in 1953, as a Talk of the Town reporter, and contributed to the magazine until 1991. A collection of her stories on the country life, *The Wildlife Stories*, was published in 1980, and *The Burning Bed*, her book on a murder trial in Dansville, Michigan, was later made into a film.

JOHN MCPHEE began contributing to *The New Yorker* in 1963. He has since written more than a hundred pieces for the magazine, among them a Profile of Bill Bradley, an examination of modern cattle rustling, and several multipart series on subjects like Alaska, the writing process, and a stint with the Swiss Army. He is the author of twenty-eight books, all of them based on his *New Yorker* writings, including *Annals of the Former World*, which won the 1999 Pulitzer Prize for general nonfiction. He has taught writing at Princeton University since 1975, and in 1982 was awarded Princeton's Woodrow Wilson Award for service to the nation.

THOMAS MEEHAN joined *The New Yorker* in 1958, and went on to contribute comic fiction and several Talk of the Town pieces to the magazine. He has received the Tony Award for Best Book of a Musical three times, for his work on *Annie*, *Hairspray*, and *The Producers*.

VED MEHTA was a staff writer for *The New Yorker* from 1961 to 1994. He has written more than twenty books, including an eleven-volume autobiography, *Continents of Exile,* which documents his loss of sight at age three and his later journey to the U.S., where he attended Pomona College and Harvard University. He won a MacArthur fellowship in 1982.

JAMES MERRILL (1926–1995) published his first poem in *The New Yorker,* included here, in 1957. Among his collections are *Divine Comedies* (1976), which won a Pulitzer Prize, and *The Changing Light at Sandover* (1982).

W. S. MERWIN's poetry first appeared in *The New Yorker* in 1955, and the magazine has since published close to two hundred of his poems and short stories. Merwin is a two-time winner of the Pulitzer Prize in Poetry, for his collections *The Carrier of Ladders* and *The Shadow of Sirius.* From 2010 to 2011, he served as the seventeenth poet laureate of the United States.

JONATHAN MILLER is an English theatre director, actor, author, and physician. He is known for his role in the comedy revue "Beyond the Fringe," which also featured Peter Cook, Dudley Moore, and Alan Bennett, and for his prolific direction of operas, including *Rigoletto* (1982). He has also been the writer and presenter of several BBC documentaries.

LEWIS MUMFORD (1895–1990), a social theorist, cultural critic, and historian, wrote *The New Yorker*'s architecture column, The Sky Line, from 1931 to 1963. He is the author of numerous books, including *The City in History* (1961), which won a National Book Award.

HOWARD NEMEROV (1920–1991) was the United States poet laureate from 1963 to 1964 and again from 1988 to 1990. "The Triumph of Education" was his first contribution to *The New Yorker.* His *Collected Poems* (1977) won a National Book Award and a Pulitzer Prize.

EVAN OSNOS became a staff writer at *The New Yorker* in 2008, and began reporting from China for the magazine the same year. His book, *Age of Ambition* (2014), won a National Book Award in nonfiction.

GEORGE PACKER became a staff writer for *The New Yorker* in 2003 and covered the Iraq War for the magazine. His books include *The Assassins' Gate,* which was named one of the ten best books of 2005 by the *New York Times,* and *The Unwinding,* which won a 2013 National Book Award in nonfiction.

SYLVIA PLATH (1932–1963) graduated from Smith College and later attended Cambridge University on a Fulbright Scholarship. Beginning with "Mussel Hunter at Rock Harbor," in 1958, *The New Yorker* published twenty-eight of Plath's poems, as well as excerpts from her journals. In 1982 she won a posthumous Pulitzer Prize for her *Collected Poems*. She is also the author of a semi-autobiographical novel, *The Bell Jar*.

DAVID REMNICK has been editor of *The New Yorker* since 1998. He joined the magazine as a staff writer in 1992, and has since written more than a hundred pieces. He is the author of *Lenin's Tomb* (1993), for which he won a Pulitzer Prize, *The Devil Problem* (1996), *Resurrection* (1997), *King of the World* (1998), *Reporting* (2006), and *The Bridge* (2010).

ROBERT RICE (1916–1998) was a contributor to *The New Yorker* between 1947 and 1965. He wrote more than a dozen Profiles for the magazine, on subjects including Mort Sahl, Mike Nichols and Elaine May, and Dave Brubeck.

HAROLD ROSENBERG (1906–1978) was the art critic for *The New Yorker* from 1962 to 1978, and contributed more than a hundred pieces to the magazine, including a dozen book reviews. He covered the careers of Mark Rothko, Frank Stella, and Saul Steinberg, among others, and in 1952 coined the term "Action painting," for what soon became known as Abstract Expressionism.

LILLIAN ROSS became a staff writer at *The New Yorker* in 1945, and over the course of her career wrote hundreds of pieces, contributing to nearly every section of the magazine. She is the author of several books, including *Picture* (1952), *Portrait of Hemingway* (1961), and *Here but Not Here* (1998).

RICHARD H. ROVERE (1915–1979) joined *The New Yorker* in 1944 and wrote the magazine's Letter from Washington from 1948 until his death. His books include *The American Establishment and Other Reports, Opinions, and Speculations* (1962) and *Waist Deep in the Big Muddy* (1968).

MURIEL RUKEYSER (1913–1980) was an American poet and political activist, whose work frequently grappled with social violence, Judaism, and the Vietnam War. She is the author of over a dozen collections of poetry, as well as a work of criticism, *The Life of Poetry* (1949).

XAVIER RYNNE (1914–2002), a pseudonym for Francis X. Murphy, was a writer and Redemptorist priest. He wrote more than twenty books, and is known for his *New Yorker* stories on the meeting of the Second Vatican Council.

KELEFA SANNEH has been a staff writer for *The New Yorker* since 2008. He came to the magazine from the *New York Times,* where he had been the pop-music critic since 2002, and his writing has appeared in *The Source, Rolling Stone, The Village Voice,* and "Da Capo Best Music Writing" in 2002, 2005, 2007, and 2011.

WINTHROP SARGEANT (1903–1986) was a writer, critic, and violinist. In 1930, after stints playing with the New York Symphony and the New York Philharmonic, he abandoned his musical career to become a writer. From 1949 to 1972, he wrote the Musical Events column for *The New Yorker,* and he continued to contribute to the magazine until his death.

JONATHAN SCHELL (1943–2014) wrote for *The New Yorker* from 1967 to 1987. He wrote his first piece for the magazine, "The Village of Ben Suc," when he was twenty-three years old, and went on to contribute hundreds of Notes and Comment pieces for the magazine. In 1982, *The New Yorker* serialized his book about the perils of nuclear proliferation, *The Fate of the Earth,* which was nominated for a Pulitzer Prize and the National Book Award.

ANNE SEXTON (1928–1974) began publishing poems in *The New Yorker* in 1959. Her books of poetry include *To Bedlam and Part Way Back* (1960), *All My Pretty Ones* (1962), and *The Book of Folly* (1972).

ISAAC BASHEVIS SINGER (1904–1991) was a leading figure in the Yiddish literary movement, and the 1978 recipient of the Nobel Prize in Literature. His first story for *The New Yorker,* "The Slaughterer," was published in 1967, and he was a frequent contributor of fiction to the magazine until his death. He is the author of more than a dozen novels, and his short story collection, *A Crown of Feathers and Other Stories,* won the National Book Award in 1974.

L. E. SISSMAN (1928–1976) was a regular contributor of poetry and book reviews to *The New Yorker.* An advertising executive by day, Sissman's collections include *Dying: An Introduction* (1968) and *Scattered Returns* (1969).

MURIEL SPARK (1918–2006) contributed fiction, poetry, and personal histories to *The New Yorker* from 1960 until 2003. "The Ormolu Clock," collected here, was her first story in the magazine, and *The New Yorker* devoted nearly an entire issue to her sixth novel, *The Prime of Miss Jean Brodie*. She is the author of twenty-two novels, two of which, *The Public Image* (1968) and *Loitering with Intent* (1981), were shortlisted for the Man Booker Prize.

GEORGE STEINER, a critic and philosopher, wrote 134 articles for *The New Yorker* between 1966 and 1997, many of which were collected in *George Steiner at The New Yorker* (2009). The author of dozens of works of fiction and nonfiction, he has written extensively about the Holocaust, as well as the relationship between language, literature, and society. He has taught at the University of Oxford, Harvard University, and Princeton University, and is currently Extraordinary Fellow of Churchill College at Cambridge University.

JAMES STEVENSON was on the staff of *The New Yorker* for over three decades, contributing reportage, fiction, and over two thousand cartoons and eighty covers. He is the author and illustrator of over a hundred children's books.

MAY SWENSON (1913–1989) was an American poet and playwright. *The New Yorker* published dozens of her poems from 1954 until 1990. She is the author of several poetry collections, including *A Cage of Spines* (1958), *Iconographs* (1970), and *Collected Poems* (2013).

CALVIN TRILLIN has been a regular contributor to *The New Yorker* since 1963, when he published "An Education in Georgia," excerpted here. More than three hundred of Trillin's pieces have appeared in the magazine, spanning comic casuals, reporting, and varied nonfiction. Between 1967 and 1982, he wrote a series of *New Yorker* pieces from around the U.S., leading to two collections, *U.S. Journal* (1971) and *Killings* (1984). He is the author of eighteen books, and his food writing has been collected in *American Fried* (1974), *Alice, Let's Eat* (1978), and *Travels with Alice* (1989).

GEORGE W. S. TROW (1943–2006) joined *The New Yorker* in 1966 and wrote for the magazine for the next three decades, contributing short fiction, Talk of the Town pieces, and critical essays. In 1980, the magazine devoted an entire issue to his essay "Within the Context of No-Context."

He is the author of a collection of short stories, *Bullies* (1980), a novel, *The City in the Mist* (1984), several plays, and two books of criticism.

KENNETH TYNAN (1927–1980) was born in London and made his name as a theatre critic at the London *Observer*. He began writing for *The New Yorker* in 1958, contributing theatre reviews and Profiles on subjects such as Johnny Carson, Tom Stoppard, and Mel Brooks. His books include *Curtains* (1961), *The Sound of Two Hands Clapping* (1975), and *Show People* (1979).

JOHN UPDIKE (1932–2009) contributed fiction, poetry, essays, and criticism to *The New Yorker* for a half century. He is the author of twenty-two novels, including *Rabbit Is Rich* (1981) and *Rabbit at Rest* (1990), both of which won a Pulitzer Prize, as well as fifteen books of short stories, seven collections of poetry, five children's books, a memoir, and a play. His sixth collection of nonfiction, *Due Considerations* (2007), contains more than seventy book reviews and essays that first appeared in the magazine.

JOSEPH WECHSBERG (1907–1983) began writing for *The New Yorker* in 1943, and from 1958 to 1973 wrote the magazine's Letter from Berlin. He is the author of *Homecoming* (1946), *The Best Things in Life* (1951), and *Trifles Make Perfection* (1998), among other books.

E. B. WHITE (1899–1985) produced more than eighteen hundred stories for *The New Yorker* between 1925 and 1976. Though he contributed light verse, casuals, essays, and cartoon captions, he was most known for his Comments, which helped define the magazine's light, intellectual style. He is the author of several children's books, including *Stuart Little* (1945), *Charlotte's Web* (1952), and *The Trumpet of the Swan* (1970), and in 1959 he edited and updated William Strunk, Jr.'s *The Elements of Style*, which has since been published in four editions. He received a Presidential Medal of Freedom in 1963 and an honorary Pulitzer Prize in 1978.

THOMAS WHITESIDE (1918–1997) wrote for *The New Yorker* between 1950 and 1991. His 1970 article "Defoliation," about Agent Orange, led to the curtailment of the herbicide's use. His books include *The Withering Rain* (1971), *Selling Death* (1971), and *The Blockbuster Complex* (1981).

ELLEN WILLIS (1941–2006) was an American essayist, activist, and cultural critic. In 1968, she became *The New Yorker*'s first pop music critic, and over the next seven years contributed dozens of reviews to the magazine. She went on to write for *The Village Voice, Rolling Stone,* and *The Nation,* and in 1997 she founded the Cultural Reporting and Criticism program at New York University. Her writings on music, feminism, and politics were collected in *Beginning to See the Light* (1981) and *The Essential Ellen Willis,* which won the 2014 National Book Critics Circle Award for criticism.